06

WARFIGHTERS II

The Story of the U.S. Marine Corps Aviation, Weapons, and Tactics Squadron One

WP
BULLDOGS
04
WP
164566
MARINES
VMA-223
BULLDOGS

WARFIGHTERS II

The Story of the U.S. Marine Corps Aviation, Weapons, and Tactics Squadron One

Written and Photographed by

Rick Llinares & Chuck Lloyd

Schiffer Military/Aviation History
Atglen, PA

Dedication

This book is dedicated to our fathers, both of whom served proudly in our countrys armed forces.
Thanks for all the encouragement and support over the years.

Rick Llinares Sr.- 2nd Class Petty Officer
USS Independence/CVW-7 USN Active Duty - 1958-1960
ECMO-MAD United States Navy Reserve - 1960-1964

USS Independence - Carrier Air Wing 7 - 1960

Sergeant Charles D. Lloyd, Sr.
US Marine Corps, 1st Marine Air Wing
14, July 1952 - 13, July 1956
Korea - Japan February 1953 - April 1954

1st Marine Air Wing- "Semper Fi"

Book Design by Ian Robertson.

Copyright © 1997 by Rick Llinares & Chuck Lloyd.
Library of Congress Catalog Number: 97-00000

All rights reserved. No part of this work may be reproduced or used in any forms or by any means – graphic, electronic or mechanical, including photocopying or information storage and retrieval systems – without written permission from the copyright holder.

Printed in China.
ISBN: 0-7643-0329-5

We are interested in hearing from authors with book ideas on related topics.

Published by Schiffer Publishing Ltd.
4880 Lower Valley Road
Atglen, PA 19310
Phone: (610) 593-1777
FAX: (610) 593-2002
E-mail: Schifferbk@aol.com
Please write for a free catalog.
This book may be purchased from the publisher.
Please include $3.95 postage.
Try your bookstore first.

Acknowledgments

As was the case with our first book in the Warfighter series, this second installment could not have been completed without the generous assistance of a great many people. The degree of support extended to us by the many officers, NCO's and enlisted personnel was nothing short of exceptional.

To the best of our ability, we have attempted to include all those that gave us their time and talent over the many months we worked with them on Warfighters II. There were of course several individuals that embraced the idea for the book, and made it happen. To them, we are especially grateful and would like to single them out for wonderful support.

First and foremost is **Colonel John Castellaw**, former Commanding Officer at MAWTS-1. Running a squadron as important as MAWTS-1 is demanding, yet the Colonel made himself and the resources of the entire unit available to us. The photo requirements for a book of this type are significant to say the least. One of the toughest jobs at MAWTS-1 is that of Operations Officer. **Major Dave Wilson** juggled not only the demanding flight schedule for the WTI, but also the many requests we made of him.

Both **Major Myckelby** and **Major Malavet** for all of their time in crafting the 'Marines to the Rescue' chapter.

Many of the photos taken were during flights with VMGR-252, a KC-130 unit based at MCAS Cherry Point, North Carolina. One particular individual, **Captain Ron DoMainge** truly enabled us to be in a position to capture Marine Air in action.

Without a doubt, the heroes on this project have to be the unsung officers and enlisted personnel at **Public Affairs Officers and Aviation, Manpower and Support**. We constantly made demands on these people and their support in large part made 'Warfighters II' happen.

At Public Affairs -Headquarters, US Marine Corps - We would like to thank General Stanley, Major Ohwermahle, **Captain T.V. Johnson**, Fred Carr. In New York, Sgt. Kyle Olson, Lt. Christopher Lewis (Deputy Director), Colonel F. Patrick Ahern and Major Roseann Sgrignoli (Director). At MCAS New River, Lt. Sarah Quimby.

At Aviation, Manpower and Support -
We would also like to thank Major Webster, Captain Newman, SSGT Behan and MSGT Crews.

MAWTS-1:
Colonel Keith Stalder (CO), Lt. Colonel Love (XO)
Operations: Captain Leo Kilgore.
Administrative Department: CWO H.L. Miller
Academics Department: Major W.L. Niblock (Department Head), Major Ashby, Major E. Follstad, Major Malavet.
TACAIR: Major Downey, Major T.S. Clark, Major J. Brow, Captain D.G. Chandler, Major M.B. Norman, Major T.C. Moore.
Assault: Captain D.J.Andersen (AH-1W), Major R.F. Hedelund (CH-46E), Major F. Usry (AH-1W), Captain M.W. Young (CH-53), Captain Bob Tobin.
Aviation Development Tactics and Evaluation (ADT &E) - Major A.E. Kolkmeyer, Major L.A.Wright, Lt. W.E. Schutt (USN).
Ground Combat: Major S.F. Snyder
Aviation Ground Support: Major G.S. Thomas
Maintenance: Major W. Smith
Logistics: Major D.L. Hofsetter
Command, Control & Communications: Major Cianciolo

Public Affairs Offices at:
MCAS Yuma
MCAS Cherry Point
MCAS Beaufort
MCAS New River
Quantico - Sgt. Chris Cox

Commandant of the Marine Corps -
General Charles C. Krulak, CMC
Commandants Staff Group
Sgt. J.D. Powell

Commanding Generals of the Marine Air Wings -
Generals Knutson, Ryan and McCorkle and their staffs.

HMX-1
Colonel Fred Geier (CO), Lt. Colonel Mike Conklin (XO), Lt. Colonel Gerry Hammes, Major Mosher, Captain Sean Killeen, Sergent Major George Amos, Master Gunnery Sergent Thomas Downey.
Presidential Helicopter Pilots: Lt. Colonel Kevin Delmor, Major Gary Strasmann, Major Greg Siesel, Major O'Donnell (OT&E), Major Mark Peters (OT&E), Lt. Andrews (OT&E).
Marine One Crew Chiefs: Sgt. C.B. Reis, Sgt. R.L. Rood, Sgt. W.M. Scovell, Sgt. N.J. Gatewood, Sgt. W.D. Surike, Sgt. J.P Delbalso, SSgt. M.D. Carter, Sgt. D.T.Roseman, SSgt. Friend (OT&E),
Lance Corporal Ward (Adjutants Office)
White House Military Office

Air Stations:
MCAS New River - Colonel R.J. Wallace (CO MAG-49), Lt. Colonel Ronald W."The OX" Ochse (XO MAG-29), Lt.Colonel J.T. Hardwick, Lt. Colonel Ishbein.
HMLA-269 - Lt. Colonel Spencer (CO)
HMM-263 - Lt. Colonel Bartels (CO).
Lt. Colonel Mike Duva
HMH-464 - Lt.Colonel House (CO), 1st Lt. Koronek, Captain Pfannenstein, SSgt. Nordstrom, SSgt. Hansen, LCPL Rivera, LCPL Aiken.

MAG-49, Det B - Captain Mike King and the Yankees.

MCAS Beaufort -
VMFA (AW) - 224 'Bengals' - Lt. Colonel Jeff White, Major Mitchell, Major Pace
VMFA (AW) - 322 'Moonlighters' - Captain "Shades" Oakley, Major Tolomeo,
VMFA-451 'Warlords'
MAG-31 - Captain "Grape" Welch, Captain Baget.

MCAS Cherry Point -
VMGR-252 - Lt. Colonel R.H. Bell, Captain Pietila, Captain Patrick, Captain Kay, and all of the OTIS Marines.
VMAQ-1 'Screaming Banshees' - Captain Bonzo, Captain Denney, Major Boyer and the aviators of VMAQ-1.
VMA-542 'Tigers' - Captain Forrest, Captain Bagnato, Captain Lancaster.

MCAS Yuma -
Major Brad Stocker and the 'Snipers' of VMFT-401

Illustrators - For those interested in purchasing these, and other illustrations from the artists you can reach them at:

Lisa Venema (800) 758-3530

Mark Styling an English artist via his U.S. agent Warren E. Thompson, 7201 Stamford Cove, Germantown, TN 38138. These lithographic prints measure 20" x 23.5" and cost $70 for one, or $60 each for two including shipping. Please make all checks payable to Warren Thompson.

Colonel Charles Waterhouse (USMCR-ret.) - Copies of his wonderful book titled "Marines and Others" can be ordered for $75 plus shipping/handling charges by calling (908) 738 -1804

Andrew C. Whyte
Mr. Whyte provided the painting of the USMC O'Grady Rescue Mission. Full size lithographs of the painting and other fine works by Mr.Whyte can be purchased from: Andrew Whyte Galleries, 39 Stonecrop Road, Norwalk, CT 06851-1812. 203-847-2855

J. Walter Thompson (Advertising Agency for the USMC) -
Teresa McGregor, USMC Account Representative, Chris Hall, David White.

Marine Corps Recruiting Command, Washington, D.C.-
Major General Klimp, Colonel Clyde H. Slick (Chief of Staff), Lt. Colonel Robert E. Wilson (Asst. Chief of Staff for Advertising).

Marine Corps Historical Foundation, Quantico, VA -
The entire staff.

USMC Aviation Association, Quantico, VA -
The entire staff.

Sikorsky Corporation
Bill Tuttle

Bell Textron Corporation
Pat Rever

Marine Corps Aces Listing
Dr. Frank J. Olynyk

SES Homeworks
Special thanks to Saundra E. Salaam for technical assistance with information systems and graphics design.

The Garandfather, Inc.
Special thanks to Tom Byrne for providing the M1 Garand rifles and for his hitorical consultation on the history of the USMC. Tom Byrne, Oak Beach NY 516-422-0711: M1 Garand rifles and parts.

John F. Kennedy Library, Boston MA
Mr. Alan Goodrich

The White House
President Clinton
Mr. Robert McNeely, Director, White House Photographic Services

Neither the United States Marine Corps nor any other component of the Department of Defense has approved, endorsed, or authorized this product/service/activity.

...and of course, our wives Susan and Kate, for all of their sacrifices as we write, photograph, and edit a book of this magnitude.

Dash 2 Aviation Photography -
For those readers that would like to correspond with the authors, you may do so by writing us at Dash 2 Aviation Photo - PO Box 2785, North Babylon, NY 11703. For those interested in stock photos or in purchasing the Dash 2 'Above & Beyond' aviation calendar, please send a check for $12.95 plus $2.95 shipping and handling to the same address.

Authors Notes

In as much as Marine Corps aviation is about airplanes and helicopters, the real essence of this amazing military organization lies within its people—the officers, NCO's and enlisted personnel. Attributes such as sacrifice, courage, humility and devotion to country and duty were universally displayed by the Marines we had the honor of meeting. From the Commandant to the youngest Marine, these values and qualities are consistently exhibited. This is not mere hyperbole, but the simple truth as we experienced first hand.

In some respects, the mission and value of the Marine Corps is not completely understood by most people. To ask the average American citizen about the role and importance to America of the Marine Corps, one would rarely get a complete or correct answer.

Throughout much of America's history, when it has come time to pay the bill for freedom, the Marines have always taken the check. We, the citizens of the United States, tend to take for granted the sacrifices these officers and enlisted personnel make to protect our country. Needless to say, we shouldn't, for their sacrifices are not small and should never be taken for granted.

At any given time, Marine Expeditionary Units operating aboard amphibious assault ships throughout the globe stand ready to protect American interests or project American power. In some instances, they go directly in harm's way to defend the basic liberties of others, usually when internal strife in their country poses a threat to basic humanitarian needs. The Marine Corps has come to be known informally as America's 911 force. It's an accurate, worthy nickname, and a great responsibility. One they deserve, and are proud of.

Our primary goals in constructing this book are to properly and accurately present the value and capabilities of Marine aviation and its elite training squadron, MAWTS-1. Ask any Marine aviator to tell you about their aircraft or themselves and you will get the same simple answer, *"my aircraft and I have one mission, support the young Marine infantryman on the ground".* Unlike any other aviation service in the world, this has always

Section of EA-6B Prowlers with VMAQ-1 lead a pair of F/A-18's during an exercise off the South Carolina coast.

been, and will remain, their main purpose. There is obviously so much more to the Marine Corps than just its Aviation Combat Element (ACE). The scope of Warfighters II, however, is primarily focused on Marine aviation and MAWTS-1.

Warfighters II is segmented into five main parts. The Preface and Introduction were written by two of the most important and impressive Marine aviators—Lieutenant General Terrence R. Dake (Deputy Chief of Staff for Aviation) and Colonel John Castellaw (former Commanding Officer of MAWTS-1). Their words serve as a strong 'big picture' view on Marine Air, MAWTS-1 and the Weapons and Tactics Instructors the squadron creates.

Part One, titled 'The United States Marine Corps, contains three chapters that serve to introduce the reader to the Corps, its organizational layout, and the critical Marine Air Ground Task Force (MAGTF). Chapter three provides the Commandant of the Marine Corps, General Charles C. Krulak's vision for the Corps into the next century. No book on Marine aviation would be complete without first covering these items. A most unique aspect within these chapters is the artwork that we were granted permission to use for "Warfighters II". This archival material obtained from the Corps advertising firm, J. Walter Thompson, includes some of the most compelling images of the Marine Corps. Similarly, we were granted the privilege of using a number of paintings by Colonel Charles Waterhouse, USMCR(ret). These truly beautiful works of art convey much more about Marine history than any photo could.

Part Two describes the rich history and the current state of Marine aviation in detail. Two of the most interesting chapters in this book are those that cover the Six Functions of Marine Air and the multi-faceted HMX-1 squadron. These chapters are necessary to one's ability to fully understand how Marine Air fulfills its mission. We have intentionally written these two chapters in great detail. It would be an injustice to do otherwise. To the best of our knowledge, this book will be the first one to cover the "Six Functions" and "HMX-1" so thoroughly.

The numerous chapters within Part Three cover the Marine Aviation Weapons and Tactics Squadron-One, (MAWTS-1), and the Weapons and Tactics Instructor (WTI) course and its curriculum in great detail. Also included is a chapter of Marine Corps Air Station Yuma, the home of MAWTS -1. Chapter ten, 'Voices from the Past', contains personal insights from the three Commanding Generals of the Marine Corps active Air Wings, all of whom were former MAWTS-1 commanding officers. Wherever possible, we feel it's more interesting to have the experts tell their own story. In our view, one of the most compelling aspects of this book can be found in chapter eleven—the role of the Marine Corps in the rescue of downed USAF pilot Captain Scott O'Grady. We were given the opportunity to speak directly with those that planned and executed it, and their story is extraordinary.

Section Four contains chapters dedicated to each of the active duty fixed and rotary wing aircraft the Marine Corps operates. We have deliberately tried not to make this a dry, detailed technical analysis of the airplanes, but rather a broad, and hopefully interesting introduction to these remarkable aircraft and their capabilities.

The last section of this book contains a look at the main priorities for the future of Marine aviation. Lastly, we decided to include a chapter titled 'The Parting Shot'. Our goal here was to try to answer the question often posed to us by friends and family—*'So what's it like to fly in Marine jets and helo's?'* We fully recognize the rare privilege and 'once in a lifetime' opportunity we were given to strap on an F/A-18, CH-46E and KC-130. Hopefully, we can accurately describe the experience to you.

For those that are interested, we included some text relating to the challenges we faced in photographing Marine aircraft in action. We hope that we can place you, the reader, in the aircraft with us as we took to the skies with the Marines. The appendices contain very specific data for those that would like to get into the details of the MAWTS-1 curriculum. Suffice it to say, any mistakes in this work are the sole responsibilities of the authors.

Rick Llinares
Chuck Lloyd

Preface

The Marine Corps exists because the American people would not have it any other way. Marine Aviation is defined by its responsiveness, flexibility and decisiveness in conflict. When the North Korean Army swept through Seoul and surged toward Pusan in the early days of the Korean War, experts said that no force could rush into a theater teetering on the brink of collapse, engage a numerically superior enemy, and stop its advance. But that is exactly what the First Provisional Marine Brigade did. That Marine Air Ground Task Force (MAGTF), with Marine Aircraft Group 33 fully integrated, established a precedent of successful crisis responses that Americans now take for granted.

Marine aviation is uniquely Marine. No other aviation organization is capable of providing a full bodied spectrum of war fighting capabilities—like close air support, anti-air warfare and assault support—from the sea or austere expeditionary airfields ashore, like the Marines. Marine aviators pride themselves in being Marines first. As Second Lieutenants we train in basic infantry skills. This initial focus on infantry operations develops professional relationships which serve as the foundation for all future employment as the air component of the Marine combined arms team. Marine aviators serve with infantry units as the ground combat commander's aviation expert. Leading Tactical Air Control Parties as a Forward Air Controller (FAC), an aviator is responsible for coordinating close air support and assault support. When a Marine ground commander calls for air, he rests assured that the Marine aviator providing the support understands his needs and will always be there for him—on time, day or night, rain or shine.

In the late 1970's, the Marine Corps realized that it needed an organization to standardize aviation training. Marine Aviation Weapons and Tactics Squadron-1 (MAWTS-1) was formed at that time and tasked with training experienced mid-level aircrews in the art of warfare. Aircrews at the MAWTS-1 Weapons and Tactics Instructors (WTI) course receive formal classroom and flight instruction on how to best support the ground commander in the execution of his mission. Standardization of tactics, planning, and training concepts taught by MAWTS-1 has vastly enhanced Marine aviation's ability to support the Ground Combat Element (GCE). Since the inception of MAWTS-1, Marine aviation has distinguished itself in operations in Grenada, Lebanon, Libya, Desert Shield/Storm, Somalia, Haiti, and the former Yugoslavia.

Lieutenant General Terrence R. Dake (Deputy Chief of Staff - Aviation).

The 31st Commandant, General Charles Krulak, stated that *"Aviation is fundamental to the future of the Marine Corps. Without the 'A' there is no MAGTF."* Marines pride themselves on being most ready when the nation is least ready. We are and will continue to be America's force of choice--a certain force for an uncertain world. As the world enters a new millennium, Marine aviation will continue to support the needs of our Corps and Country—in any clime and place.

Terrence R. Dake
Lieutenant General, US Marine Corps
Deputy Chief of Staff for Aviation

Contents

Introduction

Marine Aviation is uniquely Marine. Alone among the world's military services, the United States Marines are a true air-ground team built around one reserve and three active divisions paired with one reserve and three active air wings. Ask a Marine what he or she is, and the answer will be "Marine", not "pilot" or "infantryman". This common bond and focus begins with The Basic School, attended by all Marine Officers, where history and traditions are imbued in each individual. This shared heritage continues with aviators and ground officers serving together in staff positions, deploying together in Marine Air-Ground Task Forces (MAGTFs) and learning together in higher level schools. The result is a group of men and women devoted to a common purpose and known by the single name, Marine. Such has been the case since the Marine Corps obtained aircraft.

The advent of Marine aviation occurred simultaneously with the birth of the modern Marine Corps. Among the many famous battlefields of our Corps, none has more importance than the wheat fields around Belleau Wood in June of 1918. Winning them the sobriquet "Teufelhunden", or "Devildogs", the Marine Brigade's victories in northern France signaled the transformation of the Marine Corps from a small naval guard force to an expeditionary force capable of a wide range of military operations. Less well known is the fact that Marine aviation also premiered in World War I, beginning a Devildog aviation tradition noted for tactical innovation. This innovation characterized the Marine development of close air support, aerial re-supply, and air evacuation of ground forces during the "Banana Wars" in Central America and the Caribbean. The role of Marine aviation continued to grow larger with the great amphibious operations in the Pacific during World War II. In Korea, the refinement of Marine Air Ground operations was profoundly demonstrated by both fixed and rotary wing aircraft in the heroic defense of the Pusan perimeter and the introduction of the vertical assault. By Vietnam, Marine aviation had achieved equal partnership with the ground components of the Marine Air Ground Task Force. Following Vietnam, farsighted Marine leaders sought to capture the spirit of innovation that prevailed during the war and channel it into an institutionalized framework. This framework, as a result of Marine Aviation Readiness Project 19, came into existence as the Weapons and Tactics Squadron One (MAWTS-1).

Activated in 1978, MAWTS-1 is charged with managing the Weapons and Tactics Training Program, developing aviation tactics, and producing Weapons and Tactics Instructors (WTI's). The WTI's are men and women who are superb instructors, who understand tactics, both air and ground, who are skilled in mission planning, and who know threat capabilities cold. MAWTS-1 produces WTI's during the twice yearly Weapons and Tactics Instructor courses attended by students from all American military services and from selected foreign countries. The WTI course is the only true joint-combined graduate level school of aviation tactics in the United States.

Needless to say, WTI's and MAWTS-1 are near and dear to my heart. It has been over 15 years since I graduated in Weapons and Tactics Class 2-81, a class which represented the first generation of Marine aviators who, rather than learning tactics in the crucible of war, learned instead from the new institution of MAWTS-1 and the recently implemented Weapons and Tactics Training Program. In the years since, first as a squadron WTI, then as a WTI customer, a squadron Commanding Officer, and, finally, as the Commanding Officer of MAWTS-1, I have seen the value of MAWTS-1 in producing the instructors, both officer and enlisted, both men and women, who ensure Marine Aviation's Combat Readiness. The proof of MAWTS-1's value to the Marine Corps can be seen in those who have achieved fame in recent conflicts. Colonel Spot Kurth, winner of the Navy Cross in the Gulf War, was a WTI and MAWTS-1 instructor. Warrant Officer Mike Durrant, U.S. Army, who was a hero in Somalia, is a WTI and returns often to lecture at MAWTS-1. Major Joachim Malavet, a WTI and planner of the Captain Scott O'Grady rescue in Bosnia, is now a MAWTS-1 staff instructor.

Marines do not stand on past accomplishment, but eagerly look to the future. The beginning of a new era, known as the "End of the Long Peace" to the Europeans and as the "post-Cold War" to us Americans, has resulted in a shift of our nation's security paradigm. Our military missions, by necessity, are now more nebulous, our tasks less well defined, and our actions subject to more pronounced limitations. The hard truth remains that, even with the paradigm shift, Marines, sailors, airmen, and soldiers are subject to being wounded and killed in waging peace just as in waging war. This time of violent peace requires our military to conduct a wide range of missions. To meet their challenges, more than ever, WTI's with flexible, nimble, open minds are needed to assist in planning these wide ranging operations and in training our aviation units in all services and in providing the air leadership.

Today, Marines remain forward deployed worldwide. Some are aboard ships operating with both our Marine Expeditionary Units (Special Operations Capable) and our Navy Carrier Battle Groups. Others are flying from airfields on foreign shores ensuring that our Nation's security interests are defended and that hope and freedom are protected. From sea or shore bases, the training and spirit of the WTI's shape the actions of these forward deployed forces and thus help to ensure success to the Marines.

Colonel John G. Castellaw

Colonel John G. Castellaw (MAWTS -1 Commander) 1994-1996

PART 1
The United States Marine Corps

For 200 years, when it's come time to pay the price for the freedom we Americans enjoy, the United States Marines have always picked up the check. Painting by Colonel Charles Waterhouse (USMCR-ret.).

1

The United States Marine Corps

When America's leaders are confronted with a crisis that requires the possibility of military intervention, they are said to ask two questions: Where are the carriers? and; How quickly can we send in the Marines? The United States Marines are one of America's most formidable weapons; the most respected and feared amongst our enemies. *"Semper Fidelis or Semper Fi"—Always faithful,* suggests immediately that the Marines are a unique breed of Warfighters. In over two hundred and twenty years of advancements in warfighting doctrine and technology, the most lethal weapon in the American arsenal is still a Marine with a rifle.

The magnificent Iwo Jima memorial to the Marine Corps at Arlington National Park, Washington D.C. The inscription reads 'IN HONOR AND MEMORY TO THE MEN OF THE UNITED STATES MARINE CORPS WHO HAVE GIVEN THEIR LIVES TO THEIR COUNTRY SINCE 10 NOVEMBER 1775'

The entire Marine Corps is dedicated to supporting the Marine on the battlefield. Major General William H. Rupetus illustrates below, the Marines dedication to their most valued weapon. He recites the ethos that all Marines are taught to be a rifleman and are required to maintain proficiency with the current issue of rifle in the Corps.

"MY RIFLE"
The Creed of a United States Marine
By Major General William H. Rupetus, USMC.

This is my rifle. There are many like it, but this one is mine. My rifle is my best friend, it is my life. I must master it as I must master my life.

My rifle, without me is useless. Without my rifle, I am useless. I must fire my rifle true. I must shoot straighter than my enemy who is trying to kill me. I must shoot him before he shoots me. I will...

My rifle and myself know that what counts in this war is not the rounds we fire, the noise of our burst, nor the smoke we make. We know that it is the hits that count. We will hit...

My rifle is human, even as I, because it is my life. Thus, I will learn it as brother. I will learn its weaknesses, its strength, its parts, its accessories, its sights, and its barrel. I will ever guard it against the ravages of weather and damage as I will ever guard my legs, my arms, my eyes, and my heart against damage. I will keep my rifle clean and ready even as I am clean and ready. We will become part of each other. We will...

Before God I swear this creed. My rifle and myself are the defenders of my country. We are the master of our enemy. We are the saviors of my life. So be it, until victory is America's and there is no enemy, but Peace!

The M1 Garand rifle was one of the most significant developments in modern infantry warfare. A Garand in the hands of a United States Marine was the most feared weapon on the battlefield. All Marines, regardless of their Military Occupational Specialty (MOS), are trained to be riflemen. The M1 Garand was used by the Marines throughout World War II and Korea. The three M1 Garand rifles picutred are in the stacked arms position.

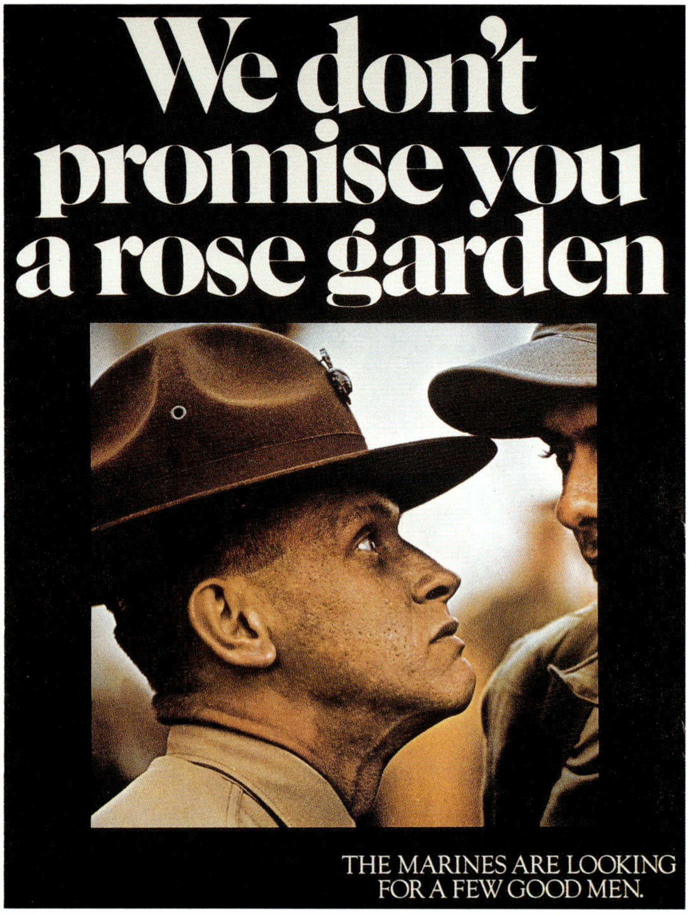

Origins & Battle History

In October 1775, a convened Second Continental Congress established a Naval Committee that was tasked with debating the merits of a proposition to create a Continental Navy and Marines.

The committee drafted a resolution to this effect, sponsored by John Adams, that established the Continental Marines and marked the birth date of the United States Marine Corps and on November 10, 1775, it was passed by Congress. It read:

> *- that two Battalions of Marines be raised consisting of one Colonel, two Lt.Colonels, two Majors & Officers as usual in other regiments, that they consist of an equal number of privates with other battalions; that particular care be taken that no person be appointed to office or inlisted into said battalions, but such as are good seamen, or so acquainted with maritime affairs as to be able to serve to advantage by sea, when required. That they be inlisted and commissioned for and during the present war between Great Britain and the colonies, unless dismissed by order of Congress. That they be distinguished by the names of first & second battalions of American Marines, and that they be considered a part of the number, which the continental Army before Boston is ordered to consist of.*

Serving on land and sea, these first Marines distinguished themselves in a number of important operations, including the Marines first amphibious raid into the Bahamas in March 1776, under the command of Captain Samuel Nicholas. Captain Nicholas was the first commissioned officer in the Continental Marines and remained the senior Marine officer throughout the American Revolution. Later promoted to Major, Nicholas is considered to be the first Marine Corps Commandant. The Treaty of Paris signed in April 1783 brought an end to the Revolutionary War and the existence of the Continental Navy and Marines.

Following the Revolutionary War and the formal re-establishment of the Marine Corps on July 11th, 1798, Marines saw action in the War with France (1798-1800) when they landed in Santo Domingo and took part in many operations against the Barbary pirates along the shores of Tripoli (1801-1815).

Marines participated in numerous naval operations during the War of 1812 as well as participating in the defense of Washington at Bladensburg, Maryland, in 1814 and fought alongside Andrew Jackson in the defeat of the British in New Orleans in 1815. The decades following the War of 1812 saw the Marines protecting American interests around the globe in the Caribbean (1821-1822), Falkland Islands (1832), Sumatra (1831-32), off the coast of West Africa (1820-61) and in operations against the Seminole Indians in Florida (1836-42).

During the Mexican War (1846-48), Marines seized enemy seaports on both the Gulf and Pacific Coasts. While landing parties of Marines and sailors were seizing enemy ports along the coast, a battalion of Marines joined General Scott's army at Puebla, fighting to the 'Halls of Montezuma' in Mexico City.

Marines served on land and sea in the Civil War (1861-1865). The primary participation of the Marines in the Civil War was with the Navy. A battalion of Marines fought at Bull Run. During the later part of the 19th century, Marines made numerous landings throughout the world, the heaviest action being in the Orient and in the Caribbean. Following the Spanish-American War (1898), the Marines performed with valor in Cuba, Puerto Rico, Guam, the Philippines, the Boxer Rebellion in China and other regions of Central America.

On a lighter note, during 1880, John Philip Sousa was appointed the band leader of the United States Marine Corps Band. Sousa transformed the band into a national treasure reflecting the pride of the Marine Corps, writing numerous marches for the Corps. His most famous was Semper Fidelis, the only march authorized for a branch of the American military service by Congress. Semper Fidelis was adopted as the Marine Corps motto in 1883. The inscription Semper Fidelis was put on a ribbon clenched in the *eagles* beak on the Marine emblem and has remained.

In World War I the Marine Corps distinguished itself on the battlefields of France as the 4th Marine Brigade and earned the title of 'Devil Dogs' for heroic actions in 1918. Marine Corps aviation played a part in this war effort, flying day bomber missions over France and Belgium. The Marines paid a heavy toll with more than a third of the 30,000 Marines killed or wounded in six months of intense fighting.

With the news of another island 'secure', the Marine infantryman of the Pacific theater raises a toast. Painting by Colonel Charles Waterhouse (USMCR ret.)

In the Pacific theater during World War II, the Marine Corps conducted a great many amphibious assaults on Japanese held islands. These now famous landings in places like Peleliu, Tarawa, Iwo Jima, Okinawa were almost always bloody, dangerous affairs and served to create the current Marine personna. Painting by Colonel Charles Waterhouse (USMCR ret.)

During the two decades before World War II, the Marine Corps began to develop in earnest its doctrine, equipment and the organization needed for amphibious warfare. The value of these efforts was later realized at battles on Guadalcanal, Bougainville, Tarawa, New Britain, Iwo Jima and Okinawa, to name a few.

On October 3, 1944, Admiral Nimitz was ordered to mount an invasion of Iwo Jima and Okinawa in early 1945. Iwo Jima was a Hell-hole for the Marines. The assault on Iwo Jima was code-named *'Detachment'*. The mission objective was to gain control of the two airfields on Iwo Jima and provide the U.S. Army Air Forces (AAF) with fighter bases. These fields were in an ideal location to provide escort services to B-29's and was an ideal emergency landing site for aircraft damaged over Japan.

The geography of Iwo Jima was less than ideal for an amphibious assault. Iwo Jima's terrain consisted of black volcanic ash, rocky hills, miles of beach and a six hundred foot mountain named Mount Suribachi. On the southern part of the island, on a plateau named Motoyama, were the airfields. The Japanese had fortified the island for nearly a year and amassed a troop force of more than 21,000 men. Knowing they would face superior naval and air forces, the Japanese commander General Kuribayashi de-

"The wind has just switched, breaking the sky over Suribachi into herringbone shapes. Then it is our turn, and we are transported to a different world. The mortars and machine guns follow us in. Suribachi looms gray, threatening and ugly. Everything is painted in a gray value scale of smoke, devoid of color except for violent flashes of light and flame, sound and fury blended into one continuous roar. And the sun does not shine". 'The Bar Man' painting and caption by Colonel Charles Waterhouse (USMCR ret.) from his masterpiece 'Marines and Others'.

vised a positional defense system, making it nearly impossible for anything other than small concentrated attack forces to approach the airfields.

The Japanese built hundreds of concrete blockhouses and thousands of emplacements and a network of thousands of caves as defense positions linked by tunnels to supply the troops.

On the morning of February 19, 1945, the 4th and 5th Marine Divisions moved toward the beaches of Iwo Jima. The Japanese troops held their fire until the initial assault wave was ashore. By nightfall, the Marine assault divisions established a beachhead approximately 3,000 yards long and up to 1,500 yards in depth. The Marines packed over thirty thousand

"No other winters were as cold or as bleak as those in Korea. The nights were long and bitter; and strong language, as well as bullets, are directed to the Chinese Communist troops surrounding the 1st Marine Division as they hold off, break through, and decimate several enemy divisions on their march to the sea." "Last of the Rear Guard" Painting and caption by Colonel Charles Waterhouse (USMCR-ret.).

men, armor and supplies into the beachhead while under intense artillery fire, while suffering nearly 2,300 casualties.

The Marines fought for every inch of the island for the next four days. On February 23, 1945, the Marines encountered heavy fighting as they approached Mount Suribachi. The 28th Marines sent patrols to the summit and captured Mount Suribachi. A small American flag was raised by the Marines to announce their success. Secretary of the Navy, James V. Forrestal, who was observing the operation said: "The rising of that flag on Suribachi means there will be a Marine Corps for the next five hundred years." Shortly after the first flag was raised, another patrol arrived at the summit and six Marines raised a larger flag. This is the historic scene captured by Associated Press photographer Joe Rosenthal. Two of the six Marines were later killed battling for control of Iwo Jima.

The fighting continued for two more weeks against relentless resistance of an opposing force ordered to die in place and kill as many Marines as they could. On March 16, 1945, the Marines gained control of Iwo Jima. General Kuribayashi's 21,000 men died in place as ordered. The Japanese killed nearly 26,000 Marines, 2,798 members of the Navy and 37 members of the Army. Admiral Nimitz reflected that on Iwo Jima; "uncommon valor was a common virtue".

By the end of the war in 1945, the Marine Corps had grown to include six divisions, five air wings and supporting troops attaining a strength of 485,113 personnel. Once again the Marines paid a heavy price. The war was tough on the Marines—87,000 dead and wounded, with eighty-one Marines earning the Medal of Honor, of which twenty-four Medals of Honor were awarded for valor at Iwo Jima.

While Marine units were taking part in post-war occupation of Japan and North China, studies were being conducted at the Marine base in Quantico, Virginia, to determine the advantages the helicopter would bring to the Corps warfighting doctrine.

In September, 1950, the Marines landed at Inchon, Korea, proving that the doctrine of amphibious assault was still viable and necessary. After the recapture of Seoul, the Marines advanced to the Chosin Reservoir only to see the Chinese Communists enter the war. Finally, in 1955, after years of offensives, counter-offensives, endless trench warfare and occupation duty, the last Marine ground troops were withdrawn from the Korean War effort, having more than 25,000 Marines killed or wounded.

In July 1958, a brigade-sized force landed in Lebanon to restore order. During the Cuban Missile Crisis in October 1962, a large Marine amphibious force was marshaled but not deployed. In April 1965, a brigade of Marines landed in the Dominican Republic to protect Americans and provide evacuation services.

The landing of the 9th Marine Expeditionary Brigade at DaNang in 1965 marked the beginning of Marine engagements in Vietnam. By the summer of 1968 following the enemy's Tet Offensive, the Marine Corps strength in Vietnam rose to a peak of approximately 85,000. The Marine withdrawal began in 1969 as the South Vietnamese began to assume a larger role in the fighting. The Vietnam War was the Marine Corps longest engagement, killing well over 13,000 Marines and wounding in excess of 85,000.

In July 1974, the Marines aided in the evacuation of U.S. Citizens and foreign nationals during the unrest in Cyprus. The following year the Marines evacuated embassy staffs, American citizens and refugees in Phnom Penh, Cambodia and Saigon. During May 1975, the Marines played an integral role in the rescue of the crew of the SS *Mayaguez* captured off the coast of Cambodia.

The later part of the 1970's saw the Marine Corps assume an increasingly significant role in defending NATO's northern flank as amphibious unites of the 2nd Marine Division participated in exercises throughout northern Europe. The Marine Corps also played a key role in the development of the Rapid Deployment Force, a multi-service organization created to insure a flexible, timely military response around the world when needed. The Maritime Propositioning Ships (MPS) concept was developed to enhance this capability by pre-staging equipment needed for combat in the vicinity of the designated area of operations, and reduce response time as Marines travel by air to linkup with MPS assets.

Marines fought honorably in our country's longest war. "The M60 in Nam" commemorates their sacrifices. Painting by Colonel Charles Waterhouse (USMCR-ret.).

In many respects, the Korean conflict was no different than those before, or since - Marines fought bravely in the most adverse of conditions, and died. In total the conflict cost America 4,262 of it's finest Marines. Their spirit can be seen in "Flanker on the March to Hungnam", a painting by Colonel Charles Waterhouse (USMCR- ret.).

The 1980's brought an increasing number of terrorist attacks on U.S. embassies around the world. Marine Security Guards, under the direction of the State Department, continued to serve with distinction in the face of this challenge. In August 1982, Marine units landed at Beirut, Lebanon, as part of the multi-national peace-keeping force. For the next nineteen months these units faced the hazards of their mission with courage and professionalism. In October 1983, Marines took part in the highly successful, short-notice intervention in Grenada.

As the decade of the 1980's came to a close, Marines were summoned to respond to instability in Central America. Operation Just Cause was launched in Panama in December 1989 to protect American lives and restore the democratic process in that nation.

Less than a year later, in August 1990, the Iraqi invasion of Kuwait set in motion events that would lead to the largest movement of Marine Corps forces since World War II. Between August 1990 and January 1991, some 24 infantry battalions, 40 squadrons, and more than 92,000 Marines deployed to the Persian Gulf as part of Operation Desert Shield. Operation Desert Storm was launched 16 January 1991, the day the air campaign began. The main attack came overland beginning February 24th when the 1st and 2nd Marine Divisions breached the Iraqi defense lines and stormed into occupied Kuwait. Meanwhile, the threat from the sea in the form of two Marine Expeditionary Brigades held in check some 50,000 Iraqis along

Crewman of UH-1 stand beside their aircraft before a flight from MCAS Yuma.

Marine at the ready during exercises at The Basic School located at Quantico, Virginia.

Section of slick (unarmed) F/A-18 Hornets with the 'Red Devils' of VMFA-232 over the Pacific Ocean during an air combat maneuvering training sortie. The Hornet serves in Marine fighter/attack units that are designated (VMFA).

the Kuwait coast. By the morning of February 28, one hundred hours after the ground war began, almost the entire Iraqi Army in the Kuwaiti theater of operations had been encircled with 4,000 tanks destroyed and forty-two divisions destroyed or rendered ineffective.

Overshadowed by the events in the Persian Gulf during 1990-91 were a number of other significant Marine deployments demonstrating the Corps flexible and rapid response capabilities. Included among these were the non-combatant evacuation operations in Liberia and Somalia to rescue civilians and diplomats, as well as humanitarian lifesaving operations in Bangladesh, the Philippines and Northern Iraq.

In December 1992, Marines landed in Somalia marking the beginning of a two-year humanitarian relief operation in that famine-stricken and strife-torn nation. In another part of the world, land and carrier-based Marine Corps fighter-attack squadrons and electronic warfare aircraft supported Operation Deny Flight in the no-fly zone over Bosnia-Herzegovina. During April 1994, Marines once again demonstrated their ability to protect American citizens in remote parts of the world when a Marine task force evacuated 142 citizens from Rwanda in response to civil unrest in that country.

Closer to home, Marines went ashore in September 1994 at Cap Haitian, Haiti, as part of the U.S. force participating in the restoration of democracy in that country. During this same period Marines were actively engaged in providing assistance to the Nation's counter-drug effort, assisting in battling wild fires in the western United States, and aiding in flood and hurricane relief operations.

Today's Marine Corps stands ready to continue in the proud tradition of those who so valiantly fought and died at Belleau Wood, Iwo Jima, Chosin and Khe Sanh. As stated by the Corps' 31st Commandant, General Charles C.Krulak:

"*Our warfighting legacy is one of duty, strength, sacrifice, discipline, and determination. These themes are cornerstones of the individual Marine and of our Corps. Indeed, they are woven into the very fabric of our battle color. However, while we reflect on our past, let us also rededicate ourselves to a future of improvement. For, as good as we are now, we must be better tomorrow. The challenges of today are the opportunities of the 21st century. Both will demand much of us all.*"

It is impossible to do justice to the many accomplishments, sacrifices and valor of the Marines in this short space. The Marines are a proud group of warfighters—they have earned that pride in blood. Marines have indeed earned the respect of friend and foe. Every American can be proud

The most dangerous weapon in the world - a Marine and his rifle. Battle tested, combat proven in places like Belleau Wood, Tarawa, Iwo Jima, the Chosin Resevoir, Khe San and Khafji.

Fighter Pilot, Warrior, Marine Aviator. Unlike other services, every Marine aviator is first schooled as an infantry platoon leader, capable of leading Marines in combat. The emphasis on understanding the role and requirements of the ground combat element remains with every aviator throughout their career. It is what separates Marine Air and its aviators from every other military organization.

"The Strife is O'er, the Battle Done" - This subject was commissioned by a major veterans publication as a cover to commemorate the end of the war (World War II). It shows a Marine, head bowed, face reflecting the exhaustion and relief he feels upon hearing that the battle is truly done, and the war is finally over. The original sketch was designed with the kneeling Marine, and a large, smoldering pillbox, with some legs in the smoke. It was suggested that I remove the pillbox and legs, and put a tank in the background instead — and that I should also get rid of the rifle. I could go along with all the suggestions except for the rifle, which needed to stay for a couple of good reasons. First, a Marine's rifle is his best friend and constant companion, and to be caught without it could result in a deck court martial. Second, it made for a vital counterpoint of composition. The statement "there are no atheists in foxholes" may not be a valid one for everyone. It is for the artist, however; and every area of this painting — the composition, color, mood and gesture — mirror personal experience of his direct conversations with God in situations of this nature. Caption and painting by Colonel Charles Waterhouse (USMCR - ret.).

that people of such uncommon valor are commonly found in the United States Marines—that our values, way of life and freedom are guarded by the Corps.

History has shown that after the heat of battle subsides, the cry again rises for less military spending and cutbacks. The Marine Corps is America's best bang for the buck. They are lean and mean and maximize every American's taxpayer dollar. Marines take what they get, integrate it into the Corps, add their Esprit-de Corps, and the result is the greatest group of warfighters on the globe. Combining a long and proud heritage of faithful service with the leadership and resolve to face tomorrow's challenges will keep the Marine Corps the "best of the best."

The official seal of the United States Marine Corps

The Eagle: Representing America
The Globe: Representing The Marines Global Commitment
The Anchor:: Representing The Marines Sea Traditions

An Overview Of The United States Marine Corps Organization Is Outlined On The Proceeding Pages

The Marine Hymn
Arranged by John W. Schaum
Official Song of United States Marine Corps

From the halls of Montezuma
To the shores of Tripoli;
We fight our country's battles
In the air, on land and sea.

First to fight for right and freedom
And to keep our honor clean,
We are proud to claim the title
Of United States Marines.

Our flags un-furl'd to every breeze
From dawn to setting sun;
We have fought in every clime and place
Where we could take a gun.
In the snow of far-off northern lands
And in sunny tropic scenes,
You will find us always on the job
The United States Marines.

Here's health to you and to our Corps
Which we are proud to serve;
In many a strife we've fought for life
And never lost our nerve.
If the Army and the Navy
Ever gaze on Heaven's scenes,
They will find the streets are guarded
By United States Marines

Marine Corps Total Force

Active: 174,883
*Reserve: 42,077
FY 1996 Total: 216,960

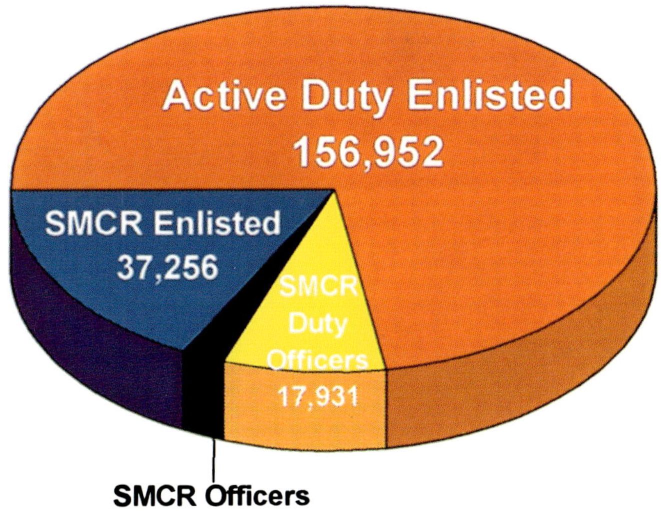

Marine Corps Reserve

FY 1996 Ready Reserve Total 101,358

FY 1996 IRR Total: 59,281
FY 1996 SMCR Total: 42,077

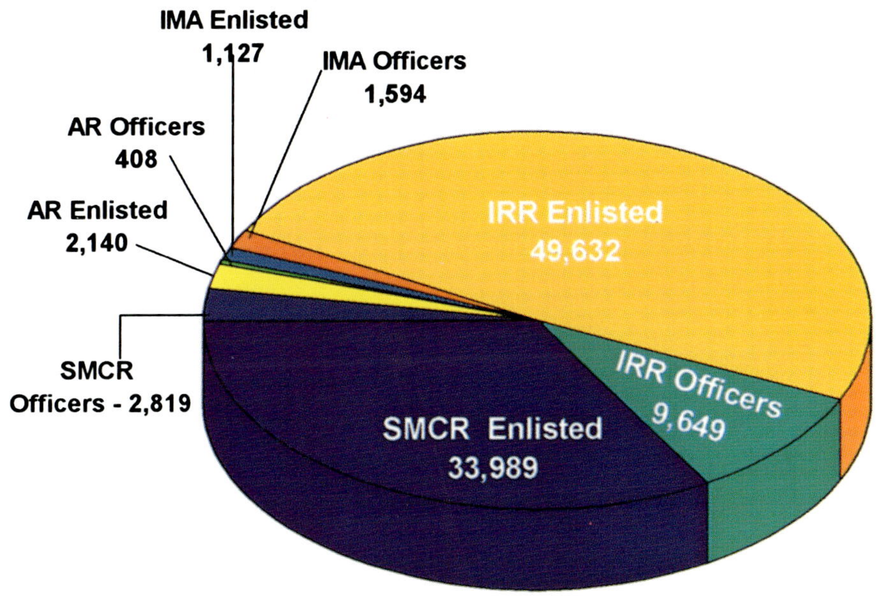

Major Marine Corps Installations

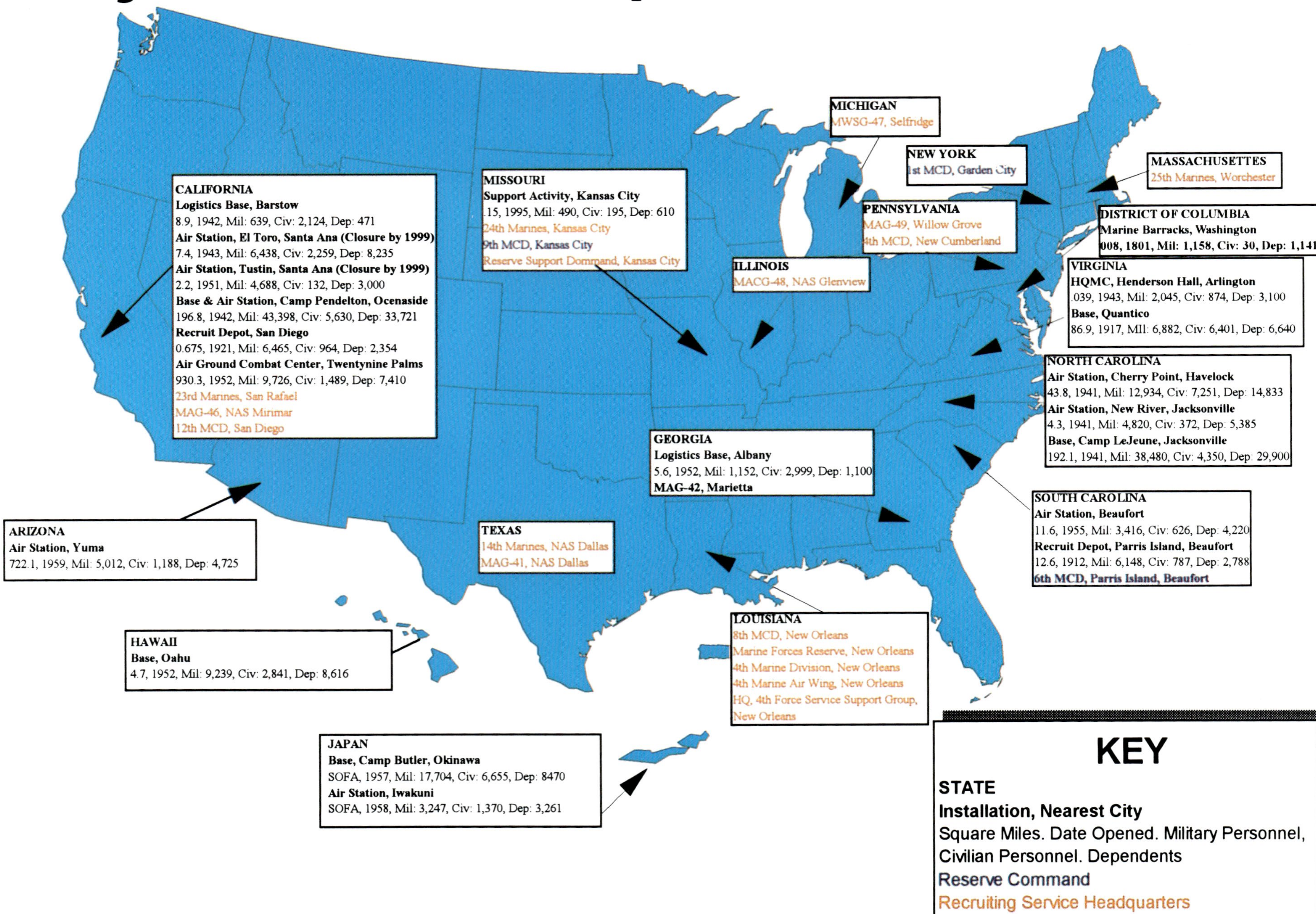

U.S. Marine Forces ATLANTIC

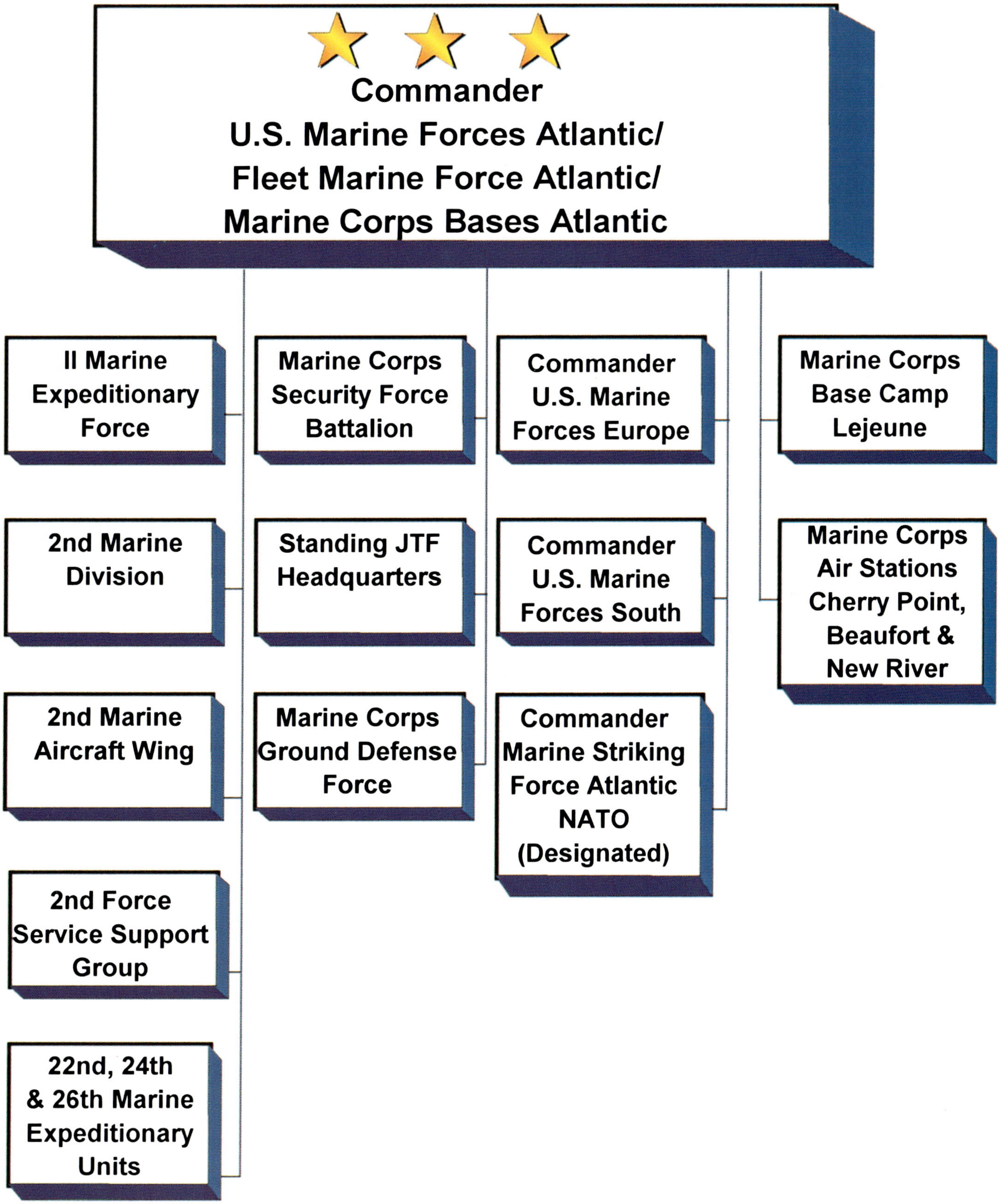

U.S. Marine Forces PACIFIC

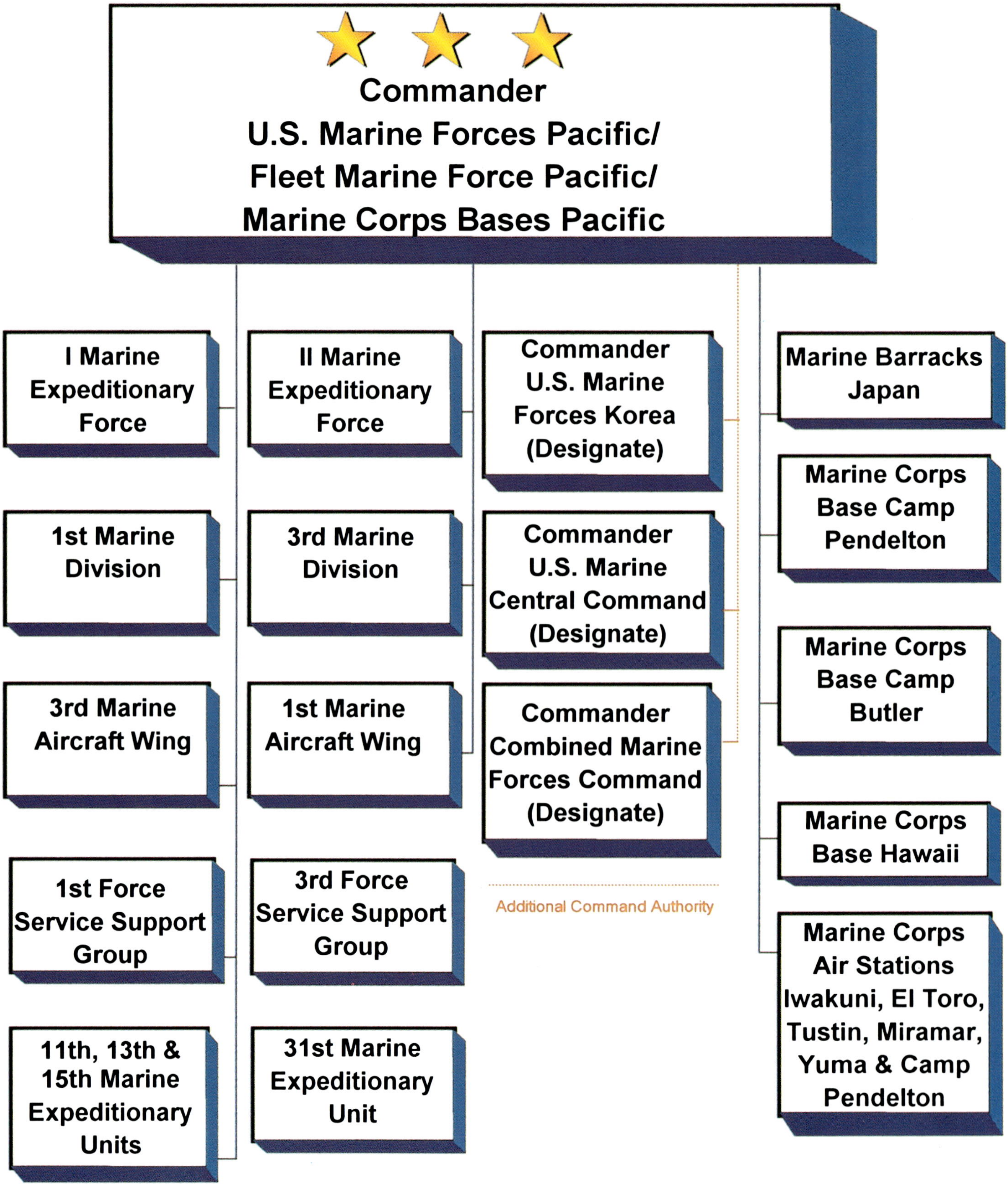

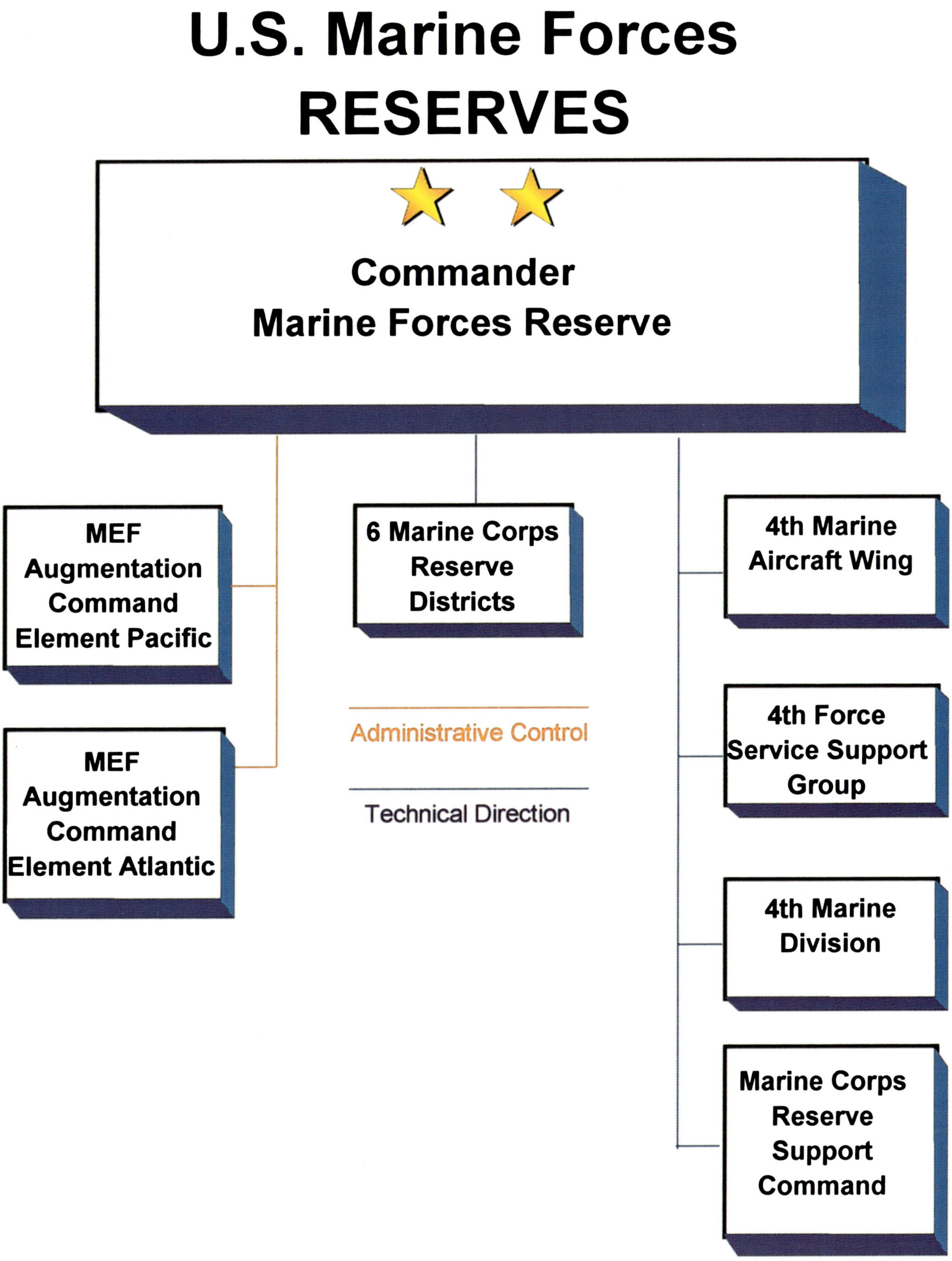

U.S. Marine Forces
RESERVES
Commander
Marine Forces Reserve
MEF Augmentation Command Element Pacific
MEF Augmentation Command Element Atlantic
6 Marine Corps Reserve Districts
Administrative Control
Technical Direction
4th Marine Aircraft Wing
4th Force Service Support Group
4th Marine Division
Marine Corps Reserve Support Command

Supporting Establishments

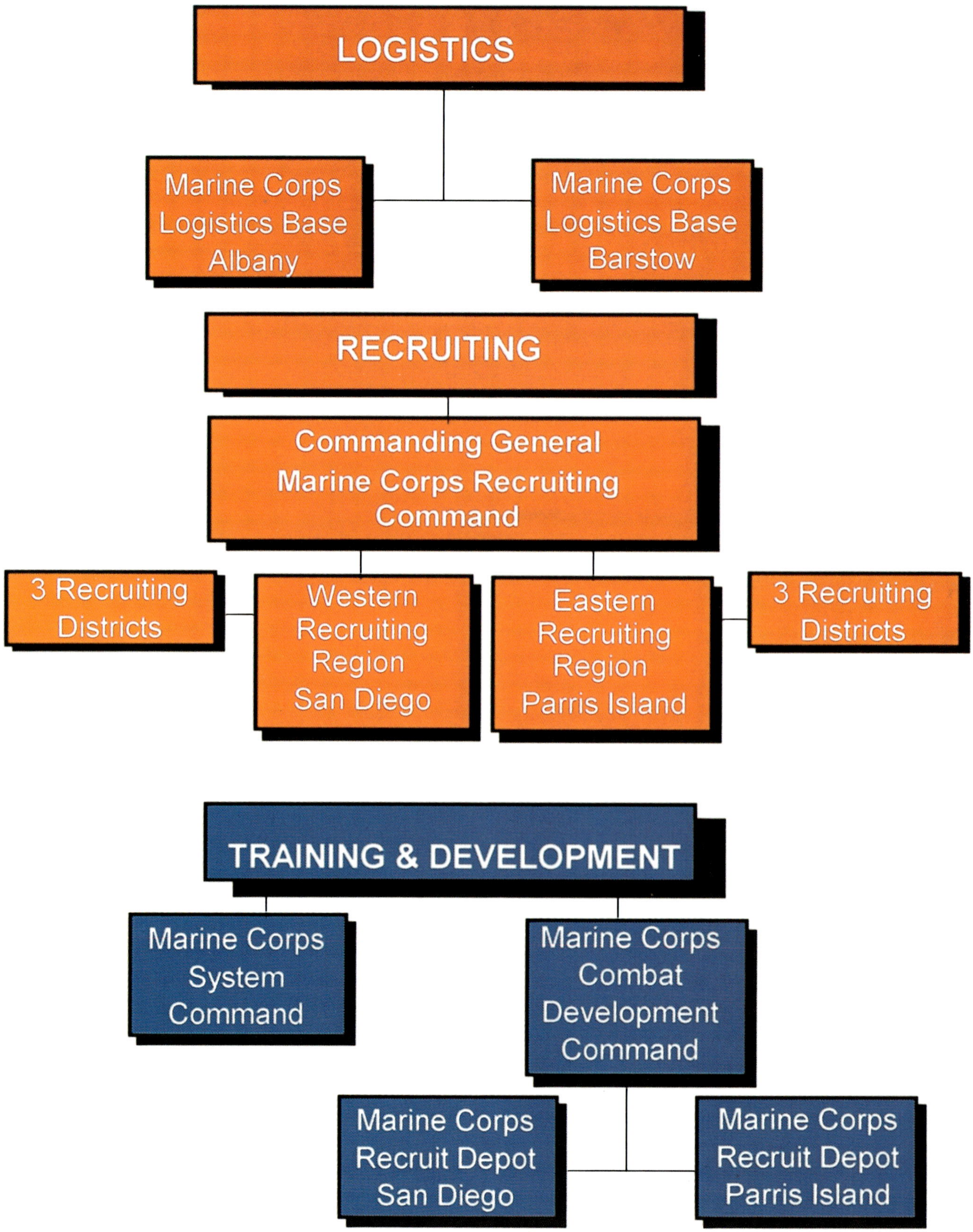

STATES MARINE CORPS

Commandants
United States Marine Corps

1st	Maj Samuel Nicholas	1775-1781	17th	LtGen Thomas Holcomb	1936-1943
2nd	LtCol William Ward Burrows	1798-1804	18th	Gen Alexander Vanderfrift	1944-1947
3rd	LtCol Franklin Wharton	1804-1818	19th	Gen Clifton B. Cates	1948-1951
4th	LtCol Anthony Gale	1819-1820	20th	Gen Lemuel C. Shepherd Jr.	1952-1955
5th	Col Archibald Henderson	1820-1859	21st	Gen Randolph McCall Pate	1956-1959
6th	Col John Harris	1859-1864	22nd	Gen David M. Shoup	1960-1963
7th	BGen Jacob Zeilin	1864-1876	23rd	Gen Wallace M. Greene Jr.	1968-1971
8th	Col Charles G. McCawley	1876-1891	24th	Gen Leonard F. Chapman Jr.	1968-1971
9th	MajGen Charles Heywood	1891-1903	25th	Gen Robert E. Cushman Jr.	1972-1975
10th	MajGen George Elliott	1903-1910	26th	Gen Louis H. Wilson	1975-1979
11th	MajGen William P. Biddle	1911-1914	27th	Gen Robert H. Barrow	1979-1983
12th	MajGen George Barnett	1914-1920	28th	Gen Paul X. Kelly	1983-1987
13th	MajGen John A Lejeune	1920-1929	29th	Gen Alfred M. Gray	1987-1991
14th	MajGen Wendell Neville	1929-1930	30th	Gen Carl E. Mundy Jr.	1991-1955
15th	MajGen Ben H. Fuller	1930-1934	31st	Gen Charles C.Krulak	1995-Present
16th	MajGen John H. Russell	1934-1936			

Sergeants Major of the Marine Corps

1st	SgtMaj Wilber Bestwick	1957 - 1959
2nd	SgtMaj Francis D. Ruber	1959 - 1962
3rd	SgtMaj Thomas J. McHugh	1962 -1965
4th	SgtMaj Herbert J. Sweet	1965 - 1969
5th	SgtMaj Joseph W. Dailey	1969 - 1973
6th	SgtMaj Clinton A. Puckett	1973 - 1975
7th	SgtMaj Henry H. Black	1975 - 1977
8th	SgtMaj John R. Massaro	1977 - 1979
9th	SgtMaj Leland D. Crawford	1979 - 1983
10th	SgtMaj Robert E. Cleary	1983 - 1987
11th	SgtMaj David W. Sommers	1987 - 1991
12th	SgtMaj Harold G. Overstreet	1991 - 1995
13th	SgtMaj Lewis G. Lee	1995 - present

HISTORY

Award, Campaign, Service and Expeditionary Streamer Entitlement to the Battle Colors of the Marine Corps

1. Presidential Unit Citation (Navy) Streamer with six silver and two bronze stars
2. Presidential Unit Citation (Army) Streamer with one silver oak leaf cluster
3. Joint Meritorious Unit Award
4. Navy Unit Commendation Streamer with 25 silver stars
5. Valorous Unit Award (Army)
6. Meritorious Unit Commendation (Navy-Marine Corps) Streamer
7. Meritorious Unit Commendation(Army) Streamer
8. Revolutionary War Streamer
9. Quasi-War with France Streamer
10. Barbary Wars Streamer
11. War of 1812 Streamer
12. African Slave Trade Streamer
13. Operations Against West Indian Pirates Streamer
14. Indian Wars Streamer
15. Mexican War Streamer
16. Civil War Streamer
17. Marine Corps Expeditionary Streamer with 12 silver stars, one bronze star, and one silver "W"
18. Spanish American Streamer
19. Philippine Campaign Streamer
20. China Relief Expedition Streamer
21. Cuban Pacification Streamer
22. Nicaraguan Campaign Streamer
23. Mexican Service Streamer
24. Haitian Campaign Streamer with one bronze star
25. Dominican Campaign Streamer
26. World War I Victory Streamer with one silver and one bronze star, one Maltese Cross, and Siberia and West Indies Clasp
27. Army of Occupation of Germany Streamer
28. Second Nicaraguan Campaign Streamer
29. Yangtze Service Streamer
30. China Service Streamer with one bronze star
31. American Defense Streamer with one bronze star
32. American Campaign Streamer
33. European-African-Middle Eastern Campaign Streamer with one silver and four bronze stars
34. Asiatic-Pacific Campaign Streamer with eight silver, and two bronze stars
35. World War II Victory Streamer
36. Navy Occupation Service Streamer with "Europe" and "Asia"
37. National Defense Service Streamer with two bronze stars.
38. Korean Service Streamer with two silver stars
39. Armed Forces Expeditionary Streamer with four silver stars and two bronze stars.
40. Vietnam Service Streamer with three silver and two bronze stars
41. Southwest Asia Service Streamer with three bronze stars
42. Philippine Defense Streamer with one bronze star
43. Philippine Liberation Streamer with two bronze stars
44. Philippine Independence Streamer
45. French Croix De Guerre Streamer with two palms and one gilt star
46. Philippine Presidential Unit Citation Streamer with two bronze stars
47. Korean Presidential Unit Citation Streamer
48. Republic of Vietnam Armed Forces Meritorious Unit Citation of the Gallantry Cross with Palm
49. Republic of Vietnam Meritorious Unit Citation Civil Actions Streamer with Palm

Official Photo—U.S. Marine Corps

Official Photo—U.S. Marine Corps

All photos official and by authority of U.S. Marine Corps

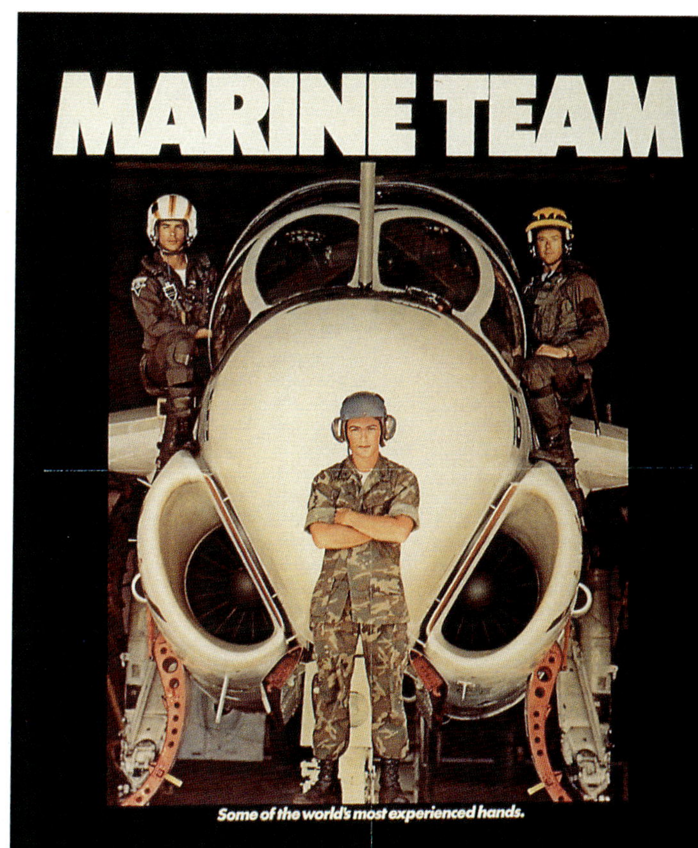

2

The Marine Air-Ground Task Force (MAGTF) - America's 911 Force

The U.S. Marine Corps is unique among military organizations and to fully understand the capabilities, mission and role of today's modern Marine Corps, a thorough look must be taken at its organizational structure. This uniqueness comes from their ability to wield a highly capable, integrated, single force consisting of combined air, ground and support elements that can fulfill the mission requirement independently, and in the most difficult of circumstances. Herein also lies its greatest strength, which is its unparalleled flexibility to respond to a wide variety of situations immediately, hence the Corps distinction as ***America's 911 Force***. Based on the proven track record of the Marines, one of the first questions asked by senior government officials in times of crisis is, "Where is the nearest MAGTF (Marine Air-Ground Task Force)?"

Soldiers of the Sea

The Marines have always been, and will continue to be an expeditionary force. This means the Corps must be prepared to conduct the full range of

F/A-18D with the 'Moonlighters' of VMFA (AW) - 332 banking sharply over the Atlantic Ocean. At the controls are Major R. "Moose" Shayne (pilot), and Captain Steve "Gargoyle" Hoyle (weapons sensors officer). The multi-mission Delta provides the MAGTF with a variety of capabilities in either the fighter or attack role, as well as reconnaissance.

The USS Nassau with CH-46's, UH-1's, CH-53's and AV-8B's on deck. Amphibious Ready Groups (ARG) are highly mobile, and are home to Marine Expeditionary Units (MEU) that project American power when and where needed.

combat operations in a forward area where there may be little, if any, U.S. presence. Often serving aboard U.S. Navy ships, the Marines are also, by nature, amphibians, i.e., soldiers of the sea. More often than not, Marines will begin their combat operations from seaborne platforms, and once having established a land presence by securing a beachhead, move forward from there. Operating in this environment presents challenges both operationally and logistically unlike those faced by most other modern military organizations. To the Marines, this forms the basis for how they are organized, how they train and how they select and utilize their weapons.

Organization

The Marine Corps combat operating forces are basically divided into two areas, Marine Forces Atlantic (COMMARFORLANT) and Marine Forces Pacific (COMMARFORPAC). Under the Atlantic Forces is the II Marine Expeditionary Force located at facilities within both North and South Carolina. The Pacific Forces are I Marine Expeditionary Force in California and III Marine Expeditionary Force in a forward deployed manner in Okinawa and Japan.

Under current American Department of Defense plans, the defense of US interests worldwide is based on the geographic segmentation of what are called CINC's (Commander in Chiefs). Large segments of the globe are partitioned with senior most officers responsible for all American combat forces in the given area of responsibility as tasked by the Joint Chiefs Of Staff under direct authority of the President.

There are five major CINC's which are USCINCA (United States Proper), USCINCEUR (Europe), USCINCSOUTH (South America), USCINCPAC (Pacific) and USCINCCENT (Mid-East). The Marine Corps provides the forward presence, crisis response and fighting power available to the CINC's. Marine Forces, Atlantic (COMMARFORLANT) supports USCINCA, USCINCEUR and USCINCSOUTH. Similarly, Marine Forces, Pacific (COMMARFORPAC) supports USCINCPAC and USCICNCENT.

The Marines are organized in a manner consistent with their primary requirement—which is to be ready to meet any threat or fulfill any mission immediately, to be a force in a constant state of readiness. As such, they are basically divided into three major categories.

*** Reserves**
*** Supporting Establishment**
*** Operating Forces**

Reserves - As an organization which expands the Marines total force structure, the reserves, like the active duty, consist of a balanced force of assets. Reserve units are present in ground, aviation and combat service support units. The quality and warfighting capability of these reserve units is extremely high and as such, they can supplement and reinforce active units in case of conflict.

Supporting Establishment - As the name implies, this organization with over 30,000 Marines provides a full range of support to the Corps. This includes staff personnel at the major Marine facilities, and also, support through the Recruiting, Combat Development and Systems Commands in addition to that provided to Headquarters, U.S. Marine Corps.

Operating Forces - This is the major element of the Marine Corps and represents the vast majority of its assets. In fact, seventy percent of all the Marines active duty forces are assigned to the three elements of the Operating Forces.

Table 1- Three Elements of the U.S. Marine Corps Operating Forces

Marine Corps Security Forces
Marine Security Guard Battalion
Fleet Marine Forces

Marine Corps Security Forces (MCSF) - These include roughly 4,000 Marines that are located at naval installations and in detachments aboard U.S. naval vessels in order to provide and maintain the highest level of security. In addition, the MCSF contains a Fleet Anti-terrorism Security Team (FAST). The FAST unit can deploy to high threat locations, provide security for nuclear fueling operations, and respond to any crises.

Marine Security Guard Battalion - These detachments of Marines are responsible for protecting 127 American embassies and consulates in 115 different countries around the globe.

The Fleet Marine Force (FMF) - The FMF is the highest structure and consists of a balanced force of land, air and service support elements. The FMF provides its actual operating forces through its Marine Air-Ground Task Forces, or MAGTF's (pronounced mag-taff). The MAGTF consists of combined arms made up of infantry, artillery, aviation, reconnaissance, engineer and logistical components. These individual elements are taken from Marine Divisions (MarDiv's), Marine Air Wings (MAW's), and Force Service Support Groups (FSSG's). The MAGTF's are formed based on the specific tasks of a given mission and are not permanent entities since they are dissolved once the mission is completed.

The MAGTF is a complete package of forces which can be totally self sufficient, but also being able to be integrated into a larger joint, naval or combined force. Rarely will a MAGTF act in a completely isolated manner. Fast reaction to crisis situations makes the MAGTF an important tool and its flexible organization allows the MAGTF to effectively complete the tasked mission.

MARINES
156469

CH-46E Sea Knight with HMM-263 skirts just above the waves near it's home base at MCAS New River, the home of Marine Air Group's 26 and 29. This low level maneuver is used when Marine forces conduct a water insertion.

The many hard-fought lessons learned in the Pacific during the Second World War were instrumental in forming the basis for today's Marine combat strategy and organization. The first modern MAGTF was formed in 1950. The First Provisional Marine Brigade, which was comprised of the 5th Marines, Marine Air Group thirty three (MAG-33), and its supporting forces were a critical element in the defense of the Pusan area in Korea. This successful fledgling outfit became the model for the modern MAGTF.

Every MAGTF consists of four elements, are expeditionary in nature and are detailed in the table below :

Table 2 - MAGTF Structure

Command Element
Ground Combat Element
Aviation Combat Element
Combat Service Support Element

Command Element (CE) - Provides command, control and coordination for planning and execution of operations. The CE will include communications and radio battalions, force reconnaissance, remotely piloted vehicle (RPV), intelligence, and air/naval gunfire liaison companies, counterintelligence teams and platoons for tactical deception, topography and interrogation.

Ground Combat Element (GCE) - Conducts all ground operations in support of the MAGTF mission and is formed around infantry organizations and reinforced with artillery, reconnaissance, armor and engineer forces. The GCE can vary in size and composition from small teams to one or more Marine Divisions and include normally three infantry and one artillery regiments, tank, light armor infantry, assault amphibian, combat engineer and reconnaissance battalions.

Aviation Combat Element (ACE) - Conducts air operations in support of the MAGTF mission. It is formed around an aviation headquarters and can vary in size from an aviation detachment to one or more Marine Aircraft Wings. Assets of the ACE include both rotary and fixed wing Marine Aircraft Groups (MAG's), a Marine Air Control Group (MACG), Marine Wing Support Group (MWSG) and refueler transport aircraft along with tactical electronic warfare aircraft.

Combat Service Support Element (CSSE) - Provides the full range of combat service support functions. It is formed around a combat service support headquarters and may vary in size and composition from a support detachment to one or more Force Service Support Groups. Typically, the CSSE includes battalions for maintenance, engineer support, supply, motor transport, landing support and medical/dental.

There are three different types of MAGTF's: the Marine Expeditionary Force (MEF) and with it, the Marine Expeditionary Brigade, also known as the (MEF fwd); Marine Expeditionary Unit (and the Special Operations Capable MEU (SOC); and the Special Purpose MAGTF, each of which are expeditionary forces.

Table 3 - Types of MAGTF's*

(1) Marine Expeditionary Force (MEF) - The principal warfighting organization, usually commanded by a Lieutenant General and can vary in size from less than one, to multiple divisions and aircraft wings. By far the MEF is the largest of all MAGTF types and is designed to deploy in a self sufficient manner for at least sixty days. A subset of the MEF is the Marine Expeditionary Brigade (MEB). Normally the MEB consists of a reinforced infantry unit, a single air group and a brigade service support group. The MEB serves as a forward echelon portion of a MEF and can remain in a forward deployed position for an extended period of time. The designation of the MEB has recently been changed to MEF (Forward). The MEF (Forward) is larger than a Marine Expeditionary Unit, but smaller than an MEF. It is usually employed as the forward echelon of an MEF.

(2) Marine Expeditionary Unit (MEU) - The MEU consists typically of an infantry battalion, a composite helicopter squadron that includes fixed wing assets (usually six AV-8B's) and a command and control element. Usually, a MEU is commanded by a Colonel. This is by far the most common type of MAGTF and is the one normally deployed continuously aboard amphibious ships stationed in the Mediterranean Sea and Pacific Ocean while also visiting the Caribbean Sea and Indian Ocean.

MEU Special Operations Capable MEU (SOC) - All forward deployed MEU's have completed highly specialized training and are designated Special Operations Capable, or MEU (SOC). Some of the capabilities of MEU (SOC's) include noncombatant evacuation operations and other selected maritime special purpose missions. These missions, both general purpose expeditionary missions and special operations tasks require rapid planning. The scope of the effort in terms of support, operational reach and coverage is what determines the special operations capability.

(3) Special Purpose MAGTF (SPMAGTF) - The Special Purpose MAGTF is utilized to fulfill very specific missions in which either a MEU or a MEF would be too large for. They are capable of handling a wide range of duties and are distinguished on a geographic basis

To fully understand how the MAGTF is able to fulfill its 'force in readiness', rapid response commitments regardless of the exact nature of the specific mission, a closer look at the composition of the most common MAGTF, the MEU, is essential.

Table 4 - MEU Composition

(1) Command Element - This includes the MEU headquarters.

(2) Aviation Combat Element - Every ACE contains a Composite Squadron which is based around the Marine Medium Lift Helicopter (HMM) squadron. The Composite Squadron designated HMM (REIN) contains both aircraft and detachments from four support squadrons:

A. Aircraft

Aircraft	Number
CH-46E	**12**
CH-53E	**4**
AH-1W	**4**
UH-1N	**3**
AV-8B	**6**

B. Support Squadron Detachments

MATCS (Marine Air Traffic Control Squadron) - Establish and control expeditionary airfields.

MACS (Marine Air Control Squadron) - Establish and control all aircraft movement from ship to shore and inland areas.

LAAD (Low Altitude Air Defense) - Defend the MEU and its assets from enemy air threats with shoulder fired Stinger missiles.

MWSS (Marine Wing Support Squadron) - Establish remote refueling sites.

(3) Ground Combat Element - Reinforced Battalion which includes:

-Infantry Battalion (3 rifle Companies, 1 weapons Company)
-Artillery battery (7 M198 Howitzers)
-Tank Platoon (4 M1A1 tanks)
-Reconnaissance Platoon
-Engineering Platoon
-Light Armored Vehicle (LAV) Platoon - 7 LAV's

(4) MEU Service Support Group - Consists of detachments from the following:

Supply Battalion	Engineer Battalion	Motor Transport Battalion
Dental/Medical Battalion	Maintenance Battalion	Landing Support Battalion

The MAGTF Characteristics and Capabilities

The primary characteristics of the MAGTF are:

* Readiness for Expeditionary Service
* Strategically Mobile - deployable by amphibious shipping, strategic airlift, and sea lift
* Capability for Forcible Entry - when deployed upon amphibious shipping, the MAGTF will need this capability to launch an amphibious assault
* Capability for Independent Action
* Sea, Land and Air Coordination
* Flexible
* Logistically Balanced
* Achieve Tactical Surprise
* Forward and Sea Based
* Compatibility with Naval, Joint and Combined Operations

There are a number of consistent capabilities that each type of MAGTF has regardless of its exact order of battle and size. Current Marine literature states them as follows:

The potent AH-1W serves as the dedicated assault support attack gunship operating from amphibious assault ships.

* Operate as a component of a joint task force
* The ability to enter a battle at night
* Operate under adverse weather conditions
* Operate from over the horizon
* Seek out, engage, destroy or capture the enemy in a rural or urban environment
* Conduct operations in hostile nuclear, biological and chemical environments

As stated previously, but worth repeating, the basic underlying characteristic of the MAGTF is the ability to conduct the full range of combat operations for indefinite, i.e., significant periods of time as an expeditionary force. As such, the ability of the MAGTF to be self sufficient or sustainable is critical to its success. Each of the three major MAGTF's are assigned the necessary supplies to last a pre-determined period of time.

Table 5 - MAGTF Sustainability

Marine Expeditionary Force (MEF) - 60 days
Marine Expeditionary Unit (MEU) - 15 days
Special Purpose MAGTF - As the given situation demands

The Marine Corps has developed the Maritime Pre-positioning Forces (MPF) program which enhances the MAGTF's ability to be as responsive as possible. Under the MPF program, three squadrons are located within over a dozen Navy vessels and are strategically positioned within the Mediterranean Sea and both the Indian and Pacific Oceans. This ingenious program places, in a forward position, the necessary equipment and supplies to support a 17,000 Marine force for 30 days. With the assistance of KC-130 aircraft, supplies can also be positioned to a specific area. As the Marines demonstrated in the early stages of Operation Desert Shield, this can be invaluable in formulating a credible combat ready force immediately.

Amphibious Ready Groups (ARG)

As stated previously, the Marine Corps maintains its critical status as America's 'force in readiness' for deployment at a moment's notice anywhere on the globe. To accomplish this, the MAGTF relies on the U.S. Navy's fleet of amphibious assault ships, of which there are over thirty-five. These ships are deployed in units of between three and five in what is called Amphibious Ready Groups, or ARG's. To maintain the three MEU's which must be continuously deployed, a total of twelve ARG's are required.

Table 6 - Types of Large Deck Amphibious Assault Ships (Amphib's)

(1) Helicopter, Dock Landing (LHD)
(2) Helicopter, Attack Landing (LHA)
(3) Helicopter, Landing Platform (LPH)

The official magazine of the U.S. Marine Corps, *Marines*, defines the mission of each of ARG's and these three types of ships as being "to *transport and land assault forces ashore by use of Landing Crait Air Cushion (LCAC), conventional landing craft and helicopters. The main purpose of forward deployed ARG's and the three MEU's that they carry is to be ready to wage war, or enforce peace, before a crisis develops into a conflict*".

Section of AV-8B Harrier II Plus jump jets with VMA-542 flown by Captain Chuck "Bags" Bagnato and Captain David W. "Burt" Lancaster as they roam in one of the restricted warning areas off the South Carolina coast. The Harriers unique ability to operate close to the front lines make it the perfect close air support aircraft for the MAGTF.

3

A Marine Corps For The 21st Century

The Second Continental Congress put forth a resolution that was passed on 10, November 1775 creating the Marine Corps. Now, over two hundred years later, the United States Marine Corps is unquestionably the finest military organization in the world. Painting by Colonel Charles Waterhouse (USMCR - ret.)

In many ways the challenges that the Marines face today mirror those of the post World War II era. Then, as now, America stands alone as the greatest military superpower—the only nation capable of winning a war anywhere on the globe. Today, just as the period after World War II, our nation feels safe in setting aside a percentage of our warfighting capabilities because the threats we face seem distant or fuzzy, rather than close and clear at hand. A major lesson learned in the decade that followed World War II and that America is relearning in this decade, is that one decisive victory will not guarantee peace everywhere and will not protect America from future threats or preclude future foreign commitments.

General Charles C. Krulak, the 31st Commandant of the Marine Corps, will lead and prepare the Marine Corps for the 21st Century. The two most important things that the Marine Corps does for the nation is to make Marines and to win battles. General Krulak believes that the Marines must continually return to the strategic concept that makes the Corps a unique institution within America's military establishment. That concept, articulated by Congress, reflects the ethos of the Marine Corps:

"The Marine Corps within the Department of the Navy shall be so organized as to include not less than three combat divisions and three air wings, and such other land combat, aviation and other services as may be organic therein. The Marine Corps shall be organized, trained and equipped to provide fleet marine forces of combined arms, together with supporting air components, for service with the fleet in the seizure of defense of advanced naval bases and for the conduct of such land operations as may be essential to the prosecution of a naval campaign.

"In addition, the Marine Corps shall provide detachments and organizations for service on armed vessels of the Navy, shall provide security detachments for the protection of naval property at naval stations and bases, and shall perform such other duties as the President may direct. However, these additional duties may not detract from or interfere with the operations for which the Marine Corps is primarily organized."

"The Marine Corps shall develop, in coordination with the Army and the Air Force, those phases of amphibious operations that pertain to the tactics, techniques, and equipment used by landing forces.

"The Marine Corps is responsible, in accordance with integrated joint mobilization plans, for the expansion of peacetime components of the Marine Corps to meet the needs of war."

The Congressional Conference Report that supported the final legislation clearly explained the background behind their strategic concept and went on to say that history...

"has finally demonstrated the vital need for the existence of a strong force in readiness. Such a force versatile, fast-moving, and hard-hitting will constantly have a very powerful impact in relation to minor international disturbances...

Such a force can prevent the growth of potentially large conflagrations by prompt and vigorous action during their incipient stages...

The nation's shock troops must be the most ready when the nation generally is least ready...to provide a balanced force in readiness for a naval campaign and, at the same time, a ground and air striking force ready to suppress or contain international disturbances short of large-scale war."

THE FUTURE DIRECTION OF THE MARINE CORPS

The words of the 82nd Congress, so carefully crafted and articulated provide the Marines with the foundation they will need to move into the 21st century. Marines have long been known as innovators and improvisers. Krulak believes the Marines ethos, together with their strategic concept, innovation and improvisation will serve as the foundation upon which they will continue to build upon, the Marines institutional objectives and translate them into a vision for the Marine Corps of the 21st century.

The next century will likely be characterized by crisis and conflict. It will place heavy demands on America's military services; demands that will require deep reservoirs of military skill, intellect, and innovation. This uncertain horizon creates an even more pressing imperative for a military force that can remain versatile and yet act decisively in the face of such uncertainty—a force that can quickly and surely anticipate change and adapt to a new reality. The Marine Corps has always been that versatile, decisive force—and they are planning to continue being that force.

The Marines will be well prepared to handle a variety of missions; trained and equipped to defeat any enemy. The Marine Corps will be recognized, not just in the United States, but globally, as the premier crisis response force—ever ready to project the power and influence of the United States from the sea to any foreign shore. Here, crisis is defined as ranging from a military attack against our nation or its interests, to acts of political violence against Americans abroad, to those operations currently falling under military operations other than war.

In these areas, the Marine Corps will be first on the scene, first to fight, first to quell disturbances, and first to help. The Marine Corps will be the nation's force of choice—a certain force for an uncertain world. No matter what the crisis or the threat, the nation will have one thought: "Send in the Marines."

Operating forward, in fully capable combined arms teams, the Marine Corps will be America's legion—on the scene, ever ready to protect the nation's interests. They will remain fundamentally naval and expeditionary in character, as comfortable on the seas as on the land and in the air. With the Navy, the Marines will be able to go anywhere rapidly and project force across any shore against any foe, sustaining themselves from sea or land bases.

Marines will continue to be a force rich in history and traditions, ingrained with the highest values of honor, courage, and commitment. They will be a total force, active and reserve, able to effectively integrate a full range of capabilities—the Marine Corps as well as those of other services, agencies, and nations—into a unified and focused instrument of national power. The Marines will continuously exploit the latest technologies, concepts, and methods to enhance their operational effectiveness. The Marine Corps has always been and will be an economical force, able to get more from less.

This superb armed force will be composed of the world's finest military professionals; disciplined, motivated, dedicated warriors—stronger, smarter Marines, filled with the values that have served them well throughout our history, and infused with the agility of mind and body that will be required in future conflicts. They will be educated to act intelligently and independently; trained to seek responsibility, required to be accountable

Commandant of the United States Marine Corps - General Charles C. Krulak

and molded to act with boldness and individual initiative. The Marine Corps will continue to be a learning organization that creates individuals who not only can adapt to changing situations, but who can anticipate and even activate them. As an organization, they will be self-critical, quick to identify shortcomings, and relentless in their efforts to improve. Marines moral character, courage, and ethical values will dominate any location or operational area with the unconditional certainty that the Marine Corps is a force for good.

The future Marine Corps will give our nation an unbeatable force, composed of highly capable men and women, bound by the unbreakable bond of their unique spirit, possessing a singular focus—to serve the nation as its force of choice. Every element of the Marine Corps will receive continuous review to warrant that the Corps is prepared for the evolving needs of the 21st century. Innovation and the Marines warfighting capabilities will be in the forefront of this preparation.

Innovation

A key objective of General Krulak's planning is to encourage creativity and innovation to ensure that the Marines retain an adaptive and flexible naval force able to anticipate events and win wars across the spectrum of conflict. General Krulak will continue to foster an institution that does not restrict or limit the opportunity of any Marine to think creatively and to develop new ideas. Marines must be seen, respected, and depended upon to innovate and improvise.

The development of forces for expeditionary duty in the first part of this century, the development of the Fleet Marine Force and amphibious warfare doctrine in the 1930's, the push for the development of the helicopter and Vertial/Short Takeoff (V/STOL) technology, and the success of our Maritime Prepositioning Force program are all representative of innovations that have changed the character of war. These innovations were the result of creative thinking; thinking by sergeants and corporals, captains and lieutenants, generals and colonels; thinking by Marines who, as others have said, "Think beyond the moment, live beyond the day."

WARFIGHTING

Marines exist today because the American people expect their Marines to provide them with a lean, ready, and professional fighting force: a force that guarantees success when committed.

As good as they are today, they will need to be even better tomorrow. General Krulak will achieve this through the strength of innovation, ingenuity, and a willingness to continually adapt to changes across the spectrum of conflict. Marines are not afraid of reaching outside of the traditional realms of defense acquisition or technology. Neither are they totally wed to their current organization or operational outlook. A primary ethos of the Marine Corps, above all, is to remain focused on being ready when called.

The Marine Corps remains the nation's naval, combined arms, expeditionary force in readiness.

While Marines stand ready to perform "such other duties as the President may direct," the reason the Corps exists is what it has always been—warfighting. With capabilities inextricably linked to structure, General Krulak feels it is vital that the organization be designed with one goal in mind: success on the battlefield.

Marine Corps operational forces will continue to be organized as Marine Air Ground Task Forces (MAGTFs), with the Marine Expeditionary Force (MEF) as the principal warfighting organization. Necessary combat power will be provided to the committed MEF through global sourcing by the Total Force: one force consisting of Marine Forces, both active and reserve.

Jointness is a key warfighting principal and capability. It is more about headquarters and command elements than it is about the capabilities of any individual unit. With their experience in coordinating the elements of a MAGTF and the jointness inherent in the Marines relationship with the Navy, the Marine Corps possesses the resident expertise necessary to effectively coordinate ground, air, and sea forces. Augmenting this expertise, Marines will continue to be assigned to joint staffs. The Marine Corps must provide a fully capable, expeditionary, Joint Task Force (JTF) Headquarters organized and equipped to move out on a moment's notice to meet the uncertainties of a chaotic new world.

The nation's ability to project influence and military forces over great distances depends upon adequate strategic mobility forces. Marine expeditionary forces must continue to have a number of deployment options including amphibious lift, maritime prepositioning shipping, self-deployment, and strategic airlift. In a world in which America's ability to base forces overseas is declining, the ability to project power and conduct sea-based operations will be crucial.

The Marines remain concerned about the adequacy of amphibious lift to meet the nation's crisis response and forward presence requirements. Planner's will work closely with the Chief of Naval Operations and his staff to ensure that there are adequate numbers of the right types of ships, with the right capabilities, to meet national requirements. Amphibious ships do not simply enhance deployment options, they provide the world's only self-sustaining forcible entry capability. Amphibious ships limit the requirement for a support infrastructure ashore, allowing the naval forces to remain at sea indefinitely. The Marines believe they provide the essential versatility needed to adapt to the uncertain international landscape envisioned in the 21st century. To provide the required presence and deploy highly capable Marine expeditionary forces with an over-the-horizon launch capability, the Marines plan to maintain the capability of twelve Amphibious Ready Groups, each built around a large deck, in the active force.

The Marine Corps Maritime Prepositioning Force (MPF) concept provides America with a unique capability and is key to the rapid deployment of large-scale sustainable Marine forces. MPF flexibility is increased through innovative loading and deployment options. The Marines will continue to explore MPF employment options which support specific mission requirements as well as review other enhancements to MPF.

There is a growing need for a strategic organization that is manned, trained, and equipped to counter the growing biological-chemical (Bio-Chem) terrorist threat. The Marine Corps will have such an organization that will be centrally located, available and globally sourced to Marine Force Commanders and National Command Authorities for duties that the President may direct. This Bio-Chem Unit will be manned with properly skilled and trained personnel possibly to include civilian experts. It will be equipped with state-of-the-art detection, monitoring, and decontamination equipment, and it will be suited for operations in a wide range of military-civilian contingencies.

The Navy and Marine Corps will provide the nation with naval expeditionary forces shaped for joint operations operating forward from the sea and tailored for national needs. For the Navy, this strategic direction represents a fundamental shift away from open-ocean warfighting on the sea toward joint operations conducted from the sea. It also offers the distinct opportunity to integrate further the maritime warfighting capabilities that the Naval Services bring the nation. The Marines unique maritime character is as important to defining our Marine Corps ethos as is the individual Marine, recruit and officer training, and the basic tenet of "every Marine a rifleman." Separately and collectively, these elements are what set the Marines apart from other fighting forces.

"Forward...From The Sea" is the Navy and Marine Corps doctrine that defines their vision for expeditionary naval service in the operational and tactical levels of war. The Marine Corps contribution to Forward...From The Sea is "Operational Maneuver From the Sea" (OMFTS)—a philosophy and guide for current and future power projection ashore. OMFTS couples maneuver doctrine with technological advances in speed, mobility, firepower, communications, and navigation to achieve a seamless transition from ship to shore and the rapid movement inland to exploit enemy weaknesses. OMFTS is far more than just "ship to shore" movement, it is a new concept of naval warfare which covers the full spectrum of conflict. It is not simply a theoretical construct of the new maritime battle-space, but rather, reflects a fundamental re-orientation toward the littoral regions, complemented by advanced capabilities provided by new equipment which the Marines will continue to develop and invest in the 21st century.

The requirement for the Marines to be America's forward presence forces will continue into the next century. Forward operating MAGTFs will continue to provide Unified Commanders with a unique crisis response capability. While the Marine Corps will retain the capability to deploy MAGTF's tailored for specific missions of limited duration, the Marine Expeditionary Unit (Special Operations Capable) (MEU(SOC)), forged and tested in real-world contingencies, remains the benchmark for a forward operating Marine force. It is the "jewel" in the Marine crisis response crown and must be kept ready, relevant, and capable. Marine Corps planners will continuously take a hard look at both the MEU(SOC) and their overall amphibious requirements.

Tactical mobility will continue to be a vital part of the Marines warfighting doctrine. One of the keys to achieving decisive actions is mobility. Without the ability to move rapidly, forces cannot concentrate to fight and then disperse. To preserve the advantage which speed provides, the Marines will continue to improve their tactical mobility. From the combat load of the individual Marine to major weapons systems, improved battlefield mobility will be a paramount concern. This requires the acquisition of not only lightweight weapons systems, but also of advanced technology mobility assets in quantities sufficient to ensure a mobility advantage on the future battlefield.

Investments will also continue in Command and Control. The Marine Corps believes they must reach and execute effective military decisions faster than their adversaries, in any conflict setting, on any scale. Command and control processes and systems will reflect their warfighting philosophy. Decision making that focuses on speed and creating tempo, mission control that focuses on low level initiative, simple planning processes and orders writing techniques that are measured by the quality of the intent, all require a command and control system that is both flexible and adaptable. The Marines are going to focus on Command and Control improvements in technologies and the processes for Marines to interact with the technology.

Processes are what commander's do; systems exist only to support the commander's needs. The Corps commanders understand that no matter how well Marines understand warfighting concepts or how well they can perform tactical procedures, if they do not utilize the right command and control processes or build the fight systems to support them, they will not succeed.

Ground Combat will be another area of continued investment. The Marine Corps will continue to pursue enhancements which maximize the capabilities of ground combat forces. The entire spectrum of technologies that provide and enhance speed, protection, tactical mobility, and lethalness on the battlefield will be explored, especially those that maximize the advantage and effects of maneuver.

These include not only advanced technologies for ship to shore movement, but also the technologies which support Marines in the field. Their clothing and individual equipment have a direct and immediate impact on survivability, lethality, and mission accomplishment. Every effort will be made to provide more durable, less bulky, lighter, and more comfortable individual equipment. Personal equipment will receive significant investments such as new combat boots, infantry shelters, sleeping bags, as well as giving individual Marines capabilities they do not currently posses such as GPS Sensor packs, digital communications at the lowest levels, fire-and-forget weapon systems capable of taking out the most formidable opponents, improved chemical and biological detection and protection equipment.

Aviation will be a primary sphere of investment. Marines always keep in mind that the specific language in the Congressional Conference Report called for both a ground and air striking force to be "most ready when the nation...is least ready...to provide a balanced force in readiness..." That will continue according to General Krulak.

Marine aviation will remain capable of providing effective support to MAGTF across the spectrum of conflict. To enhance its expeditionary utility, we will continue to reduce the number of type/model series aircraft with a goal of achieving an all Short Take-Off/Vertical Landing (STOVL) aviation component while maintaining state of the art capabilities in air to ground and air to air combat.

Aviation modernization initiatives to enhance night and adverse weather effectiveness, to improve aircraft supportability, reliability and maintainability, and to reduce strategic lift dependency remain essential to meeting warfighting requirements. With all the shift in naval focus from open-ocean operations to operations in the littoral, integration of Marine squadrons into carrier air wings, which has ample historical precedent, will continue to the extent it maximizes naval aviation capabilities. Marine Corps aviation planners want to ensure that the unique capability which Marine tactical aviation provides to the MAGTF—providing support to the ground forces in an expeditionary environment—remains the key signature of Marine aviation.

In preparing for the 21st century, the primary tenant of planning will be to preserve those elements of the Marine Corps which have continuing relevance and quickly jettison those which do not. What serves them well today might not be what is needed for tomorrow. The Marine Corps will keep an eye on the future and rapidly adapt to meet the challenges put before them.

"The lifeblood of our Corps is the individual Marine."

GENERAL CHARLES C. KRULAK, COMMANDANT OF THE UNITED STATES MARINE CORPS

Marines

General Krulak has a great affection for the young Marine that is today, and has always been, the foundation of the US Marine Corps.

PART 2
Marine Air

Precise flying is needed by all involved as a pair of AV-8B's with VMA-214 and VMA-231 refuel from a VMGR-252 KC-130F over the Chocolate Mountain range near MCAS Yuma. The Hercules crew maintain a stable platform for the Harrier pilots to fly their refueling probes into the baskets that stream from the KC-130's wing mounted housing. Marine aircrews routinely conduct fixed wing refueling like this at altitudes as low as 500 feet.

4

The History of Marine Aviation

'Final Attack of the Scooter' - For many years the A-4 Skyhawk was the mainstay of Marine light attack (VMA) squadrons as seen in this stunning depiction of a VMA-124 'Skulls' A-4M dropping four Snakeye retarded bombs on the ranges outside MCAS Yuma. The unit was activated on September 7, 1942 and was the first to receive the F-4U Corsair. By the end of the Second World War, the unit had amassed an impressive record in countless campaigns producing three aces, including Ken Walsh, the first Corsair pilot to receive the Medal of Honor. After the war, the unit was redesignated as a Reserve unit. The squadron operated the A-4 'Scooter' for a great many years before turning them in for the F/A-18 Hornet. Illustration by Mark Styling.

The origins of Naval and Marine Corps aviation began on November 14, 1910, on the deck of the USS *Birmingham* off the coast of Hampton Roads, Virginia. The Curtiss Airplane & Motor Company demonstrated the potential capabilities of aircraft by having a test pilot named Eugene Ely fly off the USS *Birmingham* to the opposite shore to Willoughby Spit. Aircraft technology was very much in its infancy and the practical utilization of the airplane by the military had many skeptics in Congress and in the Navy.

The president of the Curtiss Airplane & Motor Company, Glenn Curtiss, believed in aircraft technology and the utility to warfighters. Curtiss put a program together in conjunction with the Navy to train a pilot at his expense and the Navy accepted. Lieutenant T.G. Ellyson became the Navy's first aviator and he was officially designated Naval Aviator 1.

Impressed by Ellyson's progress, technological advances and some forward thinking, the Navy asked for and received a Congressional appropriation of $25,000 to establish a training camp near the Naval Academy in Annapolis, Maryland, and the purchase of three hydroplanes; one from the Wright Company and two from Curtiss Airplane & Motor Company. Hydroplanes were selected to provide a greater margin of safety to the early aviators in the event of an engine failure

In 1911, Marine Corps Lieutenant Alfred A. Cunningham, an aviation enthusiast with experience in ballooning, took the personal initiative to begin experiments with the airplane. He leased the aircraft named 'Noisy Dan' for twenty-five dollars per month at his own expense from a civilian aviator. Cunningham experimented with the aircraft for about a year, gaining knowledge but no flight time. Although 'Noisy Dan' never actually became airborne, Cunningham's enthusiasm continued to soar despite ridicule and disappointments for his efforts.

Seeing the progress being made by the Navy, Marine Corps Commandant, Major General William P. Biddle, came to the conclusion that the aircraft would be of great benefit to the Corps emerging Advance Base Force concept. Lt. Alfred A. Cunningham was ordered to report to the aviation camp the Navy had established for flight training. Cunningham reported in on May 22, 1912, a date which is now recognized as the birthday of Marine Corps aviation.

Shortly after reporting to the aviation camp, he was ordered to serve a brief expeditionary duty. In June, he returned to the Navy aviation camp only to find that there were no aircraft in serviceable condition to allow his training to commence. Cunningham requested and received permission to go to the Burgess Company plant in Marblehead, Massachusetts, to begin his actual flight training. His instruction was conducted by the manufacturer, which consisted of two hours and forty minutes of flight instruction. On August 20, 1912, Lt. Alfred A. Cunningham took his solo flight, making him the fifth naval aviator, and he became the first marine aviator, designated Marine Aviator 1.

Cunningham spent his next twenty-five years in Marine aviation retiring as a Lt. Colonel. His contributions to Naval Aviation and the Marine Corps can not be measured. Cunningham pioneered aviation in the Corps when the contributions of the aircraft were recognized by only a few men of broad vision. He experienced many personal risks and sacrifices which brought little glory to him or his family when he was alive. His efforts contributed to the toll of Japanese aircraft destroyed by Marine aviators and served as the foundation of success for the Marines accomplishments in Desert Storm, and these accomplishments will forever stand as Cunningham's monument.

He could not have envisioned the striking power of Naval aviation as it is today, but he must have had aspirations for it in his relentless efforts to advance aviation in the Marine Corps. His spirit exists in all of Marine aviators and he is honored at Marine Corps Air Station (MCAS) Cherry Point, which named its airfield after him. On August 1944, a U.S. Navy Destroyer was given one of the most illustrious names in Naval Aviation—that of Alfred Austell Cunningham.

Marines contributed to the early development of naval aviation, whose stalwart aviators participated in some of the earliest experiments—bombing from a naval plane (Bernard L.Smith); taking off by catapult from a battleship underway (Alfred A. Cunningham); and looping a seaplane (Francis T. Evans).

When the United States entered the first World War on April 6, 1917, Marine aviation consisted of only six Marine officers, designated naval aviators, one warrant officer and forty-five enlisted men. Six months later, the First Marine Aeronautic Company was organized. It was destined to make history by becoming the first American flying unit of any branch of the American military to go overseas completely trained and equipped. On January 9, 1918, the company of twelve officers and one hundred thirty-three enlisted men were transferred to Ponta Delgada, on the Island of Sao Miguel for active duty. The First Marine Aeronautic Company flew seaplanes on anti-submarine patrol in the Azores area for the remainder of the war.

Expansion and development began for marine aviation back in the United States. For a brief period, the Marines used Navy airfields at Mineola, NY; Cape May, NJ; Lake Charles, LA; and Coconut Grove, FL. In April 1918, the Marines got their first airfield at the Curtiss Flying Field in Miami, Florida, which was renamed the Marine Flying Field.

With the move to Miami came the formation of the 1st Marine Aviation Force, composed of a headquarters detachment and four landplane squadrons. This organization was ordered almost immediately to prepare to sail for France. By July 30, 1918, three Marine Squadrons, composed of 101 officers and 657 enlisted men, arrived in France, followed by the fourth in October. Upon their arrival, the Marine squadrons became the Day Wing of the Northern Bombing Group, while two Navy squadrons made up the Night Wing. That was the first instance of wing and group organization in naval aviation. The group, however, was the higher echelon, whereas in World War II the order was reversed.

The Marine pilots, like most American airmen in France, faced a most perplexing problem—no aircraft. While they awaited delivery of their planes, they were assigned to British squadrons wherein they got their first taste of combat in DeHavilland aircraft (DH's). It was not until September 23 that the Marines received their first DH in France.

Although the Armistice came soon after marine aviation arrived, the Marines performed creditably despite a shortage of planes and time. They shot down at least four, possibly as many as twelve, German planes. They performed the first recorded food dropping mission when they replenished a French regiment isolated for several days in the front lines on the Western Front. For that accomplishment, three pilots were awarded the Distinguished Service Medal; their observers received the Navy Cross, at that time a lower rated decoration. Two Medals of Honor were awarded a pilot (2dLt. Ralph Talbot) and his observer (GySgt. Robert Guy Robinson) for shooting down two enemy planes against overwhelming odds. In World War I, a total of 282 officers and 2,180 enlisted men served in marine aviation. Of this number, about one half served overseas.

In tribute to perhaps the most famous Marine aviator, Major Gregory 'Pappy' Boyington of World War II fame. His unit, the 'Black Sheep' of VMA-214, have long since traded in their Corsairs, and now operate the AV-8B Harrier II.

Shortly after its return from France, Marine Air began demobilizing. In February 1919, the 1st Marine Aviation Force was disbanded at Miami, and the following month witnessed the dissolution of the First Marine Aeronautic Company, which had served in the Azores. Remaining personnel at Miami were transferred in the summer of 1919 to Paris Island and Quantico, and the Marine Flying Field at Miami was abandoned on September 25. The following year, marine aviation had but sixty-seven pilots and suffered a still further reduction in 1921, when its pilot strength dropped to forty-three.

Yet, between World Wars, the Marine Corps was the only United States military service that actually saw combat. Marine air served in Santo Domingo from February 1919 until July 1924; in Haiti form March 1919 to August 1934; and in Nicaragua from 1927 to 1933. Throughout those years, the handful of Marine pilots was not only experiencing combat, but was also contributing radically new tactics to both ground and air warfare. In Nicaragua, Marine pilots led by Major Ross E. Rowell were the first to use dive-bombing against an organized enemy (Sandino's rebels); again in Nicaragua, they were the first to employ air-to-ground communications in combat; and there, they were the first to transport troops and supplies by air.

Marine pilots evacuated wounded in Haiti and Santo Domingo in the early 1920's, utilizing two modified DH's designed by a marine aviator. But the most well known of the evacuation missions occurred during the fighting in Nicaragua. General Christian F. Schilt, on January 6-8, 1928, made ten hair-raising flights, under fire, landing on a makeshift airfield in Quilali, to rescue eighteen seriously wounded Marines who had been ambushed by the enemy. For his 'almost superhuman skill' Schilt was awarded the Medal of Honor.

At home during those years of so-called peace, Marine aviators ardently and arduously labored to increase their knowledge of and proficiency in aeronautics. They flew record-breaking flights, established speed records, won safety awards, dispatched medicine and supplies to areas stricken by earthquakes and hurricanes, and experimented in blind flying, aerial cartography and photography.

As naval tactics changed, it became necessary for marine aeronautical organization and aviation tactics to change also. From 1931 to 1934, VS-14M and VS-15M, the first Marine squadrons to become part of the fleet air organization, were aboard the carriers Saratoga and Lexington. On December 8, 1933, a step of vital importance was taken with the organization of the Fleet Marine Force, a unit constituted as an integral part of the United States fleet. The development of the Fleet Marine Force brought about many changes in the organization of Marine aviation.

The next organizational change of importance to Marine aviation came in 1935, when the aviation section was divorced from the Division of Operations and Training and became an independent section under the Major General Commandant. On April 1, 1936, it became a division under a Director of Aviation. The director of the new division served as an adviser to the Commandant on all aviation matters, and as a liaison officer between the Marine Corps and the Navy's Bureau of Aeronautics. Unlike the Marine Corps infantry and artillery, which drew their equipment from both Army and Navy (in addition to supplying much of their own), Marine aviation depended solely on the Navy for its aircraft and all other aviation gear.

On June 30, 1939, there were 210 officers and 1,142 enlisted men on active duty in Marine aviation. By June 1940, Congress authorized the Navy's 10,000 plane program of which Marine aviation was allotted 1,167. Plans were made for the establishment of four groups of eleven squadrons each. Following landing exercises in 1941, it was estimated that a single division making an amphibious landing would require twelve fighter, eight dive-bomber, two observation, and four utility squadrons. Although the 1st and 2nd Marine Aircraft Wings were commissioned in July 1941, when war came five months later there was still only one group in each wing—Marine Aircraft Group 11 at Quantico and Marine Aircraft Group 21, with some units at Ewa and others at Wake Island.

The Pearl Harbor attack liquidated all but one of the forty-eight Marine aircraft at Ewa—the one to escape was a transport sent to Ford Island for repairs. The personnel of Marine Aircraft Group VMF-231 organized and directed the defense of their field so well that they were able to keep it open throughout the attack, thus rendering assistance to Army and Navy aircraft unable to reach their own stations for servicing; they downed a Japanese plane with a ground gun; and they had a lower percentage of battle casualties (4 killed, 13 wounded) than any other field air station under attack in the area.

The last of the twelve Marine planes at Wake were destroyed on December 22. Yet, with a maximum of only five planes, seven having been destroyed in the initial attack on December 8, Wake pilots sank the destroyer *Kisaragi* and shot down seven planes before their last aircraft was destroyed. Then, the twenty unwounded survivors of the squadron's complement of sixty-one joined the ground troops and fought as infantrymen until they were killed or captured.

Shortly after mid-December, seventeen Marine SB2U's (Vindicators), of VMSB (Marine Dive Bomber Squadron)-231, led by a Navy PBY, reached Midway after a spectacular flight of no less than ten hours from Pearl Harbor—the longest mass overwater single-engined flight recorded to date. On December 25, 1941, Midway received fourteen Marine F2A-3's (Brewster Buffaloes) from Marine Fighter Squadron 221 to augment Midway's dive-bombers.

Marine pilots were outnumbered and their aircraft outclassed by the Japanese Zero as the Battle of Midway unfolded in June, 1942. The Marines at Midway were unsurpassed in valor. In the Marines first engagement with the Japanese Zero's, ten of twenty-five fighter pilots survived the first encounter and thirteen of the twenty-seven dive-bombers and their crews were lost. Captain Richard E. Fleming, a Marine Pilot, posthumously received the Medal of Honor for diving his flaming bomber onto the deck of the Japanese cruiser *Mikuma*. This set the *Mikuma* on fire, crippling her in the water, and making her easy prey to the U.S. Navy carrier based aircraft, which later sunk her.

The importance of aviation to Marine tactics was graphically demonstrated at Guadalcanal, where one of the first objectives of the assault was a partially completed Japanese airfield, later named Henderson Field. Appalling shortages of everything earned Guadalcanal the nickname 'Operation Shoestring.' Despite the lack of supplies and personnel, Marine aviators based at Henderson Field devastated the overwhelming opposition from the Japanese Air Force and forever shattered the myth that the Japanese pilots and their Zero's were invincible.

After Guadalcanal, Marine aviators fought their way through the Soloman Islands until none of the enemy airfields remained operable. Marine Corsairs, called Whistling Death by the Japanese, relentlessly pursued the enemy. Carrier based Marine aircraft attacked the Philippines and went on to provide four Aircraft Groups to support U.S. Army troops fighting in the Philippines. In February 1945, Marine carrier aviators supported fellow Marine ground troops at Iwo Jima, adding a new element to Marine aviation doctrine. Marine pilots went on to attack Tokyo and Okinawa.

Marine aviators emerged from World War II as a tough and gritty cadre who advanced their warfighting capability and reputation for valor and character. Twenty-nine year old fighter pilot Major Gregory R. Boyington, better known as "Pappy" to his squadronmates, contributed to the legends of Marine aviation. Boyington was engaged in combat, flying his F4U Corsair when he heard a squadron mate inquire over the radio as to his location—Boyington is said to have replied: "I've got five Zeros surrounded.", asked; "Where are they?"; Boyington replied: "Outside this cloud they've got me in!" He was also known to taunt Japanese pilots over the radio to *"come up and fight!"*

Major Boyington took command of VMF-214 with a colorful reputation for having pilots known as brash brawlers that some considered undesirable. Boyington rallied the squadron which took the moniker "Black Sheep" and went into action in the Solomons in 1943. By the end of 1943,

"Pappy Gets Three" celebrates the Marines top ace after his third kill. Painting by Colonel Charles Waterhouse (USMCR ret.)

Major Boyington had amassed twenty-six kills. On January 3, 1944, Boyington led the Black Sheep on a sortie and scored two more Zero kills, making him the leading Marine Corps Ace—a record that still stands today. Boyington's wingman was shot down in the engagement and Pappy had to jump from his burning Corsair. Floating in the water, Boyington was taken prisoner by a Japanese submarine and sent to a prison camp in Japan for the next twenty months.

When Boyington was reported missing, his intrepid squadron mates braved a storm to search for him with no success. Boyington was awarded the Medal of Honor and listed as missing in action. After the Japanese surrender in 1945, American pilots flew over Japanese prison camps dropping supplies to the repatriated Americans. Boyington was discovered alive when a pilot saw the name 'BOYINGTON' painted on the roof of one of the camp huts that housed the pilots.

Major Gregory R. Boyington was a tough, gritty Marine aviator who earned his fellow aviators' admiration for his skills and determined leadership as a warrior. The Marine Black Sheep squadron VMF-214 is now known as the VMA-214 Black Sheep squadron. The Black Sheep honor Boyington and his legacy by adorning his name on one of their AV-8B Harriers.

Marine aviators shot down their first enemy plane at Wake Island and the last of World War II at Okinawa. During this period, Marine aviators scored 2,355 shoot downs, produced one hundred twenty-one aces, five of whom downed twenty or more aircraft—Boyington, Foss, Hanson, Walsh and Aldrich. World War II brought about a record level of Marine aviation units which included five air wings, thirty-one aircraft groups, one hundred forty-five aircraft squadrons and the peak rise in personnel in Marine aviation was 125,162.

On September 7, 1945, the Yokosuka airfield was occupied by Marine Aircraft Group 31, becoming the first aviation unit to operate on Japanese soil. Following the Japanese surrender, Marine Corps aviation units were moved from the Philippines to North China performing peacetime occupational services through January 1949.

During the short peace between 1945-1950, Marine aviation returned to the task of peacetime preparedness. Heavy emphasis was placed on familiarizing Marine aviators with carrier operations. The helicopter revitalized and reshaped the Marine aviation warfighting capability in the area of amphibious warfare. This new weapon was put to use in the Korean War.

Marine aviation gave an outstanding performance in Korea, first when they went into action in support of the 1st Provisional Marine Brigade in the Pusan Perimeter. Next came the Inchon landing by the 1st Marine Division, with squadrons of the 1st Marine Aircraft Wing providing close air support from carriers during the amphibious assault and later from Kimpo Airfield. Following the collapse of North Korean resistance in early October 1950, air-lifted elements of the 1st Marine Aircraft Wing occupied the seaport town of Wonsan. During the latter part of November and early part of December 1950, when the 1st Marine Division was fighting its way through hordes of Chinese Communist Forces from the Chosin Reservoir area to Hamhung, aircraft of the Navy, Air Force, and Marine Corps supplied the division by airdrops and evacuated more than 5,000 casualties. Marine aircraft, aided by those of the Navy, provided brilliant close air support, an important factor in the 1st Marine Division's breakout of the enemy trap and its fighting withdrawal to Hamhung.

Between August 1950 and July 27, 1953, units of the 1st Marine Aircraft Wing flew more than 118,000 sorties, of which more than 39,500 were close support missions. Marine helicopter squadrons, during the same period, evacuated almost 10,000 personnel.

One of the most famous Marine aviators to emerge from Korea was Major John H. Glenn, a combat pilot in World War II and Korea. While on an exchange tour with the Air Force's 25th Fighter Squadron, Glenn was credited with three MiG-15 kills. Glenn was known as a determined, loyal and aggressive pilot who later went on to become one of America's first astronauts and a Senator representing the State of Ohio.

The end of the Korean War brought about post-war cost cutting, however the Marines, being the first to arrive in Korea in 1950, were also the last to leave the region. Elements of the 1st Wing remained on station in the Far East, where they bolstered the air defense of Taiwan in the latter part of 1958. The 2nd Marine Aircraft Wing, stationed at Cherry Point, North Carolina, provided squadrons for duty aboard carriers of the Sixth Fleet in the Mediterranean. These units, as well as Marine helicopters and airlift transports, figured as part of the Marine Corps force-in-readiness in the Lebanon operation in the summer of 1958.

The helicopter remained at the center of the Marine Corps aviation program, having demonstrated its value in Korea. A focused effort in Marine aviation was to evolve the role helicopters would have in addressing their amphibious-warfare challenges. The Marines focused on the Sikorsky HR2S/CH-37 and the HUS/UH-34. While the Corps focused on refining the role of the helicopter, several new fixed-wing aircraft would emerge into the Marine Corps. By the beginning of the sixties, the A-4, F-8 and the F-4 were integrated into Marine aviation squadrons, and their predecessors were relegated to reserve units. The Marines also began purchasing the C-130 as a replacement for the C-47. Others to emerge would be the Grumman A-6A Intruder, the Bell UH-1E Huey, Vertol CH-46 and the Sikorsky CH-53A.

Known as 'The Longest War', Vietnam occupied America between 1964-73. In August 1964, American destroyers were attacked off the coast of North Vietnam by Communist patrol boats which prompted the United States to commence air strikes against the patrol boat bases—this became known as the Gulf of Tonkin incident. In January 1965, the Marines 9th Expeditionary Brigade was stationed off the South Vietnamese coast near Da Nang. In February, enemy attacks prompted the United States to order the 1st Light Anti-aircraft Missile Battalion into Da Nang. A Marine C-130 flew in HAWK missiles and in March of 1965, the Marines stormed ashore into Da Nang. By April of 1965, the first tactical fixed wing units began to arrive in Vietnam, which consisted of fifteen McDonnell F-4B Phantoms from VMFA-531. The war continued to escalate and by the middle of 1965, the USS *Oriskany* (CV-34) was in place with an Air Wing. By the end of her tour in November, the Marine aviators on the *Oriskany* flew 1,588 sorties. By the end of 1965, Marine Corps aviation was in place in Vietnam with major facilities in Da Nang and Chu Lai. During this period, thousands of sorties had been flown in support of ground operations.

In 1966, the Marines got their first RF-4B's to replace the RF-8A Crusaders. The RF-4B was introduced by the Air Force as a reconnaissance version of the F-4. The Navy ended their acquisitions of the RF-4B's and allocated forty-six to the Marines. The RF-4B had an increased power plant consisting of two engines and provisions for a two man crew. New capabilities were brought into Marine air as well, which included a variety of imagery sensors for day and night use.

In November of 1966, the Grumman A-6A Intruders brought new capabilities to the Marines in Vietnam such as a highly advanced bombing computer, all weather night attack capabilities and the ability to deliver thousands of additional pounds of bombs compared to the A-4. The EA-6A entered the Marines inventory about the same time. The EA-6A provided

Early recruiting poster for Marine Air.

The oldest squadron in the Marine Corps, VMA-211 'The Ace of Spades' as depicted in this Lisa Venema illustration.

The mighty Phantom (like this VMFA-134 'Smokes" F-4S) served as the Corps frontline fighter for years. Illustration by Lisa Venema.

invaluable electronic jamming capabilities to be used against the growing network of efficient North Vietnamese radar sites. The Marines also deployed the F-8E for two years, flying 718 combat missions.

The helicopter community received its first CH-46 Seaknight helicopters on March 8, 1966. A total of twenty-seven were deployed and put into combat operations immediately, followed by an additional twenty-four in June. Another new helicopter arrived in late December to replace the aging CH-37. Sikorsky introduced the CH-53A Sea Stallion—the largest operational helicopter in the U.S. military inventory.

During the heavy combat operations of 1967, the only Medal of Honor to be awarded to a Marine Corps aviator occurred. On August 19, Captain Stephen W. Pless, a UH-1 pilot with VMO-6, responded to a rescue call. Four Marines were pinned down by forty to fifty Viet Cong on a nearby beach. Arriving at the scene, Pless made repeated strafing runs with rockets and machine guns before landing to pick up the Marines on the ground. After the four men had scrambled aboard his damaged Huey—Pless sustained shrapnel hits from debris from his own ordnance because he was flying so low. Pless attempted liftoff four times before his overloaded helicopter remained in the air, all the while under heavy fire. He made it on the fourth try and brought his helicopter and men home. Captain Pless was presented with his Medal of Honor in 1969 at ceremonies in the White House and was later promoted to the rank of Major, the youngest in the Marine Corps. His two crewmen and co-pilot were awarded the Navy Cross.

In July 1968, the OV-10A Bronco arrived in Da Nang as a light-armed reconnaissance aircraft. The OV-10A resembled a World War II fighter with twin propellers and tailbooms. The Marines deployed the OV-10A as a helicopter escort and reconnaissance aircraft. During 1968, 47,436 combat sorties were flown by fixed-wing aircraft and helicopter sorties doubled from the previous year to 639,194.

The primary role of Marine Corps aviation in Vietnam was dedicated to close air support and the role of augmenting or supporting larger strike groups. The opportunities for Marine aviators to kill MiGs were extremely limited. The Marines had that opportunity only three times in Vietnam, two while Marine pilots were on exchange duty with the Air Force. The first was on December 17, 1967 when Captain Doyle D. Baker shot down a MiG-17 from his F-4D. The second was on August 12, 1972 by Captain Larry Richard and Navy Lt.Commander Mike Ettel flying an F-4E which claimed a MiG-21.

The third opportunity arose off the USS *America* CV-66 when on duty at Yankee Station. On September 11, 1972, two VMFA-333 F-4Js were patrolling the skies near Phuc Yen. The lead aircraft flown by the squadron executive officer, Major Lee Lasseter and Radar Intercept Officer, Captain John Cummings. Cummings got a radar fix on two MiG-21s and Lasseter turned the flight rapidly into the oncoming MiGs, fired a missile and destroyed one of the MiGs. The second MiG retreated and the two Phantoms turned back toward the *America.* The second MiG returned and attacked Lasseter's wingman. Lasseter fired another Sidewinder, damaging the MiG, but not destroying it—the F-4Js again headed for the *America.* Enroute, Lasseter's F-4J was hit by a SAM and his wingman's aircraft, flown by Captain A.S. Dudley and RIO Lt. J.W. Brady, was damaged by flak and in grave danger of running out of fuel. Both crews ejected and were picked-up by a helicopter and flown back to the *America.* Although both aircraft were lost, this represented the first and only kill by a Marine Corps aviator. Major Lasseter was awarded the Alfred E. Cunningham Award as the top Marine aviator of 1972.

The 'Longest War' came to an end on April 29, 1975, when orders were given to execute operation Frequent Wind—the evacuation of Saigon. In over forty sorties during a period know as the 'Night of Helicopters', the Marines brought out over 2,000 people from Saigon. On April 30, 1975, the 'Longest War' came to an end for America and the Marines.

Back home in the United States, the Marine Corps continued to work on the Harrier program, which offered the Marines tactical jet speed and weapons capabilities and the ability to get right in the fight with the troops. Technical and political problems delayed the Harrier's introduction into the Corps, but issues were resolved and the Marines received their first Harriers in February 1971. The Marines continued to fly the same helicopters for the next two decades with significant upgrades.

The Marines needed to replace the F-4 Phantom and initially the F-14 Tomcat seemed like a good candidate. However, technical and maintenance issues, politics and financial considerations precluded the selection of the Tomcat for the Marines. The decision was made to extend the use of the Phantoms until the F-18s became available. The F-18 Hornet provided the Marines with light-attack and air combat capabilities to replace the F-4s.

US Marine Corps Aircraft - Primary Fixed Wing

Manufacturer	Designation	Role	Date Introduced
De Havilland	DH-4	Fighter	1918
Curtis	JN	Trainer	1920
Boeing	FB-1	Fighter	1925
Douglas	DT-2	Observation	1925
Loening	OL	Observation	1923
Curtiss	F6C	Fighter	1927
Ford	RR-5	Transport	1927
Vought	02U	Observation	1927
Curtiss	F8C	Fighter	1928
Sikorsky	RS-1	Utility	1931
Vought	03U	Observation	1932
Boeing	F4B-3	Fighter	1934
Curtiss	F8C	Fighter	1934
Great Lakes	BG-1	Bomber	1936

Manufacturer	Designation	Role	Date Introduced
Grumman	F3F-1	Fighter	1937
Brewster	F2A	Fighter	1940
Brewster	SB2A	Bomber	1940
Douglas	SBD	Bomber	1941
Curtiss	SBC	Bomber	1941
Curtiss	SB2C	Bomber	1941
Grumman	F4F	Fighter	1941
Vought	SB2U	Attack	1942
Vought	F4U	Fighter	1942
Grumman	F6F	Fighter	1943
Douglas	C-47	Transport	1945
Grumman	F7F	Fighter	1945
McDonnell	FH-1	Fighter	1946
McDonnell	F2H	Fighter	1949
Grumman	F9F	Fighter	1950
Fairchild	C-119	Transport	1952
Douglas	F3D	Fighter	1952
North American	FJ-2	Fighter	1954
Douglas	AD-1	Attack	1955
Grumman	F9F	Fighter	1956
Douglas	F4D	Fighter	1957
Vought	F8U	Fighter	1958
Lockheed	KC-130	Transport	1960
Grumman	A-6	Attack	1964
Grumman	EA-6A	Electronic Warfare	1966
McDonnell Douglas	F-4	Fighter	1966
North American	OV-10	Observation	1968
McDonnell Douglas	A-4	Attack	1970
McDonnell Douglas	AV-8	Attack	1971
Grumman	EA-6B	Electronic Warfare	1972
Beech	C-12	Transport	1972
McDonnell Douglas	F/A-18	Fighter/Attack	1980
McDonnell Douglas	F/A-18D	Night Attack	1989

US Marine Corps - Primary Rotary Wing Aircraft

Manufacturer	Designation	Role	Date Introduced
Sikorsky	H-19	Transport	1950
Sikorsky	H-37	Assault	1950
Sikorsky	H-34	Transport	1954
Bell	HTL	Utility	1958
Bell	UH-1	Utility	1964
Boeing	CH-46	Assault/Transport	1964
Sikorsky	CH-53	Assault/Transport	1966
Bell	AH-1	Attack	1968
Sikorsky	VH-3	Transport	1975
Sikorsky	VH-60	Transport	1989

United States Marine Corps Aces

Ace	Victories
1. Gregory Boyington	28
2. Joseph J. Foss	26
3. Robert M. Hanson	25
4. Kenneth A. Walsh	21
5. Donald N. Aldrich	20
6. John L. Smith	19
7. Marion E. Carl	18.5
8. Wilbur J. Thomas	18.5
9. James E. Swett	15.5
10. Harold L. Spears	15
11. Edward O. Shaw	14.5
12. Archie G. Donahue	14
13. James N. Cup	13**
14. Robert E. Galer	13**
15. William P. Marontate	13
16. Kenneth D. Frazier	12.5**
17. Harold E. Segal	12
18. E.A. Trowbridge	12**
19. Phillip C. DeLong	11 1/6 (13 1/6)
20. William N. Snider	11.5
21. Harold W. Bauer	11
22. Loren D. Everton	10
23. Donald H. Sapp	10***
24. Jack E. Conger	10
25. Herbert H. Long	10
26. Jefferson J. De Blanc	9
27. Christopher L. Magee	9
28. Thomas H. Mann, Jr.	9
29, Edmund F. Overend	9*
30. F.C. Thomas, Jr.	9
31. Gregory K. Loesch	8.5
32. John L. Morgan, Jr.	8.5
33. William N. Case	8
34. Fred E. Gutt	8
35. Edwin J. Hernan, Jr.	8
36. George L. Hollowell	8
37. Charles M. Kunz	8
38. Nathan T. Post	8
39. Authur T. Warner	8
40. Donald K. Yost	8
41. John F. Dobbin	7.5
42. Joseph L. Narr	7
43. Robert M. Baker	7**
44. William P. Brown	7
45. Dean Caswell	7
46. William E. Crowe	7
47. Henry B. Mamilton	7
48. Alvin J. Jensen	7
49. Robert W. McClurg	7
50. Jeremiah J. O'Keefe	7
51. Robert G. Owens	7
52. Jack Pittman, Jr.	7**
53. Joseph H. Reinburg	7
54. John W. Ruhsam	7
55. Robert Wade	7 (8)
56. G.M.H. Williams	7
57. Paul A. Mullen	6.5
58. Roger A. Haberman	6.5
59. Dewey F. Durnford	6 1/3 (6 5/6)
60. Joseph V. Dillard	6 1/13
61. Francis A. Terrill	6 1/12
62. George C. Axtell, Jr.	6
63. Robert Baird	6
64. John F. Bolt, Jr.	6 (12)
65. Creighton Chandler	6
66. Arthur R. Conant	6
67. Eugene Dillow	6
68. Jefferson D. Dorroh	6
69. Frank C. Drury	6
70. Don H. Fisher	6
71. Robert B. Fraser	6
72. Sheldon O. Hall	6
73. John C. Hundley	6
74. Charles C. Jones	6
75. John McManus	6
76. Gilbert Percy	6
77. Francis E. Pierce, Jr.	6
78. Zenith A. Pond	6
79. Perry L. Shuman	6
80. Robert F. Stout	6
81. Howard J. Finn	6
82. Herbert J. Valentine	6
83. Milton N. Vedder	6
84. Herman Hansen	5.5
85. William L. Hood	5.5
86. Floyd C. Kirkpatrick	5.5
87. Joseph P. Lynch	5.5
88. John B. Maas	5.5
89. Frederick R. Payne, Jr.	5.5
90. Wallace E. Sigler	5 1/3
91. Julius W. Ireland	5 1/3
92. Hugh McJ. Elwood	5 1/6
93. Stuart C. Alley, Jr.	5
94. Frank H. Presley	5
95. Donald L. Balch	5
96. Frank B. Baldwin	5
97. Oscar M. Bate	5
98. Richard L. Braun	5
99. William A. Carlton	5
100. Leonard K. Davis	5
101. Cecil J. Doyle	5
102. Charles W. Drake	5
103. William Farrell	5
104. Paul J. Fontana	5
105. Kenneth M. Ford	5
106. Freeman	5
107. Albert C. Hacking	5
108. Charles Kendrick	5
109. H.A. McCartney, Jr.	5
110. Selva E. McGinty	5
111. Edwin L. Olander	5
112. Donald C. Owen	5
113. Hyde Phillips	5
114. Robert B. Porter	5
115. George H. Foske	5
116. Ernest A. Powell	5
117. Orvin H. Ramlo	5**
118. H.V. Scarborough, Jr.	5
119. Robert B. See	5
120. Stanley Synar	5
121. G.L. Weissenberger	5
122. Albert P. Wells	5
123. Michael R. Yunck	5
124. John Andre	4 (5)
125. Wayne W. Laird	4.5
126. Raymond Scherer	4.5

* Both Boyington and Overend are credited with six planes while with the Flying Tigers in China.

** Indicates unresolved problems with documentation.

*** Since WW II, Sapp changed his name to Stapp.

( ) Total indicated in parentheses include Korean War Victories

Note: The Marine Corps has never compiled an "official" list of its fighter aces. This list is the unofficial record compiled by Dr. Frank J. Olynyk.

5

Marine Air

Hornet driver banks his F/A-18C away from MCAS Yuma during a practice sortie for the bi-annual Weapons and Tactics Instructors course conducted by MAWTS-1.

Head on view of the immensely capable F/A-18D night strike fighter. The Marines developed the D model in order to replace it's aging A-6E Intruder, RF-4 Phantom and O/A-4 Skyhawk aircraft. There are 72 Deltas in the Corps inventory within 6 active squadrons.

"The only excuse for aviation in any service is its usefulness in assisting troops on the ground to successfully carry out their operations" Major Alfred A. Cunningham - the US Marine Corps first aviator.

These words were spoken decades ago, at a time when Marine Air was in its infancy, yet they still convey the singular purpose of aircraft in the Corps to this very day, and into the foreseeable future.

The aviation community within the Marine Corps is very unique among military organizations. While it is highly varied, with a mix of fixed wing aircraft and helicopters (referred to as rotary aircraft), it is a fully integrated force with only one goal in mind—support the Marine ground combat infantryman. To accomplish this, the Marine Corps operates some of the most sophisticated aircraft within the American arsenal. No other air force can compare with the Marines ability to effectively operate such a variety of assets from austere forward air fields, aircraft carriers or amphibious assault ships. The Marines will deploy aboard these amphibious assault ships named after famous World War Two campaigns in the Pacific such as the USS *Tarawa*, *Saipan*, *Iwo Jima* and others. These vessels will be 'home' for the Marine Expeditionary Unit (MEU) and its composite squadron made up of AV-8B Harriers and helicopters. In addition, Marine F/A-18 and EA-6B squadrons will serve within Navy air wings that deploy aboard large deck aircraft carriers.

Marine aviators are trained along with U.S. Navy aviators, but that's where the similarity ends. From the moment they are commissioned as officers, they are Marines first, and as such, they spend a fair amount of time receiving instruction on the basics of Marine ground operations long before they sit in their first airplane. Much of this is completed during instruction at the Basic School located at Quantico, Virginia. During this intensive six month course, the newly commissioned 1st Lieutenant will be taught what it means to be part of America's elite fighting force. The tremendous spirit and unity which has come to exemplify the Marines is born at this school. Here the officer is taught how to be a competent leader of men, of Marines. The motto, *Semper Fidelis*, or simply *Semper Fi*, (Latin for always faithful) becomes a code the officer lives by throughout the rest of their career, and more often than not, their entire life. After graduation from the Basic School, the officer, if selected, is sent off to begin aviation training.

F/A-18D carrying a pair of AGM-88 HARM's pitches away from a single seat F/A-18C.

This VMAQ-3 'Moondog' EA-6B Prowler photographed during a WTI training mission is still wearing the markings from a recent deployment with the USS America. The Marines were instrumental in the creation and introduction of the Prowler when they initially converted their A-6 Intruders to the EA-6A electronic warfare aircraft.

Marine Air - Organization

As defined within the Marines official planning document for its aviation element, the Aviation Plan, or AVPLAN, the mission of Marine Aviation is *"to participate as the supporting Aviation Combat Element (ACE) of Marine Forces in the seizure and defense of advanced naval bases and for the conduct of such land operations as may be essential to the prosecution of a naval campaign. A collateral mission of Marine Corps aviation is to participate as an integral component of naval aviation in the execution of such other Navy functions as the fleet commanders may direct."*

The major organizational component of the Marines aviation assets is the Marine Air Wing, or MAW, of which there are four (three active duty 1st, 2nd and 3rd MAW, and a single reserve, the 4th MAW). Usually, a given MAW will consist of a number of individual Marine Air Groups, or MAGs, that are geographically segmented and reside at different air stations. The Marine Air Wings normally contain a composite force of fixed and rotary wing MAGs. The MAG will contain squadrons of either fixed wing assets or rotary, but will not have both. Usually, the typical squadron will contain between six and twenty-two aircraft depending on the type.

As mentioned previously, the larger squadrons will detach a certain number of their aircraft and personnel, called DETs, in order to meet operational commitments. The MAG may or may not include more than one aircraft type. In addition to active flying squadrons, the MAG may include Stinger anti-aircraft assets, and other aviation support entities such as the MALS (Marine Aviation Logistics Squadron). In fact, the ACE's ability to deploy rapidly for extended periods of time is in large part based on the quality of the Corps Aviation Logistics Support Program.

Marine aviation also contains a strong emphasis on Air Defense and Anti-Air equipment as defined within 'The Six Functions of Marine Air'. This includes the Stinger and Hawk anti-air missile systems. In almost every case, the large Marine Corps Air Stations are located relatively close to a large Marine ground facility or Camp. For obvious logistical and operational reasons, this enhances the ongoing training needed to enhance combat effectiveness in the air-ground concept. As an expeditionary, sea going force, most stateside Marine facilities are situated on either the east or west coasts.

When the MAGTF is formed and air assets are assigned for deployment aboard one of the assault ships, a Medium Helicopter Squadron (HMM) will be re-designated as a composite squadron with the addition of six AV-8B Harriers. Lt. Colonel John T. Hardwick (Commanding Officer of HMM-365) describes the composite squadron as follows *"the squadron will consist of the normal complement of helicopters up until the unit deploys as part of a MEU. At that time, we will add a complement of six AV-8Bs from an active duty squadron."*

Table 1 - Marine Air Wings

1st Marine Air Wing (1stMAW) - As part of Marine Forces Pacific, the 1st MAW is headquartered at Iwakuni, Japan and directly supports the 3rd Marine Division. The 1stMAW is by far the most forward deployed of all the Wings. It contains the smallest complement of actual aircraft. In order to fulfill its commitments, the 1stMAW will utilize assets from other MAWs in the form of the Unit Deployment program (UDP). Under this program, 2DMAW and 3DMAW squadrons will rotate for six month deployments to forward positions assigned to the 1stMAW.

2nd Marine Air Wing (2DMAW) - Headquartered at MCAS Cherry Point, North Carolina, and responsible to Commander Marine Forces Atlantic, the 2nd MAW directly supports the 2nd Marine Division and the 22nd, 24th and 26th MEUs.

3rd Marine Air Wing (3DMAW) - Headquartered at MCAS El Toro, California, the 3rd MAW directly supports the 1st Marine Division as part of the Marine Forces Pacific.

4th Marine Air Wing (4thMAW) - The 4th MAW is the only reserve air wing and is headquartered in New Orleans, Louisiana.

In recent years there has been some reshuffling of Marine Corps Air Stations (MCAS) as a result of the ongoing downsizing throughout the entire U.S. military establishment. Traditionally, on the east coast, there are three primary bases which would compare with the Navy's master jet bases. Atlantic forces assigned to 2DMAW include both MCAS Cherry Point and MCAS New River, both of which are located on the eastern shore of North Carolina. Cherry Point is the home of MAG-14 with its large compliment of AV-8Bs, the entire EA-6B community and two KC-130 units including the training squadron. MCAS New River is home to two MAGs (MAG-26 and 29) and is the single largest rotary wing facility. Further south on the southern coast of South Carolina is MCAS Beaufort, which houses MAG-31 which contains a large mix of F/A-18 Cs and Ds.

On the west coast, forces assigned to 3DMAW are located at MCAS Yuma, Arizona, which contains MAG-13 consisting entirely of Harriers. Yuma, with its splendid year round flying conditions in the southwestern most corner of the state, is also the home to Marine Aviation Weapons and Tactics Squadron One (MAWTS-1), and the reserve F-5E unit, the 'Snipers' of VMFT-401. The remainder of 3DMAW air stations are located in southern California. The Marines plan to phase out their El Toro facility and will place all MAG-11 Hornet units for the 3DMAW and the Hercules unit and MAG-16's inventory of CH-53s at the Navy's former master jet base, NAS Mirimar, San Diego. This was a result of their previous home MCAS Tustin being closed. MAG-39, with its AH-1s and UH-1s reside at MCAS Camp Pendelton, California, as well as the CH-46 units assigned to MAG-16. The Marines maintain a small, austere facility in the desert of lower California called 29 Palms. This facility, with its negligible accommodations, is used for many of the Corps ongoing Capabilities Exercises (CAPEXs).

For its forward deployed commitments in the Pacific, the Marines operate under the 1st MAW, a series of facilities in Hawaii (MCAS Kaneohe Bay) and in Japan at MCAS Iwakuni and Futenma. The reserve Wing, the 4th MAW, has no dedicated facilities. In most cases, the units are attached to either an MCAS, a naval air station or, in some cases, a civilian air facility.

The Marines reserve community assigned to 4th MAW has its forces located at a number of facilities throughout the continental United States as detailed in Table 2. The 4th MAW contains a variety of aircraft including the F-5E, CH-53D, F/A-18A, CH-46E and KC-130.

'Ace of Spades' AV-8B banks gently over a turquoise colored Atlantic Ocean. The unit, VMA-231, is attached to the 2nd Marine Air Wing (MAW), 14th Marine Air Group (MAG). During the ground phase of the Gulf War, AV-8B's were the most forward deployed tactical strike aircraft, at times as close as 35 miles from the Kuwaiti border. Now that's close air support.

A pair of KC-130T Battleherks with the 'Yankees' of VMGR-452 located at Stewart, NY. The capable Hercules provides critical aerial refueling and transport capabilities to Marine Air.

Rotary wing muscle Marine Corps style comes in the form of the AH-1W Cobra. The Cobra community is split between Marine Corps Air Stations Pendleton in California, and New River in North Carolina.

Table 2 - Marine Air Wing (Bases and Assigned Marine Air Groups)

Marine Air Wing	Bases	Assigned MAGs
1st MAW	Futenma and Iwakuni Japan, Kaneohe, Hawaii	MAG 36, MAG-12, MACG-18, MWSG-17
2DMAW	Cherry Point, Bogue, New River, North Carolina,	MAG-14, MAG-26,
	Beaufort, South Carolina, Quantico, Virginia	MAG-29, MAG-31, MACG-28, MWSG-27
3DMAW	El Toro, Camp Pendleton, Miramar, 29 Palms California, Yuma, Arizona	MAG-16, MAG-13, MACG-38,MWSG-37, MAG-39
4thMAW	Stewart, NY, NAS Dallas, Texas, NAS Willow Grove	MAG-49, MAG-46, MAG-41, MAG-42, MACG-48, MWSG-47

Marine Aircraft

Fixed Wing

Currently, much of the Marines inventory of front line aircraft are state of the art. The Marines operate five major fixed wing aircraft with many variants.

Table 3 - Current Marine Fixed Wing Aircraft

Aircraft	Mission	Number in Service	
		Active	Reserve
AV-8B Harrier II/II+	Close Air Support	154	0
TAV-8B Harrier	Trainer	12	0
F/A-18 A/B/C Hornet	Multi-Role Fighter	230	48
F/A-18D Hornet	Strike Fighter	95	0
EA-6B Prowler	Electronic Warfare	20	0
KC-130 Hercules	Transport/Refueler	44	24
F-5E Tiger II	Fighter	0	12

This CH-46E PHROG banks sharply during a range sweep mission over the North Carolina coastline. The PHROG will fly over the range in order to clear out any misguided fisherman before Marine ground units begin live fire artillery training.

The venerable UH-1N Huey in-flight.

Section of CH-53E Stallions with HMH-464 in echelon formation. Note the FLIR (Forward Looking Infra Red) pods located on the left side of the nose. These systems along with night vision goggles, provide a highly effective night capability. In a fluid campaign such as Desert Storm, the ability to fight at night allows the Corps to deny the enemy any refuge the darkness may offer.

The primary multi-role fighter attack aircraft is the highly versatile McDonnell Douglas F/A-18 Hornet. The Corps has in its inventory the A,B,C and D variants of the aircraft and has replaced three different aging aircraft with the mighty Hornet, (the A-6E Intruder, RF/F-4 Phantom and OA-4 Skyhawk). The Hornet is operated in greater numbers than any other aircraft in the Marines inventory. Of particular interest is the D model that the Marines developed into their primary night attack deep strike aircraft.

To date, the Marines are the only American service to successfully employ the McDonnell Douglas AV-8B Harrier II vertical short takeoff and landing aircraft (V/STOL). The latest variant of the Harrier jump jet, the II Plus night attack jet, provides the Corps with a close air support platform that can operate closer to the main battle lines than any other fixed wing aircraft available. The Marines aggressively and somewhat independently went after obtaining this British aircraft and made it their own. It has proven to be rugged, reliable and capable of doing everything asked of it—much like the Marine Corps itself.

The Northrop/Grumman EA-6B Prowler is found in fair numbers within Marine Air Wings and provides the full spectrum of electronic warfare capability. This highly advanced variant of the Grumman A-6 Intruder was actually developed by the Corps during the Vietnam War when the Intruder variant was modified and dubbed the EA-6A. Recognizing the benefits to their operations with the availability of an electronic warfare platform, the Marines worked with the Navy to further develop the design and the Prowler was born.

The last fixed wing aircraft operated by active duty Marine units is the venerable Lockheed KC-130 Hercules, which is used by the Corps to fulfill critical requirements for troop and material transport, and aerial refueling for enhanced force projection of both fixed and rotary wing resources.

Of particular interest is the use of the Northrop F-5E Tiger II by the Marines dedicated adversary training squadron, the 'Snipers' of VMFT-401 which is a reserve unit based at MCAS Yuma, Arizona. The highly maneuverable, simple Tiger offers a viable air combat threat for training purposes of all active duty Marine aircrews, regardless of airframe.

Table 4 - Marine Corps Fixed Wing Prefixes and Squadrons

Prefix	Designation	Aircraft Type
VMA	**Marine Attack Squadron**	**AV-8B Harrier**
VMA-513, VMA-214, VMA-311, VMA-542, VMA-211, VMA-223, VMA-231		
VMAT	**Marine Attack Training Squadron**	**TAV-8B Harrier**
VMAT-203		
VMFA	**Marine Fighter Attack Squadron**	**F/A-18 A,B,C Hornet**
VMFA-124, VMFA-131, VMFA-134, VMFA-235, VMFA-251, VMFA-312, VMFA-314, VMFA-321, VMFA-232, VMFA-323, VMFA-451, VMFA-112, VMFA-122, VMFA-115, VMFA-212		
VMFA (AW)	**Marine All Weather Fighter Attack Squadron**	**F/A-18 D Hornet**
VMFA(AW)-121, VMFA(AW)-225, VMFA(AW)-242, VMFA(AW)-533, VMFA(AW)-224, VMFA(AW)-332		
VMFAT	**Marine Fighter Attack Training Squadron**	**F/A-18 A,B,C,D Hornet**
VMFT-101		

Section of F-5E Tiger II's with the 'Snipers' of VMFT-401 returning to MCAS Yuma after an early morning hop. The squadron is a reserve unit and is the only dedicated adversary training squadron within the Marine Corps. The units Operations Officer, Major Brad 'Embo' Stocker, is flying the lead aircraft #12, with Major Greg 'Ajax' Gaff at the controls of #04.

Prefix	Designation	Aircraft Type
VMFT	**Marine Fighter Training Squadron**	**F-5E Tiger II**
VMFT-401		
VMAQ	**Marine Tactical Electronic Warfare Squadron**	**EA-6B Prowler**
VMAQ-1, VMAQ-2, VMAQ-3, VMAQ-4		
VMGR	**Marine Aerial Refueler Transport Squadron**	**KC-130 Hercules**
VMGR-152, VMGR-252, VMGR-234, VMGR-352, VMGR-452		
VMGRT	**Marine Aerial Refueler Transport Training Squadron**	**KC-130 Hercules**
VMGRT-253		

One look says it all. This AV-8B Harrier II pilot, Captain Roger 'Corndog' Cordell with VMA-223 prior to closing the canopy for a daytime flight. Most Marine aviators wear the camouflage cover over their helmet. This is done in part out of respect for the Marine infantryman they are responsible for supporting.

A TAV-8B Harrier taxies back after practicing several vertical landings at one of the hot pads at MCAS Yuma. The Corps only AV-8B training squadron are the 'Hawks' of VMAT-203 at Cherry Point. The unit operates a mix of single seat and TAV-8B two seat aircraft. Only a dozen of the two seat variant are in operation and they are always busy training future Harrier pilots.

Dash 2 in this section of VMAQ-4 'Seahawk' EA-6B Prowlers, pitches away from his flight leader high over the clouds near MCAS Cherry Point, North Carolina.

Rotary Wing

The Marines inventory of aircraft contains a tremendous number of helicopters of various types and while perhaps less glamorous than their fixed wing brethren, they are essential to the success in supporting Marine ground personnel and objectives. Currently, the Marine rotary wing inventory includes four major types which fulfill the troop transport, assault support, anti-armor, anti-personnel requirements.

Table 5 - Current Marine Rotary Wing Aircraft

Aircraft	Mission	Number in Service Active	Reserve
AH-1W Cobra	Attack	116	30
UH-1 Huey	Utility/Assault Support	70	15
CH-46 Sea Knight	Assault Support	236	24
CH-53 Stallion	Transport/Assault Support	174	16

The Bell Textron AH-1W Cobra is unquestionably one of the finest attack helicopters in the world. The maneuverable two man Cobra carries a wide variety of air to ground ordnance and provides escort duties for assault support troops. The Cobra began its life as a U.S. Army aircraft. The Marines quickly recognized the contribution the Cobra would make and have dramatically improved the aircraft over the years.

The Marines have in fact brought the use of helo's to an art form and rely quite heavily on several older, rugged workhorses for the critical assault support role. Both the Bell Huey UH-1 and Boeing CH-46 helicopters are the oldest helicopters operated by the Marines and have served admirably for three decades and many combat operations. Both aircraft fulfill assault support and general utility roles. These two aircraft will in all likelihood, however, be replaced by the new Bell Boeing V-22 Osprey.

The last helicopter operated by the Marines is the huge Sikorsky CH-53 Stallions which can carry large numbers of troops in its spacious cabin. The Stallion also can fulfill critical material transport needs which includes the movement of supplies and artillery.

Mutual support, a key attribute of Marine Air, as demonstrated by these 4th Marine Air Wing F/A-18's and KC-130.

Table 6 - Marine Corps Rotary Wing Prefixes and Squadrons

Prefix	Designation	Aircraft Type
HMLA	**Marine Light Attack Helicopter Squadron**	**UH-1 Huey, AH-1 Cobra**
HMLA-167, HMLA-169, HMLA-267, HMLA-269, HMLA-367, HMLA-369, HMLA-773, HMLA-775		
HMH	**Marine Heavy Helicopter Squadron**	**CH-53D/E, UH-1**
HMH-361, HMH-362, HMH-363, HMH-366, HMH-461, HMH-462, HMH-463, HMH-464, HMH-465, HMH-466, HMH-769, HMH-772		
HMM	**Marine Medium Helicopter Squadron**	**CH-46E**
HMM-161, HMM-162, HMM-163, HMM-164, HMM-165, HMM-166, HMM-261, HMM-262, HMM-263, HMM-264, HMM-265, HMM-266, HMM-268, HMM-364, HMM-365, HMM-764, HMM-764, HMM-774		
HMT	**Marine Training Helicopter Squadron**	**CH-46E, CH-53, AH-1, UH-1**
HMT-204, HMT-301, HMT-302, HMT-303		
HMX	**Marine Helicopter Squadron**	**VH-46, VH-3D, VH-53, VH-60**
HMX-1		

Two ship of VMFA (AW) - 332 F/A-18D Hornets thunder across a tranquil slate gray sea.

Warriors in the Desert (Marine Aviation in the Gulf War)

The rapid deployment capability so critical to Marine Corps operations was put to the test during the Gulf War. The deadly serious, real life scenario that was unfolding in the region was just the kind of event the Marine Air-Ground Task Force (MAGTF) was designed for. With the onset of Operation Desert Shield, Marine Corps forces were quickly mobilized and within ten days an initial combined force was in the Gulf area. In less than one month, almost half a million Marine troops were poised for action. To no one's surprise, the Marines were the first American service to completely deploy all necessary assets in the region. The scope of "Warfighters II" does not include a detailed account of the actual ground war. In broad terms, the Marine Corps was given the assignment of conducting feints in the form of decoy amphibious assaults on the Kuwaiti shoreline. The objective being to draw enemy attention and forces east, away from the main attacking forces of the 1st and 2nd Marine Divisions from positions in Saudi Arabia directly to the south of Kuwait.

In the early morning hours of the first day of the ground offensive, February 24th, 1991, also known as G Day, elements of the 1st and 2nd Marine Divisions breached the Iraqi defenses in lower Kuwait with a direct frontal assault. The 1st, 3rd, 4th and 7th Marines, all elements of the 1st Marine Division penetrated deep into Kuwait and secured the days main objective of Al Jaber airfield.

On G +1, the 1st Marine Division continued its attacks this time on the Burgan oilfields while consolidating its positions around the Al Jaber airport. By day's end, they would claim the destruction of over eighty enemy tanks and the capture of significant numbers of Iraqi POWs. The 2nd Marine Division was continuing its push north with success. By G +2, both the 1st and 2nd Divisions were advancing as far north as Kuwait International Airport and the city of Al Jahra, respectively. The 2nd Division also took up blocking positions at Mutla Ridge northwest of Al Jahra blocking the Iraqi escape route north to Basrah. By G +3, the 1st Marine Division consolidated its positions at the Kuwaiti Airport as did the 2nd Divisions at Al Jahra.

By G +4, combat operations ceased. Marine forces had claimed the destruction or capture of 1,040 enemy tanks, 608 enemy armored personnel carriers, the destruction of 432 artillery pieces with 1,050 enemy KIA and over 20,000 POWs. All in 100 hours of combat! Marine casualties due to ground action were five killed and forty-eight wounded.

<u>Table 7 - Deployed Marine Forces to the Persian Gulf</u>

1st Marine Expeditionary Force
1st Marine Division
2nd Marine Division
1st Force Service Support Group
4th Marine Expeditionary Brigade
5th Marine Expeditionary Brigade
13th Marine Expeditionary Unit

<u>Total Number of Marines deployed to the Gulf = 92,000+</u>

24 Infantry Battalions
19 Fixed Wing Squadrons
21 Helicopter Squadrons

A two ship of PHROGS just over the surface prepare to insert troops into the water.

Marine aviation played a large role in the War and every type of aircraft the Corps operated was employed in large numbers as listed in Table 8. The 3rd Marine Air Wing with Marine Air Groups 11, 13, 16, 26, 40 and 50 were utilized. The aircraft operated from a variety of Amphibious Assault Ships carrying the 4th and 5th Marine Expeditionary Brigades and the 13th Marine Expeditionary Unit in the Gulf and from land bases at Sheikh Isa, Bahrain and King Abdul Aziz airbase Al Jubail, Saudi Arabia.

HMM-263 CH-46E PHROG prepares to land in small landing zone near MCAS New River.

Table 8 - Marine Corps Aviation Assets In The Gulf

Aircraft	Unit(s)
AV-8B	VMA-231, VMA-311, VMA-331, VMA-542, DetB VMA-513
F/A-18A/C	VMFA-212, VMFA-232, VMFA-235, VMFA-314, VMFA-333, VMFA-451
F/A-18D	VMFA(AW)-121
A-6E	VMA(AW)-224, VMA(AW)-533
EA-6B	VMAQ-2
OV-10A/D	VMO-1, VMO-2
KC-130F/R/T	VMGR-252, VMGR-352, VMGR-452
AH-1J	HMA-773, HMA-775, HMLA-169, HMLA-269, HMLA-367, HMLA-369
UH-1N	HML-767, HMLA-269, HMLA-367, HMLA-369
CH-46E	HMM-161, HMM-164, HMM-165, HMM-261, HMM-263, HMM-265, HMM-266, HMM-268, HMM-365, HMM-774
CH-53A/D/E	HMH-362, HMH-461, HMH-462, HMH-463, HMH-464, HMH-465, HMH-466, Det A HMH-772

***Non flying assets included MALS-13, MALS-14, MALS-16, MALS-24, MALS-26, MALS-39, MACG-38, MWSG-37, MAG-40 and 50 Support Units.**

Marine Air - Combat Mission Descriptions

By and large, these were the forces that Marine Air was directly supporting once the ground offensive kicked off. A more specific identification of the missions flown by Marine aviation assets is described below.

Suppression of Enemy Air Defenses (SEAD)

The attack and debilitation of the Iraqis air defense network was termed SEAD, or Suppression of Enemy Air Defenses. This mission involved deep strikes into Iraq with F/A-18s and A-6Es under the watchful, protective eye of Marine EA-6Bs. The support the Prowlers offered was so critical to the attack aircraft that they always accompanied them into hostile airspace.

AH-1W Cobra hovers over a group of devastated ground vehicles after a rocket attack in the range north of MCAS Yuma, Arizona. The Cobra represents the state of the art in Marine rotary wing attack aircraft.

There's more to Marine Air than just aircraft. The Corps contains a dedicated number of Marine Air Control Groups (MACG) which are units that employ ground based air defense radar and missile systems.

Insignia of the 4 Marine Air Wings, or MAW's. The 1st, 2nd and 3rd MAW's are active duty with the 4th MAW being a reserve wing.

Battlefield Preparation

During the air offensive in preparation for the ground assault, Marine fixed wing assets flew a variety of missions both in Kuwait and Iraq. Initially, the aircraft flew interdiction missions to reduce the warfighting capability of the Iraqis. This included attacks against both ground forces and air defense sites. American military planners had segmented the air campaign into three separate phases which included the destruction of the strategic enemy installations, the destruction of the Iraqi air defense system and the preparation of the battlefield.

This included the destruction of Iraqi ground forces and their supporting armor and artillery. This was handled by F/A-18 Hornets, A-6E Intruders, AV-8B Harriers, EA-6B Prowlers and AH-1W Cobras. These aircraft would rely on primarily 'dumb' ordnance such as Mark 82 500 pound and Mark 83 1,000 pound bombs, AGM-88 High speed Anti-Radar Missiles (HARM), Mark 20 Rockeye cluster bombs, 2.75 inch rockets, AGM-65 Mavericks and TOW missiles. The enemy wasn't safe from Marine aircraft day or night. The extensive night training that is emphasized by Marine Air paid off as many of these missions were conducted under cover of darkness.

Close Air Support

The direct support of Marine ground forces, the cornerstone of Marine aviation was handled by the full complement of Marine aircraft. The AV-8B and AH-1W were particularly active in this role as well as A-6Es and F/A-18s.

Marine ground forces saw significant resistance during the ground offensive, especially in fighting Kuwait City and other parts of southern Kuwait, as well as Khafji, located in northern most Saudi Arabia. During the first day of the ground offensive, G Day, 3DMAW aircraft flew 671 sorties in direct support of the I Marine Expeditionary Force. Marine aircraft destroyed over forty Iraqi tanks and several armored personnel carriers.

Fly Marines

Light Attack helicopter squadrons designted HMLA like the 'Gunrunners' of HMLA - 269 fly both the UH-1N and AH-1W.

This kind of close air support would continue during G +2, G +3 and G +4. On G+2, 3dMAW assets concentrated on enemy artillery and armor in the areas near Kuwait Airport and Al Jahra in direct support of the 1st and 2nd Marine Divisions. By G+3, Marine aircraft harassed the withdrawing Iraqi forces.

Forward Air Control (Airborne) FACA & Tactical Air Coordinator (Airborne) TACA

The airspace in which the Marines operated was broken out into Air Control Zones. These areas were separated into squares. Intelligence as to what the enemy's forces were comprised of and their activities was handled in large part by Marine OV-10 Broncos and F/A-18Ds. The faster moving F/A-18Ds conducted Tactical Air Coordinator (Airborne)—(TACA) and Forward Air Controller (Airborne)—(FACA) missions. Among other things, the F/A-18D's spotted for enemy artillery and naval gunfire. The Hornets would fire 2.75 inch rockets and white phosphorous along with 20 mm cannon fire on suspected targets. Priorities for the Hornet crews in these roles are detailed in Table 9. The Hornet crews utilized NVGs in order to conduct these missions at night. During the ground battle, Hornet crews would fly ahead of coalition forces to mark targets for a variety of allied aircraft to strike.

Table 9 - F/A-18D TACA & FACA Priorities

Artillery and Rocket Launchers
Armor
Troops
Trench Lines

Aerial Refueling Support

Marine KC-130s were of critical importance in supporting the fixed wing aircraft to and from the targets. This, of course, included supporting large strike packages of Navy and Marine aircraft. By all measures, this was a 'tanker war' in that the huge strike packages of coalition aircraft could not have operated without the support of USAF KC-10s, KC-135s, US Navy KA-6s, S-3s and Marine KC-130s. Of particular interest was the use of Herks to keep F/A-18Ds aloft for extended periods in their Forward Air Controller (FAC) role.

Assault Support

The Marines conducted a single large scale helicopter airborne assault on February 25th, when Marine forces stormed the burning Burgan oilfields. All rotary wing assets were utilized heavily during the conflict. The CH-46, CH-53 and UH-1s flew a great many transport missions from land and seaborne bases.

6

The Six Functions of Marine Corps Aviation

By definition, assault support provides combat assault transport of troops, supplies, and equipment. Troop assault is its primary function, and the CH-46 has been filling this role for years.

The Six Functions of Marine Corps Aviation are:

1. **Aerial Reconnaissance**
2. **Anti-air Warfare**
3. **Assault Support**
4. **Control of Aircraft and Missiles**
5. **Electronic Warfare**
6. **Offensive Air Support**

Weapons and Tactics Instructors (WTIs) selected to attend the WTI course at MAWTS-1 receive graduate levels of education in all six areas in the "Generic" phase of the MAWTS-1 curriculum.

As you read on, keep in mind the words of Alfred A. Cunningham, the Marine Corps first aviator: "*The only excuse for aviation in any service is its usefulness in assisting troops on the ground to successfully carry out their operations.*"

The Marine Air Ground Task Force (MAGTF) is organized to meet the continuing demands of modern combat by coordinating a diverse array of assets under the control of a single commander. Marine aviation adds a unique capability and dimension to the MAGTF by dramatically increasing its firepower, mobility and area of influence. Support for the MAGTF has been the focus of Marine aviation for nearly eighty years. This common theme links the Six Functions of Marine aviation and establishes the foundation for aviation support.

Function One - Aerial Reconnaissance

Historical Overview

Throughout the history of armed conflict, opposing forces have sought to control the high ground. The reason is simple: better observation and fields of fire. With the advent of aerial platforms, it was soon found that one could obtain observation of the enemy and terrain without necessarily paying the price of taking the high ground. The French experimented with military observation balloons as early as the 1790's. Observation balloons became very popular in the American Civil War. By 1914, with the outbreak of World War I, aircraft were designed solely for aerial reconnaissance. The aerial engagements that occurred between pilots and observers were waged with pistols, carbines, hand grenades and even shotguns. The concept of aerial reconnaissance had not yet been embraced by the more conservative general staffs of the era. The dense "fog of war" blinded the opposing forces, placing their trust in cavalry patrols rather than aerial reconnaissance.

As technology improved during World War II, hand held cameras were no longer used as was the case during World War I. Cameras were mounted in a variety of aircraft including the P-38, P-51, and the larger B-24. One of the more successful Pacific campaigns of World War II was the conquest of Tinian. Major General Harry Schmidt was of the opinion that photographic reconnaissance 'left nothing to be desired'. The reconnaissance effort included seven dedicated aerial photo missions which were flown by various Army Air Corps and Naval units. From these, excellent mosaic maps of the entire island were constructed and distributed to all echelons down to battalion commanders. In the Fourth Marine Division, not only the Commanding General and his staff, but all regimental and battalion commanders and even some company commanders made several flights over the island in order to familiarize themselves with the terrain on which they would have to fight. Based on aerial photos, the intelligence section estimated the enemy troop strength to be 11,350 (within 550 of the actual number of Japanese on the island). Aerial reconnaissance greatly reduced unknown risks for the Tinian operation.

In Normandy, one of the great concerns prior to Operation Overlord was the possibility of the German army reinforcing the beaches at Normandy. A reconnaissance mission using new night photography equipment under huge strobe lights was deployed to determine if the Germans were prepared for an attack at Normandy on the night prior to the invasion to reduce the unknown risks of the operation.

The tactics associated with aerial reconnaissance progressed tremendously during World War II.

Early in the war, reconnaissance aircraft were slow but very stable photography platforms. These aircraft often went unarmed and unescorted. Needless to say, many were lost due to enemy action. Later in the war, faster and better armed aircraft were utilized. In the case of the P-38 and the P-51, the ability to self-protect increased survivability substantially.

In the Korean and Vietnam eras, Marine aviation evolved into the jet age and aerial reconnaissance capabilities also increased. Radar imaging came into being, as did the ability to image areas at night with new infrared technology. Electronic reconnaissance also evolved during this time. During this time period, unmanned reconnaissance vehicles came into their own.

The versatile F/A-18D Hornet can fulfill the Forward Air Control and Reconnaissance role.

The Unmanned Aerial Vehicle (UAV), is one of the tools used by Marine Aviation to conduct Aerial Reconnaissance.

Numerous unmanned vehicles were used during the Vietnam War. They were used on high risk missions over North Vietnam and made a large number of flights over the Chinese mainland.

Air Reconnaissance

When a commander commits his troops to battle, he does so with certain risks. The ultimate purpose of any type of reconnaissance is to reduce the commander's unknown risks. Aerial reconnaissance is broken down into two categories, strategic and tactical.

Strategic Reconnaissance is the gathering of information that is used to affect policy on the national or international level. This information is used by strategic planners and is conducted mostly by National or Theater assets. Some USMC aircraft are utilized in this role to a limited extent, but not as their primary mission.

Tactical Reconnaissance is the use of air vehicles to obtain information concerning terrain, weather, and the disposition, composition, movement, installations, lines of communications, electronic and communication emissions of enemy forces. Also included are artillery and naval gunfire adjustment, and systematic and random observation of ground battle areas, targets, and/or sectors of airspace. There is currently no manned aircraft in the Marine Corps that performs tactical air reconnaissance as a primary mission. The Pioneer Remotely Piloted Vehicle (RPV) system is assigned to the Unmanned Aerial Vehicle (UAV) company of the Survallance Reconnaissance Intelligence (SRI) group in each Marine Expeditionary Force (MEF). The Pioneer system is the only dedicated air reconnaissance system in service with the USMC.

PRESENT DAY CAPABILITIES

Unmanned Aerial Vehicles

Currently, the MAGTF has only one asset that performs aerial reconnaissance as its primary mission—the Unmanned Aerial Vehicle, managed by Unmanned Vehicle Companies. The mission of the UAV Company is to conduct day and night UAV operations in support of the MAGTF.

Tasks included in the mission are to:

1. Detect, recognize, identify, and locate targets in support of the MAGTF.
2. Assist in the adjustment of indirect fire weapons.
3. Conduct real-time reconnaissance, surveillance, and intelligence collection.
4. Provide support for rear area security.
5. Assist in Search and Rescue (SAR), helo route and Landing Zone (LZ) reconnaissance, and Bomb Damage Assessment (BDA).
6. Provide airborne radio relay (this capability does not presently exist).
7. Identify follow-up requirements and develop UAV tactics and techniques.

The advantages and capabilities of the Unmanned Aerial Vehicles (UAV) include:

- Real-time information via Remote Receive Station (RRS)
- Small visual, Infrared (IR), and radar signature
- No risk to aircrew
- Day TV Camera/Night FLIR Sensor

A pair of VMFA-451 'Warlord' Hornets at your six. The F/A-18C is the primary air combat fighter fulfilling the air superiority role within the Anti-Air Warfare function for the Corps.

The disadvantages and limitations of UAV's are:

- You must have line of sight between UAV and Ground Control Station (GCS)
- Relatively small field of view
- Must establish communication between Marine Air Command Control Systems (MACCS) agencies and ground control stations
- Large embarkation footprint
- Unique fuel requirement

Aircraft

The Aviation Combat Element (ACE) of the MAGTF has no assets that perform air reconnaissance as its primary mission. All aircraft are assigned the secondary mission of visual reconnaissance. The EA-6B is a multi-mission aircraft whose primary mission is Electronic Attack (EA), however, it is capable of electronic warfare support measures. It should be noted that the electronic warfare support capability of the EA-6B is significantly reduced while conducting EA simultaneously.

The AH-1W Night Targeting System (NTS) is an upgrade to the AH-1W and has added significant tactical reconnaissance capabilities to any MAGTF. Improved day optics allow for television recording with up to thirty-four magnification, while the Forward-Looking Infra-Red (FLIR) has added nighttime capability with up to twenty-five times magnification capabilities.

FUTURE DEVELOPMENTS

1. Joint Source Imagery Processing System (JSIPS) is a system currently under joint development (with the USAF as the lead service). It will augment the Marine Corps present capability to produce imagery and to collect data from varied sources. JSIPS consists of a multiple van setup which will increase the logistical requirements for its employment. The Marine Corps will, with JSIPS, increase their Tactical Exploitation of National Capabilities (TENCAP) possibilities.

2. Beginning in 1991, certain F/A-18D aircraft were designated as being 'reconnaissance capable'. This means that the airframe is able to accept a reconnaissance pallet in place of the internal gun pod. In excess of thirty aircraft are configured for reconnaissance, however with the recent cancellation of the Advanced Tactical Air Reconnaissance System (ATARS), a replacement system has been identified. Modifications to the APG-65 radar on the F/A-18D will allow for a limited radar reconnaissance capability.

3. The introduction of UAV's into the Marine Aircraft Wing's dramatically improved UAV availability and reliability. The current plan for Marine Corps UAV's is to extend the service life of the Pioneer system.

Marine aviators never lose track of the fact that intelligence will drive operations during war time. As Winston Churchill so wisely put it, "However absorbed a commander may be in the elaboration of his own thoughts, it is sometimes necessary to take the enemy into account."

The Bell/Textron AH-1W Cobra a fearsome sight to enemy ground forces and is used for Assault Support.

Function Two - ANTI-AIR WARFARE

Historical Overview

From WWI to present day, Anti-Air Warfare (AAW) has been an integral part of Marine aviation and an essential ingredient to success. Historically, this function has been required with varying degrees of intensity depending upon the extent and nature of the enemy air threat. Marine forces have not had to actively counter a meaningful enemy air threat since WWII. Today, however, the sophistication and magnitude of anti-air weapons systems available to even third world countries pose a serious threat to any mission the Corps is assigned to.

Anti-Air Warfare (AAW)

AAW is the action that is required to destroy or reduce the enemy air and missile threat to an acceptable level. There are two general types of AAW: Offensive AAW (OAAW) and Air Defense. OAAW constitutes operations conducted against enemy air or air defense systems before they can launch or assume an attacking role. OAAW operations in or near the objective area consist mainly of air attacks to destroy or neutralize hostile aircraft, airfields, radars, air defense systems, and supporting areas. Air defense consists of defensive measures designed to destroy attacking enemy aircraft or missiles or to nullify or reduce the effectiveness of such attack. Air defense can be further broken down into two categories: active air defense and passive air defense.

1. Active air defense is direct defensive action taken to destroy attacking enemy aircraft or missiles or to nullify or reduce the effectiveness of such an attack. It includes such measures as the use of aircraft, interceptor missiles, air defense artillery, non-air defense weapons in an air defense role and electronic countermeasures.

2. Passive air defense constitutes all measures, other than active air defense, taken to minimize the effects of hostile air action. These measures include the use of cover, concealment, camouflage, deception, dispersion, and protective construction.

OAAW objectives include weakening the enemy's offensive air capability to a manageable level, thereby gaining access to a zone of airspace for a specified time frame to allow friendly air operations and local air superiority in conjunction with friendly operations. These objectives can be incorporated into three specific areas: preemptive measures, suppression of enemy air defenses (SEAD), and local air superiority measures. OAAW is defined by three specific tasks, each with its corresponding objective.

The CH-46E is still the Corps main assault support aircraft, capable of delivering up to eighteen combat ready Marines where needed. As such, it is a critical element of the Six Functions of Marine Air.

The U-1N is an exceptionally versatile aircraft capable of providing a wide range of tasks including Command and Control support and MEDEVAC duties.

1. Preemptive Measures- The objective is to weaken the enemy air threat before the enemy can make effective use of their air defense systems (air-to-air elements, ground-to-air elements, and support C3 structure) and prevent attainment of MAGTF objectives. Preemptive measures are required in the early phase of an amphibious operation and in sustained operations ashore. Preemptive measures allow subsequent air and ground operations to proceed without prohibitive interference. Preemptive measures can include:

   - Air strikes on enemy airfields to destroy or damage aircraft, facilities, and logistic support.

   - Attacks on command and control facilities and surveillance systems.

   - Air strikes on the enemy's aircraft supply and support, such as railroads and convoys.

   - Offensive air-to-air sweeps to search out and destroy enemy aircraft.

2. Suppression of Enemy Air Defenses (SEAD)- The objective of SEAD is to gain access to a defined zone of airspace that will allow MAGTF operations to proceed. SEAD may become periodic in nature, applied at a critical time that will allow air and ground forces to proceed without prohibitive interference from the enemy's air defense systems. SEAD is an important part of any campaign and the MAGTF must plan a coordinated effort against the enemy air defense threat. Sustainability of a coordinated GCE/ACE SEAD plan is a function of asset availability. SEAD will include the following strategy mix:

   - Direct confrontation of the enemy's air defense with ground forces.
   - Direct confrontation of the enemy's air defense with air forces.
   - Direct confrontation of the enemy's air defense with naval forces.
   - Command and Control Warfare (C2W)

3. Local Air Superiority Measures- Even with successful application of preemptive measures and SEAD, a residual air threat may still exist. This threat may be of such a nature and magni-

tude that friendly air operations are still possible and survivable with proper application of local air superiority measures. The objective of local air superiority measures is to prevent the enemy residual air threat from affecting the execution of friendly operations to the point of prohibitive interference in a specific zone of action.

Local air superiority measures may be used separately or in conjunction with preemptive measures and SEAD. Local air superiority measures can include:

- The use of offensive combat air patrols
- Escort and self-escort tactics
- The use of aircraft onboard countermeasures and maneuvers

Air Superiority

The primary purpose of AAW is to gain and maintain AIR SUPERIORITY. Air superiority is 'that degree of dominance in the air battle of one force over another which permits the conduct of operations by the former and its related land, sea, and air forces at a given time and place without prohibitive interference by the opposing force." The significant points for analysis in the preceding definition are "prohibitive interference" and "at a given time and place." In planning the conduct of an operation, the requirement exists to address these points in detail. For example, the single greatest vulnerability of an amphibious task force is during the ship-to-shore movement. Once forces are ashore, vulnerability still exists, but to a lesser degree. Therefore, the term "prohibitive interference" is relative to "a given time and place" and must be analyzed for each phase of a particular operation. The greater the scope of the operation, the more encompassing this analysis must be. The question arises as to the precise meaning of the term "prohibitive." A prohibitive level of interference exists for each phase or element of an operation beyond which success is improbable. The lack of success of any particular aspect of an operation is not necessarily characterized by abject failure. It may be limited to levels of damage or interference which, if received, will seriously jeopardize the accomplishment of the assigned mission. Consequently, analysis of the major facets of the operation determines the level of interference which is prohibitive. Once this determination is reached, the required AAW measures to minimize this "prohibitive interference" can be ascertained.

The principles which have evolved from years of experience are: destruction in depth, mutual support, and centralized command and decentralized control. The application of these principles is necessary to achieve and preserve air superiority.

1. Destruction-in-Depth is considered the most important principle of AAW. The primary goal is to destroy the enemy air threat at its source. The area required to ensure destruction-in-depth is designated as the Air Defense Sector. The Air Defense Sector consists of the vital area, the destruction area, and the surveillance area. By means of operation plans and orders, the Air Defense Sector is made known to subordinate units of the MAGTF and to interested external commands. Effective communications range, detection range, weapons range (friendly and enemy), and the relative danger from an air or surface attack all govern the expansion or contraction of this area.

Vital Area is a designated area or installation to be defended by air defense units. It contains the facilities, units, and installations necessary for the MAGTF to accomplish its mission. The outward edge or boundary of the vital area is always the reference point in applying destruction-in-depth principles. There may be one or more vital areas, depending on the scope of the operation. The probable method of air delivery, the anticipated weapons to be used by the enemy, and an overall standoff range by which enemy air attacks must be destroyed are examined in determining and designating the vital area. The vital area corresponds with designated Air Defense priorities.

Destruction Area is an area in which it is planned to destroy or defeat the enemy airborne threat. It begins at the edge of the vital area. The size of the destruction area will depend upon the situation; however, the goal of every air defense system should be to make the destruction area as large as possible. The three factors which normally determine the size of the destruction area are the capabilities of the air defense weapons system, engagement sequence, and surveillance capabilities. The destruction area is normally divided into four geographical subdivisions: the missile engagement zone, crossover zone/line, fighter engagement zone and base defense zone. The missile engagement zone is that geographical division of the destruction area where surface-to-air missiles have primary responsibility for destruction of airborne targets. It is normally established to include the maximum range of the surface-to-air missile system. The cross over zone/line is that area in which a target normally ceases to be an air intercept target and becomes a surface-to-air missile target. The use of a cross over zone/line may not be necessary with aircraft utilizing Inertial Navigation System (INS) manning the Fighter Engagement Zone (FEZ). The Fighter Engagement Zone is that part of the destruction area in which interceptor aircraft have the responsibility for destroying airborne targets. The Base Defense Zone is an air defense zone established around an air base and limited to the short range air defense weapons system defending that base.

Surveillance Area is the area in which air search, detection, and tracking are accomplished. It must extend beyond the destruction area to allow enough time for warning and identification so that reaction time will permit engagement as the target reaches the destruction area. This surveillance area is not coincidental with the destruction area as it is not limited by intercept positive control restrictions. Further, the destruction area is oriented totally toward the assigned air defense sector of responsibility, while the surveillance area might extend into another air defense sector. Special visual zones in specific avenues of approach may be used beyond the vital area or surrounding installations to further supplement surveillance coverage. The surveillance area must be large enough to provide maximum reaction time and a maximum number of engagements and destruction with minimum penetration of the vital area.

2. Mutual Support is the concept which involves the simultaneous engagement of a target by multiple elements of the same type weapon. In this way, the MAGTF increases the probability of preventing the penetration of the vital area by hostile aircraft or missiles. Proper location and/or employment of assets ensures that each target is within range of several AAW elements. This integrated and overlapping pattern of mutual support and continuity of engagement minimizes any reduction in effectiveness of the AAW system resulting from the loss of one or more of its elements.

3. Centralized Command and Decentralized Control is the third principle of AAW and offers the best means of achieving economy of forces while minimizing reaction time and vulnerability to losses. Coordinated operations and economy of force require centralized command. To achieve a system that has minimum reaction time, maximum damage resistance, and inherent self-sufficiency requires the capability to function under decentralized control.

The Anti-Air Warfare System: Successful accomplishment of AAW requires that the total capability of the MAGTF be merged into a single, flexible AAW system. This system must be capable of operating independently or as an integral part of the overall amphibious task force or joint task force AAW system. An effective AAW system integrates all available assets and requires that the tasks of surveillance, control, and weapons employment be performed.

1. Surveillance- This is concerned with detecting, locating, and identifying hostile targets on the ground and in the air and transmitting this information to a control agency.

2. Control- Is the function of directing and coordinating the employment of weapons systems involved in destroying the enemy air capability. The AAW system should also provide the means to maintain positive control over friendly air support operations to prevent mutual interference in the AAW of missions.

3. Weapons Employment- Involves the effective utilization of assets to destroy or reduce the enemy's capability for an air attack.

Over the years, equipment and procedures have evolved to ensure that the required degree of air superiority can be attained. The Marine Air Command and Control System (MACCS) is capable of integrating all AAW assets into an effective air defense system. It permits centralized coordination and supervision of air operations at the highest level, but also has the flexibility to permit decentralized control by subordinate agencies so that immediate threats can be engaged.

AAW is a vital role for all Marine Aviators in order for the Marines to achieve the required degree of air superiority. In combat, one of the major factors affecting their success is the enemy threat. The Marines ability to cope with this ever-changing threat can only be improved through the training, planning and integration of tactics provided by the WTI's to the Fleet Marines.

Function Three - ASSAULT SUPPORT

ASSAULT SUPPORT

Assault support provides the MAGTF commander the ability to concentrate his strength against selected enemy weaknesses using speed and surprise. It provides operational and tactical mobility as well as logistics support to the MAGTF. The MAGTF commander bases his decision about the extent and use of assault support on the following Mission, Enemy, Terrain and Weather, Troops and Fire Support-Time, Space & Logistics (METT-T-SL) considerations:

- MAGTF's mission and concept of operations.
- The enemy's capability to interrupt movement of assault support assets.
- The effect of terrain and weather on assault support missions.
- Helicopter availability and lift capability.
- Time available for planning, rehearsal and briefing.

A CH-53E Stallion comes in for a landing near the rugged terrain north of MCAS Yuma. The Stallion can carry up to fifty-five combat equipped Marines over great distances.

Tactical Aerial Refueling is a key component of the Six Functions, as demonstrated by this VMGR-252 KC-130.

The MAGTF commander uses assault support to focus combat power at the decisive place and time to achieve local combat superiority. Using assault support, the commander can rapidly concentrate forces or redeploy those forces as necessary. It allows him to apply and sustain combat power and strike the enemy where he is unprepared. This function comprises those actions required for the airlift of personnel, supplies and equipment into or within the battle area by helicopters or fixed wing aircraft. These are the general categories of assault support:

1. Combat assault operations
2. Aerial delivery
3. Aerial refueling
4. Air evacuation
5. Tactical Recovery of Aircraft and Personnel (TRAP)
6. Air logistical support
7. Battlefield illumination

Assault support operations may be tactical, logistic or administrative in nature. As with any operation conducted by the MAGTF, assault support requires detailed, coordinated and concurrent planning at all echelons to increase operational efficiency and the chances for success.

Helicopter Missions and Tasks

Marine helicopters provide air mobility of personnel, supplies and equipment, combat utility support, close air support and other air support for the landing force during ship to shore movement and within the objective area during subsequent operations ashore. Tactical missions generally consist of helicopter-borne assaults to seize critical terrain, isolate enemy formations, attack an enemy's flank/rear or conduct raids or patrols. Administrative and logistical missions include supply or re-supply of troops, movement of equipment, messenger and liaison service, and casualty and prisoner of war evacuation. The specific missions of the different helicopter squadrons are listed below:

1. Marine Medium Helicopter Squadron (HMM: 12 CH-46E): The HMM squadron, operating medium lift helicopters, is organized to conduct operations as an entire squadron. This is the mainstay of the Marine Corps troop lift capability.

   Mission: The mission of the HMM is to provide assault support of combat troops, supplies and equipment during amphibious operations and subsequent operations ashore.

Mission Tasks:

- Provide combat assault support of troops, supplies and equipment. Troop assault is the primary function, and movement of supplies and equipment is secondary.

- Conduct assault support for evacuation operations and other maritime special operations.

- Provide support for mobile Forward Arming and Refueling Points (FARPs).

- Provide airborne control and coordination for assault and assault support operations.

- Maintain a self-defense capability to counter ground-to-air and air-to-air threats.

- Maintain the capability to operate from amphibious shipping, other floating bases, and austere shore bases as required.

- Maintain the capability to deploy and conduct extended range operations, employing auxiliary internal aircraft refueling (appropriate assigned aircraft).

- Maintain the capability to operate at night, in adverse weather, and under instrument flight conditions at extended ranges.

- Augment local Search and Rescue (SAR) assets and provide aero medical evacuation of casualties from the field to suitable medical facilities or other aeromedical aircraft.

- Perform organizational maintenance on assigned aircraft in all environmental conditions.

2. Marine Heavy Helicopter Squadron (HMH: 16 CH-53E or 8 CH-53D): The HMH squadron, operating heavy lift helicopters, is organized to conduct operations as either an entire squadron or in detachments operating under the control of another command element.

Mission: The mission of the HMH is to provide assault support of equipment, supplies and combat troops during amphibious and subsequent operations ashore. This is the only heavy lift asset for the Marine Corps.

Mission Tasks:

- Provide combat assault support of heavy weapons, equipment, supplies, and troops. Movement of heavy weapons, equipment, and supplies is the primary function, and troop assault is secondary.

- Conduct tactical retrieval and recovery operations for downed aircraft, equipment, and personnel (TRAP).

- Conduct combat assault and assault support for evacuation operations and other maritime special operations.

- Provide support for mobile forward arming and refueling points either in the form of a Rapid Ground Refueling (RGR) platform or re-supply for an established FARP.

- Augment local search and rescue (SAR) assets and provide aero medical evacuation of casualties from the field to suitable medical facilities or other aeromedical aircraft.

- Provide airborne control and coordination for assault support operations.

- Maintain a self-defense capability to counter ground-to-air and air-to-air threats.

- Maintain the capability to operate from amphibious shipping, other floating bases, and austere shore bases as required.

- Maintain the capability to deploy and conduct extended range operations, employing auxiliary internal aircraft refueling (appropriate to assigned aircraft).

- Maintain the capability to operate at night, in adverse weather, and under instrument flight conditions at extended ranges.

- Perform organizational maintenance on assigned aircraft in all environmental conditions.

3. Marine Light/Attack Helicopter Squadron (HMLA: 18 AH-1W/9 UH-1N): The HMLA squadron, operating both utility and attack helicopters, is organized to conduct operations as either an entire squadron or in detachments operating under the control of another command element.

Mission: The mission of the HMLA is to provide combat assault helicopter support and attack helicopter fire support and fire support coordination for aerial and ground forces during amphibious operations and subsequent operations ashore. Support is provided in relation to specific aircraft tasks.

Mission Tasks:

Specific Utility Helicopter Tasks

- Provide an airborne command and control platform for command elements.

- Augment local Search and Rescue (SAR) assets and provide aero medical evacuation of casualties from the field to suitable medical facilities or other aeromedical aircraft.

- Conduct combat assault and assault support for evacuation operations and other maritime special operations.

- Maintain an offensive weapons capability for air-to-ground threats and self-defense capabilities for air-to-air threats.

Specific Attack Helicopter Tasks (Offensive Air Support)

- Conduct point target/anti-armor operations.

- Conduct anti-helicopter operations.

- Provide point and limited area air defense to counter threat aircraft.

- Conduct armed and visual reconnaissance.

- Augment local search and rescue assets.

Combined Attack/Utility Helicopter Squadron Responsibilities and Tasks

- Provide armed escort, airborne control and coordination for vertical assault support operations.

- Control, coordinate, and provide terminal guidance for supporting arms to include offensive air support, artillery, mortars, and naval surface fires.

- Provide fire support and security of forward and rear area forces.

- Maintain the capability to operate from amphibious shipping, other floating bases, and austere shore bases as required.

- Maintain the capability to operate at night, in adverse weather, and under instrument flight conditions at extended ranges.

- Perform organizational maintenance on assigned aircraft in all environmental conditions.

Fixed Wing Missions and Tasks

Fixed wing operations contribute to the support of the MAGTF in a manner similar to helicopters. Fixed wing aircraft are employed to deliver troops, equipment and supplies to areas beyond the range and lift capacity of the helicopter. They also provide medical evacuation, airborne command and control, illumination and in-flight refueling.

1. Marine Aerial Refueling/Transport Squadron (VMGR: 12 KC-130): The VMGR squadron, operating the 'Battleherk', is organized to conduct operations as an entire squadron or as two six aircraft detachments. This is the aerial refueling platform for the Marine Corps.

   Mission: The mission of the VMGR is to provide aerial refueling service in support of Fleet Marine Forces; provide assault air support for personnel, equipment and supplies; and to conduct other air operations as may be directed.

Mission Tasks:

- Provide aerial refueling service.

- Provide assault air support of air landed troops and combat cargo between a logistic air head and small combat fields in the objective or battle area.

- Perform air delivery of combat cargo and emergency re-supply, to include airdrop into the objective area during night and all weather conditions.

- Provide a capability of long range direct delivery of high priority material and personnel to alleviate an emergency combat situation wherein other means of suitable air transport are not readily available.

- Provide casualty evacuation from fields within the objective area or battle area.

- Provide up to intermediate level maintenance of assigned aircraft and avionics equipment peculiar to those aircraft.

- Provide aircraft for airborne direct air support center (DASC)/command post functions when required for special operations.

Mission Categories: Assault support missions are divided into two categories: pre-planned and immediate. Both types of missions are executed in response to specific requests by elements of the MAGTF.

Pre-planned Missions: Pre-planned missions provide, by far, the most economical and efficient use of assets. In order to effectively employ assault support assets, the MAGTF commander must establish priorities and study the needs of the MAGTF. Pre-planned missions are requested far enough in advance to allow coordination between the requester, the supporting unit, and fire support/ air command and control agencies.

Scheduled Missions: These types of missions are requested in advance and permit detailed mission planning and close coordination with the appropriate MAGTF elements. Scheduled missions are executed at a specific L-Hour or Time on Target (TOT). This type of mission allows permission planning to be conducted well prior to takeoff.

On Call Missions: These types of missions apply to helicopters as well. The critical elements in this category are location and time. Assets must be positioned close enough to provide a timely response. For on-call missions, only the time for execution must be relayed. Keeping helicopters airborne, awaiting activation, is not an efficient means of reducing response time. However, staging assets (strip alert) at forward operating bases (FOB) or forward arming and refueling points (FARP) will meet this requirement. Good intelligence and proper planning should identify periods of vulnerability and "strip alert assets can cover these time periods." Recent experience has demonstrated that placing assets on strip alert for extended periods of time is counterproductive and ultimately reduces efficiency.

Immediate Missions: Immediate missions are those which arise suddenly and can not be planned, in detail, in advance. They are launched in support of any requesting unit within the MAGTF. In order to efficiently support the immediate needs of MAGTF units, the commander will generally allocate some of his assets to provide an immediate response through the Direct Air Support Center/Helicopter Direction Center(DASC/HDC). The DASC/HDC may divert airborne assets from missions of lower priority or launch them from a FOB or FARP in response to an immediate request. Normally, very little detailed planning can be accomplished in advance of these missions. Therefore, the request must include the same detailed information provided in a pre-planned request.

Asset Allocation

Allocation of assault support assets will be determined by a number of factors. They normally include aircraft availability, lift requirements, aircraft capabilities, threat analysis, escort and fire support requirements, time, space and logistical requirements, and unit proficiency level. When determining asset allocation, the following considerations are also be considered:

1. Ground Considerations. Responsibilities for the GCE receiving assault support are:

- To maintain tactical integrity of units, insofar as loading space allows, for commitment in the objective area.
- To properly prepare and identify equipment to be air transported.
- To determine which equipment is to be assigned to rear and follow-up echelons.
- To prepare appropriate air movement plans and forms according to the capabilities of the aircraft involved.
- To establish the priority of loads and movement considering available aircraft and the intended tactical employment once landed.
- To ensure the accomplishment of the specialized training required for embarkation, aircraft ditching, in-flight safety, and unloading.

2. Air Considerations. Responsibilities for the ACE are:

- To provide troop units with aircraft availability and capacities according to type.
- To assign aircraft serials and schedules for takeoffs and landings in accordance with identified troop unit mobility.
- To provide adequate ground handling for securing equipment in the marshaling area.
- To provide for in-flight safety and other advisory services where aircraft are concerned.

Employment Considerations

Direct Support vs. General Support: Assault support assets are usually employed in general support of the MAGTF. However, consideration can be given to direct support of MAGTF elements for a particular phase of an operation or a specified period of time.

There will be trade-offs to this type of support. A major planning factor will be logistical support for the aviation assets. Generally speaking, direct support will involve frequent movement and operation from austere sites. Logistical support will be a constraining factor. However, in certain scenarios, direct support may be the most responsive means of providing aviation support to elements of the MAGTF.

General Helicopter Characteristics: The ground commander does not normally have a detailed knowledge of helicopter characteristics. Aviation personnel, on the staff, offer a source of specific information which might become necessary. In any event, the ground commander should possess a general awareness of fundamental characteristics and the effect of the environment on helicopter operations (Fig 3-1).

Capabilities. Helicopters generally possess the following capabilities:

- Vertical ascent/descent into and out of clear but unprepared landing areas for loading and unloading.
- Load or discharge troops and cargo while hovering.
- Achieve a degree of cover and concealment by use of terrain features and vegetation.
- Provide significant speed, mobility, and flexibility of movement in the battle area.
- Perform shuttle services, bypassing obstacles insurmount able to ground vehicles.
- Operate from all types of aircraft carriers as well as platforms upon or alongside amphibious ships.
- Operate under conditions of low ceilings and reduced visibility or during periods when surf conditions prohibit waterborne movement by small craft.
- Transport supplies rapidly to ground units.
- Load troops and cargo from ships underway.
- Transport personnel and cargo to areas inaccessible by other means.

Limitations. The following limitations apply to helicopters:

- Greater logistic support required in terms of fuel, maintenance, and support personnel than with other means of support.

Two 'Yankee' Battleherks in tight formation over the mountains of lower New York state.

- Noise or rotor wash may compromise position or create difficulty in communications and vision.

- Operations are restricted under icing conditions, heavy wind, and periods of poor lunar illumination.

- Lift capabilities are directly affected by altitude, humidity, and temperature.

- Internal loads require careful calculation for safe weight and balance.

- Helicopters are vulnerable to antiaircraft fire, surface-to-air missiles, and supporting arms and small arms fire of both enemy and friendly forces. Coordination with friendly supporting arms is of paramount importance.

- Large-scale operations require good visibility, illumination and adequate landing areas.

General Fixed Wing Characteristics: As with helicopters, the ground commander may not have a detailed knowledge of fixed wing characteristics. Generally, the limited number of Marine transport aircraft available will restrict operations to those conducted in conjunction with amphibious assaults, support of operations ashore or contingency plans established by appropriate commanders.

KC-130 Capabilities and Limitations:

1. The KC-130 can provide rapid ground refueling (RGR) for both helicopters and AV-8Bs at FARPs and forward road sites. A KC-130 can fly 200nm, land on a 4000' dirt or highway strip and give away 45,000 pounds of fuel.

2. The DASC(A) is an airborne extension of the MACCS, in particular the ground DASC. It can serve to extend UHF/VHF communications coverage of the C-3 system, provide a limited echelon capability to the DASC and/or conduct DASC functions in a designated sector. The DASC(A) utilizes the UYQ-3A van.

3. The KC-130 can work out of unimproved short fields, day or night, utilizing the PPN-119 radar beacon for terminal guidance. The PPN-119 also provides terminal guidance for night or bad weather cargo and para-ops.

4 In a permissive environment, the KC-130 can be used to deliver flares for battlefield illumination.

5 The KC-130 will require standoff or dedicated fighter escort in the tanker role if threat dictates.

6 The KC-130 can provide up to 58,000 lbs. fuel (give away) during aerial refueling operations.

The assets listed above perform the assault support function of Marine Aviation. It was George C. Marshall who said, "When the smoke cleared away, it was the man with the rifle who settled the final issue of the field." Marine Corps assault support is the means to get that rifleman to the fight!

Function Four - CONTROL OF AIRCRAFT AND MISSILES

Control of aircraft and missiles encompasses the coordinated employment of facilities, equipment, communications, procedures, and personnel in order to enable the Air Combat Element (ACE) commander to plan, direct, and control the efforts of the ACE to support the MAGTF.

The agencies of the Marine Air Command Control Systems (MACCS), as depicted below, are essential to the conduct of the control of aircraft and missiles. Additionally, although the Tactical Air Control Party (TACP) and other airborne controllers are not part of the administrative chain of the Marine Air Control Group, they are considered to be integral elements of the MACCS. Marine Wing Communications Squadron (MWCS) is the agency which ties the MACCs together to include ACE operations.

Introduction and Phase-In of the MACCS Elements: Having commenced the amphibious landing, a description of the phase-in of the MACCS elements and the inter-relationship which will exist between the Navy agencies afloat and our MACCS agencies arriving ashore is in order. Also, a brief description of those agencies in terms of capabilities, functions and equipment will be addressed. The first of these will be the Low Altitude Air Defense (LAAD) elements coming ashore.

1. LAAD sections may initially come ashore with the Ground Combat Element (GCE), in direct support, providing coverage of the maneuver forces. Notionally, a LAAD battery consisting of three platoons would be assigned to a Marine Expeditionary Force-Forward Deployed MEF(Fwd) - nine sections of five teams each - with the firing potential for 180-270 Stinger missiles (load out for each team is normally six missiles) plus reserves. LAAD sections supporting the assault may collocate and coordinate their activities with the Forward Air Controller (FAC) to deconflict supporting friendly Offensive Air Support (OAS) aircraft from potential threat aircraft. These sections will be controlled by their platoon commanders located in the Fire Support Coordination Center/Direct Air Support Center (FSCC/DASC). The LAAD commander or his representative would provide hostile early warning alerts from the Tactical Air Command Center (TACC) afloat. As the MAGTF foothold is expanded, Stinger sections would also operate in general support of the MAGTF, providing area coverage for vital areas such as airfields, port facilities or beach support areas important to the amphibious operation.

   The mission of LAAD is to provide close-in, low altitude air defense protection of the MAGTF.

The Stinger shoulder mounted weapon is devastatingly accurate against enemy aircraft. Marine Low Altitude Air Defense (LAAD) Battalions use it to provide close in, surface to air defense of forward combat areas.

Stinger specifications:
- Weight - 34.51 lb
- Length - 60"
- Guidance - IR/UV Homing
- Maximum Altitude - 10,000'
- Minimum Altitude - < 500'
- Maximum Speed - MACH 2+

LAAD is an integral part of the integrated air defense system, covering areas that other elements of the air defense system are unable to defend.

The next agency ashore would most likely be the Fire Support Coordination Center (FSCC). Although the FSCC is not part of the MACCS, its inclusion in this discussion is significant because of the relationship between the FSCC and its MACCS counterpart, the Direct Air Support Center (DASC).

There are FSCCs at every level of battalion-size and larger forces. In short, the mission of the FSCC is to provide coordination of supporting arms: ground artillery, surface fire support, and air assets. The battalion FSCC coming ashore with the initial assault wave would immediately assume a limited degree of authority to coordinate supporting arms against targets of opportunity. Until the senior level FSCC is phased ashore in subsequent assault waves and control and coordination of supporting arms is passed ashore, the Supporting Arms Coordination Center (SACC), onboard the LPH/LHA (assault landing crafts) will exercise overall control and coordination of supporting arms assets. To aid in air support coordination, the DASC will come ashore and locate with the senior FSCC.

The DASC is the principle air control agency responsible for the conduct of tactical air and assault support operations directly supporting the ground forces. The DASC answers directly to the Tactical Air Control Center (TACC afloat) when control is afloat or the Tactical Air Command Center (TACC ashore) when control is ashore.

Involved with all six functions of Marine aviation with regard to their interface with the Ground Combat Element (GCE), the DASC is closely associated with assault support and offensive air support operations. Keep in mind that the DASC does not have a radar and as such, must rely on procedural control measures. Previously agreed upon and promulgated control points, altitudes, airspeeds, and other routing measures as well as positive single channel communication with aircraft will be used in order to move aircraft from one location to another in support of the ground forces.

Based on the level of air activity as well as the size of the GCE, the DASC will be task organized, and may take the form of radio/operations configured (Highly-Mobile Multi-purpose Multi-wheeled Vehicle (HMMWV), a truck mounted or KC-130 configured AN/UYQ-3A, or the DASC (AN/TSQ-155). The DASC - FSCC interface is crucial to the integration of air support with other supporting arms. The DASC does not receive copies of the pre-planned Tactical Air Request/Assault Support Request (TARs/ASR) since it is not involved in formulating the Air Tasking Order (ATO). The DASC is responsible, however, for executing the ATO by adjusting preplanned schedules or diverting airborne assets at the request of the GCE. Further, the DASC is the agency responsible to locate and assign assets for immediate air support requests. Launch authority for offensive air support and assault support aircraft may be delegated to the DASC by the Senior Watch Officer (SWO) within the TACC to expedite the fulfillment of air support requests.

As elements of the MACCS continue ashore and the MAGTFs vital area continues to enlarge, LAAD air defense will most likely be augmented by HAWK firing platoons.

The first elements of the HAWK firing platoon may echelon to their initial firing positions ashore. The element consists of a Battery Command Post (BCP), Continuous Wave Acquisition Radar (CWAR), High Powered Illumination (HPI) radar, and launchers. Although limited in its surveillance and firepower (due to the CWAR's 10,000 ft. search ceiling and single HPI fire control radar), the fire unit can provide an all-weather, day or night air defense capability to the landing force against low altitude air attacks. The remaining Pulse Acquisition Radar (PAR) and HPI of the firing platoon are subsequently moved ashore, augmenting acquisition to medium altitude and increasing the unit's engagement capability.

An additional HAWK firing platoon is landed as soon as possible to improve the air defense system ashore. The platoon will further extend radar coverage and increase firepower (additional High Power Illuninators) (HPIs)), providing balanced coverage and weighted firepower toward expected enemy air attack directions. All reporting will be to the Sector Antiair Warfare Commander (SAWC), Seaward, aboard ship over the Antiair Warfare Coordination and Reporting (AAW C&R) net, until the Tactical Air Operations Center (TAOC) comes ashore to assume responsibility as Sector Antiair Warfare Coordinator (SAWC) for the landward section.

About the same time as the initial HAWK firing platoon arrives, an Early Warning/Control (EW/C) capability may be deployed in the form of a TPS-63 radar and AN/TYQ-23 Tactical Air Operations Module (TAOM) in order to augment the naval force's radar surveillance picture over land and provide cueing to USMC Ground Based Air Defense (GBAD). An EW/C is usually the first element of the TAOC to come ashore.

The mission of the EW/C is primarily surveillance, detection and identification of air targets. The EW/C can be assigned to control the interception of hostile air targets, provide navigational assistance to friendly aircraft or provide cueing to HAWK/LAAD. The overriding consideration is that this is a limited capability and cannot perform all the tasks of a full TAOC.

Due to limited assets, AAW control will never be phased ashore to the EW/C except in specified sectors for short periods. As with the HAWK, all reporting responsibilities will be to the Anti-Air Warfare Commander (AAWC) aboard ship.

The Air Traffic Control (ATC) detachment is the primary terminal air control agency within the MACCS. The role of the ATC detachment is to provide continuous, all weather radar/non-radar approach, weather radar/non-radar approach, departure, enroute and tower Air Traffic Control services within assigned controlled airspace to friendly aircraft. The ATC detachment accomplishes this role by supporting the MAGTF with up to four ATC detachments at four main air bases and/or up to four Marine ATC Mobile Teams (MMT) at four air facilities/air sites. The ATC detachment will be integrated into the air defense system as appropriate.

Each ATC detachment is capable of providing all-weather Air Traffic Control services. Typically control of MAGTF aviation assets within assigned airspace is coordinated between the ATC detachment and the TAOC under the cognizance of the TACC. Each ATC detachment may provide a single Marine, Air Traffic Control, Mobile Team (MMT). Employment of the MMT may cause some degradation to Air Traffic Control services normally provided by the ATC detachment.

Normally, an MMT will be composed of four Marine air traffic controllers and two technicians. MMTs can provide continuous non-radar air traffic control services for up to seventy-two hours. During amphibious operations, MMTs may be established ashore initially and eventually be built up into full ATC detachments. The equipment an MMT may use at an airfacility/airsite is scenario dependent and may include the Remote Landing Site Tower (RLST) system, and the Marine Remote Area Approach and Landing System (MRAALS).

The RLST is a mobile system mounted in a HMMWV. This system features an extensive communications package and an organic Global Positioning System (GPS).

The AN/TPN-30A MRAALS is a lightweight microwave landing system which provides azimuth and DME information out to a 40 nautical mile radius, and glidescope/localizer information within 10 nautical miles for appropriately equipped aircraft.

The ATC detachment's equipment for a FOB main air base includes the Marine Air Traffic Control and Landing System (MATCALS), NAVAIDs, control tower, and mobile power.

Marine Air Traffic Control and Landing System (MATCALS). The ATC detachment at a main air base, with MATCALS, provides continuous radar approach, departure, and enroute air traffic control services within its assigned airspace out to a radius of 60 nautical miles. Consisting of three subsystems, MATCALS collects, evaluates and displays data, makes control decisions and disseminates information. The three subsystems of MATCALS are:

The Air Traffic Control Subsystem (ATCS)- a two-dimensional (60 nautical mile) surveillance radar. The ATCS is Identification, Friend or Foe (IFF) capable. Radar and IFF information are processed and forwarded to other agencies via TADIL-B and voice.

The All-Weather Landing Subsystem (ALS)- operating in a linear mode, is a 10 nautical mile, phased array, precision approach radar which provides Automatic Carrier Landing System (ACLS) Mode I, Mode II, and Mode III approach services for FOB all-weather landings. ACLS data exchange with appropriately configured aircraft is accomplished via TADIL-C; and

The Control and Communication Subsystem (CCS)- functions as a collection point for radar data produced by the ATCS and the ALS. The CCS, having a single or dual shelter capability, provides operator Processor Display Set (PDS) consoles, each with its own communications capability. The PDS consoles serve as operational work stations for the crew members. In addition to the intercom and switchboard circuits, the CCS provides access to high frequency (HF), ultrahigh frequency (UHF) AM, and very high frequency (VHF) AM/ FM circuits. The CCS has the capability to automatically exchange certain elements of command, tactical intelligence, and situation data with other ATC detachments, TAOCs and the TACC via TADIL-B.

NAVAIDS. The ATC detachment at a main air base will also possess a dual-channel Tactical Aid to Navigation (TACAN) with Distance Measuring Equipment (DME) NAVAID. This TACAN with DME provides standard high altitude navigational/position information as well as non-precision approach information to aircrews.

Control Tower. The control tower contains the radios and equipment necessary to provide control of friendly aircraft and ground personnel in and around a main air base. As the force beachhead is expanded and additional units of the MACCS are phased ashore, the EW/C will be built-up to a full TAOC in order to provide surveillance, weapons control, and traffic management of the ACE's aviation assets. Those are:

The TAOC is characterized by three surveillance radar's, one TPS-59, and two TPS-63s. It also has operations modules containing the scopes, communications and tactical data links necessary to provide surveillance, weapons control, and airspace/traffic management of its assigned sector. With the TAOC established ashore, the commander of the landing force (CLF) may declare that he is prepared to assume AAW responsibilities in a designated sector.

The next element ashore, the MAGTF TACC is designated a Tactical Air Direction Center (TADC) until the MAGTF commander assumes control of the tactical air operations in the Amphibious Objective Area. The TADC is a function which is established for a given period of time and for a specified purpose; usually that of coordinating air operations in a given area of responsibility (Landward sector of AOA). While this TADC is being built, the Navy still retains overall control of our aviation assets through the TACC afloat.

Once all control functions have been passed ashore to the MACCS, the command of the MACCS will also shift ashore. At that point, the TADC becomes a Tactical Air Command Center (TACC).

The role of the TACC is to function as the senior MAGTF air command and control agency and to serve as the operational command post of the ACE commander or his designated representative; the Senior Watch Officer (SWO). The SWO can direct, supervise, control, and coordinate all MAGTF tactical air Operations.

The Navy TACC then reverts to a subordinate TADC status and proceeds with their tasking. All of this movement ashore has taken some time. Typically, establishing a complete MACCS as described may take from 18-21 days. This could increase if severe opposition to the amphibious landing is encountered.

Marine Wing Communications Squadron (MWCS). The MWCS is the primary communication organization within the Marine Aircraft Wing (MAW), and is a subordinate squadron within the Marine Air Control Group (MACG).

The Marine Wing Communications Squadron (MWCS) is tasked to install, operate, and maintain expeditionary communications for the ACE of a MEF.

MWCS consists of a Headquarters and two MWCS Detachments. MWCS-18 consists of a Headquarters element and one MWCS Detachment. Each detachment is made up of a Detachment Headquarters and six operational platoons.

At the present time, HQMC has not officially promulgated a mission statement or concept of employment. The concepts presented here are presently under evaluation by the MWCS in the FMF. The following missions will be fulfilled by the MWCD, regardless of it's organization.

- Assist in the systems planning and engineering of ACE communications for command and control of the MAGTF aviation assets.

- The MWCS is tasked with providing Communication Control (COMM-CON) for the ACE.

- Provide the senior MAGTF ACE Operations Systems Control Center (OSCC) for the ACE communication system.

- Provide the senior airfield OSCC at up to two airfields per detachment.

- Provide digital backbone communication in support of the ACE, Command Element (CE), expeditionary airfields, and the primary agencies of the MACCS for up airfields.

- Provide tactical automated switching and telephone services for the ACE CE and Tactical Air Command Center (TACC) at one airfield and up to three additional airfields as required.

- Provide electronic message distribution for the ACE CE, primary MACCS agencies, and tenant units at up to four airfields.

- Provide external radio communication support for ACE operation as required.

- Provide Deployed Wide Area Network (DWAN) and Deployed Local Area Network (DLAN) server support for the ACE CE and primary MACCS agencies.

- Provide calibration and repair of all ground common Test Measurement Diagnostic Equipment (TMDE) within the ACE.

- Provide cryptographic repair services for all ground common and MACCS assigned communication security equipment within the ACE.

- Provide 3d echelon maintenance support for ground common communication electronics equipment held by MWSG units.

The MAGTF is task organized with the MACCS agencies necessary to perform the six functions of Marine aviation. They are organized and equipped to support amphibious operations and subsequent operations ashore. The employment of Fleet Marine Forces requires the close integration of air and ground operations to succeed on the modern battlefield.

The HAWK missile system provides the punch to the Marine Air Command and Control System (MACCS) that handles the Control of Aircraft and Missiles function. The supersonic missile contains a 300 pound high explosive warhead.

Function Five - ELECTRONIC WARFARE (EW)

Electronic Warfare (EW) is one of the most misunderstood functions of Marine Aviation. Electronic warfare is an essential element of combat power. Its contribution lies in exploiting enemy weakness, protecting freedom of action, and reducing security and communication vulnerabilities. A modern military force depends on electronics for command and control of forces and employment of weapon systems. Because of this dependence on electronic devices, Marine forces, as well as enemy forces, are vulnerable to actions which can reduce the effectiveness of these devices or gain intelligence from them. An electronic warfare system that enables the commander to degrade the effectiveness of enemy electronic activities is a powerful weapon that can be used to support both offensive and defensive operations. Hence, electronic warfare could be the critical factor in deciding victory or defeat.

EW is defined as, "Any military action involving the use of electromagnetic and directed energy to control the electromagnetic spectrum or to attack the enemy." In plain language, electronic warfare is denying the enemy effective use of the electromagnetic spectrum while retaining its friendly use. Electromagnetic energy is, "Forms of radiant energy such as radio waves, infrared radiation, light waves, X-rays, gamma rays and cosmic rays." By virtue of the above definitions we all, regardless of Military Occupational Specialty (MOS), participate in EW because we all employ one or more forms of electromagnetic energy in the conduct of our assigned missions.

Divions of Electronic Warfare:
There are three basic divisions of EW:

1. Electronic Warfare Support (ES): "That division of EW involving actions taken under direct control of an operational commander to search for, intercept, identify, and locate sources of radiated electromagnetic energy for the purpose of immediate threat recognition." Thus, ES provides a source of information required for immediate decisions involving electronic counter measures, electronic counter-counter\-measures, avoidance, and tactical employment of forces. How does this relate to you when flying and you get strobes on your RHAW gear indicating that you might be targeted? Depending on the scenario, your reaction to the strobes will be anything from looking out in that direction to a SAM break. This is one way of utilizing ES in a tactical aircraft, and shows why EW is important to all aviators, regardless of aircraft type.

2. Electronic Attack (EA): "That division of EW involving the use of electromagnetic or directed energy to attack personnel, facilities, or equipment with the intent of degrading, neutralizing, or destroying enemy combat capability." There are two components of EA:

- Actions taken to prevent or reduce an enemy's effective use of the electromagnetic spectrum, such as jamming and electromagnetic deception.

- Employment of weapons that use either electromagnetic or directed energy as their primary destructive mechanism (lasers, RF weapons, particle beams).

3. Electronic Protection (EP): "That division of EW involving actions taken to protect personnel, facilities, and equipment from any effects of friendly or enemy employment of electronic warfare that degrade, neutralize, or destroy friendly combat capability."

- Preventive Measures. Actions taken during training, planning, and establishment of communication and non-communication electronics systems. Examples of this would be: Have Quick radio, brevity, code words, blinking, and EA training.

- Remedial Measures. Countermeasures taken when confronted with electronic countermeasures. Examples of this would be: localize the jammer (ES) and then engage it, switching frequencies, burn through, etc..

Electronic warfare cannot take or hold ground, destroy a tank or aircraft, or repel an attack. It can, however, confuse, deceive, delay, disorganize, and target the enemy when integrated into the concept of operations. When all other considerations are equal, victory may go to the force that effectively integrates electronic warfare into their concept of operations.

Function Six - OFFENSIVE AIR SUPPORT (OAS)

Offensive Air Support is defined as, "those air operations conducted against enemy installations, facilities, and personnel to directly assist the attainment of MAGTF objectives by the destruction of enemy resources or the isolation of his military force." This presentation will serve to familiarize you with OAS and the MAGTF's potential application of its capabilities.

History
Command of the battlefield has been a goal that commanders throughout history have strived to attain and maintain. With the introduction of "flying machines", this battlefield now included the airspace over it. Balloons were first used extensively in combat for observation and artillery direction during the Civil War. From that time on, commanders have used aircraft to influence the battlefield and achieve their objectives. Attack aviation was initiated in earnest during the First World War, where sustained efforts in Armed Reconnaissance and Strategic Bombing were made by the major participants. From the initial application in 1914 to the present, offensive air support has increased in importance, and in some examples, constituted the deciding factor between victor and vanquished.

Offensive Air Support Functions (OAS)
Combined Arms: The MAGTF's inherent combat power is enhanced by the concept of combined arms. Combined arms is the full integration of arms in such a way, that in order to counteract one, the enemy must make himself more vulnerable to another. To accomplish this, a task organized MAGTF will integrate its aviation assets with its organic fire support assets, to effectively support the MAGTF scheme of maneuver.

OAS operations apply firepower against our opponents' war making and sustaining capabilities. This firepower may be applied for one of two functions; either the neutralization or destruction of the assigned target(s).

03
MARINES

VMAQ-2 'Panther' on the hunt near Yuma. The EA-6B handles the full range of Electronic Warfare (EW).

13 VK
VMFA(AW)-121
MARI

On patrol at sunrise, this VMFA (AW) -121 'Green Knight' F/A-18D sports the large AGM-88 HARM missile on a wing pylon. The HARM is extremely effective against surface air defense sites and can still locate and destroy them after their radar's have been turned off. During activities in support of Operation Deny Flight over Bosnia, Marine F/A-18D units carried this weapon while flying from Aviano Air Base, Italy.

- Destruction: Destruction missions destroy enemy forces, equipment, supplies, and installations. Destruction of the target may be difficult to achieve and are contingent upon the threat, target composition, MAGTF aviation assets and available weapons.

- Neutralization: Neutralization missions render areas, weapons, or enemy forces ineffective for a specified time. Neutralization may be applied when we cannot afford to dedicate the assets to destroy our opponent, or when we decide that the most efficient application of force would be to "shut him down" for a set period of time, rendering the requirement for destruction unnecessary.

The MAGTF commander utilizes OAS throughout the operational spectrum to assist in attaining MAGTF objectives. "The MAGTF commander shapes the battlefield by focusing combined arms against critical enemy vulnerabilities. The destruction or neutralization of these targets creates the conditions for decisive action. The firepower, mobility, and flexibility provided by OAS are critical in establishing favorable conditions for deep, close, and rear operations."

OAS categories

USMC OAS operations are divided into two major categories; CAS (Close Air Support) and DAS (Deep Air Support).

- CAS: CAS is defined as; "air action against hostile targets which are in close proximity to friendly forces and which require detailed integration of each air mission with the fire and movement of those forces." The MAGTF commander depends upon CAS to provide a major proportion of his firepower due to the MAGTF's structural deficiencies in artillery support.

- DAS: DAS can be conducted in the form of either armed reconnaissance or air interdiction. The MAGTF commander utilizes DAS to shape the battlefield. DAS is defined as "air action against enemy targets at such a distance from friendly forces that detailed integration of each mission with fire and movement of friendly forces is not required." Contrary to popular opinion, DAS can be conducted on both sides of the Fire Support Coordination Line (FSCL). When DAS is required short of the FSCL, coordination with the friendly forces is required.

- Air Interdiction: Air interdiction is defined as; "Air operations conducted to destroy, neutralize, or delay the enemy's military potential before it can be brought to bear effectively against friendly forces at such a distance from friendly forces that detailed integration of each air mission with the fire and movement of friendly forces is not required."

This VMA-214 Harrier is lightly loaded with a clean set of wing stations. The AV-8B is the primary Close Air Support (CAS) aircraft which falls under the Offensive Air Support function.

Harrier and Hornet, fixed wing firepower for the Aviation Combat Element or ACE.

Armed Reconnaissance: Armed reconnaissance is defined as "locating and attacking targets of opportunity, i.e., enemy material, personnel, and facilities, in assigned general areas or along assigned ground communication routes, and not for the purpose of attacking specific/located briefed targets." (Joint Pub 1-02) Given the structural weaknesses in the MAGTF's deep targeting capability, armed reconnaissance offers the MAGTF commander a capability to address mobile enemy force structure targets enroute to the battlefield.

Mission Classifications

The ACE executes OAS missions as either; pre-planned or immediate air support. The ACE executes both types of support in response to specific requests.

1. Pre-planned missions: Pre-planned missions are either scheduled or on call. MAGTF/ACE planners will estimate the offensive air support required for different evolutions. With this estimate of anticipated support, OAS assets will be tasked to provide support at a specific time or be "on the ready" to provide support when the MAGTF scheme of maneuver requires it. The use of pre-planned missions allows the MAGTF commander to manage his limited OAS assets more efficiently.

   Pre-planned Scheduled: This type of mission is scheduled to be executed at a specific time. The MAGTF commander may use a scheduled CAS mission to provide support for a planned attack, where the attack pilots have a specific TOT and target. The pre-planned scheduled classification is not restricted to CAS missions alone. Air interdiction missions or armed reconnaissance missions may be assigned specific Time On Target (TOT) or Time On Station (TOS) as pre-planned scheduled OAS.

   - Pre-planned On-call: In many cases on-call missions represent the most efficient use of MAGTF OAS assets. On-call missions are pre-loaded and pre-briefed for a particular target array/location and then placed in an appropriate ground/air alert condition. The pilots anticipate a launch based upon their alert status. As the MAGTF order of battle dictates, the alert status will be upgraded, and if required for an attack mission, the aircraft will be launched.

2. Immediate Missions: Immediate missions can be utilized to meet unexpected OAS requirements. The immediate classification is utilized to meet fire support needs that could not be pre-planned by the ACE planners. The immediate JTAR may be filled by diverting an attack element from a pre-planned mission. While the ordnance load may not be tailored to the specific target array, the shock value of the diverted aircraft's ordnance effects may be enough to achieve the desired result. While immediate missions are utilized to cover unexpected needs, the ACE planners must assume that they will be required to cover battlefield contingencies. In this light, ordnance loads should be utilized that cover the majority of expected target types identified in the IPB process.

OAS Capabilities and Limitations: OAS represents a large percentage of the MAGTF's combat power. The MAGTF commander relies upon OAS to attack targets that other supporting arms cannot, due to capability or availability. The MAGTF should integrate the fires of all its assets to achieve a combined arms effect. Historically, the fires provided by attack aviation assets have provided capabilities against targets that the GCE weapons could not address.

OAS Capabilities
- Variety of attack
- Observation
- Responsiveness
- Flexibility
- Radius of action
- Firepower and mobility
- Accuracy
- Morale

OAS Limitations
- Limited visibility
- Weather
- Target acquisition
- Target identification
- Time on station
- Radius of action
- Communications
- Enemy defenses

Requirements for Effective OAS: The concepts/conditions listed below are considered essential to conduct effective OAS. The MAGTF attack aviation assets can conduct OAS operations without one (or several) of these requirements, but the results of these efforts will not be as great as if all were present. Results could be degraded in terms of aircraft survivability, weapons accuracy, and weapons effect.

1. Air superiority
2. Suppression of enemy air defenses (SEAD)
3. Cooperative weather
4. Effective targeting
5. Effective weaponry
6. Capable platforms/sensors
7. Responsive C3
8. Proficient players

OAS Assets

- C3 System: The MACCS described in the Control of Aircraft and Missiles brief is essential to the successful conduct of USMC OAS operations. It is this system, that ensures that the required attack aviation assets get to the appropriate customer, in the shortest possible time. Since these agencies were covered in great detail already, we will move on to OAS and the MAGTF's attack aviation assets.

2. OAS Attack Aviation Assets.

- The taxpayers have given the MAGTF an attack aviation force with tremendous capabilities. There are three different platforms that the ACE may utilize to provide OAS for the MAGTF. These plat forms are the AH-1W Cobra, the AV-8 Harrier, and the F/A-18 Hornet. Additionally, the primary terminal control platforms; the F/A-18D and UH-1N may be utilized in OAS operations as *shooters* when not required as a terminal control platforms.

The MAGTF commander utilizes OAS as an integral part of his combined arms team. OAS constitutes a large percentage of the MAGTF's combat power making up for a structural deficiency in artillery assets. Historically, the U.S. Marines have been on the cutting edge of attack aviation innovation.

Armed & Very Dangerous **- The weapons load out of these VMFA (AW) - 224 'Fighting Bengal' F/A-18D's clearly displays the versatility of the aircraft. For Close Air Support (CAS) and Suppression of Enemy Air Defense (SEAD) missions, the lead aircraft is carrying AGM-65 Mavericks on the outboard wing pylons and AGM-88 HARM's on the inboard wing pylons. If an airborne threat arises, it can be dispatched with either the long range AIM-120's under the fuselage, or AIM-9's on the wingtips. Dash 2 is sporting a mix of AIM-9, AIM-7 and AIM-120 missiles for close in and beyond visual range (BVR) encounters. The centerline fuel tanks add range to the Night Strike Hornet.**

7

Marine Helicopter Squadron One

Marine One takes off from the south lawn of the White House, transporting President Clinton to Air Force One located at Andrews AFB for his journey to the Democratic National Convention. The Sikorsky VH-3D is flown by the Presidents helicopter pilot, Marine Helicopter Squadron One Commanding Officer, Colonel Fredrick J. Geier, Co-Pilot Captain Sean C. Killeen. The Marine One Crew Chief aboard is SSgt.Carter. (Sunday, August 25, 1996)

Sikorsky S-58 (H-34 Seahorse) The U.S. Navy contracted with Sikorsky to produce a prototype helicopter for anti-submarine duty. Production of the S-58 eventually totaled 1,821 helicopters, more than any other single aircraft type.The U.S.Marines used the UH-34D Seahorse utility transport, the UH-34E with amphibious gear and the VH-34D for executive transport. The helicopter in the above photo is one of the few remaining VH-34Ds, used to transport the President of the United States. The VH-34D is located at the Marine Corps Museum in Quantico, VA, USA.

Engine:	One 1,525 HP Wright R-1820-84 Radial
Crew:	Two Pilots, Twelve to Eighteen Passengers
Speed:	123 mph at sea level
Ceiling:	9,500 Feet
Range:	280 miles at 98 mph
Armament:	Provision for anti-submarine weapons in the SH-34
Weight:	8,275 lbs. Gross Weight: 14,000 lbs

Colonel Geier ready for his mission, awaiting the arrival of the President of the United States. This is the view the President typically sees his pilot from as he steps aboard Marine One. The relationship between a President and his helicopter pilot is always professional and cordial. Marine One Pilots are responsible for the safe and effective transportation of the President, requiring enormous amounts of planning, coordination and several classified elements of the mission to protect a President.

The Marine Corps first helicopter squadron was commissioned in 1947 as Marine Helicopter Squadron One (HMX-1). The squadron's initial mission was to pioneer an entirely new concept in air operations: To evaluate and test the theory of transporting Marines to a battle zone by helicopter. This early mission has evolved into the current developmental testing of new helicopter systems and products destined for the Fleet Marine Force. Undoubtedly the most visible mission this squadron performs is Presidential support in either a VH-3D or VH-60N "White Top" helicopter. Whenever the President of the United States flies on a helicopter anywhere around the world, it is a helicopter and pilot from HMX-1. The squadron's moniker is the "*Night Hawks - The First and the Finest.*"

Origins

The United States Marine Corps took its first serious look at the helicopter in 1932. A team evaluated the Pitcairn Autogyro, a rotary-winged aircraft, and determined that the technology had not yet reached a practical state for their use in combat. This assessment was primarily based on its limited payload capabilities. In 1939, Igor I. Sikorsky successfully demonstrated his rotary-winged VS-300 and recaptured the imagination of the United States Armed Forces, proving that rotary-winged aircraft had evolved to a practical stage. Sikorsky modified early designs for the U.S. Army, deploying the helicopter for rescue and observation missions in the Pacific during the later part of World War II. The helicopter industry began to grow rapidly with other players emerging such as Piasecki and Bell. Frank Piasecki designed the first experimental helicopter for the Navy called the XHRP. The XHRP was a tandem rotored, banana-shaped aircraft designed to carry a nine-hundred pound payload.

The eighteenth Commandant of the Marine Corps, General Vandegrift, was quick to realize the impact that the helicopter might have on Marine warfighting doctrine and was impressed by Lieutenant General Geiger's thinking on how atomic weapons would alter future tactics. Lieutenant General Geiger was a witness to early atomic weapon tests and was deeply concerned about the weapons capability to quickly destroy a Marine invasion force. He successfully urged General Vandegrift to pursue the helicopter as a component of traditional amphibious landing tactics.

A special board was convened under the leadership of Major General R.C. Shepherd to draw up the initial design specifications for a Marine Corps helicopter. The Marines envisioned a helicopter that could travel two to three hundred miles at a speed of one hundred knots carrying 5,000 pounds of payload at an altitude between 4,000 and 15,000 feet. In December 1946, the Shepherd board recommended formal research of the helicopter and the establishment of a Marine helicopter squadron for training and indoctrination. The Commandant quickly endorsed the board's recommendations and forwarded them to the Chief of Naval Operations (CNO). Postwar budgetary constraints limited the initial efforts; however, approval was given to create a Marine helicopter development squadron.

A perfect approach to the White House. Marine One is piloted by Marine Helicopter Squadron One, Executive Officer (XO), Lt.Colonel Mike Conklin. Squadron XO's are the driving force in Marine Corps aviation squadrons. XO Conklin works tirelessly to execute the CO's orders, keeping the largest and oldest helicopter squadron in the Marine Corps in a constant state of readiness. The Commanding Officer of Marine Helicopter Squadron One reports to three entities; Headquarters Marine Corps—The Commandant, The White House and the Chief of Naval Operations. The CO must ensure that the squadron is prepared to execute of their missions, requiring strong leadership and diplomacy. The XO acts as a *Chief of Staff* who follows in the CO's wake to deal with the operational realities and the hard line to enforce the CO's wishes.

On November 22, 1947, the Commandant of the Marine Corps issued the following order:

M302045Z
FM CMC
TO COMDTMUCS QUANT
INFO CNO
CINCLANTFLT
COMNAVAIRLANT
CG AIRFMFLANT
HMX-1
UARE
BT
CNO 221341Z NOV 47 NOTAL QUOTE
EFFECTIVE 1 DEC 47 FORM AND COMMISSION MARINE HELICOPTER SQUADRON ONE SHORT TITLE HMX-1. OPERATIONAL AND ADMIN CONTROL ASSIGNED CMC. MCAS QUANT TO FURNISH LOGISTIC SUPPORT. REVISE AS FOLS X OPERATIONAL AND ADMINISTRATIVE CONTROL FOR MARINE HELICOPTER SQUADRON ONE CMM
MCAS QUANT ASSIGNED MCAS QUANT VICE CMC X CNO CONCURS

BY CFN 221351Z NOV 47 1 DEC 47 HMX-1
30 / 2045Z APR REEPEM
TOR: 1027Z / 01 MAY 58 / BGR
DIST: CO / S-3 (ACT) ADJ / HMX-1 / FILE 302045Z

This one paragraph message started a revolution in Marine Corps aviation and in Marine Corps tactical doctrine. On December 3, 1947, the Commandant of the Marine Corps issued the following mission to Marine Helicopter Squadron One: "Develop techniques and tactics in connection with the movement of assault troops by helicopter in amphibious operations; evaluate a small helicopter as a replacement for the present OY type aircraft to be used for gunfire spotting, observation, and liaison missions in conjunction with amphibious operations." HMX-1 began with seven officers and three enlisted men under the leadership of then Colonel Edward C. Dyer, and quickly grew to eighteen pilots and eighty-one enlisted men. Colonel Dyer selected Quantico as the site to base HMX-1 due to the proximity of the Sikorsky and Piasecki manufacturing plants in Connecticut and the Marine Corps training schools at Quantico, Virginia. In the spring of 1948, HMX-1 received its first helicopters, five Sikorsky HO3S's, and then commenced pilot training and qualifications.

The whole point of commissioning the squadron and putting it into action was to develop a new concept for amphibious warfare. HMX-1 was charged with the task of determining if the helicopter was a viable platform to move Marines from ship to a Landing Zone (LZ) ashore, i.e., to execute a heliborne assault. HMX-1 wasted no time in executing its mission by engaging in one of the Marine Corps Schools' annual exercises, Operation Packard II. HMX-1's role in this operation was to participate in the amphibious assault by carrying troops over water to specified shore points, simulating a regimental combat team being air-lifted by a Marine helicopter air group.

The squadron's pilots began work-ups for Operation Packard II, flying the HO3S-1's at the maximum loads with the center of gravity at the

Marine One flying along the Potomac River, flown by Marine One Helicopter Pilot, Lt.Colonel Delmour. Marine Helicopter One selects it's pilots from the top ten percent of Marine Corps aviators. Lt.Colonel Delmour will leave the squadron shortly to take command of a CH-53 squadron in Hawaii.

maximum fore and aft limits. The HO3S-1 carried only three troops in addition to the crew, but the operation would eventually shape the developing doctrine of vertical assault.

On May 18, 1948, HMX-1 pilots flew their five HO3S-1's from Quantico to Norfolk, Virginia, and then embarked aboard the carrier USS *Palau* (CVE-122) at pier side. The initial fly-on was described by HMX-1's Commanding Officer, Colonel Dyer as "A complete shambles. There were sailors running all over the place in mortal danger of walking into tail-rotors, and the Marines were totally disorganized as well. It was complete bedlam, there was no organization and no real system developed."

Colonel Dyer and the Commander of the USS *Palau*, Captain Bob Dixon, met that evening to remedy a clearly dangerous situation. They adopted the procedures being used for fixed-wing aircraft. The next day these procedures were put in place which resulted in safe and functional operations. According to Colonel Dyer, the only thing remaining was to "devise a systematic method of embarking the troops." Specific routes were developed to move Marines from their berthing compartments on the ship to the aircraft positions, minimizing the dangers of the flight deck. This same basic system is still used today, with painted foul lines on the ship's deck to guide the scurrying Marines.

On May 23, 1948, the first airborne ship-to-shore movement began at Onslow Beach, Camp LeJeune, North Carolina. The first wave of the assault began with all five HO3S-1's taking off from the USS *Palau* and thirty minutes later arriving in the landing zone. HMX-1 pilots made continuous flights, putting sixty-six Marines in the right place at the right time.

The squadron proceeded to develop and demonstrate a number of other helicopter capabilities, including the laying of communications wire and the spotting of artillery fire. Pilot training and the investigation of the helicopter's warfighting capabilities continued, such as the testing of an airborne public address system for air-to-ground communications, rules for formation flight, and evasive tactics to be used against enemy aircraft.

A year later, in May of 1949, HMX-1 participated in Operation Packard III. HMX-1 deployed eight Piasecki HRP's, three Sikorsky HO3S's, and a single Bell HTL. The squadron and aircraft performed beyond expectations. Flying over choppy seas which swamped several landing craft, the Piasecki HRP's quickly put two hundred-thirty troops and 14,000 pounds of cargo in the designated landing zone. These troops went on to seize a tactically significant road junction five miles inland. The Bell HTL was embarked on an LST and the three Sikorsky HO3S's were shore based to provide search and rescue capabilities. The performance of the helicop-

Marine One flies past the picturesque Jefferson Memorial, flown by Presidential Helicopter Pilot, Major Shaw.

ters and crews was considered a tremendous success for HMX-1. This success was a key factor in the integration of the helicopter into the Marine Corps.

Korea

The June 24, 1950, invasion of South Korea by North Korea compelled President Harry S. Truman to respond to the United Security Council's request "to render every assistance" by ordering the U.S. Seventh Fleet and air units to assist the South Korean government. Six days after President Truman authorized the use of American troops, Headquarters Marine Corps directed HMX-1 to transfer eight officers and thirty enlisted personnel to MCAS El Toro for assignment to Korea. Among them was Captain Victor A. Armstrong who would later return at HMX-1 in 1959 as the Commanding Officer, and the Marine Corps second Presidential helicopter pilot.

The expansion of the American role in Korea began the rapid introduction of helicopter squadrons into the Fleet Marine Force, as well as additional missions for HMX-1. Pilot training and additional experimental work with helicopters included such things as mounting litters on the skids of helicopters to assist in the evacuation of wounded, and attaching rocket launchers to the skids. These results paved the way for the UH-1E (Huey) gunship later used in Vietnam. Other experiments included dropping bombs from helicopters, advancing the search and rescue doctrine, instrument flying techniques, command and control doctrine, anti-submarine warfare, heavy-lift capabilities, aircraft camouflage, and extensive modifications and developments in helicopter design in conjunction with the manufacturers. The advancement of the helicopter has continued for nearly fifty years, increasing the usefulness to the Marines, limited only by the imagination of HMX-1, the Fleet Marine Force, and budgetary constraints.

Executive Flight maintenance personnel work under the direction of Marine One Crew Chief Sgt. Roseman to keep the President's helicopter *Good To Go!*

The Presidential Mission

In 1957, HMX-1 unexpectedly acquired another important mission: Transporting the President of the United States. Previously, the squadron had conducted only operational tests and evaluations of helicopters from various manufacturers to determine their utility as a means of emergency evacuation for the President.

On September 7, 1957, President Eisenhower was vacationing at his summer home in Newport, Rhode Island, when his immediate presence was required at the White House. Typically, a return trip to Washington from Rhode Island required an hour ferry ride across the Naragansett Bay to the awaiting Air Force One. The airplane flight to Andrews AFB required forty-five minutes, then another twenty minute motorcade ride to the White House.

Recognizing the immediate need for his presence in Washington, President Eisenhower resorted to his military experience and directed his aide to find a way to get him to Air Force One in a more expeditious manner. The aide informed the President that he had an emergency helicopter available that could be used to fly him to Air Force One. President Eisenhower approved the idea and HMX-1 was tasked to get the job done. HMX-1 pilot Major Virgil D. Olson flew a Sikorsky HUS-1A (UH-34) and picked up the President. This helicopter was on station in Rhode Island to serve as a platform for the Emergency Response mission the squadron assumed. The President was flown across Naragansett Bay in about seven minutes. While climbing up the stairs of Air Force One, President Eisenhower asked his aide why the helicopter was not used in this capacity all the time. This brief trip on the in the UH-34 helicopter was the first time the squadron had ever flown the President. Shortly after that trip, the President's naval aide contacted HMX-1 and asked them to evaluate the possibility of safely landing a helicopter on the south lawn of the White

President Eisenhower receives a in-flight briefing from a Marine One Crew Chief.

President John F. Kennedy being briefed by MGySgt. A.J. Himmelberger. Both photos courtesy of HMX-1.

President Kennedy's son John, Jr., at the controls of Marine One. Both photos courtesy of HMX-1.

Mrs.Kennedy and daughter Caroline in Marine One. Both photos courtesy of HMX-1.

House for the purpose of transporting the President. HMX-1 conducted preliminary evaluations and conducted test flights which determined that there was ample room for a safe landing and departure on the south lawn. Initially, the Air Force was given the mission of transporting the President using a helicopter that proved to be too small and slow. The Marines were given back the mission utilizing the HUS-1A (UH-34). Shortly thereafter, formal procedures were finalized, and HMX-1 began flying the President to and from the south lawn of the White House to Andrews AFB.

The Executive Flight Detachment at HMX-1 has one of the most familiar missions in the Marine Corps worldwide. The call sign used by HMX-1 when the President is on board a Marine helicopter is "Marine One" which is derived from the Presidency. The aircraft that carries the President always takes the name of the respective branch of the service flying the President. When a president boards a fixed wing aircraft flown by the Air Force, it becomes Air Force One, when the President flew in an Army helicopter, it was called Army One. The United States Marines Corps is currently the only branch of the American military that provides helicopter transportation to the President of the United States. This mission has evolved from Eisenhower's brief seven minute flight to very sophisticated presidential and presidential support missions. In 1976, the United States Marine Corps was assigned the sole responsibility and mission of transporting the President of the United States of America. *Marine Helicopter Squadron One*, still uses the HMX-1 moniker on its squadron patches out of a sense of pride and historical prominence in helicopter aviation.

Marine Helicopter Squadron One, Chain-of-Command

Marine Helicopter Squadron One is one of the largest aviation squadrons in the United States Marine Corps and has a unique chain-of-command. The Commanding Officer of HMX-1 has three separate and distinct chains of commands, unlike any other unit in the Marine Corps, illustrated in *Figure One* (below).

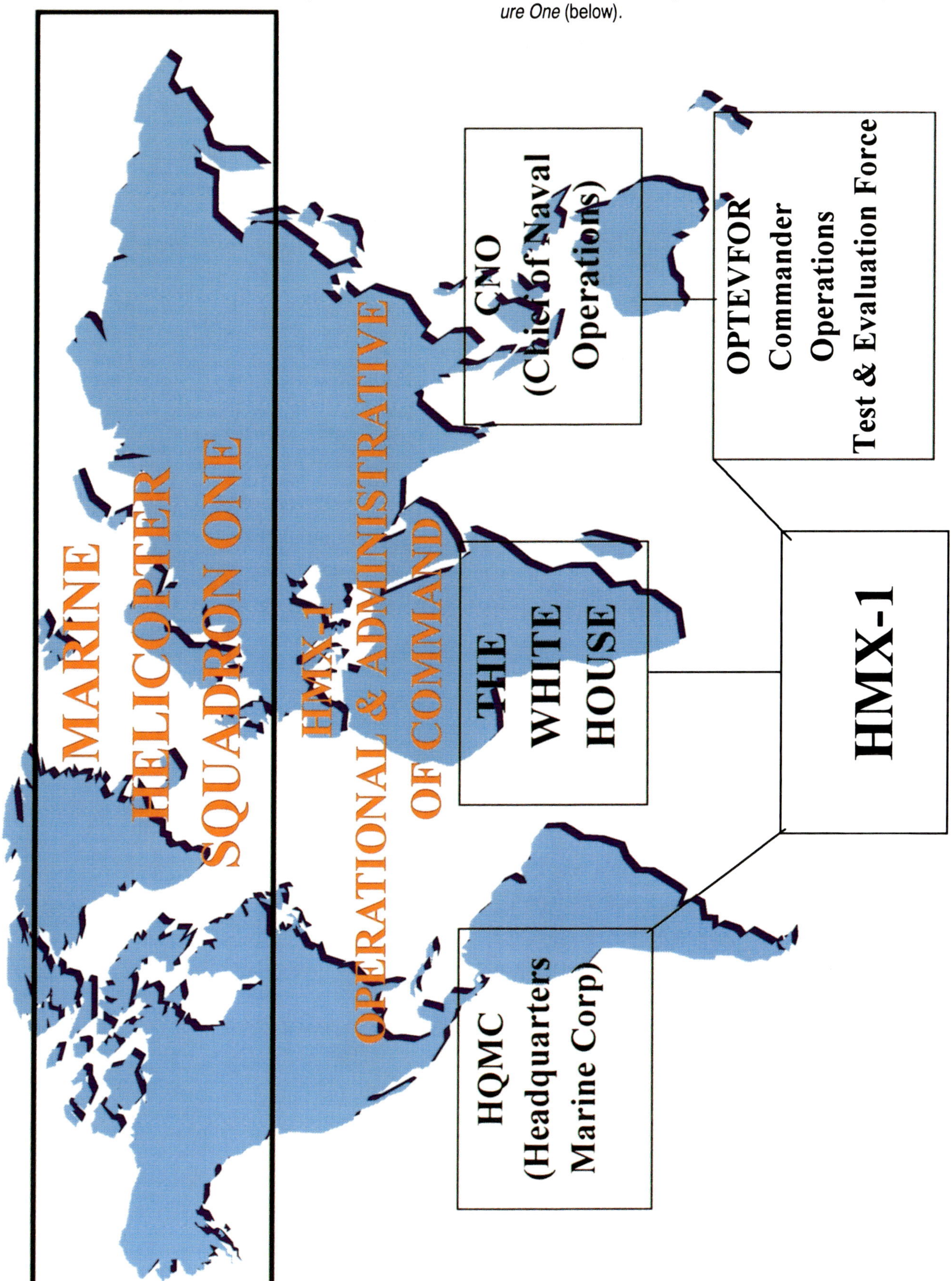

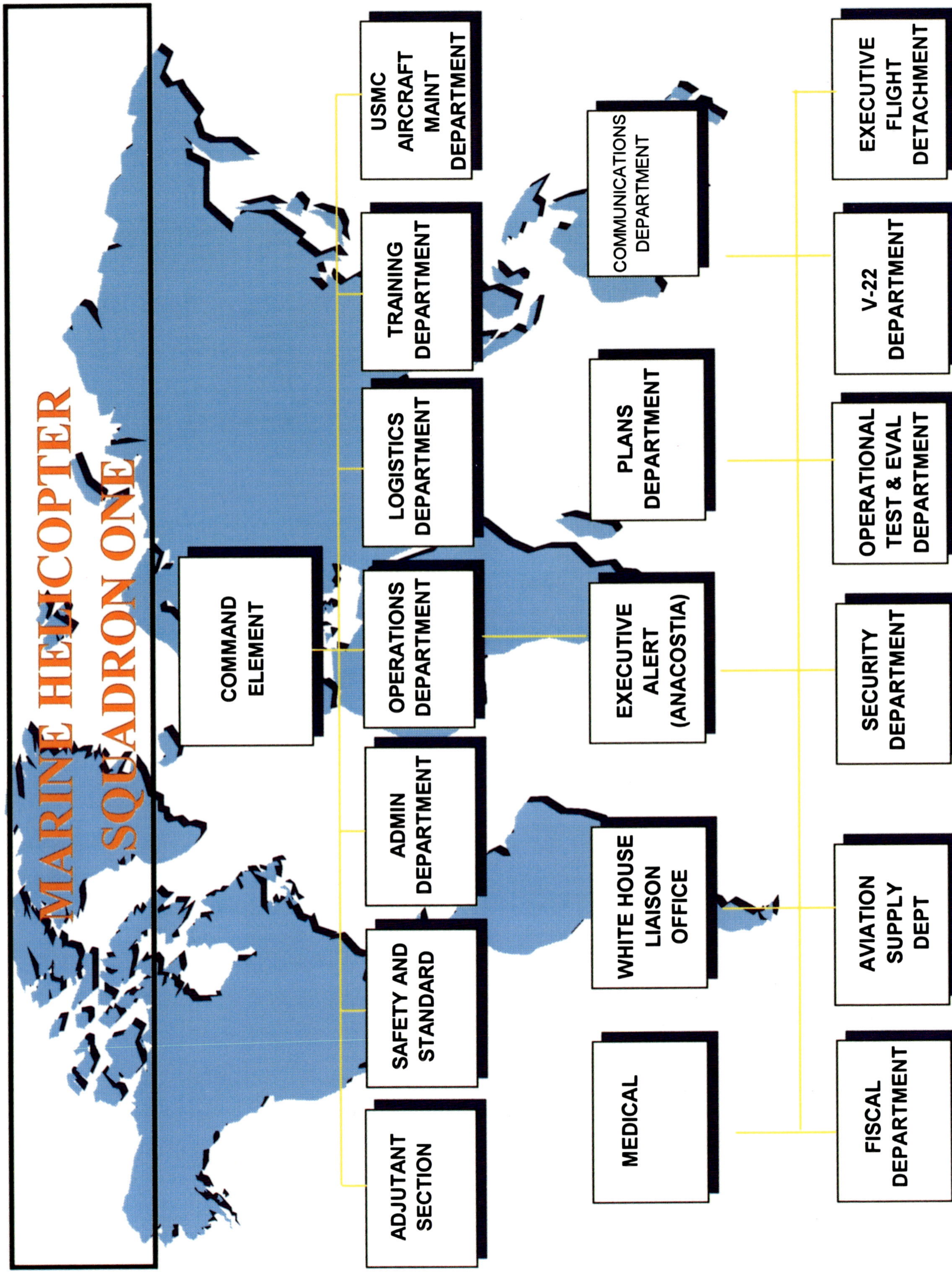
MARINE HELICOPTER SQUADRON ONE
COMMAND ELEMENT
ADJUTANT SECTION
SAFETY AND STANDARD
ADMIN DEPARTMENT
OPERATIONS DEPARTMENT
LOGISTICS DEPARTMENT
TRAINING DEPARTMENT
USMC AIRCRAFT MAINT DEPARTMENT
MEDICAL
WHITE HOUSE LIAISON OFFICE
EXECUTIVE ALERT (ANACOSTIA)
PLANS DEPARTMENT
COMMUNICATIONS DEPARTMENT
FISCAL DEPARTMENT
AVIATION SUPPLY DEPT
SECURITY DEPARTMENT
OPERATIONAL TEST & EVAL DEPARTMENT
V-22 DEPARTMENT
EXECUTIVE FLIGHT DETACHMENT

The Marine Corps chain of command goes from the Commandant of the Marine Corps (CMC) to the Deputy Chief of Staff for Aviation (DC/S A) and then straight to Marine Helicopter Squadron One. DC/S A issues orders for all tasks that Marine Helicopter Squadron One is to execute in conjunction with Marine Corps activities. Marine Helicopter Squadron One also has a separate chain-of-command, reporting to the White House. All Presidential missions and Presidential support missions are received directly from the White House Military Office. Finally, the squadron's Commanding Officer receives orders for the Operational Test and Evaluation department directly from the Commander of Operational Test and Evaluation Force in Norfolk, Virginia.

Marine Helicopter Squadron One Organization

Marine Helicopter Squadron One is the largest helicopter squadron in the Marine Corps. Most helicopter squadrons in the Fleet Marine Forces vary from one hundred and twenty Marines to just over three hundred in a composite squadron that is preparing for shipboard deployment. Marine Helicopter Squadron One has over seven hundred personnel assigned. The squadron has all the typical sections that you'd find in every other squadron throughout the Marine Corps. These are Administration (S1), Intelligence/Security (S2), Operations (S3), Logistics (S4), Safety and Standardization (DSS), and a Maintenance Department.

Departments normally found at the Marine Aircraft Group (MAG) level or at adjacent commands include Medical, Fiscal, and Supply. These departments are internally incorporated into HMX-1. The squadron has two flight surgeons and five additional medical personnel who deploy on Presidential trips and provide medical support to the squadron and Air Facility at Quantico. The squadron has a dedicated Fiscal and Aviation Supply Department as HMX-1 is the only aviation unit assigned to MCAF Quantico. The Safety and Standardization Department is similar to that found in a composite helicopter squadrons with several different types of aircraft, each requiring a standardization program. Marine Helicopter Squadron One also maintains a classified facility in Washington, D.C.

The Operations Department responsibilities include local training flights for pilot qualifications and ensuring all pilots remain proficient in all aspects of aviation. They publish daily flight schedules, coordinating with operational test and evaluation to schedule their tests. They also provide all the airlift support for the Marine Corps Combat Development Command schools located at Quantico. Additionally, they produce trip lists assigning squadron Marines to the various worldwide Presidential support missions. Operations at Marine Helicopter Squadron One is a daunting task, executing and planning missions while keeping up with the ever-changing scenarios they face on a daily basis.

Presidential Helicopter Pilot, Major Strasmann, flies a VH-60N on a routine training flight through Washington D.C.

Colonel Geier at the controls of Marine One

Marine One Crew Chief stands at the foot of Marine One awaiting the President.

Departments that are unique to the Presidential helicopter squadron include the Communications Department, the White House Liaison Office, the Plans Department, and the Security Department. The Communications Department has seventeen Communication Systems Operators (CSO's) who are assigned a specific crew mission in the VH-60N. This crew member is responsible for providing instantaneous worldwide communications capability for the President. In conjunction with the Presidential support mission, several HMX-1 officers are assigned to the White House Liaison Office. These Marines work with the White House Advance Staff and the White House Military Office in the planning of trips. They do all the logistical preparation for the squadron's detachment and coordinate with local law enforcement agencies, Secret Service, FAA, and other personnel on-site ready to brief the mission to the squadron detachment when they arrive. The Plans Department manages the classified planning portion of all Presidential missions. Marine Helicopter Squadron One has its own company sized Security Department, made up entirely of Marine Corps Military Police. They provide security at the squadron's facilities at Quantico, the Anacostia Alert facility, and every HMX-1 trip site where the Presidential helicopters are used. A security detachment is an integral part of every Presidential mission, providing twenty-four hour security for the aircraft.

Marine Helicopter Squadron One Missions

* Provide helicopter transportation for the President of the United States; Vice President of the United States; Members of the President's Cabinet and Foreign Dignitaries, as directed by the Military Assistant to the President.

* Provide Helicopter Emergency Evacuation Support.

* Plan, Execute, and Report On Independent Operational Tests and Evaluations (OT&E) of helicopters and Related Systems for Naval Services.

* Provide Support For The Commanding General, Marine Corps Combat Development Command (MCCDC) for the development of helicopter tactics, techniques and landing force equipment, as well as providing support for student demonstrations and helicopter indoctrination.

* Provides Support As Directed By the Commandant of the Marine Corps.

Sikorsky VH-60N on the flightline along the historic hangars of HMX-1.

The Few, The Proud, *The Chosen*. Only the best crew chiefs in the Marine Corps can apply to be a crew chief in Marine Helicopter Squadron One. After serving a year in the squadron executing support missions and awaiting their Top Secret clearance in what is affectionately known as the *'Greenside'* of the squadron, Crew Chiefs can move to the Executive Flight part of the squadron affectionately known as the *'Whiteside'* of the squadron. Executive Flight Crew Chiefs are then nominated by their peers and selected by the current Marine One Crew Chiefs. Currently the Marine One Crew Chiefs are *(left to right)*; Sgt. C.B. Reis, Sgt. R.L. Rood, Sgt. W.M. Scovell, Sgt. N.J. Gatewood, Sgt. W.D. Surike, Sgt. J.P. Delbalso, SSgt. M.D. Carter, Sgt. D.T.Roseman

MARINE HELICOPTER SQUADRON ONE

Only The Best Need Apply

Marine Helicopter Squadron One pilots are all volunteers; Marines with a proven track record who have already made their mark in the fleet. To the uninformed, hard-charging Marine pilot in the Fleet Marine Forces, a tour of duty with HMX-1 might appear to be a plush billet as a VIP pilot - nothing could be further from the truth. For those who want to join the squadron, it's not an easy place to get into. Pilots are required to have a minimum of 1,500 flight hours before they can apply to the squadron. Applicants in all Military Occupational Specialties have to pass the extremely stringent security clearance requirements. The slightest indiscretion can eliminate an applicant from consideration. To obtain this clearance, applicants are subjected to a very intensive background investigation which some people just can't pass. This is not to suggest that Marines who are not selected for a tour in Marine Helicopter Squadron One are not capable of making significant contributions to the Marine Corps.

All officers accepted into Marine Helicopter Squadron serve a four-year tour in the squadron. Pilots are *checked-out,* or qualified, by the squadron's senior pilots in the CH-53E or CH-46E and, in some cases, will need to make a transition. During their first year in the squadron, all pilots are put through rigorous training syllabi for both of the Executive Transport helicopters, the Sikorsky VH-3D and VH-60N. The pilots then serve as co-pilots in the VH-3D and VH-60N and once they amass one hundred hours in each aircraft and 2000 total flight hours, they are eligible to be designated as White House Helicopter Aircraft Commanders. This makes them eligible to fly as an Aircraft Commander in support of White House Missions. The Presidential Pilot, currently Colonel Frederick J. Geier (Commanding Officer of Marine Helicopter Squadron One from June 1995 through June 1997), is authorized to designate up to eight additional pilots as Presidential Command Pilots. Of these eight pilots, five receive additional designation as Marine One Pilots who are authorized to serve as helicopter Aircraft Commanders when the President is embarked on a Marine Helicopter.

Serving with Marine Helicopter Squadron One is a challenging and rewarding experience that returns Marines of all MOS's to the Fleet with a career's worth of meticulous planning skills and acute attention to detail. Invaluable experience is gained in the decision making process when it comes to the utilization, deployment, and redeployment of squadron assets. Marine Helicopter Squadron One pilots routinely do more flying under Instrument Flight Rules than most Fleet Marine Force pilots as a result of traveling across the country in support of the numerous Presidential support trips.

In the Fleet Marine Forces, Marines can be deployed for six months or more away from their home duty station. Marines in HMX-1 are deployed for much shorter periods of time with little or short notice, for a week or two at a time for an average of one hundred to one hundred-fifty days per year. It goes without saying that the time away from home increases dramatically during the Presidential election campaigns.

Feedback from FMF squadron commanders highlight they are pleased to have former HMX personnel join their squadrons. They return to the Fleet Marine Force with greater experience and expertise. Their "can do" attitude and esprit de corps can be contagious.

There's a strong tie between Marine Helicopter Squadron One and the Fleet Marine Forces in recognition of the caliber of the Marines returning to the fleet. A majority of the Marines from Marine Helicopter Squadron One return to the Fleet as a squadron's Maintenance Officer, Operations Officer, Executive Officer, or Commanding Officer. Of interest, Lieutenant Colonel Tarbutton, who served a previous tour of duty at Marine Helicopter Squadron One, was the Air Mission Commander of the Marine Corps rescue of Air Force Captain Scott O'Grady in Bosnia.

Marine Helicopter Squadron One supports the MAWTS-1 classes in Yuma, AZ, in various capacities. The squadron will frequently send members to the MAWTS-1 Aviation Development of Tactics and Evaluations (ADT&E) from the Operational Test and Evaluation (OT&E) department. OT&E members brief the MAWTS-1 classes on current state of the art projects and emerging technologies that Fleet aviation might see over the next five year period. If the assets are available, the squadron will send one or two of their CH-53E's or CH-46E's with the actual equipment being evaluated, mounted on the airframe for the students to see and at times fly for a hands-on perspective.

Marine Helicopter Squadron One segments its missions into two distinct areas of the squadron: The Executive Flight Detachment; known as the Cage or the *White Side* (Presidential Missions) and the Support Missions; know as Stake or the *Green Side* (OT&E, MCCDC, and Commandant of the Marine Corps Missions).

Executive Flight Detachment of Marine Helicopter Squadron One

The White side or Cage of Marine Helicopter Squadron One currently employs two types of aircraft that are not used anywhere else in the Marine Corps - the Sikorsky VH-3D, the primary Presidential helicopter, and the Sikorsky VH-60N, which is the executive version of the UH-60 "Blackhawk." The V designates the aircraft as configured for use by VIP's. The helicopters HMX-1 has used to transport Presidents have included the following:

Aircraft	Dates	Presidents Served
UH-34	1957 - 1962	Eisenhower, Kennedy
VH-3A	1963 - 1977	Kennedy, Johnson, Nixon, Ford, Carter
VH-1N	1976 - 1989	Ford, Carter, Reagan, Bush
VH-3D	1976 - present	Carter, Reagan, Bush, Clinton*
VH-60N	1988 - present	Reagan, Bush, Clinton*

* Although not designated a Presidential asset, the CH-46E has been utilized by President Clinton to view flood damage on four occasions.

The Sikorsky VH-3D is the primary Presidential helicopter capable of transporting fourteen people. This aircraft is also used to transport the Vice President and visiting Heads of State. Each helicopter has a three-man crew consisting of pilot, copilot, and crew chief. The Sikorsky VH-3A helicopter was first put into service at HMX-1 in 1962. While the VH-3D was put into service over twenty years ago, it looks as though it just rolled off Sikorsky's manufacturing line. To keep these aircraft in their superior condition, they are put through a very extensive Special Progressive Aircraft Rework (SPAR) at predetermined intervals. Additionally, every three to four years there is a complete review of the communication and navigation systems. Even though the cockpit is state of the art, the fuselage and the general air frame is of an older design.

The Sikorsky VH-60N seats up to eleven passengers and is used for various White House missions. The VH-60N is smaller then the VH-3D and, because it folds easily for loading onto a C-5, it is ideal for overseas assignments on very short notice. The Marines at HMX-1 can prepare a

Marine One and Marine Two in position at Andrews AFB, MD, in front of Air Force One.

Marine One arrives at Air Force One with President Clinton.

President William Jefferson Clinton looking out the door of a Marine Helicopter Squadron One CH-46E. President Clinton is the only President to have flown in a CH-46E. Mr. Clinton flew in the CH-46E, first in Iowa when he was observing the flood damage and again in Georgia, using the CH-46E for the same purpose. President Clinton has made a total of four flights in the CH-46E. Official White House photo.

Historical.

CH-46E

VH-60N

VH-60N in less than two hours for a C-5 load. It takes approximately 45 minutes per helicopter to load on the Air Force transport. Reverse the process with a single hour of penalty time, add transit time to deployment site and HMX-1 is ready for its support mission. The VH-60N is ideally suited for this short notice mission.

Sikorsky VH-3D Overview

* The VH-3 helicopter, derived from the Sikorsky Aircraft S-61 series, was developed as an antisubmarine sensor carrier for the U.S. Navy.

* The aircraft is seventy-two feet, eight inches long and sixteen feet, ten inches high with a maximum gross weight of 20,500 pounds.

* Two General Electric T-58 gas turbine turboshaft engines drive the sixty-two foot diameter, five blade main rotor which rotates at approximately two-hundred revolutions per minute. A ten foot diameter tail rotor provides directional control.

* The VH-3D cruises at speeds up to 140 nautical miles per hour and can travel as far as 330 miles without refueling, depending on the number of passengers it is carrying.

* The VH-3D is equipped with a VIP cabin interior.

Sikorsky VH-60N Overview

* The VH-60N is built upon the basic UH-60A Black Hawk airframe and powered by T700-GE-401 engines.

* Improvements and enhancements include;
  - -SH-60B improved durability gearbox
  - -HH-60A rotor brake
  - -125 gallon internal auxiliary fuel tank
  - -SH-60B modified AFCS and airspeed indicator
  - -Folding stabilator
  - -Cabin soundproofing
  - -Cabin radio operator station
  - -Extensive avionics ugrades
  - -VIP cabin interior

Executive Flight Maintenance

The squadron's VH-3D and VH-60N helicopters are maintained by a dedicated maintenance section which is known as Executive Flight Maintenance or White Side maintenance. They also aptly refer to themselves as *Cage Maintenance* because of the security requirements in this area. Marines have to go through an elaborate security network just to get into the maintenance compound. Marines assigned to White Side maintenance say that while working in this facility, there they feel like they're in a cage, so they refer to it as the cage maintenance department. Security and procedures are leading edge inside and outside the facility, with the perimeters patrolled by very serious minded armed Marines. The maintenance hangars are old but well kept. The tools that are used by White Side maintenance personnel are arranged with surgical precision. White Side maintenance personnel are fully trained by the manufacturer's factory personnel. Marines attend special schools for the VH-60N and for the VH-3D since they are unique to HMX-1 and the Marine Corps.

Marine One Crew Chiefs

The most visible White Side Marine to the public is the Marine in a Dress Blue uniform positioned by the door of the Presidential helicopter. Upon the Presidents arrival or departure they render a crisp salute and return to the position of attention. These Marines are known as Marine One Crew Chiefs.

The selection process for the Marine One crew chief is as selective and stringent as that used to select the Marine One pilots. When an opening happens in the Cage, a crew chief is transferred from the Greenside Maintenance department and the process begins.

A helicopter crew chief is responsible for the aircraft's upkeep. Under the watchful eye of Maintenance Control and quality assurance, he ensures that all maintenance cycles and inspections on the aircraft are completed. The crew chief is the one who "signs off" the helicopter, stating it is safe and ready for flight. Without a crew chief's signature on the aircraft, it is not cleared for flight. If any maintenance is performed after the crew chief signs off the aircraft he must reinspect it and sign it off again.

In addition to their flying duties, crew chiefs in the Marine Corps are expert mechanics. Once assigned to the cage, crew chiefs select the VH-3D or VH-60N as their aircraft of choice. Sikorsky factory trained instructors teach them about all the helicopters systems. They gain hands on experience under the watchful eye of experienced Marines. Then they complete Crew Member Training (CMT), including written and oral exams as well as a check ride prior to being designated crew chiefs in their respective aircraft. Crew chiefs are only designated in a single helicopter type at any one time.

The above qualifications are true of all crew chiefs throughout the Marine Corps. In the Fleet Marine Forces, crew chiefs typically are tasked with transporting Marines, gear and equipment.

Marine One Crew Chiefs have the primary responsibility for transporting the President. Other Cage crew chiefs transport Vice President, Senators and Congressmen, foreign dignitaries and other official guests. Because their mission allows them to operate in close proximity to the President, all Cage Crew Chiefs assigned to the White Side must also pass a rigorous background investigation and receive a security clearance.

USAF Colonel Robert D. 'Danny' Barr, Air Force One Presidential Pilot (left) confers with USMC Presidential Pilot, Colonel Geier, on the last minute planning details of a mission.

Marine Helicopter Squadron One Executive Officer (XO) Lt. Colonel Mike Conklin in front of a *Greenside* CH-46E.

A small percentage of Marine Helicopter Squadron One Crew Chiefs do not come from the fleet. Some Marines come right out of Basic Helicopter School and earn their first experience as a crew chief at HMX-1. All Marines are initially assigned to the Greenside Maintenance Department where they serve as crew chiefs for six months to a year on missions ranging from test and evaluation, to providing helicopter support for the various commands at Quantico, including The Basic School and Officer Candidates School. Once they have hands-on experience working with the squadron and obtain their final security clearance, the are eligible to move to the White Side.

Selection of the Marine One Crew Chiefs

Marine One Crew Chiefs are nominated by their peers from the White Side of Marine Helicopter Squadron One. There might be ten crew chiefs that are eligible and qualified at any moment for a single Marine One Crew Chief position. A White Side crew chief must have a minimum of one year experience as a crew chief in a VH helicopter before being considered as a Marine One Crew Chief. As a slot opens, a small panel made up of crew chiefs convenes and reviews the performance of all crew chiefs. The panel evaluates the Marine's initiative, technical knowledge and levels of motivation and espirt-de-corps. A short list of three candidates is compiled and put to a vote. The results are compiled and given to a Maintenance Officer who puts them in a memorandum and forwards his recommendation to the Commanding Officer who approves or disapproves the selected candidate. The Marine One Crew Chief serves in this assignment for a period of one year. This limitation is imposed primarily due to the high potential for burn-out in this position and the impact travel may have on families. It is a very prestigious position that all White Side Marines aspire to—it is an excellent motivator.

Every quarter, the selection process starts over again. At year's end, the new Marine One Crew Chief takes over. The outgoing crew chief goes back to the White Side and continues crewing for the Vice President and other White House missions. The four crew chiefs rotate back to the White Side on a quarterly basis. This way there are always three Marine One Crew Chiefs who have experience in Presidential lifts. Former Marine One Crew Chiefs provide an outstanding instructional base for the new Marines assigned to the Cage.

XO Conklin completes the final items on the check list inside the cockpit of his CH-46E.

All In A Day's Work

The Marine One Crew Chiefs rotate shifts, taking turns crewing for Marine One helicopters. They work two days on, two off, and every other weekend. On long-distance trips, two crew chiefs are required, so they can rotate flights. Short trips, known as hops, include flights to and from the White House to Camp David, MD, or to Andrews Air Force Base, MD—home of Air Force One— the President's Boeing 747. Overnight trips can be to anywhere in the country or overseas, anywhere that the President's business takes him. Air Force One flies the President to his destination, and Marine One provides the helicopter transportation around the local area once the President arrives.

Presidential business takes the Commander-in-Chief all over the world, and wherever he goes, an HMX-1 helicopter and crew travels with him. Overseas trips require that the Presidential helicopters be transported to the final destination inside an Air Force C-5 Galaxy aircraft. Transporting the VH-3D and VH-60N overseas in a C-5 is a familiar task to the Marine One Crew Chiefs, albeit a challenge that requires extensive planning and coordination to guarantee that the helicopters are prepared and at the Presidents disposal when required. The C-5 can transport up to three VH-3's at one time.

Preparing the helicopters for disassembly and tearing them down for flight on a C-5 is serious business requiring precision planning and a significant effort. It that takes 12-16 hours to prepare the VH -3D helicopter for a C-5 flight. The flight to their final destination may be twelve or more hours. Upon arrival, the Marine One Crew Chief is responsible to get the helicopter off the plane and into a secure location. The crew chief will rest or start the 12-16 hour build up process to ensure the helicopters are ready upon the President's arrival. Before the President flies on the rebuilt aircraft, it must log five hours of penalty time. It is then eligible to be signed-off as ready for a VIP flight. The Marine One Crew Chiefs then change into their Dress Blue uniforms and stand ready to perform their crew chief duties.

A mission-ready helicopter at Marine Helicopter Squadron One must be available for the President twenty-four hours a day. Marine One helicopters must always be in an 'up' status (available for flight) and remain that way. This involves an all-hands effort - hydraulics, avionics, maintenance control and ground support equipment. The following is a day in the life of a Marine One Crew Chief:

The crew chief is one of the first to arrive, usually before dawn; this is known as the *early show.* The Marine One Crew Chief spends hours preflighting and cleaning the aircraft, readies his Dress Blue uniform, boards the helicopter and flies with the crew to the Anacostia alert facility. The crew briefs and stands-by to depart for the White House when required to transport the President to his destination. While waiting up to several hours for the President to return to the aircraft, the Marine One crew chief cleans the aircraft again, whether it needs it or not. The President is then flown back to the White House and the Marine One helicopter returns to the squadron in Quantico, VA, where post-flight maintenance is performed. The helicopter is cleaned again, this time from top to bottom, inside and out. This final cleaning is an all-hands effort by Marines in White Side Maintenance Department. Depending on the flights destinations and Presidential mission conducted, a Marine One Crew Chief may not finish his workday until mid-night. If something breaks down and needs to be fixed the Marine One crew chief stays until the helicopter is good to go. Marine One Crew Chiefs have an enormous amount of pride and professionalism in the execution of their duties. They understand that they are entrusted with the responsibility of providing the President with safe transportation.

Colonel Geier (*standing*) reviews final briefing details of a mission with XO Lt.Colonel Conklin, Major Bernard Jr, Major DeVore, Major Hanson and Major Martinez in the squadron Ready Room.

Support Mission or *The Green Side*

The Marines assigned to the *Green Side* of the squadron fly the CH-53E and the CH-46E. When not supporting a Presidential mission, these aircraft and personnel work with the Marine Corps Combat Development Command (MCCDC), located at the Marine Corps base in Quantico, Virginia. The MCCDC has the responsibility of managing the Combat Development Process (CDP) for the Marine Corps. The CDP encompasses all the activities and organizations that are required to produce, improve and sustain a combat-ready Marine Air Ground Task Force for current and future deployments.

Marine Helicopter Squadron One works with the MCCDC and the schools under its command to provide new Ground Combat Marines with indoctrination training for helicopters and the assault tactics and capabilities in-flight, ingressing and egressing out of landing zones for missions such as the TRAP, Tactical Recovery of Aircraft and Personnel are included. Advanced training is supported in Fast Rope missions, where Marines repel out of a low hovering helicopter at low levels to the ground below. MCCDC maintains a training facility called Combat Town, were HMX-1 Marines participate in the training of assault troops in hostage rescue scenarios and urban assault tactics.

Support Maintenance

Greenside Maintenance provides the maintenance for Marine Helicopter Squadron One's CH-53E's, CH-46E's, and aircraft on loan to the Operational Test and Evaluation Department such as a UH-1 Huey. Up-time, the availability of the squadron's aircraft, is the primary focus of the Maintenance Department in order for the squadron to execute its missions. It takes an extremely focused and professional effort to keep the modern and sophisticated helicopter ready for flight. Tenacity and pride are critical elements for a successful Maintenance Department, especially with a set of missions as diverse as those in Marine Helicopter Squadron One.

Master Gunnery Sergeant Thomas Downey, known as *'LTD-Little Tommy Downey'*. Downey is amongst the best Master Gunnery Sergeants in the Marine Corps who keeps the squadrons CH-53Es, CH-53Ds, CH-46Es and UH-1 on loan to the Operational Test and Evaluation (OT&E) department in top condition in the Maintenance Department. Downey is a *'Marines Marine'* who will retire from the Marine Corps in 1997 after thirty years of service to the Corps—*Semper Fi!*

Operational Test & Evaluation (OT&E)

Mission

* Conduct Operational Test and Evaluation of United States Marine Corps helicopters and associated systems. Currently these are conducted on the CH-46E, CH-53E, UH-1N and the V-22 (Note: OT&E tasks are conducted for the AH-1 Cobra in conjunction with the U.S. Navy Air Test & Evaluation Squadron One (VX-1).

OT&E conducts field testing and evaluations of the actual equipment that is targeted to go into the Fleet Marine Force under realistic conditions. Any item or key component of weapons, equipment or munitions are evaluated for the purpose of determining their operational effectiveness and suitability for use in combat. Operational tests and evaluations are conducted with a focus on how the typical operator and maintainer will use the piece of equipment, and that the equipment is representative of the targeted production unit. The tests are conducted in an environment that is representative of the threats which the Marines using the equipment will face.

Programs are evaluated in the context of program management, costs, schedule performance, general systems performance, operational test characteristics and the performance in operational settings. Elements that make

Major Bruce Houser (pilot) and Co-Pilot Major Timothy Fitzgerald fly a CH-53D in a loose formation off a CH-46E piloted by Major Andrew O'Donnell and Co-Pilot Major Matthew 'Gerry' Glavy. The mission objective is to indoctrinate new Marines to the helicopters and the ingress/egress procedures in a Landing Zone. Similar missions are also flown by Marine Helicopter Squadron One for advanced training missions such as the TRAP (Tactical Recovery of Aircraft and Personnel).

a program successful are high levels of communication and interaction with private industry and contractors, Congress, the Office of the Secretary of Defense, Project Management, Inter-service Operational Test groups and the user community in the Fleet Marine Force. OT&E receives its tasking orders from the Chief of Naval Operations via the Operational Test and Evaluation Force (OPTEVFOR) and the Commandant of the Marine Corps (CMC). *Figure Three* illustrates the Marine Helicopter Squadron One OT&E reporting structure, *Figure Four* illustrates the OT&E organizational structure, and *Figure Five* illustrates a typical project OT&E cycle.

OT&E Products and Services
OT&E provides the following products and services to the Fleet Marine Force:

* Test Reports
* Operational Tactics Guides
* Tactics Manuals (TACMAN) Input
* MAWTS-1 Weapons and Tactics Instructor (WTI) Course briefings, dem onstrations and support to the instructors and Academic Department at MAWTS-1
* *NightHawk News* and *NightHawk Newsletter* - Professional Journals and newsletters

In OT&E, the actual piece of equipment that is targeted to go into the Fleet Marine Force undergoes a myriad of operational tests following developmental testing and evaluation at NAS Patuxent River. OT&E validates that the piece of equipment is in fact compatible with the targeted airframe and the Marines in the fleet who are going to maintain and use it. Marine Helicopter Squadron One's OT&E evaluates whether the equipment that was certified in a pristine test environment will work operationally in the fleet. The results are reported to Commander Operational Test & Evaluation Force.

OT&E Division Programs
The following is a sample of the OT&E Programs:

CH-46 Programs

Current	Future
* Night Vision Goggle Head-up Display (NVG HUD)	* Common Automatic Recovery System (CARS)
* Communication-Navigation Control System (CNCS)	* Tactical Aircraft Mission PlanningSystem (TAMPS)
* Digital Clock Upgrade	* AN/ARC 220 HF Radio

CH-46 Communication Navigation Control System (CNCS) for the CH-46 brings the cockpit into the nineties, providing digital displays and consolidation of communication and navigation equipment. These upgrades will also assist the community of CH-46 pilots in the transition to the V-22. The Tactical Aircrew Mission Planning System (TAMPS) works in conjunction with CNCS allowing aircrews to improve ready room planning. Chock to chock planning to determine how a mission is flown, including routes, and consolidated threat rings are put into the Data Transfer Module. This is done on a full sized keyboard as opposed to entering the data on a small keypad in a confined cockpit. Pilots carry the portable Data Transfer Module to the aircraft. The computer will integrate into the HUD and show the navigational and flight information for the CH-46.

CH-53 Programs

Current	Future
* External Air Transport Certification (EAT)	IR Expendables
* Night Vision Goggle Head-up Display (NVG HUD)	
* Global Positioning System (GPS)/ARC 210 Radio	
* Semi Rigid Deployable Wing	
* Helicopter Night Vision System (HNVS) - *Completed*	
* Ground Proximity Warning System (GPWS) - *Completed*	

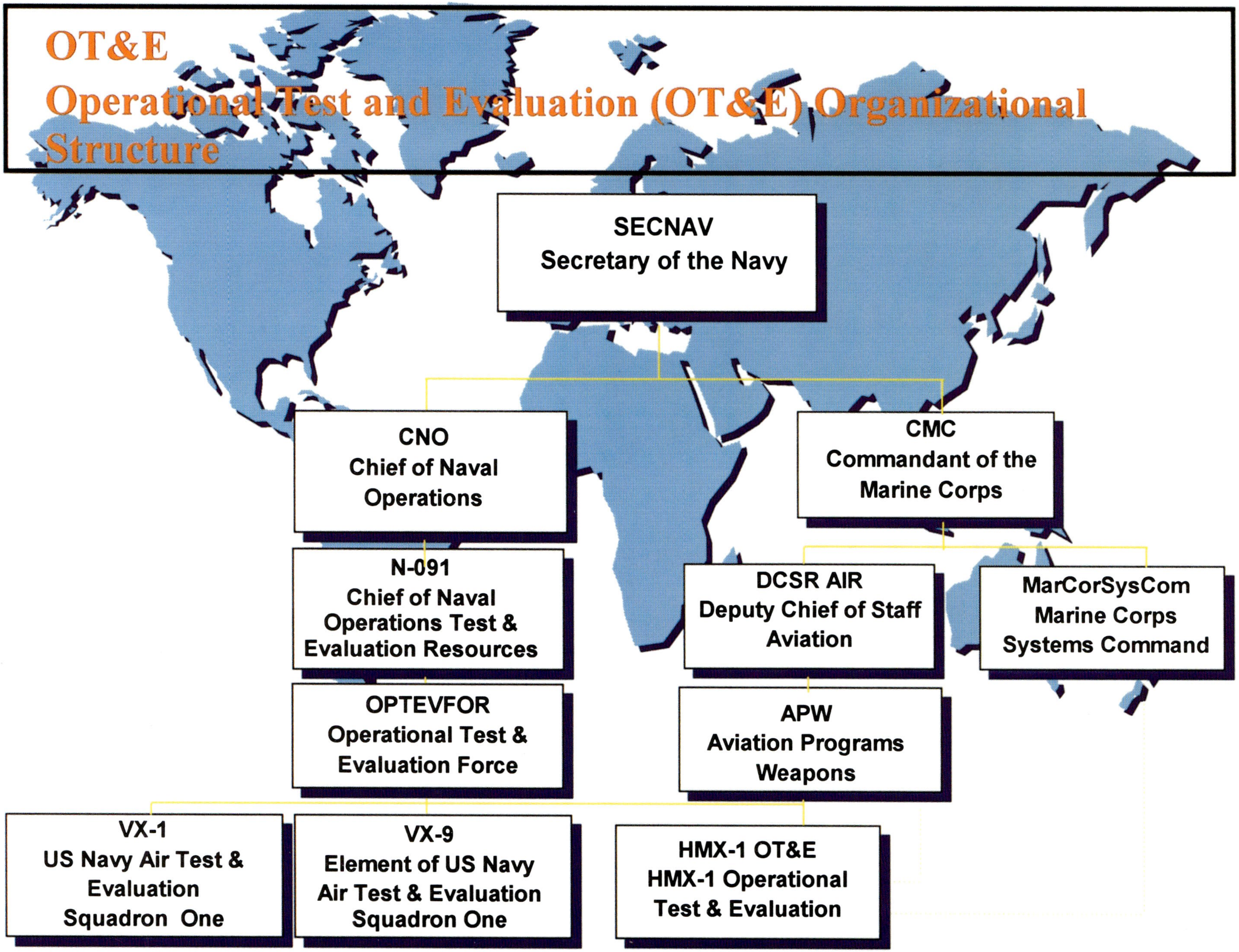
OT&E
Operational Test and Evaluation (OT&E) Organizational Structure
SECNAV
Secretary of the Navy
CNO
Chief of Naval Operations
CMC
Commandant of the Marine Corps
N-091
Chief of Naval Operations Test & Evaluation Resources
DCSR AIR
Deputy Chief of Staff Aviation
MarCorSysCom
Marine Corps Systems Command
OPTEVFOR
Operational Test & Evaluation Force
APW
Aviation Programs Weapons
VX-1
US Navy Air Test & Evaluation Squadron One
VX-9
Element of US Navy Air Test & Evaluation Squadron One
HMX-1 OT&E
HMX-1 Operational Test & Evaluation

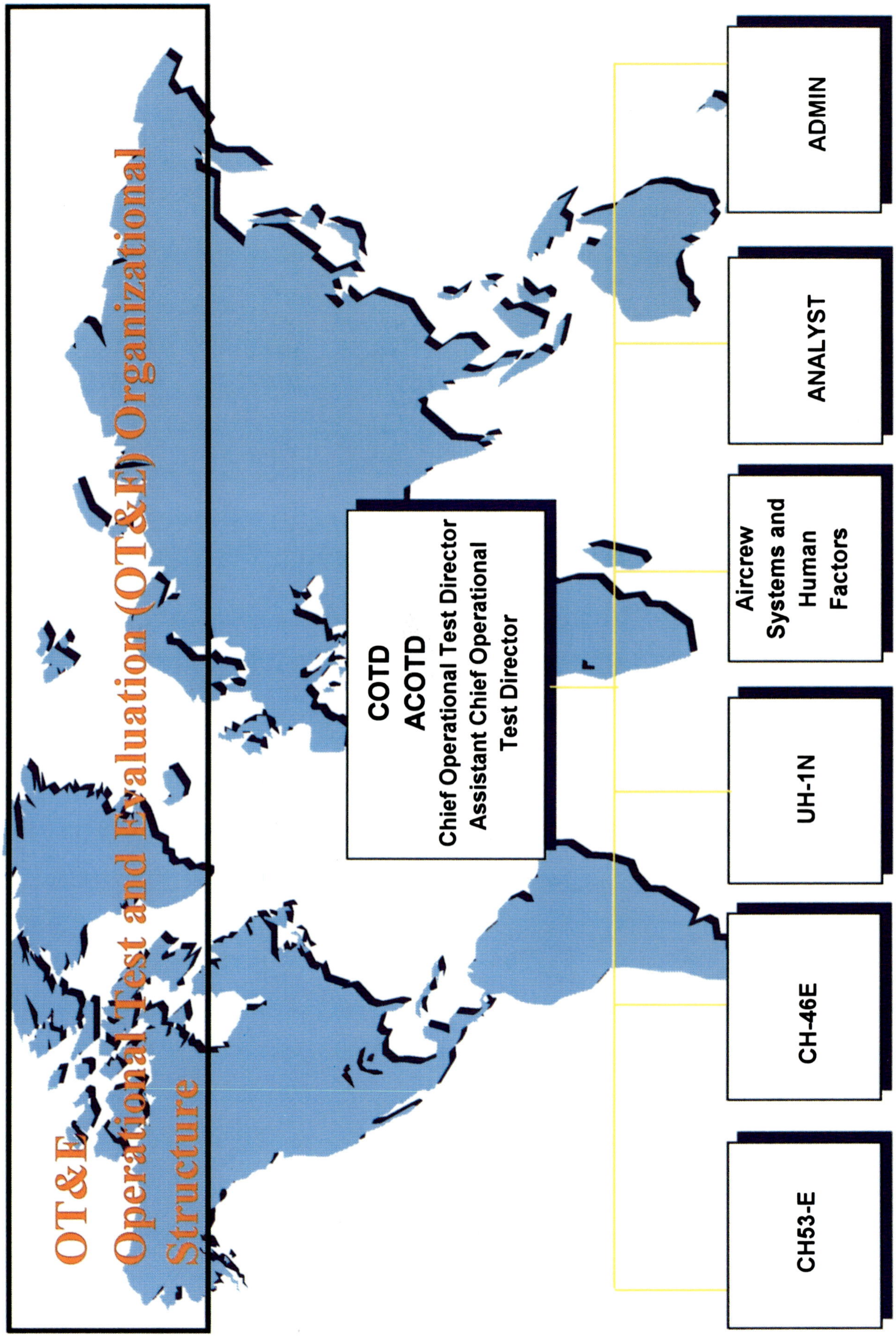
OT&E
Operational Test and Evaluation (OT&E) Organizational Structure
COTD
ACOTD
Chief Operational Test Director
Assistant Chief Operational Test Director
CH53-E
CH-46E
UH-1N
Aircrew Systems and Human Factors
ANALYST
ADMIN

OT&E

Acquisition Milestones and Phases

When mission need requires material solution. Mission Needs Statement prepared by user.	Evaluated feasibility of alternative concepts. Determine most promising concept or solution.	Design system(s) and demonstrate critical technologies and processes. Early prototypes.	Mature and finalize selected design. Validate production processes. Test and evaluate system.	Produce and field system. Monitor mission performance. Support fielded system. Modify and upgrade as required.	
PREMILESTONE	**PHASE 0**	**PHASE 1**	**PHASE II**	**PHASE III**	**PHASE IV**
Determination of Mission Need	**Concept Exploration and Definition**	**Demonstration and Validation**	**Engineering and Manufacturing Development**	**Production Approval**	**Operations and Support**

MS 0 Concept Studies Approval	MS I Concept Demonstration Approval	MS II Development Approval	MS III Production Approval	MV IV* Major Modification Approval
Approval to enter Phase 0. Exit Criteria approved.	Approval to enter Phase I. Program initiation. approved. Exit criteria approved.	Approval to enter Phase II. LRIP approved. Development baseline approved. Exit criteria approved.	Approval to enter Phase III. Production baseline approved.	Approval to modify system still in production. Mods > $115M RDTE or >$540M procurement (FY-90$)

Maintenance work being conducted on the aging CH-46E. Crew Chiefs keep Marine Helicopter Squadron One CH-46s in pristine condition.

UH-1N Programs

Current

* UH-1N Block Upgrade (Search Light Cover Shell, NVG HUD SDC Software Upgrade
* Four Bladed UH-1N
* Night Vision Enhancement (NVE) and Communication Navigation Systems Enhancements
* Electronic Warfare Suite (AN/AVR-2 Laser Detecting System. AN/APR-39A (V2) Radar Detecting Set and the AN/AAR-47 Missile Warning System Software Upgrades

Future

* Electronic Warfare Suite (AN/AAR-47 Missile Warning System Processor Upgrade
* Cargo Hook and Hoist
* ComNav Phase B Block Upgrade
* HH-1N GPS Integration
* Torque Monitoring System

Aircrew Systems Programs

Current

* AR-SCBR/NVG Compatibility
* Communications Earplug
* HGU-84/P helmet
* High Output Tube (HOT) ANVIS
* Microphone/Finger NVG lights
* Laser Interference Filters
* Aim-1 Laser Sight

Completed

* Aircrew Integrated Recovery Survival Armor Vest and Equipment (AIRSAVE)
* Helicopter Emergency Egress Device (HEED)
* Field Marker Lighting (FML)
* ANV-20/20 NVG Assessor
* Wireless Intercommunications System

Future

* OMNIBUS IV NVG
* Helmet Mounted Displays
* Low Profile Floatation Collar
* Laser Eye Protection

Major Michael Sparr pilots a CH-46E with Co-Pilot Captain William Conley on a mission toward *Combat Town* in Marine Corps Base at Quantico.

Crew Chief prepares a CH-53 for flight.

The Aircrew Systems Division focuses on human factors issues that result from the man-machine interface. Operational Test and Evaluation of aircrew systems can include items such as cockpit display type and layout, Heads-Up Displays, Helmet Mounted Displays, anthropometrics, crash/water survivability, Night Vision Systems, Laser Systems and associated eye protection, and any Aviation Life Support System.

OT&E flight equipment efforts are directed towards providing the aircrew with a streamlined, integrated, mission compatible system that is fully functional and meets the operational requirements without causing undue physical discomfort and degrading mission performance.

There Is No Monopoly On Good Ideas

Traditionally major programs require a long lead time for new systems to enter the Fleet. However, there is no monopoly on good ideas which come in a variety of channels in various scopes. One example of a simple and effective device that required little effort to evaluate and distribute to the Fleet is the NVG compatible lip light. Activated by pressing a microphone switch with the lip, it allowed pilots to read maps and publications without taking hands off the controls. Fleet Marines often channel systems or new

Trooplift of USMC Lieutenants attending Marine Corps Universities at Quantico.

capabilities to OT&E for evaluation. If an idea looks like it can enhance the Marines' capabilities and the cost is right, OT&E will poll the Fleet on the idea to determine if the fleet desires to generate an operational requirement or an operational need statement. Figure Four illustrates the typical evaluation process for a new piece of equipment.

Getting The Biggest Bang For The Buck

Marines are trained to improvise, adapt and overcome any obstacles that stand in the way of accomplishing a given mission. Marine Helicopter Squadron One's OT&E applies this ethos to the challenge of providing the Fleet Marine Forces with the required equipment for their missions while staying within their tight budgetary constraints.

An example of this is the Forward Looking Infra-Red (FLIR) system. The Commanding Officer explains; *"We did the operational test and evaluation for that entire FLIR system on the CH-53 and determined that it could be a valuable asset to the Fleet operationally. However, because of the tight budget restrictions that we're operating under now; a full roll-out of the FLIR system was prohibitive. Rather than canceling the entire program, we recommended that the Marine Corps install all the hardware and wiring required to support the FLIR system in every CH-53 in the Fleet and use the remaining funds to purchase a limited amount of FLIR packages. This allowed the Marines to introduce a valuable warfighting tool into the Fleet and keep the program moving forward, with the ability to move the capability where it could be leveraged to achieve a given mission and provide a foundation for growth in the future. Once additional funding becomes available (just over a million dollars a copy), we can readily deploy the technology."*

XO Conklin speaks to a CH-46E crew preflighting the aircraft.

CH-46E in the Zone

"There's no doubt that we get the biggest bang for the buck and I think a lot of it comes from the professionalism of the Marines throughout the Fleet. We don't sit back and complain because we don't have a state of the art radio in one of our Fleet aircraft. We say okay, this is the radio I have—how can I use it to maximize its capability? We would always like additional and more sophisticated equipment, but we're not going to waste any time waiting for better equipment.

We're going to use what we have to its maximum capability while we have it. Because even if we had the money for extra equipment, the war's not going to wait for us. In OT&E, we operate under the premise that if something happens, the Fleet Marines need to have the equipment and be trained and prepared in the systems that they have. OT&E operates to ensure that the Marines are prepared to fight the threats that will emerge in the future wars."

A Visit To Marine Helicopter Squadron One

V-22

The Marine Corps is preparing for a technological leap into the twenty-first century with the introduction of the tilt-rotor V-22 Osprey. The V-22 Osprey has more than four times the range and flies twice the speed of the CH-46. OT&E works with the Chief of Naval Operations and the United States Air Force to evaluate the operational effectiveness of the V-22 and prepare the CH-46 community for a transition to the V-22. *Figure Six* illustrates the organizational structure of the V-22 department.

Marine Helicopter Squadron One V-22 Department Head, Lt.Colonel Gerry Hammes, with members of his team preparing for a mission in a CH-46E. The CH-46 community will move many of its younger pilots into the V-22 community.

The United States Marines conjure up the image for most people as a cadre of highly motivated warfighters who are proud of their heritage, renowned for their warfighting capabilities, and represent all that is great about America. It should come as no surprise to anyone that the Marines in Marine Helicopter Squadron One embrace all the traditional ethos of the United States Marines Corps and its core values—they are just a bit more intense. One could easily imagine that espirit-de-corps is operationally tested and evaluated for the purpose of taking this particular ethos to new levels.

To reach Marine Helicopter Squadron One you need to drive through beautiful tree lined access roads of the Quantico Marine Corps Base, located in Virginia. Range Road leads you through a well groomed base and over a hill. As you reach the crest of the hill, visitors get their first glimpse of an unassuming array of aircraft hangars constructed in the 1940's with super glossy Marine green helicopters on the flightline. This is the original and only home of Marine Helicopter Squadron One.

Major Mark Peters working in the squadron's Nitelab on his Night Vision Goggles.

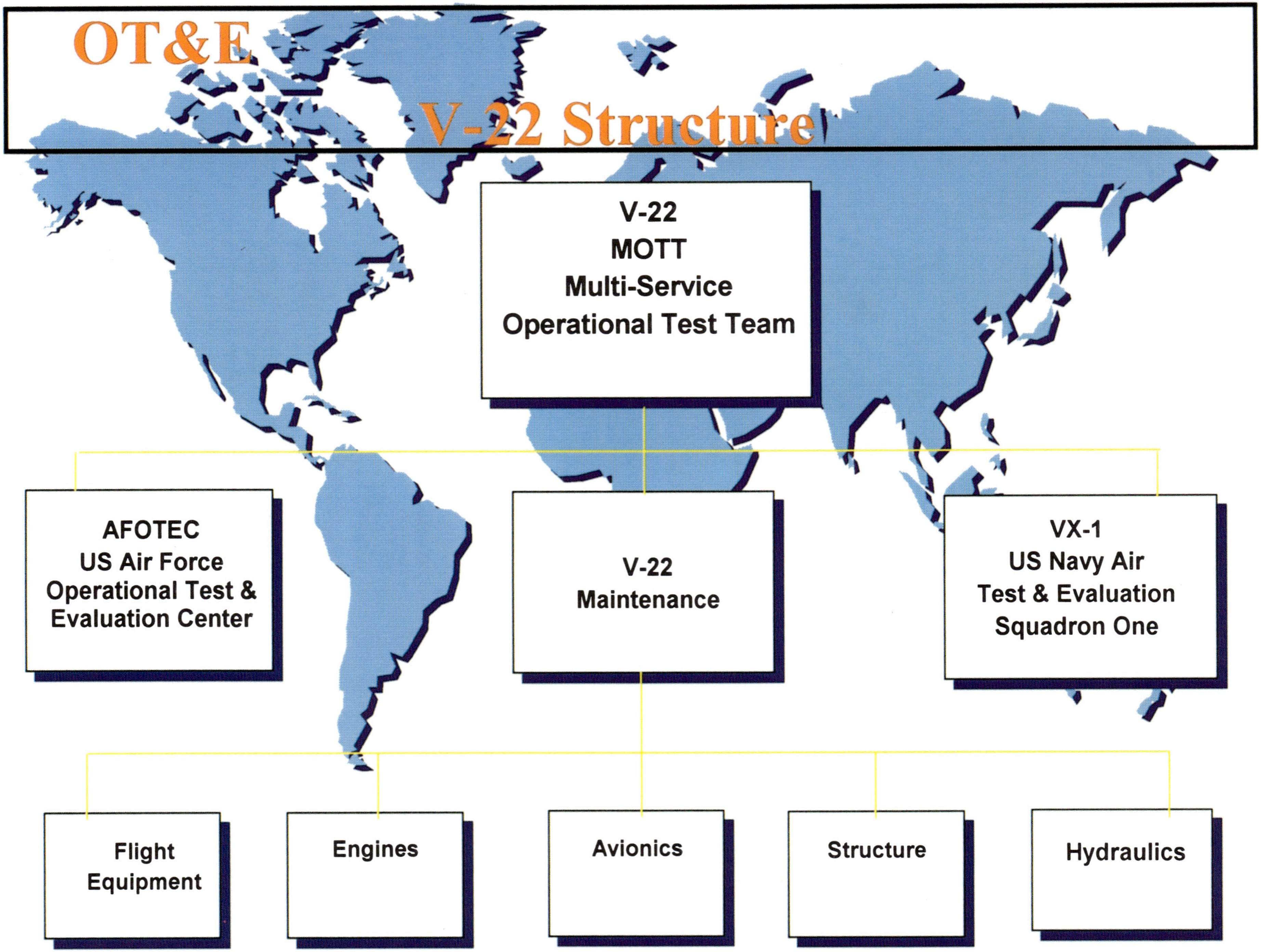
OT&E
V-22 Structure
V-22
MOTT
Multi-Service
Operational Test Team
AFOTEC
US Air Force
Operational Test &
Evaluation Center
V-22
Maintenance
VX-1
US Navy Air
Test & Evaluation
Squadron One
Flight
Equipment
Engines
Avionics
Structure
Hydraulics

VH-3D, VH-60N, CH-46E and CH-53E led by Presidential Helicopter Pilot Major Siesel down the historic HMX-1 tarmac.

As you wind down the hill, you approach the first of many security check points guarded by an armed Marine in razor sharp, creased camouflaged fatigues. After your credentials are thoroughly checked and scrutinized and you have professed your love for the United States of America, the Marine sentry crisply steps back and says in a booming voice, "Welcome Aboard!" The intensity and volume of this young Marine is enough to make *Lincoln* leap to his feet some thirty miles away from his monument chair.

As you proceed to the squadron, you see signs that announce "Do Not Enter—Deadly Force Authorized" with more armed Marines patrolling the inside perimeters of the fenced in the compound. Immediately you form an impression that these people are very different from you and that it will be wise to follow their rules. As you approach the main hangar which houses the squadron offices and Ready Room, an escort appears who obviously was trained by, and works for, the same Marine at the front gate. Immediately, you are taken to the Commanding Officer's office, walking through the historic halls of the squadron whose walls depict the history of helicopter aviation and HMX-1.

Walking up the stairs to the Commanding Officer's office, one immediately discovers where the Marine at the front gate learned his intonation. Once the CO concluded his phone call, the authors were introduced to Colonel Frederick J. Geier. The CO maintains the same office used by first CO of HMX-1, Colonel Edward C. Dyer. Memorabilia and historical photographs from the past fifty years decorate the office, from President Eisenhower to President Clinton.

Colonel Geier provided us with a walking tour of the entire squadron. As each *hatch* is opened and each room entered, he is greeted by Marines jumping to their feet and barking *Attention On Deck*—standing ready for the Commanding Officer's next order.

Espirit de Corps

Marines in the Marine Helicopter Squadron One view their billet as a great opportunity to execute their duties and have a strong sense of the honor in being able to serve the President of the United States and the Marine Corps. Everyone in the squadron has a strong sense of commitment, from the adjutant to the pilots to all the maintenance shop personnel. The aircraft stay 'up' because everyone in the squadron works on an extremely professional and highly motivated level. There's a standard of excellence that's been passed down from generation to generation to the new Marines coming into the squadron who are expected to maintain it. This standard of excellence means an incredible amount of hard work, total attention to detail, and a lot of pride. The aircraft in the entire squadron appear to have just rolled off the manufacturers lines. The sight of maintenance workers hovering around and on top of the squadron's helicopters around the clock is commonplace. Most prevalent though is the *attitude* of everyone at the squadron, they are indeed The Few, The Proud, The Marines... The *First and the Finest.*

Sikorsky VH-60N on a training mission. The VH-60N is a variant of the UH-60A Black Hawk airframe with a VIP cabin interior. The VH-60N is air transportable by C-130, C-141 and C-5 aircraft for long distance Presidential trips.

Marine One departing from the south lawn of the White House.

U.S. MARINE CORPS
E PLURIBUS UNUM
EXECUTIVE
FLIGHT
DETACHMENT

OT&E

NightHawk News

A Professional Journal of Marine Helicopter Operational Test and Evaluation

Volume 12, Issue #1 *January 1996*

In this issue:

V-22: Operational Test OT-IIB Completed
CH-53D: GPS/AN/ARC-21(V)
CH-53E: Tactical Bulk Fuel Distribution System
CH-46: Communication Navigation Control System
UH-1N: Block Upgrade

The Nighthawk News is the professional journal of HMX-1.

PART 3
MAWTS-1

One of the roles within Ant-Air Warfare is the Suppression of Enemy Air Defenses (SEAD). This F/A-18D Hornet rolls in on a target displaying a pair of AGM-88 High speed Anti-Radar Missiles (HARM).

8

Marine Aviation Weapons And Tactics Squadron-1 (MAWTS-1)

Current MAWTS-1 Commanding Officer Colonel Keith "Shadow" Stalder (pilot) and former Operations Officer Major Dave "Who" Wilson (Naval Flight Officer) prior to taking this F/A-18D on a WTI mission.

MAWTS-1 is about fighting and winning - in the air and on the ground where ever U.S. Marines may find themselves. The tradition of excellence and focus on the imperatives of beating the enemy in war found in this squadron embody an ethic quite at home with that of the Marine Corps itself. Nothing is more important than that - winning battles and our country's wars. Marine aviation exists only to support the Marine on the ground and without aviation the Marine Corps is only a very light, infantry force. Aviation is the Marine Corps secret weapon and MAWTS-1 is Marine Aviation's secret weapon.

The graduates of our Weapons and Tactics Instruction course are among the most knowledgeable and well trained fighting professionals in the world today. The regional CINCs, (Commander In Chief's) our sister services and USMC unit commanders know that. Whenever the balloon goes up, these men and women can be counted on to take the fight to the enemy.

Among our many challenges is a solemn duty to carry the flames of tactical excellence and a threat based focus to training, so that future generations of Marines never forget that, above all, we must be ready to fight and win.

As America approaches the 21st century, and our Armed Forces are employed more frequently in peacekeeping and presence missions it is vital that our military institutions preserve and protect the fundamental habits, attitudes and practices which will guarantee victory in combat. We do that here at MAWTS-1.

- Colonel K.J. Stalder, USMC
MAWTS-1 Commanding Officer 1996

Colonel Stalder joined the Marine Corps in 1972, was designated a Naval Aviator in February 1975 and was assigned to VMFAT-101 as an F-4 pilot. Having served twenty-five years in Marine aviation, Colonel Stalder arrived at MAWTS-1 as the Executive Officer on August 17, 1995, taking command of MAWTS-1 on May 17, 1996.

MISSION OF MAWTS-1

The mission of MAWTS-1 is to provide standardized training in all aspects of employment of Marine aviation units towards the accomplishment of their assigned mission; provide assistance in the development of aviation weapons and tactics, as directed and assist in preparing aviation units for evaluation, as requested.

MAWTS-1 is responsible for the following tasks in Marine aviation:

* Manage the Marine Corps Weapons and Tactics Training Program.
* Manage the Weapons and Tactics Instructor (WTI) Course to include, but not be limited to the following:

  - Develop, update and present the WTI Course to all aviation and appropriate ground units.

  - Develop, update and promulgate WTI training support curriculum and media.

  - Conduct periodic liaison visits to all aviation units to provide WTI refresher training, information on new developments and review training support curriculum and unit training.

  - Coordinate and supervise the development and presentation of formal courses of instruction and standards in aviation weapons and tactics for tactical and training squadrons.

  - Provide training for deployed and remotely located squadrons as required.

Former Assistant Operations Officer, Captain Leo "Killer" Kilgore preflights this CH-46E.

Former Operations Officer Major Dave "Who" Wilson in his office at the MAWTS-1 building. The "OP's O" has among the most demanding jobs especially during the bi-annual Weapons and Tactics Instructor course. In addition to keeping all the aircraft flying, he had to deal with two very persistent author/photographers. He graciously fulfilled our many requests, allowing us to capture Marine Air in action.

The Plankholder plaque. A 'Plankholder' is "an individual who is permanently attached to MAWTS-1 as an instructor for the longest continuous period of time".

- Provide representation to Tactical Manual Conferences, Marine Air Command and Control System (MACCS) Conferences, Training and Readiness Conferences, and other meetings of a technical or tactical nature concerning airborne weapons and tactics.

- Maintain liaison with appropriate commands within the U.S. Navy, U.S. Air Force, U.S. Army and other military or technical organizations, including foreign services as may be required to ensure that aviation tactics and courses of instruction are current and appropriate.

- Provide representation to the Marine Corps mid and long range study groups as directed.

- Provide representation and input as directed for formulation and review of Marine Corps doctrinal publications.

- Represent Headquarters Marine Corps (HQMC) as directed in other U.S. services studies relating to aviation weapons and tactics matters.

- Publish and distribute a Marine Corps Aviation Weapons and Tactics newsletter.

- Maintain a library of publications on current technical and tactical aviation information.

From this mission statement, Marine Aviation Weapons and Tactics Squadron-1 received its marching orders to make an impact on Marine aviation weapons, tactics and training. The primary objective for the squadron is to increase combat readiness of Marine Corps aviation units. For the past twenty years, MAWTS-1 has diligently executed their mission, consistently providing the Fleet Marine Force with professional Weapons and Tactics Instructors (WTI).

Building 406 at MCAS Yuma, the 'Home of MAWTS-1'.

Origins of MAWTS-1

The origin of Marine Aviation Weapons and Tactics Squadron-1 (MAWTS-1), can be traced to the aftermath of World War II when Marine pilots were first assigned to Navy Composite Squadrons (VCs). These squadrons which operated from shore bases and carriers, were assigned the special weapons delivery mission. In 1952, with the introduction of improved weapons and aircraft, the Marines were reassigned to Marine Special Weapons Delivery Units (SWDUs) on each coast. These units were short lived because their mission was given to attack squadrons in 1953. Special Weapons Training Units (SWTUs) were then formed to provide necessary training to the attack squadrons. During the 1960's conventional weapons delivery was added to the curriculum of the SWTL's, but the emphasis on special weapons delivery remained.

In response to the growing mission, the size of the SWTUs was increased, and they were redesignated as Marine Air Weapons Training Units: MAWTULant at Cherry Point, North Carolina, and MAWTUPac at El Toro, California. These units continued to expand throughout the sixties in types of aircraft and curriculum. There was also a significant increase in Fleet Marine Force squadron interaction with the introduction of Mobile Training Teams and participation of the MAWTUs in the Operational Readiness Inspections (ORI).

After the Vietnam conflict, the Commandant of the U.S. Marine Corps (CMC) recognized a need for advanced weapons and tactics training in all of Marine Corps aviation. During 1975, a high level study group, Project 19, was formed at Headquarters Marine Corps to determine requirements for the enhancement and standardization of aviation training. The recommendations of Project 19 were implemented in early 1976 with the establishment of the Marine Corps Weapons and Tactics Training Program (WTTP).

The cornerstone of the WTTP was the development of a graduate level Weapons and Tactics Instructor (WTI) Course and the placement of WTI graduates in training billets in every tactical unit in Marine Corps aviation. In late 1976 and early 1977, separate WTI Courses were conducted by MAWTUPac and MAWTULant. Consolidated WTI Courses were subsequently conducted at Marine Corps Air Station, Yuma, AZ, by a combined MAWTU staff in May 1977 and February 1978. Due to the overwhelming success of the consolidated WTI Courses, the Commandant of the Marine Corps commissioned Marine Aviation Weapons and Tactics Squadron One at Marine Corps Air Station, Yuma, Arizona, on June, 1978.

The inscription for the dedication of the MAWTS-1 building reads 'This building is dedicated to the memory of all Marines who have given their lives in the development and advancement of Marine Aviation Tactics and Weapons Systems'.

The WTI Course is a fully integrated course of instruction for highly experienced and fully qualified officers from all aviation communities. Officers from infantry and ground supporting arm units also attend the course to ensure appropriate air ground interface. The academic syllabus includes instruction in threat analysis, tactics, weapons system employment, aviation training management, and integrated operational planning. The flight syllabus reinforces the academic learning objectives with hands-on experience. Briefing and debriefing techniques and airborne instructional skills are reviewed and tactics and weapons systems employment are evaluated. The course culminates in a fully integrated combined arms exercise encompassing all functions of Marine Corps aviation in support of a Marine Air Ground Task Force. The Final Exercise (FINEX) is completely planned, executed and debriefed by the WTI students.

Since its commission in 1978, MAWTS-1 has conducted two WTI courses per year, producing Marine WTI graduates, sister service graduates, and foreign officer graduates. The WTI course is a consistently dynamic and expanding evolution. Recent milestones include the introduction of the F/A-18, AV-8B, and CH-53E to the WTI course. Additionally, there have been many improvements to the overall WTTP: the establishment of a Commanders' Weapons and Tactics Training Course (Senior Officers' Course) with a flight phase, supplemental courses of aviation instruction at both the Marine Corps Amphibious Warfare School and Command and Staff College, and a Marine Amphibious Unit Special Operations Course. A separate Aviation Development, Tactics and Evaluation Department (ADT&E) was established in June 1983 to provide a nucleus of aviation expertise in all functional areas of Marine Corps aviation. Responsive to Headquarters, Marine Corps, Marine Corps Development and Education Command, and the Fleet Marine Force, this department has already provided many significant contributions to Marine Corps aviation.

MAWTS-1 has provided instructional support for the U.S. Navy's Intermediate Level Light Attack Weapons School, Strike Fighter School and Medium Attack Weapons School. Prior to the establishment of the Navy Strike Warfare Center, MAWTS-1 provided academic and flight instruction for Carrier Air Wings, Replacement Air Groups, and Navy Fleet Squadrons. MAWTS-1 maintains close, mutually beneficial, liaison with the aviation and tactics schools of the U.S. Army and U.S. Air Force, as well as those of Allied Nations. Initial liaison established with the Israeli Air Force and Central Tactics and Trials Organization of the Royal Air Force has recently developed into an "operator to operator" relationship and forum, through which the exchange of information is easily accomplished. This fertile environment has spawned many innovative and unique tactical developments for the naval service.

Since its establishment, MAWTS-1 has been staffed by individuals of superior aeronautical and tactical expertise, instructional abilities and professionalism. From northern Europe to the Caribbean and the western Pacific, MAWTS-1 has responded to the needs of the Fleet Marine Force. The WTI Course is recognized as the most comprehensive graduate level aviation course of instruction in the world today. It is through the dedication and untiring efforts of its personnel that MAWTS-1 has earned its reputation as the Vanguard of Marine aviation. The squadron was recognized by the Secretary of the Navy in awarding a Navy Unit Commendation for sustained superior performance in all facets of Marine Aviation. In 1986, MAWTS-1 was named Marine Corps Aviation Association Special Category Squadron of the Year.

MAWTS-1 Organizational Overview

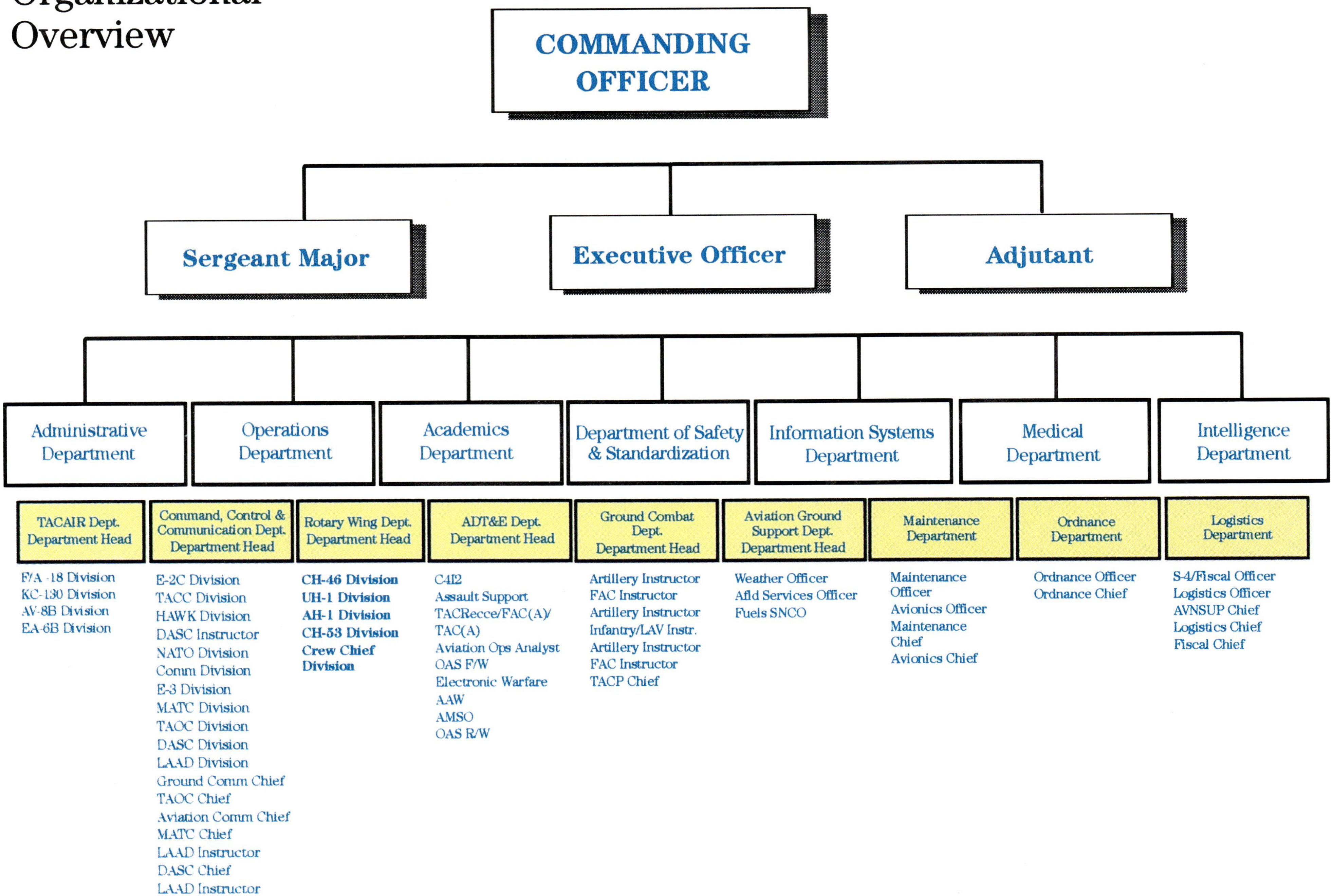

In order to accomplish it's broad mission, MAWTS-1 has consistently been staffed with Marine officers of superior aeronautical and tactical expertise, fleet experience, instructional abilities and professionalism. All functional areas of Marine aviation, as well as the ground combat arms are represented on the staff. The squadron is organized as outlined in Table-1.

Table-2 MAWTS-1 Commanding Officers

Commanding Officer	Date of Command	Transferred Command
Lieutenant Colonel Howard L. DeCastro	June 1, 1978	June 27, 1980
Colonel Bobby G. Butcher	June 27, 1980	August 6, 1982
Colonel Clyde L.Vermilyea	August 6, 1982	June 8, 1984
Colonel Randy H. Brinkley	June 8, 1984	July 11, 1986
Lieutenant Colonel Frederick McCorkle	July 11, 1986	June 10, 1988
Colonel Michael D. Ryan	June 10, 1988	June 15, 1990
Colonel Michael P. Delong	June 15, 1990	May 28, 1992
Colonel Bruce Barry Knutson, Jr.	May 28, 1992	June 3, 1994
Colonel John G. Castellaw	June 3, 1994	May 17, 1996
Colonel Keith J. Stalder	May 17, 1996	*Present Commanding Officer*

Lieutenant Colonel Howard L. DeCastro

Lieutenant Colonel Bobby G. Butcher

Lieutenant Colonel Clyde L.Vermilyea

Lieutenant Colonel Randy H. Brinkley

Lieutenant Colonel Frederick McCorkle

Colonel Michael D. Ryan

Colonel Michael P. Delong

Colonel Bruce Barry Knutson, Jr.

Colonel John G. Castellaw

AVIATION DEVELOPMENT TACTICS AND EVALUATION

During 1983 it was recognized that the increasing involvement of MAWTS-1 personnel in mission tasks not related to the Weapons and Tactics Training Program (WTTP) was diminishing the overall impact and effectiveness of the WTTP. The solution to this problem was the creation of the ADT&E Department. It was originally staffed by extending the normal tour length of who could perform the tasks associated with the development and evaluation of aviation weapons, weapons systems, training, doctrine and tactics.

Current Commanding Officer of MAWTS-1 Colonel Keith "Shadow" Stalder.

The members of ADT&E are a diverse and dedicated group of professionals who are involved in just about everything as it relates to their mission area or aircraft type. In fact, the hardest thing becomes taking too much on. It becomes a balance between directed projects, and projects which may or may not materialize. The ADT&E department monitors all the advanced weapons programs and aircraft to make sure that the Marine aviation perspective and tactics are not overlooked. ADT&E is one of the most challenging and dynamic departments in MAWTS-1. The officers assigned to ADT&E may not get as much flight time as their contemporaries in their respective divisions, but they leave this division knowing that they have had a serious impact on the readiness and future of Marine Air.

Mission

The goal of the ADT&E Department within MAWTS-1 is to perform those tasks assigned by the Commanding Officer that fall within the MAWTS-1 mission or are assigned by CMC. Projects assigned to ADT&E do not adhere to any functional boundary or specific topic. Particular branches within the Operations Department will be assigned training course development, TACMAN and Fleet Support missions. ADT&E will respond to assigned tasking that has immediate, mid-term and long range impact on Marine aviation, and combat readiness. In all cases, this impact will manifest in the form of new equipment, training improvements and/or changes to tactics.

Under the mission statement for MAWTS-1, the Commanding Officer, as directed by CMC, provides assistance in the development and evaluation of aviation training, tactics and doctrine weapons, weapon systems and command and control equipment. ADT&E fulfills this function through the following tasks:

1. Manage and coordinate Marine Corps input to the Navy Tactical Development and Evaluation (TAC D&E) programs as it relates to aviation and aviation issues. MAWTS-1 is a formal member of this community. ADT&E conducts qualitative assessments of hardware or tactics in order to develop techniques and procedures, and maintains a close relationship with Naval or other services test and evaluation communities.

2. Develop mission need statements and review Operational Requirement Documents relating to aviation and aviation command and control. ADT&E is MAWTS-1's primary link to the requirements and acquisition communities within the Navy and Marine Corps. ADT&E is responsible in this area to maintain close coordination with existing and proposed weapons or weapons systems programs that have not reached Initial Operational Capability (IOC) within the Fleet Marine Forces.

3. Publish WTI course lessons learned for dissemination to fleet units and service lesson learned data bases.

4. Coordinate Marine Corps representation in aviation related Foreign Military Exploitation (FME) programs.

5. Maintain liaison with appropriate commands within the United States Navy, United States Air Force, United States Army, and other military or technical organizations, including foreign services, when authorized, to ensure that aviation tactics and course of instruction are current and appropriate.

6. Provide representation and input to CG MCCDC for formulation and review of Marine Corps tactical and doctrinal publications.

7. As directed, provide representation for the Marine Corps in other U.S. military service studies related to the employment of aviation weapons and tactics, and aviation training.

ORGANIZATION
ADT&E is organized around the Six Functions of Marine Aviation, with specialists filling the following billets:

Command Control Communications Computer and Intelligence (C4I)
Rotary Wing Offensive Air Support (R/W OAS)
Fixed Wing Offensive Air Support (F/W OAS)
Anti-Air Warfare (AAW)
Electronic Warfare (EW)
Assault Support
FAC(A), TAC(A), Air Reconnaissance
Operations Analyst
Aeromedical Safety Officer
Automated Data Processing Officer

Each of the officers assigned to these billets are duty experts in the doctrine and tactics associated with these functions of Marine Air. They are experienced fleet operators who apply their knowledge of Marine Aviation in the development of new tactics. After assignment to ADT&E they are given training in aviation acquisition fundamentals and TAC D&E methods. They maintain close working relationships with other Navy, Marine and DOD organizations which may have an impact on the future of Marine Air. Officers assigned to ADT&E are selected by nomination from the Department Heads within the Divisions at MAWTS-1. They conduct projects and monitor programs as directed by the Commanding Officer, the ADT&E Department Head, or by their own initiative. They work closely with their contemporaries within each of the Divisions in MAWTS-1 and their flying communities. ADT&E instructors fully participate in the training of students during the WTI course and during fleet support evolutions.

The Flight OP's area at MAWTS-1 is constantly manned by instructors and details both the TACAIR and ASSAULT SUPPORT flight schedule.

Cooperation and coordination in the resolve of special tasking or projects between branches within the Operations and ADT&E Department are critical. The ADT&E Department will periodically brief the Operations Department on on-going projects to ensure adequate communications between departments.

ADT&E Night Imaging & Threat Evaluation (NITE) Lab Facility
The MAWTS-1 ADT&E Night Imaging & Threat Evaluation (NITE) Lab Facility, located at MCAS Yuma, was the first dedicated aircrew Night Vision Device (NVD) ground training facility in the United States Armed Forces. The concept of the facility was developed at MAWTS-1 during the mid-1980's as a low cost way to establish a vehicle for administration of the critically important introductory ground school training briefs on the use of various NVD sensors. MAWTS-1 trained the first USMC aircrew on the use of NVD's in a proof-of-concept demonstration in December 1987. The fleet's need for this type of training was instantly acknowledged and has led to a proliferation of these facilities throughout the Unites States Marine Corps and Navy. MAWTS-1 through the ADT&E Department will have the sole responsibilities to create and manage all curricula for Night Vision Devices for the Marine Corps and Navy.

The NITE Lab facilities support three primary NVD training courses: the NITE Lab NVG Indoctrination Training Course designed to be administered to aircrews during their first exposure to NVG training and typically occurs prior to their Night Vision Goggle familiarization flights; the NITE Lab NVG Refresher Training Course designed for experienced NVG aircrews as follow-on training; and a NITE Lab FLIR (Forward-looking Infra-Red) Training Course which is an indoctrination to thermal imaging, taken prior to specific systems training.

The guiding premise of the NITE Lab training programs is to provide aircrews with a basic exposure to:

- Night Vision Goggles or FLIR system capabilities
- Critical environmental factors that influence sensor performance
- Hands-on preflight adjustments of Night Vision Goggle sensors
- Hands-on performance demonstrations of the Night Vision Goggle sensors

Training is provided by lecture, hands-on demonstration and exposure to NVG's capabilities by viewing an extremely detailed terrain board model, capable of lighting changes, power lines and mountain types. The Marine Corps and Navy NITE Labs are located at:

Table-3: United States Marine Corps NITE Labs

USMC Site	Parent Command
MCAS Yuma AZ	MAWTS-1
MCAF Quantico, VA	HMX-1
MCAS Camp Pendleton, CA	MAG 39
MCAS Tustin, CA	MAG 16
MCAS New River, NC	MAG 29
MCAS Cherry Point, NC	MAG 14
MCAS Beaufort, SC	MAG 31
MCAS Futema, Okinawa	MAG 36
MCBH Kancohe Bay	ACE Kaneohe Bay

Table-4: United States Navy NITE Labs

USN Site	Parent Command
NAS North Island, CA	HSWINGPAC
NAS Lemoore, CA	ASTC Lemoore
NAS Whidbey Island, WA	CVWP
NAS Oceana, VA	SWATSLANT
NAS Patuxent River, MD	ASTC Patuxent River
NAS Cecil Field, FL	ASTC Cecil Field
NAS Norfolk, VA	ASTC Norfolk
NAS Fallon, NV	NSAWC

NITE LAB

Tactics are continually refined and improved as demonstrated by these two AH-1W Cobra WTI's.

A Sample of current ADT&E Projects:

Assault Support
Assault Support specialists participate in the on-going development and evaluation of the MV-22 and are involved in the development of the MV-22 Operational Tactics Guide (OTG). Specific projects involving assault support issues include the UH-1N Navigational Thermal Imaging System (NTIS), Aircraft Survivability Equipment (ASE), and the review of the H-1 Operational Requirements Document (ORD). Additional responsibilities include serving as the USN/USMC model manager for the Combat Visual Identification System (CVIS), the USMC Aviation Multi-function Electronic Warfare Trainer (AMEWT), and the design of the MAWTS-1 Electronic Classroom Upgrade.

Fixed-Wing Offensive Air Support
The Fixed-Wing specialists participate in the on-going Aircrew Systems Advisory Panel (ASAP) for the Joint Strike Fighter (JSF) focusing on pilot workload assessments, cockpit designs, sizing of displays, and helmet-mounted sighting systems. Specific projects in support of the AV-8B Harrier have included participation in operational evaluation of GPS integration for the Radar Harrier, the Automatic Target Hand-off System (ATHS), the Forward Observer Forward Air Controller (FOFAC) device, and the AV-8B Tactical Manual.

Rotary-Wing Offensive Air Support
Specific projects in support of the AH-1W Cobra included participation in the review of the 4BN/4BW Operational Requirements Document (ORD), the development of the HMLA Computer Based training systems, the Helicopter Expendable Test conducted by VX-9, and the AH-1W Tactical Manual. Additionally, the RW-OAS Specialist was responsible for the execution of the inaugural combined Naval Air Warfare Night Vision Steering Group and the corresponding Executive Steering Committee.

Anti-Air Warfare
Projects in support of the F/A-18 Hornet include participation in the development of the Multi-function Information Distribution System (MIDS), the AIM-9X Helmet Mounted Cueing System(HMCS), and the Hornet Design Advisory Groups. Additionally, the AAW Specialist is involved in the on-

going development of Tactical Aircraft Mission Planning System (TAMPS) and the upgrade of the Tactical Aircrew Combat Training System (TACTS).

Tactical Air Coordinator (Airborne), Forward Air Controller (Airborne), Reconnaissance

Projects related to aerial reconnaissance and terminal controller capabilities included participation in the Operational Assessment of the Advanced Tactical Airborne Reconnaissance (ATARS), the production of the ORD for the Digital Communications System (DCS), and the tactical demonstration of the use of IR LUU-2 Paraflares. Additionally, the TAC(A), FAC(A), Recce Specialist is involved in the development of the Joint Direct Attack Munition/Joint Stand-Off Weapon (JDAM/JSOW) and the F/A-18D Tactical Manual.

Electronic Warfare

Projects in support of the EA-6B Prowler included the execution of a tactical demonstration and evaluation of the use of Night Vision Goggles (NVGs) by EA-6B aircrews, followed by the development of the corresponding Mission Needs Statement. Additional EA-6B related projects include the employment of chaff corridors, and the refinement of High-speed Anti-Radiation Missile (HARM) employment and tactics. The EW Specialist also continues to focus on Information Warfare & Command, Control Warfare (IW/C2W), Joint Suppression of Enemy Air Defenses (J-SEAD) and tactical aircraft survivability equipment (ASE) issues.

Aero Medical Safety

As the USN/USMC Night Imaging and Threat Evaluation (NITE) Lab Model Manager, the Aero Medical Safety Officer (AMSO) is responsible for the curriculum development, standardization, and certification of 17 Navy/Marine Corps NITE Labs. Specific projects in support of the evaluation and development of Night Vision Devices (NVDs) include the execution of numerous evaluations on various NVGs, pre-flight focus devices, recording systems, and the tactical jet and helicopter NVD Tactical Manuals. Additionally, the AMSO is involved in the development of LASER threat countertactics and LASER safety procedures that have been incorporated in various Tactical Manuals.

Command, Control, Communications, Computers and Intelligence, Interoperability

Projects in support of the Marine Corps C4I capability include the execution of tactical demonstrations of the equipment upgrades being fielded throughout the Marine Air Command and Control System (MACCS) to include the Advanced Tactical Air Command Central, the High Mobility Downsized Direct Air Support Center, the Air Defense Communications Platform, and the Avenger. Additionally, the C4I specialists are involved with the issues of the Contingency Theater Automated Planning System (CTAPS), the Air Tasking Order (ATO), and the Joint Force Air Component Commander (JFACC).

Aviation Operations Analyst

The Aviation Operations Analyst (AOA) is responsible for the production of the Weapons and Tactics Instructor Course Summary of Observations, which provide an in-depth review of the lessons learned from briefing-execution-debriefing phases of each of the major flight evolutions. The AOA is also responsible for the review of the Qualitative Assessments and Tactical Demonstrations conducted during each WTI course. Additionally, the AOA is involved in the USMC Modeling and Simulation development, the design of the MAWTS-1 Electronic Classroom Upgrade, and the rotary-wing aspect of the Tactical Aircraft Mission Planning System (TAMPS).

MAWTS-1 Weapons and Tactics Instructor Course Personnel and Equipment

The MAWTS-1 Squadron does not own all the aircraft and personnel that is required to conduct the Weapons and Tactics Instructors (WTI) Course. MAWTS-1 obtains personnel and equipment from commands throughout the Fleet Marine Force for the classes. The MAWTS-1 WTI offers units from Marine Air Control Groups a unique opportunity to participate in exercises that employ all the Six Functions of Marine aviation to an entire Marine Air Command and Control System, and a fluid scenario based on realistic schemes of maneuver and threat scenarios. To accomplish this MAWTS-1 brings in all the personnel and equipment to establish a Marine Expeditionary Force Forward Air Combat Element (MEF(FWD) ACE). This requires support from Marine Air Control Groups and Marine Aircraft Groups in the form of maintenance and supply personnel and all necessary equipment. Participants are selected at a planning conference two years in advance of the specified WTI class dates.

MAWTS-1 Maintenance Department

In order to facilitate the semi-annual Weapons and Tactics Instructors (WTI) Course, it is imperative that safely flyable, properly configured aircraft be provided to the students and instructors. This monumental task is accomplished with a MAWTS-1 Maintenance Department consisting of a core of twenty permanently assigned personnel. They are responsible for the building, conducting, and disassembly of one of the largest Maintenance Departments in the Marine Corps, consisting of an average of over five hundred Maintenance Technicians supporting in excess of seventy-five aircraft from every fixed wing and rotor wing type/model/series in the Marine Corps inventory.

The MAWTS-1 maintenance core, under the direction of the Aircraft Maintenance Officer, is responsible for molding all support elements to include: aircraft, personnel, tools, test equipment, technical publications and support equipment from around the Marine Corps into a homogenous, effective and safe WTI Maintenance Department in the span of less than a week. What makes this possible is the creation of a maintenance blueprint in the form of a Maintenance Information Guide, Maintenance Milestone Checklist, Table of Organization Chart, Maintenance Instructions, Stan-

Above and Next Page (Left Column). The unsung heroes of Marine aviation are the enlisted personnel that keep the aircraft flying and the flight gear ready to wear.

MAWTS-1 insignia

The journal of Marine Aviation Weapons and Tactics, 'The Talon' is published quarterly by the squadron and represents the most up to date information on the subject.

dard Operating Procedures, Safety Survey and After Action Reports that take into consideration current instructions of all four Marine Aircraft Wings and the peculiar aircraft mix for each WTI course.

Months before the first aircraft arrives the planning begins. The Aircraft Maintenance Officer is responsible for overseeing every step in the process. Each document is meticulously screened for correctness. The aircraft configuration is decided upon and requested. A planning conference is held to determine the number of aircraft and students that will be participating. The numbers and qualifications of technicians is determined by aircraft mix and number. A Table of Organization conference is held to inform the Fleet of the requirements. This is then used to request technicians by rank and qualifications. Over 1400 Test and Measurement System (TAMS) items, 390 tool containers consisting of more than 20,000 tools, and 200 pieces of Support Equipment will be requested and tracked.

In addition, when the course begins the MAWTS-1 Maintenance Corps is responsible for supervising every aspect of maintenance and the flight schedule. The Maintenance Chief is responsible for all personnel issues. The fixed and rotor wing Quality Assurance Chiefs coordinate the arrival, inventory, acceptance and departure of every aircraft, in addition to overseeing every aspect of the flying evolutions. The Tool and TAMS NCOIC hold training for personnel to ensure proper inventory, acceptance and transfer of the hundreds of tools and Test and Measurement Equipment required to support the aircraft. The Flight Equipment NCOIC is responsible for maintaining all flight equipment and performing all thirty day inspections on night vision goggles.

The Data Analyst is responsible for processing in excess of 10,000 documents and the timely return of this data to parent commands, produc-

Graduates of the MAWTS-1 Weapons and Tactics Instructor course wear the WTI patch.

ing the Table of Organization, any special presentations and trend analysis for the course. The Maintenance Administration Chief and clerks are responsible for producing all written correspondence and instructions. The Avionics Officer and Chief are responsible for ensuring qualified Avionics Technicians and special avionics equipment is requested and tracked. To include all security clearances, Communications Security Equipment and Electronic Countermeasures Equipment is provided. Once again, the Aircraft Maintenance Officer is responsible for the entire evolution until all aircraft and personnel are returned to their home base and the entire process begins again.

MAWTS-1 Weapons and Tactics Instructor Course Student and Instructors' Nominations

Prospective students considered to attend the MAWTS-1 WTI course are first expected to be mature, career oriented Marines who have demonstrated exceptional capabilities as ground and airborne instructors. The WTI graduates have enormous responsibilities when they return to their units in the Fleet Marine Forces and the entire Marine Corps looks to the WTI's to manage the level of readiness. As such, the unit or squadrons Commanding Officer evaluates the students potential and then nominates the individual for attendance. The MAWTS-1 departments select the students based on merit, Fleet Marine Force requirements and resource availability.

Prospective WTI Instructors must first be WTI graduates. The MAWTS-1 Divisions and Departments evaluate the students total performance as a WTI student, the nominees performance in the Fleet Marine Forces and the performance of their unit or squadron members that the WTI is responsible for. The Division Heads forward the nominees from the Departments to the MAWTS-1 Commanding Officer for final approval. Once approved, the billet as an Instructor is generally two years. It is interesting to note that almost all of the MAWTS-1 Commanding Officers, typically Colonels, have all gone on to become Generals and to lead Marine Corps Air Wings.

Academic Division

The Academic Department is responsible to liaison with Fleet Marine Forces and is tasked to work with the Fleet to create and modify content for the Weapons and Tactics Instructors Courses. The syllabi is reviewed for each WTI class with the Fleet Marine Forces. The Academic Department is also responsible for publishing a journal for the Fleet Marine Forces called *The Talon.*

The Talon

The Talon is the professional Journal of Marine Aviation Weapons and Tactics. As such, it represents a forum for exchanging tactical ideas and discussing the most current issues in Marine Aviation. *The Talon* is published on a quarterly basis as an unclassified journal and a classified version is published for the purpose of discussing various secret topics such as threat issues that are pertinent to aviation commands.

Major Mark Mykleby is a recent USMC WTI and TOPGUN graduate. WTI students are amongst the top aviators in the Marine Corps. Most students find the flight planning to be the most challenging aspects in the WTI syllabi and enjoy flying with and against the top Marine Corps aviators. Major Mark Mykleby is currently flying F/A-18C's with VMFA-251.

SSgt. N.F. Doyle, Captain R.F. "Nuke" Premo, Sgt. L.G. Hinton, LCpl. M.M. Garcia, Sgt. R.A.E. Walker, Major W.L. "Nut-Z" Niblock, Cpl. K.K. Griffin, Major D.N. "Gimp" Ashby, Major E.A. "Viking" Follstad.

9

MAWTS-1 WTI Curriculum

The dual role, two seat F/A-18D Hornet, a.k.a., The Night Stalker - can carry a wide variety of air to air and air to ground weaponry on it's nine external stations. One aircraft, multiple missions - maximum capability for Offensive Air Support.

VF-32 F-14 Tomcat flies wing on this VMFA (AW) - 533 F/A-18D during a recent WTI course.

The Weapons Tactics Instructor (WTI) curriculum is hosted by the MAWTS-1 Squadron bi-annually in September and March. The curriculum has evolved over the past twenty years, keeping pace with the increasing range and lethality of the weapons employed by the Marine Corps. The curriculum has also had to rapidly adjust to the dynamic threat profiles that the Marines must plan for.

The objective of the course is to *'train the trainer* and graduate a fully qualified individual in his specific Military Occupational Specialty (MOS) who returns to his unit as the primary weapons and tactics instructor. The students benefit from the tactical expertise of the MAWTS-1 staff and students from the Fleet Marines and those accepted from the U.S. Navy, Army, Air Force and the British Royal Air Force. Each branch of the service and MOS bring a unique perspective to the application of air power in achieving various mission objectives. The graduate level courses offered by MAWTS-1 provide the students with a focused syllabus to meet the integration requirements for Joint and Combined operations.

Academics

The first half of the course centers on an academic foundation, and is presented in three phases. The first portion of academics targets an audience that includes Marines from all MOS's and representatives from sister services and allies. The "Generic" phase includes instruction in the Six Functions of Marine Aviation, intelligence assets and the threat. The next block of instruction is common academics, that is, classes focused on more specific topics to aviation communities, including TACAIR, Rotary Wing, and Command, Control and Communications (C3). The other departments at MAWTS-1, Aviation Ground Support, Ground Combat and Intelligence students attend classes with these other communities to increase their understanding and effective employment of Marine aviation. The final block of instruction leading up to the flight phase is specific academics, which include blocks of instruction on aircraft, weapons and agency specific topics. The academic phase concludes with the Marine Air Command and Control System (MACCS) tour. The MACCS Tour highlights the integration of all Six Functions of Marine Aviation by having every student observe each MACCS agency tactically deployed. Aggressor aircraft are employed throughout the tour to illustrate information flow and the engagement sequence of MACCS agencies and their associated weapon systems.

The TACAIR department common curriculum, which includes students from the F/A-18 A/C/D, F-14, AV-8B, EA-6B and KC-130 communities, focuses on Anti-Air Warfare (AAW), Offensive Anti-Air Warfare (OAAW), Offensive Air Support (OAS), and fixed wing weapons employment tactics. The specific courseware goes into greater detail about each community's weapons systems employment and tactics. It is during the specific phase of instruction that the aircrew are fully exposed to the intricacies of detailed mission planning for their platform. The F/A-18 and AV-8B students cover in great detail the capabilities and employment of their specific weapons systems, target area tactics, and the Joint Munitions Effectiveness Manual (JMEMS). The EA-6B students study jamming employment, optimization, and effectiveness, and tactical HARM tailoring and employment. The KC-130 students are exposed to both the TACAIR and Assault Support curriculum, as well as their specific classes that include tanker employment, air drop techniques, track management and the use of their Aircraft Survivability Equipment (ASE).

The MAWTS-1 Assault Support Department (ASD) conducts the Marine Corps Weapons Tactics and Training Program by incorporating the five Type/Mode/Series (T/M/S) helicopters (CH-46E, CH-53D, CH-53E, UH-1N, AH-1W) during the WTI course. The average WTI Assault Support student class represents a cross section of Marine aviation, while additionally blending elements of Special Operations Forces such as the Army's Task Force 160th, Air Force Pavelow/Pavehawk, and Navy Combat Search and Rescue units. All the students benefit from the diverse pilot backgrounds represented by the different Type/Mode/Series participating in the class. The objective is to build a solid foundation on each prospective WTI's capability to Plan, Brief, Execute and Debrief an integrated, tactical vertical assault. To meet this goal, the focus of effort concentrates on providing graduate level instruction to participating aircrew (pilots and crew chiefs).

The goal during assault support academics is to ensure students receive tactical academic instruction on each mission they will encounter in the flight phase. The rotary wing common curriculum includes classes on Rapid Response Planning, Offensive Air Support Precision Guided Munitions (OAS PGMs), Aircraft Survivability Equipment (ASE), Infra-Red Man-Portable Air Defense Systems (MANPADS), Tactical Recovery of Aircraft and Personnel (TRAP), etc. The common curriculum ends with an "Assault Support Symposium" and a Mission Planning Exercise culminating with an Air Mission Commander's (AMC) brief. Specific aircraft community academics focus on unit level training, readiness doctrines and classroom instructor techniques..

The C3 Department at MAWTS-1 includes divisions for each agency of the Marine Air Command and Control System (MACCS). Specifically, they are the Tactical Air Command Center (TACC), Direct Air Support Center (DASC), Tactical Air Operations Center (TAOC), Marine Air Traffic Control (MATC), Ground Based Air Defense (GBAD) which includes HAWK

Low level tactics are part of the Harriers curriculum as demonstrated by this VMA-211 AV-8B.

and Stinger divisions, and Communications. Additionally, the C3 staff includes an E-2C Naval Flight Officer (NFO), USAF E-3 AWACS controller and a British Royal Air Force liaison officer. The goal of the C3 staff is to provide instruction on aviation command and control, realizing that it is the foundation for the effective execution and integration of all Six Functions of Marine aviation. The MACCS WTI must have an appreciation for his system as well as the unique integration requirements for the conduct of effective Joint and Combined Air Operations.

The C3 common academic syllabus focuses on the agencies of the MACCS, Joint/Integrated Combat Airspace Command and Control (J/ICAC2) and pertinent classes from the TACAIR and Rotary Wing syllabus necessary to support the integration of Marine Aviation. The curriculum also presents a two day Marine Aviation Planning Problem (MAPP) based on a potential regional contingency. The students are required to plan the MACCS employment in this Joint/Combined operational contingency. During the MAPP, the students must recognize and plan for integration with host nation and joint C2 structure, analyze the Rules of Engagement (ROE), and plan for MACCS asset employment. At the conclusion of the common phase, the C3 students also progress to the specific curriculum that further delves into the intricacies of each MACCS agency's employment. At the completion of the Academic Phase, all WTI students are ready to progress into the flight phase of the course.

The Flight Phase

The Flight Phase of WTI follows in reverse order of the academic phase, that being specific, common, and generic. Each community has an established specific flight schedule or series of events that reinforce the lessons from the academic phase. A student will complete a series of syllabus hops in his aircraft, or events in an individual agency before proceeding to the integrated evolution's that encompass the common and generic portions of the flight phase. The centerpiece of flight phase comes together when we demonstrate the effective use of fire power and mobility inherent in Marine Expeditionary Force (MEF) operations.

During the TACAIR specific flight phase students will execute weapons employment and weapons delivery profiles commensurate with their platform. They will also practice executing their specific role as they would in larger, integrated operations. Similarly, the Assault Support Department conducts its specific flights. For example, the CH-46 and UH-1 Divisions conduct an airfield seizure while the CH-53 and AH-1 Divisions conduct a long range raid in conjunction with an enroute Rapid Ground Refueling (RGR) by KC-130. The flight phase for the C3 Department begins with a Marine Integrated Systems Training Exercise (MISTEX) which is conducted by supporting field units. The MISTEX is designed to ring out all the communications nets and data links that will be employed throughout the flight phase, while also integrating the supporting agencies who are often represented by all four Marine Aircraft Wings. After the MISTEX, the WTI students and field units participate in their specific evolution's that include a Ground Based Air Defense Exercise (GBAD) for the air defense oriented units of the MACCS, and a Fire Support Exercise for the Direct Air Support Center (DASC), Tactical Air Control Party (TACP) and artillery units.

Once the specific portion of the flight phase is finished, the course shifts to the integrated (common) flight evolution's combining aircraft and agencies within similar mission areas to perform Anti-Air Warfare (AAW), Offensive Anti-Air Warfare (OAAW), Offensive Air Support (OAS) and Assault Support Tactics (AST) exercises. The common phase is executed in the same way that an anticipated contingency operation will unfold. AAW and OAAW exercises are executed to gain and maintain air superiority. During AAW, students must work through the intricacies of transition to war Rules of Engagement (ROE), followed by wartime division sized operations. Fighter aircraft are employed along with ground based weapons, HAWK and Stinger, to provide an Integrated Air Defense System (IADS) for the Yuma vital area. During OAAW, TACAIR students plan an offensive air strike on the Integrated Air Defense System, provided by the C3 assets, in a true force on force evolution. At the debrief for the OAAW exercise, all students have a greater respect for the capabilities of both the ground based assets of the MACCS, as well as the aircraft weapons employed by Marine aircraft. Also, during OAAW, national assets are applied by the Intel students during their collection planning and execution. The blend of these assets, along with organic MAGTF assets, like the Pioneer Unmanned Aerial Vehicle (UAV) system, expose the students to a full range of resources available to the aviation planner.

Following the establishment of air superiority, the effort shifts to the conduct of Offensive Air Support. Close air support is executed throughout this four day exercise as the threat continues to become more sophisticated, and students are exposed to a higher degree of complexity. Building upon that foundation, the fundamentals of armed reconnaissance are executed during both day and night in various threat levels. Fixed wing and rotary wing integration in the target area is emphasized in order to maximize each aircraft's capabilities and minimize their limitations. Additionally, Radio Battalion is employed at the Opposing Force (OPFOR), in order to disrupt communications and gain vital elements of information. Using this resource, the students can evaluate their ability to conduct operations and casualty plans based on a threat employing radio electronic combat (REC).

The Assault Support common flight phase is accomplished through the conduct of the Assault Support Tactics (AST) exercises, each emphasizing the integration of helicopter assets with TACAIR and C3 for each mission. During the first Assault Support Tactics, a Non-combatant Evacuation Operation (NEO) is executed on Night Vision Goggles (NVG) the NEO includes an average of 50 aircraft. To enhance realism, a Marine infantry company conducts the extraction site security and organization, to include volunteer role players acting as non-combatants.

The second Assault Support Tactics evolution is a large scale day mission designed to instill confidence in our ability to conduct large scale helicopter-borne operations. It includes an artillery battery insertion followed by a single wave, battalion sized helicopter-borne lift. Assault Sup-

The capabilities and employment of the KC-130 are essential to Marine Air, and are covered in detail within the TACAIR curriculum.

04
CB
158030
VMAQ-1
MARINE
04
01
CB
160786
VMAQ-1
MARINES

The huge, menacing Prowler is among the most complex and expensive assets flown by the Marines. This section of EA-6B's belong to the 'Screaming Banshees" of VMAQ-1.

Huey crew member guides this UH-1 out from the static flightline.

port Tactics-3 builds on the Assault Support Tactics-2 scenario. The students are given the mission during a field planning exercise. By sunset, they brief the mission: An immediate company extraction from one site, and a reinforcement mission at another LZ. For this exercise, students must employ the rapid response planning techniques taught in academics. The planning is complicated by having to coordinate night fixed wing CAS and C2 from an E-2C Hawkeye. Both fixed wing assets are based at different locations. Their planning and integration must be accomplished without the luxury of physical collocation. The final Assault Support Tactics is a simultaneous NVG raid conducted at sites located in both Phoenix and El Centro. The students must be able to coordinate the execution of events at sites separated by almost two hundred fifty miles. Assault Support Tactics-4 rounds out the Military Operations in Urban Terrain (MOUT) training package presented in academics.

The Naval Expeditionary Force Exercise (NEFEX) and Final Exercise (FINEX) evolution's focus on the total integration of assets performing the Six Functions of Marine Aviation. NEFEX is the introduction of 'Brown Water Ops', MEU/ARG/CVBG and Joint integration. NEFEX builds on the integration process by incorporating a long range strike with a helicopter-borne raid, a SpecOps direct action mission, and Navy Combat Search and Rescue. To illustrate the complexity of this exercise, the long range strike includes F/A-18C/D's, KC-130s, F-14's, EA-6B's, an E-2C, and a KC-10. Concurrently, as assets from TF 160th allow, a direct action mission is executed with the Army Special Operations Force pilots against an airfield being held by terrorists with hostages. As night falls, the assault helicopters launch a large scale raid (120 Marines) that incorporates attached and detached rotary and fixed wing escort, close air support, electronic attack, and airborne C2. This culminates in very large integrated live fire exercise located in the ranges northwest of Yuma. During the flight window, a downed pilot is simulated which requires the Tactical Air Commander to launch the Tactical Recovery of Aircraft and Personnel/Combat Search and Rescue assets for his recovery.

Following the successful completion of NEFEX, the Marines land and enable Joint and Combined assets to operate with host nation support. FINEX focuses on the MEF (Fwd) sector that has been established (based on an area of responsibility assigned by the Joint Force Commander and Joint Force Air Component Commander) as it matures into a Joint Operation. Our Intelligence Department and Ground Combat Department have developed a scenario that gives breadth and depth to the battlefield while focusing on specific mission requirements requested from each division. FINEX at WTI is a rare occasion for all assets of Marine Aviation to execute integrated operations short of an actual contingency. All Six Functions of Marine Aviation are executed by ground agencies and weapons systems, fixed and rotary wing aircraft, and unmanned aerial vehicles (UAVs). The inclusion of the E-3, AWACS enhances the flight operation by providing surveillance and control of Combat Air Patrol (CAP) aircraft within the Army and Marine sector. The AWACS is an outstanding example of enhancing Marine understanding of integration requirements with joint assets. The AWACS provides fighter control, and as well provides command and control for a helicopter-borne assault.

At the conclusion of the course, the newly qualified WTI is ready to return to his parent command and assume the role of unit training manager and tactics instructor. While normally associated with flying squadrons and MACCS units, the remaining WTI graduates will also return to

HMM-265 Commanding Officer, Lt. Colonel J.T. Hardwick, brings this PHROG in for a landing.

Rear aspect photo of the AH-1W on a low level flight.

their MWSS, MALS, and intelligence billets, as well as ground combat units to pass on their knowledge with a better understanding of the employment and integration requirements of the Six Functions of Marine Aviation.

There are over 2,000 Marines and one hundred aircraft supporting the flight phase of WTI. An entire Marine Air Command and Control System (MACCS) is deployed, along with artillery, infantry and CSSD units to create as realistic an exercise as possible. Additionally, aviation maintenance Marines deploy to support approximately 35 fixed wing and 50 rotary wing aircraft assigned to MAWTS-1 for the conduct of the course. An additional 20-25 aircraft provide bogey support, Airborne Early Warning, Command and Control, etc... On average, a typical course will log well over 3,000 flight hours, and is executed around the clock six days per week.

Advanced Academic Curriculum

Over and above WTI there are three advanced curriculum courses embedded within the course: the Tactical Air Commanders Course, the MEU/SPMAGTF ACE Commanders Course and the Squadron/Battalion Commanders Course. The Tactical Air Commanders Course is designed for senior Aviation Commanders who are serving in billets where they may serve as the ACE commander for exercises or an operational contingency. The courseware focuses on the MACCS, as well as joint service C2 integration. During the flight phase, these senior officers then have the opportunity to exercise as the TAC. The MEU/SPMAGTF ACE Commanders course is focused toward the composite squadron commander and operations officer. The curriculum encompasses mission specific material on all the assets that are attached to the MEU ACE. Emphasis is placed upon command and control, including both the Amphibious Task Force and combined CVBG/ARG command structure, as well as joint asset integration. The Squadron/Battalion Commanders course is designed for commanders from all elements of the MAGTF. The course is structured to increase their understanding of aviation command and control, emerging weapons, tactics and threats that they may encounter as senior leaders.

Fleet Support and Tactics Development

Between WTI classes, MAWTS-1's charter directs the squadron to "develop tactics" and provide "fleet standardization." This two part process requires the individual divisions to maintain consistent dialogue with corresponding fleet units. Each department has several training programs that provide training to units and in a reciprocal mode MAWTS-1 instructors receive feedback which further influences subsequent training. The following is a list of the types of training provided:

Assault Support Department

Night Systems Instructor Certification
Air Combat Instructor Certification
Defensive Measures Instructor Certification
Terrain Flight (TERF) Instructor Certification
Aerial Gunnery Instructor Certification

TACAIR Department

Night Systems & Tactics Instructor Certification
Air Combat Tactics Instructor Certification
Marine Division Tactics Course (with Tactical Air Operations Center (TAOC) Division)
Weapons Training Officer Course
Forward Air Controller (Airborne) Instructor Certification
Tactical Air Coordinator (Airborne) Instructor Certification
Defensive Tactics Instructor Certification
Low Attitude Tactics Instructor Certification

Academic

MEU ACE Training Course
CAX GCE/ACE Mobile Training Course
Mobile Training Teams tailored to specific unit needs.

The MAWTS-1 Commanding Officer has the authority to certify instructors per the Training and Readiness Manual, Weapons Training and Tactics Program, and MAWTS-1 Course Catalog. Unit commanders have the authority to designate instructors following appropriate syllabus and certification flights.

In addition to the instructor certification MAWTS-1 provides for the fleet, division instructors attend various Operational Advisory Groups (OAGs), Mission Area Analysis Conference working groups, and conferences to help define requirements and priorities pertaining to tactics, weapons and acquisitions. MAWTS-1 actively participates in training and readiness issues and development. MAWTS-1 falls under MCCDC and as a result maintains a close relationship with the Standard Branch, MCCDC. We provide advisors to MCCDC during T & R Manual, Volume 1 conferences and appropriate subsequent Volume (2 through 5) conferences.

Both the Rotary Wing and Fixed Wing Departments within MAWTS-1 are actively involved with the upkeep and improvement of their Type/Model/Series aircraft Tactical Manual. This program has been a standard in the fixed wing community and recently has been initiated throughout the rotary wing community. Concurrently, the C3 Department is actively involved in the transformation of the MCCS: introduction of the Advanced Tactical Air Command Center (ATACC), High Mobility Downsized DASC (HMD), Air Defense Communications Platform (ADCP), Avenger Weapons System and the Contingency Theater Aviation Planning System (CTAPS). Our collective efforts have one goal - promoting the effective implementation and integration of tactics and capabilities within the structure of Marine Aviation.

Aviation Development Tactics and Evaluation (ADT&E)

To enhance the squadron's association and integration with other services and agencies, MAWTS-1's Aviation Development Tactics and Evaluation (ADT&E) Department was created in 1983. ADT&E's charter is to coordinate MAWTS-1's efforts in developing and evaluating tactics and hardware in all areas of Marine aviation. Examples of their recent efforts include the initial steps in developing an MV-22 Osprey operational tactics guide, chairing the Night Vision Goggle Steering Group, Joint SEAD doctrine development, the incorporation of the Contingency Theater Aviation Planning System (CTAPS) and the Tactical Aircrew Mission Planning System (TAMPS) as mission planning and execution tools, as well as tracking all current aircraft/agency improvements, system modifications, and emerging technologies and tactics. During WTI 2-96, MAWTS-1 will conduct twelve tactical development and evaluation projects. MAWTS-1 is dedicated to the development and expanded use of night vision devices (NVDs-night vision goggles and thermal imagining systems). The fundamental position on NVD's at MAWTS -1 is "they are not only tactical, they are practical."

MAWTS-1 and individual unit Weapons and Tactics instructors are an essential tool in the success of Marine aviation employment. Beyond a doubt, the U.S. Marine Corps will be equipped with the appropriate weapons and tools to conduct all operations from operations other than war and

The huge CH-53E is the largest helicopter flown within the American military.

In-Trail formation of heavily armed 3rd MAW AV-8B Harriers with 'The Great American Bulldogs' of VMA-223 operating near Quantico in support of The Basic School. Each Harrier is carrying (6) live Mark 82 500 pound bombs. During the Gulf War, Harriers flew over 3,300 combat sorties while maintaining a mission capable rate of 90%.

low intensity conflict to a major regional conflict. However, when the tools or airframes fall short, the responsibility for success falls on the individual Marine. MAWTS-1 and the WTI have proven to be a valuable tactics instructor since the inception of the Weapons and Tactics Training Program and they will remain the leaders of Marine aviation employment into the 21st century.

A Curriculum At-A-Glance

The CH-46 Division - Major Robert F. 'Fuzzy' Hedelund, Division Head

WTI Students are taught that Medium Assault Support is the linchpin of Marine aviation. The CH-46 community is known as Marine Medium Helicopter Squadrons (or HMM's). The mission of Marine Medium Helicopter squadrons in the fleet is to provide assault transport of combat troops in the initial waves and follow-on stages of amphibious operations and subsequent operations ashore.

The goal for MAWTS-1 CH-46 students and instructors is to provide the fleet with standardized training in all aspects of the employment of Marine aviation toward the accomplishment of their assigned mission; to provide assistance in the development of aviation weapons and tactics, as directed; and to assist in the evaluation of other aviation units as requested.

The Weapons and Tactics Instructor course curriculum for the 'Phrog' Division (and for all communities) revolves around a simple concept. All communities are together for the first week of academics. This week is called the Generic Week, providing formal instruction on the facets of Marine Aviation that are 'generic' to all of Marine aviation. From Aviation Ground Support to Electronic Attack, all students spend that first week together in

'Toad Hall' (large lecture hall) studying at the graduate level about the Six Functions of Marine Aviation and various other topics. After successfully completing the generic test, they move on to the next phase of their academic training.

The next week, fixed wing students and rotary wing students go their separate ways as Common Week begins. During this phase of academics, topics that are unique to the Assault Support community are presented to give all rotary wing students a common foundation once flying starts. The objective is to ensure a common ground of knowledge for all those WTI's going back to the fleet. Again, a common exam is given and the final week of academics is ready to begin.

Specific Academics for the CH-46 Division comprises the last week prior to the flight phase, which includes Aircraft Survivability Equipment, Assault Support Planning and Training Management. This phase of academics provides the CH-46 WTI student with the tools to go back to his fleet squadron and carry on the business of preparing his squadron for combat. Tactical employment of the HMM squadron is the WTI's primary role and is responsible to the squadrons Commanding Officer for accomplishing that task.

Finally, after three weeks of books, slides, videos, and tests the students are ready for the flight phase. Just as academics came in three phases, so does the flight phase. Only now, the reverse order of specifics, Common (Assault Support Tactics) and Generics and Final Exercises (FINEX) are used to build upon the knowledge gained during the academic phases. The tactics taught are refined and progress in a building block approach toward integration into the next phases.

Once the CH-46 Division students learn to 'fight the 46', they move on to flying and fighting as an assault package. Assault Support Tactics (AST's) are a forum for integrating those assets that typically are restricted to the helicopter and KC-130 community. Assault Support Rotary Wing Escort, Combined Arms Integration, Military Operations on Urban Terrain, and Non-Combatant Evacuation Operations are hallmarks of the AST's.

Finally, the culmination of all learning at WTI, is the Final Exercise or FINEX. In several days, the entire student body; TACAIR (Fixed Wing), Assault Support, Ground Combat, Aviation Ground Support, C3, Intelligence - all functions of Marine Air come together to participate, plan, brief and execute a series of evolution's designed to task and reinforce the knowledge gained over the last six weeks.

There are several challenging aspects of the course for students and instructors. For the students, the academic phase can be a great, and in a few cases, an insurmountable challenge. The academic curriculum is graduate level and presumes that students come armed with a solid base of training and knowledge. The greatest challenge for the students comes in the flight phase. Students fly every day during the first, or specific week of flying. Emphasis is on basic tactics, teamwork, and rapid planning, all with an eye toward building proactive flight leadership. Early missions concentrate on the basics—fire support coordination, integration with escort assets, defensive measures versus air and ground threats, and fast-paced, rapidly changing scenarios.

During the second week of flying, flight packages become larger as all Assault Support communities come together. Students are placed in leadership billets ranging from Air Mission Commander (AMC) to Assault

Marine Corps F/A-18C fighter rolls in on a target during a training mission over the Yuma range complex.

Hornet driver and wingman prepare for takeoff from MCAS Yuma during an early morning hop.

Flight Leader (AFL). Performance is closely monitored as students move through the phases of the mission—planning, briefing, and execution. Mission scenarios are carefully constructed by MAWTS-1 instructors to challenge the students ability to lead and think on their feet. During the final week of flying all assets come together to plan, brief, and execute in support of Marine Expeditionary Force (MEF) and Joint Force objectives.

Instructor challenges parallel what the students face, from a different perspective. For the academic phase, instructors are 'on the stage' giving classes. The delivery of these classes represents the culmination of hundreds of hours of research, study, and rehearsal by each instructor. The goal during the academic phase is clear—provide unparalleled platform instruction.

During the flight phase, instructors must guide the students progress during their planning cycle without actually dictating the plan. The MAWTS coordinator has carefully developed a mission scenario that is designed to test specific abilities of the students and reinforce specific learning objectives. Students are not given the plan up front. They must develop their plan according to the stated mission and enemy situation.

MAWTS-1 instructors are hand picked from Fleet Marine Force units. The most significant prerequisite for a potential instructor is they must be a WTI Graduate. Upon arrival at MAWTS-1 the new instructor is immersed in the Squadron Instructor Training program, which ensures thorough knowledge of the mission and operating procedures of the squadron. A new instructor will spend their first WTI class assisting lead instructors during academic and flight phases.

Sortie At-A-Glance: Operation High Noon

The sortie evolution known as 'High Noon' is AST II, or Assault Support Tactics II. It will be the second major evolution the rotary wing students face, and is designed to test the ability to conduct a battalion helicopter-borne lift. This evolution will be conducted over a period of two days: one day for deliberate planning, and execution on the second day.

"Situation: A race for the Blue Mountain airfield is occurring. A Red Armor Reconnaissance Battalion (MRB), lead element of the 2d Motorized Rifle Regiment (MRD), is approaching from the Northwest over relatively flat terrain. A Green Mechanized Infantry Battalion is close, on the Southern side of the Chocolate Mountains, but is having difficulty traversing the terrain and small groups of Red Anti-mech Teams have been found in the vicinity. It appears as though the Red forces will get to the airfield first. If the Red forces are able to capture and hold Blue Mountain, they will have effectively stopped Green's lines of communication north of the Chocolate Mountains and severely inhibit future operations. Compounding the problem is the fact that a Green Rifle Company is positioned on the airfield and faces imminent annihilation. By nightfall, they will move to a reverse slope defensive position on the eastern end of Blue Mountain."

The Navy's F-14 Tomcat has become a key participant in the WTI course. The Tomcat works in concert with Marine Hornets extremely well in the Deep Air Support role. The F-14's long range and beyond visual range air to air missiles protect the Marine strike force. Recently, Navy Tomcat units have begun delivering general purpose and precision guided ordnance as the aircraft expands it's capabilities into the air to ground role.

U.S. Navy 'Swordsman' F-14 in high visibility paint scheme banks over the outskirts of Yuma.

The student Air Mission Commander (AMC) has his planning team assembled. His 'key players' include representatives from all rotary wing platforms, several TACAIR communities, Ground Combat, Aviation Ground Support, Intel, and C3. He has been given the operations order for the mission. It will be a joint operation involving USMC, Navy, Army and Air Force assets. Marine aircraft assets will include CH-46E, CH-53E, AH-1W, UH-1N, AV-8B, F/A-18C, and KC-130. Army assets from the 160th Task Force, include MH-60s and MH-47's. The Navy will bring an E-2C to the fight and the Air Force will provide two B-52's. The AMC will have a combination of 35 aircraft to perform his mission.

*"Mission: At L-Hour (*L-Hour defined: in amphibious operations, is the time at which the first helicopter of the helicopter-borne assault package touches down in the Landing Zone (LZ). L-20 means twenty minutes before the first helicopter hits the LZ and L+20 means twenty minutes after the helicopter hits the LZ) *conduct a heliborne insert of 2nd Battalion 18th Marines in the vicinity of Blue Mountain in order to reinforce the Green Assault Reconnaissance Company, and hold Blue Mountain until relieved."*

Planning is slow to begin as the AMC assembles his team. Operations of this scale are not widely performed in the fleet, therefore the learning curve for all players is initially very steep. The students begin their mission analysis, focusing on the objective area where the Marines want to be inserted. There will be two primary LZ's, on opposite sides of Blue Mountain. The student Battalion Operations officer briefs his scheme of maneuver once he is on the ground. Marine aviation exists to support the MAGTF (Marine Air Ground Task Force) objectives. Success in this mission means putting the Marines on the ground in the right place, at the right time, with the fire support they need. Therefore, all players listen intently as the Ground Combat rep discusses his actions on the ground as he points to the map.

Next, the student Assault Flight Leader (AFL) and Escort Flight Leader (EFL) discuss with the ground rep how they will support his scheme of maneuver. The AFL is in charge of the assault helicopter flight, which will consist of ten CH-46E's, three CH-53E's, and two MH-47's. His main task is to plan how that package is going to get the Marines to their zones on time. He must do this in the face of a potential air and ground threat. Since this will be a daytime mission he must plan his ingress to the objective area carefully, using terrain and low level flight as much as possible to protect his flight. The EFL is in charge of the attack helicopter assets which will include four AH-IW's and three UH-IN's. His main tasks are to protect the assault package on the way to the LZ's and provide fire support for the Marines on the ground once they are inserted.

Another key player in the planning stage is the Fire Support Coordinator (FSC). This is an officer assigned to the Marine battalion. Upon conducting a quick mission analysis, the FSC begins to match his fire support assets against the briefed threat. He begins to formulate a plan for fire support in the objective area. He knows there is enemy in the area, and he knows that an enemy force is approaching the objective, Blue Mountain. He must work closely with the fixed wing aviators, rotary wing aviators, and artillery liaison officer to develop a plan for fire support that will pre-

Close air support is a heavily emphasized element within the TacAir curriculum of both the Harrier and Hornet divisions.

pare the landing areas and protect the Marines on the ground. Timing will be critical, and the FSC will spend the next few hours scheduling his fires from artillery, fixed wing, and rotary wing assets.

The next eight hours are spent planning this mission. Key players refine their plan and prepare their briefs. Meanwhile, subordinate planning cells are spread throughout the building, working on their specific areas. The instructors, one of whom is paired with each key player, help to keep the planning moving along in an integrated manner. The assault pilots plan their routes, and actions in the objective area. They must plan to move the package from the airfield to a pick-up zone where the Marines will be waiting. They will plan to launch in order to make the assigned L-hr. If they are early, they risk flying into friendly bombs dropped by close air support aircraft or artillery. If they are late, they put the Marines on the helo's at risk because the longer the delay after prep fires have ended, the longer the enemy has the chance to re-group. They must be on time.

The helo attack pilots are planning how they will escort the packages along the route. They must do this but also must put "eyes on" the objective area well before the assault package arrives. The EFL will split his assets to do this. In conjunction with the FSC, he will plan to have a Forward Air Controller Airborne FAC(A) in a Huey near the objective area, who from his vantage point will be able to control fixed wing, rotary wing, as well as artillery fires.

The heavy assault student players (Marine CH-53E's and Army 47's) are planning for an artillery lift. They will launch well ahead of the rest of the package, fly to an M-198 gun position well inside friendly lines, and move those guns and their crews and their ammo closer to the objective area, from where they will be able to support the heliborne insert. They must then plan for an aerial refueling operation with the KC-130, so that they can join the rest of the assault package in the pick-up LZ before the first wave of Marines launches for their LZ.

Fixed wing close air support (CAS) players are planning, in conjunction with the rotary wing attack assets, artillery, FAC(A), and FSC, how they will support the insert. They figure out on station times, weapons loadouts, routing, and terminal control procedures. They must also work with the KC-130 crew to establish an aerial refueling track, which will serve to extend the jets' on station time.

Meanwhile, C3 students are sorting out frequencies, routing, and airspace issues. There will be many aircraft in a very small area during the mission, and the C3 student must be prepared to brief exactly what altitudes, tracks, routing, frequencies, and a myriad of other issues pertinent to the mission. The Navy E-2C students are planning how they will support the lift with their inherent command and control capability from the Hawkeye. This will serve to be a key asset as the mission unfolds. From a track around 20k, he will be able to pass back and forth critical information from

MAWTS-1 instructor Major J.D. Downey in 'Vault 403'.

Deep strike missions with multiple aircraft are complex and require significant planning which is taught and perfected at MAWTS-1.

Harrier formates on a Prowler. Weapons and Tactics Instructors are expert not only in their own aircraft, but the tactics and strengths of all Marine aviation assets.

the operators performing the mission to the Tactical Air Commander back in his command center.

The planning effort goes on and finally the day ends with the mission brief. After 8-10 hours of planning, the students are ready to deliver the brief. The brief is designed to give everyone participating a good idea for the *big picture* of what is supposed to happen.

Air Mission Commander's Brief:
First, the ground commander outlines his intent:

"The Red MRB is moving fast towards Blue Mountain without the benefit of air or supporting arms. I see this as the enemy's critical vulnerability. I intend to exploit this critical vulnerability by inserting a helicopter-borne battalion into the Blue Mountain area to reinforce the Green Company while simultaneously pummeling lead elements of the MRB with combined arms. Endstate: Maximum damage inflicted on approaching Red MRB, Green Company reinforced and the Blue Mountain area held until relieved by Green Armor Battalion."

With the ground commander's intent clear, the AMC now outlines how he will accomplish his mission. He does this by breaking the mission down into phases.

In Phase One, MAG-80 heavy lift assets and their escorts will conduct an artillery lift lifting three M-198's, their equipment, ordnance, and Marines from Siphon 10 to a gun position in the vicinity of the Little Mule Mountains in order to provide artillery fire support in Blue Mountain.

In Phase Two, heavy lift assets and their escorts will refuel/rearm and assemble with remaining lift assets and escorts to pick up the 2nd Battalion / 18th Marines (2/18—is a notional unit designation / acronym for 2nd Battalion / 18th Marines) at LZ Blackbird.

In Phase Three, at L-hour, MAG-80 will conduct a helicopter-borne insert of 2/18 to Blue Mountain in order to reinforce and hold that area until relieved.

In Phase Four, heavy lift assets will reconstitute and lift the artillery package from Little Mule Mountains to gun position nine and then return to force. All other assets will refuel if required and return to force. The Marines will be prepared to conduct follow-on missions in support of 2/18. The Air Mission Commander's brief lasts about an hour as the AMC and his staff explain generally how each phase will be accomplished.

Section of AV-8B's refuel from a VMGR-252 'Raider' KC-130.

The U.S. Navy E-2C plays a large role in WTI courses. This Hawkeye belongs to VAW-120 and was photographed while operating from its home base at NAS Norfolk.

The most critical portion of the brief is the explanation of actions in the objective area. During this mission, fixed wing aircraft will be dropping bombs, artillery will be firing, rotary wing attack assets will be firing missiles, rockets, and guns. Finally, the assault helicopters will be firing their guns on approach to the LZ. None of these fires will be simulated. It will all be live fire, therefore detail at this phase of the brief is critical.

Then follow-on briefs are conducted with individual packages in separate ready rooms. For the AFL, this is his opportunity to explain to his assault pilots what he intends to happen in explicit detail. His brief will last about forty-five minutes. At the completion of this brief, individual crews are armed with a significant amount of information. They know both the "big picture" from the AMC's brief, which allows them to have an understanding of where other assets are around the battlefield, and how their individual tasking contributes to the overall mission. They should know at this point, at any time during the mission the following: what formation they are flying, and at what altitude and airspeed, what frequencies to monitor, what their weapons conditions are, fields of fire for their assault gunners, what the positions of the escorts are, what radio calls need to be made and by who, exactly where they are along the route and if they are on time, relative positions of other assets such as the E-2C, fixed wing CAS players, and artillery, and they must be prepared to execute immediate action if faced by numerous contingencies.

Mission Execution

Finally it's time to execute Operation High Noon. The AFL leads his flight of ten out of the air station to the pick-up zone. Here the rest of the assault package, which has completed the artillery lift, joins in zone. At exactly 1110, or L-20, the assault package lifts with a flight of fifteen. Enroute formation is loose combat cruise to provide dispersion in case of an air threat. The escort package positions itself at the front and back of the formation, ready to respond to any enroute air or ground threat. At this point, the AFL, who is in the lead CH-46, is a busy man. The MAWTS instructor flies the aircraft so the student can concentrate on leading his flight, navigation, timing, and radio procedures. Since timing is critical, the student provides constant feedback to the pilot at the controls, telling him to speed up or slow down as necessary. He relies on his map and uses the portable GPS for back-up. The package is flying at fifty feet above ground level, so communications with line of sight radios is a challenge. The AFL uses the E-2C to pass information to the AMC.

The area preparation is to begin at L-15. At L-15 artillery begins firing pre-planned series onto specific target areas around the objective area. The assault flight is approaching the LZ via assigned routing. Starting at L-10, F/A-18 and AV-8B aircraft are targeting areas within two to three klicks from the LZ with 500 and 1000 lb. bombs, napalm, and rockets. At L-6 the assault flight splits into two elements and head for their respective LZ's.

'Moonighters Over UDBINA' Illustration by Mark Styling - On the afternoon of Monday, November 1994, the largest NATO airstrike ever assembled hit the Croatian airfield at Udbina. Over 65 NATO aircraft participated in the forty-five minute strike, whose purpose was to deny the Krajina Serbs the use of the airfield to launch bombing and strafing sorties against the Bosnian Muslims. VMFA (AW)-332, the Moonlighters were operating out of Aviano Air base, Italy, as part of Operation Deny Flight/Provide Promise. They played a major role in the mission which was in support of UN Protection Forces. The Moonlighters F/A-18D were the first NATO aircraft to strike with AGM-88 HARM and AGM-65 Maverick missiles. They were tasked with the SEAD role, specifically the suppression of SA-6 surface to air missiles. WTI's played a critical role in the planning and execution of these types of missions.

The B-52's are passing overhead on their low altitude bomb run. From L-5 to L-2 the B-52's run in for sequential drops of their racks of Mk-82 500 lb. bombs. At L-1 attack helicopters, from their attack positions adjacent to the LZ's, are firing rockets and guns toward the enemy. The assault package is on short final, and their gunners open up with .50 cal on both sides of the formation. Soon after touching down, the assault package lifts for their egress, still covered by the attack helo's.

On the egress back to pick up the second wave, the package is hit with surface to air missile fire as they cross a ridge, and the radio comes alive. "Amp flight break right, SAM launch, flares flares!" The flight disperses into terrain as countermeasure flares eject from the aircraft. The flight will reconstitute at the next checkpoint, and the AFL will determine if he still has the assets he needs to complete the second wave.

F/A-18 FLIGHT DESCRIPTION GUIDE

Sortie Name	Mission	Sortie Description	Training Objective	Ordnance
SIM-1	LAT Refresher/Special Weapons Employment (1.0)	F/A-18 simulator sortie to provide instructor and student warmup, practice LAT rules, and special weapons switchology.	1. Warm up simulator 2. Practice advanced LAT maneuvers. 3. Special Weapons switchology/displays.	1. AGM-65 E/F 2. Walleye (ER/DL) 3. AGM-88 4. LGB
AG-1	Air-to-Ground-1 (2.0)	AG-1 is designed to give the PWTI a day air-to-ground and aerial refueling refresher. In addition, armed reconnaissance techniques will be practiced.	1. Warm up sortie. 2. Practice medium/high angle dive deliveries. 3. Practice low/high angle pop deliveries. 4. Practice strafe. 5. Practice day aerial refueling 6. Practice armed reconnaissance.	1. (1) CATM-9M (M9C) 2. (12) MK-76 (B76) 3. (200) 20MM TP (G20P) 4. (20) ChafF(C144) 5. (10) Flares (F27)
AG-2	Air-to-Ground-2 (2.0)	The AG-2 sortie is designed to give the PWTI a night air-to-ground/aerial refueling refresher. In addition, LUU-2B/B delivery and "flare bombing" will be practiced.	1. Practice night ordnance delivery in the F/A-18 a. Radar DBMS/MSAR bombing b. TFLIR bombing 2. Practice night aerial refueling 3. Practice LUU-2B delivery 4. Practice bombing using artificial illumination.	1. (6) MK-76 W/Night Spot Charge (B76) 2. (2) LUU-2B/B (F1) 3. (20) Chaff (C144) 4. (10) Flares (F27)
LAT-1	Low Altitude Tactics-1 (1.0)	Basic low altitude tactics sortie for non-LAT qualified PWTI's. LAT-1 is the first of four sorties required for initial LAT qualification. All USN PWTI's will fly LAT-1.	1. Reacquaint or introduce the PWTI with the low altitude environment, low altitude maneuvering and instructional techniques. 2. Practice flight environment assessment, basic LAT maneuvers, section maneuvers, and simulated target attacks.	1. (1) CATM-9M (M9C) 2. (20) Chaff (C144) 3. (10) Flares (F27)
LAT-2	Low Altitude Tactics-2	Basic and advanced three dimensional LAT sortie. LAT-2 is the second of four sorties required for initial LAT qualification. All USN PWTI's will fly LAT-2.	1. Develop proficiency in basic LAT maneuvers. 2. Introduce advanced maneuvers and dive recovery rules.	1. (1) CATM-9M (M9C) 2. (20) Chaff (C144) 3. (10) Flares (F27)
LAT-3	Low Altitude Tactics-3	Basic and advanced three dimensional sortie. LAT-3 is the third of four sorties required for initial LAT qualification. All USN PWTI's will fly LAT-3.	1. Develop proficiency in advanced LAT maneuvers. 2. Introduce threat counter tactics.	1. (1) CATM-9M (M9C) 2. (20) Chaff (C144) 3. (10) Flares (F27)
LAT-4	Low Altitude Tactics-4	Advanced maneuvering proficiency and introduction to the chase position for conventional LAT. LAT-4 is the fourth of four sorties required for initial LAT qualification. USN PWTI's will fly LAT-4.	1. Review all LAT maneuvers 2. Introduce the PWTI to the chase position for conventional LAT.	1. (1) CATM-9M (M9C) 2. (20) Chaff (C144) 3. (10) Flares (F-27
LATI Check	Low Altitude Tactics (Instructor) Check Ride (1.0)	The purpose of LAT(1)-1 is to practice LAT chase instructional techniques, and will serve as a LAT(1) stan check for those who have already been designated as LAT(1)'s in their squadrons.	1. Practice instructional techniques and LAT chase. 2. LAT(1) stan check	1. (1) CATM-9M (M9C) 2. (20) Chaff (C144) 3. (10) Flares (F27)
SCT	SAM Counter Tactics (SCT) (1.0)	The purpose of the SCT sortie is to gain proficiency in SCT maneuvering and practice section coordinated attacks in a high threat, low altitude environment. In addition the use of Sam Counter Tactics in a medium altitude environment will be introduced.	1. Understand the flight dynamics and principles involved in the development of the SCT maneuver. 2. Develop proficiency in the SCT maneuver as a single aircraft. 3. Practice section coordinated attacks and perform maneuvers required to survive the in high threat, low altitude environment	1. TACTS POD (TACTS 2. CATM-9M (M9C) 3. Chaff (C144) 4. Flares (F27)

Sortie Name	Mission	Sortie Description	Training Objective	Ordnance
SWD-1/2	Specific Weapons Delivery-1/2 (1.0)	The purpose of the Special Weapons sorties is to provide the PWTI with the opportunity to employ one or more of the non-conventional weapons available to the F/A-18. The scenario for the SWD sorties will be controlled in order to allow the PWTI to practice weapons switchology, display interpretation, and launch/release, in a relatively benign environment.	1. Introduce/practice WALLEYE delivery. 2. Introduce/practice LGB/LGTR delivery. 3. Introduce/practice "buddy lase" techniques for LGB/LGTR and LMAV deliveries. 4. Introduce/practice HARM delivery. 5. Introduce/practice Rockeye delivery 6. Introduce/practice Maverick delivery.	1. CATM-9M (M9C) 2. WALLEYE (BW1T/BW2T/BWE1T/ BWE2T) 3. HARM (M88T) 4. MAVERICK (M65ET/M65FT) 5. LGTR (LGTR) 6. Rockeye (BRET) 7. Chaff (C144) 8. Flares (F27)
DAS-1	Deep Air Support-1 (3.0)	DAS-1 is a day VFR coordinated strike by the F/A-18 class against a target complex defended by an enemy IADS including air-to-air and surface-to-air threats. The class will be tasked with updating and executing a preplanned mission which simulates a 5027 scenario for a UDP squadron. All asset allocation will be dictated in the ATO (provided in the LOI in appendix (c)) to allow the PWTI's to concentrate on specific mission planning details. In addition the scenario will dictate a weapon-to-target match and ingress route/altitude.	1. Large Force Planning to include: a. Launch sequence Plan b. Accurate fuel planning c. Tanking plan 2. Counter IADS plan to include: a. Effective fighter plan to deal with airborne threats b. Effective SEAD plan to deal with surface threats. c. Effective use of on board self protection systems. 3. Weaponeering to include: a. Effectiveness of fragged ordnance load b. Optimum delivery profiles 4. Intelligence utilization to obtain desired information a. BTG's are provided 5. Safe and tactically sound target area tactics a. Utilize a 1:50,000 map to do detailed target area planning b. Plan detailed ordnance delivery parameters and attack profiles. c. Determine sun angle and azimuth, and target area winds. d. Construct a detailed, oblique target depiction of the target areas for each attack axis. 6. Specific weapons objectives a. Long range Walleye ERDL employment b. Buddy/self lase delivery 7. Accurate bomb hit assessment. 8. Appropriate briefing and inflight guide construction.	1. CATM-9M (M9C) 2. WALLEYE (BWE1T) 3. HARM (M88T) 4. LGTR (LGTR) 5. MK-83/84 INERT (B3PL/B4PL) 6. Chaff (C144) 7. Flares (F27)

Sortie Name	Mission	Sortie Description	Training Objective	Ordnance
DAS-2	Deep Air Support-2 (3.0)	DAS-2 is a long range out-of-area night strike against a target defended by an enemy IADS. The sortie will require re-strike, and potentially post-strike, tanking and sensor acquisition of the target. NVG's will be used by qualified aircrew.	1. Large Force Planning to include: a. Launch sequence plan b. Accurate fuel planning c. Tanking plan 2. Counter IADS plan to include: a. Effective fighter plan to deal with surface threats c. Effective use of on board self protection systems 3. Weaponeering to include: a. Proper weapons-to-target matching b. Optimum delivery profiles 4. Intelligence utilization to obtain desired information. 5. Safe and tactically sound target area tactics a. Utilize a 1:50,000 map to do detailed target area planning 6. Specific weapons objectives a. LGTR (simulated LGB) employment 7. Accurate bomb hit assessment 8. Appropriate briefing and inflight guide construction. 9. Accurate debrief	1. LGTR (LGTR) 2. CATM-9M (M9C) 3. Chaff (C144) 4. Flares (F27) 5. Captive HARM (M88C) 6. TACTS pod (TACTS)
AAW-1	Anti-Air warfare-1 (1.8)	AAW-1 is designed to give the PWTI's the opportunity to integrate all aviation assets into an IADS to provide a point defense of the MAGTF area of responsibility (AOR) for a specified time frame. Hornet shop PWTI's will conduct point defense missions under the control of the MACCS.	1. Conduct effective CAP procedures to protect the vital area for the vulnerability window. 2. Conduct effective combat intercepts. 3. Valid weapons employment. 4. Survive. 5. Attrite the threat and protect the vital area. 6. Identify leakers. 7. Assist the C^3 systems in maintaining a complete recognized air picture (RAP) and in managing the CAP. a. Utilize datalink b. Utilize effective communications	1. CATM-9M (M9C) 2. Chaff (C144) 3. Flares (F27)
AAW-2	Anti-Air Warfare-2 (1.8)	AAW-2 is designed to give the PWTI's another opportunity to integrate all aviation assets into an IADS to provide a point defense of the MAGTF area of responsibility (AOR) for a specified time frame. Hornet shop PWTI's will conduct point defense missions under the control of the MACCS. PWTI's will be expected to apply lessons learned during the AAW-1 evolution.	1. Conduct effective CAP procedures to protect the vital area for the vulnerability window. 2. Conduct effective combat intercepts. 3. Valid weapons employment 4. Survive. 5. Attrite the threat and protect the vital area. 6. Identify leakers 7. Assist the C^3 system in maintaining a complete recognized air picture (RAP) and in managing the CAP. a. Utilize datalink b. Utilize effective communications.	1. CATM-9M (M9C) 2. Chaff (C144) 3. Flares (F27)

Sortie Name	Mission	Sortie Description	Training Objective	Ordnance
OAAW	Offensive Anti-Air Warfare (2.0)	The OAAW evolution is designed togive the PWTI the opportunity to exercise strike and SEAD planning to target an "enemy" IADS. This is a force-on-force exercise pitting the TacAir PWTI's against the C^3 PWTI's. The ultimate goal of OAAW is to accomplish the TacAir PWTI mission while preventing the C^3 PWTI's from accomplishing their mission.	1. Properly employ HARM to prevent friendly losses to HAWK missiles. 2. Conduct weaponeering to achieve required damage to IADS. 3. Employ stand-off/precision weapons.	1. CATM-9M (M9C) 2. TACTS Pod (TACTS) 3. Chaff (C144) 4. Flares (F27) 5. Captive Walleye (BWE1C) 6. Captive HARM (M88C) 7. ALE-43 (C43)
OAS-1	Offensive Air Support-1 (2.0)	OAS-1 is designed to allow the PWTI to practice Armed Reconnaissance procedures-comm, navigation, timing, target acquisition - in a day VFR dynamic threat environment. A complete MACCS will be established including a SCAR platform. Most PWTI's can expect to fly two sorties during the evolution with F/A-18D PWTI's practicing SCAR on their second sortie.	1. Provide section/division Armed Reconnaissance in a dynamic threat environment. 2. Acquire targets utilizing SCAR "talk-on's", laser designations, and/or WP marks. 3. Select appropriate weapon-to-target match. 4. Deliver fuzed weapons with a CEP less than 50 meters. 5. Provide effective visual mutual support in the target. a. Acquire threat simulators (smokey SAMS) 100% of the time. b. React appropriately to RWR. 6. Provide accurate and timely inflight reports via the C^3 system to ensure that the TAC is able to maintain SA on the battle. 7. Practice SCAR procedures. (F/A-18D only) 8. Provide effective self illumination of selected targets with LUU-2 paraflares.	1. MK-82 (B2PPS) 2. MK-83 (B3PPS) 3. 20 MM (G20P) 4. CATM-9M (M9C) 5. 2.75" WP Rockets (R7W) 6. LUU-2 B/B (F1) 7. Chaff (C144) 8. Flares (F27) 9. FLIR/LDT if available
OAS-2	Offensive Air Support-2 (2.0)	OAS-2 is designed as a stepping stone for OAS-1. During the day the PWTI will be forced to contend with a limited number of radar guided SAM's which will elevate the threat over OAS-1. For the night portion of the sortie the threat will be decreased to allow low threat CAS and Armed Reconnaissance. Once again most PWTI's can expect to fly two sorties during the evolution with F/A-18D PWTI's practicing FAC(A) or SCAR on one of their sorties.	1. Provide section/division CAS in a high threat environment. 2. Acquire targets utilizing FAC/FAC(A) laser designations and/or WP marks 3. Select appropriate weapon-to-target match. 4. Deliver fuzed weapons with a CEP less than 50 meters. 5. Provide effective visual mutual support in the target. a. Acquire threat simulators (smokey SAMS) 100% of the time. b. React appropriately to RWR. 6. Provide effective self illumination of selected targets with LUU-2 paraflares. 7. Provide accurate and timely inflight reports via the C3 system to ensure that the TAC is able to maintain SA on the battle. 8. Practice high threat day and low threat night (FAC(A) procedures. (F/A-18D only)	1. MK-82 (B2PPS) 2. MK-83 (B3PPS) 3. 20 MM (G20P) 4. LUU-2B/B (F1) 5. 2.75" WP Rockets (R7W) 6. CATM-9M (M9C) 7. Chaff (C144) 8. Flares (F27) 9. FLIR/LDT if available

Sortie Name	Mission	Sortie Description	Training Objective	Ordnance
OAS-3	Offensive Air Support-3 (2.0)	OAS-3 is designed as another stepping stone from OAS-2. During the day the PWTI will be forced to contend with a notional weather deck which forces the assets into low altitude tactics. For the night portion of the sortie the weather will mysteriously clear allowing for all altitude tactics. PWTI's should expect MIJI from Radio Bn during the evolution. Once again most PWTI's can expect to fly two sorties during the evolution with F/A-18D PWTI's practicing FAC(A) on one of their sorties.	1. Provide section CAS in a high threat environment. 2. Acquire targets utilizing FAC/FAC(A) laser designations and/or WP marks. 3. Select appropriate weapon-to-target match. 4. Deliver fuzed weapons with a CEP less than 50 meters. 5. Provide effective visual mutual support in the target. a. Acquire threat simulators (smokey SAMS) 100% of the time. b. React appropriately to RWR. 6. Provide effective self illumination of selected targets with LUU-2 paraflares. 7. Provide accurate and timely inflight reports via the C^3 system to ensure that the TAC is able to maintain SA on the battle. 8. Practice high threat day and medium threat night (FAC(A) procedures. (F/A-18D only).	1. MK-82 live/inert (B2PPS/B2PPS) 2. MK-83 live/inert (B3PPS/B3PPS) 3. 20 MM (G20P) 4. 2.75" WP Rockets (R7W) 5. LUU-2B/B (F1) 6. CATM-9M (M9C) 7. Chaff (C144) 8. Flares (F27)
OAS-4	Offensive Air Support-4 (2.0)	OAS-4 is the final evolution in the OAS cycle and is designed to allow execution of low threat CAS tactics. No mark, "talk on" targeting will be the norm though WP marks may be used when needed. As always, most PWTI's can expect to fly two sorties during the evolution with F/A-18D PWTI's practicing FAC(A) on one of their sorties.	1. Provide section/division CAS in a low threat environment 2. Acquire targets utilizing FAC/FAC(A) "talk-ons", laser designations, and/or WP marks. 3. Select appropriate weapon-to-target match. 4. Deliver fuzed weapons with a CEP less than 50 meters. 5. Provide effective visual mutual support in the target. a. Acquire threat simulators (smokey SAMS) 100% of the time. b. React appropriately to RWR. 6. Provide effective self illumination of selected targets with LUU-2 paraflares. 7. Provide accurate and timely inflight reports via the C^3 system to ensure that the TAC is able to maintain SA on the battle. 8. Practice low threat day and night (FAC(A) procedures. (F/A-18D only).	1. MK-83 inert (B3PPS) 2. MK-84 inert (B4PL) 3. 2.75" WP rockets (R7W) 4. 20 MM TP (G20P) 5. LUU-2B/B (F1) 6. CATM-9M (M9C) 7. Chaff (C144) 8. Flares (F27) 9. FLIR/LDT if available

Sortie Name	Mission	Sortie Description	Training Objective	Ordnance
FINEX-1	Final Exercise One - (2.0)	Final Exercise One is designed to integrate all functions and assets Marine aviation into a joint operations scenario. The scenario for FINEX has a MAGTF ashore as a subordinate unit in a joint force and the ACE subject to tasking from the Joint Forces Air Component Commander (JFAC) as well as the MAGTF Commander. The MAGTF area of responsibility (AOR) is the R-250&N/S and R-2301E/W. Hornet shop PWTI's will be tasked with planning and executing all functions of Marine Aviation in support of MAGTF and JFC missions.	1. Plan and execute a long range strike, AAW, OAAW, CAS, Armed Recce, FAC(A), TAC(A), SCAR and Helo Escort to support JFC and MAGTF mission objectives. 2. China Lake strike specific training objectives: a. Conduct low altitude aerial refueling in conjunction with a range critical mission. b. Conduct SEAD operations to protect the strike package from the enemy IADS. c. Conduct weaponeering to provide required effects on target. d. Strike intended DMPI's on time. e. Provide timely bomb hit assessment and/or bomb damage assessment to the JFC Commander. 3. R-2301 specific training objectives: a. Provide point defense of the MAGTF AOR from enemy aircraft. b. Locate targets of opportunity and relay to the TACC via the C^3 system. c. Deliver ordnance on target, on time. d. Conduct On-call OAAW to allow effective armed reconnaissance.	1. MK-83 inert (B3PPS) 2. LGTR (LGTR) 3. 2.75" WP rockets (R7W) 4. LUU-2 (D-22B) 5. Chaff (C144) 6. Flares (F27) 7. CATM-9M (M9C) 8. FLIR/LDT as available
FINEX-2	Final Exercise Two - (2.0)	Final Exercise Two is designed to integrate all functions and assets Marine aviation into a joint operations scenario. The scenario for FINEX has a MAGTF ashore as a subordinate unit in a joint force and the ACE subject to tasking from the Joint Forces Air Component Commander (JFAC) as well as the MAGTF Commander. The MAGTF area of responsibility (AOR) is the R-2301E/W. Hornet shop PWTI's will be tasked with planning and executing all functions of Marine Aviation in support of MAGTF and JFC missions.	1. Plan and execute a long range strike, AAW, OAAW, CAS, Armed Recce, FAC(A), TAC(A), SCAR and Helo Escort to support JFC and MAGTF mission objective. 2. Hill strike training objectives: a. Conduct medium altitude aerial refueling in conjunction with a range critical mission. b. Conduct SEAD operations to protect the strike package from the enemy IADS. c. Conduct weaponeering to provide required effects on target. d. Strike intended DMPI's on time e. Provide timely bomb hit assessment and/or bomb damage assessment to the JFC Commander. 3. R-2301 specific training objectives: a. Provide point defense of the MAGTF AOR from enemy aircraft. b. Locate targets of opportunity and relay to the TACC via the C^3 system c. Deliver ordnance on target, on time d. Conduct On-call OAAW to allow effective armed reconnaissance.	1. MK-83 inert (B3PPS) 2. LGTR (LGTR) 3. 2.75" WP rockets (R7W) 4. LUU-2(D-22B) 5. Chaff (C144) 6. Flares (F27) 7. CATM-9M (M9C) 8. FLIR/LDT as available

Sortie Name	Mission	Sortie Description	Training Objective	Ordnance
FINEX-3	Final Exercise Three (FINEX-3) - (2.0)	Final Exercise Three is a continuation of the scenario of FINEX-1/2. A planning day between flight operations is allocated to allow the PWTI's to incorporate lessons learned in FINEX-1/2. In addition new tasking from the JFC Commander will be promulgated during the FINEX-3 inbrief.	1. Plan and execute AAW, OAW, CAS, Armed Recce, FAC(A), TAC(A), SCAR and Helo Escort to support JFC and MAGTF mission objectives. 2. Provide point defense of the MAGTF AOR from enemy aircraft. 3. Locate targets of opportunity and relay to the TACC via the C^3 system. 4. Deliver ordnance on target, on time. 5. Conduct On-call OAAW, to allow effective armed reconnaissance.	1. MK-83 inerts (B3PPS) 2. LGTR (LGTR) 3. 2.75" WP rockets (R7W) 4. LUU-2 (F1) 5. Chaff (C144) 6. Flares (F27) 7. CATM-9M (M9C) 8. FLIR/LDT as available.

AH-1W FLIGHT DESCRIPTION GUIDE

Flight	Ordnance	Learning Objective	Conduct	Key Indicators
Day Warmup	20mm	1. Evaluate the IUT's knowledge of TERF techniques, to include power checks, low level, contour and NOE flight, masking/unmaksing, bunts, rolls, NOE quickstops and comfort margins. 2. Evaluate TERF navigation. 3. Evaluate weapons systems knowledge. 4. Establish a thorough, detailed objective area plan. 5. Evaluate section tactical maneuvers.	The IUT will occupy either during the flight. Mission brief and the objective area plan will be given by the MAWTS-1 Instructor.	1. Evaluate TERF and tactical formation flying skills. 2. Effective objective area plan and brief. 3. Accurate TERF navigation.
FW/RW ACM	CAIM-9, TACTS pod, chaff and flares.	1. Introduce the ACM environment. 2. Introduce ACM crew coordination. 3. Introduce FW, RW ACM principles, capabilities and limitations.	The conduct of flight and line numbers of this evolution will be briefed by MAWTS-1 instructors. The WTI students will brief the bogeys and training rules and will occupy the rear seat during this flight. Fly the aircraft to achieve either the most advantageous defensive or offensive position to employ air-to-air weapons.	1. Flight leadership and safety. 2. Wingman awareness and safety. 3. Proper employment of air-to-air weapons and tactics. 4. Defensive positioning. 5. Terminology and crew coordination. 6. Lookout doctrine. 7. Basic Airwork.
Ninja's Box 1	CATM-9, chaff, flares	1. Emphasize the importance of crew coordination and weapons system selection and operation while conducting point-target destruction in a realistic threat environment. 2. Operate in a confined objective area against medium to high ground and air threats.	The IUT may occupy either seat during the Ninja's Box. Aircraft will depart as a flight to the range, where the students will separate into either single aircraft or sections, one north, one south. IAW briefings and score cards, each aircraft will attempt to engage specific targets from an advantageous attack position, while avoiding detection by the threat. Proper execution requires the crew to correctly navigate, employ weapons, avoid detection, engage targets and complete the mission within the specified time frame. Decoy flares will be utilized to simulate weapons employment.	1. Navigate and crew coordination. 2. Weapons system switchology and selection. 3. Interpretation of threat and tactics utilized. 4. Time Management.
Night Warmup	20mm, rockets	1. Detailed route and objective area planning. 2. Evaluate NVG target ID and ordnance delivery. 3. Evaluate NVG navigation. 4. Refresh NVG flying skills.	The IUT will occupy either seat during this flight. The flight will emphasize objective area planning. The IUT will be evaluated on all facets of the AH-1W weapons systems as well as instructional techniques.	1. Refresh NVG flying skills. 2. NVG navigation. 3. Accurate ordnance delivery. 4. Effective objective area plan and brief. 5. BDA

Flight	Ordnance	Learning Objective	Conduct	Key Indicators
Day Battledrill	20mm, rockets, PGMs, Sidearm	1. Plan and execute generic AH-1W missions. 2. Execute PPOC and immediate AH-1W missions (from FMFM 5-35) as directed by appropriate controlling agencies. 3. Incorporate available fire support assets to accomplish missions. 4. Stress crew coordination, flight tactics, tactical flexibility and accurate weapons delivery.	The flight will be flown with MAWTS instructors acting as high bird and controlling agencies. General guidance will be issued Sat 5 Oct. Mission Commanders will be responsible for developing smart packs, the OAS brief, and a simple game plan. Using available S-2 assets and battlefield handovers, the IUT will execute assigned missions received from the controlling agencies utilizing all available assets.	1. Accurate navigation and timeless. 2. Target and mission analysis, tactics utilized, ordnance delivery. 3. Use of available fire support assets. 4. Tactical control and flexibility. 5. Effective threat countertactics. 6. HEADWORK AND S A.
NTAC1	20mm, rockets, PGMs	1. Introduce joint attack helicopter integration during medium threat point-target destruction operations. 2. Introduce combine FW and RW strike tactics with emphasis on terminal area target analysis. 3. Plan and execute a detailed objective area with coordinated weapons employment and target destruction. 4. Introduce tactics and control procedures specific to a point-target attack. 5. Navigate to an attack position on NVGs. 6. Deliver accurate PGM fire under illumination.	The IUT will occupy the front seat during this flight, and will navigate a pre-planned route to a target area. Conduct a point-target coordinated attack on a ground target.	1. Planning, briefing and AP selection. 2. NVG navigation. 3. Integration of AV-8B assets into mission plan. 4. Timely and accurate ordnance delivery / BDA.
NTAC II	20mm, rockets	1. Navigate pre-planned, multi-leg, long distance routes. 2. Plan and execute 3 OAS missions (2 DAS, 1 CAS) in 3 separate obj. areas. Execute assault escort, FW OAS control, and utilize EA-6B support. 3. Utilize MEU (SOC) rapid planning contingency guidelines. 4. Coordinate fuel and ordnance requirements for mission execution with KC-130 and CH-53/MH-47 RGR support at improved and unimproved sites.	The IUT will occupy either seat during this flight. Within rapid planning guidelines, the IUT will plan 2 air interdiction and 1 CAS mission focusing on 3 separate obj. areas. The MAWTS Coordinator will provide a majority of the planning requirements. The IUT is responsible for briefing the 3 obj. areas, the RGR plans, and leading the mission.	1. Intelligence integration / target study. 2. Objective area analysis / planning. 3. FW/RW OAS / SCAR mechanics and flow. 4. Accurate weapons delivery and BDA. 5. Targeting and weaponeering. 6. RGR planning.

Flight	Ordnance	Learning Objective	Conduct	Key Indicators
NTAC III (Night Battledrill)	20mm, rockets, Illum, PGMs	1. The IUT will plan, brief and lead a RW CAS mission executing PPOC and immediate mission as directed by controlling agencies. 2. Stress crew coordination, tactics on NVGs under LLL conditions, tactical flexibility and accurate ordnance delivery. 3. Incorporate available fire support assets for mission accomplishment.	The flight will be flown as student-to-student flights as much as possible. MAWTS instructors will acta as high bird and controlling agencies. Using available S-2 assets and battlefield handovers, the IUT will execute assigned missions utilizing all available support assets.	1. Flight leadership and flexibility. 2. Crew coordination and coordination with available assets. 3. Accurate navigation and timeliness. 4. Tactics chosen 5. HEADWORK AND S. A. 6. Accurate ordnance delivery. 7. BDA
NTAC IV	20mm, rockets, PGMs	1. Refine AH-1W point-target mission planning and execution 2. Conduct detailed objective area planning and briefing. 3. Refine tactics and control procedures specific to multiple PGM employment during a point-target attack. 4. Navigate to an attack position on NVGs. 5. Deliver accurate PGM fire.	The IUT will occupy the front seat during this flight, and will navigate a pre-planned route to a target area. Conduct a point-target coordinated attack on a ground target.	1. Planning, briefing and AP selection. 2. NVG navigation. 3. Simple, effective, multiple PGM employment. 4. Timely and accurate ordnance delivery / BDA.
Ninja's Box II / Shadow Guns	CATM-9, 20mm, rockets, chaff, flares	1. Emphasize the importance of crew coordination and weapons system selection and operation while conducting point-target destruction in a realistic threat environment. 2. Operate in a confined objective area against medium to high ground and air threats. 3. Employ the principles of air-to-air gunnery.	The IUT may occupy either seat during the Ninja's Box. Aircraft will depart as a flight to the range, where the students will separate into either single aircraft or sections, one north, one south. IAW briefings and score cards, each aircraft will attempt to engage specific targets from an advantageous attack position, while avoiding detection by the threat. Proper execution requires the crew to correctly navigate, employ weapons, avoid detection, engage targets and complete the mission within the specified time frame. Decoy flares will be utilized to simulate weapons employment. The IUT will occupy the rear seat during the shadow gunnery portion of the evolution. Set-up and conduct of air-to-air gunnery will be emphasized, focusing on handling the aircraft to obtain proper firing solutions in a simulated ACM environment.	1. Navigate and crew coordination. 2. Weapons system switchology and selection. 3. Interpretation of threat and tactics utilized. 4. Time Management.

Flight	Ordnance	Learning Objective	Conduct	Key Indicators
AST I	20mm, rockets, PGMs	1. Brief and lead a RW escort mission under low to medium threat conditions. 2. Integrate with other assault support assets. 3. Integrate with GCE for fire support. 4. Integrate OAS with escort.	The IUT will occupy either seat during this evolution. Use appropriate control measures to ensure the assault support assets arrive at the designated LZ within 30 seconds of the L-Hour. Plan routes and attack positions to best defeat the threat.	1. Escort flight leadership. 2. AMC Coordination, briefing and control of the package. 3. Detailed, coordinated and deconflicted fire support plan. 4. Precision timing and navigation. 5. Accurate ordnance delivery, to include a responsive plan to bring live fire onto enroute and objective area pop-up ground threats. 6. BDA
AST II	20mm, rockets, illum, PGMs	1. Rapid planning for a RW CAS and escort mission under low to medium threat conditions. 2. Plan routes and attack positions to accomplish the mission under the existing ROE.	The IUT will occupy either seat during this flight. Use appropriate measures to ensure the assault support package arrives at the correct LZ within 30 seconds of the L-Hour. Provide escort and RW CAS as appropriate to support the GCE scheme of maneuver.	1. Flight leadership. 2. RW / FW integration and execution. 3. Integration with C3 agencies and the GCE. 4. Coordination with the assault support package. 5. Accurate ordnance delivery. 6. Plan and execution abide by the ROE. 7. Information flow through the C3 system.
AST III	20mm, rockets, PGMs	1. Brief and lead a RW CAS escort mission under medium to high threat conditions. 2. Conduct planning under hasty conditions in the field. 3. Coordinate with other assault support assets. 4. Coordinate with the GCE to best support their scheme of maneuver.	The IUT will occupy either seat during this flight. Use field conditions at a FARP, plan and execute the assigned mission to ensure the assault support package arrives at the correct LZ within 30 seconds of the L-Hour Plan routes and attack positions to best defeat the threat.	1. Flight leadership. 2. Detailed, simple plan. 3. RW CAS and escort tactics. 4. Integration with C3 and the GCE. 5. Accurate ordnance delivery, to include responsive live fire in support of the transports. 6. BDA.
OAS III	20mm, rockets, PGMs	1. Brief and lead a RW OAS mission under medium to high threat conditions. 2. Integrate and coordinate with the GCE and other CAS/DAS assets.	The IUT will occupy either seat during this flight. Use appropriate control measures to ensure that ordnance is delivered on target within -10 to +10 seconds of the assigned TOT/TTT. Plan routes and attack positions to best defeat the threat.	1. Flight leadership. 2. Employment of RW CAS assets in the OAS environment. 3. Integration with C3 and the GCE. 4. Coordination with other CAS assets. 5. Accurate and timely ordnance delivery. 6. FAC(A) procedures. 7. BDA.

Flight	Ordnance	Learning Objective	Conduct	Key Indicators
OAS IV	20mm, rockets, PGMs	1. Brief and lead a RW DAS mission under high threat conditions 2. Integrate and coordinate with the GCE and other DAS assets. 3. Perform DAS / SCAR to fill gaps in FW DAS coverage.	The IUT will occupy either seat during this flight. Use appropriate control measures to ensure that ordnance is delivered on target within -10 and +10 seconds of the assigned TOT/TTT Plan routes and attack positions to best defeat the threat. Coordinate / Control Armed Reconnaissance assets to engage specified targets.	1. Flight leadership. 2. Employment of RW DAS within the OAS environment. 3. Integration with C3 agencies and the GCE 4. Coordination with other DAS assets. 5. Accurate and timely ordnance delivery. 6. FAC(A) procedures. 7. BDA. 8. DAS / SCAR
Finex 1	20mm, rockets, illum, PGMs	1. Plan, brief and lead the flight to accomplish the assigned missions. 2. Coordinate with all available assets in establishing a detailed mission plan to best support the MAGTF GCE scheme of maneuver. 3. Coordinate a fire support plan that ensures maximum fire support with detailed integration and deconfliction.	The IUT will occupy either seat during this evolution. Provide AH assets to support the GCE scheme of maneuver, assault support assets, RW CAS and all other requirements from the ACE commander's Concept of Operations and guidance.	1. Flight leadership. 2. Planning Coordination. 3. Tactics utilized and asset allocation 4. Mission accomplishment.
Finex II	20mm, rockets, PGMs	1. Plan, brief and lead the flight to accomplish the assigned missions. 2. Coordinate with all available assets in establishing a mission plan to best support the MAGTF GCE scheme of maneuver. 3. Coordinate a fire support plan that ensures maximum fire support with detailed integration and deconfliction.	The IUT will occupy either seat during this flight. Provide AH assets to support the GCE scheme of maneuver, assault support assets, RW CAS and other requirements from the ACE commanders's Concept of Operations and Guidance.	1. Flight leadership. 2. Planning Coordination. 3. Tactics utilized and asset allocation. 4. Mission accomplishment.
Finex III	20mm, rockets, PGMs	1. Plan, brief and lead the flight to accomplish the assigned missions. 2. Coordinate with all available assets in establishing a mission plan to best support the MAGTF GCE scheme of maneuver. 3. Coordinate a fire support plan that ensures maximum fire support with detailed integration and deconfliction.	The IUT will occupy either seat during this flight. Provide AH assets to support the GCE scheme of maneuver, assault support assets. RW CAS and other requirements from the ACE commander's Concept of Operations and guidance.	1. Flight leadership. 2. Planning Coordination. 3. Tactics utilized and asset allocation. 4. Mission accomplishment.

COMMAND, CONTROL & COMMUNICATIONS (C3)
Curriculum Overview

During each evolution, one of the C3 students is designated and serves as the Marine Air Control Group Operations Officer (S-3). The remaining students are assigned as battalion or squadron operations officers for each of the units within the MACG/MACCS. Each student is provided with an intelligence scenario, a mission statement, Commander's Intent, and a concept of employment and confirmation briefing formats.

The student MACG S-3 and his staff will work with the other community planners to develop a concept of employment to support the selected course of action. The student staff will brief the Tactical Air Commander (TAC) for final approval. Upon final approval by the TAC, the C3, ASD, and TACAIR staffs will submit the frags for the development of the Air Tasking Order and MACCS agency/unit operations orders.

Specific Evolution student learning objectives are listed below.

GROUND BASED AIR DEFENSE (GBAD) I & II

The GBAD week consists of a series of two training evolutions. Each evolution is centered on the requirements to maximize integration of GBAD assets to successfully defend designated air defense priorities against a dedicated threat. To enhance student and unit training, each evolution is recorded on TACTS for play-back and detailed debriefing purposes.

The focus of the evolutions is two-fold. First, C3 students are given the opportunity to develop their combat mission planning skills and agency briefing skills. Additionally, the students, serving in the capacity of a battalion or squadron S-3, are tasked with conducting a critical evaluation of the execution of their plan. The intent is to develop those skills that enable a WTI graduate to return to his home unit capable of planning integrated training and the critically evaluating and forthrightly debriefing unit execution to ensure improved unit training. The secondary focus is to provide an opportunity for the deployed MACG units to conduct realistic and challenging integrated training against a sophisticated threat.

The scenario will involve two separate but evolving snapshots in time. Each snapshot will present varied training opportunities, but all will focus on the requirement to successfully defend designated air defense priorities, using only ground based assets, from enemy air attack.

Marine units utilize advanced radar systems to keep track of enemy air activity.

A. Student Learning Objectives include:

1. Refine combat mission planning skills with emphasis on planning for both air defense operations and control of aircraft and missiles.
2. Refine briefing techniques when serving in the capacity of a battalion or squadron S-3.
3. Develop ability to critically evaluate execution of a briefed plan.
4. Refine debriefing skills to ensure critical issues are addressed in sufficient detail to enable identification of training shortfalls and ensure progression of unit combat training.
5. Improve familiarity with unit T&R syllabus and MCCRES standards. Be able to integrate the T&R syllabus and MCCRES standards requirements into the training process, and identify training requirements that can be linked to other agencies training.

B. Unit Learning Objectives

1. Conduct integrated ground based air defense training, in defense of designated air defense priorities, against a briefed threat.
2. Refine ability to critically evaluate training readiness with respect to mission assignment and integration requirements.
3. Maximize integration of the air defense system (TAOC, HAWK, LAAD, ATC). Concentrate on voice and data link connectivity and streamlining flow of critical information.
4. Exercise Sector Anti Air Warfare Coordinator (SAAWC) management of the air defense sector.
5. Maximize use of the CI/D net as a constant EW broadcast net with the TAOC as net control.
6. Refine HAWK Tactical Officer (TO) to TAOC Missile Controller (MC) interface and HAWK Radar Operator (RO) to TAOC Surveillance Operator (SO) interface.
7. Refine HAWK Platoon COC concepts and LAAD integration.
8. Exercise engagement decision making under both the centralized and decentralized modes of control.
9. Exercise appropriate authentication and encryption procedures in response to an Electronic Warfare Support (ES) and Imitative Communications Deception (ICD) threat.
10. Execute the briefed RADCON plan.

HMX-1 CH-46 practices troop insertion in the urban warfare setting duplicated at Combat Town in Quantico, Virginia.

After picking up a group of Marines, these two PHROG's kick up some desert upon departure.

Section of Cobra's protect this UH-1N as it comes in for a landing.

11. Effectively translate published Rules of Engagement and briefed firing doctrine into timely engagement decision making.

12. Exercise missile resupply procedures.

13. Exercise integration of the Remote Engagement Section (RES) and CWAR Sensor Acquisition Section (SAS).

14. Exercise passive defense measure.

ANTIAIR WARFARE (AAW) I & II

The AAW flight syllabus is designed utilizing a building block approach, wherein the evolution builds upon knowledge previously acquired during specific flight evolutions (GBAD). Upon completion of this common training block, both C3 and TACAIR students should understand the planning, integration, and airspace/air defense control measures required to conduct AAW operations in a modern battle space. The following learning objectives are accomplished.

1. Plan and execute two realistic five hour day to night AAW exercises in defense of designated air defense priorities under attack by a coordinated strike force.

Combat ready Marines around an HMX-1 CH-46E.

2. Combat Air Patrol (CAP) management and control of fighter aircraft.

3. CAP relief on station when required.

4. Control of HAWK/LAAD assets to include coordination and deconfliction of engagements between SAM and fighters.

5. Management of tanker assets.

6. Establish, disseminate, and activate RADCON measures to counter the briefed ARM threat.

7. Plan and execute appropriate airspace control measures to include Minimum Risk Routing (MRR).

8. Provide effective information flow for dissemination of weapons/ equipment status, weapons control status, air defense warning conditions, threat system status, states of alert, engagement results, and Theater Missile Defense Warning Messages.

9. Conduct all functions of Command and Control.

10. Manipulation and dissemination of the rules of engagement.

OFFENSIVE ANTIAIR WARFARE (OAAW)

The overall objective of the C3 Students for OAAW is to destroy the enemy's aviation power and will to fight, and provide air defense of the established air defense priorities. This is the only force on force flight evolution within the WTI syllabus. Forces are delineated as Red Forces (TACAIR Students) and Blue Forces (C3 Students). Blue forces are tasked to employ effective passive and active air defense measures and casualty procedures to ensure that the capability exits within the ACE to protect the established air defense priorities against subsequent strikes. The following learning objectives are accomplished:

1. Assess the threat to include, but not limited to enemy strike/fighter, aircraft, ordnance, tactics, and electronic warfare capability.

2. Build an Integrated Air Defense system (IADS) to defend the stated air defense priorities through a detailed analysis of friendly capabilities to include surveillance, identification, weapons, and weapons employment.

3. Formulate an aggressive integrated plan to exploit the capabilities of the surveillance assets and surface to air weapons systems organic to the MACCS.

4. Develop a communications plan that will integrate our air defense assets with sufficient redundancy and ensure key data links are maintained by priority.

5. Formulate an emissions control and radiation control plan that will maximize survivability of our surveillance assets while maintaining an appropriate recognized air picture.

6. Develop a realistic deception plan that will increase the survivability of our forces. This plan must be integrated with the radiation control plan, communications plan and active/passive measures to increase its effectiveness.

7. Establish appropriate Rules of Engagement to include friendly and hostile ID criteria, weapons control status, firing doctrine and other procedures that ensure maximum effectiveness of the IADS by minimizing reaction time and preserving assets.

8. Develop, coordinate, and plan for the execution of a Tactical Recovery of Aircraft and Personnel (TRAP) mission.

ASSAULT SUPPORT TACTICS 1-4

1. Community integration between the Ground Combat Element, TACAIR, Assault Support and C3.

2. Develop effective mission planning skills focusing on time management, the efficient use of assets, conducting an accurate threat analysis, develop a tactically sound aircraft route structure, and accurate fuel planning.

3. Plan for the effective flow of combat information throughout the effective employment of the MACCS in general and the Direct Air Support Center (DASC) and DASC(A).

4. Provide Command & Control of rotary wing assets. Maintain status of assets during emissions control and normal launch and recovery operations.

5. Exercise communication both internal and external to assault support flight operations.

6. Manage assets dedication to tactical recovery of personnel and equipment.

7. Plan and provide for positive communications between air support aircraft, control agencies, and the ground combat element.

The huge CH-53E is a critical element of rotary assault support.

A pair of UH-1 Huey's cavort near MCAS New River.

8. Employ the DASC(A) as an Airborne Mission Commander Platform.

OFFENSIVE AIR SUPPORT 1-4

The OAS flight evolution utilizes a logical flow to simulate a probate war scenario. Upon completion of this training block the involved TACAIR, R/W, C3 and GCE students should understand the planning, integration, and weapons system optimization measures required to conduct OAS operations (in concert with the other functions of USMC aviation) on the modern battlefield.

1. Effectively utilize the Marine Air Command and Control System to conduct Armed Recce in support of MAGTF objectives.

   a. Effectively use covered communications and COMSEC procedures.

   b. Understand the procedures established to pass vital intelligence, mission results, and target area information.

   c. Understand the problems associated with and the techniques for locating and neutralizing or destroying known and pop-up air defense threats in support of both Armed Recce and CAS.

   d. Understand the planning requirements for executing Armed Recce and SCAR in a dynamic threat environment.

2. Effectively utilize the Marine Air Command and Control System to conduct responsive CAS for the Ground Combat Element (GCE).

   a. Utilize the MACCS to launch and divert aircraft for scheduled and on call CAS missions as required by the GREEN/BLUE GCE.

   b. Effectively use covered communications and COMSEC procedures.

   c. Utilize the MACCS to proactively manage ground alert aircraft.

   d. With the TACC managing the ATO, conduct PPS, PPOC and Immediate CAS, sourcing missions from both airborne and strip alerts.

   e. Develop a destruction area and routing plan which supports CAS requirements and provides the flexibility to maintain air defense for the designated air defense priorities.

   f. Introduce and integrate a DASC(A).

   g. Formulate procedures for the detailed reporting of mission results and "vital intelligence".

h. Develop the required channels to pass and utilize this information by follow on missions and to build the target area(s) situational awareness.

i. Develop and submit preplanned JTARS for designated TAIs.

j. Conduct the planning, coordination and integration required to successfully execute day and night close air support in a dynamic threat environment in support of the MAGTF concept of operations.

k. Understand the planning and integration requirements for TACAIR, Assault Support, and C3 in the conduct of Offensive Air Support operations.

l. Identify critical elements of information and utilize established procedures for that information to flow through the MACCS.

m. Understand the problems associated with and the techniques for locating and neutralizing or destroying known and pop-up air defense threats.

n. Understand the planning and integration required to defend the air defense priorities within an air defense sector while conduction OAS missions.

o. Process Battle Damage Assessments in conjunction with the intelligence cell at the TACC.

p. Utilize the Air Boss in the management of strip alert aircraft and aircraft turn around.

q. Maintain status of FARP(s) in support of forward based air support assets.

s. Process immediate request for CAS in a timely and accurate manner.

t. Employ the DASC(A) and the E-2C as a deep battle manager.

FINEX I-II

1. Introduce all students to the air operations planning conducted in the ACE Future Operations Section (FOS), requiring the integration of all Six Functions of Marine aviation.

2. To analyze the MAGTF mission, the ACE mission, the ground scheme of maneuver, the threat, and the available ACE assets.

Camouflage netting helps conceal the Marines ground to air defenses.

Cobra fires rockets while on the move. Assault support, AH-1W style.

3. Develop a plan that will accomplish the ACE's objectives in support of the MAGTF and JFACC tasking.
4. Allocate resources to accomplish each mission.
5. Understand the coordination required between the ACE staff and FMF units to allow those units to plan tactical missions.
6. To use sound tactics when planning and executing each mission during the evolution.
7. Successfully accomplish assigned missions.
8. Analyze our ability to conduct MAGTF level ACE operations.
9. Provide the control of aircraft and missiles to integrate the Six Functions of Marine Aviation.
10. Overall MACCS Integration to manage AAW, OAS, Air Reconnaissance and Electronic Warfare assets concurrently.
11. Employ the MACCS with overextended lines of communication.
12. Plan for the overall airspace management with Six Functions of Marine aviation conducted simultaneously.
13. Develop and execute a MACCS Casualty Plan.
14. Integrate Joint Airborne Early Warning Assets.

10

Voices From The Past

Perhaps for one of the only occasions in recent history, the Commanding Generals, or CG's, of each of the active duty Marine Air Wings are former MAWTS-1 Commanding Officers. These individuals offer a unique historical perspective as to how MAWTS-1 has developed over time and its current value to Marine Air and the Corps. As well, their personal reflections offer insight into the type of Marine officer that has lead and built MAWTS-1 into the superb school it has become.

Brigadier General B. B. Knutson - Commanding General 1st Marine Air Wing

"Validation of the value of MAWTS-1 occurred in wartime...the whole concept stood the test and was validated in spades. And still is, I cannot imagine the rescue of USAF Captain Scott O'Grady being done so smoothly without a WTI program."

I served as the Commanding Officer of MAWTS-1 from the 28th of May, 1992 until June the 2nd, 1994. Previously, I was the Executive Officer of the squadron from September, 1991 until May, 1992. Fleeting up has been the case since the squadrons second commander (Bobby Butcher) gave command to the third CO (Jake Vermilyea). I had a previous tour at MAWTS-1 in 1978-1982 as an F-4 Phantom instructor and was also the F-4 Shop Head for two years and Operations Officer for EWCAS (a joint test between the Marine Corps and USAF at Nellis Air Force Base 1981-82).

The curriculum at MAWTS-1 was in good shape when I first arrived. The basic underlying framework for the course was rock solid having not really changed since 1978, and still hasn't. General DeLong was my predecessor, but he skipped two WTI's due to Desert Shield/Storm and then conducted two in the Fall of 1991 and Spring of 1992. At that time, the instructors were solid, and maintenance, logistics and safety were in good shape. I brought in a new Operations Officer, Major (now Lt. Colonel) Charlie Mitchell who greatly helped smooth out the students planning to real execution cycle. We worked hard through my years as CO to increase the realism and to also make the training scenarios more demanding and stressful in regards to planning and using Marine Air. Especially in Marine helicopter operations where we lifted some restrictive range limitations. We also had some of our innovative instructors develop realistic and demanding scenarios for the rotary wing training evolutions.

The major improvements however that were made during my tenure as CO were first started under General DeLong. This concerned getting more out of the course for the same overall investment by the Marine Corps. For example, with the same investment of people and aircraft, we crafted and instituted embedded courses within the WTI course. WTI used to just be for Aviation Officers. Before my time, the GCE course was instituted and the Helo Crew Chief course, and both paid off big. We added courses for the KC-130 Loadmaster and Navigator, DASC Crew Chief, Stinger (LAAD) Section Leader and Helo Gunner. The GBAD (Ground Based Air Defense Exercise) was also imbedded in the WTI to give the deployed air defense assets intense training. Another significant and lasting accomplishment was the unraveling and straightening out of the funding line for MAWTS-1 which aided in the budgeting process. Another initiative that was started while I was CO, but was brought to fruition under Colonel John Castellaw was the TAC (Tactical Air Commander) Course. So by having the same rough investment, we were able do a great deal more quality, (and much needed), training for the FMF (Fleet Marine Force).

The curriculum changes during my stay as CO concerned the increased emphasis on Precision Guided Munitions (PGM's) weaponeering and their integration into schemes of maneuver for the Fixed Wing elements. We also introduced and refined fixed wing and Cobra integration and simultaneous close air support. More emphasis on closer integration of helicopter operations, EA-6B employment, the use of UAV's, as well as involving all aviators with intelligence was instituted.

I cannot understate the importance of the WTI program. The training in Marine Aviation before MAWTS-1 and after is like the difference between Michael Jordan's jump shot and mine - simply night and day. As I commanded MAWTS-1, the brilliance of the Marines who conceived the program some fifteen years before revealed itself to me each day. From FMF standardization, to putting teeth into tactics, techniques and procedures training to OT & E of aviation Programs, to developing aviation planners of the future, there is absolutely no comparison to any program in the Marine Corps or any of the sister services.

The validation of the MAWTS concept occurred in wartime, in Desert Shield/Storm. What the WTI's did there is a matter of official record. The whole concept stood the ultimate test and was validated in spades. And it still is. I cannot imagine the rescue of Captain Scott O'Grady being done so smoothly without a WTI program. Moreover, the training one receives while being part of MAWTS-1, whether as an instructor or commander cannot be duplicated. One does not know his own profession until he teaches it to others.

Brigadier General Bruce Barry Knutson - Commanding General 1st Marine Air Wing.

Major General Michael D. Ryan - Commanding General 2nd Marine Air Wing.

Major General Michael D. Ryan - Commanding General 2nd Marine Air Wing

"Whenever the potential exists for any of our forward deployed units to go in harms way, the first call is "WTI's forward". The ability of MAWTS-1 WTI's to plan and lead integrated, complex air operations makes them standout's among their contemporaries."

In May of 1977, I was assigned as the first AV-8A instructor to Marine Aviation Weapons Training Unit, Pacific (MAWTUPAC). This unit, the forerunner of Marine Aviation Weapons and Tactics Squadron One (MAWTS-1), was based at MCAS El Toro, California. I was in a small branch of the unit based at MCAS Yuma, Arizona along with two F-4 Phantom and one A-4 Skyhawk instructors.

Both MAWTUPAC and its East Coast counterpart, MAWTULANT, were hard at work attempting to implement "Project 19". This was the 19th in a series of some 100 projects that the Marine leadership at Headquarters, U.S. Marine Corps had developed to modernize and revitalize the tactical viability of Marine Air. It turned out to be the most innovative, most all encompassing, and most impactive project of the group – by far. The result was the concept of the Marine Weapons and Tactics Training Program (WTTP), a program designed to permeate every aspect of our aviation training with a standardizing, building block approach to tactical excellence while improving aviation safety at the same time. Key to the success of this program was its management by Marine Aviation Weapons and Tactics Squadron One through the development of the Weapons and Tactics Course conducted twice a year at MCAS Yuma. These courses were designed to "train the trainer". We would take one aircrew per year from every squadron in the Corps, bring them to Yuma along with aircraft and maintenance men sufficient to the task, and put them through a very intense ground and airborne school to ensure that: they were the best in their own weapons platforms; they knew how their community fit in to the overall fabric of the Marine Air Ground Task Forces ability to fight as a combined arms, assault support team; they had the skills and teaching materials to go back to their individual squadrons and prepare them for combat as well. Over the last twenty years this WTI concept has become world renowned within U.S. and foreign air forces while, at the same time, bringing Marine aviation to a significantly higher state of readiness and combat capability.

Those early months, when we were developing and experimenting with the WTI "infant", provided a singular experience for all of us involved. Fashioning a service-wide training program for all USMC aviation communities (F-4, A-4, A-6, AV-8, EA-6, KC-130, OV-10, CH-46, CH-53, UH-1, AH-1, C3) to guarantee the ability to fight and win as an integrated team with our ground combat element Marines in any clime or place on a moments notice was truly heady stuff for a group of some thirty Captains and Majors led by a maverick Lieutenant Colonel named Ray Hanle (MAWTUPAC) and then Howard DeCastro (first Commanding Officer of MAWTS-1). Needless to say, we attacked the mission with a vengeance, convinced that right was on our side! Throughout the communities that embraced the WTTP concept, MAWTS instructors and WTI's began to be referred to in the same terms as the Jedi Knights in the popular movie "Star Wars". Throughout Marine aviation, at least at the company grade officer level, we all knew that "the force was with us". But there were others who referred to MAWTS instructors negatively, as the "guys with the black patch and the black T-shirts". Unfortunately, the latter were usually those who were in charge at the squadron level.

As I was leaving MAWTS in early 1980, I realized that, even though the WTI program had almost universal support at the General Officer level and at the company grade level from the very beginning, the "iron" Majors, Lieutenants Colonels, and Colonels had strongly resisted changing a system within which they had succeeded. Squadron COs often complained that the WTI in their squadron was too "expensive" to make (the WTI class required aircraft and maintenance personnel to be deployed to Yuma for seven weeks twice a year). But the most oft-repeated complaint was that the WTI's were too hard too control, were too aggressive, and pushed to conduct training that was unsafe.

When I returned to MAWTS in 1987, privileged to be selected to serve as the executive officer for one year and then commanding officer, much of that was behind us. In fact, as you would expect, WTI's had "inherited" Marine aviation since many of those first WTI's had risen to become operations officers and commanding officers.

Another singular trend was also developing. The infantry leadership of the Marine Corps was discovering MAWTS. And they loved it! More and more infantry General Officers were visiting MAWTS at the invitation of aviation leaders. By 1988, it was time to bond the WTI course closer to our ground Marines. All Marines live to the precept that "every Marine is a rifleman", and as aviators we felt very strongly that Marine airpower should always focus on its contribution to the Marine Air Ground Task Force, and not attempt to be a force on its own. And so, in 1988, we began in earnest to integrate a small number of infantry officers into the WTI class as students. That continues today.

The future for the WTTP the WTI program, and MAWTS is bright. Whenever the potential exists for any of our forward deployed units to go in harms way, the first call is "WTI's forward". (In Bosnia for a lengthy period, even the USAF required mission commanders to be USMC WTI's.) The ability of WTI's to plan - and lead - integrated, complex air operations, whether to rescue Captain Scott O'Grady or to lead strikes on enemy airfields and SAM sites, makes them standouts among their contemporaries. But the true value of the WTI can be easily overlooked. Above all else, HE TRAINS THE SQUADRON.

His value as a planner and flight leader can be short lived and only partially effective if his squadron cannot execute. It is because of his skills as a trainer responsible for implementing the entire WTTP that we continue to excel in combat air operations.

Major General Fred McCorkle - Commanding General 3rd Marine Air Wing.

Major General Fred McCorkle - Commanding General 3rd Marine Air Wing

"As one of the Marine Corps Assistant Commandants once said, "WTI's are national assets" and I truly believe that. MAWTS-1 is the only place that brings all the necessary people and assets together in one place, in a realistic training scenario, and replicates how we go to war...this gives our nation great flexibility in the way in which we would go to war and fight to win."

MAWTS-1 was started after Vietnam in order to bring increased standardization to Marine Air. It now has been operating for almost twenty years and perhaps the biggest benefit the unit brings to our Corps is this ability to provide "consistency" in all our aviation units. This cannot be overstressed. In fact, a previous Secretary of the Navy once said "If you look at the big deck Navy, we have twelve carriers and their air wings, each operating independently. With the Marine Corps there is one unit, MAWTS-1, that sets the standards for Marine aviation." Each year of existence has brought about new changes in the way we do business, but the one thing which has remained consistent is standardization for the 'fleet'.

One of the most significant changes made when I first joined MAWTS-1 as CO concerned the use of Night Vision Goggle (NVG) training for the rotary wing aircraft. The average helicopter pilot arrived as a WTI student with about fifteen hours on NVG's, when I left, it had increased to almost 100 hours, now some eight years later it's in excess of 180 hours. When you look at how effective Marine Air was throughout Operation Desert Storm, in particular helicopter operations at night, we wouldn't have been able to even come close to the level of effectiveness without the standardization and training on NVG's stressed at MAWTS-1.

On the fixed wing side, there had been a strong emphasis on low level tactics with missions being flown at altitudes as low as 100 feet or below. At MAWTS-1 we changed this in the mid 1980's and began flying at higher altitudes (around 16,000 feet). This was high enough to be out of the range of most ground based, shoulder mounted missiles, and small arms fire, and we felt we could shut down the other threats with our EA-6B's etc. During the Gulf War, we were fortunate in not losing a single F/A-18 or A-6 and this was due (at least in part) to the tactics which were taught at MAWTS-1.

What MAWTS-1 does is train the trainer, or train the instructor. The WTI accumulates many invaluable lessons during his training and then goes back to his unit and passes this knowledge to Fleet Marine Forces.

During my tenure at MAWTS-1, we worked very hard to build as many WTI's as possible so we had a large number of aircraft visiting during the course, usually over 100. We would go from a squadron of less than 150 people before a WTI course began, to upwards of 3,500 once its starts. That's an incredible buildup and I have to say that I was extremely fortunate in not losing a single person during this three year period.

When I was first at MAWTS in 1985, I was the Executive Officer (XO) as a Lieutenant Colonel and I went through the course for the first time! There was a fair amount of pressure on me since I didn't attend as a more junior officer and would be taking over as the CO in less than a year. I took command in 1986 and served as the Commanding Officer for the next two years.

In my opinion, MAWTS-1 is the only place that brings all the necessary people and assets together in one place, in a realistic training scenario, and replicates exactly how we go to war. Again, as we witnessed during Desert Storm, large numbers of Marine aircraft and helicopters of all types operated together and conducted complex integrated missions, just like it's taught at MAWTS-1. This gives our nation great flexibility in the way in which we would go to war and fight to win. I seldom flew at Yuma that didn't include thirty or so US Air Force aircraft acting as adversary's along with the 100 or so Marine and Navy aircraft. This allows us to get to build solid relationships with our counterparts in the sister services.

One of our previous Assistant Commandants once said "WTI's are national assets" and I truly believe that. Lt. General Mike Ryan, the USAF officer in charge of Air Forces in Bosnia would not allow a mission flown without a Marine WTI present and involved in the planning of the these flights, that says a great deal about or WTI's.

11

Marines To The Rescue-The Rescue of Captain Scott O'Grady, USAF

Major Scott C. Mykleby in the cockpit of an AH-1W.

As Recounted By
Major Joaquin Francis Malavet, USMC,
MAWTS-1 CH-53E Division Head, Yuma, AZ
&
Major Scott C. Mykleby, USMC,
HMLA-269, MAG-29, MCAS New River, NC

The United States Marines played critical roles in the dramatic rescue of United States Air Force Captain Scott O'Grady. Four of the Marines were MAWTS-1 WTI graduates; Major M.S. Ogden, Captain R.C. "Wiggy" Walkerwicz *(Deceased)*, Major S.C. Mykleby and Captain J.F. Malavet (now a Major). Lt.Colonel Gunther, who was also a mission participant in the rescue, attended the MAWTS-1 Commanders' Course.

Timing and the authors good fortune allowed us to meet with two of the MAWTS-1 WTI graduates that participated in the O'Grady rescue, Major S.C. Mykleby and Major J.F. Malavet.

Hundreds of members of the United States Armed Forces dedicated themselves to the planning and recovery of a total stranger and fellow aviator, unselfishly putting themselves in harms way to save one man. The success of the mission was a team effort and the result of many dedicated individuals, intense preparation, training and the real demonstration of the Marine Corps ethos of honor, courage, and commitment to, "never leave a man behind".

Major Joaquin "Keen" Francis Malavet is originally from Denville, New Jersey. He attended the Pennsylvania State University on an NROTC Scholarship and graduated as a commissioned Second Lieutenant in August 1985, with a Bachelor of Science Degree in Industrial Engineering (Systems Management), following his commissioning, he attended The Basic School (TBS) and in March 1986, reported to Naval flight training in Pensacola, Florida. Major Malavet earned his wings in August 1987 and chose to fly the CH-53D at Marine Corps Air Station (MCAS), Kaneohe Bay, Hawaii with HMH-463. He completed two deployments with HMM-265 and HMM-262 and flew numerous WESTPAC missions in Japan, South Korea, and humanitarian aid missions in the Republic of the Philippines. Major Malavet then served as the Air Officer for 3rd Battalion, 3rd Marines for one year before completing the flight conversion training to the CH-53E in Tustin, California. Upon completion of the CH-53E conversion training, he was transferred to HMH-464, MAG-29, MCAS New River, North Carolina in 1992. Major Malavet graduated from MAWTS-1 WTI class 1-94 as a Weapons and Tactics Instructor and transferred to HMM-263, 24th MEU (SOC) in October, 1994. Major Malavet has earned every flight leadership designation in the CH-53 D/E accumulating approximately 2,500 flight hours and over 300 hours with night vision goggles (NVG's). Major Malavet completed his tour with HMH-464 as the Squadron Aircraft Maintenance Officer and in August 1996 returned to MCAS Yuma as a MAWTS-1 instructor pilot. He is currently assigned as the CH53D/E Division Head of the Assault Support Department.

Major Scott C. (Mick) Mykleby joined the Marine Corps in 1979. He is originally from a small town in Minnesota called Wayzata. Scott graduated from the University of Minnesota in 1983, went to the United States Marine Corps Basic School and on to Flight School in 1984. Major Mykleby earned his wings on September 20, 1985 and has been flying Cobras ever since. He holds every possible Cobra designation that can be achieved in the aircraft. Major Mykleby served one tour for eighteen months as a Forward Air Controller with the First Battalion, Eighth Marines and a three year tour at NAS Whiting Field flying T-34Cs, as a fixed wing instructor at Training Squadron Three. Major Mykleby graduated from the MAWTS-1 WTI Class in October 1994 as a Weapons and Tactics Instructor and returned to MCAS New River NC, at HMLA-269 flying the AH-1W Cobra. He has approximately 2700 flight hours. The Major comes from a family with a rich tradition in Naval aviation. His younger brother, Major Mark Mykleby, also a MAWTS-1 Weapons and Tactics Instructor is a USMC F/A-18 pilot who flew over Bosnia off the USS Theodore Roosevelt and is a recent graduate of the U.S. Navy's Naval Strike Air Warfare Center TOPGUN program. The Myklebys' were greatly influenced by their father Chuck's passion for aviation, having served in he U.S. Navy as a Naval Air Crewman and Flight Engineer on P2V Neptune's and who had extensive experience with A-1 Skyraiders and A-4B Skyhawks.

Work-Up's

Major Malavet (call sign Keen) and Major Mykleby (call sign Mick) were assigned to HMM-263, which was the Aviation Combat Element (ACE) of the 24th Marine Expeditionary Unit-Special Operations Capable-MEU(SOC) in October of '94 and began preparations known as work-ups to become part of an Amphibious Ready Group (ARG). Marines go through a six month training cycle where the Aviation Combat Element (ACE), which is part of the MEU(SOC), works with the Ground Combat Element (GCE), practicing for all the potential MEU(SOC) missions. These missions can include the TRAP (Tactical Recovery of Aircraft and Personnel), evacuations of embassies, beach assaults and Maritime Interdiction Operations, where you seize control of maritime shipping for the purpose of securing a ship that may be running drugs or missiles. The six months is an intense period of coordination, planning and skill sharpening for the participants in order to increase the level of readiness up to combat levels.

Major Mykleby and Major Malavet were embarked on the USS *Kearsarge* as part of the Aviation Combat Element (ACE), as their squadron's Weapons and Tactics Instructors (WTI).

Major Malavet worked in the Operations Department as the head of the Future Operations section. The Future Operations section plans and briefs the tactics, techniques and procedures for any missions that may arise in the future. This section typically is tasked with reading enemy situation reports in order to study the threat, and then initiate detailed plans for any possible contingencies that may develop in a particular region.

The Marine Corps is tasked to be "organized, trained and equipped to provide forces of combined arms together with supporting air components for service with the fleet in the seizure and defense of advanced naval bases and for the conduct of landing operations as may be essential to the prosecution of a naval campaign." In a MEU(SOC), the Marines commit to 'standing ready to accomplish it's countries taskings an a moments notice', this is a commitment that the Marines and the leaders of the United States take very seriously.

Major Malavet:

"In order to rapidly execute all twenty-one specific MEU(SOC) missions and commitments, the Marines research possible contingency operations in theater and begin planning detailed missions early in the deployment. The Aviation Combat (ACE) future operations section (Tactics Cell) develops the specific tactical aviation plans to support these contingencies and briefs are then generated to articulate these plans. Contingency briefing folders are kept in future operations and are periodically reviewed and updated based on the evolving changes to the threat scenario. The MEU(SOC) trains to a six hour "plan-to-execute" cycle. From the moment the Commander issues the warning order and defines the mission with his intent, to the moment that the first wave of Marines launch from amphibious ships, is six hours. That is the standard to which the MEU(SOC) Marines must train, however, it is not just a training goal, but rather, an operational requirement!

This six hour timeline requires the utilization of a structured rapid response planning process which is what all MAWTS-1 WTI graduates are taught. Rapid Response Planning is the hallmark of the MEU(SOC) concept and no force in the world does it better than a Marine Air Ground Task Force (MAGTF). When the Navy/Marine Corps team deploys both the Carrier Battle Group and a Marine Amphibious Ready Group (MARG) into a particular region, the Regional Commander in Chief (CINC) has the most lethal and robust quick reaction force in the world to employ against a given threat. During our deployment into the Adriatic, U.S. Naval Admiral Leighton W. "Snuffy" Smith Jr. was "Dual-hatted" as USNAVEUR and AFSOUTH Commander. When he had the USS Teddy Roosevelt (CVN-71), USS Kearsarge (LHD-3) USS Nashville (LPD-13), and the USS Pensacola (LSD-38) in the region, it gave him a lot of flexibility to conduct multiple contingency operations including the TRAP (Tactical Recovery of Aircraft and Personnel).

My future operations section consisted of WTI's and top notch planners from all the ACE Aircraft communities including: Captain Ron "Wiggy" Walkerwicz (AV-8B), Captain Carl "Norman" Saltzseider (UH-1N), Captain Jim "Levi" Garret (CH-46E), Captain Mike "Shemp" Shenberger (CH-53E), with Major "Mick" Mykleby stepping in from his assistant operations officer duties as the AH-1W Cobra expert. The WTI's responsibilities included the continuous development and refinement of our rapid response plans as well as detailed instruction and training of junior pilots on tactics, techniques and procedures. During May of 1995, we were deployed off the coast of Sardinia in a NATO exercise called Tridente with over twenty other ships from the Italian, French, and Spanish Navies. While the 24th MEU(SOC) executed the varied and complex Tridente missions, my future operations section simultaneously continued to look at future real world missions in the former Republic of Yugoslavia as well as North Africa. Our job was to research the intelligence reports and develop courses of action for Non-Combatant Evacuation Operations (NEO), Maritime Interdiction Operations (MIO), In-Extremis Hostage Rescues (IHR), humanitarian assistance missions, operations to support United Nations Protection Forces (UNPROFOR), the Deny Flight mission, as well as amphibious assaults.

Prior to the shoot down of Basher 52, I looked very closely at our ACE specific TRAP Concept of Operations (CONOPS) and refined the 24th MEU(SOC) TRAP CONOPS which was subsequently sent to the Combined Rescue Coordination Center (CRCC) of the Combined Air Operations Center (CAOC) in Vicenza, Italy. This document outlined how the 24th MEU(SOC) planned to support the region with our TRAP capability. The CONOPS delineated the various TRAP force packages we utilize and the specific aircrew, equipment, and Marine capabilities to support each package. We presented our TRAP force packaging concept to the CRCC in order to articulate our highly flexible capabilities to respond to any TRAP contingency. For example, if a pilot had to eject out over the Adriatic, we may use an "Alpha" package consisting of a single Navy HH-46D with SAR Swimmer escorted by two UH-1N Huey Gunships. If a pilot ejected in the Littoral region off the Croatian coast, we may elect to use an "Echo" package with SEALS in Combat Rigid Raider Craft (CRRC) to execute a clandestine recovery with additional fire support assets held in a standby status. If a KC-130, EA-6B (multi-crew) or more than one aircraft is shot down with multiple ejection's and recovery locations separated by 25NM; it may require one TRAP force to cover one area while a second TRAP force covers another to recover all of the isolated personnel. This scenario may also require one TRAP force package that's flexible enough to hit two locations simultaneously. The 24th MEU(SOC) was prepared to execute all of our TRAP force packages well within the six hour "Plan-to-Execution" timeline standards.

If the 24th MEU(SOC) were to operate unilaterally for a specific contingency operation in perhaps a low intensity conflict, we always plan for TRAP as an implied mission verses specific or deliberate mission. In this case, the USS Kearsarge's Landing Force Operation Center (LFOC) exercised complete Command and Control of the TRAP mission and was the Rescue Coordination Center (RCC). In the Adriatic however, the 24th MEU(SOC) would have to operate within some of the CAOC/CRCC and Deny Flight guidelines while executing an actual mission. My future operations team worked hard to incorporate additional aviation assets that were external to the MARG (i.e. EA-6B, F/A-18C/D, A-10, AWACS, E-2C) into our TRAP mission templates.

The MAWTS-1 WTI curriculum teaches the student the complete integration of the Six Functions of Marine Aviation and how to incorporate Joint Force aviation assets into Marine tactical missions. For example, I was familiar with how the Air Force A-10's operate and could incorporate them into our mission planning if required. I had also worked with AWACS and the Navy E-2C Hawkeye C4I platforms and was familiar with their employment considerations. The TRAP force package that I spent most of my time scripting was the "Delta" TRAP. This force consisted of two CH-53E Super Stallions, two AH-1W Cobras, and two sections of AV-8B Harriers with a combat radius exceeding 125 NM. This was our most robust force and provided exceptional fire support measures to respond to the known threat. We planned to augment this force with additional assets including: F/A-18C/D High Speed Anti-Radiation Missile (HARM) Shooters, EA-6B electronic attack/support, as well as AWACS or an EC-130 Airborne Battlefield Command and Control Center (ABCCC).

The two CH-53E's give the package speed, lift, and combat survivability with the capability of deploying more than thirty-seven combat loaded Marines with various and unique combat specialties. These specialties may include Snipers, Corpsmen, security elements, FAC teams, Heavy Weapons Sections, Mortars, Fast Attack Vehicle teams, Radio Battalion Indications and Warning (I&W) specialists, etc. We could lose one CH-53E and both AH-1W Cobras due to mechanical malfunctions or precautionary landings due to hostile fire, and still "Self- TRAP" all of the Marines and vital equipment on the remaining one CH-53E Super Stallion and continue with the mission. The AH-1W is the best helicopter escort asset in the world. It is a tremendous Close Air Support platform with superb night targeting systems and expert FAC(A) trained pilots. The Marines employ this combat assault helicopter better than anyone in the world. The AV-8B's launched from the USS Kearsarge provided immediate quick response helicopter escort and CAS as well as radio relay capabilities. The AV-8B can also provide armed reconnaissance. The Delta TRAP force resembles a Rapid Force which can be employed if the fluid enemy ground order of battle is uncertain but estimated as a medium to low threat.

In examining our Delta TRAP force CONOPS, we decided to take the planning to an increased level of detail. I wrote, in prose, the general and specific TRAP templates so that all the pilots could read it and study the mission architecture. The detail included, but was not limited to the following: How we man aircraft, conduct radio checks and launch from the ship. How we join the package, conduct penetration checklists, and vary the tactical flight formations. How we authenticate the survivor, phase aircraft into the objective area, and conduct our specific fire support plan on the objective area. How we navigate, communicate, and pass critical execution checklist code words through the appropriate channels. How we would fly through IFR weather, mountainous terrain, and very low over numerous wires in-country. How we would defeat the enemy MANPADS, AAA, and Radar Sam threats. How we would avoid the threat, suppress the threat and kill the threat. Finally, how we would exploit the enemies many weaknesses to penetrate Bosnian airspace and return to the USS Kearsarge successfully accomplishing the mission. A specific example of an exploitable Bosnian Serb weakness was their lack of discipline and propensity to heavily imbibe after successful engagements during late evening and into the early morning hours. (*This became an important lesson learned after the O'Grady mission which has been put into practice in all MEU's. Major Malavet and Major Mykleby are now also the Marine Corps representatives for a Secretary of Defense commissioned three year study on the Joint Services CSAR capabilities — A team that is to develop joint tactics, techniques and procedures for the recovery of isolated personnel.)*

In addition to incorporating a significant level of detail to the Delta TRAP plan, we worked on the potential briefings for the key Billet holders which is an important aspect of the MAWTS-1 WTI training. WTI's consistently demonstrate expertise in planning, briefing, and tactically executing very complex aviation missions to support the Ground Commander. One format utilized to articulate a mission course of action is the Confirmation Brief. The Confirmation Brief can be structured in various formats depending on the type of mission and required level of detail. Delivering an ACE Confirmation Brief is an art. The briefer must articulate the entire mission profile quickly, concisely, and with the requisite level of detail to satisfy the MEU(SOC) commanders intent. At MAWTS-1 and in the Fleet Marine Force, the execution of the plan is the final result. If a MAGTF has executed the mission with tactical success, it was invariably because it had been properly planned, and all the tactical details and mission contingencies were articulately briefed. I briefed both the Confirmation Brief and specific pilot ready room briefs for the Basher 52 TRAP, within three hours after the shootdown notification as the TRAP Air Mission Commander. The Marine Rapid Response Planning Process, combined with solid briefs, and backed by the specific Marine Aircraft Tactics Manuals produced at MAWTS-1, is the MEU(SOC) ACE's lethal weapon employed to support the Navy/Marine Corps concept of "Operational Maneuver From The Sea (OMFTS).

Bosnia Heats Up

In late May, the situation started to heat up in Bosnia. On May 27th, the 24th MEU(SOC) was called off of the Sardinian coast and re-deployed to the Adriatic. The Bosnian Serbs continued to demonstrate an increased hostile threat to innocent civilians and UNPROFOR. When the Serbian strategic military targets were bombed, they began to take civilians and UNPROFOR as hostages and subsequently chained them to bridges, ordnance facilities, and other military targets. They did this as an attempted deterrent to the highly effective bombing campaign. As the 24th MEU(SOC) sailed to the Adriatic, my Future Operations section began the feverish intelligence collection and analysis of the Bosnian region. We looked very closely at the enemy ground, air, electronic, and communications order of battle focusing on the specific lines of conflict. The lines of conflict were studied closely because they would indicate hot areas with concentrated Anti-Air weaponry and would drive our specific penetration tactics. The Future Operation section WTI's conducted a great deal of specific threat analysis during this transit period. When we arrived off the Croatian coast, a CAOC team came aboard the USS Kearsarge to brief us on the Bosnian Provide Promise/Deny Flight Operations. This brief was given on the afternoon of June 2nd and was subsequently interrupted by the 1MC loudspeaker call to "Assemble the Trap Determination Team in the Phibron War Room!"

The Mission Rapid Response Planning process always begins with the Commanders Intent and follows with; mission analysis, enemy analysis, terrain and weather, troops and fire support, time available, space and logistics. (METT-T-SL) The Commanders Intent, as I recall it, is paraphrased as; employ the Delta Trap Package with its inherently more robust/flexible force structure during the cover of darkness and exploit the Bosnian Serbs inability to rapidly re-inforce the Bosanski Petrovac area. Ingress and Egress tactically utilizing speed, stealth, shock, and violence of action when necessary on the objective area. Use available external aviation assets to cover the force. If the package is opposed as we penetrate the enemy's Integrated Air Defense Systems (IADS), use decisive proportional and/or lethal force in accordance with the Rules Of Engagement for protection. Exercise rapid, aggressive actions on the objective area to successfully recover Basher 52 with no loss to the TRAP force. The Commander's intent was quite clear and drove the planning and execution direction."

O'Grady Is Shot Down - June 2, 1995

On June 2nd, 1995, Captain Scott O'Grady, USAF, was piloting his F-16 (Basher 52) over Bosnia as part of NATO's Deny Flight Missions along with his flight lead Captain Bob "Wilbur" Wright USAF, (Basher 51). Both pilots were assigned to the USAF 555th Fighter Squadron operating out of the Aviano Air Base in Italy.

During a Deny Flight sortie, Captain Wright's received a warning signal in his F-16 indicating that he was being tracked by a threat radar associated with surface to air missiles, Basher 52, flown by Captain O'Grady, showed no such indicators-the pilots checked with Magic, NATO's airborne early warning aircraft, who could not concur with the readings. The section of F-16's pressed on. Moments later Basher 52 got spiked by a threat radar and Captain O'Grady had a voice in his head set telling him to *counter, counter* (execute counter measures). A SAM exploded between Basher 52 and Basher 51, missing them. Seconds later came Basher 51s scream; Missiles In The Air! The events outpaced Captain O'Grady's ability to react, a total of nine seconds elapsed between the first radar spike and when his F-16 was blown apart, sending Captain O'Grady tumbling toward Bosnia in his ejection seat.

"On June second when the F-16 aircraft took off on their mission — prior to take-off, there was no clear indication of any SAM activity in the vicinity of the assigned Combat Air Patrol station. Based on everything the Deny Flight commanders knew at the time, they had reasonable grounds to believe that the Basher flight was going to be operating outside any known or suspected SAM rings. However, just minutes before the shootdown occurred, indications of SA-6 presence in southwest Bosnia-Herzegovina were picked up. And these reports were transmitted into the threat warning communications network.

In large measure due to garbled voice communications, the warning was not relayed to Basher flight in time for the F-16s to take precautionary actions. This first attempt was made a full three minutes before the shootdown. By the time the message could be understood, Basher 52 had been shot down..."

-General John Shalikashvili, Chairman of the Joint Chiefs of Staff's testimony before the House Committee in National Security on July 11, 1995.

Major Scott C. Mykleby

On Board The USS *Kearsarge* - June 2nd, 1995
Recounted By Major Scott Mykleby:

"I was up on the flight deck with Colonel Berndt (MEU Commander) and Captain Christopher Cole (Commanding Officer, USS *Kearsarge*), preparing to give them a familiarization flight in a Cobra; I was briefing them on the cockpit. In the middle of the brief, we were interrupted by an announcement over the ships public address system ordering the assembly of the TRAP Determination team in the Phibron war room immediately.

Colonel Berndt and Captain Cole both just kind of looked at me and then they both took off running because they had details to attend to immediately and I had to go running down below because I was assigned to be the escort flight leader for any TRAP mission that went out-I had to get into the fight and start planning. At this point we looked at the Rapid Response plans Major Malavet developed - the go/no go criteria that we had to have before we could actually execute a TRAP. In this case, one of the critical criteria was that we needed to know Captain O'Grady's position within one nautical mile. We had a general idea as to where he was, but at the time, nobody had communicated with him. By chance, a Harrier pilot on the USS *Kearsage* had a great deal of experience in skydiving and free fall parachuting. On his own initiative, he accumulated information on the

Major Joaquin F. Malavet

threat area. We knew there was an SA6 that was up there functioning pretty well that day, having downed an F-16. Scott's general location was about seven miles southeast of a town called Bosanski-Petrovac which was a big Serb stronghold at the time.

I worked with Keen on our team's Delta TRAP plan immediately- we flipped that thing up on the table and we just started plugging information into it. We satisfied all of our general requirements. Like I said we needed to know where (roughly) he was and that somebody was talking to him, confirming he was alive. Another asset that needed to be in place was a SEAD (Suppression of Enemy Air Defense) package. We didn't necessarily specify what aircraft it needed to be, because to us on the TRAP force it did not matter if it was an EA-6B or an EF-111—the SEAD team and their commanders would make that decision based on intelligence information and the threat. In our portion of the plan, we just needed to specify that all of the threat radar needed to be shut down and that we needed HARM shooters to take the radar sites out if the jamming was not effective. These capabilities would cover our backs when our TRAP team went in. People on the planning staff started making calls and getting these things set up, along with initiating briefings for all participants.

We were ready to go that night-we could have executed the TRAP. But the information from the objective area was still just too vague. We didn't have a real good verified location as to where O'Grady was at. In listening to some of the reports that Captain Bob "Wilbur" Wright, (Captain O'Grady's Section Leader) had given and who saw Scott get hit, a lot of us who had been flying for awhile thought in the back of our minds how difficult it would be to survive based on his initial report, which described the condition of the aircraft and ejection profile. He saw the cockpit section tumbling off into the clouds and had no visual on the actual ejection or evidence of a chute. Because he didn't see a chute did not mean that there wasn't one. We made the assumption he was alive. The atmosphere was very intense-controlled, but intense, with an enormous amount of rapid planning going on.

Finally the senior commanders decided that we just didn't really know enough about Scott's condition or location and they decided not to risk committing us, so we stood down and we went to an "alert 60" status. That first night actually paid some big dividends for us. It allowed us to do a dry run and start tightening up the plan and the players involved-we focused

winds and related information from the ship's weather department. He conferred with us on where O'Grady had been hit and he took the prevailing winds and the basic fall rate for a generic parachute and he gave us an estimated plot on where he thought Captain O'Grady might be. It later turned out that Captain O'Grady was within five kilometers of our initial projection of his location-five kilometers was an incredibly close estimate given several days of Captain O'Grady's escape and evasion maneuvers where he was moving each night.

Based on this assessment and other supporting data we had, we made a determination that his position was in the middle of a pretty high on what our priorities were. We had established the general brief and planning templates. When it came right down to looking at the dynamics of the objective area and the threat, we prioritized our efforts and focused on the most critical issues in order to streamline the plan.

Each successive day and night we would rebrief the mission - the Intel guys would come in and give us an Intel update on new SAM sites and radar sites that had been either added to or eliminated from the area. The plan was modified constantly as the threat and the ingress, egress, and objective area mechanics changed accordingly. The threat changed very quickly; for example, the SA6 that bagged Scott had moved several times after the shoot down. It was extremely important that we rebriefed the mission and refined the Intel every single day, keeping us focused and prepared to respond when the go-no go criteria were finally met and we were given the order to execute the TRAP mission.

June 5, 1995 - Signals From Captain O'Grady

On the fifth of June we started getting intermittent signals coming out of Bosnia. Major Nick Hall (call sign Festus), my wingman on the mission, believed it might be Scott, which we later confirmed in speaking to Scott after the rescue. At the time, we hoped that it was him, but we had to consider all the possibilities - if Scott had been seriously injured or killed, the Serbs could have taken his survival radio and might have been trying to use it. If they were familiar with the equipment, the possibility existed that the Serbs could have been trying to set up an ambush and to lure us into it. We had to consider these potential scenarios, and their implications.

The team was stood up and the TRAP team got into position on the flight deck about 2300 that night. We were actually getting in the aircraft and getting ready to go, when we were stood down again. Higher headquarters believed that we still did not know enough to risk committing the team. This is where experience and professionalism are crucial in not letting your emotions enter into the decision making process. Your emotions scream at you to engage-to get in there and save a fellow aviator. Your professionalism compels you to fall back to your training and make sound informed decisions that will ensure the success of the mission, the safety of your team and compliance with the Commander's intent. All that sounds easy, but it was tough.

June 7th, 1995 - Good To Go

On the 7th of June we'd come off the alert at 1500 and still hadn't heard anything. We did the usual things onboard ship to burn off some energy, we'd go running and PT a little bit. I finally hit the rack at about 2300. Of interest on this day, the original Air Mission Commander, Major Malavet, the guy who we had been working with throughout this whole process, was told he would have to leave the USS *Kearsarge.* Keen was sent to Italy to participate in other theatre planning, so they sent him off the ship."

Major Malavet:

"As I prepared to leave the ship on June 7th, I re-briefed the entire mission to ensure all the key flight leaders understood our course of action. Although I would depart the ship, I wanted to ensure that the mindset would not detract away from the possibility of conducting this TRAP. Basher 52 was still not positively identified as dead or alive and we could not afford to let our guard down. I turned to my roommate, Captain Paul "Tuna" Fortunato and told him that he would take my seat in the CH-53, fly with Captain Jim "Lefty" Wright and move to the Dash-2 / Wingman position. I then reviewed the mission specifics with my wingman, Major Bill "Button" Tarbutton, and told him to take the Dash-1 / Lead CH-53E position and assume the Air Mission Commander role. I told them to execute as I had briefed if Basher 52 communicated his position and status. I then proceeded to leave the USS Kearsarge for Brindisi, Italy. I left the ship under orders to liaison with the Joint Special Operations Task Force (JSOTF) and work with them on some projects and operations directly related to the Bosnian theater of action.

One of the benefits of the MEU(SOC) work-up concept is that, as all the Navy / Marine units train together, a special trust, confidence, and respect for each other's tactical prowess develops. This incontrovertible bond between your squadron mates, GCE Marines, Navy personnel, and Senior MEU(SOC) leadership is the cornerstone to the MARG's success. Major Tarbutton is a former Marine Helicopter Squadron One / HMX-1 White House presidential helicopter pilot with over 5,000 hours of flight time, a superb aviator, Air Mission Commander, and the one pilot I knew could easily step right in and lead the team! His flight leadership and CH-53E flight skills would prove to be unmatched on this mission; making all the correct, timely and tactical decisions to ensure our success!"

Major Mykleby:

"Like I said, I hit the rack about 2300 and at 0300 right on the nose they woke us up over the ships intercom system saying: assemble TRAP Determination team in the Phibron war room immediately-I woke up, looked at Festus and said you've got to be kidding me, it's three in the morning. Both Festus and I thought it was just a drill to see if we could really respond as fast as we were saying we could. While the MEU advertises the capability of a six hour response, we actually had it down to where we could launch the mission within a couple of hours.

We got into our flight suits and went running down to the war room which was packed with people; The MEU staff, mission participants, various unit commanders, Captain Cole, Commodore Schill and even the ship's Chaplain managed to squeeze in. I was still thinking it was a drill until I got to the war room and I looked in there; things were in full swing. I looked at Colonel Berndt (Colonel Martin R. Berndt, USMC, MEU commander) and as soon as I saw his face I knew that we were going. Festus went over to the ready room to take care of getting all the latest frequencies, call signs and the code words that change frequently—we had guys whose sole job was to make sure that they had all that stuff locked on and ready at a moments notice which was no small task, they did a great job!

The two co-pilots, my co-pilot, Captain Ian "Blondie" Walsh and Captain Jim "Jinx" Jenkins, Festus' co-pilot, went up on flight deck and began pre-flighting our Cobras, setting the ALE-39 programs and doing all the pre-flight checks on everything in order to start the Cobras. We received the latest Intel they had on Scott. I already had his ISOPREP data. This is data aircrews fill out whenever you're flying in a hostile area. It provides personal information that the enemy would have no way of knowing for authentication purposes.

I had already written out the questions I was going to ask him for authentication purposes on my knee board. I did not want to be fumbling with this when we were right in there on top of him. We had his location, actually I had three separate locations when we launched. They were all within a couple kilometers of each other but finally his location was pinpointed - a lot of people were working on actually pinning down his location. Just prior to us getting to the objective area, a couple of Marine F/A-18 Deltas came in right over the top of him to get a good mark on his position. One of them pretty much flew over the top of Captain O'Grady and he called out that they were over him. The F/A-18 pilots marked the location from their cockpit.

Major Bill Tarbutton, Air Mission Commander (Lead Pilot -flying the CH-53E, call sign Button) grabbed me and Major Mike Ogden (call sign Odie). Mike was the Harrier escort flight leader. He grabbed the two of us, pulled us off in the corner and said; look, we've briefed this thing, we know what we're going to do-nothing's changing. Do you guys have any questions? Tarbutton had his game face on and was pretty intense, we simply replied: no, we'll see you up on the frequency- he said all right, lets go, get up there, so we all went "upstairs" to the flight deck. The adrenaline was starting to pump a little bit, and there was still so much to do. We are trained to be professionals - we knew we had to go in and get him (Captain O'Grady). We could not allow ourselves to be thinking emotionally about the personal implications of what was about to happen, there was a complete sense of calm. Its not like you see in the movies, where everybody's high- fiving each other and slapping each other on the butt, jumping around saying "let's go downtown." There was none of that. It was pretty much silent. Everybody was focusing in on what they had to do. We could see that same attitude even among the young Marines loading onto the CH-53s, again this is where all the training and discipline paid off.

We got to the flight deck and started up. The AH-1W Cobras were the fuel critical aspect of the plan, so we needed to have as much gas on those aircraft as possible when we went in feet dry (over land). We started the Cobras, finished our checks and then right before we armed our weapons, we put the pressure hose on both Cobras again to top us off with fuel, taking as much gas as we could. We then quickly armed the weapons and launched. We actually launched three CH-53's and three AH-1W's so we had a backup for each aircraft. We went into the Starboard D holding pattern, on the Starboard side of the USS *Kearsarge,* formed up with the CH-53's and began orbiting, waiting for the push call (commence the mission) to come.

A small problem developed at this point. The TRAP plan required that the SEAD package be up and in place prior to us going feet dry. We had a misunderstanding with the SEAD package, and as the final details were being ironed out, we orbited for nearly twenty minutes. I checked and recalculated our fuel requirements for the mission, adding the holding time to the calculation. I knew we needed an hour's worth of gas to get from point A to point B, that we were committed to thirty minutes on station in the objective area and then an hour to get back out to the ship. So I'm looking at this and I'm saying okay, I've already been holding now for twenty minutes—I'm going to be BINGO at the target if I go right now. So I called Button and told him I needed more fuel, that we've been holding out there too long. Following his acknowledgment, I led all three Cobra's back down and we landed them on the *Kearsarge*, disarmed the weapons and had them top off all three Cobras with fuel again very quickly. We armed the weapons again and rejoined the CH-53's. We did about one turn in the Starboard D pattern when they gave us the push call. Button just came up on the radio and said; You want me to push-You want me to go? And the reply came: Push-Go feet dry. It was 05:43 and the TRAP team was headed into Bosnia.

We turned east and started heading inland. As we flew toward Bosnia, we completed our penetration checklists and weapons checks. We just put the guns in a fixed position and ripped off a thirty to forty round burst just to tighten the belt up, as this lessens the chance of getting a gun jam. Past experience had shown that as the gun turret moves around, it can cause a kink in the ammo belt and the rounds could get jammed up. This would have been an unacceptable occurrence on this mission. We also fired a burst of chaff and flares off each side to make sure that the chaff and flare dispensers were functioning the way they are supposed to. When we completed our checks we made a joint determination that all the primary aircraft in the mission where good to go. the back-up AH-1W and CH-53 broke off and returned to the *Kearsarge* as we headed in.

Feet Dry

Heading into Bosnia, we flew over the small islands right off the coast and then went in-country, feet dry. The weather in-country was relatively clear with a few clouds and it was very quiet. We proceeded inbound on an east, northeasterly heading. Button had been talking to Magic, a U.S. Air Force AWACS aircraft, and an AWACS controller named Captain Chris Weldon. The AWACS was not a briefed integral part of the TRAP mission, but part of the Deny Flight Operations. He told us later that he was sitting up there at his console and all of a sudden the Marines showed up on his frequency and they're driving into bad guy country. He knew at this point something was going on. The Air Force was not expecting the U.S. Marine Corps to be sent in to rescue Captain O'Grady. So, we suddenly showed up on Weldon's screen; he told us later, he put his cup of coffee down said "something big is going on here." We integrated him into the mission as our eye in the sky.

He asked a couple of quick questions to build his own situational awareness about what was happening. The AWACS began looking in front of us for any threats. Button led us deeper in-country, flying at about fifty feet above the ground at about a hundred and twenty knots, things still were pretty quiet. Suddenly Magic comes up on the radio to pass us a new location on O'Grady. This was done with a procedure called ramrod which is a system that uses code words that constantly change that are associated with ten digits. The coordinates that we had did not jive with the new ones we were receiving- when we computed it with ramrod - it put the new coordinates way out in the Adriatic some place—we knew this had to be wrong. Magic came up on the radio again and told us that we had an oil field off our nose.

So we are flying low and fast (for helicopters), rechecking the ramrod code words in a code book or 'Smart Pack' the size of a New York City telephone book and we are trying to deal with this new data about an oil field. We could not get a visual on the oil field and made the assumption that whatever it was, it had to be something bad. If it really was an oil field, the enemy probably would have it fortified with antiaircraft artillery and we did not want to risk being discovered. Button conferred with Magic, who recommended turning our formation to evade the possible threat- we concurred and took an early turn off to the northeast—the oil field turned out to be a SAM site we that we did not know about-it was a good call this early in the mission.

As we approached the coastal mountain range and started going up the side of the mountains to head deeper inland, the weather changed dramatically. As far as you could see there was a very low overcast layer of clouds, low enough in spots that we saw mountain peaks actually poking up through the clouds. Underneath the overcast layer, a thick white ground fog covered everything as far as we could see. This is the stuff like we used to get up in Minnesota where you couldn't see across your backyard—not misty, but the real thick white stuff. It was like a cloud on the ground and we couldn't see anything. We had to fly in between these two layers being careful to avoid known threats such as the active SAM sights we knew about. Our tactics to evade the SAM radar is to fly low, down in the mountains so the enemy can't see us with the radar. While we are maneuvering through the clouds I started to think if it was possible for the fog to get any worse and if it did, we would have to get up over it. As it was, we were actually flying between two SAM threat rings and there wasn't a whole lot of running room in there if the SAM radars got a fix on us.

We just kept going. I used our Global Positioning System (GPS) and continuously checked it against our maps. When we were rerouted, I could not take the time to reprogram it while dealing with the weather, so I just scrolled through the program to the last known survivor position. We had a pretty good steer with the GPS to direct us to Captain O'Grady's last known position and the AWACS also had a good lock on where he was from the F/A-18's fly-over.

We're continuing along in country and the one good thing about the ground fog was that nobody on the ground could see us. While all this is going on, about thirty minutes after we launched, the first section of Harriers flown by Major Michael Ogden (call sign Odie) and Captain Blot, (call sign Blotto and also USMC General Blot's son) take off. The Harrier guys launch and now they're heading incountry, simulating a Deny Flight sortie as a diversionary tactic against the Serbs to keep them busy and to reduce the chance of the Serbs discovering us. The Harriers reached a position known as Checkpoint America and held in an orbit at a high altitude. Our flight continued heading incountry unchallenged.

Ten Miles To The Objective Area - Authentication

Magic began giving us the range countdown to O'Grady's position (the AWACS controller calls identifying the distance to the objective area. e.g. *you are twenty-five miles to the objective area.*). In our plan, we briefed that when we reached the ten mile mark, I would lead the Cobras forward while the CH-53s held their position until we located Captain O'Grady. Our role at this point was to secure the area, authenticate O'Grady and then find him on the ground before we brought the CH-53's and infantrymen in. Button and Tuna (Captain Paul Fortunato) dropped off into a valley at the ten mile mark and we moved forward to O'Grady's last known position. The weather was deteriorating rapidly, it was really bad at this point- I can't describe it as anything else but absolutely horrible—I mean it was bad. The ground fog was really screwing with us and the overcast layer was dropping down on us as we moved forward.

Ten miles out, I switched my section (flight of two Cobra's) up to O'Grady's frequency and tried to reach him. At about eight miles out he finally heard us. I just kept saying "Basher Five Two, Bolt" (Cobras were designated as Bolt, Harriers as Boomer, CH-53s were Linus.) I was using the Bolt call sign so everybody else in the flight knew who was doing the talking. "Basher Five Two, Bolt", "Basher Five Two, Bolt." Finally it came—"Bolt, Basher Five Two - go ahead." I had to set him up for authentication so I came up on the radio and said: Basher Five Two, what's the third digit of your authentication number? All of us have a four digit personal number that we use and he came right back with *eight,* which was correct. I then asked Basher Five Two: "When you were in high school and got liquored up with your buddies, what did they call you?" His reply was the *Terrible Ten,* which matched his ISOPREP data. I said "Roger, we're inbound." With Magic's assistance, I was actually within about a mile of him. We had swung out to the northwest of where Captain O'Grady was located.

In order to get to Captain O'Grady, we had to go around a pretty big mountain and as soon as we got around it, we dropped down into an open plain area. Looking off northwest you could actually see where Bosanski-Petrovac was. You could see a couple of building tops poking up out of the fog in that direction; it was clearly evident that we were attempting to pull this mission off right underneath their noses—literally, I mean they were close. Captain O'Grady came up on the radio and told us he heard us. I told him to talk me onto his position. He started giving me directions saying; 'you need to come further southeast'. So I rolled the section right and started heading southeast. I am heading southeast and I see a small mountain coming up out of the fog and he's bringing me right towards it. I'm thinking hey, that's probably where he is going to be at. Captain O'Grady remained, and I can't emphasize this enough, he remained very professional, very tactical throughout this whole thing. He continued to provide me with important information that I needed from what he was seeing and hearing on the ground. This guy was in control, assessing the tactical situation, which was remarkable when you consider what he had gone through over the past six days. He also informed us that the night before, he had people moving around to the southeast of his position and heard sporadic small arms fire coming from that direction. He explained that he had not heard anything recently but wanted to provide us with his latest assessment of the threats. He did a terrific job!

***Mark, Mark,* You're Directly Overhead!**

I continued to ask him questions about what was going on around him. I confirmed that he was foot mobile and that he was going to be able to move on his own—that we didn't need anybody to go in there to carry him out. We came in over the top of him and I was trying to get a visual on him through that thick white ground fog. The radio popped to life with, "you're directly overhead." I went into a hard left hand turn; our position was on the north side of this mountain and looking down, I found a hole in the fog where I could see down to the ground. The wind was out of the south and it was shoving the fog up against the side of the mountain—on the leeward side there was a little pocket where you could see the ground. That's where Captain O'Grady was located. I knew geographically where he was but I still didn't know where his precise location was, nor did I have a visual on him. As we were trying to get a visual on Captain O'Grady, we were also trying to confirm that the objective area was secure and that there was no evidence of hostile activities underneath all this fog. The fog was both working in our favor and against us—it was shielding us from any enemy visual acquisition but at the same time, I could not see any movement on the ground. I asked Captain O'Grady if he had any smoke to pop; I told him I needed him to pop a smoke.

Mick Has Tally On The Smoke

We all carry little orange smoke flares in our survival flight gear. He lights the smoke off and sure enough, right on the northern edge of that little pocket in the fog, all this orange smoke came up. I was in a hard left hand turn and I was asked my Dash Two, Festus, if he saw anything — negative was the reply. Just as the negative reply came over the radio, I looked down and spotted the smoke — I said; "Mick has tally on the smoke." I had a good authentication and now I knew where Scott was physically at. I told Festus to padlock that position (don't lose sight of him). I called Magic and told him that we had good authentication. Push Linus (CH-53s) *Now!* I wanted to emphasize with my voice that I didn't have time to be screwing around in there. I needed those 53's to come to our position immediately because we had a visual on O'Grady and all the mission planning criteria had been met. This could change at any moment based on weather and our proximity to Bosanski-Petrovac. We didn't have any time to waste in there. Magic replied; Roger-*Linus Push, Linus Push.* Button and Tuna's CH-53's are headed inbound and I called Magic again to tell him to tell Button to Buster (go as fast as you can). All of our communications over the radio needed to be limited, crisp and succinct to keep things moving along without 'Clobbering' the radios.

P—u—s h - ing !

This is where the individual personalities and teamwork became invaluable to the success of this mission. Button is an experienced Air Mission Commander with great flight leadership skills—skills that are strongly reinforced during the WTI training at MAWTS-1. I think he sensed over the radio that things were getting a little intense up where we were at. His acknowledgment to my request over the radio was a drawn out, somewhat comical one word reply; *P — u - sh — ing !* We knew he was going to Buster it up to our position and it relieved the tension a bit.

Button and Tuna were on their way in and we (section of AH-1Ws) were circling left at two to three hundred feet AGL (Above Ground Level). Inside the cockpits, we're keeping O'Grady in sight, watching for any developments both inside and outside the orbit and we are looking for Button. I know I am going to have to talk Button into the Landing Zone (LZ) location because of the conditions of the terrain and weather. Suddenly I see Button's CH-53 pop out of the fog and about the same time Button sees my Cobra and calls a tally on me. I told him to keep coming toward me. I'm bringing him towards me with vectors to our position and I glance down to Captain O'Grady's position and see the hole in the fog , which is allowing us to keep a visual on him, starting to close up. Now our two Cobras can not just hover above Scott's position because we would be setting ourselves up as an easy target. So we were moving the whole time and it's getting very difficult to keep a visual on Captain O'Grady's position. Compounding our problems with the decaying weather situation, the smoke from Captain O'Grady's survival smoke began to dissipate. During our mission planning, one of the things that I fought hard for was to get smoke grenades in the front seat of the Cobras. That's an old Vietnam lesson learned, having smoke grenades in the cockpit. Vietnam helicopter pilots were successful using them for marking targets or marking survivors; I wanted them for precisely this type of scenario. I knew they would be useful if we got in there and the guy was hurt or if he was able to talk on the radio but could not move on his own or had a broken arm and could not pop a smoke.

In the front seat of each Cobra, we each had two yellow and two red smoke grenades and I was going to ask Festus to drop down and put one on O'Grady's position. Festus hears me talking to Captain O'Grady, asking him if he has another smoke to which he replied negative. Festus came up on the radio and said; *Festus has smoke.* He rolled in over O'Grady's position, did a little bit of a quick stop maneuver to slow his Cobra down and Festus just popped open his front canopy and *'John Wayned'* a smoke grenade right out the cockpit. It was one of those big yellow infantry smokes with a lot more volume than a survival vest type. Up out of the fog, this big, billowing yellow cloud comes up and I thought Button's going to be able to find that for sure. Button's approaching O'Grady's position and I told him he was on the hill off the nose of his CH-53. Button approached the hill and started setting up for a landing on the south side of it because there was a nice little pasture there. I said; "No, that's not it, you need to come over the hill, keep coming, he is on the north side." Button came around the hill and I was trying to vector him onto O'Grady as he was turning.

I got him turned around and he started to go back up the north side of the hill (operating still with terrible visibility) I said; "No, you've got to bring it back around." I just started to steer his nose. I said; "Come right, come right, come right—Okay—Roll out—Smoke's on the deck, off your nose—three hundred meters." He said; *"I don't see it. No tally."* "Okay—Just keep coming—Keep coming. Its off your nose for two hundred meters." He said; *"I don't see it. No tally. I don't see it."* Button simply could not see the yellow smoke yet, the fog was so thick. I had a better vantage point at two hundred feet and had a better view of both O'Grady's position and Button's CH-53. Button and the 53's were coming down the hill and did not have the angle because the smoke was mixing with the fog at his altitude.

Button Goes For The Deck

Button continued coming down and I said; okay Button, you have yellow smoke on the deck off your nose at a hundred meters. He didn't say anything to me but I knew he had acquired a visual, because Button then did something that I've never seen a CH-53 do before. I knew that he had a visual because all of a sudden, his CH-53 literally stood on its tail, dropped all of his speed and he rolled the nose level and went down through the fog right on top of the yellow smoke. And his Dash Two, Tuna (the second CH-53) went right down there with him. I thought okay, they've seen him and I'm still talking to Scott the whole time while I'm trying to vector Button in. Captain O'Grady continued to stay extremely professional with a tactical focus. The only time a little excitement got into his voice is when he laid eyes on those 53s coming in. At this point, Button's job is to get the CH-53's into the LZ safely, get the infantry off the 53's and get O'Grady into one of the helicopters. Festus and I have to continue to communicate with Captain O'Grady and make sure the area is kept clear of any threats to the Marines on the ground.

Captain O'Grady sees the 53s rolling in and tells me; *I see the helicopters— I see the 53s.* I asked him what his exact location was in relation to the CH-53s and he replied: *I'm at the right three o'clock.* I relayed this data to Button as he hit the LZ and everybody in the 53's cockpit started looking over that way for him. I told Scott to start moving towards them. Generally, we are taught that the survivor should sit still and let the rescue force come to him. But, based on my tactical assessment of the situation, I concluded that because I had a survivor who was mobile and in relatively good condition, with no bad guys around him, that we could save some time— I told him to start moving towards the helicopters.

I knew what the book said, but in this case I did not apply standard operating procedure. Later, during our debrief, some people said; *you know the common accepted practice is that the survivor should sit there* and that I violated that. I agreed and said it was my conscious decision to do so at the time because I believed we did not have a whole lot of time to waste. The weather was now improving rapidly too, but to the enemy's advantage; the fog was dissipating and exposing the TRAP team.

Also, during our mission planning and briefings, Button and I decided that I would make recommendations based on my assessment of the tactical situation as to how many ground force Marines should get off the CH-53's. This was a lesson learned for Button and I. Our timing on communicating this aspect of the mission was off. I told Button we actually only needed a couple of guys to get off, just for basic security while Captain O'Grady came to him. Button said; *its too late,* the ground troops in his CH-53 had already gone out the back door the second the wheels hit the ground, which is what they were trained to do. I mean as soon as they got the ramp down—those guys were out. Button radioed the ground force Marines that O'Grady would be approaching them from the CH-53's right three o'clock. The Marines starting legging it in the direction of the right three o'clock.

The Marines were running toward the right three to get Captain O'Grady and Captain O'Grady was running along a trail toward the Marines. I was telling him over the radio; keep going Basher-keep moving towards them. I was also calling Button asking him; Do you see him? Do you see him? Button told me later that I was starting to bug him. I gathered as much from is reply; ' *I'm IN the BUSHES!* And its kind of funny—Captain O'Grady kept coming up on the radio saying "I'm going as fast as I can" and I kept am telling him; keep going buddy, just keep running. He came back on the radio to *tell* me that he was wearing an orange hat, which I communicated to Button, who was able to tell the infantry guys, okay this guy's coming from the right three and he's got an orange hat on. Who else but a downed American aviator in a combat zone would be wearing a little orange hat? When he did pop out of the trees, everybody knew who he was with that hat on.

As Captain O'Grady was running along the trail to the CH-53's, the trail took a turn and so did he. The Marines on the ground were looking to the right three and Captain O'Grady came out at their left ten o'clock position between the two CH-53's, not knowing which CH-53 to run to. Sergeant Scott Pfister who was on the Dash Two CH-53 as the crew chief, saw Captain O'Grady come out of the tree line—he jumped out of his CH-53 and moved toward the advancing O'Grady. The terrain was rocky and Captain O'Grady was running toward Pfister with his pistol in his hand. Sergeant Pfister is a big Marine and was concerned about O'Grady running toward his helicopter with a loaded pistol. Pfister hit his wrist to knock the weapon from his hand and helped O'Grady aboard. Now you have to conjure up this image of Pfister being charged by a guy with a six day growth on his face and gun pointed in his direction, there was a lot of adrenaline flowing.

Sergeant Pfister had his fifty caliber machine gun in the doorway and it wasn't immediately clear to Captain O'Grady how to enter the CH-53. Pfister gave him an energetic boost at the same time the guys inside the CH-53 were pulling him in. Captain O'Grady went flying into the CH-53 and hit the far side of the CH-53 fuselage pretty hard.

Captain O'Grady later told us that that was the only time he ever actually chambered a round, locked and loaded, was when we were inbound to get him because he said nobody was going to get in between him and those helicopters-if anybody tried to stop him he was going to take them out. He also wanted that pistol when he was on the helicopter; in his view if the helicopter went down, he did not want to be back in enemy territory unarmed—he was still very much in survival mode. From the time the CH-53's landed in the LZ to the time we got him in the CH-53, a total of two minutes had elapsed based on the clock we had running in our cockpit.

They had to get the infantry back on the CH-53's So they pulled them back in and this is when I really started looking at the watch; I came up on the radio and said; Hey Button, we've been in here too long, let's get this show on the road-we've got to get out of here. As usual, Murphy's Law is coming into play, all that fog that was obscuring us is starting to dissipate and the LZ is becoming vulnerable. I was looking off towards Bosanski-Petrovac and at a pretty good road that came from the town down to our position capable of transporting a couple of truckloads of hostiles right into our position. The last thing I wanted at this time was a gun fight while we're trying to get these guys out of there.

I had the best situational awareness at this point as far as the objective area was concerned and I wanted us all out of there because we're becoming vulnerable. So they get all the infantry back together and they counted them and counted them again—because that would have been a tragedy to have gotten O'Grady out and then discover that we left one of the infantry guys on the ground-we had to make sure we had accounted for all those Marines. We got them all on the CH-53's and the fog was dissipating so fast I was really starting to get concerned about that road. I called the Harriers and told Odie "the weather's clearing down here fast-be ready to work Checkpoint America straight in." If we had to run a bombing mission, that's where I was going to bring them in from, Checkpoint America. While they're collecting everybody I called AWACS and told Magic I needed a snap to feet wet which means - I need the quickest vector to the water. He said 230. Button came up and said he needed a vector for the fastest route out of here and I gave him 230, Button replied *Lif—ting.* I formed the Cobra's up on the CH-53's and we started shagging ass out of there, just booming along as fast as we could. I called Odie and I said the 53's are out of the zone-we're out of here, and he passed that off to Magic. And we just started heading southwest. As we were egressing, the large mountain that we flew around to come in was now uncovered—the ground fog had lifted and we were underneath it now.

I was looking at my map and I told Blondie, my co-pilot, that I think we're going to have to go up through this stuff. The only way out of the valley was over to my left. That actually went out northeast and that was back into the threat area so we didn't want to be going that way. I was looking at our position and the map and about to come up on the squadron common frequency and make a recommendation to Button that we climb through the fog. Button had already made the decision. He said we're going through it and we saw the two CH-53 noses come up and they went up into the clouds. We were at the left seven o'clock and Festus and Jinx (Captain James T. Jenkins II) were up at the right five and we saw Button and Tuna head up into the fog, so we followed them up. And this is where my co-pilot Ian Walsh did a fantastic job. I was the escort flight leader so I was in the front seat with all the maps and crypto gear. Ian was the guy in the back that was flying our Cobra. I had four aircraft that I needed to be worrying about. I had great visibility in the front and would not have time to also handle mechanics of wiggling the sticks—that was Ian's job. He was going to be shooting the rockets and physically working the controls so I could concentrate on the flight leadership responsibilities.

I couldn't see this mountain in front of us and we're climbing-Ian is pulling all the power we have and we're losing air speed as we climb, we are climbing as fast as we can. I kept looking for blue sky, backing him up on the instruments and looking out in front, hoping I wouldn't see pine trees in front of the aircraft. We finally popped out at 5,500 feet and I saw blue sky. I didn't ask Ian at the time but I asked him the next day what the radar altimeter bottomed out at while we were climbing over the moutain—he said two hundred feet. So we'd come within two hundred feet of hitting that mountain in the clouds and never saw it. We never saw the damn thing, it was a good piece of flying by Ian, he did a great job. Anyway, we popped out at 5,500 feet still heading 230.

Now remember on the way in I said we ran in between those two SA6 SAM sites. What had protected us on the way in was hugging the terrain; now we're no longer down in the terrain because we had to get above the clouds and we're high now—in between these two SAM sites going as fast as we can go.

Radar Gets A Look

As soon as we popped out of the clouds, our flight of four was spread out a little bit because everybody put some separation between the aircraft going through the clouds. We tightened the formation back up and kept going. About this time a radar came up and illuminated us, taking a look at us. I thought, well, we are still working under U.S. Rules of Engagement (ROE). At some point during the mission, the rules of engagement had changed to where we were working under NATO rules of engagement. All the guys who were on the mission thought we were still working under the U.S. R.O.E. There are just some subtle differences, but based on U.S. rules of engagement at the time, the ones that I had been briefed on as escort flight leader, we could kill that radar. To sum it up, Colonel Berndt grabbed me right before we left and he said; *Mick, if anything gets in the way, take it out*-that was my ROE. Anything tries to impede us, Whack it.

So we had this radar come up and take a peek at us and I expected that the SEAD guys would pump some HARM missiles into this thing. The SEAD guys had the radar and were in position to take it out. They requested permission to fire and it was denied by CAOC. They told them to continue to jam and they knew the radar was looking at us. We were in between those SAM sites, and we (helo's) just don't have the energy that the fast movers (fixed-wing aircraft) have. I can't throttle it up to go six hundred knots and run out of there; the Cobra was limited to about 150 knots in my present configuration. Now as we got closer to the coastal mountain range, the weather suddenly cleared up. Button decided he was going to take us down close to the ground. Button just pushed the nose over and we went running down out of the mountains going as fast as we could at about fifty feet off the deck with the CH-53's.

Once we got down out of the mountains we headed across into the coastal plain area. We were a little bit worried about wires and the power line towers. The area looked like a bombed out version of post World War II Germany. There wasn't a house that hadn't been hit with something. We were zinging along out there, staying about twenty-five feet and 150 knots. This is where flying with the 53's is an escort pilot's dream. I had to ask *them* to slow down, Button was pulling so much power he was actually pulling away from me. I had to ask him a couple of times to give me some knots, because we were pulling a hundred percent torque in our aircraft and he was just opening the distance. It was getting to the point where he was getting to the outer limits of where we could protect him with our weapons—I had to keep asking him to slow down, -that's how fast we were going. It doesn't sound fast compared to an F/A-18, but at twenty-five to fifty feet, at 150 knots it gets pretty exciting.

SAM At Ten O'clock

We were flying along, going in between houses and barns and seeing people's laundry going by. I mean that's how low and how fast we were. We are about twenty miles or so from feet wet and I was following our route on the map. My head was on an a swivel the whole time to be sure there's not any threat—AWACS and the fighter cap and Harriers are in position to deal with the air threat, so we were primarily looking for ground threats. I was still at the left seven of the formation and all of sudden, I saw this grayish white corkscrew smoke trail that's perpendicular to the formation and I thought you've got to be kidding me. We're twenty miles from the water and now they're going to start shooting SAM's at us. That smoke trail was a classic sign that somebody shot an IR Sam at us. I called SAM at ten o'clock and the CH-53 guys start calling, saying they are taking fire—Right two o'clock, right three o'clock, taking small arms fire.

We were trying to determine where the fire was coming from and with the ROE that I was operating under, I was able to take out anything might impede the mission-I could whack it. The only thing I needed to have was a target-all I needed was a muzzle flash, if I could have just seen where the fire was coming from I could have put something on it to suppress it. But I had to have a target. It is not always the best thing to just start slinging ordnance all over the place when you're not sure what it will be hitting.

I asked Ian if he saw anything, muzzle flashes, tracers—He said negative. The CH-53 crews were still saying they were taking fire. I was looking ahead and I was seeing rounds impacting and explosions underneath the CH-53's. The stuff's hitting the ground underneath them. I called Button and said you're taking impacts underneath—it was a long beaten zone perpendicular to his flight path where all these rounds were hitting. The fire was tracking along the ground underneath the CH-53's, so I knew it was not just sporadic fire, somebody was definitely aiming at and tracking the CH-53's.

We still did not have a visible target. If we did, all we had to do was roll the nose about forty-five degrees right and start putting rockets on the hostiles. We were carrying high explosive rockets and also 2.75 inch Flechette Rockets which fly down range for a given distance, detonate and its like a big shotgun shell that goes off and just sprays these little steel darts all over the place. Its pretty good for suppressing anything that's shooting at your buddies. While I was looking towards Button, I saw a flash, a plume, a dust cloud and this spiraling grayish white corkscrew smoke trail coming out at me. I called "SAM in the air!" I had just seen a Serb shoot an SA7 SAM missile at me. This thing came up and it started to maneuver onto us — I can't even describe to you how fast it was. I've never had one shot at me before and I only knew what I had read in the tactics manuals. We always brief for this type of engagement, and I learned real quick that our preconceived notions of how we would deal with SAM's weren't realistic. It was so incredibly fast that I hardly had enough time to react to the event before the SAM went by us, passing under the nose of the aircraft.

I saw the guy shoot the thing, he was off to my right two o'clock. He released the weapon and when I saw it, I said "Uh-oh; I hope that's not what I think it is." I had my map in my left hand and I let go of the map to move my hand about a foot and a half to get to the flare switch on the left side of the seat armor. I hit the switch and got the flares off and the SAM basically beat me. I had to move a foot and a half and that thing got to me before I could move that far. There's a couple of different reasons why I think it missed, and I really can't get into those but suffice it to say, it did. After the SAM had gone by I went preemptive. I continued to pop flares in case they were shooting more than one at us. Button had already seen one up by his position and Tuna saw a third one get launched.

There were at least three SA7 SAM's shot against us—I was getting flares off now and we were looking for targets and the CH-53 guys were still calling fire. Festus heard me call SAMs in the air and he said he'd been looking out the front of his Cobra. He didn't see anything go by him so he figured that the guy that fired the SAM was off to the left of his nose towards the inside of the formation. Festus said he was looking towards me, watching me getting flares off and all of a sudden he heard this boom, boom, boom, sound and he felt the concussions on his aircraft. He said he thought; what the hell is that?

He looked off to the right and said he was looking right down the barrels of a ZU-23-2 anti- aircraft gun and it was just boom, boom, shooting at him. He said he could see the muzzle flashes and tracers coming out. He said tracers were going in front of the nose and over the top of his canopy. Jinx was in his back seat and basically had them cold. He was going to try and get a some twenty millimeter on him with the helmet sight system. With all the other things going on, the cord that you hook on to the back of your helmet had somehow gotten disconnected. So Jinx had these guys cold. He hits the action bar, swings his head to slew the turret, he goes to hit the trigger and the gun didn't slew because his helmet had

Major Malavet explains the finer points of the O'Grady rescue to the authors in the cockpit of the CH-53E.

gotten disconnected—by this time we had blown past these guys. I had to make a quick decision. Should we go back and take out the site or press forward? I made the decision to press forward and stay with the CH-53's. We beat the threat by blowing past it. It couldn't have been more than a minute that all this shooting was taking place, but it seemed like a half an hour as all the tracer and SAM's were flying by. I thought, now that we're past the threat, what purpose would it serve for me to roll back in to engage the AAA sites, MANPAD SAM shooters and the infantry delivering the small arms fire? The mission was to get Captain O'Grady to the *Kearsarge* and continue to protect the CH-53's. I did not know what was out in front of us either —there might have been more hostile activity. The training we receive at MAWTS-1 focuses on the Commander's Intent for the mission. In this case it was to get Scott O'Grady back out to the *Kearsarge*; it wasn't to go toe to toe with SAM and anti-aircraft artillery sites in the middle of Bosnia just for the sake of getting into a gunfight.

Speaking to Button during the debrief, he didn't want me to detach from him. Our mission (the Cobra's), was to stay with those guys and protect them from any further trouble that they might encounter. My thinking here was that we had already beaten the threat by blowing by it. An attack might have been considered retaliatory which could have further escalated various scenarios that did not need to be escalated at this point in time in Bosnia.

Now we were past the threat and we were heading out towards the sea. The CH-53's started checking for damage. Button had taken a round through one of his main rotor blade and he was getting a light indicating that the rotor blade had been hit and started to depressurize. Tuna in the Dash Two, with O'Grady on board, took a round in the tail rotor and a round had come into the crew compartment and ricocheted around, hitting Sergeant Major Angel Castro in the back. He was wearing his flak jacket and the round was pretty much spent— it thumped him pretty good but it didn't hurt him. About the same time I asked Button if I could speak directly to Magic, which he approved.

I wanted to make sure we gave a good accurate report on the location of the SAM and AAA sites, that had fired at us in case somebody else had to go through there at a later time. About this time, we got a transmission chip caution light in our Cobra, which meant the transmission gears were starting to come apart on us. Ian and I discussed the probability of us taking a hit during the shooting—neither of us believed that we took any hits. If we did take a round to the transmission case, things would start binding up back there pretty quickly. Ian was looking at the oil pressure and oil temperature and he said there were no secondary indications. It was later determined that we had been flying that aircraft so hard to keep up with the CH-53's, pulling a hundred percent torque to stay with them, that we were just chewing up the transmission.

We continued heading back out and we went over this small lake. There was a little ferry out there with cars and people on it and we came roaring by. I mean there are all these guys on the first deck drinking coffee, watching a couple of CH-53's and AH-1W's go roaring by—we could see all the heads moving and for a some reason a couple of them were waving at us. Maybe they thought it was some kind of airshow. We got feet dry again and we were getting close to reaching feet wet over the Adriatic Sea.

We came up on this little town (Zadar) and there was an airfield up there. Magic started telling us; you've got civilian traffic bearing two-eight-zero at eight miles. We looked over and there was this twin engine airliner coming at us for a landing on the field. Button says, "*Yeah, roger.*" I asked Button later about the airliner and he said; "I was busy and I had the right of way, besides, he lives here, I don't; he can wave off" — and he did. We came close to the airfield, he took one look at us and he just turned around and went in the other direction; he wasn't having any part of landing there.

Feet Wet

We finally got back over the water-feet wet!. We knew the CH-53's had been hit and we had the transmission chip light problem. I didn't say anything to Button up to this point because we were still flying and he had a lot of other things to worry about. I figured that unless it starts really causing us problems, I am not going to tell him. When we got feet wet, I came up on my radio and said I have a transmission chip light—I need to land—I need to get this thing on the deck. The USS *Kearsarge* had been monitoring most of our communications. The Captain turned the ship toward us and they were coming to us as fast as they could go. At this point, they said forget the twelve mile limit or the exclusion zone. The *USS Kearsarge* was coming up to the beach to get us if they had to. The *USS Kearsarge* turned towards us and we landed on the ship.

Normally when you land on a ship, there's not that many people up on the deck except the flightdeck crews—the usual guys that you need on deck to manage the aircraft. As we approached the *Kearsarge*, we could see that the deck was packed with people. Once we landed and we shut down, the flight deck personnel chained the aircraft to the deck. People were all over the place, but again, it wasn't like the movies. Nobody came up and hugged me and said, *"Hey, you know, you can be my wingman anytime"* or anything like that. There were no high five's or anything. We were happy to have accomplished the mission and talked about the mission details in preparation for the debriefing.

When we got off the fight deck, we turned in our personal weapons, got a drink of water and went right to the Ready Room. The Intelligence guys were there and we debriefed the mission right away so we didn't lose any of the details or forget anything. We had a mass debrief for all the guys in the MEU, the squadron, and Intelligence personnel. Captain O'Grady was taken immediately down to sick bay. The most immediate concern was to get his body temperature up and get him hydrated; the hypothermia was kicking his butt. Later that day, Major Tarbutton, Major Ogden, myself, and a couple of the other pilots went down to sick bay to see Captain O'Grady. We brought him some M&M's, a Cobra patch, other memorabilia and just shot the breeze for a little bit.

After the extensive debriefs and our visit with Scott we all seemed to be getting tired. I just wanted to drink some more water, take a shower and lay down for a while. A large single malt scotch would have been great!! I had just hit the rack and I was listening to some music, when all of a sudden there was a knock on my door and someone shouting *Get up, Get up,* the media's coming. We had to get cleaned up, get in clean flight suits, shine our flight boots and get up on the flight deck as soon as possible. A couple of helicopters full of reporters came out and it was an all afternoon event. By the time all that was done - everybody was pretty much exhausted.

The strange thing about all this was that we did not have any time to think emotionally about what we had just been through because we had so much to do that afternoon. As time went on during the day we would sit there and talk a little bit about what went on and it started to sink in as to what we had accomplished. That night, the guys on the mission kept running into each other in the passageways of the *USS Kearsarge* at two thirty in the morning—the adrenaline still hadn't worn off, and we had a difficult time relaxing. We were also beginning to realize just how lucky we had been that morning..."

Major Malavet- Brindisi, Italy

Major Malavet:

"On the morning of June 8th, I woke up in a hotel in Brindisi, Italy and turned on CNN to get an early world update. It was then that I learned of the successful TRAP mission. Captain John "Spaldo" Taylor an AV-8B pilot and squadron intelligence officer was actually the individual who told me to turn to CNN because he said, "WE DID IT!" I can't adequately describe the feeling of elation I had, knowing that my fellow Marines and the *USS Kearsarge* team succeeded in snatching Captain Scott O'Grady out of enemy territory and back into American hands. Captain Taylor and I then quickly headed to the United States Air Force Joint Special Operations Task Force (JSOTF) compound. I arrived at the JSOTF compound and was escorted into a room of tired pilots who had recently finished six hours of flying. JSOTF launched as a back-up to our TRAP mission and to cover CSAR for fixed wing assets deployed from Aviano, Italy. The USAF Special Operations personnel are highly skilled professionals who take pride in their capabilities. A couple of their MH-53J "Pavelow" pilots have also attended the MAWTS-1 WTI class. We stayed at the compound for a week discussing the tactics of the mission, the lessons learned, and how to improve joint service operations. I was able to inform the Air Force about specific MEU(SOC) capabilities which helped us plan future joint operations to support UNPROFOR in Bosnia. That week was definitely a moment of pride for the Marine Corps and the 24th MEU(SOC) team."

WTI Training At MAWTS-1 Pays Off

Major Malavet:

"The MAWTS-1 emphasis on threat analysis, exploitation of enemy weaknesses, tactical mission planning, incorporating the Six Functions of Marine Aviation, and briefing skills was credited as one of the significant factors in the successful TRAP of Basher 52."

Major Mykleby:

"During the MEU work ups we conducted the planning exactly as we were taught at MAWTS-1. When Captain O'Grady was shot down, the *USS Kearsarge* broke off from our NATO exercise because the real world called. By virtue of the training that we had at MAWTS-1 in the area of planning, we were able to get a lot done in a short period of time. We didn't branch out into small, insignificant tangential issues that could have distracted us. All the pilots that attend the MAWTS-1 WTI course's are top rated pilots and instructors—you are in some pretty experienced and knowledgeable company. We are put into real world scenarios and taught to plan in very tight time frames commensurate with the MEU's six hour response commitment. This is where the WTI student has the most significant professional growth and development.

Effective mission planning and the skills to conduct a good, concise brief so that everybody knows what their actions are and what's going to happen when we execute a mission are what a WTI graduate brings to the MEU, amongst their many other talents. Those are two of the things that I

Andy Wyte's painting of the Captain Scott O'Grady rescue. Courtesy of Andy Whyte.

personally feel made the whole O'Grady rescue a success. We did a lot of our general planning early on—all of our research and identification of the assets that we would require was done up front so we didn't have to "light ourselves on fire", trying to get that done at the last minute. Additionally, Keen took the planning to new levels of detail that ensured that we were locked on. He led the development of the TRAP brief and when we were called, we plugged the new data in and we were on our way, addressing the finer points of the execution of the mission.

Flight leadership is another set of skills that are strongly emphasized in the WTI syllabus. During the training you might be leading a flight of eight using Night Vision Goggles (NVG's) in low light level conditions, going way the heck out in the middle of no where in the desert to conduct a strike. MAWTS-1 puts you in scenarios that are as close to combat as possible, operating in extremely hazardous conditions with a large amount of aircraft and a rather complex set of scenarios. One of the desired results of attending the WTI course and returning to the fleet as a WTI graduate is, when it comes down to actually executing a mission for real in a combat situation, that you've already experienced the situation as far as you can in peace time — experiencing similar flight leadership situations and problems. You develop and perfect your style and line of thinking—How you're going to do this, how you're going to do that. It paid off for all the WTI graduates involved in the O'Grady rescue mission. Once the real rounds started to fly, I can't tell you that it was really any different than some of the high threat scenarios that we worked on back at MAWTS-1.

Major Malavet:

"The Six Functions of Marine Aviation; assault support, offensive air support, anti-air warfare, electronic warfare, air reconnaissance, and Control of Aircraft and Missiles are functions that directly support the ground commander. Our aviation TRAP template for the Basher 52 rescue was designed to support Lt.Colonel Chris Gunther's (The Trap Mission Commander) concept of recovery. The MAWTS-1 WTI graduate is considered a Marine aviation force multiplier whose enviable tactical prowess is sought by regional CINC's as well as by Marine Ground Commanders at all force levels. The importance of the WTI role in the Navy / Marine Corps OMFTS concept cannot be overstated. As we enter the 21st century with new technologies and warfighting concepts, the MAWTS-1 certified WTI will continue to ensure the ground commander is supported by the best aviation tacticians!"

Communication About How The Marines Do Business

One of the major lessons learned from the O'Grady mission was the need for other branches of the American military and Allies to understand how the Marine Expeditionary Units conduct business. This communication will continue and will be enhanced in the days ahead. An example of this need for communication is cited in the following anecdote:

During the egress portion of the O'Grady TRAP mission as the formation of CH-53's and AH-1W's were taking SAM and ground fire, a couple of USAF A-10's pilots were listening up in the stack off feet wet. The pilots just dropped out of the stack and started coming towards the Marines when they heard the Marines were taking fire. Their intent was admirable and intended to get in there to help the Marines out. But they probably wouldn't have done that if they knew that the MEU already had Harriers overhead for this purpose—the A-10's actually flew between the Harriers that were directly responsible for flying top cover for the TRAP team and were waved off..

Great Americans

Colonel R.J. Wallace, Commanding Officer of Marine Aircraft Group-Twenty Nine (MAG-29) based at MCAS New River, NC summed up the actions of the WTI graduates involved in the O'Grady Rescue best when he referred to them in the following manner:

"Ogden, Walkerwicz, Mykleby and Malavet—Gunther and Tarbutton; *All Great Americans!*
All Great Marines!"

Captain Ronald C. "Wiggy" Walkerwicz—who flew as Dash Two in the second section of AV-8B's that provided cover for the TRAP team was later tragically killed in a Harrier crash in February 1996. Captain Ronald C. "Wiggy" Walkerwicz is missed by his comrades but not forgotten. Semper Fi!

Samples of the Rapid Response Planning Process and Tactical Recovery of Aircraft and Personnel (TRAP) taught in the MAWTS-1 WTI courses are included in Appendices.

The Tactical Recovery Aircraft and Personnel (TRAP) team prepares to lift off from the deck of the USS Kearsarge (LHD 3) aboard two Marine Corps CH-53 E's to rescue USAF Captain Scott O'Grady. The TRAP team consisted of US Marines from the 24th MEU and the aircraft are assigned to HMM-263. DOD Photo by Sgt. Dave A Garten, USMC.

12

MCAS Yuma- The Home of MAWTS-1

MCAS Yuma at sundown. One of the static aircraft displayed at the front gate to the air station is this AV-8A.

Originating near Casa Grande, Arizona and reaching to points west is Highway 8, one of the more scenic stretches of road in the American southwest. Heading toward the Pacific coast and San Diego, one must first traverse through the flat open expanse of the lower Sonoran Desert past Gila Bend. Further west, the rugged Palomas and Castle Dome mountain ranges to the North and the Mohawk and Copper mountains to the South serve to frame the highway. The beauty and serenity of this inhospitable geography is captivating, and makes the desolate road a bit easier to manage. Passing through the small town of Ligurta, some thirty miles from the border of Mexico, the highway snakes into the rugged foothills. The town of Yuma lies straight ahead, and with it, the location of one of the most important facilities the US Marine Corps operates.

As the first signs of the thriving city rise from the desert, the occupants of the skies above the highway changes. The hawks that ride the thermals over the desert floor in search of food are replaced by other hunters. Hornets, Prowlers, Tigers reach for the sky, leaving behind the deafening roar of their jet engines. Cobras and Stallions pass low over the desert. Every type of warplane the Marines operate fills the skies as they head out to the controlled airspace attached to the vast ranges in southwestern Arizona. All this activity begins and ends at the Marines premier aviation training facility - ***Marine Corps Air Station (MCAS) Yuma***.

Courteous, yet serious greeting at the main gate.

Control tower at MCAS Yuma. A busy place indeed as there are over 130,000 military aircraft takeoff and landings a year at the facility.

Origins of MCAS Yuma

The air station traces its beginnings back to the 1920's, when President Calvin Cooledge authorized the United States Government to lease 640 acres of desert near the town of Yuma for use as a flying area. The area was simply called Fly Field in honor of Colonel Benjamin F. Fly who was instrumental in persuading the Government to lease the land. Initially, Fly Field served as a stop over point for two dozen aircraft involved in the cross-country New York to Los Angeles air race. The facility was under the command of the US Army and with the outbreak of hostilities during the second world war, became a key pilot training location. Hundreds of combat ready pilots were turned out under the new designation of Yuma Army Airfield.

As was the case with many wartime installations, Yuma was closed after the war ended. By the summer of 1951, the fledgling US Air Force reactivated the base until they signed it over to the Navy on January 1, 1959. Nine days later it became the newly designated US Marine Corps Auxiliary Air Station. This name would be again changed in 1962 to its current Marine Corps Air Station Yuma.

MCAS Yuma logo.

This distinctive sign announces the Corps most important air station.

The view from the top of the control tower looking to the east with the VMFT-401 'Snipers' hangar in the foreground.

The largest tenant unit at MCAS Yuma is MAG-13 with its (4) Harrier units including the 'Tomcats' of VMA-311.

In the ensuing years, the air station grew dramatically, as did Marine aviation itself. From 1969 through 1987, the primary task at Yuma was jet pilot training. Marine Corps Crew Readiness Training Group - 10 (MCCRTG-10) was involved with training crews in the primary fighter, the F-4 Phantom with VMFT-101 and the light attack jet, the A-4 Skyhawk, with VMAT-102.

The air station underwent a major change to its current status in 1987, when Marine Air Group (MAG-13) replaced MCCRTG-10 as the major tenant command. MAG-13 contains four Harrier squadrons and ushered in new era for the air station.

Search and Rescue UH-1N flightline.

12
MARINES
04
MARINES
04

VMFT-401 Sniper logo

Section of VMFT-401 'Sniper' F-5E Tiger II's heading north with the Chocolate Mountains and the Salton Sea in the background. The unit contains some of the finest fighter pilots in the world, many of whom regularly make life difficult for WTI crews.

MCAS Yuma is Harrier country on the west coast. This section of Harriers heads out at first light - the effectiveness of the camouflage is evident in this photo.

VMFT-401 'Sniper' pilot taxis in after a mission. In the highly capable hands of these air combat maneuvering specialists, the 3rd generation F-5E is still a dangerous adversary, one that even Hornet pilots don't take lightly.

One of the more striking sights immediately seen upon entering the air station is this captured Iraqi (Soviet) S-60 57MM Anti-Aircraft Gun.

The weapons dedication reads 'Citation in recognition of Harrier pilots who braved Iraqi anti-aircraft fire throughout Operation Desert Storm and the liberation of Kuwait - Iraqi (Soviet) S-60 57 MM Anti-Aircraft Gun captured by 2nd Light Anti Aircraft Missile Battalion 26 February 1991 at Ahmed Al Jabar Airbase, Kuwait'

Section of Hornets line up for the break to MCAS Yuma. At military airbases that house tactical jets, returning aircraft approach at high speed and low altitude. This expedites the landing process. Once past the midpoint of the field, they will roll into a 3g turn which bleeds off airspeed. After turning 180 degrees, the aircraft enters the downwind leg and transitions to the landing configuration by dropping the landing gear and flaps. It will then turn 90 degrees on to final approach while descending rapidly, before rolling wings level for landing.

MCAS Yuma Today

MCAS Yuma is based on the south side of the airfield which also is home to the Yuma Regional Airport with a fair amount of civilian traffic. These facilities are housed on the north side of the complex.

The facility is currently home to a number of important tenant units as listed in the chart below. As mentioned previously, its ideal weather conditions and accessible range complexes make MCAS Yuma *the* training facility for aviation.

Table 1 - Tenant Units at MCAS Yuma

MAG-13
-VMA-211 Wake Island Avengers
-VMA-214 Black Sheep
-VMA-311 Tomcats
-VMA-542 Flying Nightmares

Marine Aviation Logistics Squadron-13
Marine Aviation Weapons and Tactics Squadron-1
Marine Fighter Training Squadron-401
Marine Wing Support Squadron-371
Marine Air Control Squadron-7
1st Light Antiaircraft Missile Battalion
Combat Service Support Detachment-16

Marine Aircraft Group (MAG) -13 is part of the 3rd Marine Air Wing and was activated in March 1, 1942 at San Diego. The MAG participated directly in the Marshall Islands campaign of the second World War. After being de-activated for a short time after the war, MAG-13 was re-activated in March of 1951. The MAG moved to Kaneohe Bay, Hawaii, in early 1953 with a pair of fighter squadrons and Marine Air Control Squadron (MACS) - 2. In June of 1965, MAG-13 became a unit of the 1st Marine Air Wing at MCAS Iwakuni, Japan were it operated until 1966. The MAG returned to El Toro in October of 1970, and then re-located to its current home at MCAS Yuma in October of 1987.

Many of the squadrons that reside at Yuma have long proud histories serving the Corps and are noteworthy. The Harrier units VMA-214, VMA-211, VMA-311 and VMA-311 each served with distinction during the second World War in battles throughout the Pacific. With the outbreak of hostilities in Korea, and then Vietnam, these units would once again take their aircraft into hostile skies in support of Marine ground forces.

Table 2 - MCAS Yuma Facts

Total Population	**5,541 Military** **7,823 Dependents** **1,128 Civilian Employees**
Payroll	**$104 million for military** **$13 million for civilians**
Air Station Activity (Takeoffs and landings)	**57,000 civilian** **130,500 military**
Total Runway(s)	**13,300 feet**

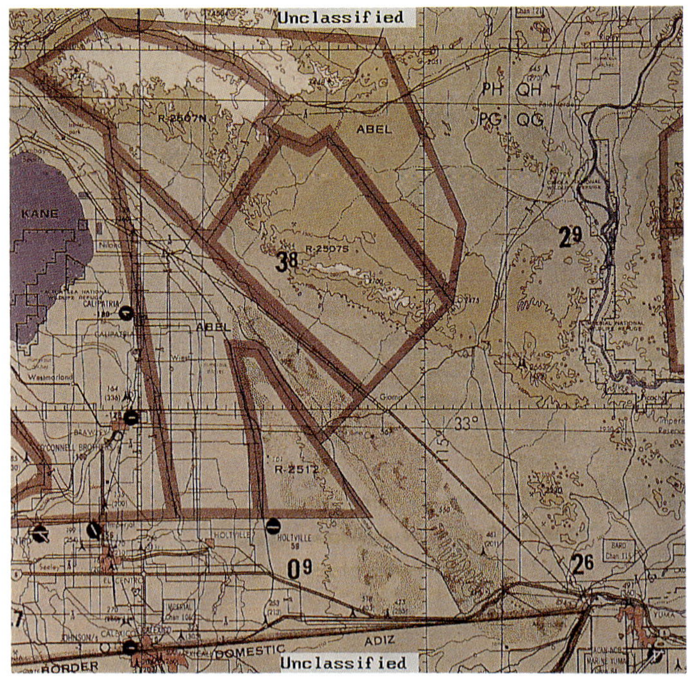

The ranges north of MCAS Yuma are located in the Chocolate mountain ranges to the east of the Salton Sea are designated R2507N (North) and R2507S (South). These are the best ranges for the delivery of live ordnance in the Marine Corps.

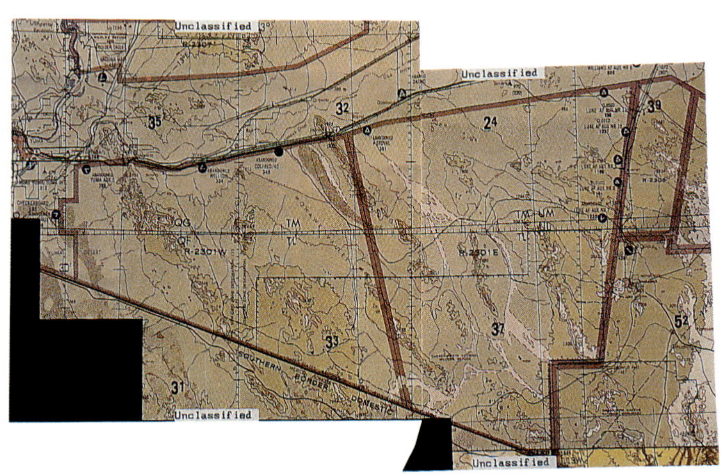

To the east of MCAS Yuma are the 2301E (East) and 2301W (West) ranges that are split by the Mohawk Valley. These ranges are restricted to inert ordnance only and for Low Altitude Training (LAT) missions. They are also highly instrumented ranges under the control of the TACTS system.

By a wide margin, MCAS Yuma is the busiest air station the Marine Corps operates, and is the second busiest in the entire naval service. Its stated mission is "to support aerial weapons training for the Atlantic and Pacific Fleet Marine Forces and Navy, and to serve as a base of operations for MAWTS-1, MAG-13 and other 3rd MAW units". In any given year, as many as fifty Marine Corps and Navy units will deploy to MCAS Yuma for training.

The 'Tomcats' of VMA-311

The 'Flying Nightmares' of VMA-513

The 'Wake Island Avengers' of VMA-211

The 'Black Sheep' of VMA-214

PART 4

U.S. Marine Corps Fixed and Rotary Wing Aircraft

'Blacksheep' and 'Wake Island Avenger' AV-8B's perform a scissors break

13

Hornets: The F/A-18 C and D

VMFA (AW)-332 F/A-18D pops self protection flares to thwart heat seeking missiles. This would most likely be followed immediately by a brutal high g turn to defeat the missile.

Origins

While now a success story for both the Marine Corps and the Navy, the F/A-18 Hornet started its life as the second choice for the USAF behind the General Dynamics F-16 Fighting Falcon. Today's Hornets are direct descendants of the Northrop YF-17 design (titled P-530 Cobra) which competed for the USAF Light Weight Fighter (LWF) program of the 1970's. The Northrop design lost to the highly capable F-16 but was by no means finished.

During the early 1970's, the Navy was looking for a low cost, multi-role aircraft which could be deployed in sufficient numbers to replace the F-4 Phantom, A-7 Corsair, and possibly at a later date, the Grumman A-6. Limited budgets, exacerbated by the high cost of the Navy's primary fleet air defense fighter, the F-14 Tomcat, necessitated a relatively inexpensive multi-purpose aircraft.

As a general rule, with the exception of the F-4, neither 'navalized' Air Force designs or the vice versa work out, e.g., the F-111. The operational differences and mission requirements of the Air Force and Navy are disparate enough to require separate aircraft. Smarting quite a bit from the loss of such a huge program as the LWF, Northrop teamed up with McDonnell Douglas to reshape the YF-17 into a serious contender for the Navy's (VFAX) lightweight multi-mission fighter requirement. This proved to be a shrewd move for Northrop as they were able to leverage McDonnell Douglas' significant experience in producing Navy aircraft, an area Northrop had limited experience in.

Distinctive unit insignia confirms that this F/A-18D belongs to the 'Hawks' of VMFA (AW) - 533.

The prospect of sales of the aircraft to the Navy, Marine Corps and possibly abroad wouldn't be a bad consolation prize. This is not to suggest that the YF-17 was incapable, far from it. The design team at General Dynamics quite astutely gambled that by sharing certain aspects of the F-16 (like the engines), with the Air Forces other major fighter, the F-15, their competitive position would be enhanced by virtue of certain economical advantages.

The Navy did conduct a competition for the winner of their now designated Navy Air Combat Fighter (NACF) program with both aircraft and among other considerations, the safety that a twin engine aircraft affords was very compelling to the Navy. The F/A-18 that first took to the skies in November of 1978 was a different airplane however than the YF-17 Cobra. As the aircraft proceeded through the rigorous deck trials it became apparent that the design was flexible enough to fulfill both the fighter and attack roles.

The marriage between Northrop and McDonnell Douglas was not a perfect one, and over time relations were strained somewhat. It was difficult for the Northrop designers to witness the modification of their pure fighter into the multi-role aircraft. This necessitated changes that limited the aircraft's ACM performance slightly, added weight, but had a major impact on the fuel capacity. This would dog the F/A-18 continually and represents its only weakness.

The Hornet Goes Operational

By February of 1981, the F/A-18 began arriving to operational squadrons from Navy's VFA-125 at Naval Air Station Lemoore, California. From the official standpoint however, the 'Black Knights' with the Marines VMFA-314 were the first fully operational unit with the Hornet.

The first variants of the Hornet to become operational were the single seat F/A-18 A and the two seat B models. Perhaps the most striking aspect of the Hornet was not from the outside, but rather, was the highly advanced cockpit layout. The avionics of the Hornet were centered around the Hughes AN/APG-65 multi-mode radar system. The 'glass cockpit' concept had become a reality in the Hornet as the many traditional switches and dials of previous aircraft were replaced by three programmable DDI's (Digital Display Indicators). The status of the aircraft's primary systems, weapons and a moving map could all be easily displayed. In addition, the pilot looked straight ahead through the Kaiser AN/AVQ-28 Heads Up Display (HUD) for real-time flight information. For truly 'heads up' flying, the Hornet also employed Hands On Throttle And Stick (HOTAS) technology to allow the pilot to control weapons and sensor systems while keeping an eye on surface and air threats.

The pilot sits inside a snug cockpit on the Martin-Baker SJU-5/6 ejection seat (the Naval Air Common Ejection Seat - NACES in the late model C and D). Visibility in the Hornet is superb since the front windscreen is a single piece unit, and the cockpit canopy is large and also a single piece design.

One of the more unusual aspects of the Hornet which contributes to its unique shape are the leading edge extensions (LEX) on the forward fuselage. The LEX's are located on both sides of the aircraft beginning just about at the beginning of the front windscreen and running aft to the mid point of the fuselage where they blend into the wings leading edge flaps. Subsequently, a small slot was added at the top of the LEX that further enhanced the Hornets superb high angle of attack maneuverability. The LEX's are separated by the main fuselage that is adorned with a distinctive

201
VMFA-32

Top view of VMFA-323 'Death Rattlers' F/A-18 Hornet carrying an AGM-65 Maverick on the port side wing pylon. The Hornet is Marine Air's 'Jack of all Trades', equally adept in the air to air and air to ground roles.

The glow of the setting desert sun highlights the distinctive lines of the F/A-18D. Currently, the 6 active duty F/A-18D units are VMFA (AW)-121 (Green Knights), 224 (Fighting Bengals), 225 (Vikings), 242 (Batmen), 332 (Moonlighters) and 533 (Hawks).

bulge at the top that carries much of the aircraft's internal fuel. As is the case with most aircraft that operate on US Navy carriers, the Hornets wings contain a fold which minimizes the amount of footprint the jet occupies.

The Hornet derives its power from its twin General Electric F404-GE-400 afterburning engines rated at 16,000 pounds of thrust each. The Hornet was never meant for very high speed flight, and the engines along with the intake design afford solid performance although it isn't blistering.

The Hornets twin vertical tails are located forward of the engines exhaust nozzles and contain a variety of antenna (both ECM and RWR) on slightly bulged fairings above the split rudder. The Hornet while at rest appears to almost squat down atop its massive main landing gar assemblies under the main fuselage. The demands placed on the airframe and landing gear during continuous carrier landings is extreme and this has always been one of the design differences between Air Force and Navy aircraft.The Hornets undercarriage is large and sturdy in appearance. The two initial operational versions of the Hornet were the single seat A and two seat B models. The two seater served strictly as a training aircraft.

Table 1 - F/A-18 Current Operational Variants

F/A-18A - Base model single seat.
F/A-18B - Two seat version of A model.
F/A-18C - Improved single seat version.
F/A-18D - Marine Corps dedicated night attack aircraft.

The improved C variant of the Hornet first flew in September of 1987 and contained a number of key enhancements, most of which were avionics related. The C model is essentially the same from the outside as the earlier A variant. The only notable differences are the addition of several small antennas that are part of the AN/ALQ-126 electronic counter measures system and AN/ALR-67 radar warning receiver located in the front of the aircraft. The A model was experiencing excessive fatigue in the twin tails due to the vortices created from the wings LEX's. As a result, the rudders were cracking prematurely. The initial fix was made which involved the use of a small metal support at the base of the inside portion of the

The beautiful Delta at rest on the Yuma ramp. Because of it's all weather capability, the F/A-18D units are designated VMFA (AW).

Major J. "Homer" Hannay (pilot) and Captain H.D. "Shades" Oakley (weapons sensors officer) in 'Attic 51' which is carrying inert 1,000 pound Mark 83 bombs on inboard wing stations. Dash 2, call sign 'Attic 52', is carrying a combination of AGM-65 Maverick and AGM-88 HARM missiles.

505
VMFA AW-224

VMFA (AW) - 224 'Fighting Bengals' insignia.

Claws of the Cat - This section of heavily armed F/A-18D's with the 'Fighting Bengals' of VMFA (AW) -224 display the many weapons options available to the Night Strike Hornet. Major Stephen "Space" Pace (pilot) and Lt. Gregory "Gomez" Smith (WSO) in the lead aircraft 'Bengal 13' watch as their wingman, 'Bengal 14' flown by Captain Brian "T-Bone" Beckwith (pilot) and Major James "Rodney" O'Hagen (WSO) pitch away.

VMFA (AW) - 332 'Moonlighter' insignia.

This 'Green Knights' Hornet taxis in after a mission. The Marines operate their inventory of F/A-18D's from three locations - MCAS El Toro which houses the sole F/A-18 training unit (VMFAT-101), and MCAS Beaufort and Miramar which contain 3 All Weather (AW) Delta squadrons each.

VMFA (AW)-533 'Hawks' F/A-18D. The D can act as a Forward Air Controller (Airborne)/Tactical Air Controller (Airborne) termed FAC(A)/TAC(A). During Operation Desert Storm, Marine F/A-18D's flew into target areas ahead of coalition strike aircraft to locate and identify high value targets.

lower rudder where it meets the fuselage. The final fix which was installed in every variant consisted of the LEX Fence (a small foot long piece of metal located forward of the wing) which disrupts the airflow before it reaches the vertical tails thereby reducing the overall stress to the surface. The main radar system, the Hughes APG-65 was upgraded to the newer APG-73 in late model C and D variants.

F/A-18D - The Night Stalker

Even as Marine fighter squadrons were replacing their F-4 Phantoms with the single seat Hornets, they were still relying on the venerable Grumman A-6E Intruder to fill the night attack requirement. As the Intruder was at the end of its operational career, a replacement would be needed. The demanding low level, night attack mission is best suited for a two man crew with a dedicated officer controlling the navigation and attack and the pilot flying the aircraft. The Marines decided to modify the two seat Hornet with a dedicated night attack avionics capability and called it the F/A-18D or simply the Delta.

As mentioned above, the greatly enhanced APG-73 is at the heart of the F/A-18D's capabilities. The APG-73 incorporates upgrades to the target data processors, computer supply units and the receiver/exciter.

The Ford AN/AAS-38 Targeting Forward Looking Infra-Red (TFLIR) pod housed under the port engine intake allows the Hornet a day and night targeting capability via infra-red technology. When used with Night Vision Goggles (NVG), the Hornet crew can effectively operate in darkness, even at low altitudes. The cockpit displays had to be re-designed in order to not interfere with the NVG's that greatly magnify available light.

The Hughes AN/AAR-50 Thermal Imaging Navigation System (TINS) consists of a pod mounted under the starboard engine intake. The cockpit

Marine Hornet Driver — First to Fight, Last to Leave.

Displaying a pristine new paint job, a section of 'Warlord' Hornets in a knife edge turn over the waters outside their home base at MCAS Beaufort, South Carolina.

Colonel Keith Stalder (MAWTS-1 Commanding Officer) at the controls of 'LATCH 436'.

This view of a VMFA-451 'Warlords' F/A-18 is definitely not the one an enemy fighter pilot wants in his rearview mirror.

in the rear seat of the D model was redesigned and include two DDI's and one Multi-Purpose Color Display (MPCD) displays with a digital moving map display that presents a wealth of information. The flight controls in the rear seat were removed and replaced with two hand controllers that allow the WSO to interface with the navigation, sensors and weapons systems easily.

The more capable avionics also increased the Hornets weapons variety with the AGM-65 Maverick anti-armor missile and the AIM-120 Advanced Medium Range Air to Air Missile (AMRAAM). The C and D variants also included a more powerful set of engines with the upgraded General Electric F-404-GE-402 Enhanced Performance Engines (EPE) that produced an additional fifteen percent of thrust.

Hornets Sting

The Hornet is truly a multi-role aircraft in that it can conduct a wide variety of both air to ground and air to air missions as detailed within the Six Functions of Marine Air. These include, basic close air support, deep strike interdiction, anti-armor, anti-personnel, Suppression of Enemy Air Defenses (SEAD) as well as air superiority . The Hornets multi-role capability allows it to engage and defeat adversary's enroute to target with Beyond Visual Range (BVR) missiles without having to unload its air to ground ordnance first.

Table 2 - Primary F/A-18 C/D Weapons Capability

Air to Ground

M61A1 20 mm cannon with 578 rounds
AGM-65 Maverick (laser and infra-red)
AGM-88 HARM
AGM-62 Walleye
AGM-84 Harpoon/E SLAM
GBU 10/12/16/24 Paveway Laser Guided Bombs
Mark 82/83/84 General Purpose Bombs
CBU-55 Fuel Air Explosive
Mark 7 Cluster Bomb Unit
2.75 inch and 5 inch Rockets
TALD - Tactical Air Launched Decoy

Rear cockpit of the F/A-18D and 'the office' for the Weapons Sensors Officer or (WSO). As a designated Naval Flight Officer, the WSO manages the weapons systems (both offensive and defensive). The 3 multi-purpose color displays provide a wealth of information to the WSO in a concise manner.

Air to Air Loadout

Location	Number of Missiles
(2) Wingtip Stations	(2) AIM-9 with (1) missile on each rail
(2) Outboard Wing Stations	(4) AIM-9 or (4) AIM-120 or (2) AIM-7
(2) Inboard Wing Stations	(4) AIM-120 or (2) AIM-7
(2) Nacelle Fuselage	(2) AIM-120 or (2) AIM-7

Note: The AIM-9 Sidewinder is a short range infra-red heat seeking missile. Both the AIM-7 Sparrow and the more advanced AIM-120 are beyond visual range radar guided missiles.

Foreign Hornets

The F/A-18 has done reasonably well in the foreign market and equips the Air Forces of eight allied countries. The largest user is Canada, followed by Australia and Spain, all of which operate the A and B variant. The Finnish Air Force utilize the C and D variants having taken receipt of their first D model in April of 1995. Kuwait, Malaysia and Switzerland also operate the C and D variants.

Table 3 - Foreign F/A-18 Operators

Country	Total	Quantity/Variants
Australia	75	(60) F/A-18A, (15) F/A-18B
Canada	138	(98) F/A-18A, (40) F/A-18B
Finland	64	(57) F/A-18C, (7) F/A-18D
Kuwait	40	(32) F/A-18C, (8) F/A-18D
Malaysia	8	(8) F/A-18D
Spain	72	(57) F/A-18A, (18) F/A-18B
Switzerland	34	(26) F/A-18C, (8) F/A-18D
Thailand	8	(4) F/A-18C, (4) F/A-18D

Table 4 - F/A -18C Specifications

Height	15ft., 3 1/2in.
Length	56ft.
Wingspan	37ft., 6in.
Weights:	
Empty	23,050 lbs.
Gross	49,224 lbs.
Maximum Speed	1,190 mph
Combat Radius	660 miles

Top down view of a "Moonlighter" F/A-18D lofting over a washed out Atlantic Ocean.

14

Harrier: The AV-8B

Head on view of a Harrier without ordnance. The Harrier has up to 7 external store stations for air to air and air to ground ordnance.

The McDonnell Douglas AV-8B Harrier II is unique among American military aircraft for two reasons. The AV-8B remains the only vertical/short take off and landing (V/STOL) aircraft in active status (the new Bell/Boeing V-22 Osprey will be the second once it enters service). This amazing capability has earned the Harrier the alternate designation in certain circles as the 'jump jet'. The second, and perhaps more interesting aspect of the Harrier is that it is the only aircraft currently operating within Americas armed forces that was at first developed abroad.

Today, the Harrier is *the* Marine Corps close air support aircraft equipping all VMA attack squadrons. The Harriers ability to deploy with composite HMM (REIN) squadrons as part of a Marine Expeditionary Unit (MEU) is critical. Serving aboard amphibious assault ships, the multi-role Harrier provides MEU commanders with a highly effective platform in which to assist ground forces. While not designed as an air combat fighter, the Harrier can credibly take care of itself with its mix of AIM-9 Sidewinders and the 25mm cannon.

Origins

The Harrier was developed initially in 1960 by the British aerospace firm Hawker Siddeley (now known as British Aerospace) under the nondescript designation P.1127. At the time, the only group within the United States that was working on a vertical takeoff aircraft was NASA with the Bell X-14 aircraft. Much of the flight testing and other related technical information on this was passed on by NASA to Hawker Siddeley. The P.1127 remained essentially a NATO sponsored effort, with Germany also involved and the design first took to the air in November of 1960.

After initial testing was conducted, a total of nine airframes were produced and delivered to an RAF squadron with pilots from the RAF and the Luftwaffe. In addition, the US Navy, Army and Air Force were also involved. Throughout 1964, the aircraft was tested rigorously under the US designation of the XV-6A Kestrel at Edwards Air Force Base, California. After some initial trouble in funding and some changes to the P.1127 design, the first production orders of the aircraft (now designated Harrier GR.Mk1) were completed in mid 1969 with the jet entering service with the Royal Air Force only.

The Harrier that entered service initially differed from the original P.1127 most notably in the improvement in design of the wing itself. The aircraft was constructed primarily of titanium and incorporated the Martin-Baker Mk 9 zero-zero ejection seat and was powered by the Pegasus 6 engine delivering 19,000 pounds of thrust through the four underbody rotating exhaust nozzles.

Marine Harrier

The U.S. Marine Corps expressed strong interest in the design as a close air support aircraft replacing the A-4 Skyhawk in the light attack role. Since so much of the emphasis on Marine aviation is placed on the support of

The McDonnell Douglas AV-8B Harrier II. During the Gulf War, the Harrier II was the first tactical strike aircraft deployed by the Corps. As many as 86 Harriers took part in the conflict from 3 squadrons, plus a 6 plane detachment that were shore based at various locations. A single squadron operated from a seaborne platform.

Dash 2 watches as his flight leader begins his roll in on a target.

Underneath view of a heavily loaded AV-8B carrying (4) inert Mark 82 500 pound bombs. The cement filled bombs will not detonate on impact, but they have the same ballistic qualities of live ordnance, so accuracy doesn't suffer.

'Tomcat 02' undergoing final pre-flight checks before taxiing out for takeoff. The unit is one of 4 located at MCAS Yuma with MAG-13.

Captain M.C. Brewster, MAWTS-1 AV-8B instructor in this 'Black Sheep' Harrier.

ground troops, the close air support (CAS) mission is considered among the most vital roles Marine aviators fulfill. To be effective in this demanding role, an aircraft needs to be rugged, maneuverable and capable of deploying sufficient quantities of ordnance in a single mission to support friendly forces. Perhaps most important of all however, a CAS aircraft must be able to spend as much time over the battlefield as possible to quickly come to the aid of ground forces in trouble.

The Harriers unique ability to operate from small, austere airfields close to the battlefield or from mobile amphibious ships located close to a developing beachhead is key to its success. Unlike traditional fixed wing assets within the air forces of other branches of the US military, the Harrier does not require long runways and airfields which usually are placed safely out of the range of enemy aircraft. The forward operating airfields that the Harrier utilizes can be extremely small without the extensive support facilities needed for most modern jet airbases. This allows the Harrier to operate very close to the battle lines thereby minimizing the time to transit to and from an air station. This translates into more time over the troops and greater responsiveness.

After reviewing the aircraft's performance at the 1968 Farnborough air show, initial orders for the Corps were placed in 1969 and contracts were issued totaling 102 single seat AV-8A and eight of the two seat TAV-8A models. It was intended initially that the aircraft for the Corps would be co-produced in the United States by McDonnell Douglas under agreement with Hawker Siddeley, however the small initial orders prevented this from occurring with the A variant.

The Second Generation

It didn't take long for both the manufacturers (primarily McDonnell Douglas with British Aerospace as a subcontractor) and the Corps to look beyond the initial A variant towards a more improved version and by the mid-1970's a new design was offered. The primary thrust of the improvements were along the lines of lowering the aircraft's weight while increasing its payload, combat radius, avionics and flying qualities.

Towards this end, the designers radically altered the Harriers wing design by increasing its wingspan and area while slightly decreasing its sweep angle. The greatest single modification to the wing relates to its actual makeup in that the AV-8B incorporates a greater amount of composite material in the wings structure which is formed by treating carbon fiber with epoxy resin. The fiber which comes in a cloth form is cut and shaped, and then subjected to intense heat and pressure during the manufacturing cycle. The result is a material which is extremely strong, yet lightweight. Up to twenty-six percent of the Harriers structural weight is composite material. In addition to being lighter, these new materials are more wear resistant and have a longer structural life than the metal parts used previously.

VMA-542 pilot Captain Chuck "Bags" Bagnato deploys a flare in spectacular style. The Harrier is unique in that it has flare dispensers on the top and bottom of the fuselage. As Captain Bagnato explains "we deploy flares and chaff depending on the threat we are facing. If the element of surpise is lost, we will pop flares during the ingress to the target, and egress. If we are not detected, then deploying flares inbound to the target would give us away, so they are used to protect us from infra-red missiles on our way out of the target area."

Another major improvement was also in the form of the addition of Leading Edge Root Extensions (LERX's) that greatly enhanced the aircraft's high angle of attack and turning capabilities. This was a development of the British testing on the impact of increasing the wings surface area.

In addition to the improvements in performance as a result of the wing redesign, other Lift Improvement Devices (LIDS) were added to the Bravo model. Under the fuselage a retractable transverse dam was fitted which along with the LIDS strakes which acts to trap engine exhaust and utilize it for additional thrust.

The cockpit and avionics of the Harrier has been improved also within the AV-8B. The integrated Hands On Throttle And Stick (HOTAS) system along with the Heads Up Display (HUD) help reduce the pilots workload, especially in the demanding low altitude, night flying regime. An improved Inertial Navigation System (INS) from Litton Industries was added. Also included was the Hughes ASB-19 Angle Rate Bombing Set which affords a higher degree of accuracy in the air to ground mission. The ejection seat was changed and actually raised a bit in order to enhance the pilots over-the-shoulder visibility.

Many other important improvements were made including the use of a more powerful engine, the Rolls Royce (which bought Pegasus) F402-RR-406 engine delivering over 21,000 pounds of thrust. The armament of the Harrier was broadened significantly with the support of the Hughes AGM-65 Maverick weapon along with Rockeye cluster bombs, Paveway precision munitions, the AIM-9M Sidewinder and the replacement of the original British ADEN cannon with the more advanced 25mm General Electric GAU-12 cannon. The cannon consists of two pods with the left one being the actual gun itself, and the right one serving as the storage container for the 300 rounds of ammunition.

Implications of the significant design improvements to the wing also impacted the weapons capability as the number of underwing hardpoints grew from four to six. In addition, the Harrier II contains one underbody hardpoint for the ALQ-164 DECM pod.

Table 1- AV-8A/B Harrier Users

United States	**Marine Corps.**
England	**Royal Air Force and Navy**
India	**Navy**
Spain	**(Navy) Arma Aerea de la Armada**
Italy	**(Navy) Aviazione per la Marina**

Night Attack Harrier

The 'Night Attack' Harrier is designed to operate under the cover of darkness through the use of the navigation FLIR, Night Vision Goggle (NVG) compatible lighting and the NVG's themselves. The enhancements to the air to ground weapons systems includes the Infra-Red AGM-65F Maverick

The only squadron that possesses the two seat TAV-8B is VMAT-203 based at MCAS Cherry Point, North Carolina. In vertical flight, the (4) exhaust nozzles are positioned downward as is evident in this photo.

which provides an independent means for the Harrier pilot to locate and engage high value hardened targets including enemy armor.

The Harriers survivability was enhanced with the increase of flare and chaff threefold with the rear fuselage upward mounted dispensers. The Night Attack is different than the basic AV-8B II in that it has the more powerful Rolls-Royce Pegasus engine designated F402-44-408. The Harrier still retains its four rotating nozzles (two on each side of the fuselage) which direct engine thrust and facilitate V/STOL flight. The 408 version of the Pegasus engine delivers 23,400 pounds of thrust.

The Radar Bird

The latest variant of the Harrier is a result of a multi-national collaboration between the United States, Italy and Spain. In September 1990, the three countries signed a memorandum of understanding that detailed the integration of the new radar system into the AV-8B.

The AV-8B Harrier II Plus or Radar Bird variant contains the new Hughes APG-65 radar providing an enhanced air to air self protection capability in addition to all the advantages of the Night Attack variant. The radar system is the same one used in the F/A-18 Hornet and is an all

Captain James 'Hoser' Blackburn watches as his wing, Captain Mike 'Calvin' Hobbs roll in over the Quantico range. The AV-8B Harrier's primary mission is close air support with general purpose bombs (on these aircraft), AGM-65 Maverick missiles and rockets.

VMA-231 'Ace of Spades' Harrier at rest on the static line at MCAS Yuma. The unit is the oldest squadron in the Marine Corps and is assigned to MAG-14 at MCAS Cherry Point, the other main facility for the AV-8B.

'Vault 401' on the prowl just after sunrise. 'Vault' is the usual call sign for Harrier flights attached to the WTI course.

weather, multi-mode sensor which contains a programmable signal processor. This high speed computer system supports a much wider variety of operating modes and weapons types. The APG-65 is resistant to ECM jamming and can detect and track airborne targets at all altitudes. The system also supports the future use of beyond visual range weapons such as the AIM-120 Advanced Medium Range Air to Air Missile (AMRAAM).

In navigation and air to ground modes, the APG-65 provides long range surface mapping which improves the target identification, location and attack capability of the AV-8B. The radar antenna and receivers for the II Plus are located in the nose which extends an additional seventeen inches than that of the regular AV-8B. Since weight balance is especially critical to Vertical/Short Take Off and Landing (V/STOL) aircraft, the majority of the APG-65's systems components are located aft of the cockpit throughout the fuselage.

Table 2 - The AV-8B Harrier II Plus Specifications

Length	**47 3/4 ft.**
Height	**11 1/2 ft.**
Wingspan	**30 1/3 ft.**
Wingarea	**238 sq.ft.**
Weights:	
Gross Takeoff	**31,000 lbs.**
Empty	**14,568 lbs.**
Maximum Speed	**660 mph**

Close up of the forward starboard exhaust nozzle and intake of this VMA-211 'Wake Island Avenger' AV-8B. Tradition runs deep within Marine Air as well as the Ground Combat Element. On December 8, 1941, Japanese forces attacked a small force of less than 500 Marines of the 1st Defense Battalion and VMF-211 fighter squadron on Wake Island. For the next several weeks the Marines fought off the Japanese, until superior forces and shortages of equipment necessitated their surrender. The squadron was later renamed so as to ensure that their sacrifice and heroism is not forgotten.

Section of Harriers in the in-trail formation over the flat expanse of the Lechuguilla Desert.

Close Air Support is *the* Harriers' purpose in life. This AV-8B is prepared for this role by sporting a pair of devastating AGM-65 Maverick anti-armor missiles on the inside wing pylons. The AGM-65 Maverick missile can destroy enemy armor with pinpoint accuracy. The 630 pound missile uses a 300 pound blast penetration warhead to penetrate the thickest armor plating. The Maverick comes in three variants, electro-optical, infra-red or laser guided.

VMA-223 pilot rolls his AV-8B pitches 90 degrees in order to display the underside of the Harrier for the camera.

Insignia of 'The Great American Bulldogs' of VMA-223.

The "Tigers" of VMA-542 now fly the advanced AV-8B Harrier II Plus. The unit dates back to March, 1944 when the squadron was commissioned as Marine Night Fighter Squadron (VMF (N)-542. The unit distinguished itself during the campaign for Okinawa with several pilots becoming the first night fighter aces. The "Tigers" would see combat in the Korean, Vietnam and Gulf wars. The unit deployed to Bahrain in support of Operation Desert Shield and within 12 hours were flying combat alert missions. Throughout the 42 days of the conflict, the "Tigers" flew more than 1,000 combat sorties.

AV-8B Division instructor Captain T.G. Bogard at the controls of this Harrier. This close up view clearly displays the large canopy and intakes of the Harrier. Underneath the aircraft's fuselage is the dual pod Avenger cannon with an ECM pod on the centerline station.

15

Prowler: The EA-6B

VMAQ-3 'Moondog' EA-6B banks away from the Chocolate Mountain range and Salton Sea.

Close up view of the cockpits of the Prowler. The pilot sits in the left front seat, with ECMO1 next to him. ECMO's 2 and 3 occupy the seats directly aft.

The Marines employ a dedicated aircraft to wage the full spectrum of electronic warfare which is defined within official MAWTS-1 publications as *"Military action involving the use of electromagnetic energy to determine, reduce, exploit or prevent hostile use of the electromagnetic spectrum and action which retains friendly use of the electromagnetic spectrum'*. In today's modern high technology battlefield, control of the electronic medium is essential to the Marine Aviation Combat Elements ability to fulfill its commitment to the MAGTF. As such, it is a critical part of the Six Functions of Marine Air.

As was made apparent during the Gulf War, the identification and destruction of an enemies command, control and communications (C3) infrastructure is a prerequisite in waging a successful air campaign - the primary goal of which is to achieve complete air superiority. To successfully execute ground combat operations, Marine Air must be able to conduct successful close air support (CAS) and assault support missions. Therefore, air superiority over the battlefield is essential. As capable as the AV-8B, AH-1W and other CAS assets may be, they weren't designed to fight 4th generation former Soviet Union fighter aircraft.

For Marine Air to provide effective CAS, an opponents ability to electronically identify threats and direct his ground and air based anti-air forces against them, must be sufficiently diminished. This includes of course his fighter/attack aircraft and anti-air defense systems.

The aircraft the Marines use to fill this requirement is the Northrop/Grumman EA-6B Prowler. The huge, four man Prowler is a highly capable electronics countermeasures variant of the venerable Northrop/Grumman A-6 Intruder attack jet. The proven EA-6B has taken to the skies over Iraq and Bosnia in recent years to protect American and allied aircraft from prying electronic eyes. With the addition of the devastating AGM-88 High

AGM-88 HARM missile on the Prowler. The weapon of choice for the SEAD role.

Former VMAQ-4 Executive Officer, Lt. Colonel Dwight Motz at the controls of 'Seahawk 5' as it glides over a solid cloud deck.

The distinctive nose section of the Prowler with its fixed refueling probe.

VMAQ-4 Prowlers with their tailhooks down as a reminder that they can, and often do deploy aboard US Navy aircraft carriers.

speed Anti-Radar Missile (HARM), the Prowler can seek out and destroy an opponents surface to air defense system affording it a viable offensive capability.

Origins

The relationship between the US Marine Corps and the Grumman Corporations EA-6B Prowler is a long and successful one. While the Marines operate a smaller number of operational EA-6B squadrons than the Navy, four in total, they were actually responsible for its creation, albeit somewhat indirectly.

In the late 1950's the Marines saw a need to replace its aging fleet of Douglas EF-10 Skynights in the electronics reconnaissance mission. The aircraft that the Marines decided upon was a modified version of their primary attack jet at the time, the Grumman A-6 Intruder. The new variant, initially designated as the A2F-1Q soon came to be known as the 'Electric 6' due to its mission profile and enhanced avionics package. The aircraft jointly developed with Grumman was initially test flown in 1963 and as a variant of the A-6, was logically designated as the EA-6A.

While the Marines began successfully employing the EA-6A, the Navy was still using the EKA-3B Skywarrior to fulfill its electronic intelligence and reconnaissance requirements. This version of the venerable 'Whale' was in dire need of an upgrade.

The EA-6A remained a two man aircraft, although it differed from the A-6 primarily due to the addition of specialized mission related avionics and antennas. The now familiar 'football' shaped fairing atop the rudder housed a myriad of antenna attached to the Bunker Ramo ALQ-86 receiver/surveillance system. The primary electronic countermeasures, (ECM) gear, i.e. communications jammers and chaff dispensers were contained in underwing pods. A total of twenty-seven EA-6A's were made available and summarily dispatched to serve in the Vietnam conflict in composite squadrons along with RF-4B Phantoms. Subsequently all EA-6A's were consolidated into a single operating unit called the Playboys of VMAQ-2, and later as part of Reserve unit VMAQ-4. As the Marines upgraded to the Prowler their inventory of EA-6A's were given to the Navy and served in several reserve VAQ units until several years ago.

In the autumn of 1966 Grumman developed at the Navy's request, a completely new version of the EA-6A, designated the EA-6B. Testing of this new prototype was lengthy and it was not until 1972 that the aircraft ready and was officially named the Prowler. The Prowler owes a great deal to its ancestor, the Intruder, and shares a great many structural components with it. Beyond the physical similarities however, it is a vastly different airplane.

CB
160786
MARINES

Major Rick "Spike" Boyer (pilot), Major James "Govna" Griffin (ECMO 1) and Captain Dean "Wedge" Ebert (ECMO 2) crew 'Banshee 01' which is followed by Captain Marshall "Hooker" Denney (pilot), Captain Andrew "Mongo" East (ECMO 1) and Captain David "Fruitbat" Perrin (ECMO 3) in 'Banshee 04'.

Close up view of the top of the EA-6B, as seen from the boom operators position of a Pennsylvania Air National Guard KC-135E

Pair of 'Screaming Banshee' Prowlers captured in a section turn. The EA-6B has five hardpoints under the wings and fuselage which can carry a combination of ALQ-99 pods, fuel tanks, and AGM-88 HARM missiles. Note the low and high visibility paint schemes of the unit logo atop the tail.

At rest on the MCAS Yuma ramp.

The Corps dedicated Electronic Warrior is the Northrop/Grumman EA-6B Prowler. The Marines operate a total of 20 Prowlers within 4 active duty squadrons.

Enter the Prowler

The Prowler is operated by a crew of four with the pilot seated in the left front cockpit responsible for flying the aircraft. Seated to his right in the right front cockpit is the lead electronics countermeasures officer, called ECMO 1 for short. ECMO 1 is primarily responsible for handling all radio communication and radar equipment. In addition, ECMO 1 controls the communications jamming system and all defensive electronic counter measures (DECM) systems. Seated in the rear cockpits are ECMO's 2 and 3 who operate the heart and soul of the Prowler, the Eaton Corporations (AIL division) ALQ-99 Tactical Jamming System, or simply TJS. The addition of the two ECMO's necessitated the lengthening of the front fuselage by four and one half feet with each crewmember seated in a Martin Baker GRUEA-7 ejection seat. In reality it's the ALQ-99 TJS with the extra two crewmembers that really makes the Prowler the effective electronic warfare platform that it is today. The crew sits high in their ejection seats which affords them outstanding visibility forward, above and to the side from the front. The ECMO's seated in back have very limited forward visibility. The canopy is large and has a gold tint which is due to a protective layer on the glass which serves to shield the crew from the radar's powerful emissions.

The ALQ-99 is a state of the art electronics countermeasures system that consists of both internal and externally housed components. The sheer complexity of the system is what mandates the two additional operators. The TJS displays and controls are located in the cockpits of ECMO's 2 and 3. The TJS main jammers are carried in under-wing and under fuselage pods. Each of the pods contain jammers and a transmitter with a steerable antenna and track receiver which directs the transmitters. Each pod has a distinctive tiny propeller located in the front which is activated by the airstream created once airborne. This propeller drives a small turbine which provides all of the necessary electrical power needed to operate the pod. As was the case with the EA-6A, the other significant characteristic of the Prowler is the large fintip fairing sitting atop the rudder. This fairing contains system integration receivers, (SIR's). The SIR's handle different frequency bands and are part of the ALQ-99 package. The TJS is modular in that the number of pods can be matched to meet the size and scope of the electronic threat to be encountered.

Typically, three pods are carried, one on the centerline under fuselage station and two on the wing hardpoints. The additional wing points can be used to carry fuel tanks or AGM-88 missiles. Standing between the jamming pods and system antennas is the main on board computer which processes all relevant signal and electronics data.

Carrying this myriad of advanced avionics, the Prowler if not visually appealing is certainly menacing in appearance. Like the A-6 the Prowler has a large nose mounted refueling probe that also includes antennas for

Quartet of VMAQ-4 Prowlers toting HARM's.

VHF communications and the defensive counter measures system. UHF and Tacan antennas also protrude from the Prowlers fuselage along with chaff and flare dispensers which all add to the Prowlers unique appearance. While the Prowler is not as maneuverable as the fighters and attack aircraft it protects, its performance is still very good. The airframe carrying a full load out of pods and tanks has a 5g limit on the structure itself.

Variants of the Prowler

Since this base model, there have been several upgrades which have been delineated into individual variants. Unlike most other military aircraft programs, the sequential letter suffix, EA-6B has remained unchanged. In order of introduction, the variants have been: Expanded Capability (EXCAP), Improved Capability 1 (ICAP 1), and Improved Capability 2 (ICAP 2).

The upgrades have been primarily internal and there is little difference in the Prowlers outward appearance from one variant to the next. The main differences have been within the avionics and engine systems. The ALQ-99 TJS has seen dramatic increases in the capabilities of its frequency band range, main onboard computer processing speed and memory size. The original engine shared with the A-6 was insufficient for the Prowler as the EA-6B is a heavier aircraft by virtue of its TJS pods and extra crewman. The engine system has been upgraded to the Pratt & Whitney J52-P-408 delivering increased power.

Within the ICAP 1 variant a vastly improved Deception Countermeasures systems was introduced which also includes one of the few physical differences between variants. The DECM system has a small antenna housed at the base of the refueling probe along with a small 'beer can' type protrusion at the back of the tail. Also the ICAP 1 supports the Automated Carrier Landing System, ACLS. Within the ICAPS 2 upgrade the Suppression of Enemy Defenses, or SEAD role was added with the inclusion of the AGM-88 HARM anti-radiation missile. This represents a significant addition to the Prowlers capability, turning the aircraft into an offensive weapons system capable of destroying enemy SAM sites. The HARM is a powerful 800 pound missile that is not only capable of destroying land based SAM sites, but can also be used in the anti-shipping role. The HARM is typically mounted on a wing mounted LAU-118 launch rail and is deployed in four variants differentiated primarily by improvements in its guidance electronics.

Marine Prowlers

The Prowler community within the Corps has grown significantly from the single active duty unit, VMAQ-2, previously known as the Playboys, but

01

Few military units have as intimidating a logo as the skull motif of VMAQ-1 on the tail of 'Banshee 01'. This, along with the lethal AGM-88 HARM missile on the left outboard wing pylon, makes the Prowler a fearsome sight.

Pristine Prowler displaying brand new paint scheme, sans squadron markings.

VMAQ-1 Screaming Banshee unit patch.

VMAQ-1 Unit insignia TAIRNGREACHT BAS - Death Fortold

now known as the Panthers. When they were the sole unit operating the Prowler, the Playboys would deploy three detachments identified by the letters X, Y and Z to fill overseas obligations. These detachments were the equivalent of sister Navy VAQ squadrons, usually with five aircraft and a total of 160 personnel assigned. In the early 1990's the Marine Corps EA-6B's were segmented into three active duty units with the addition of VMAQ-1 and 3. Later, the Seahawks of VMAQ-4 were added.

Table 1 - Marine EA-6B Prowler Units

VMAQ-1 Screaming Banshees	**VMAQ-2 Panthers**
VMAQ-3 Moondogs	**VMAQ-4 Seahawks**

Currently the Marines have a total of twenty Prowlers segmented within the four squadrons, all of which are home based at MCAS Cherry Point, North Carolina. On a rotating basis individual units will deploy to a forward area overseas under the Marines Unit Deployment Program, UDP. Most often, this will be to MCAS Iwakuni, Japan joining the 1st MAW. The entire Prowler community is under the command of the 2nd MAW, MAG-14.

Table 2 - EA-6B Prowler Specifications:

Maximum Speed	**530 knots**
Cruise Speed	**420 knots**
Max Range	
(Internal Fuel)	**1,110 miles**
Dimensions:	
Wingspan	**53 ft.**
Length	**59 ft.**
Height	**16 ft., 8 in.**
Weights:	
Empty	**34,200 lbs.**
Max	**61,500 lbs.**

16

Battleherk:
The KC-130 Hercules

VMGR-252 Herk glides across a tranquil sky.

By far the largest aircraft operated within Marine Corps Air Wings is the Lockheed KC-130 Hercules, or BattleHerk as the Marines refer to it. The Marines man their KC-130's with a crew of six - pilot, co-pilot, flight engineer, navigator up front inside the spacious cockpit, and a loadmaster and mechanic seated in back. The loadmaster and mechanic also are responsible for the activities related to passenger and material handling. This also includes the role of lookout on each of the two side rear windows during the actual aerial refueling operations.

The basic C-130 shape has changed relatively little over the many years the aircraft has been in operation. Its distinctive nose contains the radar system and protrudes slightly. As mentioned above, the cockpit is spacious and the visibility forward, up and to the side is quite good by virtue of the many segmented glass panels. A bulkhead separates the crew station from the main cargo area and the aft section of the aircraft.

While not comparable in size to the USAF's large C-17, C-141 and C-5A transport aircraft, the cargo area of the Hercules is spacious. Running the length of the cabins floor are rollers which facilitate the movement of cargo in and out of the aircraft. For strictly refueling missions, the Marines place a large auxiliary fuel tank in the main cargo area to supplement the internal load.

Thanks for the gas guys! A section of Harriers depart this OTIS KC-130 after getting topped off.

Hercules pilots often practice tight formation flying which is as demanding, if not more so, than doing it in a fighter.

VMGR-452 insignia.

Tight in trail formation by a section of VMGR-452 'Yankee' KC-130's with the 4th MAW near their home base at Stewart Airport, Newburgh, NY.

The KC-130 is a crucial element in Marine Air's ability to project power. Without it, personnel, aircraft and material cannot be positioned as needed.

Initially, the US Air Force had developed the requirements which led to the development and selection of the original C-130 Hercules in the mid 1950's. A formal requirements definition was issued by the Air Force in the spring of 1951 for a medium lift transport that could effectively operate from rough surfaces and less than ideal runways. The aircraft would primarily be a troop and material transport platform. Several major vendors responded with Lockheed's design being selected the winner. The first production model was first flown in 1955 and began flying in operational Air Force squadrons a year later.

The Navy was actually next to utilize the aircraft for operations in the unforgiving Arctic area. The aircraft, LC-130/C-130B was outfitted with skis. By the late 1950's, the Marine Corps saw in the C-130 a viable platform

This Hercules is longer than the typical KC-130 and is referred to as the 'stretch model'. In addition to a longer fuselage, it includes cockpit bunks that could handle extra crew members for long flights.

Battleherk prepares to start engines.

'Yankee' KC-130's in close formation. In addition to aerial refueling, the Battleherk delivers material and personnel anywhere on the globe.

2nd MAW Herk in action refueling a section of VMA-223 A-8B's east of Cherry Point.

from which to meet their needs for in-flight refueling. By 1957, a pair of USAF C-130A's were reconfigured and tested successfully in this role. This led to an initial procurement of forty six aircraft. The Hercules was fitted with under wing mounted fuel tanks that employed a hose and drogue setup with one on each wing.

The Hercules is powered by four Allison T56 engines fitted with the Hamilton-Standard four bladed propeller that push the aircraft up to speeds of over 250 miles per hour. The Hercules employs a large, straight wing which contains internal fuel cells and the two external fuel tanks with hose and drogue system. The KC-130 is surprisingly agile aircraft for its size.

OTIS Marines of VMGR-252 in action as Major Jim Kazin holds formation off the lead KC-130.

Cockpit of the KC-130.

Marine crews routinely take their Battleherks to very low altitudes during gut wrenching low level flights a mere two hundred feet above the ground.

Over the course of its thirty year career, the basic C-130 has fulfilled a myriad of tasks as is evident by the many modifications and variants the aircraft has had (see Table 1). The USAF has developed several unique applications for the aircraft which has led to separate variants. This is testament to the amazing versatility of the basic Lockheed design.

Table 1 - C-130 Primary Variants

Variant	User/Description
YC-130	Prototype
C-130A	Initial production version
AC-130A/F	USAF/Gunship
HC-130B	U.S. Coast Guard/Maritime Search and Rescue
C-130K	RAF/Transport, also known as C Mk.1
LC-130F	U.S. Navy/Support
KC-130 F/R/T	US Marine Corps/Refueler and Transport
MC-130E/H	USAF and ANG/Combat Search and Rescue
EC-130E/H	USAF/Command, Control and Communications Countermeasures

Several of the more interesting variants of the Hercules that have placed the aircraft in a far more offensive role are the AC-130 Spectre gunship, the MC and HC-130 Combat Search and Rescue (CSAR) and the EC-130 Electronic Warfare versions. In each variant, the basic aircraft has had highly specific, mission related improvements made to the basic design.

Table 2 - C-130 Warriors

Variant	Mission	Improvements
AC-130	Gunship	-(2) M61 20mm Vulcan cannons, (2) 7.62 miniguns, (2) 40mm cannons, AN/APS-42 radar, enhanced ECM avionics
EC-130	Electronic Warfare	-enhanced ECM and eavesdropping avionics
HC/MC-130	CSAR	-terrain following radar

Marine BattleHerk's

The Corps operates a total of sixty-eight KC-130's in three variants, the KC-130 F, R and T. Within the six functions of Marine aviation, the BattleHerk supports the critical role of Assault Support. The backbone of the Marines

895

The KC-130 Battleherk flown by VMGR-252 pilots Captain Ed "Mario" Grandinetti and Captain Charlie Miles.

VMGR-252 KC-130 flightline at MCAS Cherry Point. In addition to 252, Cherry Point is home to the Corps KC-130 training squadron VMGR(T)-253.

fixed wing transport and aerial refueling requirement is filled by the venerable Lockheed KC-130 Hercules. This workhorse of an aircraft is currently employed with the USAF, Navy, Coast Guard and Marine Corps as well as in the air forces of over fifty countries.

The first operational flights of the Marines KC-130F variant began in early 1960. By the early 1970's improved KC-130R models were ordered by the Corps. An additional ten KC-130T's were ordered in early 1983. Subsequent orders for this variant brought the total to twenty two.

Table 3 - Marine BattleHerk's

Unit/MAG	Variant	# of Aircraft	Status
VMGR-152/MAG-36	KC-130F/R	8/4	Active Duty
VMGR-252/MAG-14	KC-130F/R	8/4	Active Duty
VMGRT-253/MAG-14	KC-130F	8	Active Duty
VMGR-234/MAG-41	KC-130T	12	Reserve
VMGR-352/MAG-11	KC-130F/R	8/4	Active Duty
VMGR-452/MAG-49	KC-130T	12	Reserve

The Herk meets several essential requirements that are critical to Marine aviation's ability to support Marine ground forces. The first of which that of the tactical aerial refueler for both fixed and rotary wing assets. This capability allows Marine fighters, attack and electronic warfare assets, along with the CH-53 Stallion to project power further than would be possible on their own. It also enhances their ability to stay 'on station' near the area of operations that would need air support.

Captain Ron Domingue rolls this VMGR-252 Battleherk to display the maneuverability of the aircraft.

Refueling includes more than just air to air as far as the Marines are concerned. The KC-130 can provide Rapid Ground Refueling (RGR) for both helo's and AV-8B's at Forward Area Refueling Positions (FARPs) and forward road sites. MAWTS-1 documentation highlights the capability of the KC-130 to fly more than 200 nautical miles, land on a 4,000 foot highway or dirt strip and off-load over 45,000 pounds of fuel. This is an important capability in allowing Marines aircraft the ability to project power while operating very close to the battlefield. The KC-130 can fly into unprepared landing sites, supply the critical fuel requirements of assault support aircraft and then exit. This maximizes the ability of Marine aviation to support Marine ground forces for extended periods of time, when and where it's needed most. The KC-130 has several secondary missions including the transportation of critical material and personnel, Medevac, Search and Rescue and target area illumination with flares.

Table 4 - Specifications KC-130F

Wingspan	**132 ft., 7 in.**
Length	**97 ft., 9 in.**
Height	**38 ft., 3 in.**
Weights:	
Empty	**69,300 lbs.**
Max	**135,000 lbs.**
Range	**4,500+ miles**

Squadron insignia of VMGR-252.

17

Cobra: The AH-1W

The Cobra flown by Major S.R. Rudder AH-1W Division Head operating in the 2507S range.

Close up of the CH-46E nose and cockpit.

able tricycle landing gear system, one of which is located directly under the cockpit, with the two rear assemblies located under each of the two self sealing fuel tanks that jut from the lower rear fuselage. The rear of the CH-46 is lower than the front and the aircraft appears to squat backward, this has no doubt led to the more popular unofficial name of PHROG given to the CH-46. The CH-46 employs a fairly large rear door which troops can be deployed from.

The second variant that the Marines deployed was the CH-46D of which a total of over 270 examples were made available. The Delta model incorporated a more powerful General Electric T58-GE-10 turbo-shaft engine and cambered rotor blades.

The most current variant of the CH-46 found within Marine Air Wings is the E model. Again, the most significant enhancement was the use of a more powerful engine, the T58-GE-16. Other notable improvements included an emphasis on enhancing the aircraft's crash worthiness and survivability. The main rotors were again changed, this time glassfibre blades were utilized. When necessary, the CH-46 can pack a solid offensive punch with the addition of a fifty caliber machine guns mounted on each side of the front cabin.

Table 2 - CH-46E Specifications

Engines:	**Two 1,800 horsepower General Electric T58-GE-16 engines.**
Speed:	**166 mph maximum**
Weights:	
Empty	**11,585 lbs.**
Maximum	**24,300 lbs.**
Length:	**44 ft., 10 in.**
	84 ft., 4 in. (with rotors)
Height:	**16 ft., 8 1/2 in.**
Ceiling	**14,000 ft.**

CH-46E taxi's out from the hangars at MCAS Yuma toward the takeoff area.

Dust, heat and wind are all elements of Marine combat helicopter flight operations. This CH-46E gets it all on liftoff from one of the operating areas west of MCAS Yuma.

EG
3372
2
MARINES
EG

Depending on your perspective, this can be a welcome sight, or a fearsome one. For Marine troops awaiting extraction from the combat zone it's the former - for enemy troops awaiting attack, the latter.

CH-46E refuels at a Forward Area Refueling Point (FARP).

Late afternoon maintenance on the Yuma flightline.

Sea Knight in-flight outside MCAS New River.

Nice looking CH-46E with HMM-365 at rest on the New River flightline.

Former MAWTS-1 Assistant Operations Officer Captain Leo 'Killer' Kilgore holds this CH-46E in a hover with the Colorado River Wildlife Preserve in the background.

19

Huey: The UH-1N

UH-1N Huey operating near Pacatio Peak north of MCAS Yuma.

UH-1N from MCAS New River (home of MAG-26) operating off the North Carolina coast.

Perhaps one of the most versatile aircraft to serve within the Marine Corps is the Bell UH-1 Iroquois, also known as the Huey. The aircraft has been filling a variety of roles for the Corps since 1964, including command and control, assault support, close in fire support, observation, small unit special missions, general utility and medivac. It is probably the most widely used helicopter in the world, with more than 9,000 examples built over its long and distinguished career.

Origins

As was the case with the AH-1 Cobra, the Marine Corps filled a specific requirement within its rotary community with an aircraft first operated by the US Army. In March of 1962, the requirement for an assault support aircraft was detailed by the Corps. The aircraft chosen was very similar to the Army's UH-1B with the exception of certain minor changes in the areas of avionics and instruments and was designated as the UH-1E.

The aircraft used a single Lycoming T-53 engine which was rated at 1,100 shaft horsepower. A total of 192 UH-1E's were purchased along with twenty TH-1E's for training purposes for the Corps.

Updated Iroquois

The primary version of the aircraft in service with the Corps is the UH-1N variant. The most important distinction with this model is its Pratt and

Close up view of a heavily armed UH-1N taxiing out from MCAS Yuma. Note the large .50 caliber machine gun which allows the Huey to fulfill the assault support mission.

Trio of Huey's on a late afternoon aerial gunnery training hop during a WTI.

Section of UH-1N's cavorting off the North Carolina coast.

The Huey over the desert near Yuma.

Huey on approach to landing area near MCAS New River.

Whitney PT6T Twin Turbo engine. With the twin engines, the aircraft could operate from amphibious assault ships with a greater margin of safety in the case of a single engine failure.

The N was developed from the basic Bell Model 212 (Twin Two-Twelve) which was a joint initiative between the Canadian government, Bell Helicopters and Pratt & Whitney, Canada. This initiative sought to develop a twin turbine version of the Bell 205 (UH-1H).

The main advantage in this design was the increases safety that results from a dual engine variant. The PT6T turbo twin package included two turboshaft engines mounted side by side through a single gearbox. In addition to the increased reliability there was also a significant increase in thrust.

Another important attribute of the N is the specialized ASC-26 Communication Package. This includes one UHF and two VHF/FM radios and allows the Huey to fulfill the critical Airborne Command and Control mission. The Huey can pack a punch for assault support missions with the addition of a Defensive Armament Subsystems (DAS).

Busy UH-1 flightline during a WTI at Yuma.

Table 1 - DAS Armament Options

M-240 7.62mm machine gun
GAU-16 .50 caliber machine gun
GAU-17 7.62mm automatic gun
(2) 7 or 19 shot 2.75 inch rocket pods

Table 2 - UH-1N Specifications

Dimensions:	
Length	**57 ft.,3 in.**
Height	**14 ft., 4 in.**
Rotor Diameter	**48 ft.**
Max Speed	**126 mph**
Range	**248 miles**
Weights:	
Empty	**6,196 lbs.**
Max	**11,200 lbs.**

The Huey taxi's out for a hop.

Cockpit of the UH-1N as it chases a section of AH-1W Cobras near MCAS New River.

20

Stallion: The CH-53

An HMX-1 CH-53E silhouetted against a sun drenched river outside of Quantico, Virginia.

Certainly the most awe inspiring aircraft within the Marine Corps rotary community is the massive, Sikorsky CH-53 Stallion. Weighing in at similar levels to a fully loaded fixed wing fighter, the mammoth Stallion is the largest helicopter flown in the armed forces of the United States. The primary variant is the CH-53 ***E**cho*, although the older D model is flown by Reserve units. The multi-role Stallion is able to fulfill a variety of missions including Assault Support, Special Operations and Heavy Lift and Transport. Like the KC-130, the Stallion can fly to a FARP, land, and offload fuel for other rotary or fixed wing aircraft to utilize.

Origins

The requirements that led to the development of the Stallion date back to 1960's when the U.S. Navy began looking for a replacement for its CH-37 Mohave in the cargo transportation role. Initially designated as design S-65 by Sikorsky, the CH-53A twin engine aircraft was selected by the Navy as the winner of the HH(X) Helicopter Heavy Experimental competition in the summer of 1962. By 1966, the Marines began receiving the first of a total of 139 aircraft called the Sea Stallion. The A model performed admirably and also saw combat in Vietnam. For the Marines, the Stallion ushered in a new era in helicopter operations. The huge CH-53 was able to transport greater numbers of Marines than was possible with any previous helicopter. It also was able to carry heavier pieces of field artillery to critical areas of operation, thereby saving time and allowing field commanders to concentrate maximum firepower where needed. It also served extremely well in the aircraft recovery role during the conflict.

The CH-53A was upgraded with the more powerful T64-GE-413 engine and re-designated as the D model. In addition, the rotor blades on the Delta model were retractable that facilitated easier seaborne operations. The D variant also found use with the Navy in the vertical replenishment and transport roles as well as a new assignment as a dedicated Mine Sweeper. As an airborne mine countermeasure's platform, the newly designated MH-53D would deploy a large sled that it would drag along the surface and can clear an area of mines.

Table 1 - Variants of the CH-53

Variant	Operator	Name	Mission
CH-53A	US Marines	Stallion	Assault Transport
CH-53D	US Marines	Stallion	Assault Transport
VH-53D	US Marines	Stallion	VIP Transport (HMX-1)
CH-53E	US Marines	Super Stallion	Assault Transport
CH-53E	US Navy	Sea Stallion	Transport
RH-53D	US Navy	Sea Dragon	Mine Sweeping
MH-53E	US Navy	Sea Dragon	Mine Sweeping
MH-53J	USAF	Pave Low	Assault Transport for Special Forces

Above and next page (Top) A Stallion transporting a large cement slab slung underneath the fuselage outside of Yuma. This is used to practice the transport of heavy items like field artillery pieces.

The large interior cabin of the CH-53E.

Defensive air combat maneuvering (ACM) is a standard part of the CH-53 WTI and requires superb piloting skills. During the WTI course, CH-53 crews will fight against VMFT-401 F-5E's in order to improve lookout doctrine, crew coordination and ACM skills. The combination of low level maneuvering and skilled adversaries make for some very demanding flying.

Super Stallion

Based on their wealth of experience from the A and D models as well as previous testing, Sikorsky responded to the Navy's request for a three engine version of the Stallion in the early 1970's with the YCH-53E. This was based on the stated requirement to have the CH-53 lift 1.8 times its weight, or a downed aircraft. After initial flights in 1974, the first production aircraft entered service in 1978. The addition of the top mounted third engine was the first of several significant design changes between the A and D series and the E (which was also called the Super Stallion). Whereas the earlier variants employed a six bladed rotor, the Echo utilized a new seven bladed rotor.

Unlike the fixed refueling probe the early models had, the E had a retractable in-flight refueling probe. The aircraft was considerably bigger and more powerful than its predecessors and could thereby carry more troops and greater loads. One other minor change that discerns the A/D from the E is the canted tail assembly added to the E. The 53 Echoes used by the Navy, designated as the MH-53E, also included a vastly enlarged internal fuel capability with the addition of sponsons mounted on the fuselage.

For the Marine Corps, the E greatly enhanced the heavy lift capability of the rotary community. The Echo is able to carry up to 30,000 pounds of cargo internally or up to fifty combat ready Marines and up to 36,000 pounds utilizing an exterior sling mounted under the fuselage. This could include the recovery of downed aircraft and the transportation of ground equipment and weaponry. The latest addition to the Stallion comes in the form of a Forward Looking Infra-Red (FLIR) system that, when combined with Night Vision Goggles (NVG), affords the CH-53 crew with an effective night capability. The main FLIR sensor is housed on the forward port side of the aircraft's nose.

Table 2 - Marine Corps CH-53 Comparative Capabilities by Variant

Capabilities	Variant	
	CH-53A/D	CH-53E
External Load	20,000 lbs.	32,000 lbs.
Combat Troops	30	55
Aerial Refueling	no	yes
Shipboard Operations	no	yes
Engines	2	3
Rotor Blades	6	7
Rotor Blade/Tail Fold	no	yes

UNITED STATES MARINE CORPS

This immaculate CH-53E is assigned to HMX-1.

The massive CH-53 receives some post-flight maintenance at Yuma.

The CH-53 Echo.

The cockpit of the 53.

MAWTS-1 Executive Officer Lt. Colonel Love preparing to bring this 53 Echo (callsign Duel 164) in for a landing.

HMX-1 CH-53E over the woods outside Quantico on a clear autumn afternoon. One of the key differences between the 53D and this 53E, is the Echo's third engine located on the port side. It's highlighted in this photo by the flag that is painted on it.

Table 3 - CH-53E Specifications

Performance:	
Max	170 knots
Cruise	150 knots
Max rate of climb	2,500 feet per minute
Weights:	
Max gross	73,500 lbs.
Empty	33,373 lbs.
Height	28 ft., 4 in.
Length	99 ft., 5 in.
Main rotor diameter	79 ft.
Tail Rotor diameter	20 ft.

HMM-365 CH-53E at rest on the MCAS New River flightline. This aircraft would soon deploy with the squadron as part of the 26th MEU.

CH-53E on a low level near Yuma.

PART 5
Conclusions

HORNETS STING: This heavily armed Night Strike Hornet with VMFA (AW) - 224 sports three different weapons - the AIM-120 under the fuselage, the AGM-88 on the inboard wing pylons and the AGM-65 on the outboard wing pylons. Note the large canopy which offers superb visibility for both crewman, still an essential ingrediant to the success of a modern warplane. If this isn't enough, the jet is also carrying a pair of AIM-9's on the wingtips out of view.

21

The Future - Marine Aviation in the 21st Century

The ongoing downsizing within the American military establishment and the associated shrinking of the defense budget have posed significant challenges for the Marine Corps and its aviation element in particular. Again referring to the AVPLAN, *"the vision for the 21st century concentrates on ensuring the Aviation Combat Element (ACE) remains effective and responsive to MAGTF commanders across the spectrum of organizational capabilities as well as participating as equal partners with Navy squadrons through integration. To this end, the Marine Corps concentrates on combat systems oriented toward expeditionary operations, world instability, countering terrorism and the threat of regional war. To achieve these capabilities in a declining budget, we continue to 'neck down' the number of type/model/series (T/M/S) aircraft. This is an effort to field a credible fighting force of advanced technological systems possessing affordable capabilities, reliability and survivability."*

Table 1 - Marine Aviation Priorities for the 21st Century

(1) Introducing the MV-22 Osprey to the Fleet and accelerating its production
(2) Introduce the Joint Strike Fighter (JSF) with its Short Takeoff/ Vertical Landing (STVOL) capability to Fleet Marine Forces
(3) AH-1W Cobra 4 Bladed Remanufacture
(4) UH-1N Huey 4 Bladed Remanufacture
(5) AV-8B Harrier Remanufacture
(6) Advanced Tactical Air Reconnaissance System(ATARS)
(7) CH-53E Super Stallion
(8) Unmanned Aerial Vehicle (UAV) Plan
(9) Night and Adverse Weather Capability Enhancements

(1) Introducing The MV-22 Osprey - The Bell/Textron MV-22 is the replacement for the Marine Corps inventory of aging CH-46E and CH-53D medium assault helicopters. The Ospreys amazing tilt-rotor capability will allow it to provide the Marines with the capabilities to fight and win in the battlefields of tomorrow. The Osprey offers significant improvements over the current helicopters in the areas of survivability, speed, range, maneuverability and payload including the ability to carry twenty four combat ready Marines.

The introductions of the Osprey remains *the* number one priority for Marine Corps Rotary Wing aviation. The current plan calls for the introduction of the Osprey to Fleet Marine Squadrons in the late 1990's with production running through the year 2023, bringing the planned total of aircraft being produced to 425.

The Bell/Boeing V-22 Osprey was developed from the Bell XV-15 tilt-rotor prototype based on the Department of Defense requirement for a Joint Services Vertical Lift (JFX) aircraft in 1981. Based on funding constraints, the only service that furthered the aircraft's design was the Navy/ Marine Corps. The Marines saw obvious benefits of the V-22 as a new assault support aircraft, and detailed a requirement for 552 MV-22A's was drawn up.

The program has gone through a number of hurdles to get to its current point, and cancellation due to funding problems a never ending threat.

V-22 Osprey logo. Courtesy of Bell/Textron.

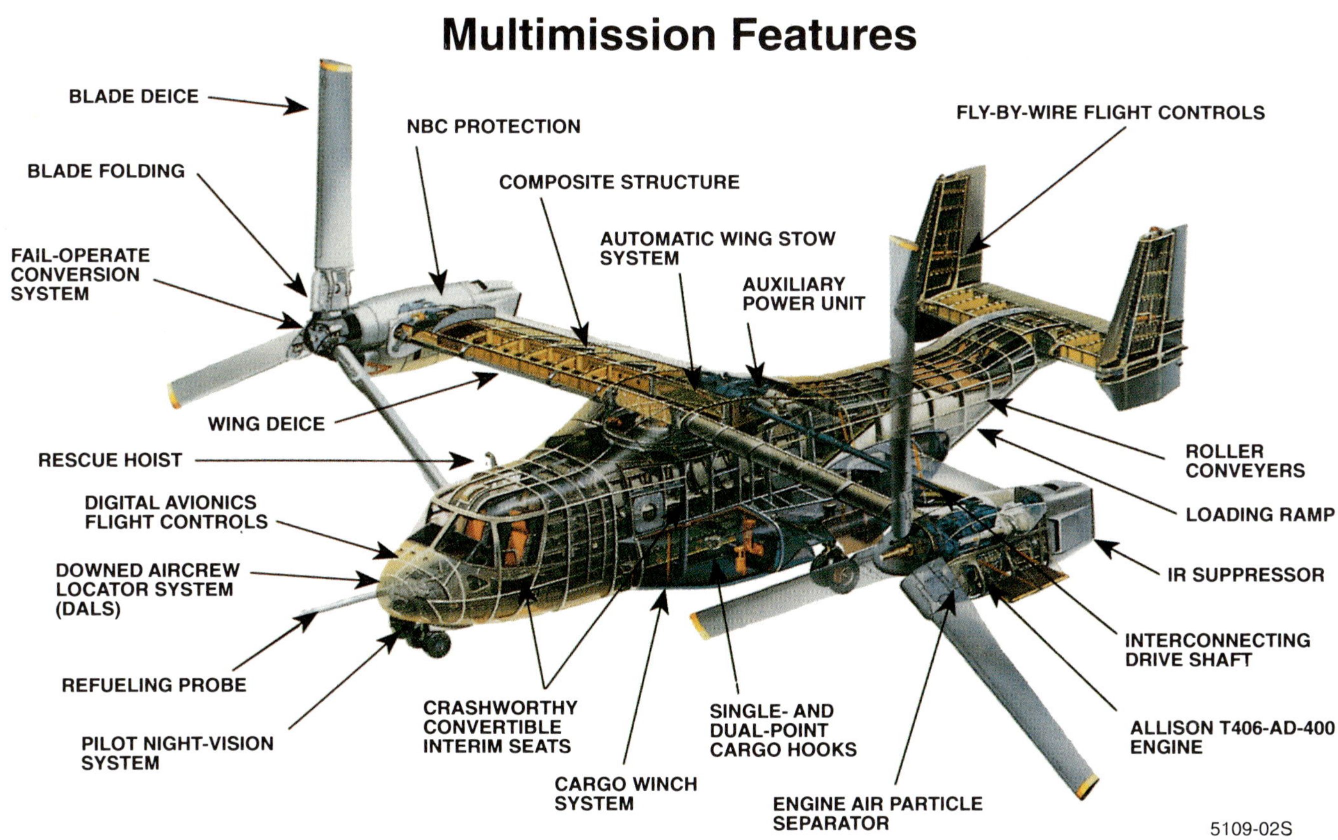

MV-22 Diagram - Courtesy of Bell/Textron.

Nonetheless, the Osprey has undergone extensive flight testing and fortunately appears to be closer than ever to becoming a reality for the Corps.

This technological marvel is a true multi-mission aircraft and represents an indispensable addition to Marine aviation. The Corps envisions the MV-22 acting primarily as an amphibious assault transport of troops, equipment and supplies. But, manufacturers documentation suggest much more as detailed in table 2.

Table 2 - MV-22A Osprey Mission Capabilities

- Assault Support
- Aerial Refueler
- Counter Terrorist Operations
- Special Forces Operations
- Fleet Logistics Support
- Strike Rescue
- Aeromedical
- Combat Search and Rescue

A very strong case could be made to justify the Osprey's use solely based on the inherent benefits of introducing such cutting edge technology. Its civilian applications are apparent, once the cost can be managed by the airline industry, especially smaller commuter airlines.

Table 3 - MV-22 Specifications

Max Speed	275 knots
Vertical Rate of Climb	1,090 feet per minute
Max Rate of Climb	2,320 feet per minute
Service Ceiling	26,000 feet
Range(Combat)	515 nautical miles
Weights:	
Empty	33,140 lbs.
Max Vertical Takeoff	47,500 lbs.
Dimensions:	
Length	57.33 ft.
Width (rotors turning)	83.83 ft.
Height	17.62 ft.

Inset Story: Flying the MV-22 Osprey Simulator

Continued internal strife has ignited a full scale civil war in this already war weary land. As the rebels continue to push pro-democratic government forces back, the fighting in the streets reaches a fever pitch. The sun begins to beat back the night sky, ushering in another bleak day. A small group of Americans, some men, but mostly women and children, rush to the rooftop of their beleaguered embassy. The handful of U.S. Marines guarding the embassy are repelling the second attack of rebel forces, but even they cannot hold out much longer. Should they fail, an uncertain fate awaits the Americans.

Peering out over the rooftop toward the ocean several miles away from this embattled capital, an unusual sight appears. First one, then two large aircraft with huge propellers splitting the dawn skies, approach. They are flanked on each side by several small helicopters. High above a sound like thunder washes over head as several camouflaged jet aircraft circle like buzzards awaiting their turn at the kill.

The supporting helicopters, Marine Corps AH-1W Super Cobras, begin firing rockets at rebel armored vehicles at the gates of the embassy. Several of the vehicles burst into flames from direct hits. As they pass overhead they split away in opposite directions and circle back to begin their second attack. Again, they fire, again the rebels forces are decimated. One of the strange aircraft approaches and as it does its small wings and engines tilt upward slowing the aircraft to a hover over the rooftop. As the first one settles down, the other circles in the distance. Should the lead aircraft take ground fire rendering it inoperable, the second will replace it. The rear cargo door of the aircraft opens, and heavily armed Marines fan out and begin firing down at the rebels. The American civilians are quickly secured inside the aircraft along with the Marines. They huge bird lifts then turns away under the protective eyes of the Cobras.

Once safely out to sea, the tension within the large cabin of the new MV-22 OSPREY eases and the welcome sight of the friendly American fleet appears on the horizon. This story, while fictional and perhaps futuristic, represents a distinct possibility in an uncertain future. It is the kind of situation that a Marine Expeditionary Unit could certainly face while forward deployed aboard an amphibious assault ship. Looking at recent history, Marines have been protecting American interests in flash points around the globe. Thanks to some advanced technology currently available, future MV-22 aviators can practice this, and many other scenarios without ever leaving the ground.

During one of our visits to MCAS New River, we were given the opportunity to fly the current version of the MV-22 simulator under the direction of Major Ray Osborn and Captain Gerald Brown, both with the MV-22/CH-46 Fleet Project Team.

With Major Osborn in the left seat and Captain Brown in the right, several programmed scenarios were displayed for our benefit. The realism of the simulator was simply incredible. With full cockpit instrumentation, the Osprey comes to life. The large panoramic view which includes the propellers adds to the sense of realism. Seated behind the pilots is an operators console. This provides an interface to the simulator software allowing it to be configured to the task at hand.

The database at the time was limited to several west coast facilities and the USS Nassau out at sea off the coast from San Diego. A variety of other aircraft can participate in the simulation including the AV-8B, AH-1W, KC-130 and other MV-22's. Initially, Major Osborn took us out from MCAS Yuma for a late night refueling mission with a Marine Hercules to the north of the facility over the Chocolate Mountain range. Having actually flown over this terrain, we can attest to the simulators authenticity.

The sense of motion is quite real as we break through a thin cloud layer and Captain Brown acquires the Hercules visually from its blinking anti-collision lights. He quickly brought us to the port side observation position. The realism of any simulator can be measured by the concentration levels the pilots maintain during the flight. After this, we break off and author Chuck Lloyd takes the left seat and dons a set of NVG's for some low level flying under the command of Captain Brown. An intrepid sole, Lloyd opts for the full motion capability and begins one heck of a ride. The realism makes this without a doubt, the worlds best video game.

The simulator is quickly reprogrammed, and author Llinares takes the controls from the right seat at 1,200 feet over the Pacific Ocean. Directly ahead is the USS Nassau steaming through the calm blue waters. Lining up on the ship, we descend to 800 feet and pass the ship on the starboard side. Snapping the stick to the left, the aircraft quickly banks to sixty degrees. The MV-22 enters the break and begins to slow as the turn bleeds off speed. The throttle on the left is brought back and the aircraft slows further. There is a small control on the throttle that controls the tilt angle of the wing which is also displayed on one of the multi-purpose displays. For visual confirmation, a quick glance outside confirms the upward movement of the wing.

Again the aircraft makes a left turn and lines up behind the ship at a half a mile away. The combination control inputs of stick, rudder, throttle and pitch proves too taxing for the author and the aircraft enters a dangerous attitude. Low and slow with an excessive sink rate is a fatal mixture for naval aviators. Llinares calls for help, and Captain Brown in the left seat stabilizes the aircraft a mere 50 feet over the water. This definitely takes some getting use to. The Captain settles the Osprey alongside the pitching flight deck and then slides over it and lands. The realism is so great that you actually feel as though you are moving up and down with the sea.

There are a great many benefits to this advanced simulator. Crew training is enhanced in a far more cost effective manner than could otherwise be realized. In addition, validation of new flight software is handled easily and safely. The variety of realistic combat scenarios that could be encountered can also be practiced.

(2) Introducing the JSF - With planned initial deliveries in the year 2007, the JSF will fulfill multiple missions previously handled by the AV-8B and F/A-18C/D. This will allow the Marines to fulfill their strategy of 'necking down' the fighter force from multiple aircraft types to one.

With the exception of the perhaps the F-4 Phantom, few fighter aircraft have successfully been deployed within the various services, although its been tried, i.e. the F-111. The unique requirements of each service are disparate enough to prevent any single design from filling all the requirements successfully. The Navy needs an aircraft that can operate effectively and withstand the rigors of life aboard an aircraft carrier. The Air Force needs an aircraft that can be deployed in large quantities without paying the penalties in weight that 'navalized' aircraft demand. The Marines need an aircraft that can operate from austere facilities and assault ships while able to support the Marine infantryman (a capability whose absence would render the aircraft of *NO* use to the Corps.)

Unfortunately, fiscal realities prevail, and affordability becomes the most important attribute. The answer to this problem is the JSF. It remains the first priority within Marine Aviation's Fixed Wing community.

(3) 4 Bladed AH-1W Cobra - The 4 bladed modernization program will extend the service life of the Cobra until the year 2020. The various enhancements that are packaged with the 4 bladed modernization will double the aircraft's range and payload. The new six station wing will allow the Cobra to carry up to sixteen Precision Guided Munitions (PGM) thereby enhancing the Cobras lethality.

(4) 4 Bladed UH-1N Huey - Enhancements to the Huey's engines, avionics and the rotor system will effectively enhance the capabilities and extend the service life of the aircraft considerably. The current plan calls for the upgrade of 100 UH-1N's to the newer 4BB configuration around 2003. A key element within the UH-1N Block Upgrade is the addition of a Night Vision Enhancement Package that will greatly increase the Huey's night fighting capability.

(5) AV-8B Remanufacture - The Marines are currently looking to upgrade seventy two of the older 'day attack' versions of the Harrier to the current radar/night attack variant. This will help meet operational commitments and force levels through 2007 until the JSF goes operational.

(6) Advanced Tactical Air Reconnaissance Vehicle (ATARS) - The ATARS system will provide a real time, digital tactical reconnaissance capability to be added to the F/A-18C/D. The self contained sensor will work in conjunction with the Hornets APG-73 radar system and will provide enhanced reconnaissance imagery.

(7) CH-53E Super Stallion - As the most capable assault transport available to the MEU, the CH-53 Echo needs several critical improvements. This includes the addition of a Helicopter Night Vision System Forward Looking Infra-Red, Night Vision Goggle Heads-Up Display, a Global Positioning System (GPS) and enhanced radios.

(8) Unmanned Aerial Vehicle (UAV) Plan - The proven effectiveness of the UAV has led Marine planners to look at more closely integrating this asset into the MAGTF scenario with the establishment of Unmanned Aerial Vehicle squadrons (VMU). Future goals call for the cohesive integration of UAV's into a common, compatible and interoperable environment.

(9) Night and Adverse Weather Capability Enhancements - Operating effectively, and safely at night is a primary goal of Marine Air. As such, there will be a continued emphasis on enhancing the current aircraft with night fighting systems. This is to include: the Night Targeting System (NTS) for the AH-1W, CH-53E Night Vision System, Radar/Night Attack for the AV-8B, Night Attack F/A-18C/D, KC-130 Night Vision System, Stinger Night Sights, and night lighting for Expeditionary Air Fields (EAF).

22

The Parting Shot - Photographers' Notes

For those that have already purchased and read *'Warfighters I - The Story of the US Air Force Weapons School and 57th Wing'*, you will notice that we have attempted to keep to the same general format within 'Warfighters II'. We decided with this second book, to add a new section called *The Parting Shot.* The idea is to express in more personal terms, the experiences we both had in creating this book.

HMX-1 and the White House

We never dreamed when we initially developed the 'Warfighters' book concept the places we would visit, and the people we would meet. For 'Warfighters II', we visited with the unique HMX-1 squadron, and were afforded unprecedented access to the unit. Most incredible of all, we had the opportunity to visit the White House and capture on film a Presidential Lift (in our case it was President Clinton's trip to the Democratic National Convention in August of 1996). To witness from the south lawn, the absolute precision in which Colonel Fred Geier, the Commanding Officer of HMX-1 landed the VH-3D on the small landing area next to the White House was incredible. After the lift, our gracious tour guide, unit Executive Officer, Lt. Colonel Mike Conklin showed us the Oval Office. Walking the same halls that Presidents Roosevelt, Kennedy, Reagan and Bush passed through as history was being made was a truly unforgettable experience.

Majors Malavet and Mykelby and the Capt. Scott O'Grady Rescue

Another memorable experience during the creation of 'Warfighters II' was the dinner we had with Major Joaquin F. Malavet and Major Scott C. Mykelby in the Officers Club at Camp LeJeune. We have met a great many officers and aviators during the last several years, none have made as strong and lasting an impression on us as these two Marines did. To listen to these men describe what it was like to plan and execute the Captain Scott O'Grady rescue was simply spellbinding. Not only for the what they said, but also, the way in which they said it. The self-effacing manner of these two heroes was incredible in light of all that they and their fellow Marines accomplished. Both officers gave us significant amounts of time from their busy schedules to describe what it was like to plan and execute this daring rescue. Heroic feats like those of these two officers and their fellow Marines aboard the USS Kearsarge make one proud to be an American.

Author Rick Llinares prior to his first flight in the F/A-18D from Yuma. Flying in the back seat of the Marine F/A-18D can be exhilarating, terrifying, confining and unsettling. It's also one hell of a ride.

Colonel Charles Waterhouse (USMCR ret.)

It is important to us both that the 'Warfighters' series is more than just a 'coffee table picture book'. Obviously, we take great pride in the photos we take, no question. But, we want 'Warfighters' to have a more enduring quality. Toward this end, the extensive text and unique artwork separate the series from many other aviation related books. As we began the final stages of our work on 'Warfighters II', we approached Colonel Charles Waterhouse (USMCR ret.) to see if he would consider allowing us to use some of his artwork within the book. After exchanging several phone calls, we visited with the Colonel and his lovely wife Barbara, in their New Jersey home.

The Colonel began his career as a private with the 3rd Platoon, C Company, 5th Engineering Battalion, 5th Marine Division that took part in the assault on Iwo Jima. During the battle, he was seriously injured in the arm. After leaving the Corps, the Colonel used the GI bill to attend art school, he also got married and raised two daughters.

His love for the Corps never diminished, and his many paintings always seemed to include images of Marines. The Corps offered him a once in a lifetime opportunity to become their 'Artist in Residence'. This included re-joining the Corps, this time with an officers commission as a Major. He quickly accepted and began painting for the Corps, his works represent some of the most compelling images ever produced concerning Marines.

To our delight, the Colonel was very enthusiastic to our request to use a sample of his works in 'Warfighters II'. Our visit with him at his home turned out to be one of the most enjoyable afternoons either of us have had. Getting the chance to speak with the Colonel and his wife about their lives as well as viewing his works in his studio was a rare privilege for both of us. One we will not soon forget. While the 'Warfighters' series concerns itself with aviation, these paintings allow us to honor and recognize the Marine infantryman in a way that photos cannot.

Author Chuck Lloyd does a little cockpit management before flight. For safety purposes, no items such as film, lens caps, batteries can remain in the cockpit postflight. A simple rule applies to tactical jet photography - take out all that you bring in. Otherwise, the entire ejection seat must be removed until the lost or misplaced object is located. Any FOD (foreign object damage) could have an impact on the operation of the ejection sequence.

Without a doubt, the best part of writing this book are the outstanding people we get to meet. Few we came across were more gracious, accommodating and helpful than Colonel Wallace, Lt. Colonel Ochse and the Marines at MCAS New River. Thanks guys.

After strapping in to the F/A-18D, there isn't much room for camera gear.

The Aviation Artists - Lisa Venema, Mark Styling, and Andrew Whyte

Although we both take great pride in our photography, we thought 'Warfighters II' would be enhanced if we could add several dramatic pieces of artwork on Marine Aviation. This was done to our satisfaction in the first 'Warfighters' book on the USAF Weapons School. In our view, the artwork adds a nice variety that balances the many photos that are in the book series. We came across the superb artwork of Lisa Venema, Mark Styling and Andy Whyte quite accidently. In all cases, actual Marine units we were flying with introduced us to the work of the respective artists. We knew right away that their talents would help make the book even better.

Andy, Lisa and Mark were very receptive to our request to use their material. All artists use different methods in capturing Marine Air, but we were thrilled to be able to incorporate their works into the book.

Flying In Marine Aircraft

Our friends and family often ask us, *'What is it like to fly in Marine jet fighters and helicopters?'*. The answer we give is often a surprise to them. We tried to capture the feelings and sensations in the segment titled *'Flying the F/A-18D Hornet and CH-53 Stallion'*. Our intent is simply to relate the experience to those that have often wondered what it must be like. The segment could just as easily be titled, *'How to fill a barf bag'*. The fact that Marine aircrew's can function in this environment is a wonder to both to us and is a tribute to their toughness and training.

Needless to say, we both consider ourselves lucky to be given the chance to fly with these fine Americans, it's an honor to say the least. In case it isn't obvious to you, the reader, we are both very enamored with the Marine Corps. These men and women sacrifice much, and often place themselves in harm's way in order to preserve our way of life. They deserve our appreciation and thanks.

Flying the F/A-18D Hornet

For us, the moment of truth, realization and sheer terror comes at two different moments. For author Rick Llinares, it comes at the entrance to

A legend in the AH-1W Cobra community is Lt. Colonel Ronald W. Ochse, known simply as "The OX". Many of the photos that we took of rotary wing assets for this book could not have been taken without Lt. Colonel Ochse' outstanding support.

the runway when the pilot tells you over the radio to *"arm your ejection seat"*. For author Chuck Lloyd, this moment occurs upon walking out to the jet. Much of the tactical photo hops were conducted during actual Weapons and Tactics Instructor (WTI) courses at MAWTS-1. After a 5:30 AM brief we would both join our respective Hornet pilots in the small building next to the visiting aircraft ramp that houses the flight gear. It all begins with putting on the g-suit, harness and flight helmet prior to flight. The flight gear is heavy and restrictive once it is properly placed on your body.

The flightline is just coming to life with maintenance personnel placing the finishing touches on the Hornets, Harriers, Prowlers and Tomcats. Walking out to the jet in full flight gear with the adrenaline kicking in is some sensation.

Climbing up the ladder and into the back seat of the Hornet is a little tricky and in the words of former MAWTS-1 Operations Officer Major Dave Wilson, *"it's a bit of a snug fit"*. The occupant in the rear seat sits fairly high and has a superb view all around. The plane captain will assist with connecting the many straps that secure your harness and g suit to the ejection seat.

The jet rumbles gently once it comes alive, and the sounds of the diagnostics fill the earphones and the smell of JP4 fuel fills your nostrils. The pilot warns you to not be alarmed at the words *'Engine Fire, Altitude'* that emanate from 'Bitching Betty', the automated voice status monitor . The busy ground crew are scrambling underneath the aircraft and the pilot asks you to bring both hands up into view while they remove the safety pins on the missiles under the jet. This prevents an inadvertent firing by hitting the wrong switch.

Once the camera gear is stowed, and the engines are running to his satisfaction, the pilot will tell you to clear your area so the canopy can be brought down and locked. At this point, you are reminded to snap your oxygen mask and place your visor down. This will protect you should we take a bird strike on takeoff. Such an occurrence isn't uncommon in military aviation and can necessitate ejection. The visor protects your eyes from the shattered canopy and bird, while the mask keeps your helmet on upon ejecting into a 150 mph plus air stream.

Once the canopy is down and locked, the feeling is slightly claustrophobic. The aircraft rolls away from its resting area and then lumbers out

The unsung heroes of this project are the officers and staff of the Public Affairs Office - Headquarters U.S. Marine Corps. 1st Row from left to right: Hattie Powell-Ray, Capt. Whitney Mason, Capt. Pat Johnson, Brigadier General Clifford Stanley, Master Gunnery Sgt. Donald Long, Capt. Michael Neumann. 2nd Row left to right: Sgt. Eric Tausch, Gunnery Sgt. Theresa Anthony, Vadya Dillon, Major Kurt Owermohle, Cpl. Jorge Vallejo, Gunnery Sgt. Patrick Fitch, Lt. Colonel Rick Dechaineau, Colonel Stuart Wagner, Capt. John "Doc" Church. Last Row: Bridgette Killkenny, Sgt. Michael Flemming, 2nd Lt. Zach Jacobson, Sgt. Kurt Sutton, Major Ken White, Major Robert Hollman, Cpl. Arturo Rivera, 2nd Lt. Mark Blumfield, Capt. T.V. Johnson, Lt. Colonel Patrick Messer, Cpl. Leo Natt, Randy Blocker, Gunnery Sgt. Don Hooper, Major Timothy O'Connor, Gunnery Sgt. Robert Taylor.

to the hold short area next to the active runway. Once cleared for takeoff by the tower, the pilot reminds you to pull the lever which arms the ejection seat. From this point on, a firm pull on the handle between your legs will rocket you clear of the aircraft, whether you want to or not.

Up until this point its been too cool, a dream come true. But this isn't all fun and games. Flying modern fighter jets is a serious and dangerous business. These amazing warplanes are complex, things both good and bad happen very fast. The training we received at NAS Patuxent River comes to mind. Remember to maintain a proper position, so the initial 20 g force from the ejection won't damage your spine. Keep your hands and arms in to prevent flailing injury. Today's modern ejection seats are so advanced and intelligent that they do all the work automatically, right up to the point when your feet hit the ground.

After receiving clearance from the tower, we pull out onto the runway and line up with the centerline. The pilot asks if your ready. Your heart is beating, almost thundering in your chest. So this is it. The prominent thought in ones head at this point is from a line by the character 'Goose' in the movie TOP GUN *"I can't believe we're doing this!"*

Colonel Waterhouse painted this self portrait of himself after he was wounded during the Iwo Jima campaign. Painting by Colonel Charles Waterhouse (USMCR-ret.)

Some pilots talk to themselves as they go through their various preflight checks. *"Okay, powers coming up and we're rolling. Systems look good we're going into afterburner. Passing 125 knots and we're going flying".* The sheer acceleration of the Hornet is unbelievable. Halfway through the brief takeoff roll, the engines are advanced from military power into full afterburner and it's like being tackled by a blitzing Lawrence Taylor.

The ground flashes by and the nose of the Hornet lifts and the aircraft skims just above the runway. Holy S*&%, this is incredible! After crossing the fence at the end of the runway, the pilot pulls the stick back and to the side and the Hornet leaps upward and over. Once we reach several thousand feet in altitude, which happens quickly by the way, the sensation of speed diminishes drastically. Flying in the back seat of the Marines fantastic F/A-18D Hornet strike fighter is an almost surreal experience.

The smoothness of the aircraft is surprising, it's almost as though we are suspended in the air. *"Hey, I don't need the barf bag after all!"* The pilot comes over the radio to tell you that the aircraft we are going to photograph (a pair of AV-8B Harriers) are off to our right. At the risk of pegging the cheese meter, a shout from the rear cockpit comes out over the radio *"Tally-Ho, two AV-8B's at our 3:00 o'clock high".* Hey, it's goofy, but how many times will you get the chance to say that in your lifetime? It is rumored that on one flight, photographer Lloyd was quoted as saying *"Goose, check the guys to the north, check the guys to the north!"*, this is what happens after watching Top Gun in excess of 75 times!

The pilot snaps the Hornet into a high g turn to the right and pulls into the Harriers in order to cut the angle so we can join on them. The sensation is very strange as the g-suit constricts around your legs in order to keep oxygen rich blood up in your head. You sink a bit in the seat, and your helmet rotates slightly downward. Time is tight, the Harriers have a time-over-target at the range that is quickly approaching. Unlike Maverick and Goose who had the *'need for speed'*, once we join and level off, we feel the *'urge to purge'*. Out comes the barf bag and there goes breakfast, dinner from the night before, and perhaps everything eaten since last Thanksgiving.

With complete precision, the Hornet pilot slides right up to the Harriers which look great. One of the biggest challenges with this type of photography is glare. Since we are sitting totally surrounded by glass, the reflection of the interior of the cockpit on the canopy can be excessive. Before the pictures are taken, some repositioning is necessary. Once this is completed and the photos are taken, the Harriers depart and one takes this opportunity to get a fresh bag. We join on a section of Hornets and take a variety of pictures of them pitching out and turning. It's now time to return and we head back to base.

The pilot comes on the radio and asks if your up for the standard fighter break over the field. We approach the field at 350 knots at 1,500 feet. Once past the mid-field point, the pilot snaps the aircraft aggressively into another 3 plus g break and turns 180 degrees to the downwind leg.

One of the best afternoons we spent during the creation of 'Warfighters II' was with Colonel Charles Watherhouse (USMCR ret.) at his home. The Colonel, along with his wife, Barbera, were gracious hosts as we discussed the use of some of his artwork within 'Warfighters II'. (left Rick Llinares, middle Colonel Charles Waterhouse (USMCR - ret.), right Chuck Lloyd.)

The gear and flaps come down and we turn 180 degrees on final approach. Once past the runway, we turn 90 degrees while descending rapidly, roll wings level and touch down.

At least the cockpit didn't get dirty.

Inside 'Stallion 1' a Sikorsky CH-53E Super Stallion, 200 feet AGL, 1500 hours PST.

Much to our surprise, the flight is fairly smooth inside the rear cargo cabin of the massive CH-53E, even at this low altitude. We are Dash 2 in this two ship section in what we mistakenly thought at first was a routine navigation hop. The first hint that this would be a memorable flight came when an F-5E Tiger II with Snipers of VMFT-401 blasted right between our section at over 400 knots.

The pilot of the Stallion rolls the helo aggressively and begins pumping out chaff which can be seen exiting behind the aircraft. The crewman in the back maintain a vigilant lookout in the hope of spotting the F-5E as he sets up for his next shot. The ability to work as a team and maintain a disciplined lookout doctrine is critical to their chances for survival against a fixed wing threat. The goal here is to keep an eye on the bogey, the other CH-53 ahead of us, the mountains and of course, the ground, until our own fixed wing guys can show up to help us. The Stallion rocks left and right as we pass even lower into a valley. The Sniper pilot is trying to get a guns solution on us. Over the radio, you can hear the urgent calls from the crew *"He's closing on our 4:00 o'clock. Chaff! Chaff! Break right, break right. Watch the mountains!"*

Finally, we are finished and we land for a quick break. The loadmaster comes up to see how we're doing, and remind us that we are going up to hit the orbiting KC-130 for a bit of in-flight aerial refueling practice. At this point we very seriously think about walking back to Yuma. We figure it's about twenty miles. *"How many snakes and scorpions could they're possibly be between here and the base?"*

Once airborne, we spot the tanker and join on its left side. As the crew begins to bring the CH-53 in to begin refueling we begin asking ourselves *"what the hell are we doing here?"* The rotors of the Stallion are awfully close to the tail of the KC-130. The pilot tries to fly the extended refueling probe into the swaying basket streaming from the wing mounted refueling pod of the Hercules. We never imagined an aircraft could move in every axis at once. Looking out the open rear cargo door, the horizon is moving up, down, left and right at a rapid rate. As our knuckles turn a whiter shade of pale, all thoughts of photography are long gone. *"Oh Lord just let us land".*

The amount of airmanship needed to pull this off is significant. Imagine, the Marines routinely practice this same maneuver at night while flying on Night Vision Goggles!

The sign outside HMX-1 leaves little room for misinterpretation.

Aerial Photography

For those readers that are interested in the photo angle, we thought we would spend a moment describing the actual picture taking end of the project. The 300 plus photos in this book were selected from over 5,000 taken. We both use Canon EOS equipment with the RS and older 630 bodies exclusively. We use a variety of lenses from Canon (L series and Ultrasonics) and SIGMA ranging from 18mm to 350mm. The film choice is Fuji, either Velvia 50 speed slide or the slightly faster 100 speed Provia. Both are excellent for aviation photography. At no point do we use any special filters or effects items. What you see, is what we saw.

Taking pictures of military aircraft in-flight from other military aircraft is a very difficult endeavor. In fact, outside of perhaps nature photography, we don't think there is a more hostile environment in which to take photographs. In the tactical jets, there is the never ending problem with glare, the tight confines of the cockpit, the restrictive flight gear, the ceaseless motion and the fact that if you lose any item, the entire ejection seat must be removed after flight. This is for safety reasons as any debris left behind, i.e., lens cap, batteries, film can pose a hazard to the next guy in case of an ejection. A further challenge is the fact that you must shoot through a one inch thick glass canopy that bows slightly and may be scratched. Any focal length beyond 50mm will render the photo fuzzy (an insidious opponent since the human eye doesn't easily detect this distortion). As mentioned previously, glare is a never ending enemy of the aviation photographer and has ruined more than one otherwise spectacular shot. For every one great photo, we probably shoot between five and ten marginal ones. One trick we use is to bring a yard of black linen cloth which we drape over our legs, torso and cockpit instrumentation. This handy device from our good friend Jan Jacobs, the editor of "The Hook" magazine works wonders.

As is plainly evident, so much of the Corps aviation concerns helicopters, and this represented an entirely different challenge from a photo perspective. Flying in Marine helo's was truly enjoyable and provides one with a far more personal sense of flight. Most of our flying and photo taking in helo's was done in warm weather conditions. With the windows open, the aircraft's engines and rotors produce a great amount of noise and wind, along with heat. Almost always the flights are at low altitudes down 'in the weeds'.

The nice part about this is that one can use longer lenses and glare isn't a problem, the bad news is the never ending vibration. The shudder

Author/Photographer Rick Llinares snaps his oxygen mask prior to a mid day F/A-18D photo flight at MCAS Yuma.

Many of the photos for 'Warfighters II' were taken during fixed wing aerial refueling missions with KC-130 units like VMGR-252. In addition to handling the mission itself, Battleherk crews provided us with outstanding support. Special thanks to VMGR-252 at MCAS Cherry Point, in particlular Captain Ron Domingue (seated in the middle of the photo), Captain J. Taylor Keeney (seated in the right of photo), Captain Patrick, Captain Kaye and the rest of the OTIS Marines. Hurrah and Thanks!

Andrew C. Whyte, Illustrator of the painting depicting the USMC rescue of USAF Captain Scott O'Grady. Andy Whyte was born in Bridgeport, CT, in 1926 and grew up with a love for aviation instilled by his father. In WWII, Mr. Whyte served with the U.S. Navy Air Force as a flight engineer/gunner in SBD's, PBY's, PBM's and PV-2's.

He spent ten years in active duty and reserve service.

Mr. Whyte attended the University of Oklahoma, majoring in Engineering. In 1951, Mr. Whyte returned to Connecticut and joined the Sikorsky Aircraft Corporation as a design engineer in the Sikorsky Advanced Design Group. He combined engineering and art in doing configuration work for all Sikorsky products. Mr.Whyte received eight aircraft design patents during his forty-one year career with Sikorsky.

Mr. Whyte is now devoting his time to Aviation Art. He is a member of the Society of Illustrators in New York City, the U.S. Air Force Art Program and is an Artist Fellow with the American Society of Aviation Artists.

speeds cannot be placed too high, say over 350, or the blades on the helo will appear to be frozen, making for a strange photo. One attempts to hold on the camera as firmly as possible, frame the photo and shoot without falling out of the aircraft.

If this all isn't too much to handle there is the additional element of adrenaline that always seems to kick in moments before the shoot. The anticipation builds, and as the aircraft first come into view the excitement level grows considerably. It just doesn't get any better.

Many of the photos in the book could not have been taken without the incredible support of the many units involved, in particular, VMGR-252 at MCAS Cherry Point. Since we both live on the east coast, MCAS Cherry Point is most accessible to us. Over the course of several critical photo visits to the base, and to MCAS Beaufort, the officers and enlisted personnel at 252 went out of their way to ensure our success. In particular, Captains DoMainge, Kaye and Patrick. Without their dedication and friendship, this book may not have been completed.

To the many Marines, both officers and enlisted that helped us capture Marine Air for 'Warfighters II' - thanks and Hurrah.

Glossary

A
AAW - Anti Air Warfare
ACE - Aviation Combat Element
ACM - Air Combat Maneuvering
ACMI - Air Combat Maneuvering Instrument/Instructor
ACTI - Air Combat Training Instructor
ADT&E - Aviation Development, Tactics & Evaluation
ADVCAP- Advanced Capability (EA-6B)
AGI - Aerial Gunnery Instructor
AGS - Aviation Ground Support
AIM - Air Intercept Missile
AMC - Air Mission Commander
AMRAAM - Advanced Medium Range Air to Air Missile
ARG - Amphibious Ready Group
ASD - Assault Support Department
ASF - Assault Flight Leader
AST - Assault Support Tactics
ATARS - Advanced Tactical Air Reconnaissance System
ATI - Adversary Tactics Instructor
ATO - Air Tasking Order, a.k.a. FRAG
AVPLAN - Aviation Plan

B
BARCAP - Barrier Combat Air Patrol
BVR - Beyond Visual Range

C
CAOC - Combined Area Operations Center
CAPEX - Capabilities Exercise
CAS - Close Air Support
CE - Command Element
CINC - Commander In Chief
CMC - Commandant Marine Corps
CRT - Cathode Ray Tube
CSAR - Combat Search and Rescue
CSSE - Combat Service Support Element
CTAPS - Contingency Theater Aviation Planning System

D
DACT - Dissimilar Air Combat Training
DASC - Direct Air Support Center
DAS - Deep Air Support
DECM - Defensive Countermeasures
DEFTAC - Defensive Tactics
DFM - Defensive Maneuvering
DMI - Defensive Measures Instructor

E
EA- Electronic Attack
EAF - Expeditionary Air Field
ECM - Electronic Counter Measures
ECMO - Electronic Counter Measures Officer
EFL - Escort Flight Leader
EVM - Evasive Maneuvering
EXCAP - Expanded Capability (EA-6B)

F
FACA - Forward Air Control (Airborne)
FARP - Forward Area Refueling Point
FINEX - Final Exercise
FLIR - Forward Looking Infra-Red
FOB - Forward Operating Bases
FMF - Fleet Marine Force
FSC - Fire Support Coordinator
FSSG - Force Service Support Group
F/W OAS - Fixed Wing Offensive Air Support

G
GCE - Ground Combat Element
GBAD - Ground Based Air Defense

H
HARM- High speed Anti-Radiation Missile
HOTAS - Hands On Throttle And Stick
HMH - Marine Heavy Helicopter Squadron
HMA - Marine Attack Helicopter Squadron
HMLA - Marine Light Attack Helicopter Squadron
HMM - Marine Medium Helicopter Squadron
HMT - Marine Training Helicopter Squadron
HMX - Marine Helicopter Squadron
HSS - Helmet Sight Subsystem (AH-1W)
HUD - Head's Up Display

I
ICAP - Improved Capability (EA-6B)
IFA - International Fighter Aircraft (F-5)
INS - Inertial Navigation System
IUT - Instructor Under Training

J
JSF - Joint Strike Fighter
JSIPS - Joint Source Imagery Processing System
JSOTF - Joint Special Operations Task Force

L
LAAD - Low Altitude Air Defense
LATI - Low Altitude Tactics Instructor
LAV - Light Armored Vehicle
LCAC - Landing Craft Air Cushion
LERX- Leading Edge Root Extension's (AV-8B)
LEX - Leading Edge Extension (F/A-18)
LHA - Helicopter, Attack Landing
LHD - Helicopter, Dock Landing
LIDS - Lift Improvement Devices (AV-8B)
LPH - Helicopter, Landing Platform
LZ - Landing Zone

M
MACG - Marine Air Control Group
MACS - Marine Air Control Squadron
MACCS - Marine Air Command and Control System
MAG - Marine Air Group
MAGTF - Marine Air Ground Task Force
MALS - Marine Aviation Logistics Squadron
MARDIV - Marine Division
MATCS - Marine Air Traffic Control Squadron
MAW - Marine Air Wing
MAWTS - As in MAWTS-1, Marine Aviation Weapons and Tactics Squadron
MCAS - Marine Corps Air Station
MCM - Multi Command Manual
MCSF - Marine Corps Security Force
MEB - Marine Expeditionary Brigade, same as MEF Forward
MEF - Marine Expeditionary Force
MEU - Marine Expeditionary Unit
MEU (SOC) - Marine Expeditionary Unit - Special Operations Capable
MISTEX - Marine Integrated Systems Training Exercise
MPF - Marine Prepositioning Force
MPCD - Multi-Purpose Color Display
MWSS - Marine Wing Support Squadron
MWCS - Marine Wing Communications Squadron

N
NACF - Navy Air Combat Fighter
NEFEX - Naval Expeditionary Force Exercise
NITE - Night Imaging & Threat Evaluation
NSFI - Night Systems Familiarization Instructor
NTI - Night Tactics Instructor
NTS - Night Targeting System
NVG - Night Vision Goggle

O
OAAW - Offensive Anti Air Warfare
OAS - Offensive Air Support
ORI - Operational Readiness Inspection

R
RAG - Replacement Air Group
RGR - Rapid Ground Refueling
ROE - Rules Of Engagement
RPV - Remotely Powered Vehicle
RRS - Remote Receive Station
R/W OAS - Rotary Wing Offensive Air Support
RWR - Radar Warning Receiver

S
SAR - Search And Rescue
SEAD - Suppression of Enemy Air Defenses
SIR - System Integration Receiver's (EA-6B)
SLAR - Side Looking Radar
SPMAGTF - Special Purpose MAGTF
SWTU - Special Weapons Training Units

T
TAC - Tactical Air Controller
TACA - Tactical Air Coordinator (Airborne)
TACAIR - Tactical Aircraft
TACC - Tactical Air Control/Command Center
TAMPS - Tactical Aircrew Mission Planning System
TAOC - Tactical Air Operations Center
TERF - Terrain Flight
TERFI - Terrain Flight Instructor
TJS - Tactical Jamming System (EA-6B)
TOT - Time On Target
TOW - Tube launched, Optically tracked, Wire guided (AH-1W)
TRAP - Tactical Recovery of Aircraft and Personnel
TSU - Telescopic Sight Unit (AH-1W)

U
UAV - Unmanned Aerial Vehicle
USAF - United States Air Force
USN - United States Navy

V
VFAX - Lightweight Multi-mission Fighter Experimental
VMA - Marine Attack Squadron
VMAQ - Marine Tactical Electronic Warfare Squadron
VMAT - Marine Attack Training Squadron
VMFA - Marine Fighter Attack Squadron
VMFA (AW) - Marine Fighter Attack All Weather Squadron
VMFAT - Marine Fighter Attack Training Squadron
VMFT - Marine Fighter Training Squadron
VMGR - Marine Aerial Refueler Transport Squadron
VMGRT - Marine Aerial Refueler Transport Training Squadron
V/STOL - Vertical/Short Takeoff and Landing
VMU - Marine Aerial Vehicle Squadron

W
WTI - Weapons and Tactics Instructor
WTO - Weapons Training Officer
WTTP - Weapons and Tactics Training Program

Appendix One: Marine Aviation Weapons and Tactics Squadron One 1996 Course Catalog

CORE CURRICULUM

WEAPONS AND TACTICS INSTRUCTOR COURSE

Course Objective: To train and certify officers as Weapons and Tactics Instructors (WTI's), capable of the following:

1. Assisting their respective unit commanders in conducting a professional aviation weapons and tactics training program which includes individual training and collective training.
2. Functioning as Combat Mission Planners with enhanced planning skills, and knowledge of how to integrate all aviation assets to promote mission success.
3. Acting as weapons and tactics coordinators for MCCRES evaluations and, when requested, assist as evaluators for MCCRES.
4. Coordinating and conducting appropriate supplementary courses applicable to their particular community.
5. Ensuring all training conducted under their supervision adheres rigidly to established safety procedures.
6. Submitting appropriate information, including post exercise/deployment reports, to assist MAWTS-1 in updating tactics and instruction.

Length: 100 - 140 classroom hours 40 - 60 flight hours

Academic Syllabus: Academic instruction is divided into three phases: generic, common and specific

1. Generic academics builds a broad foundation for all communities and includes graduate level instruction on the six functions of Marine aviation, aviation employment, tactics and integration, joint operations, and analysis of the threat.
2. Common academics provide more detailed information on Marine aviation employment, tailored to the needs of the aircraft type and command and control communities. The WTI course addresses common academics in three groups; TACAIR (fixed wing aviation), rotary wing aviation, and command, control, and communications (C3). Communities that do not fall entirely in line with these three groupings tailor their academic program as required.
3. Specific academics are tailored to the needs of the individual aircraft or command and control community. Specific academics address the weapons systems applicable to a particular aircraft or agency, employment considerations, tactics, training management, and instructor standardization and certification. Specific academics also include student presentations in order to evaluate the student's instructional abilities. Specific academics are coordinated within each division at MAWTS-1. Specific academic schedules exist for the following communities:

AV-8B	F/A-18	EA-6B	KC-130
CH-46	CH-53	UH-1 N	AH-1W
Aviation Ground	Communications	Direct Air Support Center	
Ground Combat Department	Ground Based Air Defense (GBAD)	Intelligence	UAV
Tactical Air Operations Center	Tactical Air Command Center	Marine Air Traffic Control	AEW (E-2C, E-3)

Flight Syllabus: In-flight instruction is conducted in three phases: specific, common, and final exercise (FINEX). All sorties are conducted as instructor under training (IUT) events. In conjunction with the flight phase, C3, GCD, AGS, and Intelligence students perform IUT events which comprise specific training or support the TACAIR and Rotary Wing flight syllabi. Successful completion of the events that occur during the flight syllabus is required for graduation.

1. Specific flight evolutions are tailored to the needs of the individual aircraft community. The events address weapons and tactics that increase the prospective WTI's ability to conduct instruction in mission areas specific to their MOS. Specific flight syllabi exist for the following communities:

AV-8B	F/A-18	EA-6B	KC-130
CH-46	CH-53	UH-1 N	AH-1W

2. Common flight evolutions allow aircraft from like communities (fixed wing and rotary wing) to conduct integrated operations, coordinated through the Marine Air Command and Control System. Each common flight evolution is designed to accomplish specific objectives associated with the aircraft and command and control agencies participating in the evolution. A building block approach is utilized adding to the knowledge and skills acquired during the specific flight evolution. The following flight evolutions comprise the common flight phase:
   a. Ground Based Air Defense (GBAD) evolutions center on the requirement to conduct effective combat mission planning and maximize integration of GBAD assets to defend designated air defense priorities against a multi-axis, multi-altitude threat.
   b. Antiair Warfare (MW) evolutions focus on the planning, integration, and airspace control measures required to conduct air defense of designated air defense priorities within the MAGTF AOR against a coordinated enemy strike force.
   c. Offensive Antiair Warfare (OAW) is a force on force evolution that focuses on the planning and integration required to conduct successful air operations against a sophisticated integrated air defense system.
   d. Offensive Air Support (OAS) evolutions concentrate on the planning and integration required to conduct effective fixed and rotary wing Close Air Support and Armed Reconnaissance in a dynamic threat environment in support of MAGTF objectives.
   e. Assault Support Tactics (AST) evolutions are designed to develop and evaluate the mission planning and integration skills required to conduct assault support operations across a diverse spectrum of situations and threat environment.

3. The Naval Expeditionary Force Exercise (NEFEX) builds upon the common flight evolutions and is the first evolution that brings all communities together to execute a forward presence mission utilizing Carrier Battle Group (CVBG) assets integrated with Marine Expeditionary Unit (MEU) assets and Special Operations Forces operating under a Joint Task Force Commander.

4. The Final Exercise (FINEX) is the culmination of flight training at WTI. The FINEX brings all communities together to plan and execute integrated air operations performing all six functions of Marine aviation in support of a notional MAGTF scheme of maneuver. The FINEX is designed as a comprehensive graduation evolution incorporating all of the principles, tactics and techniques previously addressed. FINEX focuses on the Aviation Combat Element staff planning process in a joint environment.

EMBEDDED CURRICULUM
GROUND COMBAT OFFICER COURSE

Course Objective: Held in conjunction with the Weapons and Tactics Instructor (WTI) Course, the course exposes Ground Combat Arms Officers to aviation planning, employment and the integration of all six functions of Marine aviation in support of a Marine Air (Ground Task Force (MAGTF) scheme of maneuver.

Length: 6 weeks

Academic Syllabus: Academic instruction coincides with the academic phase of the WTI Course. Specific syllabi will be published by MAWTS-1 prior to the beginning of each WTI Course.

AVIATION GROUND SUPPORT (AGS) OFFICER COURSE

Course Objective: Held in conjunction with the Weapons and Tactics Instructor (WTI) Course, the course exposes AGS officers to aviation planning, employment and the integration of all six functions of Marine aviation to improve support provided by the AGS community.

Length: 6 weeks

Academic Syllabus: Academic instruction coincides with the academic phase of-the WTI Course. Specific syllabi will be published by MAWTS-1 prior to the beginning of each WTI Course.

INTELLIGENCE OFFICERS COURSE

Course Objective: Held in conjunction with the Weapons and Tactics Instructor (WTI) Course, the course exposes intelligence officers to the capabilities, limitations and applicability of national intelligence systems, their role in supporting the Aviation Combat Element planning process, and intelligence requirements inherent to each of the Six Functions of Marine aviation.

Length: 6 weeks

Academic Syllabus: Academic instruction coincides with the academic phase of the WTI Course. Specific syllabi will be published by MAWTS-1 prior to the beginning of each WTI Course.

AVIATION LOGISTICS OFFICER COURSE

Course Objective: Still under development by MAWTS-1, this course, held in conjunction with the Weapons and Tactics Instructor (WTI) Course, will expose aviation logistics officers to aviation planning and employment considerations and their role in supporting the Aviation Combat Element.

Length: 6 weeks

Academic Syllabus: Academic instruction coincides with the academic phase of the WTI Course. Specific syllabi will be published by MAWTS-1 prior to the beginning of each WTI Course.

ROTARY WING WEAPONS AND TACTICS CREW CHIEF INSTRUCTOR (WTCCI) COURSE

Course Objective: To train and certify helicopter crew chiefs as Weapons and Tactics Crew Chief Instructors capable of the following:

1. Establishing and managing the Enlisted Aircrew Training Program.
2. Training and developing enlisted instructors within the squadron.
3. Providing academic and flight instruction to enlisted aircrews

Length: 40-50 classroom hours 40-60 flight hours

Upon successful completion of all academic and flight requirements, the candidate will be certified by MAWTS-1 as a Weapons and Tactics Crew Chief Instructor (WTCCI). The WTCCI designation and the additional MOS (6177) can be made as appropriate.

Academic Syllabus:

1. Academic instruction coincides with the common/specific academic phase of the WTI Course. Specific syllabi will be published by MAWTS-1 prior to the beginning of each WTI Course.
2. The WTCCI candidate will conduct a presentation, to include demonstration and practical application, from the Academic Support Package or one which the candidate has developed.

Flight Syllabus:

1. The WTCCI flight stage training is conducted in conjunction with the WTI specific, common and Final Exercise (FINEX) flight phases. All sorties are conducted as Instructor Under Training (IUT) events.
2. During the IUT events, the WTCCI candidate will demonstrate the ability to brief, instruct and critique the following flights from the MAWTS-1 Course Catalog as part of the Aerial Gunnery Instructor (AGI), Air Combat Maneuver Instructor (ACMI), Defensive Measures Instructor (DMI) and Night Systems Instructor (NSI) (as applicable to type aircraft) certification process:
   a. AGI: 540, 541, 542, 543
   b. ACMI: 580, 581, 582
   c. DMI: 580, 581, 582, 583, 584, 585
   d. NSI: 590, 591, 592, 593

KC-130 WEAPONS AND TACTICS AIRCREW (NAVIGATOR) INSTRUCTOR COURSE

Course Objective: To certify the KC-130 Navigator Instructor as a Weapons and Tactics Aircrew Instructor capable of safely conducting ground and airborne instruction in the KC-130 navigator combat qualification and full combat qualification flight syllabus as outlined in MCO P3500.15.

Length: 64 classroom hours 20 flight hours

Academic Syllabus:

1. The WTACI candidate will review and be capable of presenting classes listed in the MAWTS-1 KC-130 Specific Academic Support Package.
2. Academic instruction coincides with the academic phase of the WTI Course. Specific syllabi will be published by MAWTS-1 prior to the beginning of each WTI Course.
3. The WTACI Candidate will conduct a presentation, to include demonstration and practical application, from the KC-130 Academic Support Package, as assigned by the instructor.

Flight Syllabus:

1. WTACI Candidate flight stage training is conducted in conjunction with the WTI specific, common and FINEX flight phases. All sorties are conducted as Instructor Under Training (IUT) events.

KC-130 WEAPONS AND TACTICS AIRCREW (LOADMASTER) INSTRUCTOR COURSE

Course Objective: To certify the KC-130 Loadmaster Instructor as a Weapons and Tactics Aircrew Instructor capable of safely conducting ground and airborne instruction in the KC-130 Loadmaster combat qualification and full combat qualification flight syllabus as outlined in outlined in MCO P3500.15.

Length: 68 classroom hours 20 flight hours

Academic Syllabus:

1. The WTACI candidate will review and be capable of presenting all classes listed in the MAWTS-1 KC-130 Specific Academic Support Package.
2. Academic instruction coincides with the academic phase of the WTI Course. Specific syllabi will be published by MAWTS-1 prior to the beginning of each WTI Course.
3. The WTACI Candidate will conduct a presentation, to include demonstration and practical application, from the KC-130 Loadmaster Specific Academic Support Package, as assigned by the instructor.

Flight Syllabus:

1. WTACI candidate flight stage training is conducted in conjunction with the WTI specific, common and FINEX flight phases. All sorties are conducted as Instructor Under Training (IUT) events.

KC-130 WEAPONS AND TACTICS AIRCREW (FLIGHT ENGINEER) INSTRUCTOR CERTIFICATION COURSE

Course Objective: To certify the KC-130 Flight Engineer Instructor as a Weapons and Tactics Aircrew Instructor capable of safely conducting ground and airborne instruction in the KC-130 Flight Engineer Combat Qualification and Full Combat Qualification Flight Syllabus as outlined in outlined in MCO P3500.15.

Length: 40 classroom/fuselage trainer hours 20 flight hours

Academic Syllabus:

1. The WTACI candidate will review and be capable of presenting all classes listed in the MAWTS-1 KC-130 Specific Academic Support Package.
2. Academic instruction coincides with the academic phase of the WTI Course. Specific syllabi will be published by MAWTS-1 prior to the beginning of each WTI Course.
3. The WTACI Candidate will conduct a presentation, to include demonstration and practical application, from the KC-130 Academic Support Package, as assigned by the instructor.

Flight Syllabus:

1. WTACI candidate flight stage training is conducted in conjunction with the WTI specific, common and FINEX flight phases. All sorties are conducted as Instructor Under Training (IUT) events.

LAAD SECTION LEADERS COURSE

Course Objective: To graduate qualified individuals as LAAD Section Leaders capable of the following:

1. Planning for successful combat/peacetime operations to include:
   a. Demonstrating the ability to plan employment, brief the plan to subordinates, and successfully execute the plan.
   b. Demonstrating the ability to effectively articulate LAAD employment requirements and considerations to higher, adjacent, and supporting units.
2. Demonstrating an ability to discuss and evaluate Threat Weapon Systems and their capabilities as they pertain to LAAD operations in particular and the MACCS in general.
3. Demonstrating an ability to discuss the capabilities of each MACCS agency, and effectively integrate LAAD operations within appropriate agencies as dictated by the situation and the mission.
4. Demonstrating knowledge of the Stinger Missile system. In particular, its performance, capabilities and limitations, and their impact on the operational employment of Stinger teams and the conduct of engagements.
5. Managing and conducting section level training as part of a unit level training plan.
   a. Identifying and overcoming training deficiencies through observing subordinate elements.
   b. Conducting formal and informal evaluations.

Length: 5 weeks/104 academic hours.

Academic Syllabus:

1. Academic instruction coincides with the academic phase of the WTI Course. Specific syllabi will be published by MAWTS-1 prior to the beginning of each course.

Flight Syllabus: The purpose of the flight evolution phase is to develop planning and briefing skills and provide practical application of knowledge gained during the academics phase of the course. The students will participate as actual Section Leaders employing their sections as part of the integrated air defense system during all WTI flight evolutions. Additionally, students will have the opportunity to observe each MACCS agency during the flight evolution phase.

DASC WEAPONS AND TACTICS CREW CHIEF INSTRUCTOR COURSE (DWTCCI)

Course Objective: To train and certify combat qualified crew chiefs in the Direct Air Support Center as DASC Weapons and Tactics Crew Chief Instructors capable of the following:

1. Assisting their respective unit commanders in conducting a professional aviation weapons and tactics training program.
2. Assisting as weapons and tactics coordinators for MCCRES evaluations and when requested, assist as evaluators for MCCRES.
3. Coordinating and conducting appropriate supplementary courses applicable to the DASC.
4. Ensuring all training conducted under their supervision adheres rigidly to established safety procedures.

Length: 96 classroom hours, 20 days of practical application to include approximately 24-50 DASC hours per student (combination of DASC/DASC(A) operational hours).

Academic Syllabus: Academic instruction coincides with the academic phase of the WTI Course. Specific syllabi will be published by MAWTS-1 prior to the beginning of each course.

Flight Syllabus: Practical application begins with two MACCS Integrated Systems Training Exercises (MISTEX's) that occur immediately after academics and precede the flight evolutions. Each DWTCCI student will participate as either the Crew Chief for the evolution or as White Force Controllers. The intent is to familiarize the students with the crews and the supporting unit's SOP. During the planning phase of each flight evolution (OAS, AST, NEFEX, FINEX), students are responsible for integrating the DASC and/or the DASC(A) into the overall scheme of maneuver. They are further responsible for providing a detailed brief to the DASC crew executing the plan. During the evolution, they will sit in the position of Crew Chief in either the DASC or DASC(A).

MARINE AIR TRAFFIC CONTROL MOBILE TEAM (MMT) LEADERS COURSE

Course Objective: To train and certify air traffic controllers in the concept and employment of MMT operations. Team leaders will be capable of the following:

1. Assisting their respective unit commanders in conducting a professional MMT weapons and tactics training program.
2. Coordinating and conducting appropriate supplementary courses applicable to MMT operations.
3. Coordinating and conducting appropriate training for MMT Marine Expeditionary Unit (MEU (SOC)) operations.
4. Ensuring all training conducted under their supervision adheres rigidly to established safety procedures.

Length: 12 days of academics, followed by 3 weeks of field operations during the flight phase of the WTI course.

Academics Syllabus: Academic instruction coincides with the academic phase of the WTI Course. Specific syllabi will be published by MAWTS-1 prior to the beginning of each course.

Flight Syllabus: Practical application begins after academics during the 3rd week flight phase of the WTI Course. Operations will take place at several airfields and air sites in support of I(C-130, AV-8 and helicopter operations. Each student will serve in the billet as team leader and have an opportunity to lead, plan and execute the various missions in support of the flight syllabus of the WTI Course.

TAOC ENLISTED WEAPONS AND TACTICS COURSE (TEWTC)

Course Objective: To provide Fully Combat Qualified Tactical Air Defense Controllers (TADC) graduate level training in aviation mission planning, exercise execution, and exercise evaluation. TEWTC graduates will be capable of the following:

1. Assisting their respective unit commanders in conducting a professional a professional aviation weapons and tactics training program.
2. Assisting as weapons and tactics coordinators for MCCRES evaluations and when requested, assist as evaluators for MCCRES.
3. Coordinating and conducting appropriate supplementary courses applicable to the TAOC.
4. Provide the stability, expertise, and continuity required to successfully train a TAOC crew.

Length: 95-100 classroom hours and 3.5 weeks of practical application at the TAOC and other MACCS agencies.

Academics Syllabus: Academic instruction coincides with the academic phase of the WTI Course. Specific syllabi will be published by MAWTS-1 prior to the beginning of each course.

Flight Syllabus: Practical application begins with two MACCS Integrated Systems Training Exercises (MISTEX) that occur immediately after academics and precede the flight evolutions. Each TEWTC student will participate as White Forces personnel in both the TAOC and Simulation Cell for MISTEX. The TEWTC student will be involved in all TAOC specific evolution planning (GBAD, AAW, OAAW, FINEX), and will observe non-specific TAOC planning (AST, NEFEX) when the opportunity presents itself. During the conduct of each flight evolution, the TEWTC student will deliver the TAOC brief prior to STARTEX, and will evaluate the evolution for lessons learned while positioned at the TAOC or E/WC. TEWTC students will be exposed to other agencies of the MACCS and Marine aviation on a continual basis.

TACTICAL AIR COMMANDER'S (TAC) COURSE

Course Objective: The course is designed to familiarize senior aviators (0-5, 0-6) with the agencies and equipment the Marine Corps uses to command and control Marine Aviation, as well as, to enhance the commander's knowledge and ability to conduct combat operations in the context of the Six Functions of Marine Aviation. More specifically, the course was designed to enhance the knowledge of the TAC in the following areas:

1. How the Marine Air Command and Control System (MACCS) supports the six functions of Marine aviation.
2. The TACs relationship with the SAAWC at the TAOC, the SAD at the DASC, and other key individuals.
3. Aviation asset management, to include aircraft, MACCS agencies, and Ground Based Air Defense (GBAD) elements.
4. How the Tactical Air Command Center (TACC) operates and understand the various mediums by which information is displayed within the TACC.
5. TACC crew member responsibilities and how these crew members facilitate situational awareness and the implementation of decisions.
6. How the MACCS ties into the JCAC2 system.

Length: 14 classroom hours, 10 - 16 TACC hours (times do not include opportunities to participate in the planning and debriefing process).

Academic Syllabus:

1. Control of Aircraft and Missiles
2. The Tactical Air Command Center (TACC)
3. Marine Air Traffic Control
4. The MACCS in support Antiair Warfare
5. The MACCS in support of Direct Air Support
6. Airborne Early Warning
7. Data Link Interoperability
8. Combat Airspace
9. Joint Air Operations
10. Joint Combat Airspace Command and Control
11. ACE Communications
12. Intelligence Process/Systems
13. Contingency Theater Automated Planning System (CTAPS)
14. MACCS Tour
15. Joint Training
16. Guest Speakers

Flight Syllabus: The flight phase is integrated into the WTI flight evolutions and each officer will participate in one of three training windows. The intent is to balance system exposure with the minimum time required to accomplish objectives. Each window is ideally suited to train two officers. The TACs will serve as ACE Commanders for briefing, execution and debrief purposes during the training window they attend. The windows are as follows:

1. AAW Window. Comprised of three days: AAW-1 Plan, AAW-1 fly, and AAW-2 fly.
2. OAS Window. Comprised of five days: OAS-4 plan, OAS-3 fly, OAS-4 fly. OAS-3 fly, OAS-4 fly.
3. FINEX Window. Comprised of four days: FINEX-1 plan, FINEX-1 fly, FINEX-2 plan, and FINEX-2 fly.

MEU/SPMAGTF ACE COMMANDER'S COURSE

Course Objective: Enhance the knowledge of current or potential ACE Commanders in integrating and employing all elements of the ACE. Particular emphasis is placed on Offensive Air Support; Command, Control and Communications; and Naval Expeditionary Force integration. Provide a forum to familiarize ACE Commanders with the following:

1. Offensive Air Support planning and the integration of fixed and rotary wing aircraft in close air support and assault support missions.
2. Marine Corps and Navy command and control agencies and procedures involved in executing Assault Support and Offensive Air Support missions.
3. Sources of aviation intelligence and how it is disseminated to the MEU/SPMAGTF ACE.
4. Issues involved with integrating the MEU/SPMAGTF ACE in the Naval Expeditionary Force and Joint Task Forces.

Length: 26 classroom hours

Academic Syllabus:

1. The academic syllabus includes the following classes:
   a. Aviation Intelligence
   b. Air Support Element
   c. LAAD/STINGER
   d. MATC Mobile Team
   e. MACG Detachment Integration 3-3
   f. KC-130 Capabilities and Employment
   g. Offensive Air Support Overview
   h. Offensive Air Support Platforms
   i. FAC(A) Employment
   j. Escort Operations
   k. Offensive Air Support Fixed Wing/Rotary Wing Integration
   l. Offensive Air Support Precision Guided Munitions
   m. Mission Load Allowance
   n. EDATF
   o. SH-60B
   p. Special Operations Aviation
   q. AEW Assets
   r. CVBG Integration
   s. TACRON
2. The course includes Guest Speakers with current or recent MEU/SPMAGTF ACE experience.

MAWTS-1 COMMANDERS COURSE

Course Objective: To update squadron and battalion commanding officers, executive officers, and other senior officers on Marine aviation tactics and training, joint operations and issues concerning the employment of Marine aviation in future conflicts.

Length: 24 classroom hours

Academic Syllabus:
1. The academic syllabus is divided into three phases; generic, common, and specific.
2. Specific syllabi will be published by MAWTS-1 prior to the beginning of each course.

MOBILE TRAINING CURRICULUM
MEU ACE TRAINING COURSE (MATC)

Course Objective: To improve the ability of the composite helicopter squadron planners to organize, plan for and conduct tactical operations as may be assigned by a respective task force or MEU commander. The following specific objectives further define the scope of this course:

1. Review the current capabilities of each of the platforms and agencies resident within the MEU aviation combat element.
2. Introduce the command and control agencies and procedures involved in executing Assault Support and Offensive Air Support missions.
3. Develop the capability to effectively and systematically conduct rapid response planning, for an assigned mission within the time specified by applicable mission performance standards.
4. Examine the relationships between threat capabilities and enroute/objective area
5. Effectively complete the tasks associated with the ACE in the accomplishment of MEU combat/continqency missions as specified in MCO 3120.

Length: 28 classroom hours (3 days of academics plus 1 day planning problem)

Course Syllabus:

1. MEU (SOC) Overview
2. ACE Capabilities Briefing
3. Aviation Intelligence
4. Navy Tactical Air Control System
5. Helicopterborne Assault Key Players
6. Assault Support Mission Planning Considerations
7. Rapid Response Planning
8. Objective Area Planning
9. Offensive Air Support Planning Considerations
10. Escort Planning Considerations
11. Contingency Area Brief (SPEAR)
12. MOUT
13. NEO
14. TRAP
15. Assault Support Planning Problem (optional)

GCE TRAINING COURSE

Course Objective: To improve the Ground Combat Element (GCE) staff and subordinate unit commanders' ability to employ aviation in support of a ground operation. The following are the objectives of this course:

1. Review the current capabilities of USMC Offensive Air Support and Assault Support aircraft.
2. Provide instruction on the process and agencies involved in requesting air support.
3. Introduce the functions of various MAGTF command and control agencies responsible for executing Assault Support and Offensive Air Support operations.
4. Examine techniques used by terminal controllers to maximize the effectiveness of Close Air Support (CAS).
5. Examine, through a guided exercise, the planning process involved in air operations from the battalion through the JTF level.
6. Encourage the direct exchange of concerns and ideas between MAWTS-1 instructors and GCE officers.

Length: 16 classroom hours

Academic Syllabus:

1. The academic syllabus includes the following classes:
   a. Helicopterborne Assault Operations Planning Fundamentals
   b. Helicopterborne Assault Key Players
   c. MACCS Overview
   d. Control of Aircraft and Missiles 4-3

e. Offensive Air Support (OAS) Planning Considerations
f. OAS Fixed Wing/Rotary Wing Integration
g. OAS Precision Guided Munitions
h. FAC(A)/TAC(A) Employment
i. Terminal Control Integration
j. Planning Problem
k. Intelligence

2. The last five hours of classroom instruction consist of a guided planning problem, exercising the planning process for air support from the battalion through JTF level.
3. The course includes an air support symposium at the end of the second day of instruction.

ACE TRAINING COURSE

Course Objective: To improve the Aviation Combat Element (ACE) staff and subordinate unit commanders' ability to employ aviation in support of a ground operation. The following are the objectives of this course:

1. Review the Battlestaff Planning process and how the ACE plans operations in support of the GCE.
2. Provide instruction on the intelligence capabilities available to the ACE.
3. Introduce the requirements of the Ground Combat Element in terms of Air Support and Fire Support Coordination.
4. Provide instruction on the Marine Air Command and Control System and the process for requesting and tasking aviation.
5. Review the planning considerations required to conduct and integrate Offensive Air Support and Assault Support operations.
6. Examine, through a planning problem, the planning process required to conduct air operations in support of the GCE.

Length: 16 Classroom Hours

Academic Syllabus:

1. The academic syllabus includes the following classes:
   a. Battle Staff Planning
   b. Intelligence Systems
   c. Ground Operations and Fire Support
   d. Tasking Marine Aviation
   e. Control of Aircraft and Missiles
   f. Assault Support Key Players
   g. Assault Support Mission Planning
   h. Offensive Air Support
   i. Escort Operations
   j. OAS Fixed Wing/Rotary Wing Integration
   k. Planning Problem

MARINE DIVISION TACTICS COURSE (MDTC)

Course Objective: To provide F/A-18 aircrew and Air Intercept Controllers (AIC) with ground and airborne instruction in the doctrine, tactics, and weapons employment considerations for successfully fighting a division or more of Marine fighters in multi-bogey, complex scenarios. The course is taught at the graduate level and is instructional vice evaluation oriented.

Length: 20 classroom hours 12-15 flight hours

Course Contents:

1. The course consists of an academic and flight phase. The length of the course varies depending upon the number of student aircrew. For a two division six crew course the nominal completion time is ten to fourteen days. With approval of Group Commanders a nine crew course can be conducted in sixteen to eighteen days.
2. The course begins with an academics phase, consisting of two and one half days of lectures. This phase normally begins on Saturday morning and concludes Monday morning. Academic only students from the respective MAG(s) are encouraged to attend, but the number of available seats will be kept at a minimum to preserve the student-to-instructor ratio. When the course is conducted away from Yuma academic requirements, i.e. seating and audio visual equipment, will be given to the respective MAG. The academic syllabus begins with a MDTC Program in-brief and follows with twelve lectures to include:
   a. AI M-7
   b. AIM-1 20
   c. AI M-9
   d. Threat Aircraft
   e. Threat Tactics
   f. Intercept Control
   g. Radar Employment
   h. Fighter Missions
   i. Division Tactics
   j. Self Protect Considerations
   k. Threat Radar Missile Update
   l. Threat IR Missile Update

   In addition to these lectures, controllers will receive instruction in the following classes:
   a. AIC Inbrief
   b. AIC Briefing and Debriefing
   c. Tactical Terminology and the AIC
   d. FSU Tactics Trainer
   e. Situational Awareness and Radio Transmissions Lecture
   f. Range Brief and Area Familiarization
   g. Simulator events
   h. Control Equipment Familiarization

The lectures are taught at the graduate level and a classified take-home package containing all of the lectures is given to each individual. The academic phase concludes with a Flight Phase in-brief. Total lecture time is approximately twenty hours.

3. The flight phase, which is normally ten days, consists of ten different sorties; all of which are flown on a TACTS range. Each aircrew undergoing training will normally fly a single sortie on eight fly days and two sorties on the remaining days. During this phase each aircrew will lead a minimum of four sorties including M-581 and M-585. Student crews normally lead a total of five to six sorties. Actual responsibilities for briefing, leading, and debriefing for each aircrew under instruction will be specified by the MAWTS-1 staff during the MDTC inbrief. Students will also receive an MDTC syllabus guide which covers specific sortie requirements. The following is a list of the sorties with a brief description:

Sortie	Mission	# of a/c	Remarks
a. M 579	Prestrike Sweep	2v2	Warm-up.
b. M 580	Prestrike Sweep	4v4	MAWTS-1 IP brief/lead.
c. M 581	Sweep	4v4	Each student briefs/leads. Each division will fly this sortie once at night.
d. M582	Moving BARCAP	4v4	
e. M583	HVAA CAP	4v4	
f. M584	Self-Protect	4-8v4	Each division briefs/leads.
g. M 585	Point Defense	4vX	Each student briefs/leads.
h. M586	BARCAP	4vX	Helo intercept/attack
i. M587	Escort	4-8vX	Low altitude ingress/egress simulating adverse weather. Each division briefs/leads.
j. M 588	Prestrike Sweep/Escort	4-8vX	Each division briefs/leads.

4. If a two division course is being conducted M-581, 584, 587, & 588 will be flown twice with each division leading once. M-581 will be flown once at night unless prohibited by crew day restrictions. NVGs will be used within the guidelines of T&R volume 1 & 2. If a division is scheduled to fly twice in one day the aircrew leading the second sortie will not fly in the morning event.
5. The course length limits available training to nine student crews and four AIC students. If one to three student crews are attending the course a single division syllabus will be flown, while four to six student crews require a two division course and seven to nine student crews will require a three division course. A MAWTS-1 instructor crew is required for airborne instruction in each student division.
6. If additional seats are available in the divisions, i.e. a two division four crew course, the squadron supplying the additional aircraft may fill the slot. We require at least ACM qualified aircrew and recommend that competent individuals be selected so that training for the students is not degraded.
7. Adversary aircraft will be provided primarily by VMFT-401. Additional dissimilar adversaries will be scheduled to augment "401" and to provide a more representative fourth generation threat. MAWTS-1 will coordinate adversary and range scheduling when the course is flown out of Yuma or Miramar and will notify MAG-31 of adversary and range requirements when the course is flown out of Beaufort. Adversary aircraft will simulate the following threat aircraft:

Adversary A/C	Threat A/C	Weapons
F-5	Mig-23K/Mig-29	Archer/ApexJAlamo
F-16	Mig-29/Su-27	Archer/Alamo A/C
F-1	Mig-29/Su-27	Archer/Alamo A/C

Certification Stage

1. Successful completion of all sorties is required for graduation. The aircrew under instruction will normally brief, lead and debrief 40% of the sorties flown during the course.
2. Emphasis will be placed on briefing and debriefing, radar sorting and targeting, mutual support, communications, AIC integration and weapons employment.
3. A form of positive identification (PID), which will be delineated in the syllabus guide, will be required for all sorties.
4. FSU formations and tactics will be flown by the adversaries.
5. A face to face brief and debrief is required.
6. All sorties will be flown on a TACTS range, R-2301 (NYL), or SOA-3X & 4X (NBC).

Sortie Description

AA 579 — 2 F/A-18 vs 2 Adversaries — T&R M 229(A/C)/334(D)

Description: 2 vs 2 Prestrike Sweep

Goal: Practice section maneuvering against a dissimilar section. This sortie will be a warm-up sortie.

Requirements: Based upon the scenario provided by the MAWTS-1 instructor, the aircrew under instruction will brief, execute, analyze, and debrief the following; Two intercepts to engagements and bugouts and one short set of 15-20 NM to practice section forward quarter missile defense.

AA 580 — 4 F/A-18 vs 4 Adversaries — T&R AA 434

Description: 4 vs 4 Prestrike Sweep

Goal: Practice division tactics in support of a strike package against a dissimilar division.

Requirements: A MAWTS-1 instructor will brief, execute, analyze, and debrief two combat intercepts in a Prestrike Sweep role.

AA 581 — (N) 4 F/A-18 vs 4 Adversaries — T&R AA 434(AIC)1432(D)

Description: 4vs4 Sweep

Goal: Practice division tactics in a Sweep role against a dissimilar division. When flown at night emphasis will be placed on night flight control and intercept considerations.

Requirements:

1. Based upon the scenario provided by the MAWTS-1 instructor, the aircrew under instruction will brief, execute, analyze, and debrief two combat intercepts in a Sweep role.
2. Every student will brief, lead and debrief this sortie.
3. Every division will fly this sortie once at night.

AA 582 — 4 F/A-18 vs 4 Adversaries — T&R M 432(AIC)/433(D)

Description: 4 vs 4 Moving BARCAP

Goal: Practice division tactics as a Moving BARCAP against a dissimilar division. emphasis will be placed on CAP management.

Requirements: Based upon the scenario provided by the MAWTS-1 instructor, the aircrew under instruction will brief, execute, analyze, and debrief two combat intercepts in a Moving BARCAP role.

AA 583 — 4 F/A-18 vs 4 Adversaries — T&R M 338(A/C)/431(D)

Description: 4 vs 4 HVM CAP

Goal: Practice division tactics in support of a high value airborne asset against a dissimilar division. Emphasis will be placed on CAP management and protection of a high value airborne asset.

Requirements: Based upon the scenario provided by the MAWTS-1 instructor, the aircrew under instruction will brief, execute, analyze, and debrief two combat intercepts in a HVM CAP role.

AA 584 — 4-8F/A-18 vs 4 Adversaries — T&R M 436(A/C)/434(D)

Description: 4-8vs4 Self-Protect

Goal: Practice division tactics enroute to and returning from a target against a dissimilar division. Emphasis will be placed on the ingress and egress of a strike package into a target area.

Requirements:

1. Based upon the scenario provided by the MAWTS-1 instructor, the aircrew under instruction will brief, execute, analyze, and debrief a Self-Protect strike package into and out of a target area.
2. Each division will fly this sortie as the lead division.

AA 585 — 4 F/A-18 vs X Adversaries — T&R M 432(A/C)/433(D)

Description: 4vsX Point Defense

Goal: Practice division tactics in a Point Defense against a dissimilar unknown number of adversaries. Emphasis will be placed on CAP management and targeting multiple groups.

Requirements:

1. Based upon the scenario provided by the MAWTS-1 instructor, the aircrew under instruction will brief, execute, analyze, and debrief two periods in a Point Defense role.
2. Every student will brief. lead and debrief this sortie

AA 586 — 4 F/A-18 vs X Adversaries — T&R M 438.434(A/C)/432,436(D)

Description: 4 vs X BARCAP

Goal: Practice division tactics against a dissimilar unknown number of adversaries (Fixed Wing and Rotary Wing). Emphasis will be placed on detection, intercept and escort/attack of helicopters.

Requirements: Based upon the scenario provided by the MAWTS-1 instructor, the aircrew under instruction will brief, execute, analyze, and debrief two vul periods in a BARCAP role.

AA 587 4-8 — F/A-18 vs X Adversaries — T&R M 434(A/C)/432(D)

Description: 4-8 vs X Escort

Goal: Practice division tactics in support of a strike package against a dissimilar unknown number of adversaries. Emphasis will be placed on low altitude tactics and strike package integration.

Requirements:

1. Based upon the scenario provided by the MAWTS-1 instructor, the aircrew under instruction will brief, execute, analyze, and debrief an Escort mission into and out of a target area.
2. In order to emphasize low altitude tactics a ceiling of 10,000' will be used.
3. A minimum of two strike aircraft are required.

AA 588 — 4-8 F/A-18 vs X Adversaries — T&R M 436(A/C)/434(D)

Description: 4-8 vs X Prestrike Sweep/Escort

Goal: Practice division tactics in support of a strike package against a dissimilar unknown number of adversaries. Emphasis will be placed on integration between the Sweep, Escort and Strike divisions.

Requirements:

1. Based upon the scenario provided by the MAWTS-1 instructor, the aircrew under instruction will brief, execute, analyze, and debrief a Prestrike Sweep and Escort mission into and out of a target area.
2. Each division will fly this sortie as the lead division.
3. A minimum of two strike aircraft are required. The strike route will be provided by the MAWTS-1 instructor.
4. In the event 8 aircraft are not available, a MIGSWEEP in support of a strike will be executed.
5. A face to face brief and debrief is required.
6. Airspace: R2301 (NYL), SOA-3Xand 4X(NBC).

AIC Instructor Under Training (IUT) Stage

1. The squadron is responsible for ensuring that the controller under instruction is prepared for the course. At a minimum, the controller under instruction must be current in the following T&R sorties prior to the beginning of MDTC.
   a. FI-263, 2 vs UNK VAD X
   b. FI-264, 2 vs UNK MIGSWEEP
2. Successful completion of all sorties in the MDTC and completion of an academic test with a minimum grade of 80% is required for graduation. The controller under instruction will assist in the brief and debrief of 50% of the sorties flown during the course. Actual responsibilities for briefing and debriefing for each controller under instruction will be specified by the MAWTS-1 staff during the Flight Phase Inbrief.
3. Standardized scenarios will be provided to the students and bogies for each sortie.
4. All sorties will be flown on a TACTS Range, but controlled from the MACS tactical gear (TAOM). Equipment requirements include a minimum of (1) AN/TYQ-23, (1) AN/TPS-59, and (1) AN/TPS-63.

F/A-18 MDTC REQUEST MESSAGE

FROM: REQUESTING MAG
TO: MAWTS-1 YUMA AZ//S3//
INFO: CG MCCDC QUANTICO VA//ITE32A// APPROPRIATE CHAIN OF COMMAND//S3//
UNCLAS//NO3500//
MSGID/GENADMIN//

SUBJ: REQUEST FOR MDTC SUPPORT//
REF/A/DOC/MCOP3500.12B//
REF/B/DOC/MCOP3500.19C, CHAPTER 13,14//
REF/C/MAWTS-1 COURSE CATALOG//
POC/NAM E/RAN K/UNIT/TEL: DSNNO//
RMKS/1. IAW THE REFS, THE FOLLOWING SUPPORT IS REQUESTED:

A. TYPE SUPPORT: MDTC CERTIFICATION FOR (X) AIRCREW.
B. AIRCRAFT/SOFTWARE TYPE: (X) F/A-18A, (X) F/A-18C/(X)SOFTWARE, (X) F/A-18D/ (X) SOFTWARE.
C. COURSE LOCATION: MCAS YUMA/MIRIMAR OR MCAS BEAUFORT)
D. COURSE DATES:
2. REQUEST MAWTS-1 SCHEDULE RANGE SPACE AND ADVERSARY SORTIES FOR THE YUMA/MIRIMAR COURSE. FOR THE BEAUFORT COURSE, REQUEST MAWTS-1 NOTIFY MAG-31 OF ACADEMIC, RANGE SPACE AND ADVERSARY REQUIREMENTS.

MDTC STUDENT NOMINATION MESSAGE

FROM: REQUESTING MAG
TO: MAWTS-1 YUMA AZ//S311
INFO: CG MCCDC QUANTICO VA//TE32A//
APPROPRIATE CHAIN OF COMMAND//S3//
UNCLAS//NO3500//
MSGID/GENADMIN/(APPROPRIATE UNIT/(SHOP)/(MONTH)//
AMPN/SUBJ: SUBMISSION OF MDTC STUDENT NOMINATION//
REF/A/DOC/MCOP3500. 1 2B/-//
REF/B/MAWTS-1 COURSE CATALOG//
RMKS/1. IAW THE REFS, THE FOLLOWING NOMINEE(S) IS/ARE SUBMITTED:
A. NAME, RANK, SSN
B. UNIT/MOS/MODEL ACFT
C. TOTAL FLIGHT HOURS
D. HOURS IN MODEL
E. FLIGHT QUALIFICATIONS *(PROVIDE DESIGNATION DATES/INFO)*
(1) DIVISION LDR (PILOT)
(2) MSN CDR (WSO)
(3) ACTI
(4) NSQ/NTI
(5) TOTAL NVG HOURS
F. EXPECTED WTI COURSE DATE OR DATE WTI COMPLETED
G. SECURITY CLEARANCE/BASIS/DATE
H. SQUADRON POC/DSN
I. SQUADRON MAILING ADDRESS

MDTC AIC STUDENT NOMINATION MESSAGE

FROM: REQUESTING MACG
TO: MAWTS-1 YUMAAZ//S31C311
INFO: CG MCCDC QUANTICO VA//TE32A//
APPROPRIATE CHAIN OF COMMAND//S3//
MAG-XXIIS-311

UNCLAS//NO3500//
MSGID/GENADMIN//
SUBJ: SUBMISSION OF MDTC AIC STUDENT NOMINATION//
REF/A/DOC/MCOP3500.19C, CHAPTER 13,14//
REF/B/MAWTS-1 COURSE CATALOG//
REF/C/MSG/MAG-X)(/REQ FOR MDTC SUPT/DTG//
POC/NAMF/RANK/IJNIT/TEL DSNNO//
RMKS/1. IAW THE REFS, THE FOLLOWING NOMINEE(S) IS/ARE SUBMITTED
A. NAME, RANK, SSN (SPECIFY FEMALE)
B. MOS
C. UNIT
D. CURRENT BILLET
E. SENIOR WEAPONS DIRECTOR DATE OF DESIGNATION
F. UNIT POC
G. SECURITY CLEARANCE HELD, DATE AND BASIS FOR ISSUE
2. THE NOMINEE(S) HAS/HAVE NOT ATTENDED NFWS POWER PROJECTION COURSE (TOPGUN)CHAPTER FIVE

GENERIC ACADEMIC SUPPORT PACKAGE

Course Objective: To provide additional ground training as required by MCO P3500. 14D.

Length: 17 classroom hours

Academic Syllabus:

1. The following classes should be presented on a regular basis as part of a sound ground training plan:
   a. MAGTF Organization and Equipment
   b. MAGTF: The Amphibious Assault
   c. MACCS Part 1
   d. MACCS Part 2
   e. Intel Sources and Collection
   f. Opposing Forces Ground Tactics
   g. Basic Radar Principles
   h. Soviet Tactical Surface to Air Threat Systems (SAMS/AAA)
   i. Non-Soviet SAMS/AAA
   j. Soviet IADS
   k. Surface to Surface Threat
   1. Soviet REC
   m. Soviet Rotary Wing Technology Trends
   n. Soviet Rotary Wing Tactics
   o. Soviet Air to Ground Tactics and Weapons
   p. The Soviet Pilot
   q. Tactical Recovery of Aircraft and Personnel (TRAP)
2. The above listed classes reflect the Generic ASP as of the last MAWTS-1 update. The entire MAWTS-1 ASP is scheduled to be updated/published on CD-ROM 1 July 1996.

TACAIR COMMON ACADEMIC SUPPORT PACKAGE

Course Objective: To provide additional ground training for fixed wing aircrew on general subject matter, as required by MCO P3500.14D.

Length: 1 5 classroom hours

Academic Syllabus:

1. The following classes should be presented on a regular basis as part of a sound ground training plan:
   a. LAT Part I: Philosophy and Concepts
   b. LAT Part II: Considerations
   c. LAT Part Iil: Basic and Section Maneuvering
   d. LAT Part IV: Advanced Maneuvering
   e. LAT Part V: Instructional Techniques
   f. AAW Planning
   g. OAAW
   h. OAS Planning and Execution
   i. Terminal Control Procedures
   j. Helo Attack
   k. Escort Tactics (R/W)
   l. Air/Air Missile Countertactics
   m. SAMS/MA Countertactics
   n. JMEMS
   o. Laser Smart Weapons
   p. Escort Tactics

EA-6B SUPPLEMENTARY COURSES

EA-6B SPECIFIC ACADEMIC SUPPORT PACKAGE

Course Objective: To provide EA-6B aircrew with additional ground training as required by MCO P3500.14D.

Length: 12 classroom hours

Academic Syllabus:

1. The following classes should be presented on a regular basis as part of a sound training plan:
   a. EA-6B Burnthrough
   b. Electronic Warfare
   c. War at Sea Tactics and Planning
   d. Electronic Warfare in support of CAS (EWCAS)
   e. Maximizing Jamming Effectiveness
   f. HARM: Definitions and Employment Considerations
   g. USMC Intelligence System
   h. Electronic Protection Fixes
   i. Special Information Systems Aircraft
   j. CV NATOPS/TACPROS
   k. Battle Group Organization
   l. Effective Electronic Warfare Support (ES)
   m. USQ-1 13 Tactical Considerations

EA-6B LOW ALTITUDE TACTICS (LAT) COURSE

Course Objective: To provide EA-6B aircrew with ground instruction necessary to safely participate in LAT flight training.

Length: 5 classroom hours

Academic Syllabus:

1. The following classes will be presented to the aircrew under instruction prior to flying any combat ready or subsequent LAT sortie:
   a. LAT Part I: Philosophy and Concepts
   b. LAT Part II: Considerations
   c. LAT Part III: Basic and Section Maneuvering
   d. LAT Part IV: Advanced Maneuvering
2. The following class shall be presented to the aircrew under instruction prior to the SFAM-400 and FAM-401 sorties.
   a. EA-6B Advanced Maneuvering.
3. The academic syllabus should be reviewed annually.

EA-6B AIR TO AIR COURSE

Course Objective: To provide ground instruction enabling the EA-6B aircrew to successfully defend against a fixed wing attack and safely participate in defensive tactics (DEFTAC) training.

Length: 15 classroom hours.

Academic Syllabus:

1. The following class will be presented to the aircrew under instruction prior to flying any combat ready air-to-air sortie:
   a. Basic Air Maneuvers
2. The following classes will be presented to the aircrew under instruction prior to flying any combat qualified air to air sortie:
   a. ACM Terms and Definitions
   b. Aerodynamics in ACM and Energy Maneuverability
   c. Air to Air Weapons
   d. Defensive Maneuvering Principles
   e. Threat Assessment
   f. Preflight Preparation and Intra-cockpit Communication
   g. Briefing and Debriefing Techniques
   h. HVU Tactics
   i. Air to Air Missile Countertactics
3. The following classes should be integrated into the full combat qualification phase of training:
   a. FSU F/W Strengths and Weaknesses
   b. FSU F/W Basic Tactics Employment
   c. FSU Air to Air Missiles Part 1
   d. ROW Air to Air Missiles Part 1
4. The academic syllabus should be reviewed annually.

EA-6B LOW ALTITUDE TACTICS INSTRUCTOR (LATI) CERTIFICATION COURSE

Course Objective: To certify the EA-6B aircrew as an instructor capable of safely conducting ground and airborne instruction of the EA-6B low altitude tactics (LAT) syllabus.

Length: 5 classroom hours 6.0 flight hours.

Academic Syllabus:

1. The instructor under training (IUT) will review and be capable of presenting all classes listed in the EA-6B LAT Course.
2. The following class will be presented to the IUT prior to beginning the IUT stage of the flight syllabus:
   a. LAT Part V: Instructional Techniques

Flight Syllabus:

Instructor Under Training (IUT) Stage

1. The squadron WTI will conduct a build-up phase to prepare the IUT for certification. LAT IUT build-up syllabus codes are LAT 591 - LAT 593.
2. During the LATI build-up, the WTI will demonstrate to the IUT appropriate flight brief techniques, structure and objectives, correct chase positions, and highlight common errors in every maneuver.
3. During the LATI build-up, the IUT must demonstrate the ability to brief, lead, debrief and instruct LAT maneuvers. The LAT IUT must demonstrate a working knowledge of, and an elevated level of proficiency, in all maneuvers delineated in the EA-6B LAT syllabus defined in MCO P3500.15B with particular emphasis on safety and absolute adherence to LAT rules of conduct.

Certification Stage

1. The IUT will brief, lead, debrief, and demonstrate to the squadron EA-6B WTI or MAWTS-1 instructor the capability to provide LAT instruction. The following sortie will be flown during the certification phase:
   LAT 594 E 2EA-6B T&R: LAT 394

Goal: Certify LAT IUT in the instruction of LAT.

Requirements: The LAT IUT will brief, lead and debrief the flight IAW the requirements outlined in the LAT 394 sortie with the following exceptions:

1. IUT is responsible for section lead and will initiate turns at comfort level.
2. Pilot IUT will be evaluated with respect to chase position and procedures, section control. all LAT tasks and instructional techniques.
3. ECMO IUT will be evaluated with respect to section control, all LAT tasks, understanding of chase procedures and position, and instructional techniques.

Refresher Requirements:

1. Certified EA-6B LATI aircrew returning to the EA-6B following less than 18 months out of model will retain the LATI certification and may be designated as a LATI at the discretion of the commanding officer.
2. Certified EA-6B LATI aircrew requiring refresher training in accordance with MCO P3500.14D must complete an EA-6B LATI recertification course. Upon recertification by the squadron WTI or MAWTS-1 instructor, the LATI designation can be made by the squadron commanding officer. The following comprises the EA-6B LATI recertification course:
   a. The aircrew under instruction must satisfy all prerequisites.
   b. The aircrew under instruction must complete the LAT 594 sortie evaluated by the squadron EA-6B WTI or MAWTS-1 instructor.

Transition Requirements:

1. Aircrew designated as a LATI in an aircraft other than the EA-6B that undergo transition training in accordance with MCO P3500.14D must complete the entire- EA-6B LATI Certification Course.

Conversion Requirements:

1. Aircrew designated as a LATI in an aircraft other than the EA-6B, that undergo conversion training to the EA-6B must complete the entire EA-6B LATI Certification Course.

EA-6B DEFENSIVE TACTICS INSTRUCTOR (DEFTACI) CERTIFICATION COURSE

Course Objective: To certify the EA-6B aircrew as a DEFTACI, capable of safely conducting ground and airborne instruction of the EA-6B air to air flight syllabus outlined in MCO P3500.15B.

Length: 9 classroom hours 7.5 flight hours

Academic Syllabus:

1. The IUT will receive the following periods of instruction:
   a. EA-6B DEFTACI Program
   b. EA-6B DEFTACI Briefing Guide
   c. DEFTACI Briefing and Debriefing Techniques
2. The IUT will review and be capable of presenting all classes listed in the EA-6B Air to Air Course.
3. The IUT will successfully complete a DEFTAC instructor exam, administered by a MAWTS-1 instructor, prior to beginning the certification stage. The IUT Stage (build-up phase) may be conducted prior to successful completion of the MAWTS-1 DEFTACI examination.
4. The IUT will present to the MAWTS-1 instructor, one of the classes listed in the EA-6B Air to Air Course, as selected by the MAWTS-1 instructor, prior to finishing the certification process.
5. The MAWTS-1 instructor will present the following class to the IUT prior to the certification stage:
   a. DEFTACI Inbrief

Flight Syllabus:

Instructor Under Training (IUT) stage

1. The squadron WTI/DEFTACI will conduct a build-up phase to ensure that the IUT is prepared for certification by MAWTS-1.

2. During the build-up, the IUT will demonstrate the capability to brief, lead, debrief, and instruct basic tactical maneuvering in a multi-aircraft environment.
3. UT syllabus codes are ACM 520-ACM 522. The IUT stage will be tailored to the capabilities of the IUT and will include the IUT conducting the following sorties from an instructional viewpoint:
   a. EA-6B Basic Aircraft Maneuvering, T&R code ACM 520.
   b. EA-6B vs. EA-6B, T&R code ACM 521.
   c. EA-6B vs 1 Adversary, T&R code ACM 522.

Certification Stage:

1. The DEFTAC IUT will brief, lead, debrief, and demonstrate to the MAWTS-1 instructor the ability to conduct airborne DEFTAC instruction. Emphasis will be placed on:
   a. Briefing all basic tactical, defensive maneuvers.
   b. Conducting airborne instruction of basic tactical defensive maneuvering.
   c. Debriefing the flight evolution to include reconstruction of engagements and emphasizing lessons learned.
2. The following sorties will be flown during the certification stage:
   <u>ACM 523E</u> <u>1.7</u> <u>2 EA-6B</u> <u>T&R ACM 320</u>

Goal: To demonstrate proficiency of the skills required to instruct 1 v 1 s defensive maneuvering.

Requirement: The IUT will brief, lead, instruct, and debrief a 1v1 similar defensive tactics sortie consisting of the following items. The IUT will provide demonstration and instruction of the maneuvers from both an attacker's defender's position:

1. Eyeball calibration. Control flight to calibrate eyeballs with respect to weapons envelopes.
2. Pure, lead, and lag pursuit
3. High and low yo-yo's
4. Barrel roll
5. Guns envelope
6. Basic counters to above mentioned offensive maneuvers
7. Counters to raking and saddled guns
   <u>ACM 524 E</u> <u>1.7</u> <u>1 EA-6B vs. 1 Dissimilar Adversary</u> <u>T&RACM 322</u>

Goal: To demonstrate mastery of the instructional skills required for the conduct EA-6B defensive tactics maneuvering.

Requirement: The IUT will brief, lead, instruct, and debrief a 1v1 flight with aggressor aircraft. The IUT will demonstrate to the MAWTS-1 instructor the the ability to instruct the following set-ups:

1. Attacker less than 60 degrees angle off and less than 1.5NM
2. Attacker greater than 60 degrees angle off and less than 1.5NM
3. Guns defense drill
   a. Raking guns
   b. Saddled guns
4. Head on engagements to a forward quarter missile defense
5. Emphasis will be on defense against an attacker using all aspect IR missiles and 23 mm guns.

Refresher Requirements:

1. Certified EA-6B DEFTACI aircrew returning to the EA-6B following less than 18 months out of model will retain the DEFTACI certification and may be designated as a DEFTACI at the discretion of the commanding officer.
2. Certified EA-6B DEFTACI aircrew requiring refresher training in accordance with MCO P3500.14D must complete an EA-6B DEFTACI recertification course. Upon recertification by MAWTS-1, the DEFTACI designation can be made by the squadron commanding officer. The following comprises the recertification course.
   a. The IUT must meet all prerequisites listed previously.
   b. The IUT must complete the academic syllabus outlined previously, including the DEFTACI exam administered by the MAWTS-1 instructor.
   c. The IUT must complete an IUT flight syllabus that prepares him for recertification outlined by the squadron WTI.
   d. The IUT must complete the ACM 524 sortie, evaluated by the MAWTS-1 instructor.

Transition Requirements:

1. Aircrew designated as a DEFTACI or ACTI in an aircraft other than the EA-6B, that transition to the EA-6B, must complete the entire EA-6B DEFTACI Certification Course previously outlined.

Conversion Requirements:

1. Aircrew designated as a DEFTACI or ACTI in an aircraft other than the EA-6B, that undergo conversion to the EA-6B, must complete the entire EA-6B DEFTACI Certification Course previously outlined.

EA-6B ELECTRONIC WARFARE TRAINING PROGRAM

Course Objective: To provide EA-6B aircrew with ground instruction in the employment of the EA-6B's various weapons systems and the planning requirements for optimum employment.

Length: Variable. Depends upon the squadron's requirements.

Academic Syllabus:

1. The list below serves as a list to draw the training material from. Any or all of the below can be scheduled for instruction.
   a. Electronic Warfare
   b. IW/C2W
   c. EW Principles
   d. EP Fixes
   e. Jamming Fundamentals
   f. JATO & Effectiveness
   g. Offensive Antiair Warfare
   h. EW Targeting
   i. ACE SEAD Planning/SEAD Planning Problem
   j. USQ-113 Operations
   k. EA General Tactics
   l. USQ-1 13 Tactical Considerations
   m. HARM Tactical Employment
   n. HARM: Tactics, Targeting, & Deconfliction
   o. EWCAS
   p. HARM as a Sensor
   q. Shooter-to-Shooter Initiatives
   r. HARM Tailoring
   s. HARM: MME/MNT & Tailor Problem
   t. Considerations for Effective ES
   u. Chaff/Flare Theory and Application
   v. Mission Planning Manually
   w. Training Management
   x. Squadron Deployment Preparation
   y. Helo & Ground Support Considerations
   z. OAAW Manager/SEAD During CAS
   aa. HVM Protection Considerations
   ab. Special Systems Information Aircraft
   ac. DAS Planning and Problem
   ad. Any ASP lecture

EA-6B ELECTRONIC WARFARE MOBILE TRAINING PROGRAM

Course Objective: To expose EA-6B aircrew to the employment and optimization of the EA-6B's electronic warfare/C2W capabilities and weapons systems.

Length: 25 classroom hours/three days.

Academic Syllabus:

1. The MAWTS-1 instructor(s) will in-brief the squadron(s) on the EWMTP prior to beginning the course.
2. The Squadron(s) will receive instruction from the MAWTS-1 instructor(s) on the following classes:

a.	Chaff Corridor Applications/Theory	1.0 hrs
b.	EW Principles	1.0 hrs
c.	Jamming Technique Optimization (JATO)	3.0hrs
d.	Jamming Fundamental	1.0hrs
e.	EP Fixes	1.0hrs
f.	HARM	6.0hrs
g.	Radar Guided SAMs	1.0hrs
h.	Engagement Based Planning	2.0hrs
i.	USQ-113: Ops and Application	2.0hrs
j.	EAD in the CAS Environment	4.0hrs
k.	Electronic Attack: General Tactics	1.0hrs
l.	Considerations for Effective EW Support	1.0hrs
m.	Mission Planning Manually	1.0hrs

SAMPLE MAWTS-1 INSTRUCTOR SUPPORT REQUEST

From: (Requesting Unit)
To: MAWTS ONE YUMA AZ
INFO: CG MCCDC QUANTICO VA/TE/C462//(Appropriate Chain of Command)
UNCLASS//NO3500//
SUBJ: REQUEST FOR MAWTS-1 STAFF INSTRUCTOR SUPPORT
REF: (A) MCO 3500.12
(B) MAWTS-1 COURSE CATALOG

1. PER REFS, THE FOLLOWING SUPPORT IS REQUESTED:
   A. Type support (list specific academic instruction, supplementary courses, or certification)
   B. Aircraft Type
   C. Number of aircrew to receive Instruction/Certification
   D. Location where support will be conducted
   E. Primary inclusive dates
   F. Alternate inclusive dates
   G. Anticipated adversaries (Organization/home station)
2. (In case of ground academic instruction, the following statement must appear:)

Classroom space for the dates indicated I par 1 has been reserved and personnel receiving the requested academic instruction have been directed/sceduled to attend. (In the case of inflight instruction or certification, the following statement must appear:) The sorties required including adversary sorties for the requested inflight instruction/certification as listed in ref (B) have been planned/scheduled. Range space to conduct these sorties has been planned/scheduled.

AV-8B SUPPLEMENTARY COURSES

AV-8B SUPPLEMENTARY COURSES AV-8B LOW ALTITUDE TACTICS (LAT) COURSE

Course Objective: To provide AV-8B aircrew with ground instruction necessary to safely participate in LAT flight training.

Length: 5 classroom hours

Academic Syllabus:

1. The following classes will be presented to the aircrew under instruction prior to flying any combat ready or subsequent LAT sortie:
   a. LAT Part I: Philosophy and Concepts
   b. LAT Part II: Considerations
   c. LAT Part III: Basic and Section Maneuvering
   d. LAT Part IV: Advanced Maneuvering
   e. Low Altitude Training
2. The following class will be presented to the aircrew under instruction prior to any flight outlined in MCO P3500. 15 that requires SAM Countertactics (SCT) maneuvering:
   a. SAMS/AAA Countertactics
3. Aircrew will successfully complete the advanced maneuvering exam prior to commencing the Combat Qualified phase of LAT flight training.
4. The academic syllabus should be reviewed annually.
   Note: The LAT ASP is presently under rewrite for release during CY 96.

AV-8B BASIC CONVENTIONAL WEAPONS DELIVERY (BCWD) COURSE

Course Objective: To provide ground training for the AV-8B aircrew enabling them to employ the AV-8B in the air to ground role.

Length: 14 classroom hours

Academic Syllabus:

1. The following classes should be presented to the aircrew under instruction prior to flying any air to ground sortie that requires carriage/release of the weapon or performance of that particular maneuver
   a. Air to Ground Weapons Delivery Theory
   b. Introduction to Aircraft and Mission Publications
   c. Determination of Air to Ground Delivery Parameters
   d. Sight Angle Determination and Error Analysis
   e. Computed Weapons Theory
   f. Dual Mode Tracker
   g. Air to Ground Target Designation Methods
   h. Weapons Delivery Modes
   i. Weapons Delivery Options
   j. Weapons Delivery Techniques
   k. Weapons System Programming
   l. 25mm Guna-2
   m. Practice Ordnance and Suspension Equipment
   n. Weapons Delivery Safety Considerations
   o. Air to Ground Briefing and Debriefing
   p. Air to Ground Review
2. All classes listed above will be presented prior to the completion of the combat capable flight stage outlined in MCO P3500.15 and should be reviewed annually.

AV-8B TACTICAL CONVENTIONAL WEAPONS DELIVERY (TCWD) COURSE

Course Objective: To provide ground training for the AV-8B aircrew enabling them to employ the AV-8B in the air to ground role.

Length: 23 classroom hours

Academic Syllabus:

1. The following classes should be presented to the aircrew under instruction prior to flying any air to ground sortie that requires carriage/release of the weapon or performance of that particular maneuver:
   a. Advanced Weapon Delivery Theory
   b. Probability of Hit/Early Burst
   c. Multiple Weapons Release Planning
   d. Weapons System Limitations and Restrictions
   e. Footprinting Program
   f. Degraded Weapon Delivery Modes & Procedures
   g. Pop-up Attacks
   h. Standardized CAS Attacks
   i. Night Visual Attack and Flare Delivery
   j. Target Attack Considerations
   k. Target Area Tactics
   l. Loft Weapons Delivery
   m. Conventional Weapons: Bombs
   n. Conventional Weapons Fuzing: Bombs
   o. Conventional Weapons: GBU
   p. Conventional Weapons: Clusters
   q. Conventional Weapons Fuzing: Clusters
   r. Conventional Weapons: Rockets
   s. Conventional Weapons Fuzing: Rockets
   t. Conventional Weapons: AGM-65E
   u. Conventional Weapons: AGM-65F
   v. Operations Guide: AGM-65E
   w. Operations Guide: AGM-65F
   x. Conventional Weapons: AGM-122A
   y. Operations Guide: AGM-122A
   z. MK-43 TDD
   aa. Reactive Weaponeering
   bb. Computed Weapons Systems Integration and Optimization
2. All classes listed above will be presented prior to completion of the AV-8B combat ready stage outlined in MCO P3500.15 and should be reviewed annually.

AV-8B OFFENSIVE AIR SUPPORT COURSE

Course Objective: To provide ground instruction enabling the AV-8B aircrew to employ the AV-8B and its associated weapons systems in all threat conditions.

Length: 6 classroom hours

Academic Syllabus:

1. The following classes should be presented to the aircrew under instruction prior to flying the Combat Ready OAS phase sortie:
   MACCS PART I (MAWTS-1 ASP)
   MACCS PART II (MAWTS-1 ASP)
   a. Introduction to OAS (MAWTS-1 ASP GWTI)
   b. OAS Planning
   c. Integration of Supporting Arms
   d. AV-8BVSTOL Employment Concept
   e. Armed Reconnaissance Execution
   f. Air Interdiction Execution
   g. Close Air Support Execution
   h. Suppression of Enemy Air Defense
   i. Terminal Control Procedures (MAWTS-1 ASP)
   j. Standard CAS attack
   k. Target Area Considerations

2. The academic syllabus should be reviewed annually.

AV-8B AIR TO AIR COURSE

Course Objective: To provide ground instruction enabling the AV-8B aircrew to tactically employ the AV-8B in the air to air role and safely participate in air to air training.

Length: 30 classroom hours

Academic Syllabus:

1. The following classes will be presented to the pilot under instruction prior to flying the appropriate combat ready stage air to air sortie
   a. One versus One Basic Fighter Maneuvers
   b. 9L-3 Aerial Gunnery
   c. 9L-5 Energy Maneuverability
   d. 9L-6 Basic Fighter Maneuvers
   e. 9L-7 Two versus One
   f. 9W-8 Combat Thrust Vector Control
   g. AIM-9 MAWTS-1 ASP
   h. APG-65 M Program Mode/Considerations
   i. 14L-1 MWPlanning and Execution
   j. 14L-2 Missile Envelopes/Shot Validation
   k. 14L-3 Intercepts I.
   l. 4L-4 Combat Section Tactics
   m. 1 4L-5 Strike Escort
   n. 14L-7 Division Tactics
2. The academic syllabus should be reviewed annually.

AV-8B NIGHT ATTACK COURSE

Course Objective: To provide ground instruction necessary for the AV-8B aircrew to safely and effectively employ the AV-8B in the night attack environment

Length: 7 classroom hours

Academic Syllabus:

1. The following classes will be presented to the aircrew under instruction prior to flying the SFAM-301 sortie:
   a. Introduction to Night Attack
   b. The Digital Moving Map and Mission Display.
   c. Introduction to the Night Attack FLIR 1,2, and 3
   d. Night Attack Safety Considerations
   e. Introduction to Cats Eyes Night Vision Goggles 1 and 2
   f. AV-8 TACMAN Vol III Chapter 3 Air-to-Surface tactics
2. The following classes will be presented to the aircrew under instruction prior to flying fully combat qualified phase of training:
   a. Night LAT program and Philosophy b. Night Attack Considerations in the LAT Environment
3. The following documents should be reviewed by all aircrew prior to commencing Night Systems flight training:
   a. AV-8B Tactical Manual Vol I Sensor Information
   b. AV-8B Night Attack - Operational Tactics Guide
   c. F/A-18 Night Attack - Operational Tactics Guide
4. The academic syllabus should be reviewed annually.

AV-8B ELECTRONIC WARFARE COURSE

Course Objective: To provide ground instruction necessary for the AV-8B aircrew to recognize, interpret, and counteract the electronic warfare threat, and participate in electronic warfare training.

Length: 9 classroom hours

Academic Syllabus:

1. The following classes should be presented to the aircrew under instruction prior to flying any combat qualified electronic warfare sortie:
   a. The Electro-Magnetic Spectrum's Role in Modern Combat
   b. Expendable Countermeasures
   c. ALR-67
   d. ALQ- 16
   e. ALE-39
   f. Basic Radar Principles
   g. Threat Reaction

2. The academic syllabus should be reviewed annually.

AV-8B LOW ALTITUDE TACTICS INSTRUCTOR (LATI) CERTIFICATION COURSE

Course Objective: To certify an AV-8B pilot as an instructor capable of safely conducting ground and airborne instruction of the AV-8B low altitude tactics flight syllabus outlined in MCO P3500.15B.

Length: 7 classroom hours 3.0 flight hours 3.0 simulator hours

Academic Syllabus:

1. The instructor under training (IUT) will present all lectures listed in the AV-8B LAT Course.
2. The following classes will be presented to the IUT prior to beginning the IUT stage of the flight syllabus:
   a. LAT Part V: Instructional Techniques
   b. LAT Bandit Bounce Techniques/Responsibilities
3. The IUT will successfully complete a LATI exam, administered by the MAWTS-1 instructor or squadron WTI, prior to beginning the certification flights.

Flight Syllabus:

Instructor Under Training (IUT) Stage

1. The squadron WTI will conduct a build-up phase to prepare the IUT for certification.
2. During the LATI build-up, the WTI will demonstrate to the IUT appropriate flight briefing techniques, structure and objectives, correct chase positions, and highlight common errors in every maneuver.
3. During the LATI build-up, the IUT must demonstrate the ability to brief, lead, debrief, and instruct LAT maneuvers. The LAT IUT must demonstrate a working knowledge of, and an elevated level of proficiency in, all maneuvers delineated in the AV-8B LAT syllabus defined in MCO P3500.15 with particular emphasis on safety and absolute adherence to LAT rules of conduct.

Certification Stage

1. The LAT IUT will brief, lead, debrief, and demonstrate to the squadron WTI or MAWTS-1 instructor the capability to provide LAT instruction. The following events will be flown during the certification stage:
2. If no simulator exists, the simulator sorties may be flown in a TAV-8B or chased AV-8B.
   LATI-1 E   1.0 hrs   SIMULATOR   T&R SLAT220

Goal: Demonstrate proficiency in briefing, and flying a LAT course in the AV-8B visual simulator.

Requirements:

1. The squadron WTI or MAWTS-1 instructor will evaluate the IUT's knowledge of and proficiency in:
   a. 25 degree dive recovery using 50% rule
   b. 360 degree sustained turns at comfort level
   c. Increased task loading (IFF, ALQ, weapons, etc.)
   d. Break turns initiated from comfort level
   e. Vertical jink (20,10)
   f. SOJ (20,10)
   g. TOJ (20,10)
   h. ROJ (20,10)
   i. SAM break
   j. Guns jink
   k. Turn radius exercise
   l. AV-8B performance and handling characteristics in the LAT environment
   m. Principles of safety and rules of conduct
   n. Conduct reactive LAT circuit with active threat sites
   LATI-2 E   1.0 hrs   SIMULATOR   T&R SLAT-221

Goal: Demonstrate proficiency in briefing and executing a single aircraft LAT circuit.

Requirements:

1. The IUT will demonstrate the ability to instruct a simulator LAT sortie. The profile will include all maneuvers included in LATI-1 plus a reactive LAT circuit, called turns, and low altitude abort procedures. A mountainous data base should be utilized to demonstrate ridgeline crossings. The WTI or MAWTS-1 instructor should demonstrate dangerous, procedural, and performance errors to the IUT. The IUT should demonstrate the ability to identify and correct the "students" errors.

2. The MAWTS-1 instructor or Squadron WTI will fly the LATI-1 sortie. The MAWTS-1 instructor or squadron WTI will evaluate the IUT's knowledge and proficiency in instructing all maneuvers listed in LATI-1.
   LATI-3 E 1.0 hrs SIMULATOR T&R SOAS 241

Goal: Demonstrate the ability to brief, lead, and debrief an instructional LAT sortie.

Requirements:

1. The IUT should demonstrate the ability to plan, brief and execute a high threat (under the weather) interdiction profile. The MAWTS-1 instructor or WTI will generate a scenario that supports a mission that will have to deal with a radarfighter and radar SAM threat on the ingress and egress from the target area. Emphasis should be placed on "heavy" weaponeering, DECM, expendables programs, and threat reaction. The MAWTS-1 instructor or WTI will monitor the mission from the simulator console, inputting new threats and "situations" that the IUT will have to deal with in order to get to the target and then egress.
   LATI-4: E 1.0 hours 2 AV-8B T&R LAT 224
1. The IUT will brief, lead, and debrief an instructional LAT sortie that includes all events called for the LAT-224 sortie. Proper emphasis should be placed on IUT chase position and threat counter-tactics. The IUT shall describe the WHY and the HOW for the advanced vertical maneuvers in relation to the THREAT. The threat reaction/expendables gameplan as compared to the threat should be explained by the IUT in great detail during the brief. The MAWTS-1 instructor or squadron WTI will evaluate the following:
   a. Briefing technique, structure, and objectives
   b. Instructional content of the brief
   c. Flight leadership and control with a simulated pilot under instruction
   d. Ability to recognize errors and flight path deviations
   e. In-fiight instructional techniques
   f. Knowledge of and adherence to rules of conduct and safety considerations
   g. Debriefing technique and ability to identify and correct errors and highlight important learning objectives
   LATI-5 E 1.0 hrs 2 AV-8B T&ROAS 343

Goal: Demonstrate the ability to brief, lead, and debrief a tactical LAT sortie.

Requirements:

1. The IUT will brief, lead, and debrief a tactical LAT sortie that includes all basic LAT maneuvers, look-out doctrine and SAM/AAA countertactics. The MAWTS-1 instructor or squadron WTI will evaluate the following:
   a. Briefing technique, structure, and objectives
   b. Instructional content of the brief
   c. Flight leadership and control with a simulated pilot under instruction
   d. Ability to recognize errors and flight path deviations
   e. In-flight instructional techniques
   f. Knowledge of and adherence to rules of conduct and safety considerations
   g. Debriefing technique and ability to identify and correct errors and highlight important learning objectives
2. The IUT will demonstrate his ability to plan and brief a successful target attack, ingress and egress routing through an IADS that includes a radar SAM/ AAAthreat and the threat reaction plan for the section.
   LATI-6: E 1.0 hours 4 AV-8B T&ROAS442

1. The IUT will brief, lead, and debrief a tactical OAS-442. A primary and alternate target attack will be planned. For this check-ride a minimum of 4 aircraft are required, with emphasis placed on the division attack, and appropriate threat reaction plans. The MAWTS-1 instructor or squadron WTI will give the IUT the scenario and targets 2 hours prior to the brief. The IUT's ability to delegate responsibility, and to construct, brief, and execute a tactically viable plan will be assessed by the check pilot.

Refresher Requirements:

1. Certified AV-8B LATI pilots returning to the AV-8B following less than 18 months out of model will retain the LATI certification and may be designated as a LATI at the discretion of the commanding officer.
2. Certified AV-8B LATI pilots requiring refresher training in accordance with MCO P3500.14D must complete an AV-8B LATI recertification course. Upon recertification by MAWTS-1 or the squadron WTI, the LATI designation can be made by the commanding officer. The following comprises the recertification course:
   a. The IUT must meet all prerequisites listed previously.
   b. The IUT must complete the academic syllabus listed previously.
   c. The IUT must complete an IUT flight syllabus, outlined by the squadron WTI, that prepares him for certification.
   d. The IUT must complete the LATI written exam plus the LATI -1, LAT-2, LATI-3, LASTI-4, and LATI-5 sorties evaluated by the MAWTS-1 instructor or WTI.

Transition Requirements:

1. Aircrew designated as a LATI in an aircraft other than the AV-8B that transition to the AV-8B must complete the entire AV-8B LATI Certification Course as outlined.

Conversion Requirements:

1. Aircrew designated as a LATI in an aircraft other than the AV-8B that undergo conversion to the AV-8B must complete the entire AV-8B LAT Certification Course as outlined.

AV-8B WEAPONS TRAINING OFFICER (WTO) CERTIFICATION COURSE

Course Objective: To certify an AV-8B pilot as a WTO, capable of safely conducting ground and airborne instruction in the employment and optimization of the AV-8B's air to surface weapons and weapons systems. This air to surface syllabus is outlined in MCO P3500. 1 5B.

Length: 24 classroom hours 2 simulator hours 2 flight hours (Seven days required for an average class of four and one instructor)

Academic Syllabus:

1. The MAWTS-1 instructor will inbrief the prospective WTO prior to beginning the certification course.
2. The prospective WTO will be familiar with the information provided in all the following classes to include the WTO Handbook (March 93 edition).
   a. Systems
   (1) ADC/INS/RALT derived Height Above Target
   (2) DMT/RADAR derived Height Above Target
   (3) SMC/ACP Operation and Degraded Modes
   (4) Footprinting Program

   b. Weapons
   (1) Weapons Restrictions and Limitations
   (2) GAU-12 System
   (3) Fuzes
   (4) General Purpose Bombs
   (5) Cluster Munitions (MK-20/CBU-78)
   (6) Rockets
   (7) GBU-12/16
   (8) AGM-65E
   (9) AGM-65F
   (10) AGM-1 22A

   c. Techniques
   (1) Air to Ground Briefing and Debriefing
   (2) Sight Angle Derivation and Dive Delivery Planning
   (3) Multiple Weapons Release Planning
   (4) Systems Management in the Target Area
   (5) Cruise Climbs/Ramp Downs/Loft/Pop-ups
   (6) Reactive Weaponeering

3. The prospective WTO will be required to present four of these lessons. Depending on class size, priority lectures will come from the systems and techniques sections with the remaining lectures filled from the weapons section.

4. The prospective WTO will successfully complete the WTO workbook given at the WTO inbrief. The workbook is to be completed by certifications end and prior to WTO certificates being issued.

Flight Syllabus:

WTO Under Training Stage:
1. The squadron WTI will ensure that the WTO under training is prepared for certification by MAWTS-1. This build up will be tailored to the capabilities of the prospective WTO, and will include flights from the air to ground syllabus outlined in MCO P3500.15B as required.
2. All simulator events will include (P) WTO "hands-on" time at the console in order to evaluate knowledge base and instructional techniques.

Certification Stage:

1. The following events will be evaluated by the MAWTS-1 instructor:

   WTO-1 E SIMULATOR 0.5 hrs T&R: 211 WTO-1 E

High/Low angle MK-76/BDU-48 deliveries. The prospective WTO shall perform academic 10 and 45 degree deliveries in the AV-8B visual simulator. Emphasis will be placed on systems optimization and utilization of a systems/sensor upgrade or cascade plan in order to achieve first pass success and optimize delivery accuracy as well as off target maneuvering, expendable usage and communications. High angle release parameters should be utilized that will allow the aircraft to remain clear of a small arms and light AAA threat. Degraded mode programming and utilization will be reviewed.

<u>WTO-2 E</u> <u>SIMULATOR</u> <u>0.5 hrs</u> <u>T&R: 243/244</u>

This sortie is designed to be a reactive weaponeering review for the WTO student. The loadout will consist of 10 MK-82's with M-904 (6 sec), FMU-139 and BSU-86 High/Low drag selectable fins. Weaponeering should include both 10 and 45 degree deliveries. The PUI will be given target sets that vary in number, type and spacing with emphasis placed on reactive weaponeering in the delivery of this ordnance.

<u>WTO-3 E</u> <u>SIMULATOR</u> <u>0.5 hrs</u> <u>T&R: 212/624/625</u>

This sortie will consist of deliveries using Maverick (LASER/IR), Rockeye, Rockets, Sidearm and high angle strafe with the GAU-12. Rockeye deliveries will employ the FMU-140 fuze. This sortie is intended as a weapons familiarization sortie and weaponeering should provide for high angle releases to remain clear of a small arms and light AAA threat. Laser geometry and J-Laser terminology should be briefed and utilized as well as predicted acquisition ranges for the various sensors to be employed.

<u>WTO-4 E</u> <u>SIMULATOR</u> <u>0.5 hrs</u> <u>T&R: 240/241</u>

This sortie will consist of cruise climbs, Hi pops, Ramp downs and loft deliveries. Weapons loadout will consist of 4 X MK-83, BSU-85, M904(6) and FMU-139 fuzes. Using the attack profile worksheets, plan for deliveries using the above techniques. Emphasis should be placed on proper weaponeering, aircraft energy management and system optimization.

<u>WTO-5 E</u> <u>2 AV-8B</u> <u>1.0 hrs</u> <u>T&R: 214</u>

The prospective WTO will brief, lead and debrief a high angle (45 degree) and a low angle (10 degree) weapons consolidation sortie. The aircraft loadout will consist of 6 MK-76's and 6 BDU-48's. If BDU-48's are not available then ensure adequate low drag time of fall for the low angle deliveries. The deliveries should ensure time of fall requirements for simulated MK-904 (6 sec) and FMU-139 fuzes are met and no frag damage to the aircraft. High angle deliveries should allow a 5000' AGL "bubble" around the target to avoid simulated AAA. Delivery modes should optimize effect on target and emphasis placed on first pass success by utilization of a sensor/systems upgrade or cascade plan. Particular emphasis should be placed on briefing technique, content, structure, objectives and debrief format to include HUD video analysis and error recognition. Each delivery should be debriefed in detail.

<u>WT0-6 E</u> <u>2 AV-8B</u> <u>1.0 hrs</u> <u>T&R: 347</u>

This sortie is designed to bring the WTO syllabus, as presented thus far, to final culmination by combining classroom knowledge and practical application into a tactical scenario. The prospective WTO will brief, lead and debrief a sortie that will consist of section target area mechanics and tactics. Emphasis should be placed on target area entry, reactive weaponeering, sensor/mode cascade plan, medium altitude attack profiles, tactical communications, mutual support, dive delivery parameters, hits, off target maneuvers, target area egress and brief/debrief format. The sortie may be flown to a raked range. Target acquisition is NOT the primary goal of the sortie. Emphasis should be placed on the objectives as listed above. Deliveries should be planned that will keep the aircraft above a simulated small arms and light AAA threat. Ordnance loadout should consist of 12 MK-76's.

Refresher Requirements:

1. Certified AV-8B WTO's returning to the AV-8B following less than 18 months out of model will retain the MAWTS-1 WTO certification and may be designated as a WTO at the discretion of the commanding officer.
2. Certified AV-8B WTO's requiring refresher training in accordance with MCO P3500.14D must complete an AV-8B WTO recertification course. Upon recertification by MAWTS-1! the WTO designation can be made by the commanding officer. The following comprises the recertification course:
   a. The prospective WTO must meet all prerequisites listed previously.
   b. The prospective WTO must complete the academic syllabus listed previously, including the WTO workbook administered by the MAWTS-1 instructor.
   c. The prospective WTO must complete the WTO 1, 2, 3, 4 and 6 events, evaluated by the MAWTS-1 instructor.

Transition Requirements:

1. Aircrew designated as a WTO in an aircraft other than the AV-8B, that undergo transition to the AV-8B, must complete the entire AV-8B WTO Certification Course as outlined.

Conversion Requirements:

1. Aircrew designated as a WTO in an aircraft other than the AV-8B, that undergo conversion to the AV-8B, must complete the AV-8B WTO Certification Course as outlined.

AV-8B AIR COMBAT TACTICS INSTRUCTOR (ACTI) CERTIFICATION COURSE

Course Objective: To certify an AV-8B pilot as an Air Combat Tactics Instructor, capable of safely conducting ground and airborne instruction concerning the employment of the AV-8B in aerial combat. This air to air syllabus is outlined in MCO P3500. 1 5.

Length: 15 classroom hours 4.0/9.0 flight hours

Academic Syllabus:

1. The MAWTS-1 instructor will inbrief the IUT prior to beginning the certification course.
2. The IUT will successfully complete the ACTI exam, administered by MAWTS-1, prior to beginning the certification flights.
3. The IUT will be familiar with the information provided in the following classes prior to beginning the certification course:
   a. AV-8B TACMAN Vol I Chapter 3
   b. AV-8B TACMAN Vol lil Chapters 1 & 4
   c. Briefing and Debriefing (9L-9 CAE-Link)
   d. Al M-9 (MAWTS- 1 FWTI 1 0170)8 7,3
   e. Radar Missiles (NFWS TOPGUN Manual)
   f. Threat Aircraft (NFWS TOPC .N Manual/MCM 3-1) "
   g. Threat Tactics (NFWS TOPGUN Manual/MCM 3-1)
   h. Air to Air Missile Countertactics (MAWTS-1 CWTI 10142)
   i. ALR-67/ALQ-164 TACMAN Vol III Chapter 1
4. The IUT will be required to present the following classes:
   a. AV-8B One versus One BFM
   b. AV-8B Two versus One
   c. Combat Section Tactics
   d. Division Tactics against the Air Threat
5. The use of the ACMR is encouraged throughout the certification stage. If for some reason this excellent training tool can not be utilized, the IUT must demonstrate proficiency with the TACTS console prior to the conclusion of the certification course.

Flight Syllabus

Instructor Under Training Stage

The squadron WTI is responsible for conducting a work-up to ensure the IUT is prepared for certification by MAWTS-1. The IUT must develop the capability to brief, lead, instruct, and debrief the aerial combat sorties outlined in MCO P3500.15. This process should be tailored to the needs of the IUT. A blueprint is provided in the first chapter of the ACTI Handbook providing an overview of the ACTI Program.

Certification Stage

The IUT will brief, lead, and debrief the following sorties to demonstrate to the MAWTS-1 instructor the capability to instruct air combat tactics both in the air and on the ground. Aircraft utilized for the ACTI certification will be appropriately configured with captive carry AIM-9, AN/ALR-67, and expendables. Again, the utilization of the ACMR is encouraged for all certification sorties.

<u>ACTI-1 E</u> <u>2 AV-8B</u> <u>T&R M 274</u>

Description: BFM Instruction

Goal: Demonstrate proficiency in briefing, leading, debriefing, and teaching an instructional BFM sortie. Emphasis will be on briefing techniques, airmanship, inflight instruction, inflight leadership, and debriefing skills.

Requirements: The IUT will brief lead, and debrief an instructional BFM sortie with a MAWTS-1 instructor evaluating knowledge and proficiency in the following:

1. Briefing and instructional techniques
2. Sortie structure and objectives
3. Flight leadership and inflight instruction
4. Harrier performance and handling characteristics
5. Guns weave
6. Offensive and Defensive Perches
7. Weapons employment
8. Out of Plane maneuvering
9. Rolling and Flat scissors
10. Rear quarter missile defense
11. Expendable usage
12. Guns defense

13. High aspect pass option Consideration Gameplans
14. Disengagement techniques
15. Safety and Training Rules

<u>ACTI-2 E</u> <u>2 AV-8B and 1 Adversary</u> <u>T&R M 275</u>

Description: 2 vs 1 instruction

Goal: Demonstrate proficiency in briefing, leading, and debriefing a 2 vs 1 sortie. Emphasis will be on briefing skills, the teaching/execution of tactically sound gameplans, communication, weapons employment, and debriefing techniques.

Requirements: The IUT will brief, lead and debrief a 2 vs 1 instructional sortie with a MAWTS-1 instructor evaluating his knowledge and proficiency in the following:

1. Briefing and instructional technique
2. Sortie Structure and Objectives
3. Flight leadership and tactically sound decision-making
4. Section tactics against a single adversary from the forward quarter, beam, and rear quarter.
5. Disengagement technique
6. Debriefing structure and reconstruction accuracy
7. Safety and Training Rules

<u>ACT1-3 E</u> <u>2AV-8B and 2 Dissimilar Adversaries</u> <u>T&R AA372</u>

Description: Section Tactics Proficiency

Goal: Demonstrate proficiency in briefing, leading, and debriefing a 2 vs 2 sortie. Emphasis will be placed on briefing/debriefing skills (section, adversaries, and AIC). Formulating tactically sound gameplans, mission sortie objectives, effective communications, and valid weapons employment.

Requirements: The IUT will brief, lead, and debrief a 2 vs 2 proficiency sortie with a MATS-1 instructor evaluating knowledge and proficiency in the following:

1. Sortie objectives and briefing techniques
2. Mission objectives and gameplan formulation
3. adherence to established ROE
4. Inflight leadership and decision making
5. Radar missile defense
6. Mission awareness and gameplan execution
7. Safety and Training Rules
8. Debriefing structure/reconstruction accuracy

AIC is required and use of the ACMR is recommended. Adversaries must be radar equipped with forward quarter capabilities and authorized to engage beyond visual range. The set-ups will include a Vital Area Defense against a Strike and/or Sweep, a Strike against a Vital Area Defense, and a visual set. Adversaries should be briefed to remain as a single group.

<u>ACTI-4 F</u> <u>4 AV-8B and 2 Dissimilar Adversaries</u> <u>T&R OAS 441</u>

Description: Division Strike Tactics against an Air threat

Goal: Demonstrate proficiency in briefing, leading, and debriefing a 4 vs 2 sortie. Emphasis will be placed on briefing/debriefing skills (flight, adversaries, and AIC), mission sortie objectives, formulating tactically sound gameplans, contingency development for reaction to threat, and effective communications.

Requirements: The IUT will brief, lead, and debrief a 4 vs 2 sortie with a MAWTS-1 instructor evaluating his knowledge and proficiency in the following:

1. Sortie objectives and briefing techniques
2. Mission objectives and gameplan formulation
3. Adherence to established ROE
4. Threat reaction gameplan
5. Flight leadership
6. Mission awareness and gameplan execution
7. Debriefing technique/reconstruction accuracy
8. Safety and Training Rules

AIC is required and use of the ACMR is recommended. Adversaries must be radar equipped and capable/authorized to support radar missiles beyond visual range. Set-ups will be an AV-8B Strike against adversary air defense. The mission objectives should focus on denying the air threat while ingressing to and egressing from the target area.

Refresher Requirements:

1. Certified AV-8B ACTIs returning to the AV-8B following less than 18 months DIFDEN or out of model will retain their MAWTS-1 ACTI certification and may be designated as an ACTI at the discretion of the commanding officer.
2. Certified AV-8B ACTIs requiring refresher training in accordance with MCO-P3500.14 must complete an AV-8B recertification course before being designated by the commanding officer. The following comprises the ACTI recertification course:
   a. The IUT must meet all previously listed prerequisites
   b. The IUT must present the combat section tactics lecture and successfully pass the ACTI exam.
   c. The IUT must complete an IUT syllabus, designed by the squadron WTI, to prepare him for the recertification course.
   d. The IUT must complete the ACTI-3 and the ACTI-4 sorties evaluated by a MAWTS-1 instructor.
3. Certified AV-8B ACTIs returning to the AV-8 from a TACAIR exchange tour where he acted as an ACM flight leader will retain their MAWTS-1 ACTI certification and may be designated as an ACTI at the discretion of the commanding officer.
4. Foreign exchange pilots must complete the entire ACTI certification course and are not eligible for the recertification course.

Transition Requirements

1. Pilots designated as an ACTI in an aircraft other than the AV-8B, that transition to the AV-8B, must complete the entire ACTI Certification Course.

Conversion Requirements

1. Pilots designated as an ACTI in an aircraft other than the AV-8B, that undergo conversion to the AV-8B, must complete the entire ACTI Certification Course

AV-8B NIGHT SYSTEMS INSTRUCTOR (NSI) CERTIFICATION COURSE

Course Objective: To certify AV-8B aircrew as an instructor capable of safely conducting ground and airborne instruction of the AV-8B night systems flight syllabus outlined in MCO P3500.15B.

Length: 3 classroom hours 4.0 flight hours

Academic syllabus:

1. The instructor under training (IUT) will review and be capable of presenting the following classes during the certification stage:
   a. Night LAT Program and Philosophy b. Night Attack Safety Considerations c. AV-8B Night Tactical Employment Considerations
2. The IUT will successfully complete the NSI exam, administered by the MAWTS-1 instructor.

Flight Syllabus

Instructor Under Training (IUT) Stage

1. The squadron NSI or WTI will conduct a build-up phase to prepare the IUT for certification.
2. During the NSI build-up. the WTI or NSI will demonstrate to the IUT appropriate flight brief techniques, objectives, correct chase procedures, and night system operations.
3. During the NSI build-up, the IUT must demonstrate the ability to brief, lead, debrief, and instruct night systems flights. The NSI IUT must demonstrate a working knowledge of, and an elevated level of proficiency in, all maneuvers delineated in the AV-8B night systems flight syllabus defined in MCO P3500.15 with particular emphasis on safety.

Certification Stage

1. The NSI IUT will brief, lead, debrief, and demonstrate to the MAWTS-1 instructor the capability to provide night systems instruction.
2. The following sorties will be flown during the certification stage:

   <u>NA1-1 F</u> <u>2 AV-8B</u> <u>1.3 hrs N</u> <u>T&R 425</u>

Description: Night systems certification flight 1.

Goal: Demonstrate proficiency in briefing, chasing, instructing, and debriefing a section low altitude training mission.

Requirements:

1. The IUT will be evaluated on:
   a. Brief of night vision goggle rules of conduct
   b. Brief of night vision goggle currency requirements
   c. Brief of night terrain maneuver techniques
   d. Brief of partial system flight restrictions (threat degraded)
   e. Inadvertent night IMC entry
   f. Night chase position and communications
   g. Perceptions of pilot under instruction flight deviations

h. Debrief on cause of flight deviations
i. Pilot under instruction proficiency

NSI-2 E 2 AV-8B 1.3 hrs N T&R 315

Description: Night systems certification flight 2.

Goal: Demonstrate proficiency in briefing, chasing, instructing and debriefing a section tactical DAS mission.

Requirements:

1. The IUT will be evaluated on:
   a. Brief on optimum weapons and employment
   b. Brief on section target attack tactics
   c. Section formation on ingress, search, attack, and egress
   d. Night system management techniques
   e. Brief on FLIR and night vision goggle performance given historical performance data
   f. Section defensive reaction to air to air and surface to air threats
   g. Mission success
   h. Capability of IUT to perceive mission tasking overload
   i. Debrief of lessons learned and flight deviations

NSI-3 E 2AV-8B or NAWST 1.2 hrs N T&R 352 NSI-3

Description: Night systems certification flight 3.

Goal: Demonstrate proficiency in briefing, chasing, instructing, and debriefing a section CAS mission.

Requirements:

1. The IUT will be evaluated on:
   a. Brief on section maneuvering and tactics in night CAS
   b. Brief on optimum weapons and employment
   c. Brief on systems management techniques to include optimum use of the operator station/NAMPS to enhance overlay and card presentations
   d. Brief on night vision goggle and FLIR performance given historical performance data
   e. Defensive reactions to simulated threats, both as a single and as a section
   f. Optimum target acquisition techniques
   g. Mission success
   h. Debrief of mission execution and lessons learned

Refresher Requirements:

1. Certified AV-8B NSI aircrew returning to the AV-8B following less than 18 months out of model will retain the NSI certification and may be designated as an NSI at the discretion of the commanding officer.
2. Certified AV-8B NSI aircrew requiring refresher training in accordance with MCO P3500.14 must complete an AV-8B NSI recertification course. Upon recertification by MAWTS-1, the NSI designation can be made by the commanding officer. The following comprises the recertification course:
   a. The IUT must meet all prerequisites listed previously.
   b. The IUT must complete the NSI exam, administered by the MAWTS-1 instructor.
   c. The IUT must complete an NTI flight syllabus, outlined by the squadron WTI, that prepares him for certification.
   d. The IUT must complete the NSI-2 sortie, evaluated by the MAWTS-1 instructor.

Transition Requirements:

1. Aircrew designated as an NSI in an aircraft other than the AV-8B, that transition to the AV-8B, must complete the entire AV-8B NSI Certification Course as outlined.

Conversion Requirements:

1. Aircrew designated as an NSI in an aircraft other than the AV-8B, that undergo conversion to the AV-8B, must complete the entire AV-8B NSI Certification Course as outlined.

F/A-18 SUPPLEMENTARY COURSES
F/A-18 LOW ALTITUDE TACTICS (LAT) COURSE

Course Objective: To provide F/A-18 aircrew with ground instruction necessary to safely participate in LAT flight training.

Length: 5 classroom hours

Academic Syllabus:

1. The following classes will be presented to the aircrew under instruction prior to flying any combat ready or subsequent LAT sortie:
   a. LAT Part I: Philosophy and Concepts
   b. LAT Part II: Considerations
   c. LAT Part III: Basic and Section Maneuvering
   d. LAT Part IV: Advanced Maneuvering
2. The following class will be presented to the aircrew under instruction prior to the first flight outlined in MCO P3500.15 that requires SAM Countertactics (SCT) maneuvering. It s recommended that this class be given prior to LAT Part IV.
   a. SAMS/AAA Countertactics
3. The academic syllabus should be reviewed annually.

F/A-18 TACTICAL CONVENTIONAL WEAPONS DELIVERY (TCWD) COURSE

Course Objective: To provide ground training for F/A-18 aircrew enabling them to employ the F/A-18 in the air-to-ground role.

Length: 30 classroom hours

Academic Syllabus:

1. The following classes should be presented to the aircrew under instruction prior to flying any combat ready sortie that requires carriage/release of the weapon or performance of that particular maneuver:
   a. FLIR Tactical Employment
   b. LDT Strike Camera Operation
   c. HARM (Parts I, II, III, IV)
   d. ALE-39 Counter Measures Dispensing System
   e. Walleye Tactical Employment
   f. DAS Planning
   g. Low Altitude Weapons Delivery
   h. Use of Imagery and Target Acquisition
   i. Close Air Support (Part I and 11)
   j. AGM 65 E/F Maverick
   k. ACE SEAD Planning
   l.. OAS Planning and Execution
   m. Terminal Control Procedures
   n. JMEMS
   o. OAAW
   p. Laser Guided Bomber (Part I and 11)
2. All classes listed above will be presented prior to completion of the F/A-18 combat ready flight stage outlined in MCO P3500.15 and should be reviewed annually.

F/A-18 AIR TO AIR COURSE

Course Objective: To provide ground instruction for F/A-18 aircrew enabling them to employ the F/A-18 in the air-to-air role, and safely participate in air to air training.

Length: 27 classroom hours

Academic Syllabus:

1. The following classes should be integrated into the combat ready and combat qualified stages of the air-to-air syllabus:
   a. Briefing and Debriefing
   b. Fighter Performance and Comparison
   c. Data Link
   d. Basic Fighter Maneuvers
   e. Helicopter Attack
   f. Escort Tactics (F/W)
   g. Escort Tactics (R/W)
   h. AAW Planning
   i. Air-to-Air Missile Countertactics
   j. Radar CAP Employment
   k. AIM-9 Sidewinder
   l. ALE-39 Counter Measures Dispensing System
   m. Threat Tactics
   n. AI M-7
   o. AIM-1 20
   p. Fighter Missions
   q. Division Tactics
   r. Threat Aircraft
   s. Threat IR Missiles
   t. Threat Radar Missiles

2. The following Naval Fighter Weapons School classes should be integrated into the combat ready and combat qualified stages of the air-to-air syllabus as required:
   a. Rule of Thumb
   b. Comm Brevity
   c. Teaching and Learning
   d. Combat Gunnery
   e. IR Missiles
   f. Radar Missiles
   g. F/A-18 1v1
   h. F/A-18 Section Tactics
   i. Night Tactics
3. The academic syllabus should be reviewed annually.

F/A-18 NIGHT SYSTEMS (NS) COURSE

Course Objective: To provide ground instruction for F/A-18 aircrew enabling them to tactically employ the F/A-18 utilizing Night Systems Devices, and safely participate in NS training.

Length: 6 classroom hours

Academic Syllabus:

1. The following classes will be integrated into the Combat Ready stages of the NS syllabus:
   a. F/A-18 NS Review
   b. F/A-18 NS OAS Considerations
   c. F/A-18 NS AAW Considerations
   d. F/A-18 Night LAT Techniques
2. The academic syllabus should be reviewed annually.

F/A-18 COMBAT ARMS COORDINATION AND CONTROL (CACC) COURSE

Course Objective: To provide ground instruction for the F/A-18D crew enabling them to safely participate in CACC training.

Length: 25 classroom hours Notes

Academic Syllabus:

1. The following classes should be integrated into combat ready and combat qualified stages of CACC training:
   a. Artillery Call for Fire and Special Missions (Part I, II, III)
   b. NGF Call for Fire and Special Missions (Part III)
   c. Fire Support Coordination Measures and Agencies
   d. NTACS/SACC
   e. FAC(A) Planning and Mission Preparation
   f. FAC(A) Procedures (Part I, II, III)
   g. FAC(A) Crew Coordination
   h. MACCS (Part I, II)
   i. Request for OAS Missions
   j. Attack Helicopter Employment
   k. FAC(A) and TAC(A) Employment
   l. Visual RECCE (Part 1,11)
   m. OAS Targeting
2. The academic syllabus should be reviewed annually.

F/A-18 LOW ALTITUDE TACTICS INSTRUCTOR (LATI) CERTIFICATION COURSE

Course Objective: To certify an F/A-18 pilot as an instructor capable of safely conducting ground and airborne instruction of the F/A-18 low altitude tactics flight syllabus.

Length: 6 classroom hours 6.0 flight hours

Academic Syllabus:

1. The instructor under training (IUT) will review and be capable of presenting all lectures listed in the F/A-18 LAT Course. (LAT Part I-IV and SAMS/AAA Countertactics)
2. The following class will be presented to the IUT prior to beginning flight in the IUT stage of the flight syllabus:
   a. LAT Part V: Instructional Techniques

Flight Syllabus

Instructor Under Training (IUT) Stage

1. The squadron WTI will conduct a build-up phase to prepare the IUT for certification.
2. During the LATI build-up, the WTI will demonstrate to the IUT appropriate flight briefing techniques, structure and objectives, correct chase positions, and highlight common errors in every maneuver.
3. During the LATI build-up, the IUT must demonstrate the ability to brief, lead, debrief, and instruct LAT maneuvers. The LAT IUT must demonstrate a working knowledge of, and an elevated level of proficiency in, all maneuvers delineated in the F/A-18 LAT syllabus defined in MCO P3500.15. Particular emphasis will be placed on safety and absolute adherence to LAT rules of conduct.
4. The following two sorties comprise the IUT stage:
   LAT 575   2 F/A-18   T&R LAT 251 Description: LATI-1

Goal: Develop proficiency in briefing, performing, and chasing basic LAT maneuvers.

Requirements:

1. Circuit 1: The IUT will fly and demonstrate proficiency in the following maneuvers at comfort level, chased by the MAWTS-1 instructor or squadron WTI on an approved course:
   a. Check, navigation, and tac turns
   b. Speed rush baseline demonstration at comfort level
   c. Ridge line crossings (beam/straight ahead)
   d. Level break turns
   e. Minimum Altitude Capable
   f. The MAWTS-1 instructor or squadron WTI will demonstrate the flight environment assessment, proper flight control, and chase position for the various maneuvers.
2. Circuit 2: The MAWTS-1 instructor or squadron WTI will perform all circuit 1 maneuvers. The IUT will chase and call all turns, refining chase position, error analysis, and flight control.
3. Circuit 3: The IUT will lead a section LAT circuit performing the following (turns on this circuit will be both called and uncalled):
   a. Check, navigation, tac, shackle, in-place and cross turns
   b. Ridgeline crossing
   c. Section SCT on one leg
   d. Section target attack
   LAT 576   2 F/A-18   T&R LAT 252

Description: LATI-2

Goal: Develop proficiency in briefing, performing, and chasing advanced maneuvers.

Requirements:

1. Circuit 1: The IUT will fly and demonstrate proficiency in advanced maneuvers chased by the MAWTS-1 instructor or squadron WTI. The MAWTS-1 instructor or squadron WTI will demonstrate proper chase position and flight control. Each of the following maneuvers will be performed:
   a 50% dive recovery rule
   b. Straight ahead oblique jink
   c. Turning oblique jink
   d. Reverse oblique jink
   e. Vertical jink
   f. Threat reaction drills
      (1) Guns jink
      (2) Level S
      (3) SAM break
      (4) 3D jink
   g. One leg performing SCT
2. Circuit 2: The IUT will chase and call ail Circuit 1 maneuvers refining chase position, error analysis, and flight control.

Certification Stage

1. The LAT IUT will brief, lead, debrief, and demonstrate to the squadron WTI or MAWTS-1 instructor the capability to provide LAT instruction. The following two (2) sorties will be flown during the certification stage:
   LAT 577 E   2 F/A-18   T&R 251

Description: LATI-3

Goal: Demonstrate proficiency in briefing, executing, and chasing a tactical LAT circuit.

Requirements:

1. Circuit 1: The IUT will demonstrate proficiency, chased by the MAWTS-1 instructor or squadron WTI on a single ship tactical LAT circuit consisting of the following:
   a. 50% dive recovery rule let down to low altitude environment
   b. Check, navigation and tac turns
   c. Ridgeline crossing
   d. Demonstrate speed rush base line at comfort level

e. Minimum Altitude Capable
f. Threat reaction drills:
(1) Guns jink
(2) Level S
(3) SAM break
(4) 3D iink
g. Level break turns
h. SCT required on one leg
i. Section target attack
j. The chase pilot will introduce increased task loading at various points in the circuit e.g. radar set-up, ALQ-126 to REC/RPT, navigation system update, target designation.
2. Circuit 2: The IUT will chase the MAWTS-1 instructor or squadron WTI on a single ship tactical LAT circuit performing all maneuvers from Circuit 1.
LAT 578 E 2 F/A-18 T&R LAT 351

Description: LATI-4

Goal: Demonstrate proficiency in briefing, executing, and debriefing a section tactical LAT circuit.

Requirements:

1. Circuit 1: The IUT will chase or perform any of the maneuvers from LATI-3 as directed by the MAWTS-1 instructor or squadron WTI.
2. Circuit 2: The IUT will lead a section tactical LAT circuit consisting of the following:
   a. Uncalled check, navigation, tac, shackle, in-place and cross turns
   b. Section SCT on one leg
   c. Section target attack
   d. Ridgeline crossing
3. It is desirable to have this circuit aggressed by a similar or dissimilar bogey.

Refresher Requirements:

1. Certified F/A-18 LATI pilots returning to the F/A-18 following less than 18 months out of model will retain the LATI certification and may be designated as a LATI at the discretion of the commanding officer.
2. Certified F/A-18 LATI pilots requiring refresher training in accordance with MCO P3500.14 must complete an F/A-18 LATI recertification course. Upon recertification by MAWTS-1 or the squadron WTI, the LATI designation can be made by the commanding officer. The following comprises the recertification course:
   a. The IUT must meet all prerequisites listed previously.
   b. The IUT must complete the academic syllabus listed previously.
   c. The IUT must complete an IUT flight syllabus, outlined by the squadron WTI, that prepares him for certification.
   d. The IUT must complete the LATI-4 sortie evaluated by the MAWTS-1 instructor or squadron F/A-18 WTI.

Transition Requirements:

1. Pilots designated as a LATI in an aircraft other than the F/A-18, that transition to the F/A-18, must complete the entire F/A-18 LATI Certification Course as outlined.

Conversion Requirements:

1. Pilots designated as a LATI in an aircraft other than the F/A-18, that undergo conversion to the F/A-18 must complete the entire F/A-18 LATI Certification Course as outlined.

F/A-18 AIR COMBAT TACTICS INSTRUCTOR (ACTI) CERTIFICATION COURSE

Course Objective: To certify an F/A-18 aircrew as an Air Combat Tactics Instructor, capable of safely conducting ground and airborne instruction of F/A-18 employment and the F/A-18 air-to-air flight syllabus outlined in MCO P3500.15.

Length: 15 classroom hours 15-25 flight hours

Academic syllabus:

1. The following classes will be presented to the Prospective Air Combat Tactics Instructor (PACTI) prior to beginning the PACTI flight stage:
   a. F/A-18 ACTI Program
   b. Briefing and Debriefing
   c. F/A-18 One Versus One BFM
   d. F/A-18 One Versus One
   e. Fighter Performance and Comparison
   f. Section Maneuvering
   g. F/A-18 Combat Section Tactics
   h. Division Tactics
   i. Combat Gunnery
   j. Fighter Missions
   k. AIM-9 Sidewinder
   l. AIM-7 Sparrow
   m. AIM-120 AMRAAM
   n. Threat Tactics
2. The MAWTS-1 instructor will present the ACTI Inbrief to the PACTI prior to beginning the certification flights.
3. The PACTI will successfully complete the ACTI exam with a passing grade of 85%, administered by the MAWTS-1 instructor, prior to beginning the certification flights.

Flight Syllabus

Instructor Under Training (IUT) Stage

1. The squadron is responsible for conducting a build-up to ensure that the PACTI is prepared for certification by MAWTS-1.
2. During the PACTI IUT stage, the PACTI will demonstrate the capability to brief, lead, debrief, and instruct tactical maneuvering in a multi-aircraft environment.
3. The build-up can be tailored to the needs of the PACTI, but should include at a minimum the following:
   a. Three (3) 1 v 1 similar sorties
   b. Three (3) 2 v 2 dissimilar sorties
   c. hree (3) 2/4 v unknown (3 or more) sorties
   d. One (1) 1 v 1 warm-up sortie

Certification Stage

1. During the certification stage, weapons systems officers will not normally be responsible for stick and rudder discussions, but will be responsible for tactical application of the F/A-18, specifically crew coordination and weapon system management. When pilots and weapons system officers are undergoing the certification stage simultaneously, briefing and debriefing responsibilities will be specified by the MAWTS-1 instructor.
2. The PACTI will brief, lead, debrief, and demonstrate to the MAWTS-1 instructor the ability to conduct air-to-air instruction.
3. The following three sorties will be flown during the certification stage:
AA 571 E 1 F/A-18 vs 1 F/A-18 T&RM 223 (F/A-18 A/C)
T&R M 233 (F/A-18 D)

Description: 1 vs 1 Similar ACTI certification

Goal: Demonstrate proficiency in briefing, executing, debriefing and analyzing 1 vs 1 maneuvers. Emphasis is placed on briefing techniques, in-flight instruction, debriefing technique, recall, reconstruction and analysis.

Requirements:

1. Brief, execute, debrief, and analyze, 1 vs 1 maneuvers, designated by the MAWTS-1 instructor. from the following list:
   a. Guns weave
   b. Horizontal scissors
   c. Rolling scissors
   d. Offensive maneuvering
   e. Defensive maneuvering
   f. Missile defense
   g. CAT I/IIIIII/IV Fight
2. Two full maintenance capable (FMC) F/A-18s with operable APG-65/73, ALR, ALE, chaff/flares and CATM-9 are required.
3. The PACTI will be prepared to discuss EM considerations, one and two circle flow in terms of advantages/disadvantages, out of plane maneuvering considerations, and the impact of rate and radius.
4. F/A-18D Certification. PACTI pilots and WSOs should expect to brief 3 or 4 maneuvers each. PACTIs will debrief the maneuvers briefed for the certification.
5. Simulated loadout for the fighters will be 1 AIM-120, 1 AIM-7, 2 AIM-9 and FAMMO, or 2 AIM-7, 2 AIM-9 and FAMMO. A two shot kill criteria may be used to emphasize follow-on maneuvering.
AA 572 E 2 F/A-18 vs 2 Dissimilar Adversaries T&R M 333 or M 334

Description: 2 vs 2 dissimilar ACTI certification

Goal: Demonstrate proficiency in briefing, executing, debriefing, and analyzing basic section tactics. Emphasis will be placed in briefing skills, flight leadership, mutual support, radar sorting, communications, weapons employment, engaged maneuvering and debriefing.

Requirements:

1. Brief, execute, debrief, and analyze two combat intercepts and engagement and one visual start. The MAWTS-1 instructor will provide the fighter mission and visual set to be flown. The PACTI will develop a scenario and learning objectives for the flight.
2. Two FMC F/A-1 8s with operable APG-65/73, ALR, ALE, chaff/flares and CATM-9 are required. GCI/AIC and airspace to support engaged maneuvering must be scheduled.
3. Radar capable bogeys are required and they will be authorized to shoot BVR. Bogeys may be tasked to fly Former Soviet Union (FSU) formations and tactics. Face-to-face brief and debrief with the bogeys are required.
4. F/A-18D Certification. The briefing responsibilities will be split by the crew in order to get an even look at each PACTI. Generally, having one PACTI brief the admin through bandit brief, the other PACTI brief mission planning factors through approaching the merge, and the initial PACTI wrapping up the brief with merge/ engaged philosophy through defensive considerations (to include any visual sets) works well. Each PACTI can expect to act as the TACLEAD for 1 of the radar intercepts. PACTIs will completely debrief at least 1 run each.
5. Simulated M loadout for the fighters will be either 1 AIM-120, 1 AIM-7, 2 AIM-9 and gun or (2 AIM-7) 2 AIM-9 and gun.

Description: 2/4 vs X (3 or more) dissimilar ACTI certification

Goal: Demonstrate proficiency in briefing, executing, debriefing and analyzing section or division tactics in an unknown environment. Emphasis of the evaluation will be placed on briefing skills, flight leadership, intercept tactics, targeting and sorting, communications, weapons employment, and debriefing.

Requirements:

1. Brief, execute, debrief, and analyze a minimum of 2 radar attacks to engagement and/or bug-out. The MAWTS-1 instructor will provide the mission to be flown. The PACTI will need to create a logical training scenario to include PID criteria. A vulnerability window (i.e., 20 minutes) or specific "Fights on - KIO" may be used.
2. Two or four FMC F/A-18s with operable APG-65/73, ALR, ALE, chaff/flares, and CATM-9 are required. GCI/AIC and airspace to support engaged maneuvering must be scheduled.
3. Radar capable bogeys are required and they will be authorized BVR. Non radar bogeys may only be used as force multipliers. Bogeys may be tasked to fly FSU formations and tactics.
4. F/A-18D Certification. Briefing, execution and debriefing considerations are the same as the 2 v 2 sortie.
5. Simulated A/A loadout for the fighters will be either 2 AiM-120, 2 AIM-7, 2 AIM-9 and gun or 4 AIM-7, 2 AIM-9 and gun.

Refresher Requirements:

1. Certified F/A-18 ACTI aircrew returning to the F/A-18 following less than 18 months out of model will retain the MAWTS-1 ACTI certification and may be designated as an ACTI at the discretion of the commanding officer.
2. Certified F/A-18 aircrew requiring refresher training in accordance with MCO P3500.14 must complete an F/A-18 ACTI recertification course. Upon recertification by MAWTS-1, the ACTI designation can be made by the commanding officer. The following comprises the recertification course:
   a. The IUT must meet all prerequisites listed previously.
   b. The IUT must complete the ACTI academic syllabus.
   c. The IUT must complete an IUT flight syllabus, outlined by the squadron WTI, that prepares him for certification.
   d. The IUT must complete the ACTI exam and either the 2 v 2 M 572 or 2/4 v X M 573 sortie with a MAWTS-1 instructor.

Transition Requirements:

1. Aircrew designated as an ACTI in an aircraft other than the F/A-18, that transition to the F/A-18, must complete the entire F/A-18 ACTI Certification Course as outlined.

Conversion Requirements:

1. Aircrew designated as an ACTI in an aircraft other than the F/A-18, that undergo conversion to the F/A-18, must complete the entire F/A-18 ACTI Certification Course as outlined.

F/A-18 NIGHT TACTICS INSTRUCTOR (NTI) CERTIFICATION COURSE

Course Objective: To certify an F/A-18 aircrew as an instructor capable of safely conducting ground and airborne instruction of the F/A-18 night systems flight syllabus outlined in MCO P3500.15.

Length: 6 classroom hours 4.5 flighthours

Academic Syllabus:

1. The instructor under training (IUT) will review and be capable of presenting all lectures listed in the F/A-18 Night Systems Course.
2. The IUT will successfully complete the NTI exam, administered by the MAWTS-1 instructor prior to flying the last certification sortie.
3. References for the NTI exam are:
   a. NWP 55-5-F/A-18 TACMAN, Vol II Chapter 6 (F/A-18 Night Fighter Tactics (and Degraded Weather Considerations))
   b. MAWTS-1 Tactical Jet Night Vision Device Manual Flight Syllabus

Flight Syllabus:

Instructor Under Training (IUT) Stage

1. The squadron WTI will prepare the IUT for certification.
2. During the NTI build-up, an NTI will demonstrate to the IUT appropriate flight brief techniques, objectives, correct chase procedures, and night system onerations.
3. During the NTI build-up, the IUT must demonstrate the ability to brief, lead, debrief, and instruct night systems flights. The NTI IUT must demonstrate a working knowledge of, and an elevated level of proficiency in all maneuvers delineated in the F/A-18 night attack syllabus defined in MCO P3500.15 with particular emphasis on safety.

Certification Stage

1. The NTI IUT will brief, lead, debrief, and demonstrate to a squadron NTI or MAWTS-1 instructor the capability to provide night tactics instruction.
2. The NTI-1 and NTI-2 sorties can be evaluated by a squadron NTI or MAWTS-1 instructor. The NTI-3 sortie will be evaluated by the MAWTS-1 instructor. The following sorties will be flown during the certification stage:

<u>NTI 600 E</u> <u>2-4 F/A-18 N</u> <u>T&R: TBD</u>

Description: NTI-1

Goal: Demonstrate proficiency in briefing, instructing, and debriefing a formation and AWI training mission with emphasis on night systems management and two-plane operations with night vision devices.

Requirements: Conduct formation familiarization at medium altitude demonstrating administrative and tactical formations under various aircraft lighting conditions. Conduct multiple All Weather Intercepts versus a lights out bogey to emphasize NS sensor usage in the AAW role. Conduct post mission rendezvous and battle damage checks.

Description: NTI-2

Goal: Demonstrate tactical proficiency in planning, briefing, instructing, and debriefing a night DAS training mission. Emphasis on route selection, formation considerations, weapons delivery, and target acquisition methods using NS devices. Scenario at discretion of squadron WTI.

Requirements: Conduct a multi-plane DAS mission to a tactical ordnance range. Conduct multiple re-attacks with various delivery parameters and modes.

<u>NTI 602 E</u> <u>2 F/A-18 N</u> <u>T&R: TBD</u>

Description: NTI-3

Goal: Demonstrate proficiency in briefing, performing, and chasing basic night LAT maneuvers and section target attacks.

Requirements:

1. Circuit 1: The IUT will chase the squadron NTI/MAWTS-1 instructor in the performance of the following maneuvers:
   a. Ridge line crossings (beam/straight ahead)
   b. Level (hard/break) turns
   c. The IUT will demonstrate the flight environment assessment, proper flight control, and chase position for the various maneuvers.

2. Circuit 2: The IUT will lead a section LAT circuit performing the following:
    a. Turns (both called and uncalled)
    b. Ridge line crossing c. Simulated target attacks

Refresher Requirements:

1. Certified F/A-18 NTI aircrew returning to the F/A-18 following less than 18 months out of model will retain the NTI certification and may be designated as an NTI at the discretion of the commanding officer.
2. Certified F/A-18 NTI aircrew requiring refresher training in accordance with MCO P3500.14 must complete an F/A-18 NTI recertification course. Upon recertification by MAWTS-1, the NTI designation can be made by the commanding officer. The following comprises the recertification course:
    a. The IUT must meet all prerequisites listed previously.
    b. The IUT must complete the academic syllabus listed previously, including the NTI exam administered by the MAWTS-1 instructor.
    c. The IUT must complete an NTI flight syllabus, outlined by the squadron WTI. that prepares him for certification.
    d. The IUT must complete the NTI-3 flight evaluated by the MAWTS-1 instructor.

Transition Requirements:

1. Aircrew designated as an NTI in an aircraft other than the F/A-18, that transition to the FIA-18, must complete the entire F/A-18 NTI Certification Course as outlined.

Conversion Requirements:

1. Aircrew designated as an NTI in an aircraft other than the F/A-18, that undergo conversion to the FIA-18, must complete the entire F/A-18 NTI Certification Course as outlined.

F/A-18D FORWARD AIR CONTROLLER (AIRBORNE) INSTRUCTOR (FAC(A)I) CERTIFICATION COURSE

Course Objective: To certify F/A-18D aircrew as a Forward Air Controller (Airborne) Instructor capable of conducting ground and airborne instruction of the FAC(A) mission and capable of safely controlling CAS in close proximity to friendly troops. Emphasis will be placed on demonstration of ability to coordinate simultaneous CAS, artillery, or NSFS, while providing safety and timely control of all agencies.

Length: 20 classroom hours 4.5 flight hours

Academic Syllabus:

1. The Academic Syllabus will be the same as in the CACC course.
2. The FAC(A), under training, will successfully complete a locally generated written FAC(A) exam to include visual recognition of ground vehicles (MCCRES standards), fire support asset capabilities and fire support coordination principles.

Flight Syllabus:

Instructor Under Training (IUT) Stage

1. The squadron WTI will conduct a build-up phase to prepare the aircrew for certification. The build-up should prepare the crew to conduct day and night FAC(A) and fire support coordination missions in low, medium, and high threats. It should contain at a minimum CACC-265 through CACC-368 and CACC-461.
2. During the build-up, the WTI will demonstrate flight planning and briefing techniques, fire support coordination techniques. target area tactics and terminal control techniques. The IUT must demonstrate the ability to brief, lead, and debrief FAC(A) supporting arms coordination techniques.
3. The IUT must demonstrate proficiency in performing visual reconnaissance, controlling up to three CAS sections simultaneously, and coordinating SEAD and/or a mark in all threat environments day and night.
4. The IUT must also demonstrate knowledge of all courses and the ability to instruct those listed in the Combat Arms Coordination Course Academic Syllabus.

Certification Stage:

1. The IUT will brief, lead, debrief, and demonstrate to the Squadron WTI or MAWTS-1 instructor the ability to provide FAC(A) instruction. The following sorties will be flown:
    CACC-561 E   1 F/A-18D   T&R CACC/266

Description: FAC(A) procedures in a low or medium threat environment.

Goal: To show proficiency of FAC(A) procedures in a low or medium threat environment.

Requirements: Perform visual reconnaissance of three targets and prepare target briefs. Control three attacks by CAS aircraft using appropriate tactics. Utilize standard CAS briefing and control procedures. Deliver a mark thirty seconds prior to the TOT, and demonstrate ability to provide timely, accurate corrections for attack aircraft.

Ordnance: Seven 2.75 inch or eight 5 inch WP rockets, 20 chaff, 40 flares.

External Support Requirements: Three to six attack aircraft; optional artillery or mortar target marking agency.
    CACC-562 E   1 F/A-18D   T&RCACC/365

Description: FAC(A) procedures in a high threat environment.

Goal: To show proficiency of immediate CAS procedures in a high threat environment.

Requirements:

1. The FAC(A) crew will build a scenario creating a simulated MACCS system and an air tasking order delineating at least three CAS missions to be carried out in a high threat environment. The scenario will incorporate SEAD provided by an artillery or mortar unit.
2. The FAC(A) crew will perform visual reconnaissance on three targets, prepare target briefs, and control three separate attacks while coordinating SEAD from an artillery or mortar unit against simulated threats. The FAC(A) will coordinate/ provide the mark and timely, accurate corrections for CAS aircraft and bomb damage assessment. Authentication procedures will be utilized as necessary. Ordnance: Seven 2.75 inch or eight 5 inch WP rockets, 20 chaff, and 40 flares.

External Support Requirements: Six CAS aircraft, artillery or mortars for SEAD.
    CACC-563 E   1 F/A-18D N   T&RCACC-366

Description: Night FAC(A) procedures.

Goal: To show proficiency in night FAC(A) procedures in a low or medium threat environment.

Requirements:

1. The FAC(A) crew will build a scenario creating three known targets received through intelligence sources, a simulated MACCS system, and an air tasking order with two preplanned-on-call missions and two immediate missions to be carried out in a medium or low threat environment.
2. Prepare target briefs and control two preplanned and two immediate CAS missions. Coordinate/provide illumination and a mark for CAS aircraft. Provide timely, accurate corrections and BDA. illumination may be provided by artillery or mortars, requiring coordination with that agency.

External Support Requirements: Four to eight CAS aircraft, optional artillery or mortar unit

Ordnance Requirements: Four LUU-2 flares if FAC(A) provides illumination and eight 5 inch or seven 2.75 inch WP rockets, 20 chaff and 40 flares.

Refresher Requirements:

1. Certified FA-18 aircrew requiring refresher training in accordance with MCO P3500.14 must complete a FAC(A) recertification course. Upon recertification by MAWTS-1 or the Squadron WTI, the FAC(A) designation can be made by the Commanding Officer. The following comprises the recertification course:
    a. The refresher aircrew must review the Academic Syllabus listed previously.
    b. The refresher aircrew must complete the CACC-562 sortie evaluated by the MAWTS-1 instructor or the Squadron WTI.

Transition Requirements:

1. Aircrew designated as a FAC(A) in an aircraft, other than the F/A-18D, must complete the entire F/A-18D FAC(A) Certification Course as outlined.

Conversion Requirements:

1. Aircrew designated as a FAC(A) in an aircraft, other than the F/A-18D, must complete the entire F/A-18D FAC(A) Certification Course as outlined.

F/A-18 TACTICAL AIR COORDINATOR (AIRBORNE) INSTRUCTOR (TAC(A)I) CERTIFICATION COURSE

Course Objective: To certify an F/A-1 8D aircrew as a Tactical Air Coordinator (Airborne) Instructor capable of conducting ground and airborne instruction of the TAC(A) mission. Emphasis will be placed on demonstration of ability to coordinate with the GCE, coordinate mission assignments with DASC and TACPs and airspace management.

Length: 4 classroom hours 1.5 flight hours

Academic Syllabus:

1. The aircrew under instruction will review all classes listed in the F/A-18D CACC Course.
2. The following classes will be presented to the TAC(A)I under training prior to flying the CACC 463 sortie:
   a. TAC(A) procedures
   b. Aviation planning documents
   c. USAF and USA airspace management
   d. JFACC
3. The TAC(A)I under training will successfully complete a locally generated written TAC(A) exam.

Flight Syllabus:

Instructor Under Training (IUT) Stage

1. The squadron WTI will conduct a build-up phase to prepare the aircrew for certification. The build-up should prepare the crew to conduct TAC(A) missions in low, medium, and high threat environments. It should contain at a minimum CACC-369, CACC-462, and CACC-463.
2. During the build-up, the WTI will demonstrate flight planning and briefing techniques, target area tactics, and terminal control techniques when necessary. The IUT must demonstrate the ability to brief, lead, and debrief TAC(A) techniques.
3. The IUT must demonstrate proficiency in performing airspace management, coordinating up to three CAS sections simultaneously, and coordinating with a NARC and TACP in all threat environments.
4. The IUT must also demonstrate knowledge of all courses and the ability to instruct those listed in the Combat Arms Coordination Course Academic Syllabus, and those listed in this course.

Certification Stage

1. The IUT will brief, lead, debrief, and demonstrate to the Squadron WTI or MAWTS-1 instructor the capability to provide TAC(A) instruction. The following sorties will be flown:
   CACC-564 E 1 F/A-18D T&RCACC-463

Description: TAC(A) procedures in a medium threat.

Goal: To show proficiency of TAC(A) procedures in a MAGTF/combined operations scenario.

Requirements: Perform coordination of terminal controllers, attack aircraft, and airspace management. Receive a minimum of three targets from the FAC(A) and request and coordinate assets to destroy designated targets. As airspace manager, coordinate the movement of helicopters in conjunction with attacking assets. Prepare standard CAS briefs and assign to appropriate assets. Pass EEIs to the C3 system.

Ordnance: Seven 2.75 inch or eight 5-inch WP rockets, 20 chaff, and 40 flares.

External Syllabus Support: Multiple terminal controllers, one to four attack aircraft, supporting arms.

Refresher Requirements:

1. Certified F/A-18 TAC(A)i aircrew returning to the F/A-18 following less than 18 months out of model will retain TAC(A)I certification and may be designated as a TAC(A)I at the discretion of the commanding officer.
2. Certified F/A-18 aircrew requiring refresher training in accordance with MCO P3500.14 must complete a TAC(A)I recertification course. Upon recertification by MAWTS-1 or the Squadron WTI, the TAC(A)I designation can be made by the commanding officer. The following comprises the recertification course:
   a. Refresher aircrew must review the Academic Syllabus listed previously.
   b. The refresher aircrew must complete the CACC-564 sortie evaluated by the MAWTS-1 instructor or the Squadron WTI.

Transition Requirements:

1. Aircrew designated as a TAC(A)I in an aircraft other than the F/A-18, that transition to the F/A-18, must complete the entire F/A-18 TAC(A)I Certification Course as outlined.

Conversion Requirements:

1. Aircrew designated as a TAC(A)I in an aircraft other than the F/A-18, that undergo conversion to the F/A-18, must complete the entire F/A-18 TAC(A)I Certification Course as outlined.

KC- 1 30 SUPPLEMENTARY COURSES
KC-130 SPECIFIC ACADEMIC SUPPORT PACKAGE

Course Objective: To provide KC-130 aircrew with additional ground training as required by MCO P3500.15.

Length: 15 classroom hours

Academic Syllabus:

1. The following classes should be presented on a regular basis as part of a sound training plan:
   a. KC-130 Tactical Employment Concepts
   b. Low Level Navigation
   c. KC-130 Radar Electronic and Navigation Systems
   d. Temporary Landing Zones
   e. Tactical Aerial Refueling
   f. Battlefield Illumination
   g. Tactical Air Deliver
   h. KC- 130 LAT Maneuvering
   i. Rapid Ground Refueling
   j. ASE/DEFTAC: Crew Coordination
   k. KC-130 Threat Countertactics
   l. KC-130 Aircraft Survivability Equipment
   m. KC-130 NVG Use
   n. KC-130 Performance Limitations and Stress

KC-130 LOADMASTER SPECIFIC ACADEMIC SUPPORT PACKAGE

Course Objective: To provide KC-130 Loadmasters with additional ground training as required by MCO P3500.15.

Length: 52 classroom/fuselage trainer hours

Academic Syllabus:

1. The following classes should be presented on a regular basis as part of a sound training plan:
   Volume I: General Tactics
   a. Temporary Landing Zone Operations
   b. General Aircraft Preparation for Aerial Delivery
   c. Battlefield Illumination
   d. Rapid Ground Refueling
   Volume II: Aerial Delivery
   a. Personnel Static and Military Freefall Aerial Delivery
   b. Container Delivery System Aerial Delivery
   c. Heavy Equipment Extraction Aerial Delivery
   d. Combination and Combat Rubber Raiding Craft Aerial Delivery
   Volume III: Night Systems
   a. Night Vision Systems I
   b. Night Vision Systems II
   c. Night Vision Systems IIII (NSI Candidates)
   Volume IV: Instructor Training
   a. Student instructor Roles
   b. Student Briefing/Critique
   c. Aircrew Coordination Review
   d. Loadmaster Continuation Training

10-3 KC-130 AIRCRAFT SURVIVABILITY EQUIPMENT (ASE) COURSE

Course Objective: To provide ground instruction enabling the KC-130 Aircrews to utilize ASE.

Length: 4 classroom hours

Academic Syllabus:

1. The following classes will be presented to the aircrew under instruction prior to flying any combat ready sortie:
   a. KC-130 Aircraft Survivability Equipment
   b. IR SAM Threat to Assault Support Aircraft

c. Radar SAM Threat to Assault Support Aircraft
d. AAS Threat to Assault Support Aircraft
e. Radio Electronic Combat
f. MAGTF GBADS

2. The academic syllabus should be reviewed annually.

KC-130 LOW ALTITUDE TACTICS (LAT) COURSE

Course Objective: To provide KC-130 aircrew with ground instruction necessary to safely participate in LAT flight training.

Length: 4 classroom hours

Academic Syllabus:

1. The following classes will be presented to the aircrew under instruction prior to flying any combat ready or subsequent LAT sortie:
   a. LAT Part I: Philosophy and Concepts
   b. LAT Part II: Considerations
   c. KC-130 LAT Maneuvering
   d. KC-130 Performance Limitations/Stress
2. The following classes should be integrated into the combat qualification stage of training:
   a. KC-130 Aircraft Survivability Equipment
   b. Radar SAM Threat to Assault Support Aircraft
   c. IR SAM Threat to Assault Support Aircraft
   d. AAA Threat to Assault Support Aircraft
3. The academic syllabus should be reviewed annually.

KC-130 DEFENSIVE TACTICS (DEFTAC) COURSE

Course Objective: To provide KC-130 aircrew with ground instruction enabling them to defend against fixed wing attack and safely participate in defensive tactics (DEFTAC) training.

Length: 12 classroom hours

Academic Syllabus:

1. The following classes will be presented to the aircrew under instruction prior to flying any combat qualification DEFTAC sortie:
   a. KC-130 Threat Countertactics
   b. KC-130 Aircraft Survivability Equipment
   c. Performance Limitations and Stress
   d. ASE/DEFTAC Aircrew Coordination
2. The academic syllabus should be reviewed annually.

KC-130 PILOT/NAVIGATOR NIGHT SYSTEMS COURSE

Course Objective: To provide instruction for KC-130 pilots and navigators enabling them to safely plan and execute night systems training.

Length: 14 classroom hours

Academic Syllabus:

1. The following classes will be presented to the aircrew under instruction prior to flying any combat qualification NVG sortie:
   a. LITE Level Calendar
   b. NITE Lab
   c. KC-130 NVG use
2. The following classes should be reviewed and integrated into the NVG flight syllabus:
   a. KC-130 Radar and Electronic Systems
   b. temporary Landing Zone
   c. Tactical Aerial Refueling
   d. Low Level Navigation
   e. Rapid Ground Refueling
3. The academic syllabus should be reviewed annually.

KC-130 LOW ALTITUDE TACTICS INSTRUCTOR (LATI) CERTIFICATION COURSE

Course Objective: To certify the KC-130 pilot as an instructor capable of safely conducting ground and airborne instruction of the KC-130 LAT flight syllabus outlined in MCO P3500.15B.

Length: 4 classroom hours 7.5 flight hours

Academic Syllabus:

1. The instructor under training (IUT) will review and be capable of presenting all classes listed in the KC-130 LAT Course.
2. The following class will be presented to the IUT prior to beginning the IUT flight stage:
   a. LAT Part V: Instructional Techniques

Flight Syllabus:

Instructor Under Training (IUT) Stage

1. The squadron WTI will conduct a build-up phase to ensure that the IUT is prepared for certification.
2. During the IUT stage, a squadron WTI will demonstrate to the IUT, appropriate flight brief techniques, structure, objectives, and highlight common errors in every maneuver. The squadron WTI will emphasize safety and absolute adherence to the rules of conduct for all LST flights.
3. The squadron will ensure that the IUT demonstrates an elevated level of proficiency in all of the maneuvers delineated in MCO P3500.15 prior to recommendation for certification. The following sorties will be instructed by the squadron WTI:
   <u>LAT532</u> <u>1 KC-130</u> <u>T&R: LAT 332</u>

Goal: Reestablish currency/begin certification for the ST IUT on the ~T course. Practice flying at comfort level, terrain masking, ridgeline crossings and proper lookout doctrine. Fly in right seat.

Requirement: The IUT will brief, instruct and debrief a low altitude flight on a published MTR or closed course. Flight conduct and requirements are the same for LAT 332.
<u>LAT 533</u> <u>1 KC-130</u> <u>T&R: LAT 333</u>

Goal: Continue build-up/continue certification phase with IUT flying in left seat. IUT will establish comfort level and demonstrate proficiency in the performance of hard turns, break turns, bunt maneuvers, zoom climbs and ridgeline crossings as well as supervision of navigation and proper lookout doctrine.

Requirement: The IUT will brief, instruct and debrief a low altitude flight on a published MTR or closed course. Flight conduct and requirements are the same as for LAT 333.
<u>LAT 534</u> <u>2 KC-130</u> <u>T&R: LAT 334</u>

Goal: Finish build-up/continue certification phase with formation LAT procedures. IUT flies in right seat as wingman.

Requirement: The IUT will brief, instruct and debrief a low altitude formation flight on a published MTR or closed course. Flight conduct and requirements are the same as ST 334 except for:
1. IUT will demonstrate proper formation LAT procedures

Certification Stage

1. The IUT will brief, lead, debrief, and demonstrate to a squadron WTI or MAWTS-1 instructor the ability to conduct LAT instruction. The following sortie will be flown during the certification stage:
   <u>LAT591 E</u> <u>1 KC-130</u> <u>T&RLAT333</u>

Goal: To certify the IUT as a LATI in anticipation of designation by the squadron commanding officer.

Requirement: The IUT will brief, instruct and debrief a low altitude flight on a published MTR or closed course. Flight conduct is the same as LAT 533 and the IUT will demonstrate the proficiency and knowledge required to safely and properly instruct single ship and section LAT.

Refresher Requirements:

1. Previously certified KC-130 LATI's returning to the KC-130 following less than 18 months out of model will retain their LATI certification and may be designated as a LATI at the discretion of the squadron commanding officer.
2. Previously certified KC-130 LAT instructors who require refresher training in accordance with MCO P3500.14D must be recertified by the squadron WTI or MAWTS-1 in order to regain LATI certification. Upon regaining LATI certification, LATI designation can be made by the squadron commanding officer. The following comprises the recertification course:
   a. The IUT must meet all prerequisites.
   b. The IUT must complete the academic syllabus previously outlined.
   c. The IUT must complete the LAT 534 sortie as outlined in the IUT stage.
   d. The IUT must complete the LAT 591 sortie, evaluated by the Squadron WTI or MAWTS-1 Instructor.

Transition Requirements:

1. Aircrew transitioning to the KC-130, as defined in MCO P3500.14D must meet all prerequisites and successfully complete the entire KC-130 LATI Certification Course.

Conversion Requirements:

1. Aircrew converting to the KC-130, as defined in MCO P3500.14D must meet all prerequisites and complete the entire KC-130 LATI Certification Course.

KC-130 DEFENSIVE TACTICS INSTRUCTOR (DEFTACI) CERTIFICATION COURSE

Course Objective: To certify the KC-130 aircrew as an instructor capable of safely conducting ground and airborne instruction of the KC-130 Defensive Tactics flight syllabus outlined in MCO P3500.15.

Length: 12 classroom hours 9.0 flight hours

Academic Syllabus:

1. The instructor under training (IUT) will review and be capable of presenting the following classes prior to beginning the IUT flight stage:
   a. KC-130 Threat Countertactics
   b. Aircraft Survivability Equipment
   c. KC-130 Performance Limitations and Stress
   d. ASE/DEFTAC Crew Coordination

Flight Syllabus:

Instructor Under Training (IUT) Stage

1. The squadron WTI/DEFTACI will conduct a build-up phase to ensure that the IUT is prepared for certification by MAWTS-1.
2. During the IUT stage, the IUT will demonstrate the capability to brief, lead, debrief, and instruct tactical maneuvering in a multi-aircraft environment.
3. IUT syllabus codes are DEFTAC 595,596, and 592. The build-up will be tailored to the capabilities of the IUT and will include the IUT conducting the following sorties from an instructional viewpoint:
   a. KC-130 vs 1 Adversary, T&R Code 361
   b. KC-130 vs 1 Adversary, T&R Code 362
   c. KC-130 vs 2 Adversaries, T&R Code 363

Certification Stage:

1. The IUT will brief, lead, debrief, and demonstrate to the MAWTS-1 instructor the ability to conduct DEFTAC instruction. Emphasis will be placed on:
   a. Briefing all defensive maneuvers and set-ups.
   b. Conducting airborne instruction of the defensive maneuvers and set-ups.
   c. Debriefing the flight evolution, to include reconstruction of engagements and emphasizing lessons learned.
2. The following sorties will be flown during the certification stage:
   DEFTAC 595 E 1 KC-130 vs 1 Adversary T&R DEFTAC 361

Goal: To demonstrate proficiency of the instructional skills required for the conduct of DEFTAC 361.

Requirement: The IUT will brief, lead and debrief a 1 vs 1 defensive tactics sortie. The IUT will demonstrate single aircraft defensive maneuvers to include ranging runs, hard turns, break turns, bunts, and extension maneuvers. The IUT will also demonstrate the ability to instruct crew coordination during defensive maneuvering.

DEFTAC 596 E 1 KC-130 vs 1 Adversary T&R DEFTAC 362 10-13

Goal: To demonstrate proficiency of the instructional skills required for the conduct of DEFTAC 362. To certify the IUT in instruction of 1 vs 1 defensive maneuvering.

Requirement: The requirements for the IUT are the same as those outlined in DEFTAC 595.

DEFTAC 592 E 1 KC-130 vs 2 Adversaries T&R DEFTAC 363

Goal: To certify the IUT as DEFTACI. To demonstrate proficiency of the instructional skills required for the conduct of DEFTAC 363.

Requirement: The IUT will brief, lead and debrief a 1 vs 2 defensive tactics sortie. Emphasis will be on lookout doctrine, crew coordination and defensive maneuvering. The IUT will demonstrate proficiency in the maneuvers performed in DEFTAC 595 and 596.

Refresher Requirements:

1. Certified KC-130 DEFTACI's returning to the KC-130 following less than 18 months out of model will retain their DEFTACI certification and may be designated as a DEFTACI at the discretion of the squadron commanding officer.
2. Previously certified KC-130 DEFTAC instructors who require refresher training in accordance with MCO P3500.14 must be recertified by MAWTS-1 in order to regain DEFTACI certification. The following comprises the recertification course:
   a. The IUT must meet all prerequisites.
   b. The IUT must complete the academic syllabus previously outlined.
   c. The IUT must complete the IUT flight stage, tailored to his capabilities.
   d. The IUT will successfully complete the DEFTAC 592 sortie, evaluated by the MAWTS-1 instructor.

Transition Requirements:

1. Aircrew transitioning to the KC-130, as defined in MCO P3500.14, must meet all prerequisites and successfully complete the entire KC-130 DEFTACI certification course.

Conversion Requirements:

1. Aircrew converting to the KC-130, as defined in MCO P3500.14D, must meet all prerequisites and successfully complete the entire KC-130 DEFTACI certification course.

KC-130 PILOT/NAVIGATOR NIGHT SYSTEMS QUALIFICATION (NSQ) COURSE

Course Objective: To conduct Night Systems Training and to certify the KC-130 Pilot or Navigator as Night Systems qualified.

Length: 10 classroom hours 2 simulator hours
9 flight hours (pilots) 11 flight hours (navigators)

Flight Syllabus:

1. The basic Night Systems Qualification sorties for pilots and navigators are as follows
   Pilots SNVG 601 SNVG 602 Simulator Introduction Simulator Review/Practice

NVG 601	FAM
NVG 610	Fixed Wing Aerial Refueling
NVG 611	Rotary Wing Aerial Refueling
NVG 620	Low Level Navigation
NVG 630	Section Formation
NVG 640	Tactical Air Delivery
NVG 670	Temporary landing zone operations
NVG 671	Unimproved Temporary Landing Zone Operations
NVG 672	NVG Certification Flight

Navigators

ARNVG 610	Fixed Wing Aerial Refueling
ARNVG 611	Rotary Wing Aerial Refueling
LLNVG 620	Low Level Navigation
FRMNVG 630	Formation
ADNVG 643	Tactical Air Delivery
TLZNVG 671	Temporary Landing Zone Operations
TLZNVG 672	Self Contained Radar Approaches
TLZNVG 673	Review and Certification Flight

2. The goals, requirements, and standards for these sorties are contained in MCO P3500.15B, Chapters 10 and 11.

KC-130 NIGHT SYSTEMS INSTRUCTOR PILOT CERTIFICATION COURSE

Course Objective: To certify the KC-130 Pilot Instructor as a Night Systems Instructor (NSI) capable of safely conducting ground and airborne Pilot Night Vision Systems Training leading to Night Systems Qualification as outlined in MCO P3500.15B.

Length: 7.5 flight hours

Academic Syllabus:

1. The NSI Pilot candidate will review and be capable of presenting and/or accomplishing the following:
   a. Demonstrate the ability to teach the proper use of the LITE Level Calendar program.
   b. KC-130 NVG use

Flight Syllabus:

1. NSI Pilot candidate flight stage sorties are conducted as Instructor Under Training (IUT) events.
2. During the IUT events, the NSI Pilot candidate will demonstrate the ability to brief, instruct, and debrief the following sorties from the Pilot NSQ T&R events as build-ups to NSI certification:
   NVG 601 FAM
   NVG 611 Helo AR
   NVG 620 Nav
   NVG 630 Form
   NVG 671 TLZ

Certification Stage:

1. The NSI Pilot candidate will brief, instruct, and debrief a NVG T&R event.
2. The following sortie will be flown during the certification stage:
   NSI -593 E 2.0 hrs. 1 KC-130 N

Goal: To demonstrate proficiency of the instructional skills required to conduct Pilot Night Systems Qualification Training.

Requirement: The NSI Pilot candidate will have successfully completed the NSI Pilot/ Navigator Academic Syllabus in accordance with the MAWTS-1 Course Catalog. The NSI Pilot candidate will also have completed all five build-up flights from the NSI Pilot flight syllabus.

KC-130 NIGHT SYSTEMS INSTRUCTOR NAVIGATOR CERTIFICATION COURSE

Course Objective: To certify the KC-130 Navigator Instructor as a Night Systems Instructor (NSI) capable of safely conducting ground and airborne Navigator Night Vision Systems Training leading to Night Systems Qualification as outlined in MCO P3500.15B.

Length: 4.0 flight hours

Academic Syllabus:

1. The NSI Navigator candidate will review and be capable of presenting and/or accomplishing the following:
   a. KC-130 NVG use.
   b. Demonstrate the ability to teach the proper use of the LITE Level Calendar program.

Flight Syllabus:

1. NSI Navigator candidate flight stage sorties are conducted as Instructor Under Training (IUT) events.
2. During the IUT events, the NSI Navigator candidate will demonstrate the ability to brief, instruct, and debrief the following sorties from the Navigator NSQ T&R events as build-ups to NSI certification:
   ARNVG 610
   RNVG 611
   LLNVG 620
   ADNVG 643
   TLZNVG 671

Certification Stage:

1. The NSI Navigator candidate will brief, instruct, and debrief a Navigator NVCi T&R event.
2. The following sortie will be flown during the certification stage:
   NSI - 591 E 3 0 hrs 1 KC-130 N

Goal: To demonstrate proficiency of the instructional skills required to conduct Navigator Night Systems Qualification Training.

Requirement: The NSI Navigator candidate will have successfully completed the NSI Pilot/Navigator Academic Syllabus in accordance with the MAWTS-1 Course Catalog. The NSI Navigator candidate will also have completed a minimum of two build-up flights from the NSI Navigator flight syllabus.

KC-130 NIGHT SYSTEMS INSTRUCTOR LOADMASTER CERTIFICATION COURSE

Course Objective: To certify the KC-130 Loadmaster Instructor as a Night Systems Instructor (NSI) capable of safely conducting ground and airborne Loadmaster Night Vision Systems Training leading to Night Systems Qualification as outlined in MCO P3500.15B

Length: 4 classroom/fuselage trainer hours 6 flight hours

Academic Syllabus:

1. The NSI Loadmaster candidate will review and be capable of presenting the following classes:
   a. Night Vision Systems I, NVG Indoctrination, Introduction and Techniques b. Night Vision Systems II,
   Tactical Application of the Night Vision System
2. The following class will be presented to the NSI Loadmaster candidate prior to beginning the IUT flight stage:
   a. Night Vision Systems III - Night Systems Instructor

Flight Syllabus:

1. NSI Loadmaster candidate flight stage training is conducted in conjunction with the WTI specific and common phases, or in conjunction with Squadron Night T&R Syllabus training. All sorties are conducted as Instructor Under Training (IUT) events.
2. During the IUT events, the NSI Loadmaster candidate will demonstrate the ability to brief, instruct, and critique a minimum of one sortie each from the Loadmaster NVG basic and high crew tasking T&R events as build-ups to NSI certification:
   a. NVG Basic Syllabus
   (1) Fixed Wing Aerial Refueling T&R Code 482
   (2) Rotary Wing Aerial Refueling T&R Code 483
   (3) Low Level Navigation T&R Code 484
   b. NVG Basic Syllabus High Crew Tasking
   (1) Formation T&R Code 48
   (2) Aerial Delivery T&R Code 486
   (3) Tactical Landing Zone T&R Code 487

Certification Stage:

1. The NSI Loadmaster candidate will brief, instruct, and critique one of the Loadmasters NVG High Crew Tasking T&R event: NSQ AD, 486, or NSQ TLZ, 487.
2. The following sortie will be flown during the certification stage:
   NSI -593 E 2.0 hrs. 1 KC-130 N

Goal: To demonstrate proficiency of the instructional skills required to conduct Loadmaster Night Systems Qualification Training.

Requirement: The NSI Loadmaster candidate will have successfully completed the NSI Loadmaster Academic Syllabus in accordance with the MAWTS-1 Course Catalog. The NSI Loadmaster candidate will also have completed a minimum of two build-up flights from the NSI Loadmaster flight syllabus.

KC-130 NIGHT SYSTEMS INSTRUCTOR FLIGHT ENGINEER CERTIFICATION COURSE

Course Objective: To certify the KC-130 Flight Engineer Instructor as a Night Systems instructor (NSI) capable of safely conducting ground and airborne Flight Engineer and Flight Mechanic Night Vision Systems Training leading to Night Systems Qualification as outlined in MCO P3500.15B.

Length: 3 classroom/simulator/cockpit trainer hours 6.0 flight hours

Academic Syllabus:

1. The NSI Flight Engineer will review and be capable of presenting and/or accomplishing the following:
   a. Demonstrate the ability to teach the proper use of the LITE Level Calendar program.
   b. KC-130 NVG use.
   c. Night Vision Systems I - NVG Indoctrination, Introduction and Techniques
   d. Night Vision Systems II - Tactical Application of the Night Vision Systems
2. The following class will be presented to the NSI Flight Engineer candidate prior to beginning the IUT flight stage:
   a. Night Vision Systems III - Night Systems Instructor

Flight Syllabus:

1. NSI Flight Engineer candidate flight state training is conducted as Instructor Under Training (IUT) events.
2. During the IUT events, the NSI Flight Engineer candidate will demonstrate the ability to brief, instruct, and critique/debrief the following sorties from the Flight Engineer NSQ T&R events as build-ups to NSI certification:
   NVG - 611
   NVG - 620
   NVG - 673

Certification Stage:

1. The NSI Flight Engineer candidate will brief, instruct, and debrief a Flight Engineer NVG T&R event.
2. The following sortie will be flown during the certification stage:
   NSI - 593 E 2.0 hrs. 1KC-130 N

Goal: To demonstrate proficiency of the instructional skills required to conduct Flight Engineer/Flight Mechanic Night Systems Qualification training.

Requirements: The NSI Flight Engineer candidate will have successfully completed the NSI Flight Engineer Academic Syllabus in accordance with the MAWTS-1 Course catalog. The NSI Flight Engineer candidate will also have completed a minimum of two of the build-up flights from the NSI Flight Engineer Flight Syllabus.

ROTARY WING COMMON ACADEMIC SUPPORT PACKAGE
ROTARY WING COMMON ACADEMIC SUPPORT PACKAGE

Course Objective: To provide additional ground training as required by MCO P3500. 1 4D.

Length: 32 classroom hours

Academic Syllabus:

1. The following classes should be presented on a regular basis as part of a sound ground training plan:
   a. Tactical Formation Maneuvering
   b. Helicopter Aircrew Coordination Considerations
   c. Helicopter Escort Tactics 1
   d. Helicopter Escort Tactics 2
   e. Terrain Flight Introduction
   f. Assault Support Mission Planning
   g. Tactical Briefing and Debriefing
   h. Forward Arming and Refueling Point
   i. TRAP Mission Planning
   j. Countering the Fixed Wing Threat
   k. Night Vision Devices
   l. Introductory Night Vision Goggle Training
   m. Night Vision Goggles Tactics and Training
   n. NVG Human Factors
   o. The Night Environment
   p. Fire Support Coordination Measures
   q. Artillery, Call for Fire
   r. Naval Gunfire, Call for Fire
   s. Rotary Wing Weaponeering: Capabilities and Limitations
   t. Introduction to Helicopter Air Combat Maneuvering
   u. Missile System Theory Part 1
   v. Missile System Theory Part 2
   w. Countering the Surface to Air Threat
   x. Helo ESM/ECM Equipment 1
   y. Countering the Fixed Wing Threat
   z. Countering the Rotary Wing Threat
   aa. Shadow Gunnery
   ab. Fast Rope Operations
   ac. SPIE Rig Operations
   ad. Helocast Operations
   ae. Rappel Operations
   af. Parachute Operations

AH-1W SUPPLEMENTARY COURSES
AH-1W SPECIFIC ACADEMIC SUPPORT PACKAGE

Course Objective: To provide the AH-1W pilot with additional ground training as required by MCO P3500.14D.

Length: 13 classroom hours

Academic Syllabus:

1. The following classes should be presented to the pilot under instruction prior to flying the CCX 180 sortie:
   a. Intel Sources and Collection b. Opposing Forces Ground Tactics c. Former Soviet Union (FSU) IADS
2. The following classes should be presented to the pilot under instruction prior to flying the CRX 241 sortie:
   a. MAGTF Organization and Equipment
   b. MAGTF: The Amphibious Assault
   c. MACCS
3. The following classes should be presented to the pilot under instruction prior to flying the SWD 316 sortie:
   a. Forward Arming and Refueling Point b. NBC Threat
4. The following classes should be presented to the pilot under instruction prior to flying the AHC 360 sortie:
   a. Assault Support Mission Planning 12-1
   b. Tactical Briefing/Debriefing
   c. Surface to Surface Threat
   d. The Soviet Pilot
   e. Tactical Recovery of Aircraft and Personnel (TRAP)
5. The academic syllabus should be reviewed annually.

AH-1W TERRAIN FLIGHT (TERF) COURSE

Course Objective: To provide instruction enabling the AH-1W pilot to safely participate in TERF training.

Length: 7 classroom hours

Academic Syllabus:

1. The following class will be presented to the pilot under instruction prior to flying the Form 130 sortie:
   a. Tactical Formation Maneuvering
2. The following class will be presented to the pilot under instruction prior to flying the TERF 140 sortie:
   a. Terrain Flight Introduction
3. The following classes will be presented to the pilot under instruction prior to flying the NAV 150 sortie:
   a. Former Soviet Union (FSU) Tactical Surface to Air Threat Systems
   b. Non-FSU SAMS/AAA
4. The following classes will be presented to pilot under instruction prior to completing the TERF qualification process:
   a. Countering the Surface to Air Threat
   b. Tactical Aircrew Coordination Considerations
   c. Basic Radar Principles
5. The academic syllabus should be reviewed annually.

AH-1W AIR TO AIR COURSE

Course Objective: To provide ground instruction enabling the AH-1W pilot to safely participate in air to air training.

Length: 18 classroom hours

Academic Syllabus:

1. The following classes will be presented to the pilot under instruction prior to flying any combat ready air to air sortie:
   a. Introduction to Helicopter Air Combat Maneuvering
   b. Air to Air Gunnery (Helo)
   c. Threat Engagement (Helo/F/W)
   d. AI M-9
   e. Countering the R/W Threat
   f. Missile System Theory
   g. FSU Air-to-Air Missiles
   h. Non-FSU Air-to-Air Missiles
   i. Shadow Gunnery
2. The following classes will be presented to the pilot under instruction prior to flying the ACM 354 sortie:
   a. Air to Air Gunnery (F/W)
   b. Intercepts (Helo/FNV)
   c. Threat Engagement
   d. AN/ALE-39 Programming
   e. Countering the F/W Threat
   f. FSU R/W Technology Trends
   g. FSU R/W Tactics
   h. FSU F/W Strengths and Weaknesses
   i. FSU F/W Basic Tactical Employment
3. The academic syllabus should be reviewed annually.

AH-1W AIR TO GROUND (AG) COURSE

Course Objective: To provide ground instruction enabling the AH-1W pilot to effectively participate in air to ground training.

Length: 8 classroom hours

Academic Syllabus:

1. The following classes should be presented to the pilot under instruction prior to flying the AG 161 sortie:
   a. 20 mm Ammunition and Employment
   b. Rockets and Rocket Employment
   c. BCWD
   d. Rotary Wing Weaponeering: Capabilities and Limitations.
2. The following classes should be presented to the pilot under instruction prior to flying the SWD 211 sortie:
   a. TOW Missile System
   b. Hellfire Missile System
   c. PGM Engagement - Surface Targets
3. The following class should be presented to the pilot under instruction prior to flying the ACWD 403 sortie:
   a. FSU Air to Ground Tactics and Weapons.
4. The academic syllabus should be reviewed annually.

AH-1W ESCORT COURSE

Course Objective: To provide ground instruction enabling the AH-1 W pilot to understand escort formations and maneuvers and safely participate in escort flight training.

Length: 4 classroom hours

Academic Syllabus:

1. The following classes will be presented to the pilot under instruction prior to flying the ESC 220 sortie:
   a. Threat Engagement (Helo/Fixed Wing)
   b. Threat Engagement-Surface Targets
   c. Escort Operations
2. The academic syllabus should be reviewed annually.

AH-1W ELECTRONIC WARFARE COURSE

Course Objective: To provide ground instruction enabling the AH-1W pilot to understand defensive electronic countermeasures tactics and equipment and participate in electronic warfare flight training.

Length: 5 classroom hours

Academic Syllabus:

1. The following classes will be presented to the pilot under instruction prior to flying the SEW 300 sortie:
   a. AN/ALE-39 Programming
   b. Helo Expendables
   c. SIDEARM Missile and Employment
   d. Helo ASE
   e. FSU REC
2. The academic syllabus should be reviewed annually.

AH-1W FORWARD AIR CONTROLLER AIRBORNE (FAC(A)) COURSE

Course Objective: To provide ground instruction for the AH-1W pilot enabling them to function as a FAC(A).

Length: 10 classroom hours

Academic Syllabus:

1. The following classes will be presented to the pilot under instruction prior to flying the SEW 300 sortie.
   a. Artillery, Mortars, NSFS Capabilities and Limitations
   b. Artillery Call for Fire and Special Missions
   c. NSF, Call for Fire and Special Missions
   d. Terminal Control Procedures
2. The following classes will be presented to the pilot under instruction prior to flying the CST 420 sortie:
   a. NTACS/SACC
   b. Advanced Terminal Control Procedures (JMT Principles)
   c. Fire Support Coordination Measures and Employment
   d. MACCS
3. All classes should be reviewed annually.

AH-1 W TERRAIN FLIGHT INSTRUCTOR (TERFI) CERTIFICATION COURSE

Course Objective: To certify the AH-1W pilot as an instructor capable of safely conducting ground and airborne instruction of the AH-1W terrain flight syllabus outlined in MCO P3500.16.

Length: 7 classroom hours 4.5 flight hours

Academic Syllabus:

1. The instructor under training (IUT) will review MUO Hb5UU.14, MUZ H3bUU.1t, NWP-55-3-AH-1 Vols 1 and 2, and FMFM 5-35 (Rev. F) prior to beginning the IUT stage of the flight syllabus.
2. The IUT will review and be capable of presenting all classes listed in the AH-1W TERF Course.
3. The IUT will successfully complete the TERFI exam (found in the Rotary Wing common class, "Terrain Flight"), administered by a TERFI, prior to beginning the certification stage of the flight syllabus.
4. The IUT will present to the TERFI one of the classes listed in the AH-1W TERF Course, as selected by the TERFI, prior to finishing the certification process.

Flight Syllabus:

Instructor Under Training (IUT) Stage

1. The following flights will be instructed by a qualified and proficient
   TERFI:TERF 570 1.5 hrs 1 AH-1W

Goal: Conduct all terrain flight maneuvers with emphasis on instructional technique.

Requirements:

1. Brief and discuss crew coordination, comfort level, map preparation, low altitude emergencies, single engine operation, weapons employment, weapons delivery, weapons delivery chart data, and the illusions of terrain flight. Emphasis will focus on tactical decisions to fly TERF and reasons behind TERF profiles.
2. Review performance checks, masking/unmasking, NOE quick stops, bunts, rolls, low level, contour and NOE profiles, low altitude emergencies, and crew coordination.
   TFRF .671 1.5 hrs 1 AH-1W

Goal: Conduct terrain flight navigation in the low level, contour, and NOE profiles with emphasis on instructional techniques.

Requirements:

1. Brief and discuss TERF/navigation techniques and responsibilities, crew coordination, comfort level, low altitude emergencies, and the illusions of terrain flight. Emphasis will be on tactical use of terrain to navigate to a specific objective area, and masking/unmasking profiles. Review boundary features including lateral limits and intermediate checkpoints.
2. Review TERF/navigation techniques and responsibilities. Utilizing a 1:50,000 map, the IUT will navigate in the contour and/or NOE profile, remaining oriented within 100 meters. The route shall include a minimum of five check points and a minimum of 15 nm in the NOE and/or contour mode. The IUT must arrive at the final checkpoint within 1 minute of the planned time. Demonstrate the use of Doppler or EGI as a back-up NAVAID.

Certification Stage

1. The IUT will demonstrate to a qualified and proficient TERFI the ability to conduct terrain flight instruction.

The following sortie will be evaluated by the TERFI:
TERF 572 E 1.5 hrs 1 AH-1W

Goal: Evaluate the IUT's ability to perform and instruct all phases of terrain flight and terrain flight navigation.

Requirements:

1. Brief and discuss crew coordination, map preparation, Magellan parameters, comfort level, the illusions of terrain flight, low altitude emergencies, single engine operations, weapons delivery chart data, ALE-39 expendables employment, and TERF navigation techniques and responsibilities. Emphasis will be on instructional techniques, briefing, set-up, and control of the evolution. Review boundary features including lateral limits and intermediate checkpoints.
2. Evaluate the IUT's ability to instruct and perform performance checks, masking/unmasking, NOE quick stops, bunts, rolls, low level, contour, and NOE profiles, crew coordination, and low altitude emergencies.

3. Evaluate the IUT's ability to instruct and perform terrain flight navigation in the contour and NOE profiles using a 1:50,000 map. The IUT is required to maintain orientation along the prescribed route within 100 meters and arrive at the final checkpoint within 1 minute of the planned time. The route shall include a minimum of 5 check points and a minimum of 10 nm in the NOE mode and/or 30 nm in the contour mode.

Refresher Requirements:

1. Designated AH-1W TERFIs returning to the AH-1W that require refresher or modified refresher training in accordance with MCO P3500.14 must complete a TERFI recertification course. Upon recertification by a TERFI, the TERFI designation can be made by the commanding officer. The following comprises the TERFI recertification process:
   a. The IUT must complete all prerequisites outlined previously.
   b. The IUT must complete the TERFI exam, administered by a TERFI.
   c. The IUT must complete the TERF 572 flight, evaluated by a TERFI.

Transition Requirements:

1. Pilots designated as a TERFI in an aircraft other than the AH-1W, that undergo transition training to the AH-1W in accordance with MCO P3500.14, must complete the entire AH-1W TERFI Certification Course.

Conversion Requirements:

1. Pilots designated as a TERFI in an aircraft other than the AH-1W, that undergo conversion training to the AH-1W in accordance with MCO P3500.14, must complete the entire AH-1W TERFI Certification Course.

AH-1W AIR COMBAT MANEUVERS INSTRUCTOR (ACMI) CERTIFICATION COURSE

Course objective: To certify an AH-1W pilot as an Air Combat Maneuvers Instructor (ACMI) capable of safely conducting ground and airborne instruction of the AH-1W air-to-air flight syllabus outlined in MCO P3500.16.

Length: 18 classroom hours 11.0 flight hours

Academic Syllabus:

1. The instructor under training (IUT) will review OPNAV 3710.7, MCO P3500.14, MCO P3500.16, the AH-1W Tactical Manual Vols 1 and 2, the MCM 3-1 and the MAWTS-1 publication "Instructing the ACM Evolution".
2. The IUT will review and be capable of presenting all classes listed in the AH-1W Air to Air Course.
3. The IUT will successfully complete the ACMI exam, administered by the MAWTS-1 instructor, prior to beginning the certification stage of the flight syllabus.
4. The IUT will present to the MAWTS-1 instructor one of the classes listed in the AH-1W Air-to-Air Course, as determined by the MAWTS-1 instructor, before completing the certification stage of the flight syllabus.

Flight Syllabus:

Instructor Under Training (IUT) Stage

1. The squadron will ensure that the IUT is prepared for certification.
2. IUT flights should be flown on a TACTS range if available. The following flights will be instructed by a squadron (ACMI) or MAWTS-1 instructor:
   AA 580 1.5 hrs 2 helicopters

Goal: Review 1 vs 1 ACM tactics and instructional techniques.

Requirements:

1. Review 1 vs 1 helicopter ACM with an aggressor helicopter. Discuss energy maneuverability of adversary and friendly aircraft and the related tactical considerations. Discuss air to air gunnery procedures to include range estimation, lead requirements, and TOF considerations. Discuss the associated F-pole relationships of adversary and friendly air to air and ATGM weapons systems. Discuss appropriate capabilities and limitations of friendly and threat ATGMSs. Emphasis will be on briefing, set-up, and control of the evolution. Utilize dissimilar helicopter if available.
   AA 581 4 1.0 hrs 3 helicopters

Goal: Review 2 vs 1 ACM tactics, and instructional techniques.

Requirements:

1. Review 2 vs 1 helicopter with an aggressor helicopter. Discuss capabilities, limitations, envelopes and weapons systems of possible adversary helicopters and procedures to counter that threat. Discuss operation and utilization of the APR/ALE-39 systems and AIM-9. Discuss air to air gunnery procedures to include range estimation, lead requirements, and TOF considerations. Discuss energy maneuverability of adversary and friendly aircraft and the related tactical considerations. Discuss the associated F-pole relationships of adversary and friendly air to air/ATGM weapons systems. Emphasis will be on section maneuvering, flight leadership, gameplan development and control. Utilize dissimilar helicopter if available.

   AA 582 1.5 hrs 2 A/C (1 helo, 1 f/w)

Goal: Review 1 vs 1 ACM tactics and instructional techniques.

Requirements:

1. Review 1 vs 1 helicopter versus fixed wing ACM with fixed wing aggressor. Discuss capabilities, limitations, envelopes and weapons systems of possible adversary fixed wing aircraft and procedures to counter that threat. Discuss operation and utilization of the APR/ALE-39 systems. Discuss fixed wing air to air gunnery considerations to include range estimation, lead requirements, and TOF considerations. Emphasis will be on briefing, set-up, and control of the evolution.
   AA 583 1.5 hrs 4 A/C (2 helos, 2 f/w)

Goal: Review 2 vs 2 ACM tactics and instructional techniques.

Requirements:

1. Review 2 vs 2 helicopter versus fixed wing ACM maneuvers with fixed wing aggressors. Discuss capabilities, limitations, and envelopes of the AIM-9 missile and ATGMs. Discuss capabilities, limitations, envelopes, and weapons systems of possible adversary aircraft and procedures to counter that threat. Discuss operation and utilization of the APR/ALE-39 systems. Discuss fixed wing air to air gunnery considerations to include range estimation, lead requirements, and TOF considerations. Emphasis will be on heightened situational awareness, tactical decision making, gameplan development, and execution.

Certification Stage

1. The IUT will demonstrate to the MAWTS-1 instructor the ability to conduct air to air instruction. The following flights will be evaluated by a MAWTS-1 instructor:
   AA84 E 2.0 hrs 3 helicopters

Goal: Evaluate 1 vs 1 and 2 vs 1 ACM tactics and instructional techniques.

Requirements:

1. The IUT will brief a 1 vs 1 and 2 vs 1 helicopter versus helicopter ACM flight. The IUT will demonstrate the ability to instruct and perform helicopter versus helicopter 1 vs 1 maneuvers during the first part of the flight, and helicopter versus helicopter 2 vs 1 during the second part of the flight. Emphasis will be on instructional techniques. Utilize dissimilar helicopters as aggressors if available. 2 vs 2, if available, can be substituted for 2 vs 1.
2. The IUT will demonstrate knowledge of the capabilities, limitations, and envelopes of all weapons systems. The IUT will demonstrate knowledge of the capabilities, limitations, envelopes, and weapons systems of possible adversary helicopters and tactics to counter that threat. The IUT will demonstrate knowledge of the operation and utilization of aircraft survivability equipment. The IUT will demonstrate a working knowledge of appropriate air to air gunnery and energy maneuverability considerations and the various F-pole relationships between ATGM systems.
   AA 585 E 2.0 hrs 4 A/C (2 helos, 2 f/w)

Goal: Evaluate 1 vs 1 and 2 vs 2 ACM tactics and instructional techniques.

Requirements:

1. The IUT will demonstrate the ability to instruct and perform 1 vs 1 and 2 vs 2 helicopter versus fixed wing ACM. Emphasis will be on instructional techniques. Utilize fixed wing aggressors. The IUT will demonstrate knowledge of the capabilities, limitations, and envelopes of all weapons systems. The IUT will demonstrate knowledge of the capabilities, limitations, envelopes and weapons systems of possible adversary fixed wing aircraft and procedures to counter that threat. The IUT will demonstrate knowledge of the operation and utilization of aircraft survivability systems. The IUT will demonstrate knowledge of appropriate fixed wing air to air gunnery considerations, and energy maneuverability considerations.

Refresher Requirements:

1. Previously certified AH-1W ACMIs returning to the AH-1W requiring refresher training as defined in MCO P3500.14 must be recertified by MAWTS-1. Upon recertification, the ACMI designation can be made by the squadron commanding officer. The following comprises the recertification course:
   a. The IUT must meet all prerequisites listed previously.
   b. The IUT must successfully complete the ACMI exam, administered by the MAWTS-1 instructor.
   c. The IUT must complete the M 584 and M 585 flights, evaluated by the MAWTS-1 instructor.

Transition Requirements:

1. Pilots certified as an ACMI in an aircraft other than the AH-1W, that transition to the AH-1W as defined in MCO P3500.14, must complete the entire AH-1W ACMI Certification Course.

Conversion Requirements:

1. Pilots certified as an ACMI in an aircraft other than the AH-1W, that undergo conversion to the AH-1W as defined in MCO P3500.14, must complete the entire AH-1 W ACMI Certification Course.

AH-1W NIGHT SYSTEMS FAMILIARIZATION INSTRUCTOR (NSFI) CERTIFICATION COURSE

Course objective: To certify the AH-1W pilot as a Night Systems Familiarization Instructor (NSFI) capable of safely conducting ground and airborne instruction of night vision device (NVD) flight during the combat capable flight phase.

Length: 6 classroom hours 6.0 flight hours

Academic Syllabus:

1. The instructor under training (IUT) will review and be capable of presenting the following classes:
   a. Night Vision Systems
   b. Introductory Night Systems Training
   c. FLIR Theory and Interpretation
   d. The Night Environment
   e. Night Systems Human Factors
2. The IUT will successfully complete the NSFI exam, administered by a NSI, NSFI or MAWTS-1 instructor, prior to beginning the certification stage of the flight syllabus.
3. The IUT will present to a NSI or MAWTS-1 instructor, one of the classes listed above, as determined by the NSI or MAWTS-1 instructor, before completing the certification stage of the flight syllabus.
4. The academic syllabus will be completed within 30 days prior to beginning the certification stage of the flight syllabus.

Flight Syllabus:

Instructor Under Training (IUT) Stage

1. The squadron will ensure that the IUT is prepared for certification. The certification stage of the flight syllabus must be complete within six (6) months following the first IUT flight. If six months have elapsed since completion of any IUT flight, that flight must be reflown prior to completing the final certification flight.
2. The following flights will be instructed by a squadron NSI or MAWTS-1 Instructor:
   NVD560 2.0hrs 1AH-1W N

Goal: Conduct low work, touch and go maneuvers and emergency procedures operations utilizing NVDs under HLL conditions as defined by MCO P3400.14.

Requirements:

1. Brief/discuss NVD lighting techniques/considerations, map preparation, and NVD training restrictions.
2. Brief/discuss NVD adjustment and NVD emergencies/failures.
3. Brief/discuss NTS switchology, FLIR operation and employment, and NVG HUD operation and employment.
3. The IUT will navigate along a predetermined low level route utilizing prominent terrain features and a 1 :50,000 map, remaining oriented within 200 meters. The IUT will set-in and utilize Doppler or EGI as a back-up NAVAID.
4. Emphasize instructional techniques.
5. Flight to be conducted in an NTS AH-1W aircraft.

Refresher Requirements:

1. Previously certified AH-1W NSFIs and NVG phase I (I)s returning to the AH-1W requiring refresher training as defined in MCO P3500.14 must be recertified by a NSI or MAWTS-1 instructor. Upon recertification, the NSFI designation can be made by the squadron commanding officer. The following comprises the recertification courses
   a. The IUT must meet all prerequisites listed previously.
   b. The IUT must successfully complete the NSFI exam, administered by an NSI or MAWTS-1 instructor.
   c. The IUT must complete the NVD 562 flight, evaluated by an NSI or MAWT-1 instructor.

Transition Requirements:

1. Pilots certified as an NSI or NSFI in an aircraft other than the AH-1W, that transition to the AH-1W as defined in MCO P3500.14 must complete the entire AH-1W NSFI Certification Course.

Conversion Requirements:

1. Pilots certified as an NSI or NSFI in an aircraft other than the AH-1W, that undergo conversion training to the AH-1W as defined in MCO P3500.14, must complete the entire AH-1W NSFI Certification Course.

AH-1W NIGHT SYSTEMS INSTRUCTOR (NSI) CERTIFICATION COURSE

Course Objective: To certify the AH-1W pilot as a Night Systems Instructor (NSI) capable of safely conducting ground and airborne instruction of the AH-1W night vision device (NVD) flight syllabus outlined in MCO P3500.16.

Length: 8 classroom hours 7.5 flight hours

Academic Syllabus:

1. The instructor under training (IUT) will review and be capable of presenting all classes listed in the AH-1W Night Systems Operations Course.
2. The IUT will successfully complete the NSI exam, administered by a MAWTS-1 instructor, prior to beginning the certification stage of the flight syllabus.
3. The IUT will present to a MAWTS-1 instructor, one of the classes listed in the AH-1W Night Systems Operations Course as determined by the MAWTS-1 instructor, before completing the certification stage of the flight syllabus.
4. The academic syllabus will be completed within 30 days prior to beginning the certification stage of the flight syllabus.

Flight Syllabus:

Instructor Under Training (IUT) Stage

1. The squadron will ensure that the IUT is prepared for certification. The certification stage of the flight syllabus must be complete within six (6) months following the first IUT flight. If six months have elapsed since completion of any IUT flight, that flight must be reflown prior to completing the final certification flight.
2. The following flights will be instructed by a squadron NSI or MAWTS-1 instructor:
   NVD 590 1.5 hrs 1 AH-1W N

Goal: Conduct low work and touch and go maneuvers utilizing NVDs under HLL or LLL conditions as defined by MCO P3500.14.

Requirements:

1. Brief/discuss NVD lighting techniques, crew coordination, comfort level, map preparation, NVD training restrictions, and artificial illumination employment.
2. Brief/discuss NVD adjustment, NVD emergencies/failures, NTS switchology, FLIR operation and employment, Laser utilization, and NVG HUD operation and employment.
3. Conduct low work, touch and go maneuvers, and emergency procedure operations.
4. The IUT will navigate along a predetermined route utilizing prominent terrain features and a 1:50,000 map. The IUT will set-up and utilize Doppler or EGI as a back-up NAVAID. The IUT is to remain oriented within 200 meters.
   NVD591 1.5 hrs 1 AH-1W N

Goal: Conduct simulated emergencies and emergency related operations utilizing NVDs under HLL or LLL conditions as defined by MCO P3400.14.

Requirements:

1. Brief/discuss NVD adjustment, NVD emergencies/failures, NTS failures and troubleshooting techniques for NVG's, FLIR, and Laser.
2. Review low work, touch and go maneuvers, and emergency procedure operations.
3. If prior proficiency in emergency procedure operations has not been demonstrated in accordance with local directives, then those operations must first be conducted during the day.

NVD 592 1.5 hrs 2 or more AH-1W N

Goal: Conduct tactical formation flight and ordnance delivery in a low threat environment utilizing NVDs under HLL or LLL conditions as defined by MCO P3500.14

Requirements:

1. IUT will fly this sortie in an NTS AH-1W aircraft, if applicable.
2. Brief/discuss lead change, inadvertent IMC procedures, formation principles (tactical breakups and rendezvous), evasive actions, use of countermeasures, tactical crew coordination, and EOTDA/TISP mission planning considerations.
3. Brief/discuss NVD ordnance delivery procedures, attack patterns, tactical formations, as well as target acquisition, identification, and engagement using night systems sensors.
4. As dictated by the threat scenario, the IUT will conduct tactical formation flight during a navigation route (minimum 50 nm) utilizing a 1:250,000 and 1:50,000 mas. The IUT will set-us and utilize Doppler or EGI as a back-up NAVAID.
5. The IUT will remain oriented within 200 meters and arrive within one minute at the final checkpoint. A minimum of two legs as lead are required.
6. Based upon the IUT's terminal/target area analysis and the threat scenario, the IUT section leader will discuss/employ tactics appropriate to the threat and in accordance with current AH-1W Tactical Manual procedures.
7. Emphasis will be placed on flight tactics, NTS employment, section control, and accurate ordnance delivery utilizing hover holds, running fire, diving fire, or a combination thereof, appropriate to the scenario.
8. The IUT will videotape FLIR techniques associated with NTS tactical employment and conduct a debrief (using the video) to the instructor. NVG HUD operations and employment will be performed.

593 1.5 hrs 2 or more AH-1W N

Goal: Conduct tactical formation flight and ordnance delivery in a medium to high threat environment utilizing NVDs under low light level conditions as defined by MCO P3400.14.

Requirements:

1. Brief/discuss NVD low light level considerations and their impact upon flight ordnance delivery.
2. Brief/discuss navigation techniques, illusions of terrain flight, and crew coordination .
3. Brief/discuss NVD ordnance delivery procedures, as well as target acquisition, identification, and engagement using night systems sensors. Emphasis of brief and flight will be on tactical formations, accurate ordnance delivery, and overall level of planning/execution (objective area analysis).
4. As dictated by the threat scenario, the IUT will conduct tactical formation flight during a navigation route (minimum 50 nm) utilizing a 1:250,000 and 1:50,000 map. The IUT will set-up and utilize Doppler or EGI as a back-up NAVAID.
5. The IUT section leader will emphasize terminal area target analysis and weaponeering, as well as target area mechanics/flow.
6. The IUT will emphasize flight fire discipline, target assignment and target destruction utilizing hover holds, running fire and/or diving fire, as appropriate to the scenario.
7. At a minimum, the IUT will plan for the use of HELLFIRE, SIDEARM, or TOW missiles, as well as FW CAS, artillery, or NSFS in the execution of the assigned mission.

Certification Stage

1. The IUT will demonstrate to the MAWTS-1 instructor the ability to instruct night systems operations. The certification flight will be conducted under low light level conditions as defined in MCO P3500.14.

NVD 594 E 1.5 hrs 2 or more AH-1W N

Goal: Evaluate the IUT's ability to plan, brief, instruct, lead and debrief tactical formation flight and ordnance delivery in either low, medium, or high threat scenarios utilizing NVDs under low light level conditions as defined by MCO Plan 14

Requirements:

1. Brief/discuss NVD low light level considerations, current Marine Corps NVD directives, inadvertent IMC procedures enroute and in the terminal area, formation and aircraft lighting procedures, navigation techniques, illusions of terrain flight, and aircrew coordination.
2. Brief/discuss AH-1W Night Vision Systems, components, operation and employment in a tactical environment.
3. Brief/discuss NVD ordnance delivery procedures, attack patterns, tactical formation and movement within the objective area, and target area mechanics/ flow.
4. As dictated by the threat scenario, the IUT will conduct tactical formation flight during a navigation route (50 nm minimum) utilizing a 1:250,000 and 1:50,000 map. The IUT will remain oriented within 200 meters and arrive within one minute at the final checkpoint. A minimum of two legs as lead are required. The IUT will set-up and utilize Doppler or EGI as a back-up NAVAID.
5. Utilizing either actual or simulated CAS, artillery, or naval surface fire support, the IUT section leader will discuss/employ tactics appropriate to the threat and in accordance with current AH-1W Tactical Manual procedures.
6. The IUT will emphasize terminal area target analysis and weaponeering in the execution of this flight, as well as EOTDA/TISP mission planning considerations.
7. Emphasis will be placed upon the IUT's ability to thoroughly instruct tactical formation flight, conduct accurate ordnance delivery, and demonstrate flight leadership skills.
8. The IUT will plan for the use of either HELLFIRE, SIDEARM, or TOW missiles during the execution of the assigned mission.
9. IUT will fly this sortie in an NTS AH-1W aircraft, if available.

Refresher Requirements:

1. Previously certified AH-1W Phase II or Phase III instructors and NSIs returning to the AH-1W requiring refresher training as defined in MCO P3500.14 must be recertified by a MAWTS-1 instructor. Upon recertification, the NSI designation can be made by the squadron commanding officer. The following comprises the recertification course:
   a. The IUT must meet all prerequisites listed previously.
   b. The IUT must successfully complete the NSI exam, administered by a MAWTS-1 instructor.
   c. The IUT must complete the NVD 594 flight, evaluated by a MAWTS-1 instructor.

Transition Requirements:

1. Pilots certified as an NSI in an aircraft other than the AH-1W, that transition to the AH-1W as defined in MCO P3500.14, must complete the entire AH-1W NSI Certification course.

Conversion Requirements:

1. Pilots certified as an NSI in an aircraft other than the AH-1W, that undergo conversion training to the AH-1W as defined in MCO P3500.14, must complete the entire AH-1W NSI Certification Course.

UH-1N SUPPLEMENTARY COURSES
UH-1 N SPECIFIC ACADEMIC SUPPORT PACKAGE

Course Objective: To provide the UH-1N pilot with additional ground training as required by MCO P3500.14.

Length: 14 classroom hours

Academic Syllabus:

1. The following classes will be presented to the pilot under instruction prior to flying the TAC 260 sortie:
   a. Assault Support Mission Planning
   b. Tactical Briefing and Debriefing
2. The following classes will be presented to the pilot under instruction prior to completion of the combat qualified stage of training:
   a. Forward Arming and Refueling/Rapid Ground Refueling
   b. NBC Threat
   c. MAGTF: Organization and Equipment
   d. MAGTF: The Amphibious Assault
   e. MACCS Part 1
   f. MACCS Part 2
   g. Intel Sources and Collection
   h. Soviet IADS
   i. Surface to Surface Threat
   j. Tactical Recovery of Aircraft and Personnel
3. The academic syllabus should be reviewed annually.

UH-1N TERRAIN FLIGHT (TERF) COURSE

Course Objective: To provide ground instruction enabling the UH-1N pilot to safely participate in TERF training.

Length: 7 classroom hours

Academic Syllabus:

1. The following classes will be presented to the pilot under instruction prior to flying the TERF 170 sortie:
   a. Terrain Flight Introduction
   b. Tactical Aircrew Coordination Considerations
2. The following classes will be presented to the pilot under instruction prior to completing the TERF qualification process:
   a. Tactical Formation Maneuvering
   b. Countering the Surface to Air Threat
   c. Basic Radar Principles
   d. Soviet Tactical Surface to Air Threat Systems (SAMS/AAA)
   e. Non-Soviet SAMS/AAA
3. The academic syllabus should be reviewed annually.

UH-1N AIR TO AIR COURSE

Course Objective: To provide ground instruction enabling the UH-1N pilot to safely participate in air to air training.

Length: 16 classroom hours

Academic Syllabus:

1. The following classes will be presented to the pilot under instruction prior to flying any combat qualification air to air sortie:
   a. UH-1 N Air to Air Considerations b. AN/ALE-39 Programming c. Introduction to Helicopter Air Combat Maneuvering
2. The following classes will be presented to the pilot under instruction prior to completing the ACM qualification process:
   a. Countering the R/W Threat
   b. Countering the F/W Threat
   c. Missile System Theory Part I
   d. Missile System Theory Part II
   e. Shadow Gunnery
   f. Soviet RIW Technology Trends
   g. Soviet RIW Tactics
   h. Soviet F/W Strengths and Weaknesses
   i. Soviet F/\N Basic Tactics Employment
   j. Soviet Air-to-Air Missiles Part I
   k. Soviet Air-to-Air Missiles Part 11
   l. Non-Soviet Air-to-Air Missiles Part I
   m. Non-Soviet Air-to-Air Missiles Part 11
3. The academic syllabus should be reviewed annually.

UH-1N NIGHT SYSTEMS OPERATIONS COURSE

Course Objective: To provide ground instruction enabling the UH-1N pilot to safely participate in night vision device (NVD) training.

Length: 5 classroom hours

Academic Syllabus:

1. The following classes will be presented to the pilot under instruction prior to flying the NVG-180 sortie:
   a. Night Vision Devices
   b. Introductory Night Vision Device Training
   c. NVG Human Factors
   d. The Night Environment
2. The following class will be presented to the pilot under instruction prior to completing the night systems qualification process:
   a. Night Vision Goggle Tactics and Training
3. The academic syllabus should be reviewed annually.

UH-1 N AIR TO GROUND COURSE

Course Objective: To provide ground training enabling the UH-1N pilot to safely participate in air to ground ordnance training.

Length: 4 classroom hours

Academic Syllabus:

1. The following classes should be presented to the pilot under instruction prior to flying the AG 160 sortie:
   a. UH-1 N BCWD
   b. UH-1 N Defensive Armament Subsystem (DAS)
2. The following classes should be presented to the piiot under instruction prior to completing the combat qualified stage of training:
   a. Rotary Wing Weaponeering: Capabilities and Limitations
   b. Soviet Air to Ground Tactics and Weapons
3. The academic syllabus should be reviewed annually.

UH-1N NIGHT SYSTEMS OPERATIONS COURSE

Course Objective: To provide ground instruction enabling the UH-1N pilot to safely participate in night vision device (NVD) training.

Length: 5 classroom hours

Academic Syllabus:

1. The following classes will be presented to the pilot under instruction prior to flying the NVG-180 sortie:
   a. Night Vision Devices
   b. Introductory Night Vision Device Training
   c. NVG Human Factors
   d. The Night Environment
2. The following class will be presented to the pilot under instruction prior to completing the night systems qualification process:
   a. Night Vision Goggle Tactics and Training
3. The academic syllabus should be reviewed annually.

UH-1 N ESCORT COURSE

Course Objective: To provide ground instruction enabling the UH-1N pilot to safely participate in escort flight training.

Length: 3 classroom hours

Academic Syllabus:

1. The following classes will be presented to the pilot under instruction prior to flying the ESC 340 sortie:
   a. UH-1 N Escort Flight Leader Responsibilities
   b. Helicopter Escort Tactics I
   c. helicopter Escort Tactics III
2. The academic syllabus should be reviewed annually.

UH-1 N FORWARD AIR CONTROLLER AIRBORNE (FAC(A)) COURSE

Course Objective: To provide ground instruction enabling the UH-1N pilot to function as a FAC(A).

Length: II classroom hours

Academic Syllabus:

1. The following classes will be presented to the pilot under instruction prior to flying the FAC(A) 330 sortie:
   a. Artillery, Call for Fire and Special Missions (Part 1 and 3)
   b. NSFS, Call for Fire and Special Missions (Part 1)
   c. Terminal Control Procedures
   d. Artillery, Call for Fire
   e. NSFS, Call for Fire
2. The following classes will be presented to the pilot under instruction prior to flying any full combat qualified FAC(A) syllabus flight:
   a. NTACS/SACC
   b. Fire Support Coordination Measures
   c. MACCS Part 1
   d. MACCS Part 2
3. The academic syllabus should be reviewed annually by all UH-1N FAC(A)'s.

UH-1 N ELECTRONIC WARFARE COURSE

Course Objective: To provide ground instruction necessary for the UH-1N pilot to recognize, interpret, and counteract the electronic warfare threat, and participate in electronic warfare training.

Length: 9 classroom hours

Academic Syllabus:

1. The following classes should be presented to the pilot under instruction prior to flying the EW 300 sortie:
   a. AN/ALE-39 Programming
   b. Helo ECM/ESM Equipment
   c. Soviet Radio Electronic Combat
   d. Soviet IADS

e. Basic Radar Principles
f. Countering the Surface to Air Threat Systems
g. Soviet Tactical Surface to Air Threat Systems (AA/VSAMS)
h. Non-Soviet SAMS/AAA
2. The aircrew under instruction should review Final Report Phase IV Project
3. The academic syllabus should be reviewed annually.

UH-1N HELICOPTER INSERTION AND EXTRACTION TECHNIQUES COURSE

Course Objective: To provide ground instruction enabling the UH-1N pilot to safely participate in helicopter insertion and extraction training.

Length: 5 classroom hours

Academic Syllabus:

1. The following class will be presented to the pilot under instruction prior to flying the HIE 460 sortie:
   a. Fast Rope Operations
2. The following class will be presented to the pilot under instruction prior to flying the HIE 461 sortie:
   a. Rappel Operations
3. The following class should be presented to the pilot under instruction prior to flying the HIE 462 sortie:
   a. SPIE Rig Operations
4. The following class should be presented to the pilot under instruction prior to flying the HIE 463 sortie:
   a. Helocast Operations
5. The following class should be presented to the pilot under instruction prior to flying the HIE 464 sortie:
   a. Parachute Operations
6. The academic syllabus should be reviewed annually.

UH-1N TERRAIN FLIGHT INSTRUCTOR (TERFI) CERTIFICATION COURSE

Course Objective: To certify the UH-1 N pilot as an instructor capable of safely conducting ground and airborne instruction of the UH-1N terrain flight syllabus outlined in MCO P3500.16.

Length: 8 classroom hours 4.5 flight hours

Academic Syllabus:

1. The instructor under training (IUT) will review MCO P3500.14D, MCOP3500.16A, FMFM 5-35, NWP 55-9-UH-1, Vols 1 and 2 prior to beginning the IUT stage of the flight syllabus.
2. The IUT will review and be capable of presenting all classes listed in the UH-1N TFRF Course.
3. The IUT will successfully complete the TERFI exam (found in the Rotary Wing common class, "Terrain Flight"), administered by a TERFI, prior to beginning the certification stage of the flight syllabus.
4. The IUT will present to the TERFI one of the classes listed in the UH-1N TERF Course, as selected by the TERFI, prior to finishing the certification process.

Flight Syllabus:

Instructor Under Training (IUT) Stage

1. The following flights will be instructed by a TERFi:
   TERF 570 1.5 hrs 1 UH-1N

Goal: Conduct all terrain flight maneuvers with emphasis on briefing and instructional technique.

Requirements:

1. Review performance checks, masking/unmasking, NOE quick stops, bunts, rolls, low level, contour and NOE profiles, low altitude emergencies, and crew coordination.
2. Brief and discuss crew coordination, comfort level, low altitude emergencies, single engine operation, in-flight weight computation, and visual illusions associated with terrain flight.
   TERF 571 1.5 hrs 2 UH-1N

Goal: Conduct terrain flight navigation in the low level, contour, and NOE profiles with emphasis on briefing and instructional techniques.

Requirements:

1. Review TERF/navigation techniques and responsibilities. Utilizing a 1:50,000 map, the IUT will navigate in the contour and/or NOE profile, remaining oriented within 100 meters. The route shall include a minimum of five check points. The IUT must arrive at the final checkpoint within 1 minute of the planned time.
2. Brief and discuss TERF/navigation techniques and responsibilities, crew coordination, comfort level, low altitude emergencies, maneuver standardization, error analysis. and critique techniques.

Certification Stage
1. The IUT will demonstrate to the TERFI the ability to conduct terrain flight instruction.
2. The following sortie will be evaluated by a TERFI:
   TERF 572 E 1.5 hrs 2 UH-1N

Goal: Evaluate the IUT's ability to perform, brief, and instruct all phases of terrain flight and terrain flight navigation.

Requirements:

1. Evaluate the IUT's ability to perform and instruct performance checks masking/unmasking, NOE quick stops, bunts, rolls, low level, contour, and NOE profiles, crew coordination. and low altitude emergencies.
2. Evaluate the IUT's ability to perform and instruct terrain flight navigation in the contour and NOE profiles using a 1 :50,000 map. The IUT is required to maintain orientation along the prescribed route within 100 meters and arrive at the final checkpoint within 1 minute of the planned time. The route shall include a minimum of 5 check points.
3. Brief and discuss crew coordination, comfort level, low altitude emergencies, single engine operations, TERF navigation techniques and responsibilities maneuver standardization. error analysis, and critique techniques.

Refresher Requirements:

1. Designated UH-1N TERFI's returning to the UH-1N that require refresher or modified refresher training in accordance with MCO P3500.14 must complete a TERFI recertification course. Upon recertification by a TERFI, the TERFI designation can be made by the commanding officer. The following comprises the TERFI recertification process:
   a. The IUT must complete all prerequisites outlined previously.
   b. The IUT must complete the TERFI exam, administered by a TERFI.
   c. The IUT must complete the TERF 572 flight, evaluated by the TERFI.

Transition Requirements:

1. Pilots designated as a TERFI in an aircraft other than the UH-1N that undergo transition training to the UH-1N in accordance with MCO P3500.14 must complete the entire UH-1 N TERFI Certification Course.

Conversion Requirements:

1. Pilots designated as a TERFI in an aircraft other that the UH-1N that undergo conversion training to the UH-1N in accordance with MCO P3500.14 must complete the entire UH-1 N TERFI Certification Course.

UH-1N AIR COMBAT MANEUVERS INSTRUCTOR (ACMI) CERTIFICATION COURSE

Course Objective: To certify a UH-1N pilot as an Air Combat Maneuvers Instructor (ACMI) capable of safely conducting ground and airborne instruction of the UH-1N air to air flight syllabus.

Length: 16 classroom hours 10.0 flight hours

Academic Syllabus:

1. The instructor under training (IUT) will review the MAWTS-1 Helicopter ACM guide, FMFM 5-35 NWP 55-9-UH-1 Tactical Manual Vols 1 and 2 and the MCM 3-1
2. The IUT will review and be capable of presenting all classes listed in the UH-1 N Air to Air Course.
3. The IUT will successfully complete the ACMI exam, administered by the MAWTS-1 instructor, prior to beginning the certification stage of the flight syllabus.
4. The IUT will present to the MAWTS-1 instructor, one of the classes listed in the UH-1N Air to Air Course, as determined by the MAWTS-1 instructor, before completing the certification stage of the flight syllabus.

Flight Syllabus:
Instructor Under Training (IUT) Stage

1. The squadron will ensure that the IUT is prepared for certification.
2. IUT flights should be flown on a TACTS range if available. The following flights will be instructed by a squadron WTI or MAWTS-1 instructor:

M580	1.5 hrs	2 helicopters

Goal: Review 1 vs 1 ACM line numbers, safety considerations, tactics, briefing and instructional techniques.

Requirements:

1. Discuss air to air gunnery procedures to include range estimation, lead requirements, and 7.62/.50 cal TOF considerations. Discuss ACM safety considerations, crew coordination, and communication. Discuss spatial and situational awareness. Discuss learning objectives and enabling learning objectives.

M 581	1.5 hrs	3 helicopters

Goal: Review 2 vs 1 ACM line numbers, tactics, briefing and instructional techniques.

Requirements:

1. Discuss capabilities, limitations, envelopes, and weapons systems of possible adversary helicopters and procedures to counter that threat. Discuss operation and utilization of the.APR/ALE-39 systems. Discuss air to air gunnery procedures to include range estimation, lead requirements, and 7.62/.50 cal TOF considerations. Discuss tactical maneuvering and intra/inter plane communication and lookout doctrine.

M 582	1.5 hrs	2 A/C (1 helo. 1 f/w)

Goal: Review 1 vs 1 ACM line numbers, tactics, briefing and instructional techniques.

Requirements:

1. Discuss capabilities, limitations, envelopes and weapons systems of possible adversary fixed wing aircraft and procedures to counter that threat. Discuss operation and utilization of the APR/ALE-39 systems. Discuss fixed wing air to air gunnery considerations to include range estimation, lead requirements, and TOF considerations. Discuss ACM safety considerations, crew coordination and communication. Discuss spatial and situational awareness. Discuss learning objectives and enabling learning objectives. Review helicopter versus fixed wing (1vs1)ACM.

M 583	1.5 hrs	3 A/C (2 helos. 1 f/w)

Goal: Review 2 vs 1 ACM line numbers, tactics, briefing, and instructional techniques.

Requirements:

1. Discuss the capabilities, limitations, and envelopes, and weapons systems of possible adversary fixed wing aircraft, and the procedures to counter that threat. Discuss operation and utilization of the APR/ALE-39 systems. Discuss fixed wing air to air gunnery considerations to include range estimation, lead requirements, and TOF considerations. Discuss tactical maneuvering, intra/inter plane communication and lookout doctrine.

M 584	1.5 hrs	4 A/C (2 helos. 2 f/w)

Goal: Review 2 vs 2 ACM line numbers, tactics, briefing, and instructional techniques.

Requirements:

1. Discuss capabilities, limitations, envelopes and weapons systems of possible adversary fixed wing aircraft and procedures to counter that threat. Discuss operation and utilization of the APR/ALE-39 systems. Discuss fixed wing air to air gunnery considerations to include range estimation, lead requirements, and TOF considerations. Discuss tactical maneuvering intra/inter plane communication and lookout doctrine.

Certification Stage

1. The IUT will demonstrate to the MAWTS-1 instructor the ability to conduct air to air instruction.

M585 E	1.5 hrs	3 Helicopters

Goal: Evaluate 1 vs 1 and 2 vs 1 ACM tactics, briefing, and instructional techniques.

Requirements:

1. The IUT will demonstrate a working knowledge of the capabilities, limitations, envelopes, and weapons systems of possible adversary helicopters and procedures to counter that threat. The IUT will demonstrate a working knowledge of the operation and utilization of the APR/ALE-39 systems. The IUT will demonstrate a working knowledge of appropriate air to air gunnery and energy maneuverability considerations. Discuss ACM safety considerations. Discuss learning objectives and enabling learning objectives.

M 586 E	1. 5 hrs	4 A/C (2 helos. 2 f/w)

Goal: Evaluate 1 vs 1 and 2 vs 2 ACM tactics, briefing, and instructional techniques.

Requirements:

1. The IUT will demonstrate a working knowledge of the capabilities, limitations, envelopes and weapons systems of possible adversary fixed wing aircraft and procedures to counter that threat. The IUT will demonstrate a working knowledge of the operation and utilization of the APR/ALE-39 systems. The IUT will demonstrate a working knowledge of appropriate air to air gunnery and energy maneuverability considerations. Flight will utilize fixed wing jet aircraft. Discuss ACM safety considerations. Discuss learning objectives and enabling learning objectives.

Refresher Requirements:

1. Previously certified UH-1N ACMI's returning to the UH-1N requiring refresher training as defined in MCO P3500.14 must be recertified by MAWTS-1. Upon recertification, the ACMI designation can be made by the squadron commanding officer. The following comprises the recertification course:
   a. The IUT must meet all prerequisites listed previously.
   b. The IUT must successfully complete the ACMI exam, administered by the MAWTS 1 instructor.
   c. The IUT must complete the M 585 and M 586 flights, evaluated by the MAWTS-1 instructor.

Transition Requirements:

1. Pilots certified as an ACMI in an aircraft other than the UH-1N, that transition to the UH-1N as defined in MCO P3500.14 must complete the entire UH-1N ACMI Certification Course previously listed.

Conversion Requirements:

1. Pilots certified as an ACMI in an aircraft other than the UH-1N, that undergo conversion to the UH-1N as defined in MCO P3500.14 must complete the entire UH-1N ACMI Certification Course previously listed.

UH-1N NIGHT SYSTEMS FAMILIARIZATION INSTRUCTOR (NSFI) CERTIFICATION COURSE

Course Objective: To certify a UH-1N pilot as a Night Systems Familiarization Instructor (NSFI) capable of safely conducting ground and airborne instruction of night vision goggle (NVG) flight during basic, non-tactical maneuvering flights.

Length: 3 classroom hours 4.5 flight hours

Academic Syllabus:

1. The instructor under training (IUT) will review and be capable of presenting the following classes:
   a. Night Vision Devices
   b. Introductory Night Vision Goggle Training
   c. NVG Human Factors
   d. The Night Environment
2. The IUT will successfully complete the NSFI exam, administered by a NSI or MAWTS-1 instructor, prior to beginning the certification stage of the flight syllabus.
3. The IUT will present to a NSI or MAWTS-1 instructor, one of the classes listed above, as determined by the NSI or MAWTS-1 instructor, before completing the certification stage of the flight syllabus.
4. The academic syllabus will be completed within 30 days prior to beginning the certification stage of the flight syllabus.

Flight Syllabus:

Instructor Under Training (IUT) Stage

1. The squadron will ensure that the IUT is prepared for certification. The certification stage of the flight syllabus must be complete within six (6) months following the first IUT flight. If six months have elapsed since completion of any IUT flight, that flight must be reflown prior to completing the final certification flight.
2. The following flights will be instructed by a squadron NSI or NSFI:

NVG 560	1.5 hrs	1 UH-1N N

Goal: Conduct NVG low work, pattern work, and simulated emergencies emphasizing instructional techniques.

Requirements:

1. IUT shall demonstrate a thorough knowledge of the MAWTS-1 NVD Manual, instructor technique, NVG emergencies, safety considerations and NVG training restrictions/requirements detailed in MCO P3500.14 and MCO P3500.16.
2. Introduce and conduct low work, pattern work and simulated emergencies with emphasis on instructional techniques.
3. Emergency procedures shall include simulated single engine malfunctions, autorotations, quick stops and high speed low level autorotations. Minimum 1.2 hrs NVG time.

NVG 561	1.5 hrs	1 UH-1N N 1 3-20

Goal: Conduct NVG navigation and confined area landings emphasizing briefing and instructional techniques.

Requirements:

1. Brief/discuss NVG map preparation, NVG route cards, checkpoint identification, enroute hazards, moon angle/azimuth and shadowing. Also discuss confined area landings, crew coordination, inadvertent IMC and brownout whiteout.
2. Conduct a minimum of five confined area landings.
3. Conduct a navigation route of 50 nm or greater, utilizing both a 1:250,000 and 1 :50,000 map. The IUT is to remain oriented within 500 meters and arrive at the final checkpoint within 1 minute. Minimum 1.2 hrs NVG time.

Certification Stage

1. The IUT will demonstrate to the NSI or MAWTS-1 instructor the ability to instruct night systems operations.

NVG 562 E	1.5 hrs	1 UH-1N N

Goal: Demonstrate the ability to brief and instruct all previously introduced NSFI training.

Requirements:

1. Brief/discuss MCO P3500.14 and MCO P3500.16 training restrictions/regulations, and the MAWTS-1 NVG Manual.
2. Review low work, pattern work, and emergency procedure operations.
3. Conduct confined area landings.
4. Conduct navigation using a 1:250,000 and 1:50,000 map (minimum 50 nm), remaining oriented within 200 meters and arriving within 1 minute at the final checkpoint. Minimum 1.2 hrs NVG time.

Refresher Requirements:

1. Previously certified UH-1N NSFI's returning to the UH-1N requiring refresher training as defined in MCO P3500.14 must be recertified by a NSI or MAWTS-1 instructor. Upon recertification, the NFSI designation can be made by the squadron commanding officer. The following comprises the recertification course.
   a. The IUT must meet all prerequisites listed previously.
   b. The IUT must successfully complete the NSFI exam, administered by an NSI or MAWTS-1 instructor.
   c. The IUT must complete the NVG 562 flight, evaluated by an NSI or MAWTS-1 instructor.

Transition Requirements:

1. Pilots certified as an NSI or NSFI in an aircraft other than the UH-1N, that transition to the UH-1N as defined in MCO P3500.14 must complete the entire UH-1N NSFI Certification Course.

Conversion Requirements:

1. Pilots certified as an NSI or NSFI in an aircraft other than the UH-1N, that undergo conversion training to the UH-1N as defined in MCO P3500.14 must complete the entire UH-1 N NSFI Certification Course.

UH-1N NIGHT SYSTEMS SAR INSTRUCTOR (NSSI) CERTIFICATION COURSE

Course Objective: To certify a UH-1 N pilot as a Night Systems SAR Instructor (NSSI) capable of safely conducting ground and airborne instruction of the night vision goggle (NVG) flight syllabus outlined in MCO P3500.17.

Length: 3 classroom hours 6.0 flight hours

Academic Syllabus:

1. The instructor under training (IUT) will review and be capable of presenting the following classes:
   a. Night Vision Devices
   b. Introductory Night Vision Goggle Training
2. The IUT will successfully complete the NSSI exam, administered by the MAWTS-1/NSI instructor, prior to beginning the certification stage of the flight syllabus.
3. The IUT will present to the MAWTS-1/NSI instructor or a NSSI, one of the classes listed above, as determined by the MAWTS-1 instructor or NSSI, before completing the certification stage of the flight syllabus.
4. The academic syllabus will be completed within 90 days prior to beginning the certification stage of the flight syllabus.

Flight Syllabus:

Instructor Under Training (IUT) Stage

1. The squadron will ensure that the IUT is prepared for certification by the NSI/MAWTS-1 instructor. The certification stage of the flight syllabus must be complete within six (6) months following the first IUT flight. If six months have elapsed since completion of any IUT flight, that flight must be reflown prior to completing the final certification flight.
2. The following flights will be instructed by a squadron NSSI/NSI or MA'/VTS-1 instructor:

NVG 550	1.5 hrs	1UH-1N	N

Goal: Conduct basic operations, CALs and navigation while utilizing NVG's above .0022 LUX.

Requirements:

1. Under ambient light conditions above .0022 LUX, evaluate the IUT's ability to instruct single aircraft CAL's and navigation while utilizing NVG's. The IUT shall remain oriented within 500 meters while conducting a 25 nm navigation route above 200 ft AGL. A minimum of 2 navigation legs and 4 CALs are required. Minimum 1.2 hrs NVG time.
2. Brief and discuss NVG operations and limitations, NVG emergencies, lookout doctrine, aircraft lighting, crew coordination/comfort level, depth perception, visual illusions. waveoffs. and inadvertent IMC.

NVG 551	1.5 hrs	1 UH-1N	N

Goal: Conduct basic operations, CALs and navigation while utilizing NVGs below .0022 LUX.

Requirements:

1. Under ambient light conditions below .0022 LUX, evaluate the IUT's ability to instruct single aircraft CALs and navigate while utilizing the NVG's. The IUT shall remain oriented within 500 meters while conducting a 25 nm navigation route above 200 ft AGL. A minimum of 2 navigation legs and 4 CAL's are required.
2. Brief and discuss low light level operations and limitations, NVG emergencies, lookout doctrine, crew coordination, comfort levels, depth perception, aircraft lighting, visual illusions, waveoffs, and inadvertent IMC.

Certification Stage

1. The IUT will demonstrate to the MAWTS-1/NSi instructor the ability to instruct night systems operations.

NVG 552 E	1.5hrs	1UH-1N	N

Goal: Evaluate the IUT's ability to instruct basic operations, CAL's, and navigation while utilizing the NVG's below .0022 LUX.

Requirements:

1. Under ambient light conditions below .0022 LUX, evaluate the IUT's ability to perform and instruct single aircraft CAL's and navigation while utilizing NVG's. The IUT shall remain oriented within 500 meters while conducting a 25 nm navigation route above 200 ft AGL. A minimum of 2 navigation legs and 4 CALs are required. Minimum 1.2 hrs NVG time.
2. Brief and discuss NVG emergencies, low light level operations, effects of cultural lighting, navigational techniques, crew coordination/comfort level, waveoffs, and inadvertent IMC, and Personnel and object visual acquisition ranges.

NVG 553 E	1.5 hrs	1 UH-1N	N

Goal: Evaluate the IUT's ability to instruct basic operations, CAL's, and navigation while utilizing the NVG's below .0022 LUX.

Requirements:

1. Under ambient light conditions below .0022 LUX, evaluate the IUT's ability to perform and instruct single aircraft CAL's and navigation while utilizing NVG's. The IUT shall remain oriented within 500 meters while conducting a 25 nm navigation route above 200 ft AGL. A minimum of 2 navigation legs and 4 CALs are required. Upon arrival at the pick-up area, conduct a simulated search and survivor pick-up. Minimum 1.2 hrs NVG time.
2. Brief and discuss NVG emergencies, low light level operations, effects of cultural lighting, navigational techniques, crew coordination/comfort level, waveoffs, and inadvertent IMC, search patterns, and personnel and object visual acquisition ranges.

UH-1N NIGHT SYSTEMS INSTRUCTOR (NSI) CERTIFICATION COURSE

Course Objective: To certify a UH-1N pilot as a Night Systems Instructor (NSI) capable of safely conducting ground and airborne instruction of the UH-1N night vision goggle (NVG) flight syllabus outlined in MCO P3500.16.

Length: 5 classroom hours 11 flight hours

Academic Syllabus:

1. The instructor under training (IUT) will review and be capable of presenting all classes listed in the UH-1 N Night Systems Operations Course.
2. The IUT will successfully complete the NSI exam, administered by a MAWTS-1 instructor, prior to beginning the certification stage of the flight syllabus.
3. The IUT will present to a MAWTS-1 instructor, one of the classes listed in the UH-1N Night Systems Operations Course as determined by the MAWTS-1 instructor, before completing the certification stage of the flight syllabus.
4. The academic syllabus will be completed within 90 days prior to beginning the certification stage of the flight syllabus.

Flight Syllabus:

Instructor Under Training (IUT) Stage

1. The squadron will ensure that the IUT is prepared for certification. The certification stage of the flight syllabus must be complete within six (6) months following the first IUT flight. If six months have elapsed since completion of any IUT flight, that flight must be reflown prior to completing the final certification flight.
2. The following flights will be instructed by a squadron NSI or MAWTS-1 instructor. They can be flown under high or low light conditions, as defined in MCO P3500. 1 4:
   NVG 590 1.5 hrs 1 UH-1N N

Goal: Conduct NVG low work, pattern work and simulated emergencies emphasizing instructional technique.

Requirements:

1. The IUT shall demonstrate a thorough knowledge of the MAWTS-1 NVG Manual, instructor technique, NVG emergencies, safety considerations, and NVG training restrictions requirements detailed in MCO P3500.14 and MCO P3500. 16.
2. Introduce and conduct low work, pattern work, and simulated emergencies with emphasis on instructional technique.
3. Emergency procedures shall include simulated single engine malfunctions, autorotations, quick stops, and high speed low level autorotations. Minimum 1.2 hrs NVG time.
   NVG 591 1.5 hrs 1 UH-1N N

Goal: Conduct NVG navigation and confined area landings emphasizing briefing and instructional technique.

Requirements:

1. Brief/discuss NVG map preparation, NVG route cards, checkpoint identification, enroute hazards, moon angle/azimuth and shadowing. Also discuss confined area landings, crew coordination, inadvertent IMC and brownout whiteout.
2. Conduct a minimum of 5 confined area landings.
3. Conduct a navigation route using a 1:250,000 and a 1:50,000 map (minimum of 50 nm). IUT to remain oriented within 500 meters and arrive at the final checkpoint within one minute. Minimum 1.2 hrs NVG time.
   NVG 592 1.0 hrs 1UH-1N N

Goal: Conduct NTIS operations emphasizing instructional techniques crew coordination, and NTIS troubleshooting.

Requirements:

1. This flight may be flown in conjunction with any of the 590 series NSI IUT flights.
2. The IUT shall demonstrate a thorough knowledge of the NTIS. Brief/discuss NTIS crew coordination, discuss and demonstrate NTIS troubleshooting techniques.
3. Brief/discuss laser range finding considerations and constraints, demonstrate if able.
   NVG 593 2.0 hrs 2 UH-1N N

Goal: Conduct tactical formation flight, confined area landings, and TERF navigation on NVG's as dictated by the tactical scenario. The IUT's mission planning, flight briefing, and overall instructional technique will be evaluated.

Requirements:

1. IUT will demonstrate his instructional technique while conducting two plane (minimum) NVG navigation (50 nm minimum), confined area landings (4 minimum) and tactical formation flight in a tactical scenario. Using a 1:250,000 and a 1:50,000 map (minimum 4 points on each), the IUT will remain oriented within 500 meters and arrive within one minute at the final checkpoint. Contour flight should be utilized while navigating on the 1:50,000 map. The IUT will conduct a minimum of two in-flight lead changes using prebriefed signals.
2. Brief and discuss MCO P3500.14 and MCO P3500.16 as they apply to NVG operations, crew coordination, comfort level, in-flight lead changes, rendezvous procedures, tactical maneuvers, inadvertent IMC procedures, wave-offs, NVG formation flight, NVG lighting, NVG emergencies, NVG map preparation and the navigation route in detail. Minimum of 1.5 hrs NVG time.
   NVG 594 2.0 hrs 2 UH-1 N N

Goal: Conduct two plane (minimum) NVG navigation and ordnance delivery in a tactical scenario. The IUT's mission planning, flight briefing, and overall instructional techniques will be evaluated.

Requirements:

1. The IUT will demonstrate his instructional technique and will plan, brief and lead a two plane (minimum) NVG ordnance mission in a tactical scenario. A minimum of four navigation legs will be flown using a 1:250,000 and 1:50,000 map. NOE navigation will be utilized while on the 1 :50,000 map, staying oriented within 200 meters and arriving at the IP within one minute. A 1:50,000 map will be prepared detailing actions in the objective area. Ordnance will include rocket delivery, forward fire gun and crew served weapons.
2. Brief and discuss NVG low light level considerations, mission planning considerations, NVG tactical considerations, lost communication, scatter plan, rendezvous procedures, BCWD, combat sights, crew coordination, comfort level, and low altitude emergencies. Minimum 1.5 hrs NVG time.

Certification Stage

1. The IUT will demonstrate to a MAWTS-1 instructor the ability to instruct night systems operations. At least one of the certification flights shall be flown in an NTIS equipped aircraft. All certification flights will be conducted under low light levels as defined in MCO P3500.14.
   NVG 595 E 2.0 hrs 2 UH-1N N

Goal: Conduct two plane NVG tactical formation flight, confined area landings and navigation in a tactical scenario. The IUT's mission planning, flight briefing and execution will be evaluated by a MAWTS-1 instructor with an emphasis to be placed on instructional technique.

Requirements:

1. Under low light conditions as defined by MCO P3500.14, the IUT will demonstrate his instructional technique while conducting two plane (minimum) NVG navigation, confined area landings and tactical formation flight in a tactical scenario such as TRAP, MEDEVAC, troop insertion or extraction. During the tactical scenario, the IUT, using a 1 :250,000 and a 1 :50,000 map, will navigate a route consisting of at least 50 nm. The IUT will remain oriented within 200 meters and arrive within 1 minute at the final checkpoint. A minimum of two CALS and one in flight lead change will be conducted during the tactical scenario. A minimum of two CALS and another in flight lead change will be executed after the tactical scenario to emphasize instructional technique.
2. Brief/discuss MCO P3500.14 and MCO P3500.16 as they apply to NVG operations, crew coordination, comfort level, in flight lead change, rendezvous procedures, tactical formation flight, inadvertent IMC, wave-offs, NVG lighting, NVG emergencies, NVG map prep, and the navigation route in detail. The cockpit brief will emphasize instructional technique. Minimum 1.5 hours NVG time.
   NVG 596 E 2.0 hrs 2UH-1N N

Goal: Conduct two plane (minimum) NVG navigation and ordnance delivery in a tactical scenario. The IUT's mission planning, flight briefing, and overall instructional techniques will be evaluated by the MAWTS-1 instructor.

Requirements:

1. Under low light conditions as defined by MCO P3500.14, the IUT will demonstrate his instructional technique and will plan, brief and lead a two plane (minimum) NVG ordnance mission using a tactical scenario. A minimum of four navigation legs will be flown using a 1:250,000 and 1:50,000 map. A 1:50,000 map will be prepared detailing actions in the objective area. Ordnance will include rocket delivery, forward fire gun and crew served weapons.
2. Brief and discuss NVG low light level considerations, mission planning considerations, tactical considerations, briefing techniques, lost communication, scatter plan, rendezvous procedures, BCWD, combat sights, crew coordination, comfort level. and low altitude emergencies. Minimum 1.5 hrs NVG time.

Refresher Requirements:

1. Previously certified UH-1N NSI's returning to the UH-1N requiring refresher training as defined in MCO P3500.14 must be recertified by a MAWTS-1 instructor. Upon recertification, the NSI designation can be made by the squadron commanding officer. The following comprises the recertification course.
   a. The IUT must meet all prerequisites listed previously.
   b. The IUT must successfully complete the NSI exam, administered by a MAWTS-1 instructor
   c. The IUT must complete the NVG 595 and NVG 596 flights, evaluated by a MAWTS-1 instructor.

Transition Requirements:

1. Pilots certified as an NSI in an aircraft other than the UH-1 N, that transition to the UH-1N as defined in MCO P3500.14 must complete the entire UH-1N NSI Certification Course previously listed.

Conversion Requirements:

1. Pilots certified as an NSI in an aircraft other than the UH-1N, that undergo conversion training to the UH-1N as defined in MCO P3500.14 must complete the entire UH-1 N NSI Certification Course previously listed.

UH-1 N CREW MEMBER SUPPLEMENTARY COURSES
UH-1N CREW MEMBER ACADEMIC SUPPORT PACKAGE

Course Objective: To provide UH-1 N crew members with academic training as required by MCO P3500.14E.

Length: 22 classroom hours

Academic Syllabus:

1. The following classes shall be presented to the crew member prior to completing the combat qualified stage of training:
   a. Aircrew Responsibilities in a Tactical Environment
   b. Tactical Aircrew Coordination Considerations
   c. Introduction to Air Combat Maneuvers for Enlisted Aircrews
   d. Night Vision Goggle Training for Enlisted Aircrews
   e. Fundamentals of Aerial Gunnery
   f. Employment Fundamentals of Aerial Gunnery
   g. XM-218/GAU-16 Machine Gun
   h. Laser Safety
   i. Basic Principles of Electronic Warfare
   j. Training the Aerial Gunner
   k. Basic Principles of Escort Operations
   l. Tactical Recovery of Aircraft and Personnel
   m. Aircraft Survivability Equipment
   n. AN/ALE-39 Systems Brief For Enlisted Aircrew
   o. Forward Arming and Refueling Point
   p. Terrain Flight for Enlisted Aircrews
   q. M-240 Machine Gun
   r. Helicopter Insertion and Extraction Operations
2. The following classes contained in the UH-1 Academic Support Package shall be presented to the crew member prior to completing the combat qualified stage of training
   a. IR SAM Threat to R/W
   b. AAA Threat to R/W
   c. R/W Threat to the MAGTF
   d. F/W Threat to the MAGTF
3. The academic syllabus shall be reviewed annually.

UH-1 N CREW MEMBER TERRAIN FLIGHT (TERF) ACADEMIC COURSE

Course Objective: To provide UH-1N crew members with academic training enabling them to safely participate in terrain flight.

Length: 8 classroom hours

Academic Syllabus:

1. The following classes shall be presented to the crew members prior to flying any TERF flight:
   a. Terrain Flight for Enlisted Aircrews
   b. Tactical Aircrew Coordination Considerations
   c. Aircrew Responsibilities in a Tactical Environment
2. The following classes shall be presented to the crew member prior to flying any combat qualified TERF flight:
   a. Basic Principles of Electronic Warfare
   b. Aircraft Survivability Equipment
   c. IR SAM Threat to R/W
   d. AAA Threat to R/W
   e. AN/ALE-39 Systems Brief for Enlisted Aircrews
3. The academic syllabus shall be reviewed annually.

UH-1 N CREW MEMBER AIR TO AIR ACADEMIC COURSE

Course Objective: To provide UH-1N crew members with academic training enabling them to safely participate in air to air training.

Length: 3 classroom hours

Academic Syllabus:

1. The following class shall be presented to the crew member prior to flying any combat qualified air to air flight:
   a. Introduction to Helicopter Air Combat Maneuvering for Enlisted Aircrews
2. The following classes shall be presented the crew member prior to completing the ACM qualification process:
   a. R/W Threat to the MAGTF
   b. F/W Threat to the MAGTF
3. The academic syllabus shall be reviewed annually.

UH-1 N CREW MEMBER NIGHT SYSTEMS ACADEMIC COURSE

Course Objective: To provide UH-1N crew members with academic training enabling them to safely participate in night vision goggle (NVG) training.

Length: 2 classroom hours

Academic Syllabus:

1. The following classes shall be presented to the crew members prior to flying any night vision goggle flight:
   a. Night Vision Goggle Training for Enlisted Aircrews
   b. AIM-1 Laser Safety
2. The academic syllabus shall be reviewed annually.

UH-1N CREW MEMBER AERIAL GUNNERY ACADEMIC COURSE

Course Objective: To provide UH-1N crew members with academic training enabling them to safely participate in aerial gunnery training.

Length: 6 classroom hours

Academic Syllabus:

1. The following classes shall be presented to the crew members prior to flying any air to ground sortie:
   a. Fundamentals of Aerial Gunnery
   b. Employment Fundamentals of Aerial Gunnery
   c. XM-21 8/GAU-16 Machine Gun
   d. GAU-17A Machine Gun
   e. M-240 Machine Gun
2. The following class shall be presented to the aerial gunner prior to beginning the Aerial Gunner Instruction course:
   a. Training the Aerial Gunner
3. The Academic Syllabus shall be reviewed annually.

UH-1N CREW MEMBER ESCORT ACADEMIC COURSE

Course Objective: To provide UH-1N crew members with academic instruction on defending and escorting assault support aircraft.

Length: 3 classroom hour

Academic Syllabus:

1. The following classes shall be presented to the crew member prior to flying any fully combat qualified flight:
   a. Basic Principles of Escort Operations
   b. Tactical Recovery of Aircraft and Personnel
   c. Forward Arming and Refueling Point
2. The academic syllabus shall be reviewed annually.

UH-1N CREW MEMBER HELICOPTER INSERTION AND EXTRACTION ACADEMIC COURSE

Length: 2 classroom hours

Academic Syllabus:

1. The following class shall be presented to the crew member prior to flying any helicopter insertion and extraction flight:
   a. Helicopter Insertion and Extraction Operations
2. The academic syllabus shall be reviewed annually.

UH-1N AERIAL GUNNERY INSTRUCTOR (AGI) CERTIFICATION COURSE

Course Objective: To certify a UH-1N crew chief or aerial gunner as an Aerial Gunnery Instructor (AGI) capable of safely conducting ground and airborne instruction, in the employment of crew served weapons in all aspects of aerial gunnery flight.

Length: 2 classroom hours 6.0 flight hours

Academic Syllabus:

1. The IUT will review the MAWTS-1 Aerial Gunnery Manual.
2. The IUT will review and be capable of presenting all classes listed in the UH-1N Crew Member Aerial Gunnery Academic Course.
3. The following class shall be presented to the IUT prior to the certification stage of the flight syllabus:
   a. Training the Aerial Gunner
4. The IUT will successfully complete a written exam for each weapon system administered by an AGI, WTCCI, or MAWTS-1 crew chief instructor prior to beginning the certification stage of the flight syllabus.
5. The IUT will present to the AGI, WTCCI, or MAWTS-1 crew chief instructor one of the classes listed in the UH-1N Crew Member Aerial Gunnery Academic Course prior to completing the certification stage of the flight syllabus.

Flight Syllabus:

Instructor Under Training (IUT) Stage

1. The squadron will ensure that the IUT is prepared for certification.
2. The following flights will be instructed by an AGI, WTCCI, or MAWTS-1 crew chief instructor:

AG 540	1.5 hrs	1 UH-1	N

Goal: Develop instructional techniques during day aerial gunnery.

Requirements:

1. Evaluate instructional techniques in the usage and application of the following during day aerial gunnery:
   a. Weapons terminology
   b. Sectors of fire
   c. Lookout doctrine
   d. Weapons preparation
   e. Safety
   f. Malfunctions and stoppages
   g. Crew member responsibilities
   h. Crew served checklist application
   i. Range estimation and lead computations
   j. Situational Awareness
   k. Instructor Technique

AG 541	1.5hrs	1UH-1N	NVG

Goal: Develop instructional techniques during NVG aerial gunnery.

Requirements:

1. Evaluate instructional techniques during aerial gunnery while using NVGs, emphasizing items a - k from AG 540.

Certification Stage

1. The IUT will demonstrate to an AGI, WTCCI, or MAWTS-1 crew chief instructor the ability to instruct aerial gunnery training.

AG 542 E	1.5 hrs	2 UH-1N	NVG

Goal: Demonstrate instructional techniques during aerial gunnery weapons employment while utilizing NVGs in a multi-aircraft shoot.

Requirements:

1. Evaluate the IUT's instructional abilities during an NVG air to ground ordnance shoot using items a - k from AG 540.

AG 543 E	1.5 hrs	1 UH-1N D (NVG)

Goal: Demonstrate instructional techniques during aerial gunnery at a moving target, either a towed aerial banner, moving land target, or during shadow gunnery.

Requirements:

1. Evaluate instructional techniques during a moving target shoot emphasizing items a - k from AG 540.

Refresher Requirements:

1. Previously designated UH-1 N AGI's returning to the UH-1 N that require refresher training in accordance with MCO P3500.14E must complete a recertification course. Upon recertification by an AGI, WTCCI, or MAWTS-1 crew chief instructor, the AGI designation can be made by the squadron commanding officer. The following comprises the recertification process:
   a. IUT must meet all prerequisites.
   b. IUT must complete the AG 542 and AG 543 flights, evaluated by an AGI, WTCCI, or MAWTS-1 crew chief instructor.

Transition Requirements:

1. Crew members designated as an AGI in an aircraft other than the UH-1N that transition to the UH-1N must meet the prerequisites and complete the AG 542 and AG 543 flights evaluated by an AGI, WTCCI, or MAWTS-1 crew chief instructor.

Conversion Requirements:

1. Crew members designated as an AGI in an aircraft other that the UH-1N that undergo conversion training to the UH-1N must meet the prerequisites and complete the AG 542 and AG 543 flights evaluated by an AGI, WTCCI, or MAWTS-1 crew chief instructor.

UH-1N CREW CHIEF NIGHT SYSTEMS FAMILIARIZATION INSTRUCTOR (NSFI) CERTIFICATION COURSE

Course Objective: To certify a UH-1N crew chief as a Night Systems Familiarization Instructor (NSFI) capable of safely conducting ground and airborne instruction of night vision goggle (NVG) flight during 100 stage introductory NVG flights.

Length: 2 classroom hours 2.5 hours

Academic Syllabus:

1. The IUT will review the MAWTS-1 Night Vision Devices Manual.
2. The IUT will review and be capable of presenting all classes listed in the UH-1 N Crew Member Night Systems Academic Course.
3. The IUT will present to the NSI, WTCCI, or MAWTS-1 crew chief instructor one of the classes listed in the UH-1N Crew Member Night Systems Academic Course before completing the certification stage of the flight syllabus.
4. The IUT will successfully complete a written NSFI Exam administered by a NSI, WTCCI, or MAWTS-1 crew chief instructor prior to beginning the certification stage of the flight syllabus.

Flight Syllabus:

Instructor Under Training (IUT) Stage

1. The squadron will ensure that the IUT is prepared for certification. The certification stage of the flight syllabus must be completed within six (6) months following the first IUT flight. If six months have elapsed since completion of any IUT flight, that flight must be reflown prior to completing the final certification flight.
2. The following flight will be instructed by a NSFI, NSI, WTCCI, or MAWTS-1 crew chief instructor

NVG 560	1.5 hrs	1 UH-1N	NVG

Goal: Conduct low work and touch and go maneuvers utilizing NVGs under ambient light conditions above .0022 LUX.

Requirements:

1. Review and conduct low work, pattern work, and simulated emergencies with emphasis on instructional techniques.
2. Brief and discuss visual illusions, depth perception problems, NVG failures, lighting techniques, and NVG training restrictions.

Certification Stage

1. The IUT will demonstrate to the NSI, WTCCI, or MAWTS-1 crew chief instructor the ability to instruct night systems operations.

NVG 561 E	1.5 hrs	2 UH-1N	NVG

Goal: Evaluate the IUT's ability to instruct NVG familiarization training during CALS and NVG navigation under ambient light conditions above .0022 LUX.

Requirements:

1. Conduct CALs at an LZ which meets the special considerations for landing zones outlined in the MAWTS-1 Night Vision Device Manual.
2. Assist the pilots with navigation on a route of 50 nm at or above 200 ft AGL.
3. Brief and discuss map preparation, route planning, visual illusions, depth perception problems, NVG failures.

Refresher Requirements:

1. Previously designated UH-1 N NSFI's returning to the UH-1 N that require refresher training in accordance with MCO P3500.14E must complete the NSFI recertification course. Upon recertification by a NSI, WTCCI, or MAWTS-1 crew chief instructor, the NSFI designation can be made by the squadron commanding officer. The following comprises the recertification process:
   a. IUT must meet all prerequisites.
   b. IUT must complete the NVG 561 flight, evaluated by a NSI, WTCCI, or MAWTS-1 crew chief instructor.

Transition Requirements:

1. Crew chiefs designated as a NSFI on an aircraft other than the UH-1N, that transition to the UH-1 N must meet the prerequisites and fly the NVG 561 sortie, evaluated by a NSI, WTCCI, or MAWTS-1 crew chief instructor.

Conversion Requirements:

1. Crew chiefs designated as a NSFI in an aircraft other than the UH-1N, that undergo conversion to the UH-1N must meet the prerequisites and fly the NVG 561 sortie, evaluated by a NSI, WTCCI, or MAWTS-1 crew chief instructor.

UH-1 N CREW CHIEF TERRAIN FLIGHT INSTRUCTOR (TERFI) CERTIFICATION COURSE

Course Objective: To certify the UH-1N crew chief as an instructor capable of safely conducting ground and airborne instruction of the UH-1N terrain flight syllabus outlined in MCO P3500.16B.

Length: 2 classroom hours 3.0 flight hours

Academic Syllabus:

1. The IUT will review NWP 55-9-UH1 Tactical Manual prior to the certification flight.
2. The IUT will review and be capable of teaching all classes listed in the UH-1N Crew Member TERF Academic Course prior to beginning the IUT stage of the flight syllabus.
3. The IUT will present one of the classes listed in the UH-1N Crew Member TERF Academic Course to a WTCCI or MAWTS-1 crew chief instructor prior to finishing the certification process.
4. The IUT will successfully complete a written TERFI Exam administered by a WTCCI or MAWTS-1 crew chief instructor prior to beginning the certification stage of the flight syllabus.

Flight Syllabus

Instructor Under Training (IUT) Stage

1. The squadron will ensure that the IUT is prepared for certification. During the IUT stage a WTCCI or MAWTS-1 crew chief instructor will demonstrate to the IUT, proper TERFI techniques during TERF syllabus flights outlined in MCO P3500. 1 6B.

Certification Stage:

1. The IUT will demonstrate to a WTCCI or MAWTS-1 crew chief instructor the ability to conduct terrain flight instruction.
2. The following flights will be evaluated by a WTCCI or MAWTS-1 crew chief instructor:

TERF 570 E	1.5 hrs	1 UH-1	N

Goal: Demonstrate instructional techniques during terrain flight and navigation.

Requirements:

1. Demonstrate instructional techniques in assisting the pilot at all TERF altitudes with emphasis on lookout doctrine, crew coordination, and obstacle clearance.

TERF 571 E	1.5 hrs	2 UH-1	N

Goal: Demonstrate instructional techniques during multi-aircraft terrain flight and navigation.

Requirements:

1. Demonstrate instructional techniques in assisting the pilot at TERF altitudes with emphasis on lookout doctrine, crew coordination, navigational assistance, and obstacle clearance.

Refresher Requirements:

1. Designated UH-1 N TERFI's returning to the UH-1 N that require refresher training in accordance with MCO P3500.14E must complete a TERFI recertification course. Upon recertification by a WTCCI or MAWTS-1 crew chief instructor, the TERFI designation can be made by the squadron commanding officer. The following comprises the TERFI recertification process:
   a. IUT must meet all prerequisites.
   b. IUT must complete the TERF571 flight evaluated by a WTCCI or MAWTS-1 crew chief instruction

Transition Requirements:

1. Crew chiefs designated as a TERFI in an aircraft other than the UH-1N, that transition to the UH-1N must complete the TERF 571 flight evaluated by a WTCCI or MAWTS-1 crew chief instructor.

Conversion Requirements:

1. Crew chiefs designated as a TERFI in an aircraft other than the UH-1N that undergo conversion training must complete the TERF 571 flight evaluated by a WTCCI or MAWTS-1 crew chief instructor.

UH-1N CREW CHIEF AIR COMBAT MANEUVERS INSTRUCTOR (ACMI) CERTIFICATION COURSE

Course Objective: To certify the UH-1N crew chief as an instructor capable of conducting ground and airborne instruction of the UH-1N air to air syllabus outlined in MCO P3500. 1 6B.

Length: 2 classroom hours 4.5 flight hours

Academic Syllabus:

1. The IUT will review the MAWTS-1 Helicopter ACM Guide.
2. The IUT will review and be capable of teaching all classes listed in the UH-1N Crew Member Air to Air Academic Course prior to beginning the IUT stage of the flight syllabus.
3. The IUT will present one of the classes listed in the UH-1 N Crew Member Air to Air Academic Course to a MAWTS-1 crew chief instructor prior to the certification flight.
4. The IUT will successfully complete a written ACMI Exam administered by a MAWTS-1 crew chief instructor prior to beginning the certification stage of the flight syllabus.

Flight Syllabus:

Instructor Under Training (IUT) Stage

1. The squadron will ensure that the IUT is prepared for certification. The following flights will be instructed by an ACMI, WTCCI or MAWTS-1 crew chief instructor:
   AA 580 1.5 hrs 2 helicopters

Goal: Demonstrate instructional techniques during ACM (helo vs helo).

Requirements:

1. Demonstrate instructional techniques in the usage and application of the following during helo vs helo ACM:
   a. Common terminology
   b. Obstacle clearance
   c. Lookout doctrine
   d. Bandit/bogey information (identification, profiles)
   e. ALE-39 employment
   f. Crew chief responsibilities
   g. Understanding of training rules
   AA 581 1 .5 hrs 2 AIC. helo

Goal: Demonstrate instructional techniques during ACM (helo vs fixed wing).

Requirements:

1. Demonstrate instructional techniques in the usage and application of the following during helo vs fixed wing ACM.
   a. Common terminology
   b. Obstacle clearance
   c. Lookout doctrine
   d. Bandit/bogey information (identification, profiles)
   e. ALE-39 employment
   f. Crew chief responsibilities
   g. Understanding of training rules
   h. Closure rate

Certification Stage

1. The IUT will demonstrate to the MAWTS-1 crew chief instructor the ability to conduct air to air instruction.
2 The following flight will be evaluated by a MAWTS-1 crew chief instructor:
   M 582 E 1.5 hrs 2 A/C (2 helo. 1 f/w)

Goal: Demonstrate instructional techniques during ACM (2 helos, 1 f/w).

Requirements:

1. Demonstrate instructional techniques in the usage and application of the following during 2 helo vs fixed wing ACM:
   a. Common terminology
   b. Lookout doctrine
   c. Bandit/bogey information (identification, profiles)
   d. ALE-39 employment e. Supporting roles
   f. Crew chief responsibilities
   g. Understanding of training rules

Refresher Requirements:

1. Designated UH-1 N ACMI's returning to the UH-1 N that require refresher training in accordance with MCO P3500.14E must complete an ACMI recertification course. Upon recertification by a MAWTS-1 crew chief instructor, the ACI\/II designation can be made by the squadron commanding officer. The following comprises the recertification process:
   a. IUT must meet all prerequisites.
   b. IUT must complete the ACM 582 flight, evaluated by a MAWTS-1 crew chief instructor.

Transition Requirements:

1. Crew chiefs designated as an ACMI in an aircraft other than the UH-1N that transition to the UH-1N must complete the entire UH-1N Crew Chief ACMI Certification Course.

Conversion Requirements:

1. Crew chiefs designated as an ACMI in an aircraft other than the UH-1N that convert to the UH-1 N must complete the entire UH-1 N Crew Chief ACMI Certification Course.

UH-1 N CREW CHIEF NIGHT SYSTEMS INSTRUCTOR (NSI) CERTIFICATION COURSE

Course Objective: To certify a UH-1N crew chief as a Night Systems Instructor (NSI) capable of safely conducting ground and airborne instruction, in any ambient light level of the UH-1 N night vision goggle (NVG) flight syllabus outlined in MCO P3500.16.

Length: 2 classroom hours 6.0 flight hours

Academic Syllabus:

1. The IUT will review the MAWTS-1 Night Vision Devices Manual.
2. The IUT will review and be capable of presenting all classes listed in the UH-1N Crew Member Night Systems Academic Course.
3. The IUT will present to a MAWTS-1 crew chief instructor, one of the classes listed in the UH-1 N Crew Member Night Systems Academic Course, as determined by the MAWTS-1 instructor, before completing the certification stage of the flight syllabus.
4. The IUT will successfully complete a written NSI Exam administered by a MAWTS-1 crew chief instructor prior to beginning the certification stage of the flight syllabus.

Flight Syllabus:

Instructor Under Training (IUT) Stage

1. The squadron will ensure that the IUT is prepared for certification by MAWTS-1. The certification stage of the flight syllabus must be completed within six (6) months following the first flight. If six months have elapsed since completion of any IUT flight, that flight must be reflown prior to completing the final certification flight.
2. The following flights will be instructed by a NSI, WTCCI, or MAWTS-1 crew chief instructor. They will be flown under ambient light level conditions above .0022 LUX.
   NVG 590 1.5 hrs 1 UH-1N N

Goal: Develop IUT's ability to instruct NVG training.

Requirements:

1. Brief and discuss, weather and terrain considerations, aircraft lighting, NVG failures. crew coordination and comfort levels.
2. The IUT will assist the pilot in the conduct of low work, touch and goes, and navigation operations emphasizing instructional techniques in the following:
   a. Distance Estimation
   b. Depth perception
   c. Crew comfort level
   d. Obstacle clearance
   e. Lookout doctrine
   f. Emergency (both aircraft and goggles)
   NVG 591 1.5 hrs 1 UH-1N N

Goal: Conduct single aircraft CAL's and TERF at all altitudes emphasizing instructional techniques.

Requirements:

1. Brief and discuss NVG failures, illusions of terrain flight, crew coordination, and comfort levels.
2. Under high light conditions as defined by current Marine Corps directives, the IUT will demonstrate his instructional techniques while assisting the pilot in CALs and navigation emphasizing:
   a. Crew coordination
   b. Terrain suitability
   c. Lookout doctrine
   d. Standard Terminology
   e. Brown Outs/White Outs
   f. Closure Rates
   g. Obstacle Clearance
   h. Situational Awareness

Certification Stage

1. The IUT will demonstrate to the MAWTS-1 crew chief instructor the ability to instruct night systems operations. NVG 593 must be flown under ambient light conditions below. 0022 LUX.

NVG 592 E	1.5hrs	1UH-1N	N

Goal: Evaluate the IUT's ability to instruct NVG operations. During a two plane (minimum) NVG Navigation and Ordnance Delivery Flight.

Requirements:

1. Evaluate the IUT's ability to assist the pilot in formation flight, section CALs, ordnance delivery, and navigation at TERF altitudes emphasizing:
   a. Crew coordination
   b. Obstacle clearance
   c. Lookout Doctrine
   d. Emergency Procedures
   e. Situational Awareness
   f. Weapons Usage/Weapons Conditions/Sectors of fire
   g. Standard Terminology
   h. Instructor Technique

NVG 593 E	1.5 hrs	N2 UH-1	N

Goal: Evaluate the IUT's ability to brief and instruct section flights utilizing NVG's under low light level conditions.

Requirements:

1. Brief and discuss NVG failures, illusions of terrain flight, crew coordination, comfort levels, and standard terminology.
2. Under ambient light level conditions below .0022 LUX, the IUT will demonstrate his instructional techniques while assisting the pilot in formation flight and section CAL's at TERF altitudes emphasizing:
   a. Crew coordination
   b. Obstacle clearance
   c. Standard terminology
   d. Mission procedures
   e. Emergency procedures
   f. Situational Awareness
   g. Standard Terminology
   h. Instruction Techniques

Refresher Requirements:

1. Previously designated UH-1 N NSI's returning to the UH-1 N that require refresher training in accordance with MCO P3500.14E must complete an NSI recertification course. Upon recertification by a MAWTS-1 crew chief instructor, the NSI designation can be made by the squadron commanding officer. The following comprises the recertification course:
   a. IUT must meet all prerequisites.
   b. The IUT must complete the NVG 592 and NVG 593 sortie, evaluated by a MAWTS-1 crew chief instructor.

Transition Requirements:

1. Crew chiefs designated as an NSI in an aircraft other than the UH-1N that transition to the UH-1N must complete the entire UH-1N Crew Chief Night Systems Instructor Certification Course.

Conversion Requirements:

1. Crew chiefs designated as an NSI in an aircraft other than the UH-1N that undergo conversion to the UH-1N must complete the entire UH-1N Crew Chief Night Systems Instructor Certification Course.

CH-46 SUPPLEMENTARY COURSES
CH-46 SPECIFIC ACADEMIC SUPPORT PACKAGE

Course Objective: To provide the CH-46 pilot with additional ground training as required by MCO P3500.14.

Length: 16 classroom hours

Academic Syllabus:

1. The following class should be presented to the pilot under instruction prior to flying the NBC 261 sortie:
   a. NBC Threat
2. The following classes should be presented to the pilot under instruction prior to flying the TAC 371 sortie:
   a. Assault Support Mission Planning b. Tactical Briefing and Debriefing c. Command and Control TACC and DASC
3. The following classes should be presented to the pilot under instruction prior to completion of the combat qualified stage of training:
   a. Forward Arming and Refueling Point
   b. Fire Support Coordination Measures
   c. Helicopter Escort Tactics 1
   d. Helicopter Escort Tactics 2
   e. TRAP Mission Planning
   f. MAGTF: Organization and Equipment
   G. MAGTF: The Amphibious Assault
   h. MACCS Part 1
   i. MACCS Part 2
   j. Intel Sources and Collection
   k. Soviet IADS
   l. Surface to Surface Threat
   m. The Soviet Pilot
   n. Tactical Recovery of Aircraft and Personnel

CH-46 TERRAIN FLIGHT (TERF) COURSE

Course Objective: To provide ground instruction enabling the CH-46 pilot to safely participate in TERF training.

Length: 7 classroom hours

Academic Syllabus:

1. The following classes will be presented to the pilot under instruction prior to flying the TERF 170 sortie:
   a. Terrain Flight Introduction b. Tactical Aircrew Coordination Considerations
2. The following classes will be presented to the pilot under instruction prior to flying the FORM 231 sortie:
   a. Tactical Formation Maneuvering
3. The following classes will be presented to the pilot under instruction prior to completing the TERF 244 sortie:
   a. Countering the Surface to Air Threat
   b. Basic Radar Principles
   c. Soviet Tactical Surface to Air Threat Systems (SAMS/MA)
   d. Non-Soviet SAMS/AAA

CH-46 NIGHT SYSTEMS OPERATIONS COURSE

Course Objective: To provide ground instruction enabling the CH-46 pilot to safely participate in night vision goggle (NVG) training.

Length: 5 classroom hours

Academic Syllabus:
1. The following classes will be presented to the pilot under instruction prior to flying the NVG 180 sortie:
   a. Night Vision Devices
   b. Introductory Night Vision Goggle Training
   c. NVG Human Factors
   d. The Night Environment
2. The following class will be presented to the pilot under instruction prior to flying the NVG. 2.51 sortie:
   a. Night Vision Goggle Tactics and Training

CH-46 AIR TO GROUND COURSE

Course Objective: To provide ground training enabling the CH-46 pilot to safely participate in air to ground ordnance training.

Length: 2 classroom hours

Academic Syllabus:

1. The following classes should be presented to the pilot under instruction prior to flying the AG 281 sortie:
   a. Rotary Wing Weaponeering: Capabilities and Limitations
   b. Shadow Gunnery

CH-46 ELECTRONIC WARFARE COURSE

Course Objective: To provide ground instruction enabling the CH-46 pilot to participate in electronic warfare flight training.

Length: 3 classroom hours

Academic Syllabus:

1. The following classes will be presented to the pilot under instruction prior to flying the EW 331 sortie:
   a. ALE Programming for Transport Helicopters
   b. Helo Electronic Warfare Equipment
   c. Soviet REC.

CH-46 DEFENSIVE MEASURES COURSE

Course Objective: To provide ground instruction enabling the CH-46 pilot to safely participate in defensive measures training.

Length: 15 classroom hours

Academic Syllabus:

1. The following classes will be presented to the pilot under instruction prior to flying any defensive measures sortie:
   a. ALE Programming for Assault Helicopters
   b. ACM
2. The following classes will be presented to the pilot under instruction prior to completing the DM qualification process:
   a. Countering the R/W Threat
   b. Countering the F/W Threat
   c. Countering the Surface to Air Threat

CH-46 HELICOPTER INSERTION AND EXTRACTION TECHNIQUES COURSE

Course Objective: To provide ground instruction enabling the CH-46 pilot to safely participate in helicopter insertion and extraction training.

Length: 5 classroom hours

Academic Syllabus:

1. The following classes will be presented to the pilot under instruction prior to flying the Helicopter Insertion and Extraction Sorties:
   a. Fast Rope Operations
   b. Rappel Operations
   c. SPIE Rig Operations
   d. Parachute Operations

CH-46 TERRAIN FLIGHT INSTRUCTOR (TERFI) CERTIFICATION COURSE

Course Objective: To certify the CH-46 pilot as an instructor capable of safely conducting ground and airborne instruction of the CH-46 terrain flight syllabus.

Length: 8 classroom hours 4.5 flight hours

Academic Syllabus:

1. The instructor under training (IUT) will review and be capable of presenting all classes listed in the CH-46 TERF Course.
2. The IUT will successfully complete the TERFI exam (found in the Rotary Wing Common Class, "Terrain Flight"), administered by a TERFI, prior to beginning the certification stage of the flight syllabus.
3. The IUT will present to a designated TERFI, one of the classes listed in the CH-46 TERF Course, as selected by the TERFI, prior to finishing the certification process.

Flight Syllabus:

Instructor Under Training (IUT) Stage

1. The following flights will be instructed by a qualified and proficient TERFI:
   TERF 570 1.5 hrs 1 CH-46

Goal: Demonstrate the ability to instruct all terrain flight maneuvers including TERF external load operations with emphasis on instructional techniques.

Requirement:

1. IUT will brief and discuss crew coordination, comfort level, voice and visual signals, flight envelopes of various loads, cargo jettison procedures, low altitude emergencies, single/dual engine operations (with or without the load), inflight weight computation, and HST requirements.
2. Review performance checks, masking/unmasking, contour/low level quick stop, bunts, rolls, low level, contour, and NOE profiles, low altitude emergencies, and crew coordination. The IUT will conduct a minimum of 2 hookups and deliveries placing the load within five meters of the intended point. Review and perform rolls and bunts with external loads emphasizing requirements for early initiation of maneuvers and small corrections to prevent pilot induced oscillation.
   TERF 571 1.5 hrs 2 CH-46

Goal: Demonstrate the ability to instruct flight navigation in the NOE/contour profiles and tactical formation in the TERF environment with emphasis on instructional techniques.

Requirement:

1. IUT will brief and discuss TERF formation techniques, TERF navigation techniques and responsibilities, crew coordination, comfort level, low altitude emergencies, weapons and ALE/APR employment.
2. Review TERF formation, TERF navigation techniques and responsibilities. Utilizing a 1:50,000 map, the IUT will navigate in the contour and NOE profile, remaining oriented within 100 meters. The route shall include a minimum of five check points and a minimum of 30 NM in the contour mode and 2 NM in the NOE mode. The IUT must arrive at the final checkpoint within one minute of the planned time. The IUT will instruct tactical formation in the low level and contour profiles.

Certification Stage

1. The following sortie will be evaluated by a qualified and proficient TERFI:
   TERF 572 E 1.5hrs 1 CH-46

Goal: Evaluate the IUT's ability to perform and instruct all phases of terrain flight and terrain flight navigation.

Requirement:

1. IUT will brief and discuss crew coordination, comfort level, illusions of terrain flight, low altitude emergencies, weapons and ALE/APR employment, and TERF navigation techniques and responsibilities.
2. Evaluate the IUT's ability to instruct and perform performance checks, masking/unmasking, low level quick stops, bunts, rolls, low level, contour, and NOE profiles, crew coordination, and low altitude emergencies.
3. Evaluate the IUT's ability to instruct and perform terrain flight navigation in the contour and NOE profiles using a 1 :50,000 map. The IUT is required to maintain orientation along the prescribed route within 100 meters and arrive at the final checkpoint within 1 minute of the planned time. The route shall include a minimum of 5 check points and a minimum of 30 NM in the contour mode and 2 NM in the NOE mode.

Refresher Requirements:

1. Designated CH-46 TERFI's returning to the CH-46 that require refresher or modified refresher training in accordance with MCO P3500.14 must complete a TERFI recertification course. Upon recertification by a TERFI, the TERFI designation can be made by the squadron commanding officer. The following comprises the TERFI recertification process:
   a. IUT must meet all prerequisites outlined previously.
   b. IUT must complete the TERFI exam, administered by a TERFI.
   c. IUT must complete the TERF 572 sortie, evaluated by a qualified and proficient TERFI.

Transition Requirements:

1. Aircrew designated as a TERFI in an aircraft other than the CH-46, that undergo transition training to the CH-46 in accordance with MCO P3500.14, must complete the entire CH-46 TERFI Course.

Conversion Requirements:

1. Aircrew designated as a TERFI in an aircraft other than the CH-46, that undergo conversion training to the CH-46 in accordance with MCO P3500.14, must complete the entire CH-46 TERFI Course.

AIR DEFENSIVE MEASURES INSTRUCTOR (DMI) CERTIFICATION COURSE

Course Objective: To certify the CH-46 pilot as an instructor capable of safely conducting ground and airborne instruction of the CH-46 defensive measures flight syllabus.

Length: 5 classroom hours 3 flight hours

Academic Syllabus:

1 The instructor under training (IUT) will review the MAWTS-1 DM Guide, the CH-46 Tactical Manual Volumes 1 and 2. and the MCM 3-1.

2. The IUT will review and be capable of presenting all classes listed in the CH-46 Defensive Measures Course.
3. The IUT will successfully complete the CH-46 DMI test, administered by a MAWTS-1 instructor, prior to beginning the certification stage of the flight syllabus.
4. The IUT will present, to the MAWTS-1 instructor or DMI, one of the classes in the CH-46 Defensive Measures Course.
5. The entire academic syllabus will be completed within 90 days prior to the beginning of the certification stage.

Flight Syllabus:

Instructor Under Training (IUT) Stage

1. The following flights will be instructed by a DMI or MAWTS-1 instructor. DM- 580 1 0 2 v Ground Threat

Goal: Demonstrate the ability to instruct 2 v ground threat tactics in accordance with the MAWTS-1 DM guide.

Requirement: Review multi-aircraft DM against a ground threat. Brief and discuss the capabilities, limitations, and envelopes of the threat system. This sortie should be conducted in airspace that permits the employment of expendables.

a. Aircrew coordination/Inter flight coordination
b. Crew comfort level
c. Lookout doctrine
d. Situational awareness
e. Use of ALE-39, APR-39, ALQ-157, and MR-47
f. Tactical formation maneuvering
g. Use of RADAR horizons, RADAR masking, maneuver and chaff to defeat threat RADAR systems
h. Use of terrain masking, maneuver, IR jamming, and flares to defeat threat IR missiles

Ordnance: 40 chaff 20 flares DM581 1.0 2v1FW/RW

Goal: Demonstrate the ability to instruct 2 v 1 FW/RW DM tactics in accordance with the MAWTS-1 DM guide.

Requirements: Review helicopter 2 v 1 DM with a fixed wing or rotary wing aggressor aircraft. Brief and discuss the capabilities, limitations, and envelopes of the aggressor aircraft. Brief and discuss weapons and ASE employment. This sortie should be conducted in airspace that permits the employment of expendables.

a. Aircrew coordination/Inter flight coordination
b. Crew comfort level
c. Lookout doctrine
d. Standardized terminology
e. Situational awareness
f. DM training rules
g. Closure rate, radius of turn, and energy state
h. Use of ALE-39, APR-39, ALQ-157, and MR-47
i. Use of .50 caliber machine gun
j. DM against RW/FW aggressor
k. Supporting roles

Ordnance: 40 flares and 20 chaff

Certification Stage

1. The following flight will be evaluated by the MAWTS-1 instructor. If DM 581 was flown versus a RW aggressor, DM 582 shall be flown versus a FW aggressor. If DM 581 was flown versus a FW aggressor, DM 582 shall be flown versus a RW aggressor.
   <u>DM 582E</u> <u>1.0hrs</u> <u>2 v 1 FW/RW</u>

Goal: Evaluate 2 v 1 DM tactics and instructional techniques in accordance with the MAWTS-1 DM guide.

Requirement: IUT will brief helicopter versus helicopter/fixed wing (as appropriate) flight. Emphasis will be on instructional techniques, to include demonstrating a working knowledge of the capabilities, limitations and envelopes of that threat aircraft. Brief, discuss, and simulate weapons and ASE employment. Discuss procedures for both FW and RW aggressor. This sortie should be conducted in airspace that permits the employment of expendables.

Ordnance: 40 flares and 20 chaff

Refresher Requirements:

1. Previously certified CH-46 ACMI's returning to the CH-46 requiring refresher or modified refresher training as defined in MCO P3500.14 must be recertified by MAWTS-1. Upon recertification by MAWTS-1, the DMI designation can be made by the squadron commanding officer. The following comprises the recertification course:
   a. The IUT must meet all prerequisites listed previously.
   b. The IUT must complete the DMI exam, administered by the MAWTS-1 instructor.
   c. The IUT must complete the DM 582 flight, evaluated by the MAWTS-1 instructor.

Transition Requirements:

1. Pilots certified as an ACMI in an aircraft other than the CH-46 that transition to the CH-46 as defined in MCO P3500.14 must complete the entire CH-46 DMI certification course.

Conversion Requirements:

1. Pilots certified as an ACMI in an aircraft other than CH-46, that undergo conversion training to the CH-46 as defined in MCO P3500.14 must complete the entire CH-46 DMI Certification Course.

CH-46 NIGHT SYSTEMS FAMILIARIZATION INSTRUCTOR (NSFI) CERTIFICATION COURSE

Course Objective: To certify a CH-46 pilot as a Night Systems Familiarization Instructor (NSFI) capable of instructing in the familiarization phase (100 series) of NS/NVG flight to include low work, pattern work, navigation, and single aircraft confined area landings.

Length: 3 classroom hours 4.5 flight hours

Academic Syllabus:

1. The instructor under training (IUT) will review and be capable of presenting the following classes:
   a. Night Vision Devices
   b. Introductory Night Vision Goggle Training
2. The IUT will successfully complete the NSFI exam, administered by a NSI or MAWTS-1 instructor, prior to beginning the certification stage of the flight syllabus.
3. The IUT will present to a NSI or MAWTS-1 instructor, one of the classes listed above, as determined by the NSI or MAWTS-1 instructor, before completing the certification stage of the flight syllabus.
4. The academic syllabus will be completed within 90 days prior to the beginning of the certification stage of the flight syllabus.

Flight Syllabus:

Instructor Under Training (IUT) Stage

1. The squadron will ensure that the IUT is prepared for certification. The certification stage of the flight syllabus must be complete within six (6) months following the first IUT flight. If six months have elapsed since completion of any IUT flight, that flight must be reflown prior to completing the final certification flight.
2. The following flights will be instructed by a squadron NSI or NSFI:
   <u>NVG 560</u> <u>1.5 hrs</u> <u>1 CH-46</u> <u>N</u>

Goal: Demonstrate the ability to instruct low work and touch and go maneuvers utilizing NVG's under ambient light conditions above .0022 LUX.

Requirements:

1. IUT to brief/discuss visual illusions, depth perception problems, NVG failures and aircraft lighting.
2. Review low work to include taxi, hover, takeoffs to a hover, hover, no hover landing.
3. Review pattern work to include normal and steep approaches to hover and no hover landings. Review touch and go, full stop, running landings, and simulated emergencies.
   <u>NVG 561</u> <u>1.5hrs</u> <u>1CH-46</u> <u>N</u>

Goal: Demonstrate the ability to instruct touch and go maneuvers, CAL's, and navigation utilizing NVGs under ambient light conditions above .0022 LUX.

Requirements:

1. IUT to brief/discuss map preparation, route planning, visual illusions, depth perception problems, NVG failures, and inadvertent IMC.
2. Conduct CAL's at an LZ which meets the special considerations for landing zones outlined in the MAWTS-1 NVD manual.

3. Conduct a navigation route of 50 nm at or above 200 ft AGL. IUT must remain oriented to within 500 meters.

Certification Stage

1. The IUT will demonstrate to the NSI or MAWTS-1 instructor the ability to instruct night systems operations.
   NVG 562 E 1.5hrs 1 CH-46 N

Goal: Evaluate the IUT's ability to instruct NVG familiarization training under ambient light conditions above .0022 LUX.

Requirements:

1. Review low work, pattern work and simulated emergencies.
2. Conduct CAL's at an LZ which meets the special considerations for landing zones as defined in the MAWTS-1 NVD Manual
3. Conduct a navigation route of 50 nm at or above 200 ft AGL. The IUT must remain oriented to within 500 meters.

Refresher Requirements:

1. Previously certified CH-46 NSFI's or Phase I Instructors returning to the CH-46 requiring refresher or modified refresher training as defined in MCO P3500.14 must be recertified by a NSI or MAWTS-1 instructor. Upon recertification, the NSFI designation can be made by the HMT-204 commanding officer. The following comprises the recertification course:
   a. The IUT must meet all prerequisites previously listed.
   b. The IUT must successfully complete the NSFI exam, administered by an NSI or MAWTS-1 instructor.
   c. The IUT must complete the NVG 562 flight, evaluated by an NSI or MAWTS-1 instructor

Transition Requirements:

1. Pilots certified as an NSI or NSFI or Phase I instructors in an aircraft other than the CH-46, that transition to the CH-46 as defined in MCO P3500.14, must complete the entire CH-46 NSFI Certification Course previously listed.

Conversion Requirements:

1. Pilots certified as an NSI or NSFI in an aircraft other than the CH-46, that undergo conversion training to the CH-46 as defined in MCO P3500.14, must complete the entire CH-46 NSFI Certification Course previously listed.

CH-46 NIGHT SYSTEMS SAR INSTRUCTOR (NSSI) CERTIFICATION COURSE

Course Objective: To certify a CH-46 pilot as a Night Systems SAR Instructor (NSSI) capable of safely conducting ground and airborne instruction of the night vision goggle (NVG) flight syllabus outlined in MCO P3500.17.

Length: 3 classroom hours 4.5 flight hours

Academic Syllabus:

1. The instructor under training (IUT) will review and be capable of presenting the following classes:
   a. Night Vision Devices
   b. Introductory Night Vision Goggle Training
2. The IUT will successfully complete the NSSI exam, administered by the MAWTS-1 instructor, prior to beginning the certification stage of the flight syllabus.
3. The IUT will present to the MAWTS-1 instructor or a NSSI, one of the classes listed above, as determined by the MAWTS-1 instructor or NSSI, before completing the certification stage of the flight syllabus.
4. The academic syllabus will be completed within 90 days prior to beginning the certification stage of the flight syllabus.

Flight Syllabus:

Instructor Under Training (IUT) Stage

1. The squadron will ensure that the IUT is prepared for certification by a MAWTS-1 instructor or NSI. The certification stage of the flight syllabus must be complete within six (6) months following the first IUT flight. If six months have elapsed since completion of any IUT flight, that flight must be reflown prior to completing the final certification flight.
2. The following flights will be instructed by a squadron NSSI or MAWTS-1 instructor:
   NVG 550 1.5 hrs 1 CH-46 N

Goal: Demonstrate the ability to instruct CAL's and navigation while utilizing NVG's above .0022 LUX.

Requirements:

1. IUT to brief/discuss NVG operations and limitations, NVG emergencies, lookout doctrine, aircraft lightning, crew coordination/comfort level, depth perception, visual illusions, waveoffs, and inadvertent IMC.
2. Under ambient light conditions above .0022 LUX, evaluate the IUT's ability to instruct single aircraft CAL's and navigation while utilizing NVG's. The IUT shall remain oriented within 500 meters while conducting a 25 nm navigation route above 200 ft AGL. A minimum of 4 navigation legs and 4 CAL's are required.
   NVG 551 E 1.5 hrs 1 CH-46 N

Goal: Demonstrate the ability to instruct CAL's and navigation while utilizing NVG's below .0022 LUX.

Requirements:

1. IUT to brief/discuss low light level operations and limitations, NVG emergencies. lookout doctrine, crew coordination/comfort level, depth perception, aircraft lightning, visual illusions, waveoffs, and inadvertent IMC.
2. Under ambient light conditions below .0022 LUX, evaluate the IUT's ability to instruct single aircraft CAL's and navigation while utilizing NVG's. The IUT shall remain oriented within 500 meters while conducting a 25 nm navigation route above 200 ft AGL. A minimum of 4 navigation legs and 4 CAL's are required.

Certification Stage

1. The IUT will demonstrate to the MAWTS-1 instructor or NSI the ability to instruct night systems operations.
   NVG 552 E 1.5 hrs 1 CH-46 N

Goal: Evaluate the IUT's ability to instruct basic operations, CAL's, and navigation while utilizing the NVG's below .0022 LUX.

Requirements:

1. IUT to brief/discuss NVG emergencies, low light level operations, light pollution, navigational techniques, crew coordination/comfort level, waveoffs, and inadvertent IMC.
2. Under ambient light conditions below .0022 LUX, evaluate the IUT's ability to perform and instruct single aircraft CAL's and navigate while utilizing NVG's. The IUT shall remain oriented within 500 meters while conducting a 40 nm navigation route above 200 ft AGL. A minimum of 4 navigation legs and 4 CAL's are required.

CH-46 NIGHT SYSTEMS INSTRUCTOR (NSI) CERTIFICATION COURSE

Course Objective: To certify a CH-46 pilot as a Night Systems Instructor (NSI) capable of safely conducting ground and airborne instruction, in any ambient light condition, of the CH-46 night vision goggle (NVG) flight syllabus outlined in MCO P.Renn- 1 G

Length: 6 classroom hours 9.0 flight hours

Academic Syllabus:

1. The instructor under training (IUT) will review and be capable of presenting all classes listed in the CH-46 Night Systems Course.
2. The IUT will successfully complete the NSI exam, administered by the MAWTS-1 instructor, prior to beginning the certification stage of the flight syllabus.
3. The IUT will present, to a NSI or MAWTS-1 instructor, one of the classes listed in the CH-46 Night Systems Course, as determined by a NSI before completing the certification stage of the flight syllabus.
4. The academic syllabus will be completed within 90 days prior to beginning the certification stage of the flight syllabus.

Flight Syllabus:
Instructor Under Training (IUT) Stage

1. The squadron will ensure that the IUT is prepared for certification by MAWTS-1. The certification stage of the flight syllabus must be complete within six (6) months following the first IUT flight. If six months have elapsed since completion of any IUT flight, that flight must be reflown prior to completing the final certification flight.
2. The following flights will be instructed by a squadron NSI or MAWTS-1 instructor. They can be flown under high or low light conditions, as defined in MCO P3500. 1 4:
   NVG 590 1.5 hrs 1 CH-46 N

Goal: Demonstrate the ability to instruct low work, pattern work and single aircraft CAL's utilizing NVG's.

Requirements:

1. IUT to brief and discuss NVG failures, waveoffs, crew coordination, comfort levels, and inadvertent IMC.
2. Conduct low work to include taxi, takeoffs to a hover, and no hover landings to a prepared surface.
3. Conduct pattern work to include normal and steep approaches to a prepared surface. Review touch and go landings and simulated emergencies.
4. Conduct single aircraft CAL's to a LZ.
   NVG591 1.5 hrs 1 CH-46 N

Goal: Demonstrate the ability to instruct and conduct NVG external operations to confined areas.

Requirements:

1. IUT to brief and discuss crew coordination, comfort level, voice and visual signals, flight envelopes of various loads, cargo jettison procedures, relative position of the moon and the aircraft during hookup, pendant and load illumination techniques, LZ lighting, NVG failures, low altitude emergencies, in-flight weight computations, and HST requirements.
2. Under ambient light conditions as defines by current Marine Corps directives, the IUT will demonstrate his instructional techniques for takeoffs, precision approach, and delivery of an external load to a confined area void of visibility restrictions utilizing NVG's. The IUT will conduct a minimum of five external hookups and deliveries or until proficiency is demonstrated in placing the load within five meters of the intended point.
   NVCG 592 1.5 hrs 2 CH-46 N

Goal: Demonstrate the ability to instruct and conduct formation CAL's on NVG's, emphasizing instructional technique.

Requirements:

1. IUT will brief and discuss NVG failures, inadvertent IMC procedures, weapons procedures, illusions of terrain flight at night on NVG's, crew coordination, and comfort level.
2. Under ambient light conditions as defined by current Marine Corps directives, the IUT will demonstrate his instructional technique while performing formation CAL's.
   NVG 593 1.5 hrs 2 CH-46 N

Goal: Demonstrate the ability to instruct formation and terrain flight navigation on NVG's

Requirements:

1. IUT to brief and discuss lead change, NVG failures, inadvertent IMC procedures, formation principles (break-ups and rendezvous), illusions of night terrain flight, crew coordination, comfort level, and emergency procedures. Brief and discuss navigation principles and the employment of the ALE/APR systems, with emphasis on night considerations.
2. Under ambient light conditions as defined by current Marine Corps directives, the IUT will demonstrate his instructional technique while performing formation flight, section CAL's, and a contour navigation flight utilizing a 1:250,000 and 1:50,000 map. The IUT shall remain oriented within 200 meters and arrive within 1 minute at the final checkpoint. A minimum of four navigational legs as lead and two navigational legs as wingman are required. Include demonstrating the utilization of existing navigation systems and APRJALE countermeasures systems (if available).

Certification Stage

1. The IUT will demonstrate to the MAWTS-1 instructor the ability to instruct night systems operations. NVG 594 may be flown under high or low light conditions. NVG595 must be flown under low light conditions as defined in MCO P3500.14.
   NVG 594 F 1 5 hrs 1 CH-46 N

Goal: Evaluate the IUT's ability to instruct low work, pattern work, single aircraft CAL's, and external operations utilizing NVG's.

Requirements:

1. Evaluate the IUT's ability to brief and discuss crew coordination, comfort level, voice and visual signals, flight envelopes of various loads, cargo jettison procedures, pendant and load illumination techniques, LZ lighting, NVG failures, low altitude emergencie, in-flight weight computating and HST requirements.
2. Under ambient light conditions as defined by current Marine Corps directives, evaluate the IUT's ability to perform and instruct single aircraft CAL's, low work, pattern work, and external load operations to confined areas void of visibility restrictions, inadvertent IMC procedures, IMC waveoff to an ITO, crew coordination, and emergency procedures utilizing NVG's. The IUT will complete a minimum of three (3) external hookups and deliveries, or until proficiency is demonstrated, and place the load within five (5) meters of the intended point.
   NVG 595 E 1 5 hrs 2 CH-46 N

Goal: Evaluate the IUT's ability to brief and instruct formation flight, section CAL's, and NVG contour navigation utilizing NVG's under low light level conditions.

Requirements:

1. Evaluate the IUT's ability to brief and discuss NV Glow light level considerations, formation inadvertent IMC procedures, lead changes, tactical formation flight, illusions of night terrain flight, long range navigational techniques, crew coordination, comfort level, NVG failures, low altitude emergencies, ALE/APR-39 employment considerations, crew served weapons employment, and multiple aircraft confined area operations.
2. Evaluate the IUTs ability to instruct tactical formation flight, section CAL's, and TERF navigation utilizing the NVG's under low light level conditions. A minimum of two CAL's with four navigation legs as lead, and three CAL's with two navigation legs as wingman are required. The IUT is required to maintain orientation within 200 meters of the prescribed route and arrive within 1 minute at the final checkpoint. If available. utilize ALE/APR-39 systems and crew served weapons.

Refresher Requirements:

1. Previously certified CH-46, Phase II Instructors, Phase III Instructors or NSI's returning to the CH-46 that required refresher or modified refresher training as defined in MCO P3500.14 must be recertified by MAWTS-1. Upon recertification by MAWTS-1, the NSI designation can be made by the squadron commanding officer. The following comprises the recertification course:
   a. The IUT must meet all prerequisites listed previously.
   b. The IUT must successfully complete the NSI exam administered by the MAWTS-1 instructor.
   c. The IUT must complete the NVG 595 flight, evaluated by the MAWTS-1 instructor.

Transition Requirements:

1. Pilots certified as an NSI in an aircraft other than the CH-46, that transition to the CH-46 as defined in MCO P3500.14, must complete the entire CH-46 NSI Certification Course previously listed.

Conversion Requirements:

1. Pilots certified as an NSI in an aircraft other than the CH-46, that convert to the CH-46 as defined in MCO P3500.14, must complete the entire CH-46 NSI Certification Course previously listed.

CH-46 CREW MEMBER SUPPLEMENTARY COURSES
CH-46 CREW MEMBER ACADEMIC SUPPORT PACKAGE

Course Objective: To provide CH-46 crew members with additional ground training as required by MCO P3500.14E.

Length: 21 classroom hours

Academic Syllabus:

1. The following classes will be presented to the crew member under instruction prior to completing the combat qualified stage of training:
   a. Aircrew Responsibilities in a Tactical Environment
   b. Tactical Aircrew Coordination Considerations
   c. Introduction to Air Combat Maneuvers for Enlisted Aircrews
   d. Night Vision Goggle Training for Enlisted Aircrews
   e. Fundamentals of Aerial Gunnery
   f. Employment Fundamentals of Aerial Gunnery
   g. XM-21 8/GAU-16 Machine Gun
   h. Laser Safety
   i. Basic Principles of Electronic Warfare
   j. Training the Aerial Gunner
   k. Basic Principles of Escort Operations
   l. Tactical Recovery of Aircraft and Personnel
   m. Aircraft Survivability Equipment
   n. AN/ALE-39 Systems Brief For Enlisted Aircrew 1G 1
   o. Forward Arming and Refueling Point
   p. Terrain Flight for Enlisted Aircrews
   q. Helicopter Insertion and Extraction Operations

2. The following classes contained in the pilots Academic Support Package will be presented to the crew member prior to completing the combat qualified stage of training:
   a. IR SAM Threat to R/W
   b. AAA Threat to R/W
   c. R/W Threat to the MAGTF
   d. F/W Threat to the MAGTF
3. The academic syllabus will be reviewed annually.

CH-46 CREW MEMBER TERRAIN FLIGHT (TERF) ACADEMIC COURSE

Course Objective: To provide CH-46 crew members with ground training enabling them to safely participate in TERF training.

Length: 5 classroom hours

Academic Syllabus:

1. The following classes will be presented to the crew members under instruction prior to flying any TERF flight:
   a. Terrain Flight for Enlisted Aircrews
   b. Tactical Aircrew Coordination Considerations
   c. Aircrew Responsibilities in a Tactical Environment
2. The following classes will be presented to the crew member under instruction prior to flying any combat qualified TERF flight:
   a. IR SAM Threat to R/W
   b. AAA Threat to R/W
3. The academic syllabus will be reviewed annually.

CH-46 CREW MEMBER ELECTRONIC WARFARE ACADEMICS COURSE

Course Objective: To familiarize the CH-46 crew members with friendly and threat electronic warfare capabilities.

Length: 3 classroom hours

Academic Syllabus:

1. The following classes will be presented to the crew member under instruction prior to completing the combat qualified stage of training:
   a. AN/ALE-39 Systems Brief for Enlisted Aircrew
   b. Basic Principles of Electronic Warfare
   c. Aircraft Survivability Equipment
2. The academic syllabus will be reviewed annually.

CH-46 CREW MEMBER AERIAL GUNNERY ACADEMIC COURSE

Course Objective: To provide CH-46 crew members with academic training enabling them to safely participate in aerial gunnery training.

Length: 5 classroom hours

Academic Syllabus:

1. The following classes will be presented to the aerial gunner under instruction Drior to flying aerial gunnery flight:
   a. Fundamentals of Aerial Gunnery
   b. Employment Fundamentals of Aerial Gunnery
   c. XM-218 Machine Gun
2. The following class will be presented to the aerial gunners under instruction prior to completion of the Aerial Gunner Qualification stage:
   a. AIM-1 Laser Safety
3. The following class will be presented to the aerial gunners prior to completing the Aerial Gunner Instruction course:
   a. Training the Aerial Gunner
4. The Academic Syllabus will be reviewed annually.

CH-46 CREW MEMBER HELICOPTER INSERTION AND EXTRACTION OPERATIONS ACADEMICS COURSE

Course Objective: To provide academic training enabling the CH-46 crew member to safely participate in helicopter insertion and extraction training.

Length: 1 classroom hours

Academic Syllabus:

1. The following classes will be presented to the crew member under instruction prior to flying any HIE flights:
   a. Helicopter Insertion and Extraction Operation
      (1) Fast Rope Operations
      (2) Rappel Operations
      (3) SPIE Rig Operations
      (4) Helocast Operations
      (5) Parachute Operations
2. The academic syllabus will be reviewed annually.

CH-46 AERIAL GUNNERY INSTRUCTOR (AGI) CERTIFICATION COURSE

Course Objective: To certify a CH-46 crew chief or aerial gunner as an Aerial Gunnery Instructor (AGI) capable of safely conducting academic and airborne instruction in the employment of crew served weapons in all aspects of tactical flight.

Length: 2 classroom hours 6.0 flight hours

Academic Syllabus:

1. The instructor under training will review the MAWTS-1 Aerial Gunnery Manual.
2. The IUT will review and be capable of presenting all classes listed in the CH-46 Crew Member Aerial Gunnery Academics Course.
3. The following class will be presented to the IUT prior to the IUT certification stage of the flight syllabus:
   a. Training the Aerial Gunner
4. The IUT will successfully complete a written exam administered by a AGI, WTCCI or MAWTS-1 crew chief instructor prior to beginning the certification stage of the flight syllabus.
5. The IUT will present to the AGI, WTCCI or MAWTS-1 crew chief instructor one of the classes listed in the CH-46 Crew Member Air to Ground Course prior to completing the certification stage of the flight syllabus.

Flight Syllabus:

Instructor Under Training (IUT) Stage

1. The squadron will ensure that the IUT is prepared for certification.
2. The following flights will be instructed by a squadron AGI, WTCCI, or MAWTS-1 crew chief instructor.

AG 540   1.5hrs   1CH-46

Goal: Develop instructional techniques during day aerial gunnery.

Requirements:

1. Evaluate instructional techniques in the usage and application of the following during day aerial gunnery:
   a. Weapons terminology
   b. Sectors of fire
   c. Lookout doctrine
   d. Weapons preparation
   e. Safety
   f. Malfunctions and stoppages
   g. Crew Member responsibilities
   h. Crew served checklist application
   i. Range estimation and lead computations
   j. Situational Awareness
   k. Instructor Technique

AG 541   1.5 hrs   1 CH-46   N NVG

Goal: Develop instructional techniques during NVG aerial gunnery.

Requirements:

1. Evaluate instructional techniques during air to ground gunnery while using NVGs and AIM-1 Laser (optional) emphasizing items a - k from AG 540.

Certification Stage:

1. The IUT will demonstrate to a designated AGI, WTCCI or MAWTS-1 crew chief instructor the ability to instruct aerial gunnery training.

AG 542 E   1.5hrs   2CH-46   NNVG

Goal: Demonstrate instructional techniques during aerial gunnery employment while utilizing NVGs in multi-aircraft shoot.

Requirements:

1. Evaluate the IUT's instructional abilities during an NVG aerial gunnery flight emphasizing items a - k from AG 540.
<u>AG 543 E</u> <u>1.5 hrs</u> <u>1 CH-46 D (N)</u>

Goal: Demonstrate instructional techniques during aerial gunnery at a moving target, either a towed aerial banner, moving land target, or during shadow gunnery.

Requirements:

1. Evaluate instructional techniques during a moving target shoot using items from AR. .540

Refresher Requirements:

1. Previously designated CH-46 AGI's returning to the CH-46 that require refresher training in accordance with MCO P3500.14E must complete a recertification course. Upon recertification by an AGI, WTCCI or MAWTS-1 crew chief instructor, the AGI designation can be made by the squadron commanding officer. The following comprises the recertification process:
   a. IUT must meet all prerequisites previously listed.
   b. IUT must complete the FAG 542 and FAG 543 sorties, evaluated by a designated AGI, WTCCI or MAWTS-1 crew chief instructor.

Transition Requirements:

1. Crew member designated as an AGI in an aircraft other than the CH-46 that transition to the CH-46 must meet the prerequisites and complete the AG 542 and AG 543 sorties evaluated by an AGI, WTCCI or MAWTS-1 crew chief instructor..

Conversion Requirements:

1. Crew members designated as an AGI in an aircraft other than the CH-46 that undergo conversion training to the CH-46 must meet the prerequisites and complete the AG 542 and AG 543 sorties evaluated by an AGI, WTCCI or MAWTS-1 crew chief instructor.

CH-46 CREW CHIEF NIGHT SYSTEMS FAMILIARIZATION INSTRUCTOR (NSFI) CERTIFICATION COURSE

Course Objective: To certify a CH-46 crew chief as a Night Systems Familiarization Instructor (NSFI) capable of instructing in the familiarization phase (100 series) of NVG flights.

Length: 1 classroom hours 2.5 flight hours

Academic Syllabus:

1. The IUT will review the MAWTS-1 Night Vision Devices Manual.
2. The IUT will review and be capable of presenting all classes listed in the CH-46 Crew Member Night Systems Operations Academics Course.
3. The IUT will present to the Crew Chief NSI, WTCCI or MAWTS-1 crew chief instructor one of the classes listed in the CH-46 Crew Member Night Systems Operation Academics Course, as determined by the Crew Chief NSI, WTCCI or MAWTS-1 crew chief instructor, before completing the certification stage of the flight syllabus.
4. The IUT will successfully complete a written NSFI Exam administered by a Crew Chief NSI, WTCCI or MAWTS-1 crew chief instructor prior to beginning the certification stage of the flight syllabus.

Flight Syllabus:

Instructor Under Training (IUT) Stage

1. The squadron will ensure that the IUT is prepared for certification. The certification stage of the flight syllabus must be completed within six (6) months following the first IUT flight. If six months have elapsed since completion of any IUT flight, that flight must be reflown prior to completing the final certification flight.
2. The following flight will be instructed by a crew chief NSI, WTCCI or MAWTS-1 crew chief instructor:
<u>CC NVG 560</u> <u>1.5 hrs</u> <u>1 CH-46 N</u> <u>NVG</u>

Goal: Conduct low work and touch and go maneuvers utilizing NVGs under ambient light conditions above .0022 LUX.

Requirements:

1. Introduce and conduct low work, pattern work, and simulated emergencies with emphasis on instructional techniques.
2. Brief/discuss visual illusions, depth perception problems, NVG failures, lighting techniques, and NVG training restrictions.

Certification Stage:

1. The IUT will demonstrate to the NSI, WTCCI or MAWTS-1 crew chief instructor the ability to instruct night systems operations. The following flight will be evaluated:
<u>CC NVG 561 E</u> <u>1.5 hrs</u> <u>2 CH-46 N</u> <u>NVG</u>

Requirements:

Goal: Evaluate the IUT's ability to instruct NVG familiarization training during CALS and NVG navigation under ambient light conditions above .0022 LUX.

1. Conduct CALs at an LZ which meets the special considerations for landing zones outlined in the MAWTS-1 Night Vision Device Manual.
2. Conduct a navigation route of 50nm at or above 200 ft AGL.
3. Brief/discuss map preparation, route planning, visual illusions, depth perception problems, NVG failures, and inadvertent IMC.

Refresher Requirements:

1. Previously designated CH-46 crew chief NSI's or NSFI's returning to the CH-46 that require refresher training in accordance with MCO P3500.14B must complete an NSFI recertification course. Upon recertification by an crew chief NSI, WTCCI or MAWTS-1, the NSFI designation can be made by the squadron commanding officer. The following comprises the recertification process:
   a. IUT must meet all prerequisites previously listed.
   b. IUT must complete the NVG 561 flight, evaluated by an crew chief NSI, WTCCI or MAWTS-1 crew chief instructor.

Transition Requirements:

1. Crew chiefs designated as an NSI or NSFI on an aircraft other than the CH-46 that transition to the CH-46 must meet the prerequisites and fly the NVG 561 sortie evaluated by an crew chief NSI, WTCCI or MAWTS-1 crew chief instructor.

Conversion Requirements:

1. Crew chiefs designated as an NSI or NSFI in an aircraft other than the CH-46 that undergo conversion to the CH-46 must meet the prerequisites and fly the NVG 561 sortie evaluated by the crew chief NSI, WTCCI or MAWTS-1 crew chief instructor.

CH-46 CREW CHIEF NIGHT SYSTEMS SAR INSTRUCTOR (NSSI) CERTIFICATION COURSE

Course Objective: To certify the CH-46 crew chief as Night Systems SAR Instructor capable of safely conducting ground and airborne instruction of the night vision goggle (NVG) flight syllabus outlined in MCO P3500.17

Length: 1 classroom hours 4.5 flight hours

Academic Syllabus:

1. The IUT will review the MAWTS-1 Night Vision Devices Manual.
2 The IUT will review and be capable of presenting all classes listed in the CH-46 Crew Member Night Systems Operation Academics Course.
3. The IUT will present to the crew chief NSI, WTCCI or MAWTS-1 Crew Chief Instructor one of the classes listed in the CH-46 Crew Member Night Systems Operation Academics Course as determined by the crew chief NSI, WTCCI or MAWTS-1 Crew Chief Instructor, before completing the certification stage of the flight syllabus.
4. The IUT will successfully complete a written exam administered by the crew chief NSI, WTCCI or MAWTS-1 Crew Chief Instructor prior to beginning the certification stage of the flight syllabus.

Flight Syllabus:
Instructor Under Training (IUT) Stage

1. The squadron will ensure that the IUT is prepared for certification. The certification stage of the flight syllabus must be complete within six (6) months following the first IUT flight. If six months have elapsed since completion of any IUT flight, that flight must be reflown prior to completing the final certification flight.
2. The following flights will be instructed by a squadron Crew Chief NSSI, NSI, WTCCI or MAWTS-1 Crew Chief Instructor:
<u>CC NVG 562</u> <u>1.5hrs</u> <u>1H-46</u> <u>N</u>

Goal: Conduct basic operations, CALS, and navigation while utilizing NVG's above .0022 LUX.

Requirements:

1. Under ambient light conditions above .0022 LUX, evaluate the IUT's ability to instruct single aircraft CAL's and navigation while utilizing NVG's. The IUT shall remain oriented within 500 meters while conducting a 25 nm navigation route above 200 ft AGL. A minimum of 2 navigational legs and 4 CAL's are required. Minimum 1.5 hrs NVG time.
2. Brief and discuss NVG operations and limitations, NVG emergencies, lookout doctrine, aircraft lighting, crew coordination/comfort level, depth perception, visual illusions, waveoffs, and inadvertent IMC.

CC NVG 563	1.5hrs	1H-46	N

Goal: Conduct basic operations, CALS, and navigation while utilizing NVG's below .0022 LUX.

Requirements:

1. Under ambient light conditions below .0022 LUX, evaluate the IUT's ability to instruct single aircraft CAL's and navigation while utilizing NVG's. The IUT shall remain oriented within 500 meters while conducting a 25 nm navigation route above 200 ft AGL. A minimum of 2 navigational legs and 4 CAL's are required. Minimum 1.5 hrs NVG time.
2. Brief and discuss low light level NVG operations and limitations, NVG emergencies, lookout doctrine, aircraft lighting, crew coordination/comfort level, depth perception, visual illusions, waveoffs, and inadvertent IMC.

Certification Stage

1. The IUT will demonstrate to the NSI, WTCCI of MAWTS-1 Crew Chief instructor the ability to instruct night systems operations.

CC NVG 564 E	1.5 hrs	1 H-46	N

Goal: Evaluate the IUT's ability to instruct basic operations, CAL's and navigation while utilizing NVG's below .0022 LUX.

Requirements:

1. Under ambient light conditions below .0022 LUX, evaluate the IUT's ability to instruct single aircraft CAL's and navigation while utilizing NVG's. The IUT shall remain oriented within 500 meters while conducting a 25 nm navigation route above 200ft AGL. A minimum of 2 navigational legs and 4 CAL's are required. Minimum 1.5 hrs NVG time.
2. Brief and discuss low light level NVG operations and limitations, NVG emergencies, lookout doctrine, aircraft lighting, crew coordination/comfort level, depth perception, visual illusions, waveoffs, and inadvertent IMC.

CH-46 CREW CHIEF TERRAIN FLIGHT INSTRUCTOR (TERFI) CERTIFICATION COURSE

Course Objective: To certify the CH-46 crew chief as an instructor capable of safely conducting academic and airborne instruction of the CH-46 terrain flight syllabus outlined in MCO P3500.16B.

Length: 2 classroom hours 3.0 flight hours

Academic Syllabus:

1. The crew chief instructor under training (IUT) will review NWP 55-9-CH-46 and the CH-46 Tactical Manual Pocket Guide prior to the certification flight.
2. The crew chief IUT will review and be capable of teaching ail classes listed in the CH-46 Crew Member TERF Academics Course prior to beginning the IUT stage of the flight syllabus.
3. The IUT will present one of the classes listed in the CH-46 Crew Member TERF Academics Course to a WTCCI or MAWTS-1 crew chief instructor prior to finishing the certification process.
4. The crew chief IUT will successfully complete a written TERFI Exam administered by a WTCCI or MAWTS-1 crew chief instructor prior to beginning the certification stage of the flight syllabus.

Flight Syllabus:

Instructor Under Training (IUT) Stage

1. The squadron will ensure that the IUT is prepared for certification. During the IUT stage a WTCCI or MAWTS-1 crew chief instructor will demonstrate to the IUT, proper TERFI techniques during TERF syllabus flights outlined in MCO P3500.16B.

Certification Stage

1. The crew chief IUT will demonstrate to a WTCCI or MAWTS-1 crew chief instructor the ability to conduct terrain flight instruction.
2. The following sorties will be evaluated by the WTCCI or MAWTS-1 crew chief instructor:

CC TERF 570	E 1.5 hrs	1 CH-46

Goal: Demonstrate instructional techniques during terrain flight, navigation and external operations.

Requirements:

1. Demonstrate instructional techniques in assisting the pilot at all TERF altitudes with emphasis on lookout doctrine, crew coordination, obstacle clearance, and external operations.
   a. Standard terminology
   b. Mission procedures
   c. Emergency procedures
   d. Brown out/white out
   e. Closure rates

CC TERF 571 E	1.5 hrs	2 CH-46

Goal: Demonstrate instructional techniques during multi-aircraft terrain flight and navigation.

Requirements:

1. Demonstrate instructional techniques in assisting the pilot at TERF altitudes with emphasis on lookout doctrine, crew coordination, navigational assistance, and obstacle clearance.

Refresher Requirements:

1. Designated CH-46 crew chief TERFI's returning to the CH-46 that require refresher training in accordance with MCO P3500.14E must complete a TERFI recertification course. Upon recertification by a WTCCI or MAWTS-1, the TERFI designation can be made by the squadron commanding officer. The following comprises the TERFI recertification process:
   a. IUT must meet all prerequisites previously listed.
   b. IUT must complete the CC TERF 571 sortie, evaluated by a WTCCI or MAWTS- 1 crew chief instructor.

Transition Requirements:

1. Crew chiefs designated as a TERFI in an aircraft other than the CH-46, that transition to the CH-46 must complete the CC TERF 570, 571 sortie evaluated by a WTCCI or MAWTS-1 crew chief instructor.

Conversion Requirements:

1. Crew chiefs designated as a TERFI in an aircraft other than the CH-46 that undergo conversion training must complete the CC TERF 570, 571 sortie evaluated by a WTCCI or MAWTS-1 crew chief instructor.

CH-46 CREW CHIEF DEFENSIVE MEASURES INSTRUCTOR (DMI) CERTIFICATION COURSE

Course Objective: To certify the CH-46 crew chief as an instructor capable of conducting academic and airborne instruction of the CH-46 defensive measures syllabus outlined in MCO P3500.16B

Length: 2 classroom hours 3.0 flight hours

Academic Syllabus:

1. The crew chief IUT will review the MAWTS-1 Helicopter DM Guide.
2. The crew chief instructor under training (IUT) will review and be capable of teaching all classes listed in the CH-46 Crew Member Defensive Measures Academics Course prior to beginning the IUT stage of the flight syllabus.
3. The crew chief IUT will present one of the classes listed in the CH-46 Crew Member Defensive Measures Academics Course to a MAWTS-1 crew chief instructor prior to the certification flight.
4. The crew chief IUT will successfully complete a written DMI Exam administered by a MAWTS-1 crew chief instructor prior to beginning the certification stage of the flight syllabus.

Flight Syllabus:

Instructor Under Training (IUT) Stage

1. The squadron will! ensure that the IUT is prepared for certification. The following sorties will be instructed by a Crew Chief DMI, MAWTS-1 crew chief instructor, Squadron or MAWTS-1 Pilot DMI:
   <u>CC DM 580</u> <u>1 0 hrs</u> <u>2 V Ground Threat</u>

Goal: Demonstrate instructional techniques during a 2 V Ground Threat.

Requirements:

1. Review multi-aircraft DM against a ground threat. Discuss the capabilities, limitations, and envelopes of the threat system. Demonstrate instructional techniques in the usage and application of the following:
   a. Aircrew coordination
   b. Crew comfort level
   c. Lookout doctrine
   d. Situational awareness
   e. Use of ALE-39, APR-39, ALQ157, MR-47
   f. Tactical formation Maneuvering
   g. Obstacle clearance
   <u>CC DM 581</u> <u>1.0 hrs</u> <u>2v1 FW or RW</u>

Goal: Demonstrate the ability to instruct 2v1 DM FW/RW

Requirements:

1. Review helicopter 2 V 1 DM with a fixed wing or rotary wing aggressor aircraft. Discuss the capabilities, limitations, and envelopes of the aggressor aircraft. Discuss weapons and ASE employment. Demonstrate instructional technique during a 2 V 1 DM flight emphasizing the following:
   a. Aircrew coordination
   b. Crew comfort level
   c. Lookout doctrine
   d. Standardized terminology
   e. Situational awareness
   f. DM training rules
   g. Closure rate
   h. Use of ALE-39, APR-39, ALQ157, MR-47
   i. Use of .50 caliber machine gun
   j. DM against FW/RW aggressor
   k. Supporting roles Certification Stage
1. The following flight will be evaluated by a MAWTS-1 Crew Chief Instructor. DM 582 must be flown against other aggressor aircraft not previously utilized in DM 581.
   <u>CC DM 582 E</u> <u>1.0 hrs</u> <u>2 V 1 FW or RW</u>

Goal: Evaluate 2 V 1 tactics and instructional techniques.

Requirements:

1. The IUT will demonstrate a working knowledge of the capabilities, limitations, and envelopes of the threat vehicle. Discuss and simulate weapons and ASE employment. Discuss procedures for both FW/RW aggressor to include items a thru k from DM 581 Emphasis will be on instructional techniques.

Refresher Requirements:

1. Designated CH-46 crew chief ACMI's returning to the CH-46 that require refresher training in accordance with MCO P3500.14E must complete the entire DMI certification course.

Transition Requirements:

1. Crew chiefs designated as a DMI in an aircraft other than the CH-46 that transition to the CH-46 must complete the entire CH-46 Crew Chief DMI Certification Course as previously listed.

Conversion Requirements:

1. Crew chiefs designated as a DMI in an aircraft other than the CH-46 that convert to the CH-46 must complete the entire CH-46 Crew Chief DMI Certification Course as previously listed.

CH-46 CREW CHIEF NIGHT SYSTEMS INSTRUCTOR (NSI) CERTIFICATION COURSE

Course Objective: To certify a CH-46 crew chief as a Night Systems Instructor (NSI capable of safely conducting academic and airborne instruction, in any light condition. Of the CH-46 night vision goggle (NVG) flight syllabus outlined in MCO P3500.16B.

Length: 2 classroom hours 6.0 flight hours

Academic Syllabus:

1. The crew chief IUT will review the MAWTS-1 Night Vision Devices Manual.
2. The crew chief instructor under training (IUT) will review and be capable of presenting all classes listed in the CH-46 Crew Member Night Systems Operations Academics Course.
3. The IUT will present to the MAWTS-1 crew chief instructor, one of the classes listed in the CH-46 Crew Member Night Systems Operations Academics Course, as determined by the MAWTS-1 instructor, before completing the certification stage of the flight syllabus.
4. The crew chief IUT will successfully complete a written NSI Exam administered by a MAWTS-1 crew chief instructor prior to beginning the certification stage of the flight syllabus.

Flight Syllabus:

Instructor Under Training (IUT) Stage

1. The squadron will ensure that the IUT is prepared for certification by MAWTS-1. The certification stage of the flight syllabus must be completed within six (6) months following the first flight. If six months have elapsed since completion of any IUT flight, that flight must be reflown prior to completing the final certification flight.
2. The following flights will be instructed by a crew chief NSI, WTCCI, or MAWTS-1 crew chief instructor. They will be flown under high light conditions, as defined in MCO P3500. 1 4E.
   <u>CC NVG 590</u> <u>1.5 hrs</u> <u>1 CH-46 N</u>

Goal: Develop IUT's ability to instruct low work, pattern work and single aircraft CALs utilizing NVG's.

Requirements:

1. Under high light conditions, as defined by current Marine Corps directives, assist the pilot in the conduct of low work, touch and goes, and single aircraft CALs, emphasizing instructional techniques in the following:
   a. Depth perception
   b. Crew comfort level
   c. Obstacle clearance
   d. Lookout doctrine
   e. Emergency (both aircraft and goggles)
   f. Closure rates
   g. Brown out/White out
   h. Aircraft lighting
   <u>CC NVG 591</u> <u>1.5 hrs</u> <u>2 CH-46 N</u>

Goal: Conduct section CALs and external operations emphasizing instructional techniques.

Requirements:

1. Brief and discuss NVG failures, IMC, illusions of terrain flight, crew coordination, comfort levels. external procedures, and standard terminology.
2. Under high light conditions as defined by current Marine Corps directives, the IUT will demonstrate his instructional techniques while assisting the pilot in CALs and externals emphasizing:
   a. Crew coordination
   b. Obstacle clearance
   c. Standard terminology
   d. External operations
   e. Emergency procedures
   f. Aircraft lighting
   g. Closure rates
   h. Brown outs/White outs

Certification Stage:

1. The crew chief IUT will demonstrate to the MAWTS-1 crew chief instructor the ability to instruct night systems operations. NVG 592 may be flown under high or low light level conditions. NVG 593 must be flown under low light conditions.
   <u>CC NVG 592 E</u> <u>1.5 hrs</u> <u>2 CH-46</u>

Goal: Evaluate the IUT's ability to brief and instruct section CALs and externals utilizing NVGs.

Requirements:

1. Brief and discuss NVG failures, IMC illusions of terrain flight, crew coordination, comfort levels, external procedures, and standard terminology.
2. Under ambient light conditions as defined by current Marine Corps directives, the IUT will demonstrate instructional techniques while assisting the pilot in CALs and externals emphasizing:
   a. Crew coordination
   b. Obstacle clearance
   c. Standard terminology
   d. Mission procedures
   e. Emergency procedures
   f. Aircraft lighting
   g. Brown out/White out
   h. Closure rates

CC NVG 593 E	1.5hrs	2CH-46	N

Goal: Evaluate the IUT's ability to brief and instruct section flights utilizing NVG's under low light level conditions.

Requirements:

1. Brief and discuss inadvertent formation IMC procedures, aircraft lighting, wingman position calls, crew coordination, comfort levels, NVG failures, and low altitude emergencies.
2. Under low light level conditions, as defined by current Marine Corps directives, evaluate the IUT's ability to assist the pilot in formation flight, and navigation at TERF altitudes, emphasizing crew coordination, obstacle clearance, and emergency procedures.

Refresher Requirements:

1. Previously designated CH-46 crew chief NSI's returning to the CH-46 that require refresher training in accordance with MCO P3500.14E must complete an NSI recertification course. Upon recertification by a MAWTS-1 instructor, the NSI designation can be made by the squadron commanding officer. The following comprises the recertification course:
   a. IUT must meet all prerequisites previously listed.
   b. The IUT must complete the CC NVG 592 and CC NVG 593 sortie, evaluated by a MAWTS-1 crew chief instructor.

Transition Requirements:

1. Crew chiefs designated as an NSI in an aircraft other than the CH-46 that transition to the CH-46 must complete the entire CH-46 Crew Chief Night Systems Instructor Certification Course as previously listed.

Conversion Requirements:

1. Crew chiefs designated as an NSI in an aircraft other than the CH-46 that undergo conversion to the CH-46 must complete the entire CH-46 Crew Chief Night Systems Instructor Certification Course as previously listed.

CH-53 SUPPLEMENTARY COURSES
CH-53 SPECIFIC ACADEMIC SUPPORT PACKAGE

Course Objective: To provide the CH-53 pilot with additional ground training as required by MCO P3500.14.

Length: 24 classroom hours

Academic Syllabus:

1. The following classes should be presented to pilots under instruction prior to flying any combat ready tactics sortie:
   a. Assault Support Mission Planning
   b. Tactical Briefing and Debriefing
2. The following classes should be presented to pilots under instruction prior to completion of the combat qualified stage of training:
   a. Tactical Aerial Refueling
   b. Tactical Aircraft Recovery (TAR) and External Operations Considerations
   c. CH-53 FARP
   d. Artillery Raid Planning
   e. Forward Arming and Refueling Point
   f. NBC Threat
   g. Fire Support Coordination Measures
   h. Artillery, Call for Fire
   i. Naval Gunfire, Call for Fire
   j. Helicopter Escort Tactics 1
   k. Helicopter Escort Tactics 2
   l. MAGTF: Organization and Equipment
   m. MAGTF: The Amphibious Assault
   n. MACCS Part 1
   o. MACCS Part 2
   p. Intel Sources and Collection
   q. Soviet IADS
   r. Surface to Surface Threat
   s. Tactical Recovery of Aircraft and Personnel
3. The following classes should be presented to pilots under instruction prior to completion of the fully combat qualified stages.
   a. Missile System Theory Part I
   b. Missile System Theory Part II
   c. Shadow Gunnery
   d. Soviet R/W Technology Trends
   e. Soviet R/W Tactics
   f. Soviet F/W Strengths and Weaknesses
   g. Soviet F/W Basic Tactics Employment
   h. Soviet Air-to-Air Missiles Part I
   i. Soviet Air-to-Air Missiles Part II
   j. Non-Soviet Air-to-Air Missiles Part I
   k. Non-Soviet Air-to-Air Missiles Part II
4. All classes should be reviewed annually.

CH-53 TERRAIN FLIGHT (TERF) COURSE

Course Objective: To provide ground instruction enabling the CH-53 pilot to safely participate in TERF training.

Length: 4 classroom hours

Academic Syllabus:

1. The following class will be presented to pilots under instruction prior to flying any combat ready TERF sortie:
   a. Tactical Formation Maneuvering
2. The following classes will be presented to pilots under instruction prior to completing the TERF qualification process:
   a. Terrain Flight Introduction
   b. Terrain Flight Externals
   c. Tactical Aircrew Coordination Considerations
3. All classes should be reviewed annually.

CH-53 DEFENSIVE MEASURES (DM) COURSE

Course Objective: To provide ground instruction enabling a CH-53 pilot to safely participate in DM training and electronic warfare training.

Length: 13 classroom hours

Academic Syllabus:

1. The following classes will be presented to pilots under instruction prior to flying any combat qualification DM sortie:
   a. Introduction to Helicopter Air Combat Maneuvers
   b. Defensive Measures
   c. Countering the R/W Threat
   d. Countering the F/W Threat
   e. Aerodynamics, Air Combat, and Maneuvering
   f. AN/ALE-39 Programming
   g. APR-39 Trainer (15E36)
   h. Helo ESM/ECM Equipment
   i. Soviet REC
   j. Countering the Surface to Air Threat
   k. Basic Radar Principles
   l. Soviet Tactical Surface to Air Threat Systems (SAMS/AAA)
   m. Non-Soviet SAMS/AAA
2. All classes should be reviewed annually.

CH-53 NIGHT SYSTEMS OPERATIONS COURSE

Course Objective: To provide ground instruction enabling the CH-53 pilot to safely participate in night vision goggle (NVG) training.

Length: 6 classroom hours

Academic Syllabus:

1. The following classes will be presented to pilots under instruction prior to flying the NVG-191 sortie:
   a. Night Vision Devices
   b. Introductory Night Vision Goggle Training
   c. NVG Human Factors
   d. The Night Environment
2. The following classes will be presented prior to completing the night systems qualification process:
   a. Light Level Calender/Shadow Determination
   b. Night Vision Goggle Tactics and Training
3. All classes should be reviewed annually.

CH-53 AIR TO GROUND COURSE

Course Objective: To provide ground training enabling the CH-53 pilot to effectively conduct air to ground ordnance training.

Length: 2 classroom hours

Academic Syllabus:

1. The following classes should be presented to pilots under instruction prior to flying any combat qualified air to ground sortie:
   a. Rotary Wing Weaponeering: Capabilities and Limitations
   b. Shadow Gunnery
2. All classes should be reviewed annually.

CH-53 TERRAIN FLIGHT INSTRUCTOR (TERFI) CERTIFICATION COURSE

Course Objective: To certify a CH-53 pilot as a Terrain Flight Instructor (TERFI) capable of safely conducting ground and airborne instruction of the CH-53 terrain flight syllabus outlined in MCO P3500.16A.

Length: 8 classroom hours 2.8 flight hours

Academic Syllabus:

1. The instructor under training (IUT) will review and be capable of presenting all classes listed in the CH-53 Terrain Flight Course.
2. The IUT will successfully complete the TERFI exam (found in the Rotary Wing common class "Terrain Flight"), administered by a TERFI, prior to beginning the certification stage of the flight syllabus.
3. The IUT will present to a designated TERFI, one of the classes listed in the CH-53 Terrain Flight Course, as determined by the TERFI, before completing the certification stage of the flight syllabus.

Flight Syllabus:

Instructor Under Training (IUT) Stage

1. The squadron will ensure that the IUT is prepared for certification.
2. The following flights will be instructed by a qualified and proficient TERFI:
   <u>TERF 570</u> <u>1.0 hrs</u> <u>1 CH-53</u>

Goal: Conduct all terrain flight maneuvers and TERF navigation in the low level and contour profiles with emphasis on instructional techniques.

Requirements:

1. Review operational power checks, TERF turns, rolls, contour/low level quick stop, bunts, low level and contour profiles, low altitude emergencies and crew coordination
2. Review TERF navigation techniques and responsibilities. Using a 1:50,000 map, the IUT will navigate in the contour profile remaining oriented within 100 meters. The route shall be a minimum of 50 nm in the contour mode. The IUT must arrive at the final checkpoint within 1 minute of the planned time.
3. Brief and discuss TERF navigation techniques, crew coordination, comfort level, low altitude emergencies, weapons and ALE/APR employment, and the illusions of TERF flight.
   <u>TERF 571</u> <u>0.8 hrs</u> <u>1 CH-53</u>

Goal: Conduct all terrain flight maneuvers while flying with an external load, emphasizing instructional techniques.

Requirements:

1. Review and perform all TERF maneuvers with external loads emphasizing requirements for early initiation of maneuvers and flight profile corrections to prevent pilot induced/assisted oscillations.
2. Brief and discuss crew coordination, comfort level, voice and visual signals, flight envelopes of various loads, cargo jettison procedures, low altitude emergencies, single/dual engine operations (with or without a load), illusions of terrain flight and HST requirements.

Certification Stage

1. The IUT will demonstrate to the TERFI the ability to instruct TERF operations.
   <u>TERF 572 E</u> <u>1.0 hrs</u> <u>1 CH-53</u>

Goal: Evaluate the IUT's ability to perform and instruct all phases of terrain flight and terrain flight navigation.

Requirements:

1. Evaluate the IUT's ability to instruct and perform operational power checks, TERF turns, rolls, contour/low level quick stops, bunts, low level and contour profiles, crew coordination, and low altitude emergencies.
2. Evaluate the IUT's ability to instruct and perform terrain flight navigation in the contour and low level profiles using a 1:50,000 map. The IUT is required to maintain orientation along the prescribed route within 100 meters and arrive at the final checkpoint within 1 minute of the planned time. The route shall be a minimum of 50 nm in the contour mode.
3. Brief and discuss crew coordination, comfort level, illusions of terrain flight, low altitude emergencies, single/dual engine operations, weapons and ALE/APR employment, and TERF/navigation techniques and responsibilities.

Refresher Requirements:

1. Previously certified CH-53 TERFI's returning to the CH-53 requiring refresher or modified refresher training as defined in MCO P3500.14 must be recertified by a TERFI. Upon recertification, the TERFI designation can be made by the squadron commanding officer. The following comprises the recertification course:
   a. The IUT must meet all prerequisites listed previously.
   b. The IUT must successfully complete the TERFI exam, administered by a TERFI
   c. The IUT must complete the TERF 572 flight, evaluated by a TERFI.

Transition Requirements:

1. Pilots certified as a TERFI in an aircraft other than the CH-53, that transition to the CH-53 as defined in MCO P3500.14D must complete the entire CH-53 TERFI Certification Course previously listed.

Conversion Requirements:

1. Pilots certified as a TERFI converting within the CH-53 series that do not require refresher training as defined in MCO P3500.14D maintain their TERFI certification and may be designated a TERFI at the discretion of the squadron commanding officer.
2. Pilots certified as a TERFI in an aircraft other than the CH-53, that undergo conversion to the CH-53 as defined in MCO P3500.14D must complete the entire CH-53 TERFI Certification Course previously listed.

Requirements:

1. Evaluate the IUT's ability to instruct and perform operational power checks, TERF turns, rolls, contour/low level quick stops, bunts, low level and contour profiles, crew coordination, and low altitude emergencies.
2. Evaluate the IUT's ability to instruct and perform terrain flight navigation in the contour and low level profiles using a 1:50,000 map. The IUT is required to maintain orientation along the prescribed route within 100 meters and arrive at the final checkpoint within 1 minute of the planned time. The route shall be a minimum of 50 nm in the contour mode.
3. Brief and discuss crew coordination, comfort level, illusions of terrain flight, low altitude emergencies, single/dual engine operations, weapons and ALE/APR employment, and TERF/navigation techniques and responsibilities.

Refresher Requirements:

1. Previously certified CH-53 TERFI's returning to the CH-53 requiring refresher or modified refresher training as defined in MCO P3500.14 must be recertified by a TERFI. Upon recertification, the TERFI designation can be made by the squadron commanding officer. The following comprises the recertification course:
   a. The IUT must meet all prerequisites listed previously.
   b. The IUT must successfully complete the TERFI exam, administered by a TERFI
   c. The IUT must complete the TERF 572 flight, evaluated by a TERFI.

Transition Requirements:

1. Pilots certified as a TERFI in an aircraft other than the CH-53, that transition to the CH-53 as defined in MCO P3500.14D must complete the entire CH-53 TERFI Certification Course previously listed.

Conversion Requirements:

1. Pilots certified as a TERFI converting within the CH-53 series that do not require refresher training as defined in MCO P3500.14D maintain their TERFI certification and may be designated a TERFI at the discretion of the squadron commanding officer.
2. Pilots certified as a TERFI in an aircraft other than the CH-53, that undergo conversion to the CH-53 as defined in MCO P3500.14D must complete the entire CH-53 TERFI Certification Course previously listed.

CH-53 DEFENSIVE MEASURES INSTRUCTOR CERTIFICATION COURSE

Course Objective: To certify a CH-53 pilot as a Defensive Measures Instructor (DMI) capable of instructing the Defensive Measures (DM) academic and flight syllabus per MCO P3500.16A.

Length: 5 classroom hours 3 flight hours

Academic Syllabus:

1. The IUT will study chapter 5 of the CH-53 Tactical Manual NWP 3-22.5-CH-53 Volume I and Chapter 2 of FMFM 5-35 (Rev F) Volume II. The IUT will be familiar with the MCM 3-1.
2. The IUT will be capable of presenting all the ASP classes listed in the CH-53 DM Course.
3. The IUT will successfully complete the DMI exam, administered by a MAWTS-1 instructor or squadron WTI, prior to beginning the certification stage of the flight syllabus.
4. The IUT will present to a MAWTS-1 instructor or squadron WTI one of the classes listed in the CH-53 DM Course, prior to completing the certification stage of the flight syllabus.

Flight Syllabus:

Instructor Under Training (IUT) Stage

1. The following flights will be instructed by a DMI:
   DM 580 — 1.0 hrs — 2 v Ground Threat

Goal: Demonstrate the ability to instruct 2 v ground threat tactics in accordance with the MAWTS-1 DM Guide.

Requirement: Review multi-aircraft DM against a ground threat. Brief and discuss the capabilities, limitations and envelopes of threat systems. This sortie should be conducted in airspace that permits the employment of expendables. Discuss:

1. Aircrew coordination/Inter flight coordination.
2. Crew comfort level.
3. Lookout doctrine.
4. Situational awareness.
5. Use of ALE-39, APR-39, ALQ-157 and MR-47.
6. Tactical formation maneuvering.
7. Use of RADAR horizons, RADAR masking, maneuver and chaff to defeat threat RADAR systems.
8. Use of terrain masking, maneuver, IR jamming, and flares to defeat threat IR jamming, and flares to defeat IR missiles.

Ordnance: 40 chaff 20 flares DM 581 1.0 hrs 2v1 FW/RW

Goal: Demonstrate the ability to instruct 2v1 RW/FW DM tactics in accordance with the MAWTS-1 DM Guide.

Requirement: Review helicopter 2v1 DM with a rotary wing or fixed wing aggressor aircraft. Brief and discuss the capabilities, limitations, and envelopes of the aggressor aircraft. Brief and discuss weapons and ASE employment. This sortie should be conducted in airspace that permits the employment of expendables. Discuss:

1. Aircrew coordination/Inter flight coordination.
2. Crew comfort level.
3. Lookout doctrine.
4. Standardized terminology.
5. Situational awareness.
6. DM training rules.
7. Closure rate, radius of turn, and energy state.
8. Use of ALE-39, APR-39, ALQ-157, and MR-47.
9. Use of .50 caliber machine gun.
10. DM against RW aggressor.
11. Supporting roles.

Ordnance: 40 flares and 20 chaff Certification Stage

1. The following flight will be evaluated by a MAWTS-1 instructor. If DM 581 was flown versus a RW aggressor, DM 582 shall be flown versus a FW aggressor. If DM 581 was flown versus a FW aggressor, DM 582 shall be flown versus a RW aggressor.
   DM 582 E — 1.0 hrs — 2v1 FW/RW

Goal: Evaluate 2v1 helicopter DM tactics and instructional technique in accordance with the MAWTS-1 DM Guide.

Requirement: The IUT will brief helicopter versus fixed wing or helicopter flight. Emphasis will be on instructional techniques, to include demonstrating a working knowledge of the capabilities, limitations and envelopes of the threat aircraft. Brief and discuss weapons and ASE employment. The APR and ALE should be utilized. Discuss procedures for both FW/RW and ground threat. This sortie should be conducted in airspace that permits the employment of expendables.

Ordnance: 40 flares and 20 chaff.

Refresher Requirements:

1. Previously certified CH-53 DMIs returning to the CH-53 requiring refresher or modified refresher training as defined in MCO P3500.14 must be recertified by MAWTS-1. Upon recertification, the DMI designation can be made by the squadron commanding officer. The following comprises the recertification course:
   a. The IUT must meet all prerequisites previously listed.
   b. The IUT must successfully complete the DMI exam, administered by a MAWTS-1 instructor or squadron WTI.
   c. The IUT must complete DM 582 evaluated by a MAWTS-1 instructor.

Transition Requirements:

1. Pilots certified as a DMI in an aircraft other than the CH-53, that transition to the CH-53 as defined in MCO P3500.14, must complete the entire CH-53 DMI Certification Course previously listed.

Conversion Requirements:

1. Pilots certified as a DMI converting within the CH-53 series, that do not require refresher training as defined in MCO P3500.14, maintain their DMI certification and may be designated a DMI at the discretion of the commanding officer.
2. Pilots certified as a DMI or ACMI in an aircraft other than the CH-53, that undergo conversion to the CH-53 as defined in MCO P3500.14D, must complete the entire CH-53 DMI Certification Course previously listed.

Requirement: The IUT will brief helicopter versus fixed wing or helicopter flight. Emphasis will be on instructional techniques! to include demonstrating a working knowledge of the capabilities, limitations and envelopes of the threat aircraft. Brief and discuss weapons and ASE employment. The APR and ALE should be utilized. Discuss procedures for both FW/RW and ground threat. This sortie should be conducted in airspace that permits the employment of expendables.

Ordnance: 40 flares and 20 chaff.

Refresher Requirements:

1. Previously certified CH-53 DMIs returning to the CH-53 requiring refresher or modified refresher training as defined in MCO P3500.14 must be recertified by MAWTS-1. Upon recertification, the DMI designation can be made by the squadron commanding officer. The following comprises the recertification course:
   a. The IUT must meet all prerequisites previously listed.
   b. The IUT must successfully complete the DMI exam, administered by a MAWTS-1 instructor or squadron WTI.
   c. The IUT must complete DM 582 evaluated by a MAWTS-1 instructor.

Transition Requirements:

1. Pilots certified as a DMI in an aircraft other than the CH-53, that transition to the CH-53 as defined in MCO P3500.14, must complete the entire CH-53 DMI Certification Course previously listed.

Conversion Requirements:

1. Pilots certified as a DMI converting within the CH-53 series, that do not require refresher training as defined in MCO P3500.14, maintain their DMI certification and

may be designated a DMI at the discretion of the commanding officer.

2. Pilots certified as a DMI or ACMI in an aircraft other than the CH-53, that undergo conversion to the CH-53 as defined in MCO P3500.14D, must complete the entire CH-53 DMI Certification Course previously listed.

CH-53 NIGHT SYSTEMS FAMILIARIZATION INSTRUCTOR (NSFI) CERTIFICATION COURSE

Course Objective: To certify a CH-53 pilot as a Night Systems Familiarization Instructor (NSFI) capable of safely conducting ground and airborne instruction of night vision goggle (NVG) flight during basic, non-tactical maneuvering flights.

Length: 3 classroom hours 3.0 flight hours

Academic Syllabus:

1. The instructor under training (IUT) will review and be capable of presenting the following classes:
   a. Night Vision Devices b. Introductory Night Vision Goggle Training
2. The IUT will successfully complete the NSFI exam, administered by a NSI or MAWTS-1 instructor, prior to beginning the certification stage of the flight syllabus.
3. The IUT will present to a NSI or MAWTS-1 instructor, one of the classes listed above, as determined by the NSI or MAWTS-1 instructor, before completing the certification stage of the flight syllabus.
4. The academic syllabus will be completed prior to beginning the certification stage of the flight syllabus.

Flight Syllabus:
Instructor Under Training (IUT) Stage

1. The squadron will ensure that the IUT is prepared for certification. The certification stage of the flight syllabus must be complete within six (6) months following the first IUT flight. If six months have elapsed since completion of any IUT flight, that flight must be reflown prior to completing the final certification flight.
2. The following flights will be instructed by a squadron NSI, NSFI, or MAWTS-1 instructor:
   NVG 560 1.0 hrs 1 CH-53 N

Goal: Conduct low work, touch and goes, pattern work, and simulated emergencies under high ambient light conditions as defined by MCO P3500.14.

Requirements:

1. Conduct low work, pattern work, touch and go, and simulated emergencies per NATOPS.
2. Review single/dual engine malfunctions, simulated inadvertent IMC on landing, recovery from inadvertent IMC, hover/no-hover landings, running landings, and simulated NVG failures.
3. Brief/discuss the use of NVGs, cockpit lighting, aircraft external lighting, crew coordination, comfort level, emergency procedures while goggled, NVG failures, depth perception, scan techniques, inadvertent IMC and waveoff procedures.
   NVG 561 1.0 hrs 1 CH-53 N

Goal: Conduct externals and CALs under high light levels as defined in MCO P3500. 1 4D.

Requirements:

1. Review maneuvers in NVG 560 as required.
2. Conduct CALs at a landing area suitable for NVG operations, which is void of obstacles and restrictions to visibility.
3. Brief/discuss: Aircrew coordination, comfort level, low altitude emergencies. NVG failures, and visual illusions.
   NVG 562 1.0 hrs 2 CH-53's N

Goal: Conduct a navigation flight with two aircraft under high ambient light levels as defined by MCO P3500.14.

Requirements:

1. Conduct a contour navigation route of 50 nm or greater, utilizing both a 1:250,000 and 1:50,000 map. The IUT is to remain oriented within 500 meters and arrive at the final checkpoint within 2 minutes.
2. Brief and discuss map preparation, route planning, shadowing, and MCO P3500.14D NVG operation specifics.
3. Brief and discuss closure rates, NVG lead changes, and tactical formations.

Certification Stage

1. The IUT will demonstrate to a NSI or MAWTS-1 instructor the ability to instruct night systems operations.
   NVG 563 E 1.0 hrs 1 CH-53 N

Goal: Evaluate the IUT's ability to instruct basic NVG familiarization maneuvers, CALs, and externals under high light levels as defined by MCO P3500.14.

Requirements:

1. Under high light level conditions as defined in MCO P3500.14, evaluate the IUT's ability to perform and instruct FAM maneuvers to include taxi, hover, pedal turns, hover/no hover landings, running takeoffs and landings, normal takeoffs, externals, pattern work, CALs, and emergency procedures per NATOPS.
2. Brief and discuss the use of NVGs, visual illusions, depth perception problems, NVG failures, cockpit/aircraft lighting, map preparation, route planning, shadowing, crew coordination. comfort level, emergency procedures, scan techniques, NVG training restrictions, inadvertent IMC, waveoffs, and instructional techniques.

Refresher Requirements:

1. Previously certified CH-53 NSI's or NSFI's returning to the CH-53 requiring refresher or modified refresher training as defined in MCO P3500.14 must be recertified by an NSI or MAWTS-1 instructor. Upon recertification, the NFSI designation can be made by the squadron commanding officer. The following comprises the recertification course:
   a. The IUT must meet all prerequisites listed previously.
   b. The IUT must successfully complete the NSFI exam, administered by an NSI or MAWTS-1 instructor.
   c. The IUT must complete the NVG 563 flight, evaluated by an NSI or MAWTS-1 instructor.

Transition Requirements:

1. Pilots certified as an NSI or NSFI converting within the CH-53, that transition to the CH-53 as defined in MCO P3500.14, must complete the entire CH-53 NSFI Certification Course previously listed.

Conversion Requirements:

1. Pilots certified as an NSI or NSFI converting within the CH-53 series that do not require refresher training as defined in MCO P3500.14 maintain their NSFI certification and may be designated an NSFI at the discretion of the squadron commanding officer.
2. Pilots certified as an NSI or NSFI in an aircraft other than the CH-53, that undergo conversion to the CH-53 as defined in MCO P3500.14 must complete the entire CH-53 NSFI Certification Course previously listed.

CH-53 NIGHT SYSTEMS INSTRUCTOR (NSI) CERTIFICATION COURSE

Course Objective: To certify a CH-53 pilot as a Night Systems Instructor (NSI) capable of safely conducting ground and airborne instruction, in any ambient light condition, of the CH-53 night vision goggle (NVG) flight syllabus outlined in MCO P3500.16.

Length: 6 classroom hours 6.0 flight hours

Academic Syllabus:

1. The instructor under training (IUT) will review and be capable of presenting all classes listed in the CH-53 Night Systems Course.
2. The IUT will successfully complete the NSI exam, administered by a MAWTS-1 instructor. prior to beginning the certification stage of the flight syllabus.
3. The IUT will present to a MAWTS-1 instructor one of the classes listed in the CH-53 Night Systems Course.
4. The academic syllabus will be completed prior to beginning the certification stage of the flight syllabus.

Flight Syllabus:
Instructor Under Training (IUT) Stage

1. The squadron will ensure that the IUT is prepared for certification by MAWTS-1. The certification stage of the flight syllabus must be complete within six (6) months following the first IUT flight. If six months have elapsed since completion of any IUT flight, that flight must be reflown prior to completing the final certification flight.
2. The following flights will be instructed by a squadron NSI or MAWTS-1 instructor. Two of the IUT sorties must be flown under low light conditions.
   NVG 590 1.0 hrs 1 CH-53 N

Goal: Conduct NVG external operations to confined areas, and CALs with emphasis on instructional technique.

Requirements:

1. The IUT will demonstrate his instructional techniques for takeoffs, precision approaches, and precision delivery of an external load to a confined area utilizing NVG's. The IUT will demonstrate proficiency in hookups when available, dual point are preferred, but single point is acceptable.
2. Conduct CALs to a landing area suitable for NVG operations. Demonstrate proficiency in the execution of takeoffs, precision approaches, and no hover landings.
3. Review single/dual engine malfunctions, simulated inadvertent IMC on landing, recovery from inadvertent IMC, simulated NVG failures, and simulated emergency procedures.
4. Brief and discuss the use of NVG's, cockpit lighting, aircraft external lighting, crew coordination, NVG failure, ITOs in a dust confined area, waveoffs, crew coordination, comfort level, voice and visual signals, flight envelope of various loads, cargo jettison procedures, illumination techniques, LZ preparation, low altitude requirements, and HST requirements.

<u>NVG 591</u> <u>1.5 hrs</u> <u>2 CH-53</u> <u>N</u>

Goal: Conduct tactical formation flight, objective area landings, and TERF navigation on NVG's as dictated by a tactical scenario. The IUT's mission planning, flight briefing, execution and overall instructional technique will be evaluated.

Requirements:

1. The IUT will demonstrate his instructional technique while performing tactical formation flight, section objective area landings and a tactical navigation flight (minimum 100 nm) utilizing a 1 :250,000 and 1 :50,000 map and a tactical scenario. The IUT shall remain oriented within 200 meters and arrive within one minute at the objective. Include utilization of the GPS (if available) and APR/ALE employment. Whenever possible, include firing the XM-218 and countermeasure flares.
2. Brief and discuss lead change, inadvertent IMC procedures, tactical formation principles, illusions of night contour terrain flight, NVG waveoffs, crew coordination, comfort level, emergency procedures, XM-218/AIM-1 DLR while utilizing NVGs, effects of countermeasures on NVGs and ITOs in a dusty confined area.

<u>NVG 592 E</u> <u>2.0hrs</u> <u>2 CH-53</u> <u>N</u>

Goal: Conduct an integrated tactical flight in a medium to high threat environment, or NVG's using the CH-53 Tactical Manual as a reference for mission planning. The IUT's mission planning, flight briefing, execution will be evaluated.

Requirements:

1. The IUT will plan, brief, execute, and debrief a tactical evolution.
2. The flight will consist of at least 2 CH-53s, tactical formation flight, section objective area landings, and a tactical navigation flight utilizing a 1:250,000 and 1 :50,000 map. The IUT shall remain oriented within 200 meters and arrive with in one minute at the objective.
3. Proficiency and knowledge in the utilization of the GPS and FLIR (if available) must be demonstrated. Employment of the APR/ALE systems must be incorporated in mission planning and execution.
4. Whenever possible, include firing of the XM-218 and countermeasures.
5. Brief and discuss tactical formation considerations, map preparation, long range navigation techniques, ASE control/employment objective area analysis, threat analysis and countertactics, C3 integration, escorts/supporting arms integration, and the ground scheme of maneuver (as applicable).
6. Pilots should use the CH-53 Tactical Manual as a source document for planning. The emphasis of this flight is on tactical mission planning, briefing, execution and debriefing.

Certification Stage

1. The prospective NSI will demonstrate to a MAWTS-1 instructor the ability to instruct night systems operations. This certification flight must be flown under low light conditions as defined in MCO P3500.1A.

<u>NVG 593 E</u> <u>2.5 hrs</u> <u>2 CH-53</u> <u>N</u>

Goal: Evaluate the prospective NSI's ability to plan, brief, execute and debrief an integrated tactical flight in a medium to high threat environment on NVG's, using the CH-53 Tactical Manual standards as a reference for mission planning, briefing and execution.

Requirements:

1. Brief/discuss NVG low light level considerations, current Marine Corps NVG directives, inadvertent IMC procedures enroute and in the terminal area, formation and aircraft lighting procedures, navigation techniques, illusions of terrain flight, and aircrew coordination.
2. Brief/discuss tactical formation flight and movement of aircraft within the objective area.
3. As dictated by the threat scenario, the prospective NSI will conduct tactical formation flight utilizing a 1 :250,000 and 1 :50,000 map.
4. Proficiency and knowledge in the utilization of the GPS and FLIR (if available) must be demonstrated. Employment of the APR/ALE systems must be incorporated in mission planning and execution.
5. Whenever possible, include firing of the XM-218 and employment of countermeasures.
6. Brief/discuss threat analysis, countertactics, C3 integration, escorts/supporting arms integration, and the ground scheme of maneuver (as dictated by the tactical scenario).
7. Evaluate the prospective NSI's ability to conduct and instruct external operations as outlined in NVG-590. The externals can be conducted as a separate evolution from the tactical evolution. Brief and discussion items remain the same from NVG-590.
8. Pilots should use the CH-53 Tactical Manual as a source document for planning. Emphasis will be placed upon the IUT's ability to thoroughly instruct tactical formation flight, section landings, and externals utilizing night systems.

Refresher Requirements:

1. Previously certified CH-53 NSI's returning to the CH-53 requiring refresher or modified refresher training as defined in MCO P3500.14 must be recertified by MAWTS-1. Upon recertification by MAWTS-1, the NSI designation can be made by the squadron commanding officer. The following comprises the recertification course:
   a. The IUT must meet all prerequisites listed previously.
   b. The IUT must successfully complete the NSI exam, administered by the MAWTS-1 instructor
   c. The IUT must complete both the NVG 593 and NVG 594 flights, evaluated by the MAWTS-1 instructor.

Transition Requirements:

1. Pilots certified as an NSI in an aircraft other than the CH-53, that transition to the CH-53 as defined in MCO P3500.14D, must complete the entire CH-53 NSI Certification Course previously listed.

Conversion Requirements:

1. Pilots certified as an NSI converting within the CH-53 series that do not require refresher training as defined in MCO P3500.14 retain their NSI certification and can be designated an NSI at the discretion of the commanding officer.
2. Pilots certified as an NSI in an aircraft other than the CH-53, that undergo conversion to the CH-53 as defined in MCO P3500.14 must complete the entire CH-53 NSI Certification Course previously listed.

CH-53 CREW MEMBER SUPPLEMENTARY COURSES
CH-53 CREW MEMBER ACADEMIC SUPPORT PACKAGE

Course Objective: To provide the CH-53 Crew Members with academic training as required by MCO P3500.14E.

Length: 21 classroom hours

Academic Syllabus:

1. The following classes will be presented to the Crew Members Under Instruction prior to completing the combat qualified stage of training:
   a. Aircrew Responsibilities in a Tactical Environment
   b. Tactical Aircrew Coordination Considerations
   c. Introduction to Air Combat Maneuvers for Enlisted Aircrews
   d. Night Vision Goggle Training for Enlisted Aircrews
   e. Fundamentals of Aerial Gunnery
   f. Employment Fundamentals of Aerial Gunnery
   g. XM-218/GAU-17 Machine Gun
   h. Laser Safety
   i. Basic Principles of Electronic Warfare
   j. Training the Aerial Gunner
   k. Basic Principles of Escort Operations
   l. Tactical Recovery of Aircraft and Personnel (TRAP)
   m. Aircraft Survivability Equipment
   n. AN/ALE-39 Systems Brief for Enlisted Aircrews 18 -1
   o. Forward Arming and Refueling Point (FARP)
   p. Helicopter Insertion and Extraction Operations (HIE)

2. The following classes contained in the Pilots Academic Support Package will be presented to the Crew Member prior to completing the combat qualified stage of training.
   a. IR SAM Threat to R/W
   b. AAA Threat to R/W
   c. R/W Threat to the MAGTF
   d. F/W Threat to the MAGTF
3. The academic syllabus will be received annually.

CH-53 CREW MEMBER TERRAIN FLIGHT (TERF) ACADEMIC COURSE

Course Objective: To provide the CH-53 Crew Members with academic training enabling them to safely participate in terrain flight .

Length: 6 classroom hours

Academic Syllabus:

1. The following classes will be presented to the Crew Members Under Instruction prior to flying any TERF flight:
   a. Terrain Flight for Enlisted Aircrew
   b. Tactical Aircrew Coordination Considerations
   c. Aircrew Responsibilities in a Tactical Environment
2. The following classes will be presented to the Crew Members Under Instruction prior to flying any combat qualified TERF flight:
   a. Terrain Flight Externals
   b. IR SAM Threat to RW
   c. AAA threat to RW
3. The academic syllabus will be received annually.

CH-53 CREW MEMBER DEFENSIVE MEASURES (DM) ACADEMIC COURSE

Course Objective: To provide the CH-53 Crew Members with academic training enabling them to safely participate in defensive measures (DM) training.

Length: 5 classroom hours

Academic Syllabus:

1. The following classes will be presented to the Crew Members Under Instruction prior to flying and DM flight:
   a. Introduction to Helicopter Air Combat Maneuvering for Enlisted Aircrews
   b. AN/ALE39 system brief for Enlisted Aircrew
   c. Basics of Electronic Warfare
2. The following classes will be presented to the Crew Members Under Instruction prior to completing the DM qualification process:
   a. IR SAM Threat to R/W
   b. AAA Threat to R/W
3. The academic syllabus will be received annually.

CH-53 CREW MEMBER NIGHT SYSTEMS ACADEMICS COURSE

Course Objective: To provide the CH-53 Crew Members with academic training enabling them to safely participate in night vision goggle (NVG) training.

Length: 1 classroom hours

Academic Syllabus:

1. The following class should be presented to the Crew Members Under Instruction prior to flying any NVG flight:
   a. Night Vision Goggle Training for Enlisted Aircrews
2. The academic syilabus will be received annually.

CH-53 CREW MEMBER AERIAL GUNNERY ACADEMIC COURSE

Course Objective: To provide the CH-53 Crew Members with academic training enablinq them to safely participate in Aerial Gunnery Training.

Length: 5 classroom hours

Academic Syllabus:

1. The following classes will be presented to the Aerial Gunner Under Instruction prior to flying any Aerial Gunnery flight:
   a. Fundamentals of Aerial Gunnery
   b. Employment Fundamentals of Aerial Gunnery
   c. XM-218/GAU-16 Machine Gun
2. The following class should be presented to the Aerial Gunner under instruction prior to the Aerial Gunner qualification flight:
   a. AIM-1 Laser Safety
3. The following class should be presented to the Aerial Gunner prior to beginning the Aerial Gunner Instructor course:
   a. Training the Aerial Gunner
4. The Academic Syllabus will be received annually.

CH-53 CREW MEMBER HELICOPTER AIRBORNE INSERTION AND EXTRACTION (HIE) ACADEMIC COURSE

Course Objective: To provide academic training enabling the CH-53 Crew Members to safely participate in helicopter insertion and extraction training.

Length: 3 classroom hours

Academic Syllabus:

1. The following classes will be presented to the Crew Member prior to any HIE flight:
   a. Helicopter Insertion and Extraction Operations
      1. Fast Rope Operations
      2. Rappel Operations
      3. SPIE Rig Operations
      4. Parachute Operations
      5. Helocast Operations
2. The academic syllabus will be received annually.

CH-53 AERIAL GUNNERY INSTRUCTOR (AGI) CERTIFICATION COURSE

Course Objective: To certify a CH-53 Crew Chief or Aerial Gunner as an Aerial Gunnery Instructor (AGI) capable of conducting academic and airborne instruction, in the employment of crew served weapons in all aspects of tactical flight.

Length: 2 Classroom hours 6.0 flight hours

Academic Syllabus:

1. The instructor under training will review the MAWTS-1 Aerial Gunnery Manual.
2. The instructor under training (IUT) will review and be capable of presenting all classes listed in the CH-53 Crew Member Aerial Gunnerv Academic Course.
3. The following class should be presented to the IUT prior to the certification flight:
   a. Training the Aerial Gunner
4. The instructor under training will successfully complete a written exam administered by a AGI, WTCCI, or MAWTS-1 Crew Chief Instructor prior to beginning the certification stage of the flight syllabus.
5. The IUT will present to the AGI, WTCCI, or MAWTS-1 Crew Chief Instructor, one of the classes listed in the CH-53 Crew Member Aerial Gunnery Academic course prior to completing the certification stage of the flight syllabus.

Flight Syllabus:

Instructor Under Training (IUT) Stage

1. The squadron will ensure that the IUT is prepared for certification.
2. The following flights will be instructed by a squadron AGI, WTCCI, or MAWTS-1 Crew Chief Instructor.

   AG 540 1 — 1.5 hrs — 1 CH-53

Goal: Develop instructional techniques during day Aerial Gunnery.

Requirements:

1. Evaluate instructional techniques in the usage and application of the following during day Aerial Gunnery:
   a. Weapons terminology
   b. Sectors of fire
   c. Lookout doctrine
   d. Weapons preparation
   e. Safety
   f. Malfunctions and stoppages
   g. Crew Member responsibilities
   h. Crew served weapons checklist application
   i. Range estimation and lead computations
   j. Situational Awareness
   k. Instructor Technique

   AG 541 — 1.5hrs — 1 CH-53 — N — NS

Goal: Develop instructional techniques during NVG Aerial Gunnery.

Requirements:

1. Evaluate instructional techniques during aerial gunnery while using NVG's. Emphasizing the following:
   a. Weapons terminology
   b. Sectors of fire
   c. Lookout doctrine
   d. Weapons preparation
   e. NVG adaptability
   f. AIM-1 Laser procedures (if used)
   g. Safety
   h. Malfunctions and stoppages
   i. Crew Member responsibilities
   j. Crew served weapons checklist application
   k. Range estimation and lead computations
   l. Situational Awareness
   m. InstructorTechniques Certification Stage
1. The IUT will demonstrate to a designated AGI, WTCCI, or MAWTS-1 Crew Chief Instructor the ability to instruct Aerial Gunnery Training.
   AG 542 E 1.5 hrs 2 CH-53 N NS

Goal: Demonstrate instructional techniques during Aerial Gunnery Weapons Employment while utilizing NVG's in a multi-aircraft shoot.

Requirements:

1. Evaluate the IUT's instructional abilities during night, multi aircraft Aerial Gunnery Weanons Emplovment. Emphasizing the followinq:
   a. Weapons terminology
   b. Sectors of fire
   c. Lookout doctrine
   d. Weapons preparation
   e. NVG adaptability
   f. AIM-1 Laser procedures (if used)
   g. Safety
   h. Malfunctions and stoppages
   i. Crew Member responsibilities
   j. Crew served weapons checklist application
   k. Range estimation and lead computations
   l. Situational Awareness
   m. Instructor Technique
   AG 543 E 1.5 hrs 1 CH-53 (N NS)

Goal: Demonstrate instructional techniques during Aerial Gunnery at a moving target, either a towed aerial banner, moving land target, or during shadow gunnery.

Requirements:

1. Evaluate instructional techniques during a moving target shoot emphasizing the following.
   a. Weapons terminology
   b. Sectors of fire
   c. Lookout doctrine
   d. Weapons preparation
   e. Safety
   f. Malfunctions and stoppages
   g. Crew Member responsibilities
   h. Crew served weapons checklist application
   i. Range estimation and lead computations
   j. Situational Awareness
   k. Instructor Technique

Refresher Requirements:

1. Previously designated CH-53 AGI's returning to the CH-53 that require refresher training in accordance with MCO P3500.14E must complete a rectification course. Upon rectification by a designated AGI, WTCCI, or MAWTS-1 Crew Chief Instructor, the AGI designation can be made by the Squadron Commanding Officer.
2. The following comprises the rectification course:
   a. IUT must meet all prerequisites previously listed.
   b. The IUT must complete the AG 542 and AG 543 flights, evaluated by a designated AGI, WTCCI or MAWTS-1 Crew Chief Instructor.

Transition Requirements:

1. An AGI in an aircraft other than the CH-53 that transition to the CH-53 must meet the prerequisites and complete the AG 542 and AG 543 flights evaluated by a designated AGI, WTCCI, or MAWTS-1 Crew Chief Instructor.

Conversion Requirements:

1. Certified AGI's converting within the CH-53 series that do not require refresher training as defined in MCO P3500.14E retain their AGI certification and can be designated an AGI at the discretion of the Commanding Officer.
2. Crew chiefs designated as an AGI in an aircraft other than the CH-53 that undergo conversion training to the CH-53 must meet the prerequisites and complete the AG 542 and AG 543 flights evaluated by a designated AGI, WTCCI. or MAWTS-1 Crew Chief Instructor.

CH-53 CREW CHIEF NIGHT SYSTEMS FAMILIARIZATION INSTRUCTOR (NSFI) CERTIFICATION COURSE

Course Objective: To certify a CH-53 Crew Chief as a Night Systems Familiarization Instructor (NSFI) capable of instructing in the familiarization phase (100 series) of night vision qoqale (NVG) flights.

Length: 1 classroom hour 3.5 flight hours

Academic Syllabus:

1. The Crew Chief IUT will review the MAWTS-1 Night Vision Devices Manual.
2. The Crew Chief Instructor under training (IUT) will review and be capable of presenting all classes listed in the CH-53 Crew Member Night Systems Academic Course.
3. The IUT will present to the MAWTS-1 Crew Chief Instructor, WTCCI, or Crew Chief NSI, one of the classes listed in the CH-53 Crew Member Night Systems Academic Course, as determined by the Crew Chief NSI, WTCCI, or MAWTS-1 Crew Chief Instructor, before completing the certification stage of the flight syllabus.
4. The Crew Chief IUT will successfully complete a written NSFI exam administered by a Crew Chief NSI, WTCCI, or MAWTS-1 Crew Chief Instructor prior to beqinning the certification stage of the flight syllabus.

Flight Syllabus:
Instructor Under Training (IUT) Stage

1. The squadron will ensure that the IUT is prepared for certification. The certification stage of the flight syllabus will be completed within six (6) months following the first IUT flight . if during the certification process six months has elapsed the delinquent flight must be reflown prior to the final certification flight.
2. The following flights will be instructed by a Crew Chief NSI, WTCCI or Crew
   NVG 560 1.0 hrs 1 CH-53 N NS

Goal: Conduct low work and touch and go maneuvers utilizing NVG's under ambient liqht conditions above .0022 LUX.

Requirements:

1. Review low work, pattern work, touch and go, and simulated emergencies per NATOPS.
2. Brief/discuss visual illusions, depth perception problems, NVG failures, NVG lighting techniques, and NVG training restrictions.
   NVG 561 1.0 hrs 1CH-53 N NS

Goal: Evaluate the IUT's ability to instruct NVG familiarization training during low work, CALs, and Externals training under ambient light conditions above .0022 LUX.

Requirements:

1. Conduct CALs at an LZ which meets the special considerations for landing zones outlined in the MAWTS-1 Night Vision Devices Manual.
2. Conduct External operations emphasizing the following:
   a. Distance Estimation
   b. Depth perception
   c. Crew comfort level
   d. Obstacle clearance
   e. Lookout doctrine
   f. Emergencies (both aircraft and goggles)
   g. Standard terminology
   h. External operations (calls and setup procedures

Certification Stage

1.The IUT will demonstrate to the Crew Chief NSI, WTCCI, or MAWTS-1 Crew Chief Instructor the ability to instruct night systems operations. The following flight will be evaluated:
   NVG 562 E 1.5 hrs 2 CH-53 N NS

Goal: Evaluate the IUT's ability to instruct NVG familiarization training during Navigation and Formation flying under ambient light conditions above .0022 LUX.

Requirements:

1. Conduct a Navigation route of 50 nm at or above 200 ft AGL.
2. Brief/discuss map preparation, route planning, visual illusions, depth perception problems, NVG failures, and inadvertent IMC.
3. Conduct Formation flying emphasizing the following:
   a. Closure rate
   b. Aircraft lighting
   c. Light signals
   d. Lookout responsibilities
   e. Target fixation

Refresher Requirements:

1. Previously designated CH-53 Crew Chief NSI's or NSFI's returning to the CH-53 that require refresher training in accordance with MCO P3500.14E must complete an NSFI rectification course. Upon rectification by a Crew Chief NSI, WTCCI or MAWTS-1 Crew Chief Instructor, the NSFI designation can be made by the Squadron Commanding Officer.
2. The following comprises the rectification process:
   a. IUT must meet all prerequisites previously listed.
   b. The IUT must complete the NVG 561 flight, evaluated by a Crew Chief NSI, WTCCI, or MAWTS-1 Crew Chief Instructor.

Transition Requirements:

1. Crew Chiefs designated as an NSI or NSFI in an aircraft other than the CH-53, that transition to the CH-53 must meet the prerequisites and fly NVG 561 evaluated by the Crew Chief NSI or MAWTS-1 Crew Chief Instructor.

Conversion Requirements:

1. Conduct CALs at an LZ which meets the special considerations for landing zones outlined in the MAWTS-1 Night Vision Devices Manual.
2. Crew Chiefs designated as an NSI or NSFI in an aircraft other than the CH-53, that undergo conversion to the CH-53 must meet the prerequisites and fly the NVG 561 sortie, evaluated by the Crew Chief NSI, WTCCI, or MAWTS-1 Crew Chief Instructor.

Flight Syllabus:

Instructor Under Training (IUT) Stage

1. The squadron will ensure that the IUT is prepared for certification. During the IUT stage a TERFI, MAWTS-1 Crew Chief Instructor or WTCCI will demonstrate to the IUT, proper TERFI techniques during TERFI syllabus flights outlined in MCO PS500. 1 6B.

Certification Stage

1. The Crew Chief IUT will demonstrate to a TERFI, WTCCI or MAWTS-1 Crew Chief Instructor the ability to conduct Terrain Flight Instruction.
2. The following flights will be evaluated by a TERFI, WTCCI or MAWTS-1 Crew Chief Instructor:
   <u>TERF 570 E</u> <u>1.5 hrs</u> <u>1 CH-53</u>

Goal: Demonstrate instructional techniques during Terrain Flight and Navigation.

Requirements:

1. Demonstrate instructional techniques in assisting the Pilot at all TERF altitudes with emphasis on lookout doctrine, crew coordination, and obstacle clearance.
   <u>TERF 571 E</u> <u>1.5 hrs</u> <u>1 CH-53</u>

Goal: Demonstrate instructional techniques during Terrain Flight with external cargo.

Requirements:

1. Demonstrate instructional techniques during TERF maneuvers while transporting external cargo, emphasizing the requirements for good look out procedures to ensure cargo clearance of terrain and obstacles and stability of the cargo during maneuvers.
2. Brief and discuss crew coordination, crew comfort level, the use of standard voice calls, options to be used if loads become unstable, cargo jettison procedures, and low altitude emergencies.

Refresher Requirements:

1. Designated CH-53 Crew Chief TERFI's returning to the CH-53 that require refresher training in accordance with MCO P3500.14E must complete a TERFI rectification course. Upon rectification by a TERFI, WTCCI or MAWTS-1 Crew Chief Instructor, the TERFI designation can be made by the Squadron Commanding Officer.
2. The following comprises the TERFI rectification process:
   a. IUT must meet all prerequisites previously outlined.
   b. IUT must complete TERF 571 evaluated by a TERFI, WTCCI or MAWTS-1 Crew Chief Instructor.

Transition Requirements:

1. Crew Chiefs designated as a TERFI in an aircraft other than the CH-53, that transition to the CH-53 must complete TERF 571 evaluated by a TERFI, WTCCI nr MAWTS-1 Crew Chief Instructor.

Conversion Requirements:

1. Crew Chiefs certified as TERFI converting within the CH-53 series that do not require refresher training as defined in MCO P3500.14E retain their TERFI certification and can be designated a TERFi at the discretion of the Commanding Officer.
2. Crew Chiefs designated as a TERFI in an aircraft other than the CH-53 that undergo conversion training must complete TERF 571 evaluated by a TERFI, WTCCI or MAWTS-1 Crew Chief Instructor.

CH-53 CREW CHREF DEFENSIVE MEASURES INSTRUCTOR (DMI) CERTIFICATION COURSE

Course Objective: To certify the CH-53 Crew Chief as an Instructor capable of conducting academic and Airborne Instruction of the CH-53 Defensive Measures syllabus outlined in MCO P3500.16B.

Length: 2 classroom hours 3.0 flight hours

Academic Syllabus:

1. The Crew Chief IUT will review the MAWTS-1 Helicopter DM Guide.
2. The Crew Chief Instructor under training (IUT) will review and be capable of teaching all classes listed in the CH-53 Crew Members Defensive Measures Academic Course prior to beginning the IUT stage of the flight syllabus.
3. The Crew Chief IUT will present one of the classes listed in the CH-53 Crew Member Defensive Measures Course to a MAWTS-1 Crew Chief Instructor or MAWTS-1 Pilot.
4. The Crew Chief IUT will successfully complete a written DMI exam administered by a MAWTS-1 Crew Chief Instructor or MAWTS-1 Pilot prior to beginning the certification stage of the flight syllabus.

Flight Syllabus:

Instructor Under Training (IUT) Stage

1. The squadron will ensure that the IUT is prepared for certification. The following flights will be instructed by a DMI Crew Chief, MAWTS-1 Pilot or a MAWTS-1 Crew Chief Instructor:
   <u>DM 580</u> <u>1.0 hrs</u> <u>2 Helicopters</u>

Goal: Demonstrate the ability to instruct 2v ground threat Tactics in accordance with tha MAWTS-1 DM Guide.

Requirements:

1. Demonstrate instructional techniques during Ground to Air Defensive Measures emphasizing the following:
   a. Common terminology
   b. Obstacle clearance
   c. Lookout procedures
   d. Threat recognition (identification, profiles)
   e. ALE-39 operation/employment
   f. Crew Member responsibilities
   g. Wingmans position h. Information relay to pilots Ordnance: 40 Chaff 20 Flares nNA .ER1 1 n hrs 2v1 FW/ RW

Goal: Demonstrate the ability to instruct 2v1 RW /FW DM Tactics in accordance with the MAWTS-1 Dm Guide.

Requirements:

1. Review helicopter 2v1 DM with a rotary wing or fixed wing aggressor aircraft. Brief and discuss the capabilities, and envelopes of the aggressor aircraft. Brief and discuss weapons and ASE employment. This sortie should be conducted in airspace that permits the employment of expendables. Discuss:
   a. Common terminology
   b. Obstacle clearance
   c. Lookout procedures
   d. Threat recognition (identification, profiles)
   e. ALE-39 operation /employment

f. Crew Member responsibilities
g. Wingmans position
h. Information relay to pilots
i. Closure rate Ordnance: 40 Flares and 20 Chaff Certification Stage

1. The following flight will be evaluated by a MAWTS-1 Crew Chief Instructor or MAWTS-1 Pilot. If DM 581 was flown versus a RW aggressor, DM 582 shall be flown versus a FW aggressor. If DM 581 was flown versus a FW aggressor, DM 582 shall be flown versus a RW aggressor.
<u>DM 582 E</u> <u>1.0 hrs</u> <u>2v1 FW/RW</u>

Goal: Evaluate 2v1 helicopter DM Tactics and instructional techniques in accordance with the MAWTS-1 DM Guide.

Requirement:

1. The Crew Chief IUT will demonstrate instructional techniques in the usage and application of the followinq during helo vs fixed wing or helicopter DM flight.
   a. Common terminology
   b. Obstacle clearance
   c. Lookout procedures
   d. Threat recognition (identification, profiles)
   e. ALE-39 operation /employment
   f. Crew Member responsibilities
   g. Wingmans position
   h. information relay to pilots
   i. Closure rates

Ordnance: 40 Flares and 20 Chaff

Refresher Requirements:

1. Designated CH-53 Crew Chief DMI's returning to the CH-53 that require refresher training in accordance with MCO P3500.14E must complete a DMI rectification course. Upon rectification by MAWTS-1 Crew Chief Instructor or MAWTS-1 Pilot, the DMI designation can be made by the Squadron Commandinq Officer.2. The following comprises the rectification process:
   a. IUT must meet all prerequisites previously listed.
   b. IUT must complete the DM 582 flight evaluated by a MAWTS-1 Crew Chief Instructor.

Transition Requirements:

1. Crew Chiefs designated as a DMI in an aircraft other than the CH-53 that transition to the CH-53 must complete the entire CH-53 Crew Chief DMI certification course as previously listed.

Conversion Requirements:

1. Crew Chiefs certified as a DMI converting within the CH-53 series that do not require refresher training as defined in MCO P3500.14E retain their DMI certification and can be designated a DMI at the discretion of the Commanding Officer.
2. Crew Chiefs designated as a DMI in an aircraft other than the CH-53 that convert to the CH-53 must complete the entire CH-53 Crew Chief DMI certification course as previously listed.

CH-53 CREW CHIEF NIGHT SYSTEMS INSTRUCTOR (NSI) CERTIFICATION COURSE

Course Objective: To certify a CH-53 Crew Chief as a Night Systems Instructor (NSI) capable of conducting academic and Airborne Instruction, in any ambient light condition, of the CH-53 flight syllabus that require the use of Night Vision Goggles (NVG).

Length: 1 classroom hours 3.5flight hours

Academic Syllabus:

1. The Crew Chief IUT will review the MAWTS-1 Assault Support Night Vision Devices Manual.
2 The Crew Chief Instructor Under Training (IUT) will review and be capable of presenting the class listed in the CH-53 Crew Member Night Systems Operations Academic Course.
3. The IUT will present to the MAWTS-1 Crew Chief Instructor, the class listed in the CH-53 Crew Member Night Systems Operations Academic Course, or an equivalent self prepared class to be determined by the MAWTS-1 Crew Chief Instructor, prior to completing certification.
<u>NVG 591</u> <u>1.5 hrs</u> <u>2 CH-53</u> <u>N NS</u>

Goal: Conduct multi aircraft CALs and assist pilots during TERF Navigation emphasizing instructional techniques.

Requirements:

1. Brief and discuss NVG failures, IMC, illusions of Terrain Flight, crew coordination, crew comfort levels, and standard terminology.
2. The IUT will demonstrate instructional techniques while assisting the Pilot in CALs and navigation emphasizing instructional techniques in the foliowing:
   a. Crew coordination
   b. Terrain suitability
   c: Standard terminology
   d. Emergency procedures
   e. Brown outs/White outs
   f. Closure Rates
   g. Obstacle Clearance
   h. Situational Awareness Certification Stage

1. The Crew Chief IUT will demonstrate to the MAWTS-1 Crew Chief Instructor the ability to instruct night systems operations. A minimum of one certification flight must be fiown under low level ambient light conditions as defined in MCO P.R.Enn 14F
<u>NVG 592 E</u> <u>1.0 hrs</u> <u>2 CH-53</u> <u>N NS</u>

Goal: Evaluate the IUT's ability to instruct NVG operations.

Requirements:

1. Brief and discuss inadvertent IMC procedures, aircraft lighting, crew coordination, comfort levels, NVG failures, low altitude emergencies.
2. The IUT will demonstrate instructional techniques by assisting the pilots in single aircraft low work, and no hover landings to CALs. Emphasizing the following:
   a. Crew coordination
   b. Obstacle clearance
   c. Standard terminology
   d. Mission procedures
   e. Emergency procedures (both aircraft and NVG's)
   f. Look out Doctrine
   g. Situational Awareness
   h. Instructor Technique
<u>NVG 593 E</u> <u>1.5 hrs</u> <u>2 CH-53</u> <u>N NS</u>

Goal: Evaluate the IUT's ability to brief and instruct NVG operations during section flight.

Requirements:

1. Brief and discuss NVG failures, inadvertent IMC procedures, illusions of night terrain flight, crew coordination, aircraft lighting, comfort levels, wing mans position calls and standard terminology.
2. External operations must be conducted. The IUT must demonstrate proficiency and conduct a minimum of two lifts and drop offs. The externals, only, may be conducted under high light conditions as defined in MCO P3500.14E. Brief and discuss calls, set-up procedures, emergencies over the load, and emergencies while carrying the load.
3. The IUT will demonstrate instructional techniques while assisting the Pilots in section CALs and Navigation at TERF Altitudes. Emphasizing:
   a. Crew coordination
   b. Obstacle clearance
   c. Standard terminology
   d. Mission procedures
   e. Emergency procedures (both aircraft and NVG's)
   f. Look out Doctrine
   g. Wingmans position updates
   h. Situational Awareness
   i. Instructor Technique

Refresher Requirements:

1. Previously designated CH-53 Crew Chief NSI's returning to the CH-53 that require refresher training in accordance with MCO P3500.14E must complete an NSI rectification course. Upon rectification by a MAWTS-1 Crew Chief Instructor, the NSI designation can be made by the Squadron Commanding Officer.
2. The following comprises the rectification course:
   a. IUT must meet all prerequisites previously listed.
   b. IUT must complete NVG 592 and NVG 593 evaluated by a MAWTS-1 Crew Chief Instructor

Transition Requirements:

1. Crew Chiefs designated as an NSI in an aircraft other than the CH-53 that transition to the CH-53 must complete the entire CH-53 Crew Chief Night Systems instructor certification course as previously listed.

Conversion Requirements:

1. Crew Chiefs certified as an NSI converting within the CH-53 series that do not require refresher training as defined in MCO P3500.14E retain their NSI certification and can be designated an NSI at the discretion of the Commanding Offinrr
2. Crew Chiefs designated as an NSI in an aircraft other than the CH-53 that undergo conversion to the CH-53 must complete the entire CH-53 Crew Chief Night Systems Instructor Certification Course as previously listed.

COMMAND, CONTROL, AND COMMUNICATIONS (C3) SUPPLEMENTARY COURSES C3 COMMON ACADEMIC SUPPORT PACKAGE

Course Objective: To provide Marine Air Command and Control System (MACCS) personnel additional instruction with emphasis on maximizing employment of the MACCS. Specific areas of instruction will include MACCS agencies' capabilities and limitations, theory and concepts, threaUcounterthreat systems, and employment planning and integration considerations at both the MAGTF and Joint levels.

Length: 19.5 classroom hours

Academic Syllabus:

1 It is recommended that the following classes be presented on a regular basis as part of a sound training plan:
   a. Systems: Volume I, C3 Common ASP
      (1) TACC
      (2) TAOC
      (3) MAGTF GBAD Systems (See Generic ASP)
      (4) DASC
      (5) Marine ATC
      (6) MWCS Det
      (7) AEW (See Generic ASP, Vol II)
      (8) SIS Aircraft (9) GPS
   b. Theory: Volume II, C3 Common ASP
      (1) Tasking Marine Aviation
      (2) Tanker Management
      (3) SMWC Concepts
   c. Threat/Counterthreat: Volume III, C3 Common ASP
      (1) Threat Air To Surface Missiles (See Generic ASP, Vol III)
      (2) C2W
      (3) ARMS for Non-users
      (4) Tactical Deception and RADCON
   d. Employment Planning and Integration: Volume IV, C3 Common ASP
      (1) MACCS Data Link Interoperability
      (2) MACCS Information Flow
      (3) Control of Aircraft and Missiles Planning Considerations
      (4) MACCS Communications
      (5) MACG in Support of the MEU(SOC)
   e. Training: Volume V, C3 Common ASP
      (1) Training Management
      (2) Instructional Techniques

GROUND BASED AIR DEFENSE (GBAD) SPECIFIC ACADEMIC SUPPORT PACKAGE

Course Objective: To provide additional instruction on the operation and employment of the HAWK and Stinger Missile systems to include standardization of planning considerations and comprehensive briefing techniques in preparation for GBAD operations.

Length: 5 classroom hours

Academic Syllabus:

1. It is recommended that the following classes be presented on a regular basis as part of a sound training plan:
   a. GBAD 5 Paragraph Order
   b. Emergency Defense of the Amphibious Task Force
   c. LAAD Employment
   d. LMD Command and Control
   e. HAWK SysOps/Fidoc
   f. GBAD Plan n inq Considerations

DASC SPECIFIC ACADEMIC SUPPORT PACKAGE

Course Objective: To provide additional ground training to air support control personnel on integrating and employing the Direct Air Support Center within the MACCS.

Length: 12 classroom hours.

Academic Syllabus:

1. The following classes should be presented on a regular basis as part of a sound training plan Vol 1: Fire Support
   a. DASC-FSCC Information Flow
   b. Fire Support Planning and Coordination
   c. USMC Conventional Ordnance and PGMs
   d. Armed Reconnaissance
   e. Terminal Control: FAC(A) & TAC(A) Employment
   f. Suppression of Enemy Air Defense (SEAD)

Vol 2: Operations and Communications

   a. DASC(A) Alternate Missions
   b. Air Support Role in MW
   c. AS Communications Considerations
   d. HF Propagation and Wire Antennas
   e. GCE Communications
   f. USMC Communications/Cryptographic Capabilities

MARINE ATC SPECIFIC ACADEMIC SUPPORT PACKAGE

Course Objective: To provide air traffic controllers with additional instructon on employing the Marine ATC detachment.

Length: 8 classroom hours

Academic Syllabus:

1. It is recommended that the following classes be presented on a regular basis as part of a sound training plan.
   a. Terminal Instrument Procedures (TERPS) Overview
   b. AN/PRC-113
   c. AN/PRC-104
   d. AN/GRC-206
   *e. Air Surge Launch and Recovery (ASLAR)
   *f. Marine ATC EP
   * These do not exist as ASP's.

MWCS SPECIFIC ACADEMIC SUPPORT PACKAGE

Course Objective: To provide Marine Wing communications squadron personnel the additional instruction in the planning and employment of expeditionary communications in support of the Aviation Combat Element headquarters and the MACCS.

Length: 12 classroom hours 2 hours of practical application

Academic Syllabus:

1. Recommend that the following classes be presented on a regular basis as part of. a sound training plan:
   a. OAS Communications Considerations
   b. MW Communications Considerations
   c. HF Antenna Construction and Propagation
   d. Aircraft Communications/Cryptographic Capabilities
   e. MACCS Communications (See C3 Common ASP, Vol IV)
   f. MACCS Datalink Interoperability (See C3 Common ASP, Vol IV)
   g. Grounding and Shielding Procedures
   h. OSCC/TECHON Procedures
   i. MIOSS Communications
   j. Communications Support for Aviation Combat Element

TAOC SPECIFIC ACADEMIC SUPPORT PACKAGE

Course Objective: To provide MACS personnel with additional instruction in planning TAOC employment, and conducting air defense operations.

Length: 10 classroom hours

Academic Syllabus:

1. Recommend that the following classes be presented as part of a sound training plan:
   a. Intercept Control
   b. Fighter Missions
   c. Division Tactics
   d. Threat Aircraft
   e. Threat Tactics
   f. Briefing and Debriefing Techniques

AVIATION GROUND SUPPORT COMMON ACADEMIC SUPPORT PACKAGE

AVIATION GROUND SUPPORT COMMON ACADEMIC SUPPORT PACKAGE

Course Objective: To provide additional ground training to improve the support provided to the aviation community by the Marine Wing Support Group (MWSG) and Marine Wing Support Squadron (MWSS).

Length: 30 classroom hours

Academic Syllabus:

1. The following classes should be presented on a regular basis as part of a sound ground training plan.
   a. FARP Operations
   b. Rapid Runway Repair
   c. Methods of Crater and Spall Repair
   d. Crater Repair FOD Cover
   e. Unexploded Ordnance
   f. Minimum Operating Strip Selection and Layout
   g. Electro-Optical Tactical Decision Aids
   h. Environmental Effects on Electromagnetic Energy
   i. M-21 Arresting Gear
   j. Fresnel Lens Optical Landing System
   k. Meteorological and Oceanographic Support to the MAGTF
   l. Survey Liaison Reconnaissance Party
   m. Base Recovery After Attack
   n. Damage Assessment Teams
   o. Tactical Landing Zone Site
   p. Airfield Design and Terminology

AIR MEDICAL SAFETY COURSES
FMF OPERATIONAL FLIGHT SURGEON COURSE

Course Objective: Held in conjunction with the Weapons and Tactics Instructor (WTI) Course, the course exposes Flight Surgeons to medical planning, employment, and integration in support of the Six Functions of Marine Aviation. Since flight surgeons attending WTI have the primary function of providing medical support, this course is on a not to interfere basis with that mission.

Length: 6 weeks

Academic Syllabus:

1. Academic instruction coincides with the academic phase of the WTI Course. Specific Syllabi will be published by MAWTS-1 prior to the beginning of each WTI course. Credit for up to 35 CME hours has been approved by Health Sciences Education Training Command (HSETC).

Flight Syllabus:

1. Flight stage training is conducted in conjunction with the WTI specific, common, and Final Exercise (FINEX) flight phases. Flight surgeons participate in both supportive and training roles.

Appendix Two:
United States Marine Corps
MAWTS-1 Student Lesson Guide
Tactical Recovery of Aircraft And Personnel (TRAP)
Rapid Response Planning Process

United States Marine Corps
MAWTS-1 Student Lesson Guide
TACTICAL RECOVERY OF AIRCRAFT AND PERSONNEL (TRAP)

I. Introduction

Lesson Purpose. To present the history and fundamentals of TRAP, how TRAP relates to Joint CSAR doctrine, and to provide the WTI with the guidance to plan, coordinate, and execute TRAP at the operational and tactical levels.

The Tactical Recovery of Aircraft and Personnel is viewed as one of the most difficult planning problems facing the MAGTF commander. Yet, the TRAP mission involves planning skills no more challenging than those required in a Non-combatant Evacuation Operation (NEO), or an In-extremist Hostage Rescue (1HR) mission. By virtue of the fact we train as a task organized combined arms team, there is no service or organization in the world today better structured to conduct TRAP, or CSAR, should these be assigned as a primary MAGTF mission. The problem facing the MAGTF commander with his limited assets is the challenge of dedicating personnel, assets, and equipment to conduct dedicated TRAP as an implied mission without detracting from combat capability and readiness. However, with the proper planning and training the MAGTF commander can meet the challenge of TRAP, and in the process, enhance his combat capability, but the key to that success is that the capability must be exercised. Later in this instruction we'll look at the fundamentals and focus of TRAP, as well as key players and considerations in TRAP planning. But first, let's define our subject, examine why we conduct TRAP, and look at a historical perspective.

II. Body

A. Definitions: TRAP and CSAR

TRAP is the US. Marine Corps Mission that fulfills the requirement in Joint Pub 1.02 that "each service is responsible for providing forces capable of performing CSAR in support of its own operations in accordance with assigned functions." Joint Pub 02 defines CSAR as a specific task performed by rescue forces to effect the recovery of distressed personnel (not limited to aircrew) during wartime or contingency operations. So a question we must ask ourselves is, what is the difference, if any between TRAP and CSAR, and by answering this question we'll go a large way to defining our subject. The most commonly cited difference between the two is that TRAP does not include a specific search phase and this in turn is largely because of the Force Structure of the Marine Corps. While a MAGTF is certainly capable of search operations, its unique, task organized structure and limited assets generally preclude such a time, manpower, and asset intensive operation, in favor of higher priority missions such as the rapid build up of combat power ashore. In TRAP, the focus of effort is on the recovery phase, and launch is predicated on strict prelaunch conditions due to the asset intensive requirements of conducting a search phase. Another difference although somewhat subjective is the scope of operations, CSAR usually covering a theater operation while TRAP tends to be associated with specific mission such as a NEO. Again, to a far greater extent than the other services, TRAP, due to the nature of our missions may have to deal with the recovery of large numbers of personnel and total or partial recovery of airframes. To sum up then, TRAP is strictly a Marine Corps mission, designed under former Deputy Chief of Staff for Aviation Lt. Gen. Keith A. Smith, to "support its own operations, in accordance with its assigned functions," per JCS guidance and within the limits placed upon the Corps by it's Force Structure.

B. Why We Conduct TRAP

1. There are many reasons for conducting TRAP, first and foremost of which, is for the aircrew and their morale. American fighting men and women have throughout history gone into combat with the confidence their country would do whatever possible to prevent their capture by the enemy. Further, if captured they knew every effort would be made to repatriate them. An aircrewman, believing he will be rescued if downed over hostile territory, will be much more motivated to push himself, his crew, and his machine to the limit to accomplish the mission.

2. Another important reason for TRAP is the preservation of aircrew as a tremendous national asset and investment. The retention of aircrew as highly skilled manpower assets is crucial to our ability to conduct sustained operations.

3. Finally, a successful TRAP operation denies the enemy a valuable source of intelligence and a possible political or psychological advantage.

C. Recent Lessons Learned

1. During the Vietnam War, 321 Navy and Marine Corps aircrewmen were shot down over North Vietnam. Sixty percent of those aircrewmen reached the ground alive, but 5 out of every 6 of them were either killed or captured. 31 pilots, about ten percent, were rescued. Not a very good record. Worse still, is the shocking fact that for every 1.4 recoveries made, one CSAR aircraft was lost. Also, for every 1.8 recoveries made, one CSAR rescuer was lost. The Navy and the Marine Corps relied on hasty, and often emotional planning and tactics using whatever assets available to rescue downed aircrew. The Navy and Marine Corps were losing the battle over preservation of assets, intelligence, political advantage, and morale.

2. By comparison, 1073 Air Force pilots were shot down over Vietnam. About the same percent as USN/USMC were rescued (160 recoveries), but the Air Force ratio of recoveries to CSAR aircraft lost was 4.5 to 1, and 5.2 recoveries per CSAR rescuer lost.

The Air Forces primary rescue agent in Vietnam was the Aerospace Rescue and Recovery Service (ARRS), under the Military Airlift Command (MAC). The fact the Air Force had a specialized unit whose primary mission was CSAR was a significant contributor to the successful USAF CSAR recovery rate. Aside from the ejection location, (most Air Force ejections were over less populated areas) the prime factor in the AARS' success involved two important elements: It treated CSAR as a preplanned response to recover mission losses, and it identified aircrew and their location on the ground before attempting recovery.

3. After the Vietnam war, ARRS training shifted to local base SAR operations, and their secondary mission of aerospace recovery for the Gemini space program As U.S. political and military focus shifted to low intensity regional conflicts and special operations, Joint Special Operations Command (JSOC) units became the CSAR "duty experts". To some extent, CSAR training and operations became a victim of a force structure issue as JSOC had neither the need or desire to involve ARRS in its planning, training, or operations. This is due in part to the unique considerations of special ops, such as deniability and covertness, where typical ARRS rescues are relatively overt in nature.

4. Desert Storm had a profound effect on the thinking of CSAR, TRAP doctrine and tactics. As the air campaign intensified, CSAR became an intense concern of the joint task force commander. The problem in this war was not a lack of personnel, assets, and equipment. The most frustrating obstacles were Joint organization and planning. First, there was no standing Joint Rescue Coordination Center (JRCC) ready and trained to assume CSAR tasking and coordination. Second, there was no standing Joint doctrine to guide Joint CSAR operations.

5. For the Marines part, the closest thing to Corps doctrine on TRAP at the time was a section out of the NWP 55-9-ASH Manual, and a handful of MEU (SOC) playbooks. These scant pubs were drawn on heavily in the preparation of a contingency plan, should the Third marine Aircraft Wing (3d MAW) be called upon to conduct TRAP missions. The RCC for the Marine Corps was located at wing headquarters. There were no personnel or assets specifically dedicated to the TRAP mission, but MAG 16 was tasked to have assets and aircrews available to support TRAP/MEDEVAC.

6. The first units designated as primary theater CSAR agents were Air Force, Army and Navy Special Operations Capable units (AFSOC, ARSOC, and Helicopter Combat Support Special Squadron (HCS). Though CSAR is not the primary mission of SOC units, they were by far the best trained and equipped forces in theater to conduct the mission. CINCCENT designated CENTAF as the theater CSAR coordinator. CENTAF established and operated the Joint Rescue Coordination Center (JRCC) in Rlyahd to coordinate these missions. Because SOF aircraft were best suited to conduct long-range personnel recovery missions, the SOCCENT commander was designated as commander of combat rescue forces. SOF provided 24-hour, on call CSAR for Coalition aircrews. The Navy was responsible for CSAR beyond 12 miles offshore in the Arabian Gulf, and in the Red Sea. The Marines, meanwhile, planned for TRAP only within their limited AOR "to support its own operations, in accordance with its assigned functions."

7. There were 38 downed Coalition aircraft and many downed crew members. Several crew members ejected over or near heavily fort)fied Iraqi positions, deep inside Iraq, making recovery impossible due to distances involved or the enemy situation (launch criteria). Seven U.S. CSAR missions were launched, there were three successful recoveries, and no recovery personnel were lost to enemy action. The success of the three recoveries without loss of additional assets is directly attributable to the specific training and sophisticated equipment employed by SOF units. However, the combination of CSAR requirements and other demands for SOF assets left little room for their prlmary role of contingency missions. A parallel may be drawn with the MEU (SOC) commander who, when tasked with providing dedicated TRAP may have to sacrifice other capabilities due to his limited assets.

D. TRAP/CSAR Key Players and Agencies

1. Although much has been written about CSARtTRAP by individual services, there has never been a consolidated document defining and explaining doctrine, training, and tactics, or Joint application. However, a thread of commonalty in CSAR, TRAP operations between the services does exist. Let's look now at the CSARtTRAP key players common to all services, and later at specific TRAP fundamentals and planning considerations.

a. SAR Coordinator (SC). In all situations, the officer in tactical command (OTC) is tasked by JCS (Pub 0-2) with ultimate responsibility of CSAR in his AOR. He is the direct representative of the theater commander (i.e. CINCEUR, CINCCENT, CINCSOUTH, etc.). During Joint Operations the Commander, Joint Task Force (CJTF) will normally designate a component commander to act as the SAR Coordinator. Aboard a carrier battle group, the battle group commander is the OTC; aboard an amphibious task force, the ATF commander is the OTC; once a MAGTF has moved ashore the commander of the landing force (CLF) is the OTC, and so on.

b. Rescue Coordination Center (RCC). Known as the JRCC or Joint Search and Rescue Center (JSRC) in joint operations, or CRCC in combined ops with other nations. The RCC implements and executes CSAR, TRAP plans and missions and when working as a component RCC, is responsible to JRCC/JSRC. Final mission planning is performed here, as well as evaluation and feedback on the effectiveness of CSARITRAP plans. If you're on a carrier, the RCC will be in the CIC. Once ashore, the RCC is in t he TACC.

c. SAR Mission Coordinator (SMC). The SMC is the direct representative of the OTC or his designated SC and exercises direct control over the assigned mission. Aboard a carrier battle group the CVW (CAG) normally fills this position; aboard an amphibious task force after the MEU has phased ashore, the aviation command element performs this role.

d. Aviation Command Element (ACE). The ACE is responsible for providing planning assistance to the RCC, and for ensuring aircraft are available to meet CSARITRAP requirements. If the ACE doesn't have the required assets, external theater assets are requested through the OTC/SC. The ACE is also responsible for publishing and disseminating supplemental instructions and standardized CSAR/TRAP procedures.

e. Operational Support Board (OSB). The OSB is responsible for developing CSAR/TRAP plans for possible contingencies in theater, and is composed of representatives from each warfare community embarked (e.g. attack, fighter, hero, reconnaissance, EW, C3, Intel, SPECWAR). During Joint Operations Marine/Navy components of the Joint Force may use the Crisis Action Team (CAT) or the TRAP Determination Team to function as a component OSB. The OSB works for the SMC.

f. Intelligence Officer. The intelligence officer is responsible for providing intelligence support to the RCC and OSB. he is also responsible for collecting and updating individual evasion plans of action (EPA's) prior to every assault or strike mission, collecting and maintaining current authentication data (ISOPREP-DD form 1833) in his assigned command, and for developing and maintaining up-to-date threat and rescue zone maps. The inter officer is also tasked with providing survival, evasion, resistance, and escape (SERE) briefs prior to every mission.

g. Recovery Force. The size and composition of the recovery force should be tailored for the mission, and is based upon the SMC, RCC, and OSB's evaluation of the threat.

h. Airborne Mission Commander/Coordinator (AMC). This player may not be required in every CSAR/TRAP scenario. The AMC offers the SMC greater control over his assets, especially in over the horizon operations. The AMC is responsible for command and control of the recovery force. Taking over for the airborne on scene commander (AOSC), the AMC will provide coordination and control to the recovery force while monitoring hostile activity, and providing a communications like to the RCC. Ideal platforms for this mission are the E-2 Hawkeye or E-3 Sentry (AWACS).

i. Airborne On-Scene Commander (AOSC). The AOSC is normally the senior member of the flight that loses an aircraft. In the Vietnam era, the AOSC was virtually in charge of the rescue effort, often directing supporting arms, rescue helos, providing CAS, and communicating with the survivor while trying to prevent himself from getting shot down. Today, the AOSC is responsible for initial notification to the RCC with essential elements of information such as the location and condition of the survivor, and the threat condition.

j. Recovery Mission Commander or Rescue Mission Coordinator (RMC). The rescue vehicle commander. The RMC may be the commander of the pickup hero, the skipper of a patrol boat, or a SEAL team leader. The RMC normally has the authority to terminate a mission when required.

k. Figure 1 is a wire diagram depiction of the key personnel and agencies we've just discussed.

1. In September of 1992, 26th MEU, aboard the USS Iwo Jima was deplcyed off the coast of Bosnia in the Adriatic Sea in support of Operation Provide Promise. Their primary mission was TRAP in support of U.N. forces in the bosnian theater. Their AOR was the country of Bosnia, from one hour prior to sunrise, until one hour after sunset. Their primary TRAP "package" was two CH-53E's, escorted by two AH-IW~s, with a follow on package of two CH-46's, one AH-I W, and one UH-I N. There were also two armed reconnaissance

packages; a "light team composed of two OH-IN's with recon Marines on board, and a "heavy" team of two CH-46's escorted by two AH-IW's.

2. The Amphibious Ready Group (ARG) Commander established strict and specific launch criteria which were as follows:

a. Verification of a live survivor.
b. Survivor is not danger of immediate capture.
c. Survivor is in a "go" zone of the TRAP launch matrix.
d. Survivor location identified within 1 nautical mile.
e. Fire support assets available on call
f. Aircrew pre-mission TRAP planning complete:
(1) Survivor position plotted.
(2) Updated order of battle known.
(3) Map study completed
(4) Comm coord complete
(5) Fire support coordination complete
(6) Survivor authentication (as available).

3. The crews rehearsed various scenarios with the ARG commander, applying a go/no-go matrix based upon the pre-set launch criteria. The CINCCENTs JRCC in Rhein-Main was read in on the TRAP plan by a representative from the MEU.

4. Late on the afternoon of September 4th, an Italian C-130 was downed by ground fire near the capital of Sarajevo. The word was passed to the ARG, and although launch criteria was not entirely satisfied, the order to launch was passed by the Commander 6th Fleet. A grid for the downed aircraft was passed by Sarajevo tower based on a GCI radar plot. A British C-130 observed smoke over what they thought to be the crash site, and guided the TRAP package to the area. Both sites were searched, with no result. The area was hilly and heavily forested, making visual search difficult. The search continued until after sunset, then was terminated when the aircraft reached their pre-determined bingo.

5. When the aircraft was finally located by U.N. ground troops, there were no survivors. By the appearance of the wreckage, it was determined the aircraft disintegrated in flight. There was no crater, and wreckage was spread out for miles, with no piece larger than a desk top remaining. The searching aircraft had actually passed over the crash site several times.

6. There are several key observations to study in this case. First, the assignment of TRAP to a MEU as a primary mission is unusual.

However, as pointed out earlier a MAGTF is uniquely suited to assume the mission. The 26th MEU staff did an exemplary job of task organizing their assets to accommodate a variety of TRAP scenarios. Second, realize that national or sensitive political priorities may necessitate mod)fications to your go/no-go launch criteria. In this case, the package was launched by higher authority without verification of live survivors, into an unknown threat environment. Finally, you should understand that sometimes a search will be required. Heavy foliage, grid errors, or bad weather can complicate survivor location. In TRAP planning, the recovery is the focus of effort, but you should be prepared to conduct limited search operations.

F. TRAP Fundamentals

1. The objective of TRAP is the recovery of downed aircrew, aircraft and or equipment under a wide spectrum of threats, while limiting additional loss. The concept of TRAP is not limited to the traditional helicopter recovery. Planning considerations at the operational level should include a wide range of recovery methods and assets, from surface ship to overland pickup by GCE or SPECWAR (SEALs, RECON, etc.) assets.

2. The emphasis of TRAP is a deliberate, preplanned recovery using all available assets, coordinated by a central agency. Hasty launches and kneejerk reactions are sure to put TRAP mission accomplishment in jeopardy, and will place additional personnel at risk.

3. In any case, certain TRAP launch criteria must be set to ensure the best chance of a successful recovery, with a minimum risk of additional loss. At a minimum, the following conditions should be met:

a. Indications of a live survivor
b. Survivor not in a position of immediate capture
c. Survivors position known within 1000 meters/INM
d. Survivor's authentication information available
e. Mission planning and briefing complete
f. Any required supporting arms available, and required BDA met.

With these fundamentals in mind, let's look at some TRAP planning considerations.

G. TRAP Planning Considerations

1. In your planning there are a number of publications you should be familiar with, to include:
a. FM-FM 5-35. Assault Support Helicopter Tactical Manual, Vol. 1 (Rev. F)
b. Individual Helicopter Tactical Manuals, Vol. 1 (Draft)
c. MEU(SOC) Training Playbook (Mar '89)
d. Mission performance Standards (MPS) MCO 3501.4 Series
e. NWP 19-2 Combat Search and Rescue
f. NWP 19-2 Supplement, CSAR Planning Guide
g. NWP 19 National SAR Manual

Of these manuals, only references a thru d specifically address TRAP.

2. In the TRAP planning process, it is critical that you identify your customer(s), internal and external. What this means is, that although the focus of your planning will be within the MAGTF amphibious objective area (AOA), you should be familiar wit all the CSARITRAP assets available within the JTF Commander's AOR as well (when applicable).

3. Here are four distinct customers you should target in your TRAP planning, and some questions you should consider:

a. Higher Echelon Command and Control

(1) Joint Task Force Commander, or Officer in Tactical Command (OTC)
(a) Has the JTF Commander established a JRCC/JSRC?
(b) What are the lines of comm between the JRCC/JSRC and service RCC's?
(c) What (if any) tasking authority has the JTF assigned the JRCC/JSRC?

(2) MAGTF Commander

(a) Has an RCC been established? (b) Is it sufficiently staffed? (c) Has a SMC been designated? By name or by billet?

b. Command and Control Middle Manager
(1) Joint Rescue Coordination Center/Joint Search and Rescue Center
(a) Does an intra-service plan exist? (b) What is the Marine Corps AOR for TRAP?

(2) Service Rescue Coordination Center
(a) What is/where is the TRAP plan?
(b) Does it comply with the joint CSAR/TRAP plan?
(c) Has appropriate TRAP launch criteria been set?
(d) Has an OSB been assigned and properly staffed?

(3) E-2, E-3, C-1 30 DASC (A)
(a) What is the availability of these assets?

c. CSAR/TRAP Aircrew Member, Ground Units

(1) Helicopter
(a) Are crews aufficiently trained?
(b) Are crews properly staffed and equipped? (SAR swimmers, corpsmen, hoists and stings, etc.)
(c) Is the GCE included in the OSB and do they have contingency packages identified and trained for TRAP security etc.
(d) Have maintenance members been identified, trained and equipped for aircraft recovery and/or repair in the field?

(2) Fixed-wing
(a) Do all aircrew know their AOR and TRAP plan?
(b) Have provisions been included for CAS, RESCAP or RESCORT?

(3) SPECWAR: RECON, SEAL, SOF, etc.
(a) Are all SPECWAR forces represented on the OSB?

d. The Survivor
(1) Distressed Aircrew Member
(a) Have all aircrew received appropriate SERE training for the operational area?
(b) Are all aircrew familiar with the TRAP plan, SAFE information, ISOPREP data?

4. One aspect of TRAP planning considerations we haven't discussed is the recovery of aircraft. The Marine Corps is the only service that consolidates recovery of aircraft and personnel in one mission. Planning for the recovery of aircraft incorporates many of the same considerations as the recovery of personnel, with a few additions. The first consideration is the addition of a type aircraft maintenance representative to the OSB as a crash and salvage officer. His knowledge of aircraft systems and support equipment will greatly enhance the speed and efficiency of recovery. Your squadron Pre-Mishap Plan will also be useful as a checklist to determine what personnel and equipment will be required to effect recovery. Consideration may also have to be given to the insert of a Quick Reaction Porce for zone security with concurrent or subsequent insertion of maintenance personnel and eventual force recovery. The OTC and SMC will make the final determination of whether an entire aircraft, or certain sensitive portions will be recovered.

H. The Future of CSAR/TRAP

1. As stated earlier, Desert Storm had an Immense effect on the CSARITRAP doctrine and tactics for the joint forces employed to conduct combat rescue. As a result of Air Force Special Operation Forces (SOF) and Air Rescue Service (ARS) rescue experiences in Desert Storm, the Air mobility Command (AMC) agreed to sponsor a CSAR process Improvement Team (PIT) and tasked ARS to be the executive agent. All services were invited to attend. The first CSAR PIT met in January of 1992. Using the Total Quality management logic model, the group identified the problem and a goal.

Problem: "Joint Forces lack a single source for CSAR tactics, techniques, and procedures."

Goal: "Provide a Joint Tactics, Techniques, and Procedures (JTTP) publication containing guidance for those who plan, coordinate, support and execute CSAR missions."

2. The JTTP will target users below the joint force commanders level. The intended users include those personnel supporting the JRCC, service RCC's, and those units requiring CSAR support. This document will not replace specific service tactics manuals. A JTTP is currently out in test status (Joint Pub 3-50.21)

3. There are four additional CSAR publications which you should be aware of. As of the date of this writing, all of the following are in the test publication phase.
   a. Joint Pub 3-50, National SAR Plan (U)
   b. Joint Pub 3-50.1, National SAR Plan (U)
   c. Joint Pub 3-50.2, Doctrine for Joint CSAR (U)
   d. Joint Pub 3-50.3, Joint Doctrine for Evasion Recovery (S)

4. Since the ffrst CSAR pit there has been a recurring meeting each year providing continuity to an ever expanding participation, including all services and an increased number of contingencies, roles and missions. At the meeting issues such as funding, doctrine, roles and equipment are discussed and ways sought to improve the effectiveness of the nations CSAR response.

5. Using publications like the JTTP and the four listed above, the Marine Corps must continue to develop and strengthen our own TRAP techniques. As we don't enjoy the wealth of equipment our sister services do, we must take advantage of our and their lessons learned in order to "fight smarter, not harder."

III. Summary

A. TRAP is undoubtedly one of the most challenging missions facing the MAGTF commander today. There is no standard TRAP mission, each situation is unique. The variables and uncertainty that may be encountered, the integration of helicopter, fixed- wing, and ground forces, and the inevitable shock and flow of emotions that follow the downing of an aircraft all contribute to the challenge. A simple, concise concept of operations, a thorough contingency TRAP plan for each strike or assault mission, and rapid final planning after the initial loss will greatly reduce uncertainty and confusion during the recovery mission.

B. Only by using sound TRAP fundamentals and planning will the TRAP planner be able to achieve his ultimate goal, the expeditious return of our personnel without further loss of friendly forces.

United States Marine Corps
MAWTS-1 Student Lesson Guide
Rapid Response Planning Process

I. Introduction

A. Given the present world situation, the application of military force to alleviate both hostile and non-hostile political crises has become a common response. The Marine Expeditionary Unit (MEW) Special Operation Capable (SOC) has long been touted as the rapid reaction force of the United States Armed Forces and consequently has found itself on many occasions conducting the Rapid Response Planning process (R2P2) to an assortment of situations.

B. The old adage "a good plan can save a poor pilot, but a good pilot cannot save a poor plan" is a fundamental truth and one which MEU mission planners can easily attest to during R2P2. Given R2P2 preparation, solid and simple plans can be developed which transition easily into and flow naturally during the execution phase.

II. Body

A. Rapid Response Missions. Rapid Response Missions are characterized as short notice missions with an operational requirement. The MEU (SOC) could be tasked with launching a short notice mission at night, in adverse weather, via helicopter and/or other surface means from extended ranges. It may have an reduced Emission Control (EMCON) requirement. The goal of the Rapid Response Mission could be to inflict losses or damage, create diversions or capture or evacuate individuals. It may require temporary occupance of an objective and a planned withdrawal. Regardless of what the requirements may be a successful Rapid Response Mission will rely heavily on existence notional mission profiles and sound SOPs.

B. R2P2 Characteristics. The primary missions tactical planners within the MEU (SOC) ACE focus are Amphibious Raids, Noncombatant Evacuation Operations (NEOs), Security Operations, Tactical Recovery of Aircraft and Personnel (TRAP), Direct Action, and Humanitarian/Civil Assistance. Although these missions is very distinct in scope, the fundamentals of each and the basis for mission planning remain the same. The three characteristics of R2P2 are:

1. R2P2 is based on deliberate planning process, the only difference is that results must be achieved in a much shorter time period. R2P2 has a set procedure, one which must be initiated with little or no information. R2P2 does not relieve mission planners from the requirements of deliberate planning. Rapid Response Planners do not have the liberty to omit any steps in the deliberate planning process.

2. R2P2 must be concurrent and parallel. Because the process of deliberate planning and R2P2 are the same, with exception of the time available to complete the planning cycle, the planning cycle is abridged through the use of concurrent and parallel planning.

3. The fundamentals of R2P2 lie in the process of Assault Contingency Planning; anticipating possible missions the ACE may have to execute and deriving from that packages which address possible contingencies. In technical terms the Rapid Response Capability is built upon Notional Mission Profiles and template planning which address generic missions. These concepts can be further formalized or streamlined through the use of playbooks and SOPs. From the contingency planning process a Rapid Response Mission plan can be easily developed.

C. Operational Requirements. The operational requirement for a R2P2 is six hours from receipt of the warning order to commencement of the operation. Given the existence of notional mission profiles, contingency templates, playbooks and SOPs, six hours from receipt of the mission to commencement of a tactically sound mission is possible. Staffplanning will utilize some of that six hour standard, but remember, planning must be concurrent and parallel. Major Subordinate elements (MSE) should begin gathering required mission information and refining contingency planning long before the receipt of the warning order.

D. Developing a Rapid Response Capability. History has shown that a battle is often won long before the first shot is fired. A Rapid Response Capability is even more reliant on good preparation, and sound SOPs. There are several items which can enhance a Rapid Response Capability, many of which can be accomplished prior to the ship leaving the pier.

1. MEU(SOC! qualification. There are three phases to achieving the MEU (SOC) qualification. Time and effort expended during these three phases translates to easier subsequent Rapid Response Operations:

a. Squadron Readiness - working to refine those skills on the unit level.
b. Training with the Ground Units that will be a part of the MEU - this includes all ground units, not only the GCE, but the CSSE, SEALS, etc.
c. All elements are brought together to train to fight as a team.

2. Identify key plaYers. Key players within the MEU(SOC) should be identified early and brought into the mission planning cycle. These might include the commanding officer, operations officer, squadron WTIs, and possible AMCs, AFL, and EFL when thinking in terms of the ACE. Outside of the ACE there might be Staff members, Naval and MSE counterparts. Point of contacts should be established as early as possible with MEU(SOC) counterparts.

3. Train key players. A large portion of mission success will be determined by how effective the key players are able to accomplish mission planning tasks. Expeditionary Warfare Training Groups (EWTGs) for both coasts conduct excellent MEU(SOC) workshops. Representation at these courses by other MSEs is always very strong and it would be advantageous for key players to attend this course. These workshops allow personnel to be exposed to a unique level of planning otherwise unavailable. Coordinate visits from Special Operations Training Group (SOTG) to discuss special operations. Send key personnel to a fire support coordinators course. The ultimate goal of this training is to enhance key players knowledge and understanding of MEU(SOC) capabilities. The value of this training will pay dividends in the planning cells and subsequent phases of every operation. Finally, build redundancy by appointing alternates and ensuring they are as well trained as the primary players.

4. Create Planning Cells. Planning cells should be created with WTIs or Flight leaders, Operations representatives. Maintenance Representatives, and other desired mission essential personnel. The composition should include all the officers in the ACE and the duty checklist should specifically task all members. Each cell should have parity in their composition. The ACE should quality spread the planning cells between the primary and alternate key players. There should be no doubt as to what the cell leader requires and who is responsible for obtaining specific information or accomplishing specific tasks. Consideration should be given to the allocation of Top Secret clearances and access to CMS which match the planning cell spread.

5. Formulate Alert Postures in Port. Reality and national obligations may dictate that the squadron have a 24 hour posture, even in port. Planning cells based on duty sections can address the requirement for an alert posture during these times of possible crisis while in port. If a warning order comes to the ATF while in port, the duty section plarming cell will be the team responsible for (a) recalling the unit, and (b) beginning the planning process.

6. Develop planning Kits. Put together a planning kit full of transparencies, markers, overhead projectors, threat weapon system overlays, friendly weapon system overlays, pen, paper, etc.

7. Compile a detailed duty checklist. A duty checklist should be very specific, designating what tasks specific individuals are responsible for accomplish ing and, based on the assignment date/time, when that task is due. To aid in determining what tasks or mission planning elements are required, outside of the normal duties of smart pack coordinator and map maker, analyze your primary mission. Identify what elements are required for the primary mission, and any implied missions (TRAP, emergency extract, etc.). Ensure that the duty checklist is both operations and maintenance oriented. For example, who within the squadron maintenance shops are trained in Aircraft battle Damage Recovery (ABDR)? Have they been identified and informed of where to meet and with what equipment? Does the squadron have the proper tools and equipment set aside? If these maintenance type of questions are incorporated into the duty checklist the evolution is more likely to run smoothly.

8. Liaison with the GCE. Liaisons with the GCE and other MEU(SOC) agencies should be accomplished as soon as possible. The GCE will have standard packages for priority missions which they will want to pursue. These priority missions may or may not match the ACE priority missions. Ultimately these priority missions must match. Identify what kind of liR they require for Sparrow Hawk of Bald Eagle packages and whether squadron assets and capabilities match those requirements. The ACE must provide the GCE with the aviation expertise for their mission accomplishment. The earlier the initial liaisons with the GCE the more apt the mission priorities will match and the easier the mission planning process.

9. Identifv and Use Intelligence Sources. Identify and utilize available intelligence sources. documents such as Non-combatant Evacuation Operation Naval intelligence Support Handbook (NEONISH), contingency support Package (CSP), generic intelligence Requirements Handbook (GIRH), ACE Intelligence Cookbooks (ALC) all provide normally unavailable information on different regional areas. The joint Deployable Intelligence Support System (JDISS) can provide real time intelligence to deployed MEU(SOC)s. External Sources include:

a. SPEAR -Strike Projection Evaluation and Anti-Air Warfare research. DSN 243-3719.
b. DIA - Defense Intelligence Agency, Crisis Action Center. DSN 243-4945/ 8127.
c. MCIA - Marine Corps Intelligence Activity. DSN 294-3516/4314.
d. DMA - Defense Mapping Agency. 1-800-826-0342.

10. Develop and stick to a standard briefing format. The MEU will have a generic SOP on what the ACE should brief. Tailor that brief to the squadrons satisfaction and only alter from that brief for the benefit of mission understanding. this also applies to flight briefs. Squadron pilots should come to recognize where within a brief specific information is to be passed.

11. Be an Active Participant in the Ship load plan. A potential problem with any amphibious force is the loading of the ships. ships that are located administratively can hold much more than those loaded tactically, but as the British found out on their way to the Falklands, it can place mission accomplishment in peril. As "Soldiers of the Sea" we are not immune to such errors in planning. If the ships are loaded administrathely, unit tacticians should seek out essential gear locations once embarked and plan ahead. Embarkation deficiencies should be noted and corrected prior to the possibility of any actual contingency missions.

12. Be an Active Participant in the Mission Load Allowance (MLA!. Of utmost importance to any MEU(SOC) is the MLA. The MLA is the class V aviation ordnance which is loaded onto the ships and is utilized by the MEU in contingency operation. There are two sources of training ordnance: 1) non-Combatant Expenditure Allowance (NCEA) and 2) MLA above the required 80%. The one caveat to utilizing MLA ordnance is that the MEU must be capable of replenishing that ammunition during the deployment. The significance of the NCE is in the prepositioining requests and training like the ACE will ffght. for example ordnance can be loaded onto an LPD. This is advantageous because (1) by placing NCEA ordnance loads and pre-staging them on an LPD, HERO condition do not interrupt flight operations on the aviation class ships, and (2) the smaller deck of the LPD can be used as a "skid" FARP reducing the deck cycle constraints and freeing the aviation class ships for more conventional transport type operations. If this is the MEU plan for contingency operations then that is how the ACE will want to train. some of the questions that need to be answered prior to deployment are:

a. How does the squadron want to preposition ordnance with the ARG?
b. Does the squadron have enough ordnance personnel to dual site with the ARG?
c. What ordnance is in the MLA?
d. How does the squadron change the composition of the MLA?
e. will the ARG have the ability to restock the MLA?

13. Get Maintenance Involved. Maintenance participation is mandatory in the R2P2 process. A central maintenance coordinator should appointed Responsibilities should include the development of Basic Aircraft Kits, Maintenance Recovery Kits, and ABDR Kits. The Basic Aircraft Kits might include a five gallon water jug, MREs and several M-15 rifles; the Maintenance Recovery Kits might be as simple as an ALICE pack with common tools required to perform enough maintenance to "one shot" an aircraft back to friendly lines; and the ABDR kit could be more elaborate. the Basic Aircraft Kit should be carried on all aircraft during contingency missions. The Maintenance Recovery and ABDR Kits should be set aside and never touched until required for an actual recovery effort. The Army conducts a school at the Aviation Maintenance Officers Course at Fort Belvoir, VA for recovery of battle damaged aircraft. the Navy also conducts en Aircraft Battle Damage Recovery School, course number N-600C 8005 at NWS china Lake.

14. Exercise R2P2. The single most effective method to developing a R2P2 capability is practice. Drills within a squadron can begin long before the MEU(SOC) work up. the R2P2 SOP should be treated as a living document; flexible and subject to change as a result of new experiences and new ideas. Utilization of Tactical Exercises Without Troops (TEWTS) and Staff Exercises (STX) ~mprove both the planning and execution phase of operations. as the deployment draws near begin focusing on regional hot spots. The Squadron can study potential missions and prepare photos, maps, target lists and area folders. As GCE point of contacts are established bring them into these planning exercises.

E. Assault Continyencv Planning. The two most important fundamentals of R2P2 are notional mission profiles and sound SOPs. These tow fundamentals combined with several other mission planning elements constitute Assault Contingency Planning.

1. Determine mission priorities. The ACE must train to accomplish what it will most likely be called upon to execute. The political climate of certain nations in close proximity to where the MEU will be operating provide a focus for where attention should be placed in terms of Rapid Response capabilities. A north African country, unstable with a large US worker population may call for focusing on NEO capabilities. On the other hand, an aggressive Middle eastern country, attempting to gain the work recognition may require focus on training for in extremis Hostage rescue (IHR) or Gas and Oil Platform (GOPLAT) takedowns. This does not mean that contingency planning should be limited to several chosen missions, rather the ACE should identify priority mission and determine what effort should be expended toward their pre-mission planning. As the world events change those primary missions can be changed.

2. Notional mission. Many of the elements and implied mission within the scope of possible missions will remain the same. The same hasty TRAP package plan designed for a raid should be able to be used for IHR. a TRAP package is essential that same as a raid with a few added variables. The seam emergency extract plan can be utilized for may different mission. these plans can be fully developed prior to receipt of any mission with only a few variables to fill in. Utilize the nature of these mission to the squadron advantage and incorporate into the squadron SOPs or ply books. Effort paled into creating mission foundations will pay dividend during R2P '. Areas to focus when developing notional mission are:

a. Threat.
b. Insert/Extract Means.
c. types ofActions.
d. PersonneVEquipment/Ordnance

3. Force Packaging. Early liaison with the GCE will provide the force packing they require for specific notional mission. these packages will drive the ACE assets required to accomplish the notional missions. The two primary force packages with which to plan notional missions are:

a. Sparrow Hawk.
b. Bald Eagle

4. Template Planning. Template Planning adds another level of detail to the preparation of R2P2. These templates include common mission profiles which when developed reduce overall planning and briefing time. These templates can be added to the squadron Sops. the templates might include:

a. LZ landing profiles.
b. CAS and fields of fire profiles.
c. Hasty TRAP profiles.
d. Extract or emergency extract profiles.

5. SOPs and PlavBooks. A newly formed composite squadrons first priority should be to ensure all aircrew are utilizing the same SOPs and play books. Composite squadron SOPs should be designed to compliment all aircraft within the squadron. Standardization is the key. SOPs must compliment the MEU SOP. there are several "playbooks" which can be obtained from the respective EWTG or SOTG. They are excellent planning guides and provide information on checklists, fire support requirements, RF is for mission and standard packages for raids, TRAPs etc. Sources for squadron SOPs are:

a. FMFM 7-32 Raid Operations.
b. MEU (SOC) Playbooks.
c. U.S. Marinesin Vietnam - "The Bitter End" 1973-1975
d. EASTERN EXIT: the NEO form Mogadishu, Somalia, in January 1991 CNA.
e. "COMMANDO RAIDS: 1946-1963" Bruce Hoffman, A Rand Note.
f. MCO 3501.4 Series Mission Performance Standards.
g. Aircraft TIMIS Tactical Manuals.

6. Checkpoints and Spider Routes. If the MEU (SOC) anticipates working in a specific Area of Operation, checkpoints can be pre-plo ted and routes based on known threats and the situation can be derived. Time and distance can be developed based on mission profiles. LZs can be developed based on key terrain and possible objective areas.

7. Treat Svstems Overlavs. Based on global hot spots threat systems overlays can be developed. Not only can this be a PME tool within the ACE, but can also reduce time required for the R2P2 process.

F. Execution Checklists. The execution checklist is a standard command and control tool. The execution checklist is primarily for the use of the CATF or CFL. It provided clarity as information wends its way through the nets and agencies from the executors to the commanders. communications among the various executors can be performed using normal brevity codes and plain language (Hero Jargon). The four methods of formatting the execution checklist for a Rapid Response Capability are:

1. Execution checklists should be pre-made to fit a notional mission profiles. The MEU(SOC) playbooks provide some basic examples that can be expanded as required. Having arrived at a generic mission execution checklist will give pliability to quickly make changes s opposed to constructing an entirely new checklist from scratch.

2. The same individual should always prepare the execution checklist. This will ensure the same logic of preparation will be found in each version and reduce confusion during execution.

3. During the pre-deployment preparation this individual should make liaison with the GCE to ensure both execution checklists are mirror images. There can be only one execution checklist.

4. Word association will make the execution checklist user friendly. An aircraft down could be associated with baseball teams or terminology. "Foul Ball" could indicate an aircraft has gone down; "Double Header" might trigger a TRAP package.

G. Other Considerations. Although there are many other R2P2 considerations they are too numerous to cover, but here are a few.

1. Communications. A poor communication plan can cause mission failure whether it is in a Rapid Response or a deliberate mission. Information passed back to the command elements must be timely and accurate. Time and effort should be given to what frequencies each element of the AFT will be operating on and how they are to contact other specific agencies. Reliance upon DASC or other command and control platforms to pass information should have redundant features. Line of sight must be factored into the plan. To be effective a communication plan must be simple and cyclical in nature. Above all, come up with an ACE standard and deviate from this plan as little as possible when developing the R2P2. The communication plan should become second nature to the executors.

2. Communication Checks. As part of the maintenance checklist for R2P2, include communications checks to be conducted prior to each mission by the avionics department.

3. Covered and Uncovered Communications. Due to the present difficulties in obtaining secure communications on a unit wide basis, consideration should be given to using uncovered ("Red") communications for mission nets and covered ("Green") communications on command nets. Disciplined use of brevity codes, "hero jargon", and execution checklists should provide good OPSEC under most circumstances. In order to reduce confusion, do not deviate from an established communication practice during a rapid response mission.

4. Penetration Checklists. Serious regard should be given to penetration checklist items. Do the benefits of turning off the radar altimeter and the TACAN outweigh the benefits of being able to find the ship or avoid hitting the ground while at low altitude on NVGs?

5. Bump Plans. The bump plan and the ensuing movement of sticks can cause havoc. Simplicity, familiarization with procedures, signals and communication must be understood by all MSEs. The opportunity to rehearse embarkation and debarkation must be made available. The most important thing to remember is that mission success depends less on how many sticks get there and more on what sticks get there. When aboard ship, coordination with the Combat Cargo is essential in order to complete

a bump plan. The efficiency of Combat Cargo can have great effects on the ship deck cycle and more importantly the fuel plan. A simple bump plan which remains similar in all notional missions is a good starting point.

6. Friendlv ID. At night the distances between friendlies and the enemy tend to decrease. Consideration should be given on how to identify friendlies and marking enemy. Chemlites are frequently used to mark individual Marines. Marking of friendly perimeters is more challenging.

7. Mission Compromise. Historically Marines have not given enough thought to compromised plans. Often this is glossed over as all focus is upon ingress. If the mission is compromised, the element of surprise is lost and the energies of the enemy are now focused on preventing the completion of the mission. Consequently, the emergency extract plan needs to be planned and the overall mission "what il~d" to address that contingency.

8. War Rooms. Set up a room as an ACE war from or COC. It should be the central point for information collection for the ACE. Set up friendly and enemy situation boards and maps. Consider dividing the war room into a planning and operations side, this will aid in providing continuity as operations continue. Set up a log book for smooth pass down (receipt of message traffic, progress of missions, threat, concurrent operations, BDA, and follow-on missions.)

9. Scheduled Fliers. One of the most difficult decisions is whether key individual should fly if a big mission comes up. Certain key billets such as Operations Officer, Combat ODO, and maintenance coordinator may require that they are left off the schedule to perform other important functions. By the nature of their billets they are usually on the schedule but more important work may be accomplished in the R2P2 billets.

10. Mission Essential Personal Gear. Pre-issue as much gear as possible. Pre-issued NBC equipment, personal armor, weapons, deuce gear, and NVGs would reduce timelines. Conduct inspections on a periodic basis to ensure that gear is maintained.

11. Ordinance Loads. Pre-build ordnance loads. Establish a standard ordnance and expendable package that can be quickly drawn from the magazines for use. Pre-built ordnance loads are required for Rapid Response Missions due to extensive amounts of time required to build up ordnance.

12. Objective Area Planning. One of the most difficult things we do as leaders or billet holders is to insure that planners focus on the end goal of the mission. Planners should put the majority of the effort into what happens when we reach the objective area. SOP's will cover most actions up to the IP and past the ECP on the way out. Where things historically come unglued is during actions in the objective area. The focus of R2P2 should start in the objective area and work backwards.

G. Briefs. Mission briefing can make or break any mission. This is especially true for Rapid Response Missions. Briefers and attendees must know what should be briefed and what should not. A large delay in any brief could cause subsequent briefs to have to be abbreviated or push back a launch time.

1. Confirmation Brief. A confirmation brief is given to the CLF and CATF in order for them to understand how the chosen course of action is to be accomplished. By the very nature of the confirmation brief it is a "Big Blue Arrow" brief, with detail provided for specific phases in the operation. The planning process should be complete and the AMC brief could be given concurrently, but there are still areas susceptible to change by the CLF or the CATF.

a. The intent of the confirmation brief is:
(1) An executors/operators brief.
(2) Ensures the commanders intent has been understood.
(3) Big blue arrow brief on how the mission is going to be accomplished.
(4) Specific information covering commanders concerns
(5) Problem finder
(6) Chance for the commander to give last minute guidance.
(7) Issues the order.

b. What a confirmation brief is not:

(1) It should not be a brief requiring command approval.
(2) It is not a Course of Action brief, that has already been given by the CAT.
(3) it is not for a cast of thousands.

c. The briefer doesn't have to be the AMC but should be a key player; someone familiar with the plan and how it became the plan.

(1) Confidence in the plan is paramount. Any uneasiness in the briefer will be sensed. The briefer is selling a product; if he or she does not have faith no one will. It is better to say you don't know vise making something up. Be open to suggestions and expect changes.

(2) Neatness counts. Have the brief pre-formatted on a computer disk and create transparencies. Keep transparencies simple and legible. A picture is worth a thousand words. Do not brief items that are non-applicable.

2. AMC Brief. The AMC brief covers the mission in detail for the participating aviators. It should be detailed enough to provide insight to what all the aircraft are accomplishing, but not discuss specific inter-flight responsibili ties. In a rapid response mission time is the critical asset. The AMC brief must allow for individual flights to brief.

a. Appoint an executive officer. This individual must be able to extract information from an assortment of people and ensure those individuals are completing assigned tasked in a timely fashion. He or she must possess initiative. This individual must be able to give the brief and assist the AMC with any questions.

b. Rehearse if there is time. This should be accomplished with the GCE and other key players to ensure there are no last minute conflicts in the information being passed.

c. Try not to chanye the plan at the last minute. If the plan is changed be cognizant of how difficult it is to ensure every one gets the change. The possibility of the word not getting to all required personnel and the benefits of the change must be weighed. Surprise the enemy, not each other. Operations representatives are crucial during last minute plan changes.

d. Educate briefers on what to brief. The weather briefer on the ship will need guidance on what to brief, especially NVG considerations. Flight deck control and the Air Boss all need guidance. They are there to support the ACE. The time for training is not during a rapid response Confirmation or AMC brief.

Ways to Fail. Failure can come in many flavors. Here are a few which have plagued passed MEU(SOC)s.

1. Inadequate coordination with the ship:
a. Attendees at the brief
b. Bump plan
c. Fuel plan
d. Load plan
e. Deck cycles
f. Cross decking priorities
g. Ammunition movement times

2. Inadequate coordination with the GCE.
a. Fire support plan - target prioritizing
b. Embark plan
c. Bump plan
d. Communication plan
e. Identification of friendliest
f. Emergency extract plan

III. Summary

A. R2P2 is a procedure similar to deliberate planning with the exception of a time constraint. In order to be successful, concurrent and parallel planning must take place. The response time from receipt of mission to the first launch is six hours. Rapid Response Planning will only be successful if exercised prior to joining the MEU. LFTCPAC/LANT and SOTG are several of the organizations available to help the ACE prepare for deployment. Standardization and rehearsal are the key between the MEU and the MSEs.

Appendix Three:
How The Helicopter Flies

Fight of a helicopter is governed by the pitch or angle of its rotor blades as they sweep through the air. For climbing and descending, the pitch of all the blades is changed at the same time and in the same degree. To climb, the angle or pitch of the blades is increased. To descend, the pitch of the blades is decreased. Because all blades are acting simultaneously, or collectively, this is known as collective pitch. For forward, backward and sideways flight an additional change of pitch is provided. By this means the pitch of each blade increases at the same selected point in its circular pathway. This is known as cyclic pitch.

With these two controls in mind let us make an imaginary flight. With the engine warmed up and the rotor blades whirling above us in flat pitch, that is, with no angle or bite on the air. We are ready to start (fig. 1).

Fig. 1 Flat Pitch

We increase the collective pitch. The rotor blades bite into the air, each to the same degree, and lift the helicopter vertically (Fig. 2).

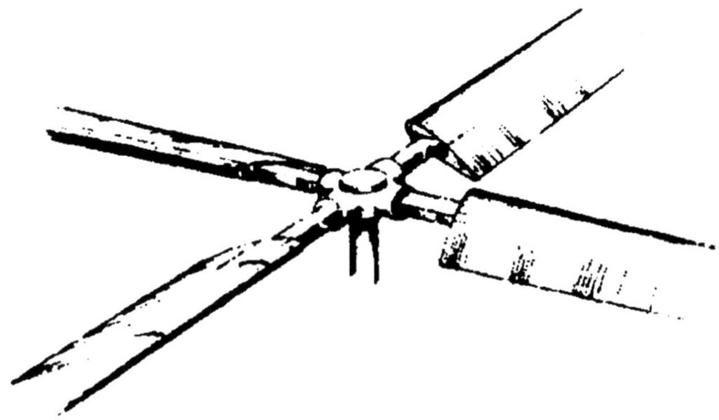

Fig. 2 Collective Pitch

Now we decide to fly forward. We still have collective pitch to hold us in the air and we adjust the cyclic pitch so that as each blade passes over the tail of the helicopter, it has more bite on the air than when it passes over the nose Fig. 3). Naturally the helicopter travels forward.

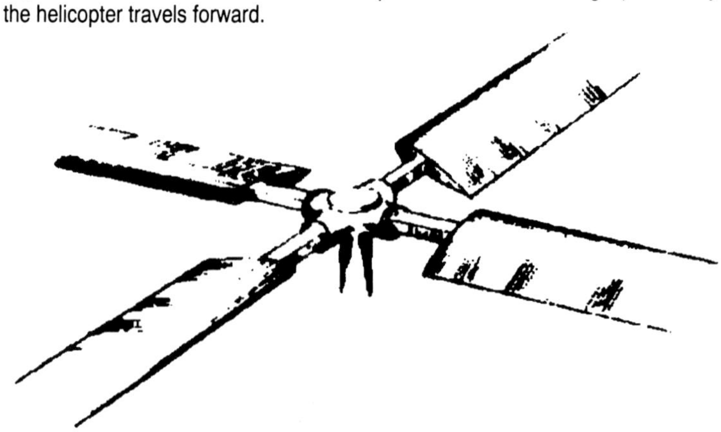

Fig. 3 CycCc Pitch

Now we decide to stop and hover motionless so we put the cyclic pitch in neutral—the rotor blades now have the same pitch throughout their cycle—and the collective pitch holds the helicopter suspended in space without moving in any direction.

In short, it is the cyclic and collective pitch which gives the helicopter its unique ability to fly forward, backward. sideways, rise and descend vertically and hover motionless in the air—making it one of the most versatile vehicles known to man.

-Courtesy of the Sikorsky Corporation.

Also from the publisher

WARFIGHTERS

A HISTORY OF THE USAF WEAPONS SCHOOL AND THE 57TH WING

Rick Llinares & Chuck Lloyd.

This is a first-hand look at how the U.S. Air Force creates its most elite, highly trained aircrews, and provides an inside look into the USAF Weapons School at Nellis Air Force Base, Nevada, one of the Air Force's most highly classified programs.
Size: 8 1/2" x 11" over 270 color photographs, unit insignia
264 pages, hard cover
ISBN: 0-7643-0044-X $49.95